# Dogmas and Dreams

CHATHAM HOUSE STUDIES IN POLITICAL THINKING
SERIES EDITOR: George J. Graham, Jr.
*Vanderbilt University*

# DOGMAS AND DREAMS
## Political Ideologies in the Modern World

Edited by Nancy S. Love
*Pennsylvania State University*

CHATHAM HOUSE PUBLISHERS, INC.
Chatham, New Jersey

Dogmas and Dreams: Political Ideologies
in the Modern World

Chatham House Publishers, Inc.
Box One, Chatham, New Jersey 07928

Copyright © 1991 by Chatham House Publishers, Inc.

*Publisher:* Edward Artinian
*Cover design:* Lawrence Ratzkin
*Production supervisor:* Chris Kelaher
*Composition:* Bang, Motley, Olufsen
*Printing and binding:* R. R. Donnelley & Sons Company

*Library of Congress Cataloging-in-Publication Data*

Dogmas and dreams: political ideologies in the modern world /
edited by Nancy S. Love

   p.   cm. —(Chatham House studies in political thinking)
Includes bibliographical references.
ISBN 0-934540-84-5
1. Political science. 2. Ideology. 3. Right and left (Political science) I. Love, Nancy Sue, 1954– . II. Series.
JA36.D64   1991
320.5–dc20                 90-19909
                             CIP

Manufactured in the United States of America
10  9  8  7  6  5  4  3  2  1

# ACKNOWLEDGMENTS

I would like to thank individually some of the teachers and students to whom I have dedicated this book. Isaac Kramnick introduced me to the study of ideologies when I assisted in his course "Liberalism and Its Critics" at Cornell University. He is a superb teacher and his influence on me was profound. My thanks here for its subtler forms, which could not be cited and included in the text itself. I also want to thank my students at Pennsylvania State University. Those enrolled in my ideologies course tested these selections and evaluated my introductions to them. Rochelle Quiggle and Lisa Leipold provided valuable research assistance and helped, along with Tracey Dolan, Ellen Foley, and Regina Moore, to prepare the manuscript.

For a project such as this, staff support is especially important. Barbara Ayalla typed much of the text. Jo Ann Harris and Debbie Price took over at critical points when it seemed it would never be completed. Darlene Irby-Adesalu supervised the whole process with grace and good humor.

At Chatham House, my thanks to Chris Kelaher for seeing this successfully through the production process and to Edward Artinian for his confidence in the project itself.

I would also like to thank the individuals and publishers who have kindly granted permission to include the following materials in this book:

Milton Friedman and The University of Chicago Press, for chapters 1 and 2 of Milton Friedman, *Capitalism and Freedom,* © 1962 by The University of Chicago.

Isaac Kramnick and *Dissent,* for Isaac Kramnick, "Equal Opportunity and the Race of Life," *Dissent* 28, no. 2 (Spring 1981): 178–87, Copyright © 1981 *Dissent.*

Michael Oakeshott, "On Being Conservative," is from *Rationalism in Politics and Other Essays,* by Michael Oakeshott. © 1962 by Michael Oakeshott. Reprinted by permission of Basic Books, Inc., Publishers, New York, and the author.

Irving Kristol, "Capitalism, Socialism, and Nihilism," is reprinted with permission of the author from *The Public Interest,* no. 31 (Spring 1973): 3–16. © 1973 by National Affairs, Inc.

Allan Bloom, "The Democratization of the University," is reprinted by permission of The Public Affairs Conference Center, Kenyon College, Gambier, Ohio.

The selections from the writings of Charles Fourier are from *The Utopian Vision of Charles Fourier* by Jonathan Beecher and Richard Bienvenu. Copyright © 1971 by Jonathan Beecher and Richard Bienvenu. Reprinted by permission of Beacon Press.

International Publishers Co., New York, granted permission to use the following: Karl Marx, "Estranged Labor," pp. 106–19 of Karl Marx, *Economic and Philosophical Manuscripts of 1844*, edited by Dirk Struik and translated by Martin Milligan (1969); pp. 29–62 of Karl Marx, *Value, Price and Profit*, edited by Eleanor Marx Aveling (1935); V.I. Lenin, section 4e, pp. 131–39, *What Is to Be Done?* (1932); V.I. Lenin, chapter 5, pp. 99–122, of *State and Revolution* (1969); Frederick Engels, excerpts from *The Origin of the Family, Private Property and the State* (1972).

Pantheon Books, for excerpts from pp. 18–27, 73–94, 135–65, from *Evolutionary Socialism* by Eduard Bernstein (1975).

Doubleday, a division of Bantam, Doubleday, Dell Publishing Group, Inc., for permission to reprint Sidney Webb, "Historic," from *Fabian Essays in Socialism*, edited by George Bernard Shaw (1967).

Dover Publications, Inc., New York, for excerpts from P.J. Proudhon, *What Is Property? An Inquiry into the Principles of Right and of Government.*

Excerpts from the writings of Mikhail Bakunin are reprinted with permission of The Free Press, a Division of Macmillan, Inc., from *The Political Philosophy of Bakunin: Scientific Anarchism*, edited by G.P. Maximoff. Copyright © 1953, 1981 by The Free Press.

Friedrich Engels, "On Authority" and "Versus the Anarchists," are reprinted from *The Marx-Engels Reader*, edited by Robert C. Tucker, Second Edition, with permission of W.W. Norton & Company, Inc. Copyright © 1978, 1972 by W.W. Norton & Company, Inc.

"Duties to Country" is reprinted from Joseph Mazzini, *The Duties of Man and Other Essays*, by permission of the publishers, J.M. Dent and Everyman's Library.

The selections from Adolf Hitler's *Mein Kampf* are from *Mein Kampf* translated by Ralph Manheim. Copyright 1943, and copyright © renewed 1971 by Houghton Mifflin Company. Reprinted by permission of Houghton Mifflin Company and Hutchinson Publishing Ltd.

"Domestic Terrorists: The KKK in the 'Fifth Era,'" pp. 5–10, is reprinted from *Klanwatch*, by permission of the Southern Poverty Law Center, Box 548, Montgomery, Alabama.

The selection by Phyllis Schlafly is reprinted from *The Power of the Positive Woman* by Phyllis Schlafly. Copyright © 1977 by Phyllis Schlafly. Used by permission of Arlington House, Inc.

The selection by Betty Friedan is reprinted from *The Feminine Mystique* by Betty Friedan, by permission of W.W. Norton & Company, Inc., and Victor Gollancz Ltd. Copyright © 1963 by Betty Friedan.

Monique Wittig, "One Is Not Born a Woman," Copyright © 1979 Monique Wittig, is reprinted by permission of Sanford J. Greenburger Associates, New York.

Heidi Hartmann, "The Unhappy Marriage of Marxism and Feminism: Toward a More Progressive Union," is reprinted from *Women and Revolution,* edited by Lydia Sargent (1981), by permission of South End Press, 116 St. Botolph St., Boston, Massachusetts 02115.

To my teachers
and
my students

# CONTENTS

# INTRODUCTION

# Ideology and Democracy

Ideology and democracy. These words share a long history. What do they mean? How are they related? Etymologically, *democracy* means rule by the people, or *demos*. Although this seems relatively clear, controversy continues over who the people are and how they should rule. *Ideology* is an even more confusing word. The *Oxford English Dictionary* provides two standard definitions. The first is descriptive or neutral: Ideology is the "science of ideas." This definition, indeed the word itself, originated with Destutt de Tracy, an eighteenth-century French philosopher. Contemporary social scientists who study ideologies as "belief systems" follow this usage. The second definition is critical or deprecatory: Ideology is "ideal or abstract speculation" and "unpractical or visionary theorizing."[1] This better fits popular usage, which includes pejorative references to ideologues as advocates, even dogmatists. Both definitions are common today, but there is some historical distance between them. As John Thompson points out, few now proudly proclaim themselves ideologues.[2] Yet Tracy and his followers once did just that. Why were they proud to be Ideologues? How did ideology become a pejorative term? In answering these questions, I also address another: Why study ideologies? These answers concern the relationship between ideology and democracy.

## The History of Ideology

The history of ideology begins with Tracy's notion that ideas originate in sensory experience and that their origins can be studied scientifically. Tracy contrasted ideology with metaphysics: "Ideology was very sensible since it supposes nothing doubtful or unknown; it does not call to mind any [supernatural] idea of cause. . . . Its meaning is very clear to everyone."[3] For Tracy, the "science of ideas" had positive political connotations. Ideology constituted a challenge to existing authorities. Philosophers and priests were superfluous if ideas were "very clear to everyone." And if everyone could understand ideas,

xiii

then everyone should discuss them and decide among them. Tracy explicitly associated his sensationalist psychology with democratic politics. He was a French revolutionary, a defender of individual freedom and representative government. A friend attested to Tracy's (and his compatriots') political aspirations: "*Ideology* they told me would change the face of the earth, and that is exactly why those who wish the world to always remain stupid (and with good cause) detest ideology and the ideologues."[4]

This history further complicates the definition of ideology by adding a third forgotten meaning. According to Tracy, ideology was a democratic philosophy, a defense of popular intelligence. The "science of ideas," today a neutral definition, originally had positive connotations and only later developed pejorative ones. Napoleon, Tracy's contemporary, first used ideology pejoratively. He referred to the Ideologues as a "metaphysical faction" and, less flatteringly, as "dangerous dreamers" and "windbags ... who have always fought the existing authorities."[5] Here, too, the term had political connotations. In his famous denunciation of ideology, Napoleon says:

> We must lay the blame for the ills that our fair France has suffered on ideology, that shadowy metaphysics. . . . Indeed, who was it that proclaimed the principle of insurrection to be a duty? Who adulated the people and attributed to it a sovereignty which it was incapable of exercising? Who destroyed respect for and the sanctity of laws by describing them, not as sacred principles of justice, but only as the will of an assembly composed of men ignorant of civil, criminal, administrative, political, and military law?[6]

Like Tracy, Napoleon links ideology and democracy, but his linkage is a negative one. With their democratic dreams, the Ideologues destroyed the illusions necessary for social order and human happiness.

Were Tracy's Ideologues a "metaphysical faction"? Was democracy a "shadowy metaphysics?" Perhaps. Tracy did regard "ideas as the only things that exist for us, the only means we have to know things."[7] He also spoke of ideology "changing the face of the earth." But this is not our concern here. History has vindicated democracy; today it is a reality. Yet history has also preserved the negative connotations of ideology. Today, Tracy would no doubt agree that democrats should not be ideologues—at least in Napoleon's pejorative sense. The continuing history of ideology reveals its incompatibility with democracy.

Karl Marx, a nineteenth-century German philosopher, took the next significant step in that history. Marx knew Tracy's work and probably adopted the term from him. Like Napoleon, Marx criticized the Ideologues' idealism; he too associated ideology with metaphysics. But Marx disagreed with Napoleon about the origins of such metaphysical illusions. He traced them to class conflict and not to democratic politics. His significant step was this socioeconomic explanation of ideology. According to Marx, ideologies have three general characteristics. They are social, functional, and illusory forms of consciousness. Marx argues that societies develop forms of consciousness suited to their historical circumstances. Class relations are the most important influences on social consciousness. Marx says, "The ideas of the ruling class are in every epoch the ruling ideas, i.e., the class which is the ruling material force of society, is at the same time its ruling intellectual force."[8] Ideologies function for the ruling class as illusions. They help legitimate that class by making its rule seem natural and its interests seem general.

In fact, every ruling class protects its own interests, and history involves conflict between classes. For Marx, then, ideology is an obstacle to democracy. It prevents the oppressed class from understanding and challenging the sources of its oppression. Indeed, Marx fears that democracy itself may become an ideology. As you see in the selections by him in this book, he distinguishes between political emancipation and human emancipation. Political emancipation grants individual rights but without eliminating economic oppression. Freedom remains illusory because economic circumstances prevent people from exercising it. For example, we are not "free to choose" where we work or the conditions under which we work if we must work to live and we live in a company town. In contrast, human emancipation involves a genuine, that is, economic and political, democracy. It involves providing people with the economic security they require to choose freely. Only after people see through the ideological illusion of rights, Marx argues, will they organize truly to emancipate themselves.

The question that arises here is: Why would people believe ideological illusions? Sigmund Freud, the next major figure in the history of ideology, offers an answer. Freud's focus is religion, not ideology, but he suggests that they have a common origin: "Having recognized religious doctrines to be illusions, we are at once confronted with the further question: may not all cultural possessions, which we esteem highly and by which we let our life be ruled, be of a similar nature? Should not the assumptions that regulate our political institutions likewise be called illusions?"[9] To understand this need for illusions, it is necessary to look briefly at Freud's psychological theory. According to Freud, the psyche has three parts: id, ego, and superego. The id contains the basic instincts, eros (libido), and thanatos (aggression). The ego mediates between those instincts and reality, balancing internal desires and external demands. The superego is the conscience, the site of internalized social values, which helps the ego control the id. For Freud, social life requires that individuals repress and/or redirect their instincts. Needless to say, this is a painful process. But, along with its many prohibitions, society provides substitute gratifications. Ideologies, the locus of social values, help to discipline individuals. But they also provide a sense of security and identity; they give life meaning. Such shared meanings, Freud argues, are fundamental for psychological well-being. According to Freud, most individuals do not really want to be free. Freedom can be frightening. Indeed, later Freudians have explained the appeal of fascism as an "escape from freedom." Freud's concept of ideology is, then, also in some tension with democracy. Ideologies allow individuals simply to accept existing values and spare them the responsibility of creating their own.

Of the many other figures in the history of ideology, I discuss only one: Karl Mannheim.[10] His work is important because he states what Marx and Freud imply: Ideology is often a conservative force in history. Mannheim's basic distinction is between ideology and utopia. In his usage, an ideological perspective values the status quo and reinforces it by obscuring other alternatives. In contrast, a utopian perspective values what does not yet exist and promotes the changes necessary to create it. Utopias also obscure; they neglect ideological (and other) barriers to change. But, whereas ideologies restrict political activity, utopias encourage it. Again, democracy, which requires an active citizenry, is incompatible with ideology.

Popular intelligence to popular illusions—that summarizes the history of ideology. Tracy's democratic philosophy is followed by Napoleon's shadowy metaphysics, Marx's false consciousness, Freud's wish fulfillment, and Mannheim's social conformity. In these later philosophies Napoleon's pejorative usage persists, but assumes a new meaning. Their recurring theme is not the association of ideology and democracy, but the opposition between them. Today, it seems, democrats should not be ideologues. So, why study ideology?

## Why Study Ideology?

Ideologies are important in modern politics. This is the standard reason for studying them. Political scientists identify several functions of ideologies. The most important is political legitimation. Ideologies outline basic values by which politics should proceed. Another function is related to this. Ideologies help to socialize individuals, giving them a shared identity. Language is a major component of this identity. Ideologies provide shared meanings that facilitate communication between individuals. Ideologies also mobilize people, whether by class, group, nation, party, race, or sex. Unlike Mannheim, political scientists argue that, in performing these functions, ideologies can be sources of stability and instability, concord and conflict. According to Roy Macridis, "The dynamics of politics . . . lie in the ideas people develop."[11] Leon Baradat concludes, "A clear understanding of current ideologies is essential to anyone who hopes to grasp the political realities of our time."[12]

This is true. We live, for better or worse, in an ideological age. Ideologies are a crucial part of the study of modern politics. But there is another, more important, reason for studying ideologies: democracy. Political scientists' standard definitions of ideology include "a set of closely related beliefs, or ideas, or even attitudes, *characteristic of* a group or community" or "a value or belief system *accepted as* fact or truth by some group."[13] These definitions parallel the neutral—and neutralized—usage included in the *Oxford English Dictionary*. They also suggest that everyone has an ideology. That *you* have an ideology. But what is it? And why do you have it? Because it is "characteristic" or "accepted"? In a democracy, this answer is inadequate. What such definitions ignore is the political problem, the problem of democracy, raised by Tracy. Ideologies not only perform certain functions. They also raise claims to truth that require justification. In a democracy, these claims should not be ascribed to you or imposed on you. They can be justified only through discussion. By studying ideologies, you can discuss their various claims and decide among them.

Even democracy—to be true to itself—must be a topic of discussion. It is not enough to be a democrat. Democracy, as John Stuart Mill tells us, does not thrive on dogma. Instead, democrats must learn to think democratically. This means resurrecting ideology as Tracy's democratic philosophy, as the demonstration of ideas. Such demonstrations are more difficult today. Most people no longer share Tracy's confidence in sensory experience. Empiricism, along with metaphysics, has lost its power. Our evaluative standards come from ourselves—from our considered, collective judgment. Nevertheless, since ideas should not be ascribed to us or imposed on us, we can specify conditions for exercising that judgment.

Jürgen Habermas has attempted to do just that. As part of his theory of democratic discourse, he describes an ideal speech situation. It includes three conditions. First, anyone should be able to raise any issue for discussion. Second, during discussions, everyone should speak sincerely and seek understanding. Third, any decisions reached should apply equally to all. Habermas describes these conditions as "symmetrical relations in the distribution of assertion and dispute, revelation and concealment, prescription and conformity among the partners of communication."[14] They are, he argues, linguistic approximations of truth, freedom, and justice. Of course, there are many obstacles to overcome before actual democracies could even approximate these ideal conditions. Without equal educational opportunities and some economic security, individuals will have neither the ability nor the energy to debate basic political values. Still, Habermas's ideal speech situation illustrates the challenges involved in thinking democratically and in recovering a positive sense of ideology.

## Political Ideology and Political Theory

Unfortunately, political theorists often denigrate the study of political ideologies. It has become customary to distinguish political ideologies from political theories. According to Roy Macridis, "What separates theory or philosophy from ideology is that while the first two involve contemplation, organization of ideas, and whenever possible, demonstration, ideology incites people to action."[15] He adds that because of their collective, active nature "ideologies are inevitably highly simplified, and even distorted, versions of the original [philosophical] doctrines."[16]

David Ingersoll and Donald Matthews agree that "ideology is rather easily distinguished from traditional philosophy." They also suggest that "what is often called the Age of Ideology came about as a reaction to classical philosophic thought and its apparent lack of concern with processes by which change could be effected."[17] Again, the distinction from theory rests on the simplification and the action orientation associated with ideology. Lyman Tower Sargent further distinguishes between political ideology (group beliefs), political theory (scientific generalizations), and political philosophy (normative theory). He admonishes students that the first term, political ideology, "should never be used in place of either of the other two terms."[18]

With the theory/ideology distinction, these authors raise an important issue: the relationship between theory and practice. They suggest that ideologies play a mediating role between theory and practice; ideologies help translate ideas into action. To explain this translation process, Macridis examines the debt political ideologies owe to political theories. How, he asks, do ideas become ideologies? He answers that history involves a dialectic between ideas and needs. Only when both converge is an ideology created. Otherwise, "heartfelt demands arising from the social body may fail for the lack of ideas; and ideas may go begging for a long time for the lack of relevance to social needs."[19] He concludes that a philosophy becomes an ideology when it provides a framework for political action to meet social needs.

Still, too much can be made of the theory/ideology distinction. Some scholars recognize that political theory is seldom above the political fray. Often the best way to understand a theory is to see it in historical context. According to Richard Ashcraft, the dominance of philosophical methods in political theory has led to the denigration of political ideologies. Ashcraft notes that these methods divorce theory from history and politics. Political theorists "link historically-rooted political theory with ideology, and great political theory with trans-historical philosophy."[20] This, he argues, is a difficult distinction to sustain. It is also a self-serving one. It allows theorists to ignore the relationship between their ideas and their context. Their work, it implies, is above politics or outside history. For this reason, political theorists do not need to be self-critical. The distinction between political theory and political ideology can, then, be undemocratic. It allows theorists to avoid thinking democratically about their assumptions, indeed about the very distinction between great philosophical and minor ideological texts. This suggests another reason to study ideologies. Reading texts historically, for their political implications, promotes a democratic political theory. It encourages theorists to consider whose interests certain ideas serve.

## How to Study Ideology

I have suggested three reasons for studying political ideologies: to understand modern politics, to think democratically, and to democratize political theory. But how should ideologies be studied? What should you look for? How should you look for it?

Regarding the first question—what to look for—you already know to explore the historical context for these political ideologies. You should also examine three aspects of the ideologies themselves. Ideologies generally include: (1) a critique of existing society, (2) a vision of a better future, (3) a strategy for getting from here to there. All three are usually informed by an underlying concept of human nature. Try to organize your reading of these texts around these components.[21]

To understand ideologies, you also need to look at them a particular way. You should practice "connected knowing."[22] Most of us are (or have learned to be) "separate knowers." Knowledge for us involves separation from the subject—here, an ideology—and mastery over it. Our epistemological stance is to doubt, to criticize. As my students tell me, they read Karl Marx to understand how he is different and why he is wrong. Genuine understanding, however, involves intimacy and equality between self and subject. A "connected knower" cares about how others understand themselves and tries to see them in their own terms. "Connected knowers" are, for the purposes of understanding, believers. To study ideologies effectively, you need to approach them this way, to enter into their different world views. Does she mean, you ask, that I should become a Marxist? Yes. And a liberal, a conservative, a fascist, an anarchist, and a feminist. At least temporarily. "Separate knowing" is extremely important; you need to develop your critical capacities. But "separate knowing" is an inappropriate way to begin studying an ideology. You need to understand a subject—and that means suspending disbelief —before you can criticize it effectively. In the process, you might also find that it has something to offer.

Studying ideologies this way is risky business. It changes people. You become aware of your own assumptions and begin to assess them. But you should demand no less of yourself. Ignorance may be bliss—but an unexamined life is not worth living. Again, democracy does not thrive on dogma.

## What Ideologies to Study

The ideologies represented here were chosen for two reasons. First, all are important in modern politics. The selections for each ideology cover both its historical origins and its contemporary manifestations. Second, these ideologies represent a range of political beliefs. As you read, disagreements will emerge. For example, conservatives and socialists will attack liberals' concept of individual freedom. Anarchists will question liberal democracy and proletarian dictatorship because both legitimate state power. Fascists will accuse liberals and socialists of denigrating the state. Feminists will suggest that the other ideologies, with the possible exception of anarchism, exclude the concerns of women and minorities. These are only a few of the differences you will discover. By studying these ideologies, by exploring their assumptions and comparing their positions, you will begin to understand political alternatives and be able to choose among them. You will learn to think democratically.

## Notes

1. *Oxford English Dictionary*, 1933, s.v. "Ideology."

2. John Thompson, *Studies in the Theory of Ideology* (Berkeley: University of California Press, 1984), 1.

3. Antoine Destutt de Tracy, "Mémoire sur la Faculté de penser," MIN (*Mémoires de l'Institut national. Classe des Sciences morales et politiques*, 5 vols. [Paris: 1798–1804]), 1:323, quoted in Emmet Kennedy, " 'Ideology' from Destutt de Tracy to Marx," *Journal of the History of Ideas* 40 (July-September 1979): 353–68, quote on 354–55. For a more extensive discussion of Tracy, see Emmet Kennedy, *A Philosophe in the Age of Revolution: Destutt de Tracy and the Origins of Ideology* (Philadelphia: American Philosophical Society, 1978).

4. Biran to Abbe Feletz, 11 thermidor X [30 July 1802], *Œuvres de Maine de Biran*, VI, 140, quoted in Kennedy, " 'Ideology,' " 357–58.

5. Quoted in Kennedy, " 'Ideology,' " 358.

6. Napoleon, "Reponse a l'adresse du Conseil d'Etat," in *Moniteur* (21 decembre 1812), 1408, quoted in Kennedy, " 'Ideology,' " 360.

7. Kennedy, " 'Ideology,' " 364.

8. Karl Marx and Friedrich Engels, *The German Ideology*, ed. C.J. Arthur (New York: International Publishers, 1977), 64.

9. Sigmund Freud, *The Future of an Illusion*, trans. W.D. Robson-Scott (New York: Liveright, 1955), 59. My remarks here parallel those of Mostafa Rejai, s.v. "Ideology" in the *Dictionary of the History of Ideas*, vol. 2, 1973.

10. Karl Mannheim, *Ideology and Utopia*, trans. Louis Wirth and Edward Shils (London: Routledge and Kegan Paul, 1948).

11. Roy Macridis, *Contemporary Political Ideologies*, 3d ed. (Boston: Little, Brown, 1986), 3.

12. Leon P. Baradat, *Political Ideologies: Their Origins and Impact*, 3d ed. (Englewood Cliffs, N.J.: Prentice-Hall, 1988), xii.

13. John Plamenatz, *Ideology* (New York: Praeger, 1970), 15; and Lyman Tower Sargent, *Contemporary Political Ideologies,* 7th ed. (Chicago: Dorsey Press, 1987), 2. Italics added.

14. Jürgen Habermas, "Towards a Theory of Communicative Competence," *Inquiry* 13 (1970): 371.

15. Macridis, *Contemporary Political Ideologies,* 3.

16. Ibid.

17. David Ingersoll and Donald Matthews, *The Philosophic Roots of Modern Ideology: Liberalism, Communism, Fascism* (Englewood Cliffs, N.J.: Prentice-Hall, 1986), 7.

18. Sargent, *Contemporary Political Ideologies,* 11. Sargent also acknowledges that many use the latter two terms interchangeably, as I do.

19. Macridis, *Contemporary Political Ideologies,* 3.

20. Richard Ashcraft, "Political Theory and the Problem of Ideology," *Journal of Politics* 42 (August 1980): 687–705.

21. Alison Jaggar, *Feminist Politics and Human Nature* (Totowa, N.J.: Rowman and Allenheld, 1983), 16.

22. For this distinction, see Mary Field Belenky et al., *Women's Ways of Knowing* (New York: Basic Books, 1986), chap. 6. These authors argue that "connected knowing" is more common among women.

*Part One*

# Liberalism and Democracy

iberal democracy. Liberalism *and* democracy; liberalism *or* democracy. How, if at all, do liberalism and democracy fit together? Most Americans are liberals, at least philosophically, and for them this is a difficult question. To answer it, they need to distance themselves, to place liberalism in historical context. Isaac Kramnick, the last author included in this part, does this. He distinguishes between two faces of liberalism. The first is progressive: liberalism against an old order. The second is regressive: liberalism as a new order. Liberal principles—individual freedom and limited government—remain the same. Depending on the context, however, their implications are dramatically different.

John Locke's *Treatise of Civil Government* represents progressive liberalism. Locke (1632–1704) lived during the Glorious Revolution, when the English Parliament deposed James II and replaced him with William of Orange. In exchange for the crown, William accepted parliamentary government and a bill of rights. Although parts of it may have been written earlier, scholars agree that Locke's *Treatise of Civil Government* is a defense of the Glorious Revolution.[1] In it he rejects hierarchical notions of society and argues that individ-

I

uals are born free and equal in a state of nature. That is, "a state of liberty, yet it is not a state of license." Individuals are free, but not to do whatever they please. A law of nature exists that "being all equal and independent, no one ought to harm another in his life, health, liberty, or possessions." But not everyone obeys this law. Conflicts frequently arise, and life is very insecure. Ultimately, the state of nature is indistinguishable from a state of war. For this reason, people form governments to protect their rights to life, liberty, and especially property.

Because Lockean government is limited to protecting those rights, it fits well with certain economic relations, for example, the free exchange of private property. Locke's individuals own themselves and hence their labor and its products. In the state of nature, everyone is free to accumulate property. But everyone does not accumulate an equal amount. In chapter 5 of his *Treatise,* "Of Property," Locke explains how accumulation eventually re-creates a hierarchy in which some labor for others.[2] This hierarchy is a meritocracy and not an aristocracy. Here, status is achieved and not ascribed. According to Locke, equal opportunity justifies unequal outcomes. As he puts it, God gave the world "to the use of the industrious and rational . . . not to the fancy or covetousness of the quarrelsome and contentious." Locke concludes that those with more property have proven themselves more rational and should also possess more rights. Women, slaves, and nonpropertied men (laborers) are neither free nor equal. Locke's sovereign people, those who expressly consent to government, are white, wealthy men. He is, then, less progressive than he initially seems.

At its origins, liberalism is far from democratic. Yet the principle of individual freedom required liberals to extend rights to those who demanded them. Gradually, liberalism has been democratized.[3] Democracy is the problem confronting John Stuart Mill (1806–73). The English Reform Acts of 1832 and 1867 expanded the suffrage, although only to more white males. Writing in the wake of these acts, Mill reveals the regressive face of liberalism, its tensions with democracy. His *On Liberty* is the classic statement of liberal toleration. In the letters on toleration, Locke had argued that religious freedom was an individual right. But Mill's defense of liberty is different. He makes a utilitarian, not a rights-based, argument for liberty. Fearing the tendency of democracy to majority tyranny, he defends liberty because it improves society. Mill says that "the only unfailing and permanent source of improvement is liberty." His basic principle, that "the sole end for which mankind are warranted, individually or collectively, in interfering with the liberty of action of any of their number, is self-protection," protects individuals from the masses.

In *Considerations on Representative Government,* Mill confronts democracy even more directly. He establishes two criteria for good government: It must simultaneously work to improve people and take people as they are.

Representative democracy, he argues, best approximates these criteria. Majority rule improves citizens and minority rights restrain them. Participation fosters social sentiments and political awareness among citizens. Mill's critique of direct democracy reveals why restraint is also necessary. Direct democracies, where the majority (i.e., the laboring class) rules, are prone to collective mediocrity and class conflict. Representation, to anticipate Madison, "refines and enlarges the public views." But representation alone is inadequate. Mill also distinguishes true from false democracy. In false democracies, the majority effectively disenfranchises the minority by outvoting it in every district. In true democracies, proportional representation guarantees some minority seats. Plural voting, another of Mill's schemes, gives the wise and wealthy additional influence.

For Mill, however, the tensions between liberalism and democracy are temporary. Writing with Harriet Taylor, late in life, he described himself as a short-term conservative, but a long-term socialist: "We were now much less democrats than I had been because so long as education continues to be so wretchedly imperfect, we dreaded the ignorance and especially the selfishness and brutality of the masses; but our ideal of ultimate improvement went far beyond Democracy, and would class us decidedly under the designation of Socialists."[4] When the people are ready, they should rule.

America's founding fathers were also acutely aware of the tensions between liberalism and democracy. Jeremy Belknap, a New England clergyman, expressed their sentiments well: "Let it stand as a principle that government originates from the people; but let the people be taught . . . that they are not able to govern themselves."[5] *The Federalist Papers*, published in New York during the ratification debates, present the Constitution as a liberal solution to democratic problems.

According to Madison, two difficulties arise in framing a government: "You must first enable the government to control the governed; and in the next place oblige it to control itself." *Federalist* no. 10 addresses the first difficulty: the vulnerability of democracy to the violence of factions. Minority factions pose little problem, since they are easily outvoted. Majority factions are a different story. Pure democracies have no cure for them. But representation allows a larger territory, making it unlikely that a majority will exist and organize. Federalism also provides the appropriate distance between representatives and constituents. State legislatures are tied to local issues; national government is freed from them. Together, representation and federalism ensure that "a coalition of a majority of the whole society could seldom take place on any other principles than those of justice and the general good." The second difficulty Madison identifies—"to oblige the government to control itself" —remains. According to Madison, the populace cannot be counted on to restrain government. The auxiliary precautions discussed in *Federalist* no. 51 —separation of powers, checks and balances—are also required. They limit government by pitting "ambition against ambition," thereby "supplying, by opposite and rival interests, the defect of better motives."

*The Federalist Papers* present the Constitution as a balance between liberalism and democracy. Government is limited by minority rights and legitimated by majority rule. Has the balance worked? Some critics argue that it has worked too well, creating an inefficient government and an apathetic citizenry. Others question liberals' confidence that competing interests create the common good.

Milton Friedman, the next author, is not among them. He explains the logic that links liberalism and capitalism: "The kind of economic organization that provides economic freedom directly, namely, competitive capitalism, also promotes political freedom because it separates economic power from political power and in this way enables the one to offset the other."[6] He praises markets for coordinating the economy and minimizing government control. Government still must enforce the rules of the game, prevent nontechnical monopolies, guard against neighborhood effects, and protect the helpless. But that is all. Anything more undermines economic and, with it, political freedom.

But are economics and politics so separate? Yes and no. After all, liberal government is limited in order to protect capitalism. (Friedman says to ensure optimality and provide incentives.) Not surprisingly, business has a privileged position in policy decisions and electoral politics.[7] Friedman recognizes this. He argues that government should cut off business and labor, rich and poor. His list of unjustifiable government interventions ranges from paying agricultural subsidies to establishing minimum wages to creating national parks. What he does not discuss are the disadvantages of markets (e.g., instability and insecurity), which prompted these programs. He simply assumes that all have an equal opportunity to succeed.

Do they? In the final selection, "Equal Opportunity and the Race of Life," Isaac Kramnick addresses this question. According to Kramnick, the freedom to compete economically parallels the freedom to participate politically. Here, too, a once progressive liberalism is now regressive. Kramnick characterizes the transformation: "A doctrine originally designed to serve the class interests of the talented 'have-nots' against the talented 'haves' now pits the talented 'haves' against the allegedly untalented 'have-nots.'" Whereas Locke attacked an old elite, Friedman defends a new one. For liberals, this is a problem. They see life as a race. Some win, some lose. Some, however, never start. Or they start late. Or they carry extra weight. Individuals are not born free and equal in a state of nature. They are born with the advantages or disadvantages of class, race, and gender. Yet only equal opportunity can justify unequal outcomes. If the race is rigged, it is unfair. Liberal principles require government action to make it fair. But they also require limited government. In short, welfare-state liberalism conflicts with laissez-faire liberalism. Both are right, and both are wrong. Each, Kramnick argues, articulates a face of liberalism.

What is to be done? Liberals could simply conclude that life is unfair. Perhaps liberalism, despite these tensions, is the best option. You may ultimately conclude that. Right now, however, it is premature. What if life is not a race? Kramnick asks, "What would a new world view look like?" The other ideologies offer answers to that question.

## Notes

1. John Locke, *Two Treatises of Government,* ed. Peter Laslett (New York: Mentor Books, 1965), introduction.

2. For a detailed discussion of this interpretation of Locke, see C.B. MacPherson, *The Political Theory of Possessive Individualism: Hobbes to Locke* (Oxford: Clarendon Press, 1962).

3. C.B. MacPherson, *The Real World of Democracy* (Oxford: Clarendon Press, 1966), chap. 1.

4. Quoted in Sanford A. Lakoff, *Equality in Political Philosophy* (Cambridge, Mass.: Harvard University Press, 1964), 130.

5. Quoted in Richard Hofstadter, *The American Political Tradition* (New York: Vintage Books, 1948), 7.

6. Friedman also notes the historical connection, i.e., all liberal-democratic countries have capitalist economies. (The obverse is not true.)

7. Charles Lindblom, *Politics and Markets* (New York: Basic Books, 1977).

# JOHN LOCKE

## *Treatise of Civil Government*

John Locke (1632–1704) lived during the Glorious Revolution of 1688 by which the English Parliament deposed King James II and replaced him with William of Orange. In the *Treatise of Civil Government* Locke defends the Glorious Revolution and the principles of individual rights and limited government it established.

## Chapter 1

3. Political power, then, I take to be a right of making laws, with penalties of death, and consequently all less penalties for the regulating and preserving of property, and of employing the force of the community in the execution of such laws, and in the defence of the commonwealth from foreign injury, and all this only for the public good.

## Chapter 2
## Of the State of Nature

4. To understand political power aright, and derive it from its original, we must consider what estate all men are naturally in, and that is, a state of perfect freedom to order their actions, and dispose of their possessions and persons as they think fit, within the bounds of the law of Nature, without asking leave or depending upon the will of any other man.

A state also of equality, wherein all the power and jurisdiction is reciprocal, no one having more than another, there being nothing more evident than that creatures of the same species and rank, promiscuously born to all the same advantages of Nature, and the use of the same facilities, should also be equal one amongst another, without subordination or subjection, unless the lord and master of them all should, by any manifest declaration of his will, set one above another, and confer on him, by an evident and clear appointment, an undoubted right to dominion and sovereignty.

5. This equality of men by Nature, the judicious Hooker looks upon as so evident in itself, and beyond all question, that he makes it the foundation of that obligation to mutual love amongst men on which he builds the duties they owe one another, and from whence he derives the great maxims of justice and charity. His words are:

"The like natural inducement hath brought men to know that it is no less their duty to love others than themselves, for seeing those things which are equal, must needs all have one measure; if I cannot but wish to receive good, even as much at every man's hands, as any man can wish unto his own soul, how should I look to have any part of my desire herein satisfied, unless myself be careful to satisfy the like desire, which is undoubtedly in other men weak, being of one and the same nature: to have anything offered them repugnant to this desire must needs, in all respects, grieve them as much as me; so that if I do harm, I must look to suffer, there being no reason that others should show greater measure of love to me than they have by me showed unto them; my desire, therefore, to be loved of my equals in Nature, as much as possible may be, imposeth upon me a natural duty of bearing to themward fully the like affection. From which relation of equality between ourselves and them that are as ourselves, what several rules and canons natural reason hath drawn for direction of life no man is ignorant." (*Eccl. Pol.* i.)

6. But though this be a state of liberty, yet it is not a state of licence; though man in that state have an uncontrollable liberty to dispose of his person or possessions, yet he has not liberty to destroy himself, or so much as any creature in his possession, but where some nobler use than its bare preservation calls for it. The state of Nature has a law of Nature to govern it, which obliges every one, and reason, which is that law, teaches all mankind who will but consult it, that being all equal and independent, no one ought to harm another in his life, health, liberty or possessions; for men being all the workmanship of one omnipotent and infinitely wise Maker; all the servants of one sovereign Master, sent into the world by His order and about His business; they are His property, whose workmanship they are made to last during His, not one another's pleasure. And, being furnished with like faculties, sharing all in one community of Nature, there cannot be supposed any such subordination among us that may authorise us to destroy one another, as if we were made for one another's uses, as the inferior ranks of creatures are for ours. Every one as he is bound to preserve himself, and not to quit his station wilfully, so by the like reason, when his own preservation comes not in competition, ought he as much as he can to preserve the rest of mankind, and not unless it be to do justice on an offender, take away or impair the life, or what tends to the preservation of the life, the liberty, health, limb, or goods of another.

7. And that all men may be restrained from invading others' rights, and from doing hurt to one another, and the law of Nature be observed, which

willeth the peace and preservation of all mankind, the execution of the law of Nature is in that state put into every man's hands, whereby every one has a right to punish the transgressors of that law to such a degree as may hinder its violation. For the law of Nature would, as all other laws that concern men in this world, be in vain if there were nobody that in the state of Nature had a power to execute that law, and thereby preserve the innocent and restrain offenders; and if any one in the state of Nature may punish another for any evil he has done, every one may do so. For in that state of perfect equality, where naturally there is no superiority or jurisdiction of one over another, what any may do in prosecution of that law, every one must needs have a right to do. . . .

## Chapter 3
## Of the State of War

16. The state of war is a state of enmity and destruction; and therefore declaring by word or action, not a passionate and hasty, but sedate, settled design upon another man's life puts him in a state of war with him against whom he has declared such an intention, and so has exposed his life to the other's power to be taken away by him, or any one that joins with him in his defence, and espouses his quarrel; it being reasonable and just I should have a right to destroy that which threatens me with destruction; for by the fundamental law of Nature, man being to be preserved as much as possible, when all cannot be preserved, the safety of the innocent is to be preferred, and one may destroy a man who makes war upon him, or has discovered an enmity to his being, for the same reason that he may kill a wolf or a lion, because they are not under the ties of the common law of reason, have no other rule but that of force and violence, and so may be treated as a beast of prey, those dangerous and noxious creatures that will be sure to destroy him whenever he falls into their power.

17. And hence it is that he who attempts to get another man into his absolute power does thereby put himself into a state of war with him; it being to be understood as a declaration of a design upon his life. For I have reason to conclude that he who would get me into his power without my consent would use me as he pleased when he had got me there, and destroy me too when he had a fancy to it; for nobody can desire to have me in his absolute power unless it be to compel me by force to that which is against the right of my freedom—*i.e.* make me a slave. To be free from such force is the only security of my preservation, and reason bids me look on him as an enemy to my preservation who would take away that freedom which is the fence to it; so that he who makes an attempt to enslave me thereby puts himself into a state of war with me. He that in the state of Nature would take away the freedom that be-

longs to any one in that state must necessarily be supposed to have a design to take away everything else, that freedom being the foundation of all the rest; as he that in the state of society would take away the freedom belonging to those of that society or commonwealth must be supposed to design to take away from them everything else, and so be looked on as in a state of war.

18. This make it lawful for a man to kill a thief who has not in the least hurt him, nor declared any design upon his life, any farther than by the use of force, so to get him in his power as to take away his money, or what he pleases, from him; because using force, where he has no right to get me into his power, let his pretence be what it will, I have no reason to suppose that he who would take away my liberty would not, when he had me in his power, take away everything else. And, therefore, it is lawful for me to treat him as one who has put himself into a state of war with me—i.e., kill him if I can; for to that hazard does he justly expose himself whoever introduces a state of war, and is aggressor in it.

19. And here we have the plain difference between the state of Nature and the state of war, which however some men have confounded,[1] are as far distant as a state of peace, goodwill, mutual assistance, and preservation; and a state of enmity, malice, violence and mutual destruction are one from another. Men living together according to reason without a common superior on earth, with authority to judge between them, is properly the state of Nature. But force, or a declared design of force upon the person of another, where there is no common superior on earth to appeal to for relief, is the state of war; and it is the want of such an appeal gives a man the right of war even against an aggressor, though he be in society and a fellow-subject. Thus, a thief whom I cannot harm, but by appeal to the law, for having stolen all that I am worth, I may kill when he sets on me to rob me but of my horse or coat, because the law, which was made for my preservation, where it cannot interpose to secure my life from present force, which if lost is capable of no reparation, permits me my own defence and the right of war, a liberty to kill the aggressor, because the aggressor allows not time to appeal to our common judge, nor the decision of the law, for remedy in a case where the mischief may be irreparable. Want of a common judge with authority puts all men in a state of Nature; force without right upon a man's person makes a state of war both where there is, and is not, a common judge.

20. But when the actual force is over, the state of war ceases between those that are in society and are equally on both sides subject to the judge; and, therefore, in such controversies, where the question is put, "Who shall be judge?" it cannot be meant who shall decide the controversy; every one knows what Jephtha here tells us, that "the Lord the Judge" shall judge. Where there is no judge on earth the appeal lies to God in Heaven. That question then cannot mean who shall judge, whether another hath put himself in a state of war with me, and whether I may, as Jephtha did, appeal to Heaven in it? Of

that I myself can only judge in my own conscience, as I will answer it at the great day to the Supreme Judge of all men.

# Chapter 5
## Of Property

26. God, who hath given the world to men in common, hath also given them reason to make use of it to the best advantage of life and convenience. The earth and all that is therein is given to men for the support and comfort of their being. And though all the fruits it naturally produces, and beasts it feeds, belong to mankind in common, as they are produced by the spontaneous hand of Nature, and nobody has originally a private dominion exclusive of the rest of mankind in any of them, as they are thus in their natural state, yet being given for the use of men, there must of necessity be a means to appropriate them some way or other before they can be of any use, or at all beneficial, to any particular men. The fruit or venison which nourishes the wild Indian, who knows no enclosure, and is still a tenant in common, must be his, and so his—i.e., a part of him, that another can no longer have any right to it before it can do him any good for the support of his life.

27. Though the earth and all inferior creatures be common to all men, yet every man has a "property" in his own "person." This nobody has any right to but himself. The "labour" of his body and the "work" of his hands, we may say, are properly his. Whatsoever, then, he removes out of the state that Nature hath provided and left it in, he hath mixed his labour with it, and joined to it something that is his own, and thereby makes it his property. It being by him removed from the common state Nature placed it in, it hath by this labour something annexed to it that excludes the common right of other men. For this "labour" being the unquestionable property of the labourer, no man but he can have a right to what that is once joined to, at least where there is enough, and as good left in common for others.

28. He that is nourished by the acorns he picked up under an oak, or the apples he gathered from the trees in the wood, has certainly appropriated them to himself. Nobody can deny but the nourishment is his. I ask, then, when did they begin to be his? when he digested? or when he ate? or when he boiled? or when he brought them home? or when he picked them up? And it is plain, if the first gathering made them not his, nothing else could. That labour put a distinction between them and common. That added something to them more than Nature, the common mother of all, had done, and so they became his private right. And will any one say he had no right to those acorns or apples he thus appropriated because he had not the consent of all mankind to make them his? Was it a robbery thus to assume to himself what belonged to all in common? If such a consent as that was necessary, man had starved, not-

withstanding the plenty God had given him. We see in commons, which remain so by compact, that it is the taking any part of what is common, and
removing it out of the state Nature leaves it in, which begins the property,
without which the common is of no use. And the taking of this or that part
does not depend on the express consent of all the commoners. Thus, the grass
my horse has bit, the turfs my servant has cut, and the ore I have digged in any
place, where I have a right to them in common with others, become my property without the assignation or consent of anybody. The labour that was mine,
removing them out of that common state they were in, hath fixed my property
in them.

29. By making an explicit consent of every commoner necessary to any
one's appropriating to himself any part of what is given in common. Children
or servants could not cut the meat which their father or master had provided
for them in common without assigning to every one his peculiar part. Though
the water running in the fountain be every one's, yet who can doubt but that
in the pitcher is his only who drew it out? His labour hath taken it out of the
hands of Nature where it was common, and belonged equally to all her children, and hath thereby appropriated it to himself. . . .

31. It will, perhaps, be objected to this, that if gathering the acorns or
other fruits of the earth, etc., makes a right to them, then any one may engross
as much as he will. To which I answer, Not so. The same law of Nature that
does by this means give us property, does also bound that property too. "God
has given us all things richly." Is the voice of reason confirmed by inspiration?
But how far has He given it us—"to enjoy"? As much as any one can make use
of to any advantage of life before it spoils, so much he may by his labor fix a
property in. Whatever is beyond this is more than his share, and belongs to
others. Nothing was made by God for man to spoil or destroy. And thus considering the plenty of natural provisions there was a long time in the world,
and the few spenders, and to how small a part of that provision the industry of
one man could extend itself and engross it to the prejudice of others, especially
keeping within the bounds set by reason of what might serve for his use, there
could be then little room for quarrels or contentions about property so established.

32. But the chief matter of property being now not the fruits of the earth
and the beasts that subsist on it, but the earth itself, as that which takes in and
carries with it all the rest, I think it is plain that property in that too is acquired as the former. As much land as a man tills, plants, improves, cultivates,
and can use the product of, so much is his property. He by his labour does, as
it were, enclose it from the common. Nor will it invalidate his right to say
everybody else has an equal title to it, and therefore he cannot appropriate, he
cannot enclose, without the consent of all his fellow-commoners, all mankind.
God, when He gave the world in common to all mankind, commanded man
also to labor, and the penury of his condition required it of him. God and his

reason commanded him to subdue the earth—i.e., improve it for the benefit of life and therein lay out something upon it that was his own, his labour. He that, in obedience to this command of God, subdued, tilled, and sowed any part of it, thereby annexed to it something that was his property, which another had no title to, nor could without injury take from him.

33. Nor was this appropriation of any parcel of land, by improving it, any prejudice to any other man, since there was still enough and as good left, and more than the yet unprovided could use. So that, in effect, there was never the less left for others because of his enclosure for himself. For he that leaves as much as another can make use of does as good as take nothing at all. Nobody could think himself injured by the drinking of another man, though he took a good draught, who had a whole river of the same water left him to quench his thirst. And the case of land and water, where there is enough of both, is perfectly the same.

34. God gave the world to men in common, but since He gave it them for their benefit and the greatest conveniencies of life they were capable to draw from it, it cannot be supposed He meant it should always remain common and uncultivated. He gave it to the use of the industrious and rational (and labour was to be his title to it); not to the fancy or covetousness of the quarrelsome and contentious. He that had as good left for his improvement as was already taken up needed not complain, ought not to meddle with what was already improved by another's labour; if he did it is plain he desired the benefit of another's pains, which he had no right to, and not the ground which God had given him, in common with others, to labour on, and whereof there was as good left as that already possessed, and more than he knew what to do with, or his industry could reach to. . . .

36. The measure of property Nature well set, by the extent of men's labour and the conveniency of life. No man's labour could subdue or appropriate all, nor could his enjoyment consume more than a small part; so that it was impossible for any man, this way, to entrench upon the right of another or acquire to himself a property to the prejudice of his neighbour, who would still have room for as good and as large a possession (after the other had taken out his) as before it was appropriated. Which measure did confine every man's possession to a very moderate proportion, and such as he might appropriate to himself without injury to anybody in the first ages of the world, when men were more in danger to be lost, by wandering from their company, in the then vast wilderness of the earth then to be straitened for want of room to plant in. And the same measure may be allowed still, without prejudice to anybody, full as the world seems. For, supposing a man or family, in the state they were at first, peopling the world by the children of Adam or Noah, let him plant in some inland vacant places of America. We shall find that the possessions he could make himself, upon the measures we have given, would not be very large, nor, even to this day, prejudice the rest of mankind or give them reason

to complain or think themselves injured by this man's encroachment, though the race of men have now spread themselves to all the corners of the world, and do infinitely exceed the small number was at the beginning. Nay, the extent of ground is of so little value without labour that I have heard it affirmed that in Spain itself a man may be permitted to plough, sow, and reap, without being disturbed, upon land he has no other title to, but only his making use of it. But, on the contrary, the inhabitants think themselves beholden to him who, by his industry on neglected, and consequently waste land, has increased the stock of corn, which they wanted. But be this as it will, which I lay no stress on, this I dare boldly affirm, that the same rule of propriety—viz., that every man should have as much as he could make use of, would hold still in the world, without straitening anybody, since there is land enough in the world to suffice double the inhabitants, had not the invention of money, and the tacit agreement of men to put a value on it, introduced (by consent) larger possession and aright to them; which, how it has done, I shall by and by show more at large.

37. This is certain, that in the beginning, before the desire of having more than men needed had altered the intrinsic value of things, which depends only on their usefulness to the life of man, or had agreed that a little piece of yellow metal, which would keep without wasting or decay, should be worth a great piece of flesh or a whole heap of corn, though men had a right to appropriate by their labour, each one to himself, as much of the things of Nature as he could use, yet this could not be much, nor to the prejudice of others, where the same plenty was still left, to those who would use the same industry.

Before the appropriation of land, he who gathered as much of the wild fruit, killed, caught, or tamed as many of the beasts as he could—he that so employed his pains about any of the spontaneous products of Nature as any way to alter them from the state Nature put them in, by placing any of his labour on them, did thereby acquire a propriety in them; but if they perished in his possession without their due use—if the fruits rotted or the venison putrefied before he could spend it, he offended against the common law of Nature, and was liable to be punished: he invaded his neighbour's share, for he had no right farther than his use called for any of them, and they might serve to afford him conveniencies of life.

38. The same measures governed the possession of land, too. Whatsoever he tilled and reaped, laid up and made use of before it spoiled, that was his peculiar right; whatsoever he enclosed, and could feed and make use of, the cattle and product was also his. But if either the grass of his enclosure rotted on the ground, or the fruit of his planting perished without gathering and laying up, this part of the earth, notwithstanding his enclosure, was still to be looked on as waste, and might be the possession of any other. Thus, at the beginning, Cain might take as much ground as he could till and make it his own

land, and yet leave enough to Abel's sheep to feed on: a few acres would serve for both their possessions. But as families increased and industry enlarged their stocks, their possessions enlarged with the need of them; but yet it was commonly without any fixed property in the ground they made use of till they incorporated, settled themselves together, and built cities, and then, by consent, they came in time to set out the bounds of their distinct territories and agree on limits between them and their neighbours, and by laws within themselves settled the properties of those of the same society. For we see that in that part of the world which was first inhabited, and therefore like to be best peopled, even as low down as Abraham's time, they wandered with their flocks and their herds, which was their substance, freely up and down—and this Abraham did in a country where he was a stranger; whence it is plain that, at least, a great part of the land lay in common, that the inhabitants valued it not, nor claimed property in any more than they made use of; but when there was not room enough in the same place for their herds to feed together, they, by consent, as Abraham and Lot did (Gen. xiii. 5), separated and enlarged their pasture where it best liked them. And for the same reason, Esau went from his father and his brother, and planted in Mount Seir (Gen. xxxvi. 6). . . .

40. Nor is it so strange as, perhaps, before consideration, it may appear, that the property of labour should be able to overbalance the community of land, for it is labour indeed that puts the difference of value on everything; and let any one consider what the difference is between an acre of land planted with tobacco or sugar, sown with wheat or barley, and an acre of the same land lying in common without any husbandry upon it, and he will find that the improvement of labour makes the far greater part of the value. I think it will be but a very modest computation to say, that of the products of the earth useful to the life of man, nine-tenths are the effects of labour. Nay, if we will rightly estimate things as they come to our use, and cast up the several expenses about them—what in them is purely owing to Nature and what to labour—we shall find that in most of them ninety-nine hundredths are wholly to be put on the account of labour.

41. There cannot be a clearer demonstration of anything than several nations of the Americans are of this, who are rich in land and poor in all the comforts of life; whom Nature, having furnished as liberally as any other people with the materials of plenty—i.e., a fruitful soil, apt to produce in abundance what might serve for food, raiment, and delight; yet, for want of improving it by labour, have not one hundredth part of the conveniencies we enjoy, and a king of a large and fruitful territory there feeds, lodges, and is clad worse than a day labourer in England. . . .

43. An acre of land that bears here twenty bushels of wheat, and another in America, which, with the same husbandry, would do the like, are, without doubt, of the same natural, intrinsic value. But yet the benefit mankind re-

ceives from one in a year is worth five pounds, and the other possibly not worth a penny; if all the profit an Indian received from it were to be valued and sold here, at least I may truly say, not one thousandth. It is labour, then, which puts the greatest part of value upon land, without which it would scarcely be worth anything; it is to that we owe the greatest part of all its useful products; for all that the straw, bran, bread, of that acre of wheat, is more worth than the product of an acre of as good land which lies waste is all the effect of labour. For it is not barely the ploughman's pains, the reaper's and thresher's toil, and the baker's sweat, is to be counted into the bread we eat; the labour of those who broke the oxen, who digged and wrought the iron and stones, who felled and framed the timber employed about the plough, mill, oven, or any other utensils, which are a vast number, requisite to this corn, from its sowing to its being made bread, must all be charged on the account of labour, and received as an effect of that; Nature and the earth furnished only the almost worthless materials as in themselves. It would be a strange catalogue of things that industry provided and made use of about every loaf of bread before it came to our use if we could trace them; iron, wood, leather, bark, timber, stone, bricks, coals, lime, cloth, dyeing-drugs, pitch, tar, masts, ropes, and all the materials made use of in the ship that brought any of the commodities made use of by any of the workmen, to any part of the work, all which it would be almost impossible, at least too long, to reckon up. . . .

46. The greatest part of things really useful to the life of man, and such as the necessity of substituting made the first commoners of the world look after—as it doth the Americans now—are generally things of short duration, such as—if they are not consumed by use—will decay and perish of themselves. Gold, silver, and diamonds are things that fancy or agreement hath put the value on, more than real use and the necessary support of life. Now of those good things which Nature hath provided in common, every one hath a right (as hath been said) to as much as he could use, and had a property in all he could effect with his labour; all that his industry could extend to, to alter from the state Nature had put it in, was his. He that gathered a hundred bushels of acorns or apples had thereby a property in them; they were his goods as soon as gathered. He was only to look that he used them before they spoiled, else he took more than his share, and robbed others. And, indeed, it was a foolish thing, as well as dishonest, to hoard up more than he could make use of. If he gave away a part to anybody else, so that it perished not uselessly in his possession, these he also made use of. And if he also bartered away plums that would have rotted in a week, for nuts that would last good for his eating a whole year, he did not injury; he wasted not the common stock; destroyed no part of the portion of goods that belonged to others, so long as nothing perished uselessly in his hands. Again, if he would give his nuts for a piece of metal, pleased with its colour, or exchange his sheep for shells, or wool for a sparkling pebble or a diamond, and keep those by him all his life, he invaded

not the right of others; he might heap up as much of these durable things as he pleased; the exceeding of the bounds of his just property not lying in the largeness of his possessions, but the perishing of anything uselessly in it.

47. And thus came in the use of money; some lasting thing that men might keep without spoiling, and that, by mutual consent, men would take in exchange for the truly useful but perishable supports of life.

48. And as different degrees of industry were apt to give men possessions in different proportions, so this invention of money gave them the opportunity to continue and enlarge them. For supposing an island, separate from all possible commerce with the rest of the world, wherein there were but a hundred families, but there were sheep, horses, and cows, with other useful animals, wholesome fruits, and land enough for corn for a hundred thousand times as many, but nothing in the island, either because of its commonness or perishableness, fit to supply the place of money. What reason could any one have there to enlarge his possessions beyond the use of his family, and a plentiful supply to its consumption, either in what their own industry produced, or they could barter for like perishable, useful commodities with others? Where there is not something both lasting and scarce, and so valuable to be hoarded up, there men will not be apt to enlarge their possessions of land, were it never so rich, never so free for them to take. For I ask, what would a man value ten thousand or an hundred thousand acres of excellent land, ready cultivated and well stocked, too, with cattle, in the middle of the inland parts of America, where he had no hopes of commerce with other parts of the world, to draw money to him by the sale of the product? It would not be worth the enclosing, and we should see him give up again to the wild common of Nature whatever was more than would supply the conveniences of life, to be had there for him and his family.

49. Thus, in the beginning, all world was America, and more so than that is now; for no such thing as money was anywhere known. Find out something that hath the use and value of money amongst his neighbours, you shall see the same man will begin presently to enlarge his possessions.

50. But since gold and silver, being little useful to the life of man, in proportion to food, raiment, and carriage, has its value only from the consent of men—whereof labour yet makes in great part the measure—it is plain that the consent of men have agreed to a disproportionate and unequal possession of the earth—I mean out of the bounds of society and compact; for in governments the laws regulate it; they having, by consent, found out and agreed in a way how a man may, rightfully and without injury, possess more than he himself can make use of by receiving gold and silver, which may continue long in a man's possession without decaying for the overplus, and agreeing those metals should have a value.

51. And thus, I think, it is very easy to conceive, without any difficulty, how labour could at first begin a title of property in the common things of

Nature, and how the spending it upon our uses bounded it; so that there could then be no reason of quarrelling about title, nor any doubt about the largeness of possession it gave. Right and conveniency went together. For as a man had a right to all he could employ his labour upon, so he had no temptation to labour for more than he could make use of. This left no room for controversy about the title, nor for encroachment on the right of others. What portion a man carved to himself was easily seen; and it was useless, as well as dishonest, to carve himself too much, or take more than he needed.

## Note

1. [Locke's reference here is probably to Hobbes' concept of the state of nature as being identical with the state of war.]

# JOHN STUART MILL

## On Liberty

John Stuart Mill (1806–73), the son of the utilitarian philosopher James Mill, grapples in these selections with the dangers of democracy. Writing in the wake of the English Reform Acts of 1832 and 1867, which expanded the suffrage, he reveals liberals' fears of majority tyranny and collective mediocrity. His major works, in addition to *On Liberty* (1859) and *Considerations on Representative Government* (1861), included here, were *Principles of Political Economy* (1848), *Utilitarianism* (1863), and *On the Subjection of Women* (1869).

## Chapter 1

The subject of this Essay is not the so-called Liberty of the Will, so unfortunately opposed to the misnamed doctrine of Philosophical Necessity; but Civil, or Social Liberty: the nature and limits of the power which can be legitimately exercised by society over the individual. A question seldom stated, and hardly ever discussed, in general terms, but which profoundly influences the practical controversies of the age by its latent presence, and is likely soon to make itself recognised as the vital question of the future. It is so far from being new, that, in a certain sense, it has divided mankind, almost from the remotest ages; but in the stage of progress into which the more civilized portions of the species have now entered, it presents itself under new conditions, and requires a different and more fundamental treatment.

The struggle between Liberty and Authority is the most conspicuous feature in the portions of history with which we are earliest familiar, particularly in that of Greece, Rome, and England. But in old times this contest was between subjects, or some classes of subjects, and the Government. By liberty, was meant protection against the tyranny of the political rulers. The rulers were conceived (except in some of the popular governments of Greece) as in a necessarily antagonistic position to the people whom they ruled. They con-

sisted of a governing One, or a governing tribe or caste, who derived their authority from inheritance or conquest, who, at all events, did not hold it at the
pleasure of the governed, and whose supremacy men did not venture, perhaps
did not desire, to contest, whatever precautions might be taken against its oppressive exercise. Their power was regarded as necessary, but also as highly
dangerous; as a weapon which they would attempt to use against their subjects, no less than against external enemies. To prevent the weaker members of
the community from being preyed upon by innumerable vultures, it was needful that there should be an animal of prey stronger than the rest, commis-
sioned to keep them down. But as the king of the vultures would be no less
bent upon preying on the flock than any of the minor harpies, it was indispensable to be in a perpetual attitude of defence against his beak and claws.
The aim, therefore, of patriots was to set limits to power which the ruler
should be suffered to exercise over the community; and this limitation was
what they meant by liberty. It was attempted in two ways. First, by obtaining
a recognition of certain immunities, called political liberties or rights, which it
was to be regarded as a breach of duty in the ruler to infringe, and which if he
did infringe, specific resistance, or general rebellion, was held to be justifiable.
A second, and generally a later expedient, was the establishment of constitutional checks, by which the consent of the community, or of a body of some
sort, supposed to represent its interests, was made a necessary condition to
some of the more important acts of the governing power. To the first of these
modes of limitation, the ruling power, in most European countries, was compelled, more or less, to submit. It was not so with the second; and, to attain
this, or when already in some degree possessed, to attain it more completely,
became everywhere the principal object of the lovers of liberty. And so long as
mankind were content to combat one enemy by another, and to be ruled by a
master, on condition of being guaranteed more or less efficaciously against his
tyranny, they did not carry their aspirations beyond this point.

A time, however, came, in the progress of human affairs, when men
ceased to think it a necessity of nature that their governors should be an independent power, opposed in interest to themselves. It appeared to them much
better that the various magistrates of the State should be their tenants or delegates, revocable at their pleasure. In that way alone, it seemed, could they have
complete security that the powers of government would never be abused to
their disadvantage. By degrees this new demand for elective and temporary
rulers became the prominent object of the exertions of the popular party,
wherever any such party existed; and superseded, to a considerable extent, the
previous efforts to limit the power of rulers. As the struggle proceeded for
making the ruling power emanate from the periodical choice of the ruled,
some persons began to think that too much importance had been attached to
the limitation of the power itself. *That* (it might seem) was a resource against
rulers whose interests were habitually opposed to those of the people. What

was now wanted was, that the rulers should be identified with the people; that their interest and will should be the interest and will of the nation. The nation did not need to be protected against its own will. There was no fear of its tyrannizing over itself. Let the rulers be effectually responsible to it, promptly removable by it, and it could afford to trust them with power of which it could itself dictate the use to be made. Their power was but the nation's own power, concentrated, and in a form convenient for exercise. This mode of thought, or rather perhaps of feeling, was common among the last generation of European liberalism, in the Continental section of which it still apparently predominates. Those who admit any limit to what a government may do, except in the case of such governments as they think ought not to exist, stand out as brilliant exceptions among the political thinkers of the Continent. A similar tone of sentiment might by this time have been prevalent in our own country, if the circumstances which for a time encouraged it, had continued unaltered.

But, in political and philosophical theories, as well as in persons, success discloses faults and infirmities which failure might have concealed from observation. The notion, that the people have no need to limit their power over themselves, might seem axiomatic, when popular government was a thing only dreamed about, or read of as having existed at some distant period of the past. Neither was that notion necessarily disturbed by such temporary aberrations as those of the French Revolution, the worst of which were the work of an usurping few, and which, in any case, belonged, not to the permanent working of popular institutions, but to a sudden and convulsive outbreak against monarchical and aristocratic despotism. In time, however, a democratic republic came to occupy a large portion of the earth's surface, and made itself felt as one of the most powerful members of the community of nations; and elective and responsible government became subject to the observations and criticisms which wait upon a great existing fact. It was now perceived that such phrases as "self-government," and "the power of the people over themselves," do not express the true state of the case. The "people" who exercise the power are not always the same people with those over whom it is exercised; and the "self-government" spoken of is not the government of each by himself, but of each by all the rest. The will of the people, moreover, practically means the will of the most numerous or the most active *part* of the people; the majority, or those who succeed in making themselves accepted as the majority; the people, consequently, *may* desire to oppress a part of their number; and precautions are as much needed against this as against any other abuse of power. The limitation, therefore, of the power of government over individuals loses none of its importance when the holders of power are regularly accountable to the community, that is, to the strongest party therein. This view of things, recommending itself equally to the intelligence of thinkers and to the inclination of those important classes in European society to whose real or supposed interests democracy is adverse, has had no difficulty in establishing itself; and in political speculations "the tyranny of the majority" is now generally included among the evils against which society requires to be on its guard.

Like other tyrannies, the tyranny of the majority was at first, and is still vulgarly, held in dread, chiefly as operating through the acts of the public authorities. But reflecting persons perceived that when society is itself the tyrant—society collectively over the separate individuals who compose it—its means of tyrannising are not restricted to the acts which it may do by the hands of its political functionaries. Society can and does execute its own mandates: and if it issues wrong mandates instead of right, or any mandates at all in things with which it ought not to meddle, it practises a social tyranny more formidable than many kinds of political oppression, since, though not usually upheld by such extreme penalties, it leaves fewer means of escape, penetrating much more deeply into the details of life, and enslaving the soul itself. Protection, therefore, against the tyranny of the magistrate is not enough: there needs protection also against the tyranny of the prevailing opinion and feeling; against the tendency of society to impose, by other means than civil penalties, its own ideas and practices as rules of conduct on those who dissent from them; to fetter the development, and, if possible, prevent the formation, of any individuality not in harmony with its ways, and compel all characters to fashion themselves upon the model of its own. There is a limit to the legitimate interference of collective opinion with individual independence: and to find that limit, and maintain it against encroachment, is as indispensable to a good condition of human affairs, as protection against political despotism.

But though this proposition is not likely to be contested in general terms, the practical question, where to place the limit—how to make the fitting adjustment between individual independence and social control—is a subject on which nearly everything remains to be done. All that makes existence valuable to any one, depends on the enforcement of restraints upon the actions of other people. Some rules of conduct, therefore, must be imposed, by law in the first place, and by opinion on many things which are not fit subjects for the operation of law. What these rules should be is the principal question in human affairs; but if we except a few of the most obvious cases, it is one of those which least progress has been made in resolving. No two ages, and scarcely any two countries, have decided it alike; and the decision of one age or country is a wonder to another. Yet the people of any given age and country no more suspect any difficulty in it, than if it were a subject on which mankind had always been agreed. The rules which obtain among themselves appear to them self-evident and self-justifying. This all but universal illusion is one of the examples of the magical influence of custom, which is not only, as the proverb says, a second nature, but is continually mistaken for the first. The effect of custom, in preventing any misgiving respecting the rules of conduct which mankind impose on one another, is all the more complete because the subject is one on which it is not generally considered necessary that reasons should be given, either by one person to others or by each to himself. People are accustomed to believe, and have been encouraged in the belief by some who aspire to the character of philosophers, that their feelings, on subjects of this nature, are better than reasons, and render reasons unnecessary. The practical principle which guides them to their opinions on the regulation of human conduct, is the feeling in each person's mind that everybody should be required to act as he, and those with whom he sympathizes, would like them to act. No one, indeed, acknowledges to himself that his standard of judgment is his own liking; but an opinion on a point of conduct, not supported by reasons, can only count as one person's preference; and if the reasons, when given, are a mere appeal to similar preference felt by other people, it is still only many people's liking instead of one. To an ordinary man, however, his own preference, thus supported, is not only a perfectly satisfactory reason, but the only one he generally has for any of his notions of morality, taste, or propriety, which are not expressly written in his religious creed; and his chief guide in the interpretation even of that. Men's opinions, accordingly, on what is laudable or blamable, are affected by all the multifarious causes which influence their wishes in regard to the conduct of others, and which are as numerous as those which determine their wishes on any other subject. Sometimes their reason—at other times their prejudices or superstitions: often their social affections, not seldom their antisocial ones, their envy or jealousy, their arrogance or contemptuousness: but most commonly their desires or fears for themselves—their legitimate or illegitimate self-interest. Wherever there is an ascendant class, a large portion of the morality of the country emanates from its class interests, and its feelings of class superiority. The morality between Spartans and Helots, between planters and negroes, between princes and subjects, between nobles and roturiers [plebeians], between men and women, has been for the most part the creation of these class interests and feelings: and the sentiments thus generated react in turn upon the moral feelings of the members of the ascendant class, in their relations among themselves. Where, on the other hand, a class, formerly ascendant, has lost its ascendancy, or where its ascendancy is unpopular, the prevailing moral sentiments frequently bear the impress of an impatient dislike of superiority. Another grand determining principle of the rules of conduct, both in act and forbearance, which have been enforced by law or opinion, has been the servility of mankind towards the supposed preferences or aversions of their temporal masters or of their gods. This servility, though essentially selfish, is not hypocrisy; it gives rise to perfectly genuine sentiments of abhorrence; it made men burn magicians and heretics. Among so many baser influences, the general and obvious interests of society have of course had a share, and a large one, in the direction of the moral sentiments: less, however, as a matter of reason, and on their own account, than as a consequence of the sympathies and antipathies which grew out of them: and sympathies and antipathies which had little or nothing to do with the interests of society, have made themselves felt in the establishment of moralities with quite as great force.

The likings and dislikings of society, or of some powerful portion of it, are thus the main thing which has practically determined the rules laid down for general observance, under the penalties of law or opinion. And in general, those who have been in advance of society in thought and feeling, have left this condition of things unassailed in principle, however they may have come into conflict with it in some of its details. They have occupied themselves rather in inquiring what things society ought to like or dislike, than in questions whether its likings or dislikings should be a law to individuals. They preferred endeavoring to alter the feelings of mankind on the particular points on which they were themselves heretical, rather than make common cause in defence of freedom, with heretics generally. The only case in which the higher ground has been taken on principle and maintained with consistency, by any but an individual here and there, is that of religious belief: a case instructive in many ways, and not least so as forming a most striking instance of the fallibility of what is called the moral sense: for the *odium theologicum,* in a sincere bigot, is one of the most unequivocal cases of moral feelings. Those who first broke the yoke of what called itself the Universal Church, were in general as little willing to permit difference of religious opinion as that church itself. But when the heat of the conflict was over, without giving a complete victory to any party, and each church or sect was reduced to limit its hopes to retaining possession of the ground it already occupied; minorities, seeing that they had no chance of becoming majorities, were under the necessity of pleading to those whom they could not convert, for permission to differ. It is accordingly on this battle-field, almost solely, that the rights of the individual against society have been asserted on broad grounds of principle, and the claim of society to exercise authority over dissentients openly controverted. The great writers to whom the world owes what religious liberty it possesses, have mostly asserted freedom of conscience as an indefeasible right, and denied absolutely that a human being is accountable to others for his religious belief. Yet so natural to mankind is intolerance in whatever they really care about, that religious freedom had hardly anywhere been practically realised, except where religious indifference, which dislikes to have its peace disturbed by theological quarrels, has added its weight to the scale. In the minds of almost all religious persons, even in the most tolerant countries, the duty of toleration is admitted with tacit reserves. One person will bear with dissent in matters of church government, but not of dogma; another can tolerate everybody, short of a Papist or a Unitarian; another, every one who believes in revealed religion; a few extend their charity a little further, but stop at the belief in a God and in a future state. Wherever the sentiment of the majority is still genuine and intense, it is found to have abated little of its claim to be obeyed.

In England, from the peculiar circumstances of our political history, though the yoke of opinion is perhaps heavier, that of law is lighter, than in most other countries of Europe; and there is considerable jealousy of direct interference, by the legislative or the executive power, with private conduct; not so much from any just regard for the independence of the individual, as from the still subsisting habit of looking on the government as representing an opposite interest to the public. The majority have not yet learnt to feel the power of the government their power, or its opinions their opinions. When they do so, individual liberty will probably be as much exposed to invasion from the government, as it already is from public opinion. But, as yet, there is a considerable amount of feeling ready to be called forth against any attempt of the law to control individuals in things in which they have not hitherto been accustomed to be controlled by it; and this with very little discrimination as to whether the matter is, or is not, within the legitimate sphere of legal control; insomuch that the feeling, highly salutary on the whole, is perhaps quite as often misplaced as well grounded in the particular instances of its application. There is, in fact, no recognised principle by which the propriety or impropriety of government interference is customarily tested. People decide according to their personal preferences. Some, whenever they see any good to be done, or evil to be remedied, would willingly instigate the government to undertake the business; while others prefer to bear almost any amount of social evil, rather than add one to the departments of human interests amenable to governmental control. And men range themselves on one or the other side in any particular case, according to this general direction of their sentiments; or according to the degree of interest which they feel in the particular thing which it is proposed that the government should do, or according to the belief they entertain that the government would, or would not, do it in the manner they prefer; but very rarely on account of any opinion to which they consistently adhere, as to what things are fit to be done by a government. And it seems to me that in consequence of this absence of rule or principle, one side is at present as often wrong as the other; the interference of government is, with about equal frequency, improperly invoked and improperly condemned.

The object of this Essay is to assert one very simple principle, as entitled to govern absolutely the dealings of society with the individual in the way of compulsion and control, whether the means used be physical force in the form of legal penalties, or the moral coercion of public opinion. That principle is, that the sole end for which mankind are warranted, individually or collectively, in interfering with the liberty of action of any of their number, is self-protection. That the only purpose for which power can be rightfully exercised over any member of a civilized community, against his will, is to prevent harm to others. His own good, either physical or moral, is not a sufficient warrant. He cannot rightfully be compelled to do or forbear because it will be better for him to do so, because it will make him happier, because, in the opinions of others, to do so would be wise, or even right. These are good reasons for remonstrating with him, or reasoning with him, or persuading him, or entreating him, but not for compelling him, or visiting him with any evil in case he do otherwise. To justify that, the conduct from which it is desired to deter him, must be calculated to produce evil to some one else. The only part of the conduct of any one, for which he is amenable to society, is that which concerns others. In the part which merely concerns himself, his independence is, of right, absolute. Over himself, over his own body and mind, the individual is sovereign.

It is, perhaps, hardly necessary to say that this doctrine is meant to apply only to human beings in the maturity of their faculties. We are not speaking of children, or of young persons below the age which the law may fix as that of manhood or womanhood. Those who are still in a state to require being taken care of by others, must be protected against their own actions as well as against external injury. For the same reason, we may leave out of consideration those backward states of society in which the race itself may be considered as in its nonage. The early difficulties in the way of spontaneous progress are so great, that there is seldom any choice of means for overcoming them; and a ruler full of the spirit of improvement is warranted in the use of any expedients that will attain an end, perhaps otherwise unattainable. Despotism is a legitimate mode of government in dealing with barbarians, provided the end be their improvement, and the means justified by actually effecting that end. Liberty, as a principle, has no application to any state of things anterior to the time when mankind have become capable of being improved by free and equal discussion. Until then, there is nothing for them but implicit obedience to an Akbar or a Charlemagne, if they are so fortunate as to find one. But as soon as mankind have attained the capacity for being guided to their own improvement by conviction or persuasion (a period long since reached in all nations with whom we need here concern ourselves), compulsion, either in the direct form or in that of pains and penalties for non-compliance, is no longer admissible as a means to their own good, and justifiable only for the security of others.

It is proper to state that I forgo any advantage which could be derived to my argument from the idea of abstract right, as a thing independent of utility. I regard utility as the ultimate appeal on all ethical questions; but it must be utility in the largest sense, grounded on the permanent interests of man as a progressive being. Those interests, I contend, authorise the subjection of individual spontaneity to external control, only in respect to those actions of each, which concern the interest of other people. If any one does an act hurtful to others, there is a *prima facie* case for punishing him, by law, or, where legal penalties are not safely applicable, by general disapprobation. There are also many positive acts for the benefit of others, which he may rightfully be compelled to perform; such as to give evidence in a court of justice; to bear his fair share in the common defence, or in any other joint work necessary to the interest of the society of which he enjoys the protection; and to perform certain acts of individual beneficence, such as saving a fellow-creature's life, or inter-posing to protect the defenceless against ill-usage, things which whenever it is obviously a man's duty to do, he may rightfully be made responsible to society for not doing. A person may cause evil to others not only by his actions but by his inaction, and in either case he is justly accountable to them for the injury. The latter case, it is true, requires a much more cautious exercise of compul-sion than the former. To make any one answerable for doing evil to others, is the rule; to make him answerable for not preventing evil, is, comparatively speaking, the exception. Yet there are many cases clear enough and grave enough to justify that exception. In all things which regard the external rela-tions of the individual, he is *de jure* amenable to those whose interests are con-cerned, and, if need be, to society as their protector. There are often good rea-sons for not holding him to the responsibility; but these reasons must arise from the special expediencies of the case: either because it is a kind of case in which he is on the whole likely to act better, when left to his own discretion, than when controlled in any way in which society have it in their power to control him; or because the attempt to exercise control would produce other evils, greater than those which it would prevent. When such reasons as these preclude the enforcement of responsibility, the conscience of the agent himself should step into the vacant judgment seat, and protect those interests of others which have no external protection; judging himself all the more rigidly, be-cause the case does not admit of his being made accountable to the judgment of his fellow-creatures.

But there is a sphere of action in which society, as distinguished from the individual, has, if any, only an indirect interest; comprehending all that portion of a person's life and conduct which affects only himself, or if it also affects others, only with their free, voluntary, and undeceived consent and participation. When I say only himself, I mean directly, and in the first in-stance; for whatever affects himself, may affect others through himself; and the objection which may be grounded on this contingency, will receive con-sideration in the sequel. This, then, is the appropriate region of human lib-erty. It comprises, first, the inward domain of consciousness; demanding liberty of conscience in the most comprehensive sense; liberty of thought and feeling; absolute freedom of opinion and sentiment on all subjects, practical or speculative, scientific, moral, or theological. The liberty of expressing and publishing opinions may seem to fall under a different principle, since it be-longs to that part of the conduct of an individual which concerns other people; but, being almost of as much importance as the liberty of thought it-self, and resting in great part on the same reasons, is practically inseparable from it. Secondly, the principle requires liberty of tastes and pursuits; of fram-ing the plan of our life to suit our own character; of doing as we like, subject to such consequences as may follow: without impediment from our fellow creatures, so long as what we do does not harm them, even though they should think our conduct foolish, perverse, or wrong. Thirdly, from this liberty of each individual, follows the liberty, within the same limits, of combination among individuals; freedom to unite, for any purpose not involving harm to others: the persons combining being supposed to be of full age, and not forced or deceived.

No society in which these liberties are not, on the whole, respected, is free, whatever may be its form of government; and none is completely free in which they do not exist absolute and unqualified. The only freedom which deserves the name, is that of pursuing our own good in our own way, so long as we do not attempt to deprive others of theirs, or impede their efforts to obtain it. Each is the proper guardian of this own health, whether bodily, *or* mental and spiritual. Mankind are greater gainers by suffering each other to live as seems good to themselves, than by compelling each to live as seems good to the rest.

Though this doctrine is anything but new, and to some persons, may have the air of a truism, there is no doctrine which stands more directly opposed to the general tendency of existing opinion and practice. Society has expended fully as much effort in the attempt (according to its lights) to compel people to conform to its notions of personal as of social excellence. The ancient commonwealths thought themselves entitled to practise, and the ancient philosophers countenanced, the regulation of every part of private conduct by public authority, on the ground that the State had a deep interest in the whole bodily and mental discipline of every one of its citizens; a mode of thinking which may have been admissible in small republics surrounded by powerful enemies, in constant peril of being subverted by foreign attack or internal commotion, and to which even a short interval of relaxed energy and self-command might so easily be fatal, that they could not afford to wait for the salutary permanent effects of freedom. In the modern world, the greater size of political communities, and, above all, the separation between spiritual and temporal authority (which placed the direction of men's consciences in other hands than those which controlled their worldly affairs), prevented so great an interference by law in the details of private life; but the engines of moral repression have been wielded more strenuously against divergence from the reigning opinion in self-regarding, than even in social matters; religion, the most powerful of the elements which have entered into the formation of moral feeling, having almost always been governed either by the ambition of a hierarchy, seeking control over every department of human conduct, or by the spirit of Puritanism. And some of those modern reformers who have placed themselves in strongest opposition to the religions of the past, have been no way behind either churches or sects in their assertion of the right of spiritual domination: M. Comte, in particular, whose social system, as unfolded in his *Système de Politique Positive,* aims at establishing (though by moral more than by legal appliances) a despotism of society over the individual, surpassing anything contemplated in the political ideal of the most rigid disciplinarian among the ancient philosophers.

Apart from the peculiar tenets of individual thinkers, there is also in the world at large an increasing inclination to stretch unduly the powers of society over the individual, both by the force of opinion and even by that of legislation; and as the tendency of all the changes taking place in the world is to strengthen society, and diminish the power of the individual, this encroachment is not one of the evils which tend spontaneously to disappear, but, on the contrary, to grow more and more formidable. The disposition of mankind, whether as rulers or as fellow citizens, to impose their own opinions and inclinations as a rule of conduct on others, is so energetically supported by some of the best and by some of the worst feelings incident to human nature, that it is hardly ever kept under restraint by anything but want of power; and as the power is not declining, but growing, unless a strong barrier of moral conviction can be raised against the mischief, we must expect, in the present circumstances of the world, to see it increase.

It will be convenient for the argument, if, instead of at once entering upon the general thesis, we confine ourselves in the first instance to a single branch of it, on which the principle here stated is, if not fully, yet to a certain point, recognized by the current opinions. This one branch is the Liberty of Thought: from which it is impossible to separate the cognate liberty of speaking and of writing. Although these liberties, to some considerable amount, form part of the political morality of all countries which profess religious toleration and free institutions, the grounds, both philosophical and practical, on which they rest, are perhaps not so familiar to the general mind, nor so thoroughly appreciated by many even of the leaders of opinion, as might have been expected. Those grounds, when rightly understood, are of much wider application than to only one division of the subject, and a thorough consideration of this part of the question will be found the best introduction to the remainder. Those to whom nothing which I am about to say will be new, may therefore, I hope, excuse me, if on a subject which for now three centuries has been so often discussed, I venture on one discussion more.

## Chapter 2
## Of the Liberty of Thought and Discussion

The time, it is to be hoped, is gone by, when any defence would be necessary of the "liberty of the press" as one of the securities against corrupt or tyrannical government. No argument, we may suppose, can now be needed, against permitting a legislature or an executive, not identified in interest with the people, to prescribe opinions to them, and determine what doctrines or what arguments they shall be allowed to hear. This aspect of the question, besides, has been so often and so triumphantly enforced by preceding writers, that it needs not be specially insisted on in this place. Though the law of England, on the subject of the press, is as servile to this day as it was in the time of the Tudors, there is little danger of its being actually put in force against political discussion, except during some temporary panic, when fear of insurrection drives ministers and judges from their propriety; and, speaking generally, it is not, in constitutional countries, to be apprehended, that the government, whether completely responsible to the people or not, will often attempt to control the expression of the opinion, except when in doing so it makes itself the organ of the general intolerance of the public. Let us suppose, therefore, that the government is entirely at one with the people, and never thinks of exerting any power of coercion unless in agreement with what it conceives to be their voice. But I deny the right of the people to exercise such coercion, either by themselves or by their government. The power itself is illegitimate. The best government has no more title to it than the worst. It is as noxious, or more noxious, when exerted in accordance with public opinion, than when in opposition to it. If all mankind minus one were of one opinion, mankind would be no more justified in silencing that one person, than he, if he had the power, would be justified in silencing mankind. Were an opinion a personal possession of no value except to the owner, if to be obstructed in the enjoyment of it were simply a private injury, it would make some difference whether the injury was inflicted only on a few persons or on many. But the peculiar evil of silencing the expression of an opinion, is that it is robbing the human race, posterity as well as the existing generation; those who dissent from the opinion, still more than those who hold it. If the opinion is right, they are deprived of the opportunity of exchanging error for truth: if wrong, they lose, what is almost as great a benefit, the clearer perception and livelier impression of truth, produced by its collision with error.

It is necessary to consider separately these two hypotheses, each of which has a distinct branch of the argument corresponding to it. We can never be sure that the opinion that we are endeavoring to stifle is a false opinion; and if we were sure, stifling it would be an evil still.

First: the opinion which it is attempted to suppress by authority may possibly be true. Those who desire to suppress it, of course, deny its truth; but they are not infallible. They have no authority to decide the question for all mankind, and exclude every other person from the means of judging. To refuse a hearing to an opinion, because they are sure that it is false, is to assume that *their* certainty is the same thing as *absolute* certainty. All silencing of discussion is an assumption of infallibility. Its condemnation may be allowed to rest on this common argument, not the worse for being common.

Unfortunately for the good sense of mankind, the fact of their fallibility is far from carrying the weight in their practical judgment which is always allowed to it in theory; for while every one well knows himself to be fallible, few think it necessary to take any precautions against their own fallibility, or admit the supposition that any opinion, of which they feel very certain, may be one of the examples of the error to which they acknowledge themselves to be liable. Absolute princes, or others who are accustomed to unlimited deference, usually feel this complete confidence in their own opinions on nearly all subjects. People more happily situated, who sometimes hear their opinions disputed, and are not wholly unused to be set right when they are wrong, place the same unbounded reliance only on such of their opinions as are shared by all who surround them, or to whom they habitually defer; for in proportion to a man's want of confidence in his own solitary judgment, does he usually repose, with implicit trust, on the infallibility of "the world" in general. And the world, to each individual, means the part of it with which he comes in contact; his party, his sect, his church, his class of society; the man may be called, by comparison, almost liberal and large-minded to whom it means anything so comprehensive as his own country or his own age. Nor is his faith in this collective authority at all shaken by his being aware that other ages, countries, sects, churches, classes, and parties have thought, and even now think, the exact reverse. He devolves upon his own world the responsibility of being in the right against the dissentient worlds of other people; and it never troubles him that the mere accident has decided which of these numerous worlds is the object of his reliance, and that the same causes which make him a churchman in London, would have made him a Buddhist or a Confucian in Peking. Yet it is as evident in itself, as any amount of argument can make it, that ages are no more infallible than individuals; every age having held many opinions which subsequent ages have deemed not only false but absurd; and it is as certain that many opinions now general, will be rejected by future ages, as it is that many, once general, are rejected by the present.

The objection likely to be made to this argument would probably take some such form as the following. There is no greater assumption of infallibility in forbidding the propagation of error, than in any other thing which is done by public authority on its own judgment and responsibility. Judgment is given to men that they may use it. Because it may be used erroneously, are men to be told that they ought not to use it at all? To prohibit what they think pernicious, is not claiming exemption from error, but fulfilling the duty incumbent on them, although fallible, of acting on their conscientious conviction. If we were never to act on our opinions, because those opinions may be wrong, we should leave all our interests uncared for, and all our duties unperformed. An objection which applies to all conduct can be no valid objection to any conduct in particular. It is the duty of governments, and of individuals, to form the truest opinions they can; to form them carefully, and never impose them upon others unless they are quite sure of being right. But when they are sure (such reasoners may say), it is not conscientiousness but cowardice to shrink from acting on their opinions, and allow doctrines which they honestly think dangerous to the welfare of mankind, either in this life or in another, to be scattered abroad without restraint, because other people, in less enlightened times, have persecuted opinions now believed to be true. Let us take care, it may be said, not to make the same mistake: but governments and nations have made mistakes in other things, which are not denied to be fit subjects for the exercise of authority: they have laid on bad taxes, made unjust wars. Ought we therefore to lay on no taxes, and, under whatever provocation, make no wars? Men, and governments, must act to the best of their ability. There is no such thing as absolute certainty, but there is assurance sufficient for the purposes of human life. We may, and must, assume our opinion to be true for the guidance of our own conduct: and it is assuming no more when we forbid bad men to pervert society by the propagation of opinions which we regard as false and pernicious.

I answer, that it is assuming very much more. There is the greatest difference between presuming an opinion to be true, because, with every opportunity for contesting it, it has not been refuted, and assuming its truth for the purpose of not permitting its refutation. Complete liberty of contradicting and disproving our opinion is the very condition which justifies us in assuming its truth for purposes of action; and on no other terms can a being with human faculties have any rational assurance of being right.

When we consider either the history of opinion, or the ordinary conduct of human life, to what is it to be ascribed that the one and the other are no worse than they are? Not certainly to the inherent force of the human understanding; for, on any matter not self-evident, there are ninety-nine persons totally incapable of judging of it for one who is capable; and the capacity of the hundredth person is only comparative; for the majority of the eminent men of every past generation held many opinions now known to be erroneous, and did or approved numerous things which no one will now justify. Why is it, then, that there is on the whole a preponderance among mankind of rational opinions and rational conduct? If there really is this preponderance—which there must be unless human affairs are, and have always been, in an almost desperate state—it is owing to a quality of the human mind, the source of everything respectable in man either as an intellectual or as a moral being, namely, that his errors are corrigible. He is capable of rectifying his mistakes, by discussion and experience. Not by experience alone. There must be discussion, to show how experience is to be interpreted. Wrong opinions and practices gradually yield to fact and argument; but facts and arguments, to produce any effect on the mind, must brought before it. Very few facts are able to tell their own story, without comments to bring out their meaning. The whole strength and value, then, of human judgment, depending on the one property, that it can be set right when it is wrong, reliance can be placed on it only when the means of setting it right are kept constantly at hand. In the case of any person whose judgment is really deserving of confidence, how has it become so? Because he has kept his mind open to criticism of his opinions and conduct. Because it has been his practice to listen to all that could be said against him; to profit by as much of it as was just, and to expound to himself, and upon occasion to others, the fallacy of what was fallacious. Because he has felt, that the only way in which a human being can make some approach to knowing the whole of a subject, is by hearing what can be said about it by persons of every variety of opinion, and studying all modes in which it can be looked at by every character of mind. No wise man ever acquired his wisdom in any mode but this; nor is it in the nature of human intellect to become wise in any other manner. The steady habit of correcting and completing his own opinion by collating it with those of others, so far from causing doubt and hesitation in carrying it into practice, is the only stable foundation for a just reliance on it; for, being cognisant of all that can, at least obviously, be said against him, and having taken up his position against all gainsayers—knowing that he has sought for objections and difficulties, instead of avoiding them, and has shut out no light which can be thrown upon the subject from any quarter—he has a right to think his judgment better than that of any person, or any multitude, who have not gone through a similar process.

It is not too much to require that what the wisest of mankind, those who are best entitled to trust their own judgement, find necessary to warrant their relying on it, should be submitted to by that miscellaneous collection of a few wise and many foolish individuals, called the public. The most intolerant of churches, the Roman Catholic Church, even at the canonisation of a saint, admits, and listens patiently to, a "devil's advocate." The holiest of men, it appears, cannot be admitted to posthumous honors until all that the devil could say against him is known and weighed. If even the Newtonian philosophy were not permitted to be questioned, mankind could not feel as complete assurance of its truth as they now do. The beliefs which we have most warrant for have no safeguard to rest on, but a standing invitation to the whole world to prove them unfounded. If the challenge is not accepted, or is accepted and the attempt fails, we are far enough from certainty still; but we have done the best that the existing state of human reason admits of; we have neglected nothing that could give the truth a chance of reaching us: if the lists are kept open, we may hope that if there be a better truth, it will be found when the human mind is capable of receiving it; and in the meantime we may rely on having attained such approach to truth as is possible in our own day. This is the amount of certainty attainable by a fallible being, and this the sole way of attaining it.

Strange it is, that men should admit the validity of the arguments for free discussion, but object to their being "pushed to an extreme," not seeing that unless the reasons are good for an extreme case, they are not good for any case. Strange that they should imagine that they are not assuming infallibility, when they acknowledge that there should be free discussion on all subjects which can possibly be *doubtful,* but think that some particular principle or doctrine should be forbidden to be questioned because it is so *certain,* that is, because *they are certain* that it is certain. To call any proposition certain, while there is anyone who would deny its certainty if permitted, but who is not permitted, is to assume that we ourselves, and those who agree with us, are the judges of certainty, and judges without hearing the other side.

In the present age—which has been described as "destitute of faith, but terrified at skepticism"—in which people feel sure, not so much that their opinions are true, as that they should not know what to do without them —the claims of an opinion to be protected from public attack are rested not so much on its truth, as on its importance to society. There are, it is alleged, certain beliefs so useful, not to say indispensable, to well-being that it is as much the duty of governments to uphold those beliefs, as to protect any other of the interests of society. In a case of such necessity, and so directly in the line of their duty, something less than infallibility may, it is maintained, warrant, and even bind, governments to act on their own opinion, confirmed by the general opinion of mankind. It is also often argued, and still oftener thought, that none but bad men would desire to weaken these salutary beliefs; and there can be nothing wrong, it is thought, in restraining bad men, and prohibiting what only such men would wish to practise. This mode of thinking makes the justification of restraints on discussion not a question of the truth of doctrines, but of their usefulness; and flatters itself by that means to escape the responsibility of claiming to be an infallible judge of opinions. But those who thus satisfy themselves, do not perceive that the assumption of infallibility is merely shifted from one point to another. The usefulness of an opinion is itself matter of opinion: as disputable, as open to discussion, and requiring discussion as much as the opinion itself. There is the same need of an infallible judge of opinions to decide an opinion to be noxious, as to decide it to be false, unless the opinion condemned has full opportunity of defending itself. And it will not do to say that the heretic may be allowed to maintain the utility or harmlessness of his opinion, though forbidden to maintain its truth. The truth of an opinion is part of its utility. If we would know whether or not it is desirable that a proposition should be believed, is it possible to exclude the consideration of whether or not it is true? In the opinion, not of bad men, but of the best men, no belief which is contrary to truth can be really useful: and can you prevent such men from urging that plea when they are charged with culpability for denying some doctrine which they are told is useful, but which they believe to be false? Those who are on the side of received opinions never fail to take all possible advantage of this plea; you do not find *them* handling the question of utility as if it could be completely abstracted from that of truth: on the contrary, it is, above all, because their doctrine is "the truth," that the knowledge or the belief of it is held to be so indispensable. There can be no fair discussion of the question of usefulness when an argument so vital may be employed on one side, but not on the other. And in point of fact, when law or public feeling do not permit the truth of an opinion to be disputed, they are just as little tolerant of a denial of its usefulness. The utmost they allow is an extenuation of its absolute necessity, or of the positive guilt of rejecting it.

In order more fully to illustrate the mischief of denying a hearing to opinions because we, in our own judgment, have condemned them, it will be desirable to fix down the discussion to a concrete case; and I choose, by preference, the cases which are least favourable to me—in which the argument against freedom of opinion, both on the score of truth and on that of utility, is considered the strongest. Let the opinions impugned be the belief in a God and in a future state, or any of the commonly received doctrines of morality. To fight the battle on such ground gives a great advantage to an unfair antagonist; since he will be sure to say (and many who have no desire to be unfair will say it internally), Are these the doctrines which you do not deem sufficiently certain to be taken under the protection of law? Is the belief in a God one of the opinions to feel sure of which you hold to be assuming infallibility? But I must be permitted to observe, that it is not the feeling sure of a doctrine (be it what it may) which I call an assumption of infallibility. It is the undertaking to decide that question *for others*, without allowing them to hear what can be said on the contrary side. And I denounce and reprobate this pretension not the less, if put forth on the side of my most solemn convictions. However positive anyone's persuasion may be, not only of the falsity but of the pernicious consequences—not only of the pernicious consequences, but (to adopt expressions which I altogether condemn) the immorality and impiety of an opinion, yet if, in pursuance of that private judgment, though backed by the public judgment of his country or his contemporaries, he prevents the opinion from being heard in its defence, he assumes infallibility. And so far from the assumption being less objectionable or less dangerous because the opinion is called immoral or impious, this is the case of all others in which it is most fatal. There are exactly the occasions on which the men of one generation commit those dreadful mistakes which excite the astonishment and horror of posterity. It is among such that we find the instances memorable in history, when the arm of the law has been employed to root out the best men and the noblest doctrines; with deplorable success as to the men, though some of the doctrines have survived to be (as if in mockery) invoked in defence of similar conduct toward those who dissent from *them*, or from their received interpretation.

Mankind can hardly be too often reminded that there was once a man called Socrates, between whom and the legal authorities and public opinion of his time there took place a memorable collision. Born in an age and country abounding in individual greatness, this man has been handed down to us by those who best knew both him and the age, as the most virtuous man in it;

while *we* know him as the head and prototype of all subsequent teachers of virtue, the source equally of the lofty inspiration of Plato and the judicious utilitarianism of Aristotle, *"i maestri di color che sanno,"* the two headsprings of ethical as of all other philosophy. This acknowledged master of all the eminent thinkers who have since lived—whose fame, still growing after more than two thousand years, all but outweighs the whole remainder of the names which make his native city illustrious—was put to death by his countrymen, after a judicial conviction, for impiety and immorality. Impiety, in denying the gods recognized by the State; indeed, his accuser asserted (see the "Apologia") that he believed in no gods at all. Immorality, in being, by his doctrines and instructions, a "corruptor of youth." Of these charges the tribunal, there is every ground for believing, honestly found him guilty, and condemned the man who probably of all then born had deserved best of mankind to be put to death as a criminal.

To pass from this to the only other instance of judicial iniquity, the mention of which, after the condemnation of Socrates, would not be an anticlimax: the event which took place on Calvary rather more than eighteen hundred years ago. The man who left on the memory of those who witnessed his life and conversation such an impression of his moral grandeur that eighteen subsequent centuries have done homage to him as the Almighty in person, was ignominiously put to death, as what? As a blasphemer. Men did not merely mistake their benefactor, they mistook him for the exact contrary of what he was, and treated him as that prodigy of impiety which they themselves are now held to be for their treatment of him. The feelings with which mankind now regards these lamentable transactions, especially the later of the two, render them extremely unjust in their judgment of the unhappy actors. These were, to all appearance, not bad men—not worse than men commonly are, but rather the contrary; men who possessed in a full, or somewhat more than a full measure, the religious, moral, and patriotic feelings of their time and people: the very kind of men who, in all times, our own included, have every chance of passing through life blameless and respected. The high-priest who rent his garments when the words were pronounced, which, according to all the ideas of his country, constituted the blackest guilt, was in all probability quite as sincere in his horror and indignation as the generality of respectable and pious men now are in the religious and moral sentiments they profess; and most of those who now shudder at his conduct, if they had lived in his time, and been born Jews, would have acted precisely as he did. Orthodox Christians who are tempted to think that those who stoned to death the first martyrs must have been worse men than they themselves are, ought to remember that one of those persecutors was Saint Paul. . . .

But, indeed, the dictum that truth always triumphs over persecution is one of those pleasant falsehoods which men repeat after one another till they pass into commonplaces, but which all experience refutes. History teems with instances of truth put down by persecution. If not suppressed forever, it may be thrown back for centuries. To speak only of religious opinions: the Reformation broke out at least twenty times before Luther, and was put down. Arnold of Bresica was put down. Fra Dolcino was put down. Savonarola was put down. The Albigeois were put down. The Vaudois were put down. The Lollards were put down. The Hussites were put down. Even after the era of Luther, wherever persecution was persisted in, it was successful. In Spain, Italy, Flanders, the Austrian empire, Protestantism was rooted out; and, most likely, would have been so in England, had Queen Mary lived, or Queen Elizabeth died. Persecution has always succeeded, save where the heretics were too strong a party to be effectually persecuted. No reasonable person can doubt that Christianity might have been extirpated in the Roman Empire. It spread, and became predominant, because the persecutions were only occasional, lasting but a short time, and separated by long intervals of almost undisturbed propagandism. It is a piece of idle sentimentality that truth, merely as truth, has any inherent power denied to error of prevailing against the dungeon and the stake. Men are not more zealous for truth than they often are for error, and a sufficient application of legal or even of social penalties will generally succeed in stopping the propagation of either. The real advantage which truth has consists in this, that when an opinion is true, it may be extinguished once, twice, or many times, but in the course of ages there will generally be found persons to rediscover it, until some one of its reappearances falls on a time when from favourable circumstances it escapes persecution until it has made such head as to withstand all subsequent attempt to suppress it.

It will be said, that we do not now put to death the introducers of new opinions: we are not like our fathers who slew the prophets, we even build sepulchers to them. It is true we no longer put heretics to death; and the amount of penal infliction which modern feelings would probably tolerate, even against the most obnoxious opinions, is not sufficient to extirpate them. But let us not flatter ourselves that we are yet free from the strain even of legal persecution. Penalties for opinion, or at least for its expression, still exist by law; and their enforcement is not, even in these times, so unexampled as to make it at all incredible that they may some day be revived in full force. . . .

Let us now pass to the second division of the argument, and dismissing the supposition that any of the received opinions may be false, let us assume them to be true, and examine into the worth of the manner in which they are likely to be held, when their truth is not freely and openly canvassed. However unwillingly a person who has a strong opinion may admit the possibility that his opinion may be false, he ought to be moved by the consideration that, however true it may be, if it is not fully, frequently, and fearlessly discussed, it will be held as a dead dogma, not a living truth.

There is a class of persons (happily not quite so numerous as formerly) who think it enough if a person assents undoubtingly to what they think true, though he has no knowledge whatever of the grounds of the opinion, and could not make a tenable defence of it against the most superficial objections. Such persons, if they can once get their creed taught from authority, naturally think that no good, and some harm, comes of its being allowed to be questioned. Where their influence prevails, they make it nearly impossible for the received opinion to be rejected wisely and considerately, though it may still be rejected rashly and ignorantly; for to shut out discussion entirely is seldom possible, and when it once gets in, beliefs not grounded on conviction are apt to give way before the slightest semblance of an argument. Waiving, however, this possibility—assuming that the true opinion abides in the mind, but abides as a prejudice, a belief independent of, and proof against, argument—this is not the way in which truth ought to be held by a rational being. This is not knowing the truth. Truth, thus held, is but one superstition the more, accidentally clinging to the words which enunciate a truth.

If the intellect and judgment of mankind ought to be cultivated, a thing which Protestants at least do not deny, on what can these faculties be more appropriately exercised by anyone, than on the things which concern him so much that it is considered necessary for him to hold opinions on them? If the cultivation of the understanding consists in one thing more than in another, it is surely in learning the grounds of one's own opinions. Whatever people believe, on subjects on which it is of the first importance to believe rightly, they ought to be able to defend against at least the common objections. But, someone may say, "Let them be *taught* the grounds of their opinions. It does not follow that opinions must be merely parroted because they are never heard controverted. Persons who learn geometry do not simply commit the theorems to memory, but understand and learn likewise the demonstrations; and it would be absurd to say that they remain ignorant of the grounds of geometrical truths, because they never hear anyone deny, and attempt to disprove them." Undoubtedly: and such teaching suffices on a subject like mathematics, where there is nothing at all to be said on the wrong side of the question. The peculiarity of the evidence of mathematical truths is that all the argument is on one side. There are no objections, and no answers to objections. But on every subject on which difference of opinion is possible, the truth depends on a balance to be struck between two sets of conflicting reasons. Even in natural philosophy, there is always some other explanation possible of the same facts; some geocentric theory instead of heliocentric, some phlogiston instead of oxygen; and it has to be shown why that other theory cannot be the true one: and until this is shown, and until we know how it is shown, we do not understand the grounds of our opinion. But when we turn to subjects infinitely more complicated, to morals, religion, politics, social relations, and the business of life, three-fourths of the arguments for every disputed opinion consist in dispelling the appearances which favor some opinion different from it. The greatest orator, save one, of antiquity, has left it on record that he always studied his adversary's case with as great, if not still greater, intensity than even his own. What Cicero practised as the means of forensic success requires to be imitated by all who study any subject in order to arrive at the truth. He who knows only his own side of the case knows little of that. His reasons may be good, and no one may have been able to refute them. But if he is equally unable to refute the reasons on the opposite side; if he does not so much as know what they are, he has no ground for preferring either opinion. The rational position for him would be suspension of judgment, and unless he contents himself with that, he is either led by authority, or adopts, like the generality of the world, the side to which he feels most inclination. Nor is it enough that he should hear the arguments of adversaries from his own teachers, presented as they state them, and accompanied by what they offer as refutations. That is not the way to do justice to the arguments, or bring them into real contact with his own mind. He must be able to hear them from persons who actually believe them; who defend them in earnest, and do their very utmost for them. He must know them in their most plausible and persuasive form; he must feel the whole force of the difficulty which the true view of the subject has to encounter and dispose of; else he will never really possess himself of the portion of truth which meets and removes that difficulty. Ninety-nine in a hundred of what are called educated men are in this condition; even of those who can argue fluently for their opinions. Their conclusion may be true, but it might be false for anything they know: they have never thrown themselves into the mental position of those who think differently from them, and considered what such persons may have to say; and consequently they do not, in any proper sense of the word, know the doctrine which they themselves profess. They do not know those parts of it which explain and justify the remainder; the considerations which show that a fact which seemingly conflicts with another is reconcilable with it, or that, of two apparently strong reasons, one and not the other ought to be preferred. All that part of the truth which turns the scale, and decides the judgment of a completely informed mind, they are strangers to; nor is it ever really known, but to those who have attended equally and impartially to both sides, and endeavoured to see the reasons of both in the strongest light. So essential is this discipline to a real understanding of moral and human subjects, that if opponents of all important truths do not exist, it is indispensable to imagine them, and supply them with the strongest arguments which the most skillful devil's advocate can conjure up. . . .

If, however, the mischievous operation of the absence of free discussion, when the received opinions are true, were confined to leaving men ignorant of the grounds of those opinions, it might be thought that this, if an intellectual, is no moral evil, and does not affect the worth of the opinions, regarded in their influence on the character. The fact, however, is, that not only the grounds of the opinion are forgotten in the absence of discussion, but too often the meaning of the opinion itself. The words which convey it cease to suggest ideas, or suggest only a small portion of those they were originally employed to communicate. Instead of a vivid conception and a living belief, there remain only a few phrases retained by rote; or, if any part, the shell and husk only of the meaning is retained, the finer essence being lost . . . .

To what an extent doctrines intrinsically fitted to make the deepest impression upon the mind may remain in it as dead beliefs, without being ever realised in the imagination, the feelings, or the understanding, is exemplified by the manner in which the majority of believers hold the doctrines of Christianity. By Christianity I here mean what is accounted such by all churches and sects—the maxims and precepts contained in the New Testament. These are considered sacred, and accepted as laws, by all professing Christians. Yet it is scarcely too much to say that not one Christian in a thousand guides or tests his individual conduct by reference to those laws. The standard to which he does refer it, is the custom of his nation, his class, or his religious profession. He has thus, on the one hand, a collection of ethical maxims, which he believes to have been vouchsafed to him by infallible wisdom as rules for his government; and on the other a set of everyday judgments and practices, which go a certain length with some of those maxims, not so great a length with others, stand in direct opposition to some, and are, on the whole, a compromise between the Christian creed and the interests and suggestions of wor[l]dly life. To the first of these standards he gives his homage; to the other his real allegiance. All Christians believe that the blessed are the poor and humble, and those who are ill-used by the world; that it is easier for a camel to pass through the eye of a needle than for a rich man to enter the kingdom of heaven; that they should judge not, lest they be judged; that they should swear not at all; that they should love their neighbour as themselves; that if one take their cloak, they should give him their coat also; that they should take no thought for the morrow; that if they would be perfect they should sell all that they have and give it to the poor. They are not insincere when they say that they believe these things. They do believe them, as people believe what they have always heard lauded and never discussed. But in the sense of that living belief which regulates conduct, they believe these doctrines just up to the point to which it is usual to act upon them. The doctrines in their integrity are serviceable to pelt adversaries with; and it is understood that they are to be put forward (when possible) as the reasons for whatever people do that they think laudable. But anyone who reminded them that the maxims require an infinity of things which they never even think of doing, would gain nothing but to be classed among those very unpopular characters who affect to be better than other people. The doctrines have no hold on ordinary believers—are not a power in their minds. They have an habitual respect for the sound of them, but no feeling which spreads from the words to the things signified, and forces the mind to take *them* in, and make them conform to the formula. Whenever conduct is concerned, they look round for Mr. A and B to direct them how far to go in obeying Christ. . . .

But what! (it may be asked) Is the absence of unanimity an indispensable condition of true knowledge? Is it necessary that some part of mankind should persist in error to enable any to realize the truth? Does a belief cease to be real and vital as soon as it is generally received—and is a proposition never thoroughly understood and felt unless some doubt of it remains? As soon as mankind have unanimously accepted a truth, does the truth perish within them? The highest aim and best result of improved intelligence, it has hitherto been thought, is to unite mankind more and more in the acknowledgment of all important truths; and does the intelligence only last as long as it has not achieved its object? Do the fruits of conquest perish by the very completeness of the victory?

I affirm no such thing. As mankind improve, the number of doctrines which are no longer disputed or doubted will be constantly on the increase: and the well-being of mankind may almost be measured by the number and gravity of the truths which have reached the point of being uncontested. The cessation, on one question after another, of serious controversy, is one of the necessary incidents of the consolidation of opinion; a consolidation as salutary in the case of true opinions, as it is dangerous and noxious when the opinions are erroneous. But though this gradual narrowing of the bounds of diversity of opinion is necessary in both senses of the term, being at once inevitable and indispensable, we are not therefore obliged to conclude that all its consequences must be beneficial. The loss of so important an aid to the intelligent and living apprehension of a truth, as is afforded by the necessity of explaining it to, or defending it against, opponents, though not sufficient to outweigh, is no trifling drawback, from the benefit of its universal recognition. Where this advantage can no longer be had, I confess I should like to see the teachers of mankind endeavoring to provide a substitute for it; some contrivance for making the difficulties of the question as present to the learner's consciousness, as if they were pressed upon him by a dissentient champion, eager for his conversion. . . .

It still remains to speak of one of the principal causes which make diversity of opinion advantageous, and will continue to do so until mankind shall have entered a stage of intellectual advancement which at present seems at an incalculable distance. We have hitherto considered only two possibilities: that the received opinion may be false, and some other opinion, consequently, true; or that, the received opinion being true, a conflict with the opposite error is essential to a clear apprehension and deep feeling of its truth. But there is a commoner case than either of these; when the conflicting doctrines, instead of being one true and the other false, share the truth between them; and the nonconforming opinion is needed to supply the remainder of the truth, of which the received doctrine embodies only a part. Popular opinions, on subjects not palpable to sense, are often true, but seldom or never the whole truth. They are a part of the truth; sometimes a greater, sometimes a smaller part, but exaggerated, distorted, and disjointed from the truths by which they ought to be accompanied and limited. Heretical opinions, on the other hand, are generally some of these suppressed and neglected truths, bursting the bonds which kept them down, and either seeking reconciliation with the truth contained in the common opinion, or fronting it as enemies, and setting themselves up, with similar exclusiveness, as the whole truth. The latter case is hitherto the most frequent, as, in the human mind, one-sidedness has always been the rule, and many-sidedness the exception. Hence, even in revolutions of opinion, one part of the truth usually sets while another rises. Even progress, which ought to superadd, for the most part only substitutes, one partial and incomplete truth for another; improvement consisting chiefly in this, that the new fragment of truth is more wanted, more adapted to the needs of the time, than that which it displaces. Such being the partial character of prevailing opinions, even when resting on a true foundation, every opinion which embodies somewhat of the portion of truth which the common opinion omits, ought to be considered precious, with whatever amount of error and confusion that truth may be blended. No sober judge of human affairs will feel bound to be indignant because those who force on our notice truths which we should otherwise have overlooked, overlook some of those which we see. Rather, he will think that so long as popular truth is one-sided, it is more desirable than otherwise that unpopular truth should have one-sided assertors too; such being usually the most energetic, and the most likely to compel reluctant attention to the fragment of wisdom which they proclaim as if it were the whole. . . .

In politics, again, it is almost a commonplace, that a party of order or stability, and a party of progress or reform, are both necessary elements of a healthy state of political life; until the one or the other shall have so enlarged its mental grasp as to be a party equally of order and of progress, knowing and distinguishing what is fit to be preserved from what ought to be swept away. Each of these modes of thinking derives its utility from the deficiencies of the other; but it is in a great measure the opposition of the other that keeps each within the limits of reason and sanity. Unless opinions favourable to democracy and to aristocracy, to property and to equality, to co-operation and to competition, to luxury and to abstinence, to sociality and individuality, to liberty and discipline, and all the other standing antagonisms of practical life, are expressed with equal freedom, and enforced and defended with equal talent and energy, there is no chance of both elements obtaining their due; one scale is sure to go up, and the other down. Truth, in the great practical concerns of life, is so much a question of the reconciling and combining of opposites, that very few have minds sufficiently capacious and impartial to make the adjustment with an approach to correctness, and it has to be made by the rough process of a struggle between combatants fighting under hostile banners. On any of the great open questions just enumerated, if either of the two opinions has a better claim than the other, not merely to be tolerated, but to be encouraged and countenanced, it is the one which happens at the particular time and place to be in a minority. That is the opinion which, for the time being, represents the neglected interests, the side of human well-being which is in danger of obtaining less than its share. I am aware that there is not, in this country, any intolerance of differences of opinion on most of these topics. They are adduced to show, by admitted and multiplied examples, the universality of the fact that only through diversity of opinion is there, in the existing state of human intellect, a chance of fair play to all sides of the truth. When there are persons to be found who form an exception to the apparent unanimity of the world of any subject, even if the world is in the right, it is always probable that dissentients have something worth hearing to say for themselves, and that truth would lose something by their silence. . . .

I do not pretend that the most unlimited use of the freedom of enunciating all possible opinions would put an end to the evils of religious or philosophical sectarianism. Every truth which men of narrow capacity are in earnest about, is sure to be asserted, inculcated, and in many ways even acted on, as if no other truth existed in the world, or at all events none that could limit or qualify the first. I acknowledge that the tendency of all opinions to become sectarian is not cured by the freest discussion, but is often heightened and exacerbated thereby; the truth which ought to have been, but was not, seen, being rejected all the more violently because proclaimed by persons regarded as opponents. But it is not on the impassioned partisan, it is on the calmer and more disinterested bystander, that this collision of opinions works its salutary effect. Not the violent conflict between parts of the truth, but the quiet suppression of half of it, is the formidable evil; there is always hope when people are forced to listen to both sides; it is when they attend only to one that errors harden into prejudices, and truth itself ceases to have the effect of truth, by being exaggerated into falsehood. And since there are few mental attributes more rare than that judicial faculty which can sit in intelligent judgment between two sides of a question, of which only one is represented by an advocate before it, truth has no chance but in proportion as every side of it, every opinion which embodies any fraction of the truth, not only finds advocates, but is so advocated as to be listened to.

We have now recognised the necessity to the mental well-being of mankind (on which all their other well-being depends) of freedom of opinion, and freedom of the expression of opinion, on four distinct grounds; which we will now briefly recapitulate.

First, if any opinion is compelled to silence, that opinion may, for aught we can certainly know, be true. To deny this is to assume our own infallibility.

Secondly, though the silenced opinion be an error, it may, and very commonly does, contain a portion of truth; and since the general or prevailing opinion on any subject is rarely or never the whole truth, it is only by the collision of adverse opinions that the remainder of the truth has any chance of being supplied.

Thirdly, even if the received opinion be not only true, but the whole truth; unless it is suffered to be, and actually is, vigorously and earnestly contested, it will, by most of those who receive it, be held in the manner of a prejudice, with little comprehension or feeling of its rational grounds. And not only this, but, fourthly, the meaning of the doctrine itself will be in danger of being lost or enfeebled, and deprived of its vital effect on the character and conduct: the dogma becoming a mere formal profession, inefficacious for good, but cumbering the ground, and preventing the growth of any real and heartfelt conviction, from reason or personal experience.

Before quitting the subject of freedom of opinion, it is fit to take some notice of those who say that the free expression of all opinions should be permitted, on condition that the manner be temperate, and do not pass the bounds of fair discussion. Much might be said on the impossibility of fixing where these supposed bounds are to be placed; for if the test be offence to those whose opinions are attacked, I think experience testifies that this offence is given whenever the attack is telling and powerful, and that every opponent who pushes them hard, and whom they find it difficult to answer, appears to them, if he shows any strong feeling on the subject, an intemperate opponent. But this, though an important consideration in a practical point of view, merges in a more fundamental objection. Undoubtedly the manner of asserting an opinion, even though it be a true one, may be very objectionable, and may justly incur severe censure. But the principal offences of the kind are such as it is mostly impossible, unless by accidental self-betrayal, to bring home to conviction. The gravest of them is, to argue sophistically, to suppress facts or arguments, to misstate the elements of the case, or misrepresent the opposite opinion. But all this, even to the most aggravated degree, is so continually done in perfect good faith, by persons who are not considered, and in many other respects may not deserve to be considered, ignorant or incompetent, that it is rarely possible, on adequate grounds, conscientiously to stamp the misrepresentation as morally culpable; and still less could law presume to interfere with this kind of controversial misconduct. With regard to what is commonly meant by intemperate discussion, namely invective, sarcasm, personality, and the like, the denunciation of these weapons would deserve more sympathy if it were ever proposed to interdict them equally to both sides; but it is only desired to restrain the employment of them against the prevailing opinion: against the unprevailing they may not only be used without general disapproval, but will be likely to obtain for him who uses them the praise of honest zeal and righteous indignation. Yet whatever mischief arises from their use is greatest when they are employed against the comparatively defenceless; and whatever unfair advantage can be derived by any opinion from this mode of asserting it, accrues almost exclusively to received opinions. The worst offence of this kind which can be committed by a polemic is to stigmatize those who hold the contrary opinion as bad and immoral men. To calumny of this sort, those who hold any unpopular opinion are peculiarly exposed, because they are in general few and uninfluential, and nobody but themselves feels much interested in seeing justice done them; but this weapon is, from the nature of the case, denied to those who attack a prevailing opinion: they can neither use it with safety to themselves, nor, if they could, would it do anything but recoil on their own cause. In general, opinions contrary to those commonly received can only obtain a hearing by studied moderation of language, and the most cautious avoidance of unnecessary offence, from which they hardly ever deviate even in a slight degree without losing ground: while unmeasured vituperation employed on the side of the prevailing opinion really does deter people from professing contrary opinions, and from listening to those who profess them. For the interest, therefore, of truth and justice, it is far more important to restrain this employment of vituperative language than the other; and, for example, if it were necessary to choose, there would be much more need to discourage offensive attacks on infidelity than on religion. It is, however, obvious that law and authority have no business with restraining either, while opinion ought, in every instance, to determine its verdict by the circumstances of the individual case; condemning everyone, on whichever side of the argument he places himself, in whose mode of advocacy either want of candor, or malignity, bigotry, or intolerance of feeling manifest themselves; but not inferring these vices from the side which a person takes, though it be the contrary side of the question to our own; and giving merited honor to every one, whatever opinion he may hold, who has calmness to see and honesty to state what his opponents and their opinions really are, exaggerating nothing to their discredit, keeping nothing back which tells, or can be supposed to tell, in their favor. This is the real morality of public discussion: and if often violated, I am happy to think that there are many controversialists who to a great extent observe it, and a still greater number who conscientiously strive towards it.

## JOHN STUART MILL

## *Considerations on Representative Government*

### Chapter 3
### That the Ideally Best Form of Government Is
### Representative Government

. . . There is no difficulty in showing that the ideally best form of government is that in which the sovereignty, or supreme controlling power in the last resort, is vested in the entire aggregate of the community; every citizen not only having a voice in the exercise of that ultimate sovereignty, but being, at least occasionally, called on to take an actual part in the government, by the personal discharge of some public function, local or general.

To test this proposition, it has to be examined in reference to the two branches into which, as pointed out in the last chapter, the inquiry into the goodness of a government conveniently divides itself, namely, how far it promotes the good management of the affairs of society by means of the existing faculties, moral, intellectual, and active, of its various members, and what is its effect in improving or deteriorating those faculties.

The ideally best form of government, it is scarcely necessary to say, does not mean one which is practicable or eligible in all states of civilisation, but the one which, in the circumstances in which it is practicable and eligible, is attended with the greatest amount of beneficial consequences, immediate and prospective. A completely popular government is the only polity which can make out any claim to this character. It is pre-eminent in both the departments between which the excellence of a political constitution is divided. It is both more favourable to present good government, and promotes a better and higher form of national character, than any other polity whatsoever.

Its superiority in reference to present well-being rests upon two principles, of as universal truth and applicability as any general propositions which can be laid down respecting human affairs. The first is, that the rights and interests of every or any person are only secure from being disregarded when the person interested is himself able, and habitually disposed, to stand up for them. The second is, that the general prosperity attains a greater height, and is more widely diffused, in proportion to the amount and variety of the personal energies enlisted in promoting it.

Putting these two propositions into a shape more special to their present application; human beings are only secure from evil at the hands of others in proportion as they have the power of being, and are, self-*protecting;* and they only achieve a high degree of success in their struggle with Nature in proportion as they are self-*dependent,* relying on what they themselves can do, either separately or in concert, rather than on what others do for them.

The former proposition—that each is the only safe guardian of his own rights and interests—is one of those elementary maxims of prudence, which every person, capable of conducting his own affairs, implicitly acts upon, wherever he himself is interested. Many, indeed, have a great dislike to it as a political doctrine, and are fond of holding it up to obloquy, as a doctrine of universal selfishness. To which we may answer, that whenever it ceases to be true that mankind, as a rule, prefer themselves to others, and those nearest to them to those more remote, from that moment Communism is not only practicable, but the only defensible form of society; and will, when that time arrives, be assuredly carried into effect. For my own part, not believing in universal selfishness, I have no difficulty in admitting that Communism would even now be practicable among the *élite* of mankind, and may become so among the rest. But as this opinion is anything but popular with those defenders of existing institutions who find fault with the doctrine of the general predominance of self-interest, I am inclined to think they do in reality believe that most men consider themselves before other people. It is not, however, necessary to affirm even thus much in order to support the claim of all to participate in the sovereign power. We need not suppose that when power resides in an exclusive class, that class will knowingly and deliberately sacrifice the other classes to themselves: it suffices that, in the absence of its natural defenders, the interest of the excluded is always in danger of being overlooked; and, when looked at, is seen with very different eyes from those of the persons whom it directly concerns. In this country, for example, what are called the working classes may be considered as excluded from all direct participation in the government. I do not believe that the classes who do participate in it have in general any intention of sacrificing the working classes to themselves. They once had that intention; witness the persevering attempts so long made to keep down wages by law. But in the present day their ordinary disposition is the very opposite: they willingly make considerable sacrifices, especially of their pecuniary interest, for the benefit of the working classes, and err rather by too lavish and indiscriminating beneficence; nor do I believe that any rulers in history have been actuated by a more sincere desire to do their duty towards the poorer portion of their countrymen. Yet does Parliament, or almost any of the members composing it, ever for an instant look at any question with the eyes of a working man? When a subject arises in which the labourers as such have an interest, is it regarded from any point of view but that of the employers of labour? I do not say that the working men's view of these questions is in general nearer to the truth than the other: but it is sometimes quite as near; and in case it ought to be respectfully listened to, instead of being, as it is, not merely turned away from, but ignored. On the question of strikes, for instance, it is doubtful if there is so much as one among the leading members of either House who is not firmly convinced that the reason of the matter is unqualifiedly on the side of the masters, and that the men's view of it is simply absurd. Those who have studied the question know well how far this is from being the case; and in how different, and how infinitely less superficial a manner the point would have to be argued, if the classes who strike were able to make themselves heard in Parliament.

It is an adherent condition of human affairs that no intention, however sincere, of protecting the interests of others can make it safe or salutary to tie up their own hands. Still more obviously true is it, that by their own hands only can any positive and durable improvement of their circumstances in life be worked out. Through the joint influence of these two principles, all free communities have both been more exempt from social injustice and crime, and have attained more brilliant prosperity, than any others, or than they themselves after they lost their freedom. Contrast the free states of the world, while their freedom lasted, with the contemporary subjects of monarchical or oligarchical despotism: the Greek cities with the Persian satrapies; the Italian republics and the free towns of Flanders and Germany, with the feudal monarchies of Europe; Switzerland, Holland, and England, with Austria or ante-revolutionary France. Their superior prosperity was too obvious ever to have been gainsaid: while their superiority in good government and social relations is proved by the prosperity, and is manifest besides in every page of history. If we compare, not one age with another, but the different governments which co-existed in the same age, no amount of disorder which exaggeration itself can pretend to have existed amidst the publicity of the free states can be compared for a moment with the contemptuous trampling upon the mass of the people which pervaded the whole life of the monarchical countries, or the disgusting individual tyranny which was of more than daily occurrence under the systems of plunder which they called fiscal arrangements, and in the secrecy of their frightful courts of justice.

It must be acknowledged that the benefits of freedom, so far as they have hitherto been enjoyed, were obtained by the extension of its privileges to a part only of the community; and that a government in which they are extended impartially to all is a desideratum still unrealised. But though every approach to this has an independent value, and in many cases more than an approach could not, in the existing state of general improvement, be made, the participation of all in these benefits is the ideally perfect conception of free government. In proportion as any, no matter who, are excluded from it, the interests of the excluded are left without the guarantee accorded to the rest, and they themselves have less scope and encouragement than they might otherwise have to that exertion of their energies for the good of themselves and of the community, to which the general prosperity is always proportioned.

Thus stands the case as regards present well-being; the good management of the affairs of the existing generation. If we now pass to the influence of the form of government upon character, we shall find the superiority of popular government over every other to be, if possible, still more decided and indisputable.

This question really depends upon a still more fundamental one, viz., which of two common types of character, for the general good of humanity, it is most desirable should predominate—the active, or the passive type; that which struggles against evils, or that which endures them; that which bends to circumstances, or that which endeavours to make circumstances bend to itself.

The commonplaces of moralists, and the general sympathies of mankind, are in favour of the passive type. Energetic characters may be admired, but the acquiescent and submissive are those which most men personally prefer. The passiveness of our neighbours increases our sense of security, and plays into the hands of our wilfulness. Passive characters, if we do not happen to need their activity, seem an obstruction the less in our own path. A contented character is not a dangerous rival. Yet nothing is more certain than that improvement in human affairs is wholly the work of the uncontented characters; and, moreover, that it is much easier for an active mind to acquire the virtues of patience than for a passive one to assume those of energy.

Of the three varieties of mental excellence, intellectual, practical, and moral, there never could be any doubt in regard to the first two which side had the advantage. All intellectual superiority is the fruit of active effort. Enterprise, the desire to keep moving, to be trying and accomplishing new things for our own benefit or that of others, is the parent even of speculative, and much more of practical, talent. The intellectual culture compatible with the other type is of that feeble and vague description which belongs to a mind that stops at amusement, or at simple contemplation. The test of real and vigorous thinking, the thinking which ascertains truths instead of dreaming dreams, is successful application to practice. Where that purpose does not exist, to give definiteness, precision, and an intelligible meaning to thought, it generates nothing better than the mystical metaphysics of the Pythagoreans or the Vedas. With respect to practical improvement, the case is still more evident. The character which improves human life is that which struggles with natural powers and tendencies, not that which gives way to them. The self-benefiting qualities are all on the side of the active and energetic character: and the habits and conduct which promote the advantage of each individual member of the community must be at least a part of those which conduce most in the end to the advancement of the community as a whole.

But on the point of moral preferability, there seems at first sight to be room for doubt. I am not referring to the religious feeling which has so generally existed in favour of the inactive character, as being more in harmony with the submission due to the divine will. Christianity as well as other religions has fostered this sentiment; but it is the prerogative of Christianity, as regards this and many other perversions, that it is able to throw them off. Abstractedly from religious considerations, a passive character, which yields to obstacles instead of striving to overcome them, may not indeed be very useful to others, no more than to itself, but it might be expected to be at least in-offensive. Contentment is always counted among the moral virtues. But it is a complete error to suppose that contentment is necessarily or naturally attendant on passivity of character; and unless it is, the moral consequences are mischievous. Where there exists a desire for advantages not possessed, the mind which does not potentially possess them by means of its own energies is apt to look with hatred and malice on those who do. The person bestirring himself with hopeful prospects to improve his circumstances is the one who feels good-will towards others engaged in, or who have succeeded in, the same pursuit. And where the majority are so engaged, those who do not attain the object have had the tone given to their feelings by the general habit of the country, and ascribe their failure to want of effort or opportunity, or to their personal ill luck. But those who, while desiring what others possess, put no energy into striving for it, are either incessantly grumbling that fortune does not do for them what they do not attempt to do for themselves, or overflowing with envy and ill-will towards those who possess what they would like to have.

In proportion as success in life is seen or believed to be the fruit of fatality or accident, and not of exertion, in that same ratio does envy develop itself as a point of national character. The most envious of all mankind are the Orientals. In Oriental moralists, in Oriental tales, the envious man is remarkably prominent. In real life, he is the terror of all who possess anything desirable, be it a palace, a handsome child, or even good health and spirits: the supposed effect of his mere look constitutes the all-pervading superstition of the evil eye. Next to Orientals in envy, as in activity, are some of the Southern Europeans. The Spaniards pursued all their great men with it, embittered their lives, and generally succeeded in putting an early stop to their successes. With the French, who are essentially a southern people, the double education of despotism and Catholicism has, in spite of their impulsive temperament, made submission and endurance the common character of the people, and their most received notion of wisdom and excellence: and if envy of one another, and of all superiority, is not more rife among them than it is, the circumstance must be ascribed to the many valuable counteracting elements in the French character, and most of all to the great individual energy which, though less persistent and more intermittent than in the self-helping and struggling Anglo-Saxons, has nevertheless manifested itself among the French in nearly every direction in which the operation of their institutions has been favourable to it.

There are, no doubt, in all countries, really contented characters, who not merely do not seek, but do not desire, what they do not already possess, and these naturally bear no ill-will towards such as have apparently a more favoured lot. But the great mass of seeming contentment is real discontent, combined with indolence or self-indulgence, which, while taking no legitimate means of raising itself, delights in bringing others down to its own level. And if we look narrowly even at the cases of innocent contentment, we perceive that they only win our admiration when the indifference is solely to improvement in outward circumstances, and there is a striving for perpetual advancement in spiritual worth, or at least a disinterested zeal to benefit others. The contented man, or the contented family, who have no ambition to make any one else happier, to promote the good of their country or their neighbourhood, or to improve themselves in moral excellence, excite in us neither admiration nor approval. We rightly ascribe this sort of contentment to mere unmanliness and want of spirit. The content which we approve is an ability to do cheerfully without what cannot be had, a just appreciation of the comparative value of different objects of desire, and a willing renunciation of the less when incompatible with the greater. These, however, are excellences more natural to the character, in proportion as it is actively engaged in the attempt to improve its own or some other lot. He who is continually measuring his energy against difficulties learns what are the difficulties insuperable to him, and what are those which, though he might overcome, the success is not worth the cost. He whose thoughts and activities are all needed for, and habitually employed in, practicable and useful enterprises, is the person of all others least likely to let his mind dwell with brooding discontent upon things either not worth attaining, or which are not so to him. Thus the active, self-helping character is not only intrinsically the best, but is the likeliest to acquire all that is really excellent or desirable in the opposite type.

The striving, go-ahead character of England and the United States is only a fit subject of disapproving criticism on account of the very secondary objects on which it commonly expends its strength. In itself it is the foundation of the best hopes for the general improvement of mankind. It has been acutely remarked that whenever anything goes amiss the habitual impulse of French people is to say, "Il faut de la patience"; and of English people, "What a shame." The people who think it a shame when anything goes wrong—who rush to the conclusion that the evil could and ought to have been prevented, are those who, in the long run, do most to make the world better. If the desires are low placed, if they extend to little beyond physical comfort, and the show of riches, the immediate results of the energy will not be much more than the continual extension of man's power over material objects; but even this makes room, and prepares the mechanical appliances, for the greatest intellectual and social achievements; and while the energy is there, some persons will apply it, and it will be applied more and more, to the perfecting not of outward circumstances alone, but of man's inward nature. Inactivity, unaspiringness, absence of desire, are a more fatal hindrance to improvement than any misdirection of energy; and are that through which alone, when existing in the mass, any very formidable misdirection by an energetic few becomes possible. It is this, mainly, which retains in a savage or semi-savage state the great majority of the human race.

Now there can be no kind of doubt that the passive type of character is favoured by the government of one or a few, and the active self-helping type by that of the Many. Irresponsible rulers need the quiescence of the ruled more than they need any activity but that which they can compel. Submissiveness to the prescriptions of men as necessities of nature is the lesson inculcated by all governments upon those who are wholly without participation in them. The will of superiors, and the law as the will of superiors, must be passively yielded to. But no men are mere instruments or materials in the hands of their rulers who have will or spirit or a spring of internal activity in the rest of their proceedings: and any manifestation of these qualities, instead of receiving encouragement from despots, has to get itself forgiven by them. Even when irresponsible rulers are not sufficiently conscious of danger from the mental activity of their subjects to be desirous of repressing it, the position itself is a repression. Endeavour is even more effectually restrained by the certainty of its impotence than by any positive discouragement. Between subjection to the will of others, and the virtues of self-help and self-government, there is a natural incompatibility. This is more or less complete, according as the bondage is strained or relaxed. Rulers differ very much in the length to which they carry the control of the free agency of their subjects, or the supersession of it by managing their business for them. But the difference is in degree, not in principle; and the best despots often go the greatest lengths in chaining up the free agency of their subjects. A bad despot, when his own personal indulgences have been provided for, may sometimes be willing to let the people alone; but a good despot insists on doing them good, by making them do their own business in a better way than they themselves know of. The regulations which restricted to fixed processes all the leading branches of French manufactures were the work of the great [Jean Baptiste] Colbert.

Very different is the state of the human faculties where a human being feels himself under no other external restraint than the necessities of nature, or mandates of society which he has his share in imposing, and which it is open to him, if he thinks them wrong, publicly to dissent from, and exert himself actively to get altered. No doubt, under a government partially popular, this freedom may be exercised even by those who are not partakers in the full privileges of citizenship. But it is a great additional stimulus to any one's self-help and self-reliance when he starts from even ground, and has not to feel that his success depends on the impression he can make upon the sentiments and dispositions of a body of whom he is not one. It is a great discouragement to an individual, and a still greater one to a class, to be left out of the constitution; to be reduced to plead from outside the door to the arbiters of their destiny, not taken into consultation within. The maximum of the invigorating effect of freedom upon the character is only obtained when the person acted on either is, or is looking forward to becoming, a citizen as fully privileged as any other. What is still more important than even this matter of feeling is the practical discipline which the character obtains from the occasional demand made upon the citizens to exercise, for a time and in their turn, some social function. It is not sufficiently considered how little there is in most men's ordinary life to give any largeness either to their conceptions or to their sentiments. Their work is a routine; not a labour of love, but of self-interest in the most elementary form, the satisfaction of daily wants; neither the thing done, nor the the process of doing it, introduces the mind to thoughts or feelings extending beyond individuals; if instructive books are within their reach, there is no stimulus to read them; and in most cases the individual has no access to any person of cultivation much superior to his own. Giving him something to do for the public, supplies, in a measure, all these deficiencies. If circumstances allow the amount of public duty assigned him to be considerable, it makes him an educated man. Notwithstanding the defects of the social system and moral ideas of antiquity, the practice of the dicastery and the ecclesia raised the intellectual standard of an average Athenian citizen far beyond anything of which there is yet an example in any other mass of men, ancient or modern. The proofs of this are apparent in every page of our great historian of Greece; but we need scarcely look further than to the high quality of the addresses which their great orators deemed best calculated to act with effect on their understanding and will. A benefit of the same kind, though far less in degree, is produced on Englishmen of the lower middle class by their liability to be placed on juries and to serve parish offices; which, though it does not occur to so many, nor is so continuous, nor introduces them to so great a variety of elevated considerations, as to admit of comparison with the public education which every citizen of Athens obtains from her democratic institutions, must make them nevertheless very different beings, in range of ideas and development of faculties, from those who have done nothing in their lives but drive a quill, or sell goods over a counter. Still more salutary is the moral part of the instruction afforded by the participation of the private citizen, if even rarely, in public functions. He is called upon, while so engaged, to weigh interests not his own; to be guided, in case of conflicting claims, by another rule than his private partialities; to apply, at every turn, principles and maxims which have for their reason of existence the common good: and he usually finds associated with him in the same work minds more familiarised than his own with these ideas and operations, whose study it will be to supply reasons to his understanding, and stimulation to his feeling for the general interest. He is made to feel himself one of the public, and whatever is for their benefit to be for his benefit. Where this school of public spirit does not exist, scarcely any sense is entertained that private persons, in no eminent social situation, owe any duties to society, except to obey the laws and submit to the government. There is no unselfish sentiment of identification with the public. Every thought or feeling, either of interest or of duty, is absorbed in the individual and in the family. The man never thinks of any collective interest, of any objects to be pursued jointly with others, but only in competition with them, and in some measure at their expense. A neighbour, not being an ally or an associate, since he is never engaged in any common undertaking for joint benefit, is therefore only a rival. Thus even private morality suffers, while public is actually extinct. Were this the universal and only possible state of things, the utmost aspirations of the lawgiver or the moralist could only stretch to make the bulk of the community a flock of sheep innocently nibbling the grass side by side.

From these accumulated considerations it is evident that the only government which can fully satisfy all the exigencies of the social state is one in which the whole people participate; that any participation, even in the smallest public function, is useful; that the participation should everywhere be as great as the general degree of improvement of the community will allow; and that nothing less can be ultimately desirable than the admission of all to a share in the sovereign power of the state. But since all cannot, in a community exceeding a single small town, participate personally in any but some very minor portions of the public business, it follows that the ideal type of a perfect government must be representative.

## Chapter 7
### Of True and False Democracy; Representation of All, and Representation of the Majority Only

It has been seen that the dangers incident to a representative democracy are of two kinds: danger of a low grade of intelligence in the representative body, and in the popular opinion which controls it; and danger of class legislation on the part of the numerical majority, these being all composed of the same class. We have next to consider how far it is possible so to organise the democracy as, without interfering materially with the characteristic benefits of democratic government, to do away with these two great evils, or at least to abate them, in the utmost degree attainable by human contrivance.

The common mode of attempting this is by limiting the democratic character of the representation, through a more or less restricted suffrage. But there is a previous consideration which, duly kept in view, considerably modifies the circumstances which are supposed to render such a restriction necessary. A completely equal democracy, in a nation in which a single class composes the numerical majority, cannot be divested of certain evils; but those evils are greatly aggravated by the fact that the democracies which at present exist are not equal, but systematically unequal in favour of the predominant class. Two very different ideas are usually confounded under the name democracy. The pure idea of democracy, according to its definition, is the government of the whole people by the whole people, equally represented. Democracy as commonly conceived and hitherto practised is the government of the whole people by a mere majority of the people, exclusively represented. The former is synonymous with the equality of all citizens; the latter, strangely confounded with it, is a government of privilege, in favour of the numerical majority, who alone possess practically any voice in the State. This is the inevitable consequence of the manner in which the votes are now taken, to the complete disfranchisement of minorities.

The confusion of ideas here is great, but it is so easily cleared up that one would suppose the slightest indication would be sufficient to place the matter in its true light before any mind of average intelligence. It would be so, but for the power of habit; owing to which the simplest idea, if unfamiliar, has as great difficulty in making its way to the mind as a far more complicated one. That the minority must yield to the majority, the smaller number to the greater, is a familiar idea; and accordingly men think there is no necessity for using their minds any further, and it does not occur to them that there is any medium between allowing the smaller number to be equally powerful with the greater, and blotting out the smaller number altogether. In a representative body actually deliberating, the minority must of course be overruled; and in an equal democracy (since the opinions of the Constituents, when they insist on them, determine those of the representative body) the majority of the people, through their representatives, will outvote and prevail over the minority and their representatives. But does it follow that the minority should have no representatives at all? Because the majority ought to prevail over the minority, must the majority have all the votes, the minority none? Is it necessary that the minority should not even be heard? Nothing but habit and old association can reconcile any reasonable being to the needless injustice. In a really equal democracy, every or any section would be represented, not disproportionately, but proportionately. A majority of the electors would always have a majority of the representatives; but a minority of the electors would always have a minority of the representatives. Man for man they would be as fully represented as the majority. Unless they are, there is not equal government, but a government of inequality and privilege: one part of the people rule over the rest: there is a part whose fair and equal share of influence in the representation is withheld from them; contrary to all just government, but, above all, contrary to the principle of democracy, which professes equality as its very root and foundation.

The injustice and violation of principle are not less flagrant because those who suffer by them are a minority; for there is not equal suffrage where every single individual does not count for as much as any other single individual in the community. But it is not only a minority who suffer. Democracy, thus constituted, does not even attain its ostensible object, that of giving the powers of government in all cases to the numerical majority. It does something very different: it gives them to a majority of the majority; who may be, and often are, but a minority of the whole. All principles are most effectually tested by extreme cases. Suppose then, that, in a country governed by equal and universal suffrage, there is a contested election in every constituency, and every election is carried by a small majority. The Parliament thus brought together represents little more than a bare majority of the people. This Parliament proceeds to legislate, and adopts important measures by a bare majority of itself. What guarantee is there that these measures accord with the wishes of a majority of the people? Nearly half the electors, having been outvoted at the hustings, have had no influence at all in the decision; and the whole of these may be, a majority of them probably are, hostile to the measures, having voted against those by whom they have been carried. Of the remaining electors, nearly half have chosen representatives who, by supposition, have voted against the measures. It is possible, therefore, and not at all improbable that the opinion which has prevailed was agreeable only to a minority of the nation, though a majority of that portion of it whom the institutions of the country have erected into a ruling class. If democracy means the certain ascendancy of the majority, there are no means of insuring that but by allowing every individual figure to tell equally in the summing up. Any minority left out, either purposely or by the play of the machinery, gives the power not to the majority, but to a minority in some other part of the scale.

The only answer which can possibly be made to this reasoning is, that as different opinions predominate in different localities, the opinion which is in a minority in some places has a majority in others, and on the whole every opinion which exists in the constituencies obtains its fair share of voices in the representation. And this is roughly true in the present state of the constituency; if it were not, the discordance of the House with the general sentiment of the country would soon become evident. But it would be no longer true if the present constituency were much enlarged; still less, if made co-extensive with the whole population; for in that case the majority in every locality would consist of manual labourers; and when there was any question pending, on which these classes were at issue with the rest of the community, no other class could succeed in getting represented anywhere. Even now, is it not a great grievance that in every Parliament a very numerous portion of the electors, willing and anxious to be represented, have no member in the House for whom they have voted? Is it just that every elector of Marylebone is obliged to be represented by two nominees of the vestries, every elector of Finsbury or Lambeth by those (as is generally believed) of the publicans? The constituencies to which most of the highly educated and public spirited persons in the country belong, those of the large towns, are now, in great part, either unrepresented or misrepresented. The electors who are on a different side in party politics from the local majority are unrepresented. Of those who are on the same side, a large proportion are misrepresented; having been obliged to accept the man who had the greatest number of supporters in their political party, though his opinions may differ from theirs on every other point. The state of things is, in some respects, even worse than if the minority were not allowed to vote at all; for then, at least, the majority might have a member who would represent their own best mind: while now, the necessity of not dividing the party, for fear of letting in its opponents, induces all to vote either for the first person who presents himself wearing their colours, or for the one brought forward by their local leaders; and these, if we pay them the compliment, which they very seldom deserve, of supposing their choice to be unbiased by their personal interest, are compelled, that they may be sure of mustering their whole strength, to bring forward a candidate whom none of the party will strongly object to—that is, a man without any distinctive peculiarity, any known opinions except the shibboleth of the party. This is strikingly exemplified in the United States; where, at the election of President, the strongest party never dares put forward any of its strongest men, because every one of these, from the mere fact that he has been long in the public eye, has made himself objectionable to some portion or other of the party, and is therefore not so sure a card for rallying all their votes as a person who has never been heard of by the public at all until he is produced as the candidate. Thus, the man who is chosen, even by the strongest party, represents perhaps the real wishes only of the narrow margin by which that party outnumbers the other. Any section whose support is necessary to success possesses a veto on the candidate. Any section which holds out more obstinately than the rest can compel all the others to adopt its nominee; and this superior pertinacity is unhappily more likely to be found among those who are holding out for their own interest than for that of the public. The choice of the majority is therefore very likely to be determined by that portion of the body who are the most timid, the most narrow-minded and prejudiced, or who cling most tenaciously to the exclusive class-interest; in which case the electoral rights of the minority, while useless for the purposes for which votes are given, serve only for compelling the majority to accept the candidate of the weakest or worst portion of themselves.

That, while recognising these evils, many should consider them as the necessary price paid for a free government is in no way surprising: it was the opinion of all the friends of freedom up to a recent period. But the habit of passing them over as irremediable has become so inveterate that many persons seem to have lost the capacity of looking at them as things which they would be glad to remedy if they could. From despairing of a cure, there is too often but one step to denying the disease; and from this follows dislike to having a remedy proposed, as if the proposer were creating a mischief instead of offering relief from one. People are so inured to the evils that they feel as if it were unreasonable, if not wrong, to complain of them. Yet, avoidable or not, he must be a purblind lover of liberty on whose mind they do not weigh; who would not rejoice at the discovery that they could be dispensed with. Now, nothing is more certain than that the virtual blotting-out of the minority is no necessary or natural consequence of freedom; that, far from having any connection with democracy, it is diametrically opposed to the first principle of democracy, representation in proportion to numbers. It is an essential part of democracy that minorities should be adequately represented. No real democracy, nothing but a false show of democracy, is possible without it.

# The Federalist Papers

*The Federalist Papers,* written by Alexander Hamilton, John Jay, and James Madison, were originally published in New York City newspapers during the debate over ratification of the Constitution. Intended as a defense of the document, they have become an authoritative interpretation of it. *Federalist* no. 10 outlines the principles of representation and federalism. *Federalist* no. 51 explains the separation of powers and checks and balances.

## *Federalist* no. 10

Among the numerous advantages promised by a well-constructed Union, none deserves to be more accurately developed than its tendency to break and control the violence of faction. The friend of popular governments never finds himself so much alarmed for their character and fate as when he contemplates their propensity to this dangerous vice. He will not fail, therefore, to set a due value on any plan which, without violating the principles to which he is attached, provides a proper cure for it. The instability, injustice, and confusion introduced into the public councils have, in truth, been the mortal diseases under which popular governments have everywhere perished, as they continue to be the favorite and fruitful topics from which the adversaries to liberty derive their most specious declamations. The valuable improvements made by the American constitutions on the popular models, both ancient and modern, cannot certainly be too much admired; but it would be an unwarrantable partiality to contend that they have as effectually obviated the danger on this side, as was wished and expected. Complaints are everywhere heard from our most considerate and virtuous citizens, equally the friends of public and private faith and of public and personal liberty, that our governments are too unstable, that the public good is disregarded in the conflicts of rival parties, and that measures are too often decided, not according to the rules of justice and the rights of the minor party, but by the superior force of an interested and overbearing majority. However anxiously we may wish that these complaints had no foundation, the evidence of known facts will not permit us to deny that they are in some degree true. It will be found, indeed, on a candid review of our situation, that some of the distresses under which we labor have been erroneously charged on the operation of our governments; but it will be found, at the same time, that other causes will not alone account for many of our heaviest misfortunes; and, particularly, for that prevailing and increasing distrust of public engagements and alarm for private rights which are echoed from one end of the continent to the other. These must be chiefly, if not wholly, effects of the unsteadiness and injustice with which a factious spirit has tainted our public administration.

By a faction I understand a number of citizens, whether amounting to a majority or minority of the whole, who are united and actuated by some common impulse of passion, or of interest, adverse to the rights of other citizens, or to the permanent and aggregate interests of the community.

There are two methods of curing the mischiefs of faction: the one, by removing its causes; the other, by controlling its effects.

There are again two methods of removing the causes of faction: the one, by destroying the liberty which is essential to its existence; the other, by giving to every citizen the same opinions, the same passions, and the same interests.

It could never be more truly said than of the first remedy that it was worse than the disease. Liberty is to faction what air is to fire, an aliment without which it instantly expires. But it could not be a less folly to abolish liberty, which is essential to political life, because it nourishes faction than it would be to wish the annihilation of air, which is essential to animal life because it imparts to fire its destructive agency.

The second expedient is as impracticable as the first would be unwise. As long as the reason of man continues fallible, and he is at liberty to exercise it, different opinions will be formed. As long as the connection subsists between his reason and his self-love, his opinions and his passions will have a reciprocal influence on each other; and the former will be objects to which the latter will attach themselves. The diversity in the faculties of men, from which the rights of property originate, is not less an insuperable obstacle to a uniformity of interests. The protection of these faculties is the first object of government. From the protection of different and unequal faculties of acquiring property, the possession of different degrees and kinds of property immediately results; and from the influence of these on the sentiments and views of the respective proprietors ensues a division of the society into different interests and parties.

The latent causes of faction are thus sown in the nature of man; and we see them everywhere brought into different degrees of activity, according to the different circumstances of civil society. A zeal for different opinions concerning religion, concerning government, and many other points, as well of speculation as of practice; an attachment to different leaders ambitiously contending for pre-eminence and power; or to persons of other descriptions whose fortunes have been interesting to the human passions, have, in turn, divided mankind into parties, inflamed them with mutual animosity, and rendered them much more disposed to vex and oppress each other than to co-operate for their common good. So strong is this propensity of mankind to fall into mutual animosities that where no substantial occasion presents itself the most frivolous and fanciful distinctions have been sufficient to kindle their unfriendly passions and excite their most violent conflicts. But the most common and durable source of factions has been the verious and unequal distribution of property. Those who hold and those who are without property have ever formed distinct interests in society. Those who are creditors, and those who are debtors, fall under a like discrimination. A landed interest, a manufacturing interest, a mercantile interest, a moneyed interest, with many lesser interests, grow up of necessity in civilized nations, and divide them into different classes, actuated by different sentiments and views. The regulation of these various and interfering interests forms the principal task of modern legislation and involves the spirit of party and faction in the necessary and ordinary operations of government.

No man is allowed to be a judge in his own cause because his interest would certainly bias his judgment, and, not improbably, corrupt his integrity. With equal, nay with greater reason, a body of men are unfit to be both judges and parties at the same time; yet what are many of the most important acts of legislation but so many judicial determinations, not indeed concerning the rights of single persons, but concerning the rights of large bodies of citizens? And what are the different classes of legislators but advocates and parties to the causes which they determine? Is a law proposed concerning private debts? It is a question to which the creditors are parties on one side and debtors on the other. Justice ought to hold the balance between them. Yet the parties are, and must be, themselves the judges; and the most numerous party, or in other words, the most powerful faction must be expected to prevail. Shall domestic manufacturers be encouraged, and in what degree, by restrictions on foreign manufacturers? are questions which would be differently decided by the landed and the manufacturing classes, and probably by neither with a sole regard to justice and the public good. The apportionment of taxes on the various descriptions of property is an act which seems to require the most exact impartiality; yet there is, perhaps, no legislative act in which greater opportunity and temptation are given to a predominant party to trample on the rules of justice. Every shilling with which they overburden the inferior number is a shilling saved to their own pockets.

It is in vain to say that enlightened statesmen will be able to adjust these clashing interests and render them all subservient to the public good. Enlightened statesmen will not always be at the helm. Nor in many cases, can such an adjustment be made at all without taking into view indirect and remote considerations, which will rarely prevail over the immediate interest which one party may find in disregarding the rights of another or the good of the whole.

The inference to which we are brought is that the *causes* of faction cannot be removed and that relief is only to be sought in the means of controlling its *effects*.

If a faction consists of less than a majority, relief is supplied by the republican principle, which enables the majority to defeat its sinister views by regular vote. It may clog the administration, it may convulse the society; but it will be unable to execute and mask its violence under the forms of the Constitution. When a majority is included in a faction, the form of popular government, on the other hand, enables it to sacrifice to its ruling passion or interest both the public good and the rights of other citizens. To secure the public good and private rights against the danger of such a faction, and at the same time to preserve the spirit and the form of popular government, is then the great object to which our inquiries are directed. Let me add that it is the great desideratum by which alone this form of government can be rescued from the opprobrium under which it has so long labored and be recommended to the esteem and adoption of mankind.

By what means is this object attainable? Evidently by one of two only. Either the existence of the same passion or interest in a majority at the same time must be prevented, or the majority, having such coexistent passion or interest, must be rendered, by their number and local situation, unable to concert and carry into effect schemes of oppression. If the impulse and the opportunity be suffered to coincide, we well know that neither moral nor religious motives can be relied on as an adequate control. They are not found to be such on the injustice and violence of individuals, and lose their efficacy in proportion to the number combined together, that is, as their efficacy becomes needful.

From this view of the subject it may be concluded that a pure democracy, by which I mean a society consisting of a small number of citizens, who assemble and administer the government in person, can admit of no cure for the mischiefs of faction. A common passion or interest will, in almost every case, be felt by a majority of the whole; a communication and concert results from the form of government itself; and there is nothing to check the inducements to sacrifice the weaker party or an obnoxious individual. Hence it is that such democracies have ever been spectacles of turbulence and contention; have ever been found incompatible with personal security or the rights of property; and have in general been as short in their lives as they have been violent in their deaths. Theoretic politicians, who have patronized this species of government, have erroneously supposed that by reducing mankind to a perfect equality in their political rights; they would at the same time be perfectly equalized and assimilated in their possessions, their opinions, and their passions.

A republic, by which I mean a government in which the scheme of representation takes place, opens a different prospect and promises the cure for which we are seeking. Let us examine the points in which it varies from pure democracy, and we shall comprehend both the nature of the cure and the efficacy which it must derive from the Union.

The two great points of difference between a democracy and a republic are: first, the delegation of the government, in the latter, to a small number of citizens elected by the rest; secondly, the greater number of citizens and greater sphere of country over which the latter may be extended.

The effect of the first difference is, on the one hand, to refine and enlarge the public views by passing them through the medium of a chosen body of citizens, whose wisdom may best discern the true interest of their country and whose patriotism and love of justice will be least likely to sacrifice it to temporary or partial considerations. Under such a regulation it may well happen that the public voice, pronounced by the representatives of the people, will be more consonant to the public good than if pronounced by the people themselves, convened for the purpose. On the other hand, the effect may be inverted. Men of factious tempers, of local prejudices, or of sinister designs, may, by intrigue, by corruption, or by other means, first obtain the suffrages, and then betray the interests of the people. The question resulting is, whether small or extensive republics are most favorable to the election of proper guardians of the public weal; and it is clearly decided in favor of the latter by two obvious considerations.

In the first place it is to be remarked that however small the republic may be the representatives must be raised to a certain number in order to guard against the cabals of a few; and that however large it may be they must be limited to a certain number in order to guard against the confusion of a multitude. Hence, the number of representatives in the two cases not being in proportion to that of the constituents, and being proportionally greatest in the small republic, it follows that if the proportion of fit characters be not less in the large than in the small republic, the former will present a greater option, and consequently a greater probability of a fit choice.

In the next place, as each representative will be chosen by a greater number of citizens in the large than in the small republic, it will be more difficult for unworthy candidates to practise with success the vicious arts by which elections are too often carried; and the suffrages of the people being more free, will be more likely to center on men who possess the most attractive merit and the most diffusive and established characters.

It must be confessed that in this, as in most other cases, there is a mean, on both sides of which inconveniences will be found to lie. By enlarging too much the number of electors, you render the representative too little acquainted with all their local circumstances and lesser interests; as by reducing it too much, you render him unduly attached to these and too little fit to comprehend and pursue great and national objects. The federal Constitution forms a happy combination in this respect; the great and aggregate interests being referred to the national, the local and particular to the State legislatures.

The other point of difference is the greater number of citizens and extent of territory which may be brought within the compass of republican than of democratic government; and it is this circumstance principally which renders factious combinations less to be dreaded in the former than in the latter. The smaller the society, the fewer probably will be the distinct parties and interests composing it; the fewer the distinct parties and interests, the more frequently will a majority be found of the same party; and the smaller the number of individuals composing a majority, and the smaller the compass within which they are placed, the more easily will they concert and execute their plans of oppression. Extend the sphere and you take in a greater variety of parties and interests; you make it less probable that a majority of the whole will have a common motive to invade the rights of other citizens; or if such a common motive exists, it will be more difficult for all who feel it to discover their own strength and to act in unison with each other. Besides other impediments, it may be remarked that, where there is a consciousness of unjust or dishonorable purposes, communication is always checked by distrust in proportion to the number whose concurrence is necessary.

Hence, it clearly appears that the same advantage which a republic has over democracy in controlling the effects of faction is enjoyed by a large over a small republic—is enjoyed by the Union over the States composing it. Does this advantage consist in the substitution of representatives whose enlightened views and virtuous sentiments render them superior to local prejudices and to schemes of injustice? It will not be denied that the representation of the Union will be most likely to possess these requisite endowments. Does it consist in the greater security afforded by a greater variety of parties, against the event of any one party being able to outnumber and oppress the rest? In an equal degree does the increased variety of parties comprised within the Union increase this security. Does it, in fine, consist in the greater obstacles opposed to the concert and accomplishment of the secret wishes of an unjust and interested majority? Here again the extent of the Union gives it the most palpable advantage.

The influence of factious leaders may kindle a flame within their particular States but will be unable to spread a general conflagration through the other States. A religious sect may degenerate into a political faction in a part of the Confederacy; but the variety of sects dispersed over the entire face of it must secure the national councils against any danger from that source. A rage for paper money, for an abolition of debts, for an equal division of property, or for any other improper or wicked project, will be less apt to pervade the whole body of the Union than a particular member of it, in the same proportion as such a malady is more likely to taint a particular county or district than an entire State.

In the extent and proper structure of the Union, therefore, we behold a republican remedy for the diseases most incident to republican government. And according to the degree of pleasure and pride we feel in being republicans ought to be our zeal in cherishing the spirit and supporting the character of federalists.

### *Federalist* no. 51

To what expedient, then, shall we finally resort, for maintaining in practice the necessary partition of power among the several departments as laid down in the Constitution? The only answer that can be given is that as all these exterior provisions are found to be inadequate the defect must be supplied, by so contriving the interior structure of the government as that its several constituent parts may, by their mutual relations, be the means of keeping each other in their proper places. Without presuming to undertake a full development of this important idea I will hazard a few general observations which may perhaps place it in a clearer light, and enable us to form a more correct judgment of the principles and structure of the government planned by the convention.

In order to lay a due foundation for that separate and distinct exercise of the different powers of government, which to a certain extent is admitted on all hands to be essential to the preservation of liberty, it is evident that each department should have a will of its own; and consequently should be so constituted that the members of each should have as little agency as possible in the appointment of the members of the others. Were this principle rigorously adhered to, it would require that all the appointments for the supreme executive, legislative, and judiciary magistracies should be drawn from the same fountain of authority, the people, through channels having no communication whatever with one another. Perhaps such a plan of constructing the several departments would be less difficult in practice than it may in contemplation appear. Some difficulties, however, and some additional expense would attend the execution of it. Some deviations, therefore, from the principle must be admitted. In the constitution of the judiciary department in particular, it might be inexpedient to insist rigorously on the principle: first, because peculiar qualifications being essential in the members, the primary consideration ought to be to select that mode of choice which best secures these qualifications: second, because the permanent tenure by which the appointments are held in that department must soon destroy all sense of dependence on the authority conferring them.

It is equally evident that the members of each department should be as little dependent as possible on those of the others for the emoluments annexed to their offices. Were the executive magistrate, or the judges, not independent of the legislature in this particular, their independence in every other would be merely nominal.

But the great security against a gradual concentration of the several powers in the same department consists in giving to those who administer each department the necessary constitutional means and personal motives to resist encroachments of the others. The provision for defense must in this, as in all other cases, be made commensurate to the danger of attack. Ambition must be made to counteract ambition. The interest of the man must be connected with the constitutional rights of the place. It may be a reflection on human nature that such devices should be necessary to control the abuses of government. But what is government itself but the greatest of all reflections on human nature? If men were angels, no government would be necessary. If angels were to govern men, neither external nor internal controls on government would be necessary. In framing a government which is to be administered by men over men, the great difficulty lies in this: you must first enable the government to control the governed; and in the next place oblige it to control itself. A dependence on the people is, no doubt, the primary control on the government; but experience has taught mankind the necessity of auxiliary precautions.

This policy of supplying, by opposite and rival interests, the defect of better motives, might be traced through the whole system of human affairs, private as well as public. We see it particularly displayed in all the subordinate distributions of power, where the constant aim is to divide and arrange the several offices in such a manner as that each may be a check on the other —that the private interest of every individual may be a sentinel over the public rights. These inventions of prudence cannot be less requisite in the distribution of the supreme powers of the State.

But it is not possible to give to each department an equal power of self-defense. In republican government, the legislative authority necessarily predominates. The remedy for this inconveniency is to divide the legislature into different branches; and to render them, by different modes of election and different principles of action, as little connected with each other as the nature of their common functions and their common dependence on the society will admit. It may even be necessary to guard against dangerous encroachments by still further precautions. As the weight of the legislative authority requires that it should be thus divided, the weakness of the executive may require, on the other hand, that it should be fortified. An absolute negative on the legislature appears, at first view, to be the natural defense with which the executive magistrate should be armed. But perhaps it would be neither altogether safe nor alone sufficient. On ordinary occasions it might not be exerted with the requisite firmness and on extraordinary occasions it might be perfidiously abused. May not this defect of an absolute negative be supplied by some qualified connection between this weaker department and the weaker branch of the stronger department, by which the latter may be led to support the constitutional rights of the former, without being too much detached from the rights of its own department?

If the principles on which these observations are founded be just, as I persuade myself they are, and they be applied as a criterion to the several State constitutions, and to the federal Constitution, it will be found that if the latter does not perfectly correspond with them, the former are infinitely less able to bear such a test.

There are, moreover, two considerations particularly applicable to the federal system of America, which place that system in a very interesting point of view.

*First.* In a single republic, all the power surrendered by the people is submitted to the administration of a single government; and the usurpations are guarded against by a division of the government into distinct and separate departments. In the compound republic of America, the power surrendered by the people is first divided between two distinct governments, and then the portion allotted to each subdivided among distinct and separate departments. Hence a double security arises to the rights of the people. The different governments will control each other, at the same time that each will be controlled by itself.

*Second.* It is of great importance in a republic not only to guard the society against the oppression of its rulers, but to guard one part of the society against the injustice of the other part. Different interests necessarily exit in different classes of citizens. If a majority be united by a common interest, the rights of the minority will be insecure. There are but two methods of providing against this evil: the one by creating a will in the community independent of the majority—that is, of the society itself; the other, by comprehending in the society so many separate descriptions of citizens as will render an unjust combination of a majority of the whole very improbable, if not impracticable. The first method prevails in all governments possessing an hereditary or self-appointed authority. This, at best, is but a precarious security; because a power independent of the society may as well espouse the unjust views of the major as the rightful interests of the minor party, and may possibly be turned against both parties. The second method will be exemplified in the federal republic of the United States. Whilst all authority in it will be derived from and dependent on the society, the society itself will be broken into so many parts, interests and classes of citizens, that the rights of individuals, or of the minority, will be in little danger from interested combinations of the majority. In a free government the security for civil rights must be the multiplicity of interests, and in the other in the multiplicity of sects. The degree of security in both cases will depend on the number of interests and sects; and this may be presumed to depend on the extent of country and number of people comprehended under the same government. This view of the subject must particularly recommend a proper federal system to all the sincere and considerate friends of republican government, since it shows that in exact proportion as the territory of the Union may be formed into more circumscribed Confederacies, or States, oppressive combinations of a majority will be facilitated; the best security, under the republican forms, for the rights of every class of citizen, will be diminished; and consequently the stability and independence of some member of the government, the only other security, must be proportionally increased. Justice is the end of government. It is the end of civil society. It ever has been and ever will be pursued until it be obtained, or until liberty be lost in the pursuit. In a society under the forms of which the stronger faction can readily unite and oppress the weaker, anarchy may as truly be said to reign as in a state of nature, where the weaker individual is not secured against the violence of the stronger; and as, in the latter state, even the stronger individual are prompted, by the uncertainty of their condition, to submit to a government which may protect the weak as well as themselves; so, in the former state, will the more powerful factions or parties be gradually induced, by a like motive, to which for a government which will protect all parties, the weaker as well as the more powerful. It can be little doubted that if the State of Rhode Island was separated from the Confederacy and left to itself, the insecurity of rights under the popular form of government within such narrow limits would be displayed by such reiterated oppressions of factious majorities that some power altogether independent of the people would soon be called for by the voice of the very factions whose misrule had proved the necessity of it. In the extended republic of the United States, and among the great variety of interests, parties, and sects which it embraces, a coalition of a majority of the whole society could seldom take place on any other principles than those of justice and the general good; whilst there being less pretext, also, to provide for the security of the former, by introducing into the government a will not dependent on the latter, or, in other words, a will independent of the society itself. It is no less certain than it is important, notwithstanding the contrary opinions which have been entertained, that the larger the society, provided it lie within a practicable sphere, the more duly capable it will be of self-government. And happily for the *republican cause*, the practicable sphere may be carried to a very great extent by a judicious modification and mixture of the *federal principle*.

# MILTON FRIEDMAN

## *Capitalism and Freedom*

Milton Friedman (b. 1912), recipient of a Nobel Prize in economics, is a professor at the University of Chicago. Described as an economic liberal, he emphasizes the relationship between capitalism and freedom. After *Capitalism and Freedom* (1962), his best-known work is *Free to Choose* (1980) written with his wife, Rose Friedman.

## Chapter 1
## The Relation between Economic Freedom
## and Political Freedom

It is widely believed that politics and economics are separate and largely unconnected; that individual freedom is a political problem and material welfare an economic problem; and that any kind of political arrangements can be combined with any kind of economic arrangements. The chief contemporary manifestation of this idea is the advocacy of "democratic socialism" by many who condemn out of hand the restrictions on individual freedom imposed by "totalitarian socialism" in Russia, and who are persuaded that it is possible for a country to adopt the essential features of Russian economic arrangements and yet to ensure individual freedom through political arrangements. The thesis of this chapter is that such a view is a delusion, that there is an intimate connection between economics and politics, that only certain combinations of political and economic arrangements are possible, and that in particular, a society which is socialist cannot also be democratic, in the sense of guaranteeing individual freedom.

Economic arrangements play a dual role in the promotion of a free society. On the one hand, freedom in economic arrangements is itself a component of freedom broadly understood, so economic freedom is an end in itself. In the second place, economic freedom is also an indispensable means toward the achievement of political freedom.

The first of these roles of economic freedom needs special emphasis because intellectuals in particular have a strong bias against regarding this aspect of freedom as important. They tend to express contempt for what they regard as material aspects of life, and to regard their own pursuit of allegedly higher values as on a different plane of significance and as deserving of special attention. For most citizens of the country, however, if not for the intellectual, the direct importance of economic freedom is at least comparable in significance to the indirect importance of economic freedom as a means to political freedom.

The citizen of Great Britain, who after World War II was not permitted to spend his vacation in the United States because of exchange control, was being deprived of an essential freedom no less than the citizen of the United States, who was denied the opportunity to spend his vacation in Russia because of his political views. The one was ostensibly an economic limitation on freedom and the other a political limitation, yet there is no essential difference between the two.

The citizen of the United States who is compelled by law to devote something like 10 percent of his income to the purchase of a particular kind of retirement contract, administered by the government, is being deprived of a corresponding part of his personal freedom. How strongly this deprivation may be felt and its closeness to the deprivation of religious freedom, which all would regard as "civil" or "political" rather than "economic," were dramatized by an episode involving a group of farmers of the Amish sect. On grounds of principle, this group regarded compulsory federal old age programs as an infringement of their personal individual freedom and refused to pay taxes or accept benefits. As a result, some of their livestock were sold by auction in order to satisfy claims for social security levies. True, the number of citizens who regard compulsory old age insurance as a deprivation of freedom may be few, but the believer in freedom has never counted noses.

A citizen of the United States who under the laws of various states is not free to follow the occupation of his own choosing unless he can get a license for it, is likewise being deprived of an essential part of his freedom. So is the man who would like to exchange some of his goods with, say, a Swiss for a watch but is prevented from doing so by a quota. So also is the Californian who was thrown into jail for selling Alka-Seltzer at a price below that set by the manufacturer under so-called "fair trade" laws. So also is the farmer who cannot grow the amount of wheat he wants. And so on. Clearly, economic freedom, in and of itself, is an extremely important part of total freedom.

Viewed as a means to the end of political freedom, economic arrangements are important because of their effect on the concentration or dispersion of power. The kind of economic organization that provides economic freedom directly, namely, competitive capitalism, also promotes political freedom because it separates economic power from political power and in this way enables the one to offset the other.

Historical evidence speaks with a single voice on the relation between political freedom and a free market. I know of no example in time or place of a society that has been marked by a large measure of political freedom, and that has not also used something comparable to a free market to organize the bulk of economic activity.

Because we live in a largely free society, we tend to forget how limited is the span of time and the part of the globe for which there has ever been anything like political freedom: the typical state of mankind is tyranny, servitude, and misery. The nineteenth century and early twentieth century in the Western world stand out as striking exceptions to the general trend of historical development. Political freedom in this instance clearly came along with the free market and the development of capitalist institutions. So also did political freedom in the golden age of Greece and in the early days of the Roman era.

History suggests only that capitalism is a necessary condition for political freedom. Clearly it is not a sufficient condition. Fascist Italy and Fascist Spain, Germany at various times in the last seventy years, Japan before World Wars I and II, tzarist Russia in the decades before World War I—are all societies that cannot conceivably be described as politically free. Yet, in each, private enterprise was the dominant form of economic organization. It is therefore clearly possible to have economic arrangements that are fundamentally capitalist and political arrangements that are not free.

Even in those societies, the citizenry had a good deal more freedom than citizens of a modern totalitarian state like Russia or Nazi Germany, in which economic totalitarianism is combined with political totalitarianism. Even in Russia under the Tzars, it was possible for some citizens, under some circumstances, to change their jobs without getting permission from political authority because capitalism and the existence of private property provided some check to the centralized power of the state.

The relation between political and economic freedom is complex and by no means unilateral. In the early nineteenth century, [Jeremy] Bentham and the Philosophical Radicals were inclined to regard political freedom as a means to economic freedom. They believed that the masses were being hampered by the restrictions that were being imposed upon them, and that if political reform gave the bulk of the people the vote, they would do what was good for them, which was to vote for laissez faire. In retrospect, one cannot say that they were wrong. There was a large measure of political reform that was accompanied by economic reform in the well-being of the masses followed this change in economic arrangements.

The triumph of Benthamite liberalism in nineteenth-century England was followed by a reaction toward increasing intervention by government in economic affairs. This tendency to collectivism was greatly accelerated, both in England and elsewhere, by the two World Wars. Welfare rather than freedom became the dominant note in democratic countries. Recognizing the implicit threat to individualism, the intellectual descendants of the Philosophical Radicals—Dicey, Mises, Hayek, and Simons, to mention only a few—feared that a continued movement toward centralized control of economic activity would prove *The Road to Serfdom,* as Hayek entitled his penetrating analysis of the process. Their emphasis was on economic freedom as a means toward political freedom.

Events since the end of World War II display still a different relation between economic and political freedom. Collectivist economic planning has indeed interfered with individual freedom. At least in some countries, however, the result has not been the suppression of freedom, but the reversal of economic policy. England again provides the most striking example. The turning point was perhaps the "control of engagements" order which, despite great misgivings, the Labour party found it necessary to impose in order to carry out its economic policy. Fully enforced and carried through, the law would have involved centralized allocation of individuals to occupations. This conflicted so sharply with personal liberty that it was enforced in a negligible number of cases, and then repealed after the law had been in effect for only a short period. Its repeal ushered in a decided shift in economic policy, marked by reduced reliance on centralized "plans" and "programs," by the dismantling of many controls, and by increased emphasis on the private market. A similar shift in policy occurred in most other democratic countries.

The proximate explanation of these shifts in policy is the limited success of central planning or its outright failure to achieve stated objectives. However, this failure is itself to be attributed, at least in some measure, to the political implications of central planning and to an unwillingness to follow out its logic when doing so requires trampling rough-shod on treasured private rights. It may well be that the shift is only a temporary interruption in the collectivist trend of this century. Even so, it illustrated the close relation between political freedom and economic arrangements.

Historical evidence by itself can never be convincing. Perhaps it was sheer coincidence that the expansion of freedom occurred at the same time as the development of capitalist and market institutions. Why should there be a connection? What are the logical links between economic and political freedom? In discussing these questions we shall consider first the market as a direct component of freedom, and then the indirect relation between market arrangements and political freedom. A by-product will be an outline of the ideal economic arrangements for a free society.

As liberals, we take freedom of the individual, or perhaps the family, as our ultimate goal in judging social arrangements. Freedom as a value in this sense has to do with the interrelations among people; it has no meaning whatsoever to a Robinson Crusoe on an isolated island (without his Man Friday). Robinson Crusoe on his island is subject to "constraint," he has limited "power," and he has only a limited number of alternatives, but there is no problem of freedom in the sense that is relevant to our discussion. Similarly, in a society freedom has nothing to say about what an individual does with his freedom; it is not an all-embracing ethic. Indeed, a major aim of the liberal is to leave the ethical problem for the individual to wrestle with. The "really" important ethical problems are those that face an individual in a free society—what he should do with his freedom. There are thus two sets of values that a liberal will emphasize—the values that are relevant to relations among people, which is the context in which he assigns first priority to freedom; and the values that are relevant to the individual in the exercise of his freedom, which is the realm of individual ethics and philosophy.

The liberal conceives of men as imperfect beings. He regards the problem of social organization to be as much a negative problem of preventing "bad" people from doing harm as of enabling "good" people to do good; and, of course, "bad" and "good" people may be the same people, depending on who is judging them.

The basic problem of social organization is how to co-ordinate the economic activities of large numbers of people. Even in relatively backward societies, extensive division of labor and specialization of function is required to make effective use of available resources. In advanced societies, the scale on which co-ordination is needed, to take full advantage of the opportunities offered by modern science and technology, is enormously greater. Literally millions of people are involved in providing one another with their daily bread, let alone with their yearly automobiles. The challenge to the believer in liberty is to reconcile this widespread interdependence with individual freedom.

Fundamentally, there are only two ways of co-ordinating the economic activities of millions. One is central direction involving the use of coercion—the technique of the army and of the modern totalitarian state. The other is voluntary co-operation of individuals—the technique of the market place.

The possibility of co-ordination through voluntary co-operation rests on the elementary—yet frequently denied—proposition that both parties to an economic transaction benefit from it, provided the transaction is bilaterally voluntary and informed.

Exchange can therefore bring about co-ordination without coercion. A working model of a society organized through voluntary exchange is a free private enterprise exchange economy—what we have been calling competitive capitalism.

In its simplest form, such a society consists of a number of independent households—a collection of Robinson Crusoes, as it were. Each household uses the resources it controls to produce goods and services that it exchanges for goods and services produced by other households, on terms mutually acceptable to the two parties to the bargain. It is thereby enabled to satisfy its wants indirectly by producing goods and services for others, rather than directly by producing goods for its own immediate use. The incentive for adopting this indirect route is, of course, the increased product made possible by division of labor and specialization of function. Since the household always has the alternative of producing directly for itself, it need not enter into any exchange unless it benefits from it. Hence, no exchange will take place unless both parties so benefit from it. Co-operation is thereby achieved without coercion.

Specialization of function and division of labor would not go far if the ultimate productive unit were the household. In a modern society, we have gone much farther. We have introduced enterprises which are intermediaries between individuals in their capacities as suppliers of service and as purchasers of goods. And similarly, specialization of function and division of labor could not go very far if we had to continue to rely on the barter of product for product. In consequence, money has been introduced as a means of facilitating exchange, and of enabling the acts of purchase and of sale to be separated into two parts.

Despite the important role of enterprises and of money in our actual economy, and despite the numerous and complex problems they raise, the central characteristic of the market technique of achieving co-ordination is fully displayed in the simple exchange economy that contains neither enterprises nor money. As in that simple model, so in the complex enterprise and money-exchange economy, co-operation is strictly individual and voluntary *provided:* (a) that enterprises are private, so that the ultimate contracting parties are individuals and (b) that individuals are effectively free to enter or not to enter into any particular exchange, so that every transaction is strictly voluntary.

It is far easier to state these provisos in general terms than to spell them out in detail, or to specify precisely the institutional arrangements most conducive to their maintenance. Indeed, much of technical economic literature is concerned with precisely these questions. The basic requisite is the maintenance of law and order to prevent physical coercion of one individual by another and to enforce contracts voluntarily entered into, thus giving substance to "private." Aside from this, perhaps the most difficult problems arise from monopoly—which inhibits effective freedom by denying individuals alternatives to the particular exchange—and from "neighborhood effects"—effects on third parties for which it is not feasible to charge or recompense them. These problems will be discussed in more detail in the following chapter.

So long as effective freedom of exchange is maintained, the central feature of the market organization of economic activity is that it prevents one person from interfering with another in respect of most of his activities. The consumer is protected from coercion by the seller because of the presence of other sellers with whom he can deal. The seller is protected from coercion by the consumer because of other consumers to whom he can sell. The employee is protected from coercion by the employer because of other employers for whom he can work, and so on. And the market does this impersonally and without centralized authority.

Indeed, a major source of objection to a free economy is precisely that it does this task so well. It gives people what they want instead of what a particular group thinks they ought to want. Underlying most arguments against the free market is a lack of belief in freedom itself.

The existence of a free market does not of course eliminate the need for government. On the contrary, government is essential both as a forum for determining the "rules of the game" and as an umpire to interpret and enforce the rules decided on. What the market does is to reduce greatly the range of issues that must be decided through political means, and thereby to minimize the extent to which government need participate directly in the game. The characteristic feature of action through political channels is that it tends to require or enforce substantial conformity. The great advantage of the market, on the other hand, is that it permits wide diversity. It is, in political terms, a system of proportional representation. Each man can vote, as it were, for the color of tie he wants and get it; he does not have to see what color the majority wants and then, if he is in the minority, submit.

It is this feature of the market that we refer to when we say that the market provides economic freedom. But this characteristic also has implications that go far beyond the narrowly economic. Political freedom means the absence of coercion of a man by his fellow men. The fundamental threat to freedom is power to coerce, be it in the hands of a monarch, a dictator, an oligarchy, or a momentary majority. The preservation of freedom requires the elimination of such concentration of power to the fullest possible extent and the dispersal and distribution of whatever power cannot be eliminated—a system of checks and balances. By removing the organization of economic activity from the control of political authority, the market eliminates this source of coercive power. It enables economic strength to be a check to political power rather than a reinforcement.

Economic power can be widely dispersed. There is no law of conservation which forces the growth of new centers of economic strength to be at the expense of existing centers. Political power, on the other hand, is more difficult to decentralize. There can be numerous small independent governments. But it is far more difficult to maintain numerous equipotent small centers of political power in a single large government than it is to have numerous centers of economic strength in a single large economy. There can be many millionaires in one large economy. But can there be more than one really outstanding leader, one person on whom the energies and enthusiasms of his countrymen are centered? If the central government gains power, it is likely to be at the expense of local governments. There seems to be something like a fixed total of political power to be distributed. Consequently, if economic power is joined to political power, it can serve as a check and a counter to political power.

The force of this abstract argument can perhaps best be demonstrated by example. Let us consider first, a hypothetical example that may help to bring out the principles involved, and then some actual examples from recent experience that illustrate the way in which the market works to preserve political freedom.

One feature of a free society is surely the freedom of individuals to advocate and propagandize openly for a radical change in the structure of the society—so long as the advocacy is restricted to persuasion and does not include force or other forms of coercion. It is a mark of the political freedom of a capitalist society that men can openly advocate and work for socialism. Equally, political freedom in a socialist society would require that men be free to advocate the introduction of capitalism. How could the freedom to advocate capitalism be preserved and protected in a socialist society?

In order for men to advocate anything, they must in the first place be able to earn a living. This already raises a problem in a socialist society, since all jobs are under the direct control of political authorities. It would take an act of self-denial whose difficulty is underlined by experience in the United States after World War II with the problem of "security" among Federal employees, for a socialist government to permit its employees to advocate policies directly contrary to official doctrine.

But let us suppose this act of self-denial to be achieved. For advocacy of capitalism to mean anything, the proponents must be able to finance their cause—to hold public meetings, publish pamphlets, buy radio time, issue newspapers and magazines, and so on. How could they raise the funds? There might and probably would be men in the socialist society with large incomes, perhaps even large capital sums in the form of government bonds and the like, but these would of necessity be high public officials. It is possible to conceive of a minor socialist official retaining his job although openly advocating capitalism. It strains credulity to imagine the socialist top brass financing such "subversive" activities.

The only recourse for funds would be to raise small amounts from a large number of minor officials. But this is no real answer. To tap these sources, many people would already have to be persuaded, and our whole problem is how to initiate and finance a campaign to do so. Radical movements in capitalist societies have never been financed this way. They have typically been supported by a few wealthy individuals who have become persuaded—by a Frederick Vanderbilt Field, or an Anita McCormick Blaine, or a Corliss Lamont, to mention a few names recently prominent, or by a Friedrich Engels, to go farther back. This is a role of inequality of wealth in preserving political freedom that is seldom noted—the role of the patron.

In a capitalist society, it is only necessary to convince a few wealthy people to get funds to launch any idea, however strange, and there are many such persons, many independent foci of support. And, indeed, it is not even necessary to persuade people or financial institutions with available funds of the soundness of the ideas to be propagated. It is only necessary to persuade them that the propagation can be financially successful; that the newspaper or magazine or book or other venture will be profitable. The competitive publisher, for example, cannot afford to publish only writing with which he personally agrees; his touchstone must be the likelihood that the market will be large enough to yield a satisfactory return on his investment.

In this way, the market breaks the vicious circle and makes it possible ultimately to finance such ventures by small amounts from many people without first persuading them. There are no such possibilities in the socialist society; there is only the all-powerful state.

Let us stretch our imagination and suppose that a socialist government is aware of this problem and is composed of people anxious to preserve freedom. Could it provide the funds? Perhaps, but it is difficult to see how. It could establish a bureau for subsidizing subversive propaganda. But how could it choose whom to support? If it gave to all who asked, it would shortly find itself out of funds, for socialism cannot repeal the elementary economic law that a sufficiently high price will call forth a large supply. Make the advocacy of radical causes sufficiently remunerative, and the supply of advocates will be unlimited.

Moreover, freedom to advocate unpopular causes does not require that such advocacy be without cost. On the contrary, no society could be stable if advocacy of radical change were costless, much less subsidized. It is entirely appropriate that men make sacrifices to advocate causes in which they deeply believe. Indeed, it is important to preserve freedom only for people who are willing to practice self-denial, for otherwise freedom degenerates into license and irresponsibility. What is essential is that the cost of advocating unpopular causes be tolerable and not prohibitive.

But we are not yet through. In a free market society, it is enough to have the funds. The suppliers of paper are as willing to sell it to the *Daily Worker* as to the *Wall Street Journal.* In a socialist society, it would not be enough to have the funds. The hypothetical supporter of capitalism would have to persuade a government factory making paper to sell to him, the government printing press to print his pamphlets, a government post office to distribute them among the people, a government agency to rent him a hall in which to talk, and so on.

Perhaps there is some way in which one could overcome these difficulties and preserve freedom in a socialist society. One cannot say it is utterly impossible. What is clear, however, is that there are very real difficulties in establishing institutions that will effectively preserve the possibility of dissent. So far as I know, none of the people who have been in favor of socialism and also in favor of freedom have really faced up to this issue, or made even a respectable start at developing the institutional arrangements that would permit freedom under socialism. By contrast, it is clear how a free market capitalist society fosters freedom.

A striking practical example of these abstract principles is the experience of Winston Churchill. From 1933 to the outbreak of World War II, Churchill was not permitted to talk over the British radio, which was, of course, a government monopoly administered by the British Broadcasting Corporation. Here was a leading citizen of his country, a Member of Parliament, a former cabinet minister, a man who was desperately trying by every device possible to persuade his countrymen to take steps to ward off the menace of Hitler's Germany. He was not permitted to talk over the radio to the British people because the BBC was a government monopoly and his position was too "controversial."

Another striking example, reported in the January 26, 1959, issue of *Time*, has to do with the "Blacklist Fadeout." Says the *Time* story,

> The Oscar-awarding ritual is Hollywood's biggest pitch for dignity, but two years ago dignity suffered. When one Robert Rich was announced as top writer for *The Brave One*, he never stepped forward. Robert Rich was a pseudonym, masking one of about 150 writers . . . blacklisted by the industry since 1947 as suspected Communists or fellow travelers. The case was particularly embarrassing because the Motion Picture Academy had barred any Communist or Fifth Amendment pleader from Oscar competition. Last week both the Communist rule and the mystery of Rich's identity were suddenly rescripted.
>
> Rich turned out to be Dalton (*Johnny Got His Gun*) Trumbo, one of the original "Hollywood Ten" writers who refused to testify at the 1947 hearings on Communism in the movie industry. Said producer Frank King, who had stoutly insisted that Robert Rich was "a young guy in Spain with a beard": "We have an obligation to our stockholders to buy the best script we can. Trumbo brought us *The Brave One* and we bought it."
>
> In effect it was the formal end of the Hollywood blacklist. For barred writers, the informal end came long ago. At least 15 percent of current Hollywood films are reportedly written by blacklist members. Said Producer King, "There are more ghosts in Hollywood than in Forest Lawn. Every company in town has used the work of blacklisted people. We're just the first to confirm what everybody knows."

One may believe, as I do, that communism would destroy all of our freedoms, one may be opposed to it as firmly and as strongly as possible, and yet, at the same time, also believe that in a free society it is intolerable for a man to be prevented from making voluntary arrangements with others that are mutually attractive because he believes in or is trying to promote communism. His freedom includes his freedom to promote communism. Freedom also, of course, includes the freedom of others not to deal with him under those circumstances. The Hollywood blacklist was an unfree act that destroys freedom because it was a collusive arrangement that used coercive means to prevent voluntary exchanges. It didn't work precisely because the market made it costly for people to preserve the blacklist. The commercial emphasis, the fact that people who are running enterprises have an incentive to make as much money as they can, protected the freedom of the individuals who were blacklisted by providing them with an alternative form of employment, and by giving people an incentive to employ them.

If Hollywood and the movie industry had been government enterprises or if in England it had been a question of employment by the British Broadcasting Corporation it is difficult to believe that the "Hollywood Ten" or their equivalent would have found employment. Equally, it is difficult to believe that under those circumstances, strong proponents of individualism and private enterprise—or indeed strong proponents of any view other than the status quo—would be able to get employment.

Another example of the role of the market in preserving political freedom, was revealed in our experience with McCarthyism. Entirely aside from the substantive issues involved, and the merits of the charges made, what protection did individuals, and in particular government employees, have against irresponsible accusations and probings into matters that it went against their conscience to reveal? Their appeal to the Fifth Amendment would have been a hollow mockery without an alternative to government employment.

Their fundamental protection was the existence of a private-market economy in which they could earn a living. Here again, the protection was not absolute. Many potential private employers were, rightly or wrongly, averse to hiring those pilloried. It may well be that there was far less justification for the costs imposed on many of the people involved than for the costs generally imposed on people who advocate unpopular causes. But the important point is that the costs were limited and not prohibitive, as they would have been if government employment had been the only possibility.

It is of interest to note that a disproportionately large fraction of the people involved apparently went into the most competitive sectors of the economy—small business, trade, farming—where the market approaches most closely the ideal free market. No one who buys bread knows whether the wheat from which it is made was grown by a Communist or a Republican, by a constitutionalist or a Fascist, or, for that matter, by a Negro or a white. This illustrates how an impersonal market separates economic activities from political views and protects men from being discriminated against in their economic activities for reasons that are irrelevant to their productivity—whether these reasons are associated with their view or their color.

As this example suggests, the groups in our society that have the most at stake in the preservation and strengthening of competitive capitalism are those minority groups which can most easily become the object of the distrust and enmity of the majority—the Negroes, the Jews, the foreign-born, to mention only the most obvious. Yet, paradoxically enough, the enemies of the free market—the Socialists and Communists—have been recruited in disproportionate measure from these groups. Instead of recognizing that the existence of the market has protected them from the attitudes of their fellow countrymen, they mistakenly attribute the residual discrimination to the market.

## Chapter 2
## The Role of Government in a Free Society

A common objection to totalitarian societies is that they regard the end as justifying the means. Taken literally, this objection is clearly illogical. If the end does not justify the means, what does? But this easy answer does not dispose of the objection; it simply shows that the objection is not well put. To deny that the end justifies the means is indirectly to assert that the end in question is not the ultimate end, that the ultimate end is itself the use of the proper means. Desirable or not, any end that can be attained only by the use of bad means must give way to the more basic end of the use of acceptable means.

To the liberal, the appropriate means are free discussion and voluntary co-operation, which implies that any form of coercion is inappropriate. The ideal is unanimity among responsible individuals achieved on the basis of free and full discussion. This is another way of expressing the goal of freedom emphasized in the preceding chapter.

From this standpoint, the role of the market, as already noted, is that it permits unanimity without conformity; that it is a system of effectively proportional representation. On the other hand, the characteristic feature of action through explicitly political channels is that it tends to require or to enforce substantial conformity. The typical issue must be decided "yes" or "no"; at most, provision can be made for a fairly limited number of alternatives. Even the use of proportional representation in its explicitly political form does not alter this conclusion. The number of separate groups that can in fact be represented is narrowly limited, enormously so by comparison with the proportional representation of the market. More important, the fact that the final outcome generally must be a law applicable to all groups, rather than separate legislative enactments for each "party" represented, means that proportional representation in its political version, far from permitting unanimity without conformity, tends toward ineffectiveness and fragmentation. It thereby operates to destroy any consensus on which unanimity with conformity can rest.

There are clearly some matters with respect to which effective proportional representation is impossible. I cannot get the amount of national defense I want and you, a different amount. With respect to such indivisible matters we can discuss, and argue, and vote. But having decided, we must conform. It is precisely the existence of such indivisible matters—protection of the individual and the nation from coercion are clearly the most basic —that prevents exclusive reliance on individual action through the market. If we are to use some of our resources for such indivisible items, we must employ political channels to reconcile differences.

The use of political channels, while inevitable, tends to strain the social cohesion essential for a stable society. The strain is least if agreement for joint action need be reached only on a limited range of issues on which people in any event have common views. Every extension of the range of issues for which explicit agreement is sought strains further the delicate threads that hold society together. If it goes so far as to touch an issue on which men feel deeply yet differently, it may well disrupt the society. Fundamental differences in basic values can seldom if ever be resolved at the ballot box; ultimately they can only be decided, though not resolved, by conflict. The religious and civil wars of history are a bloody testament to this judgment.

The widespread use of the market reduces the strain on the social fabric by rendering conformity unnecessary with respect to any activities it encompasses. The wider the range of activities covered by the market, the fewer are the issues on which explicitly political decisions are required and hence on which it is necessary to achieve agreement. In turn, the fewer the issues on which agreement is necessary, the greater is the likelihood of getting agreement while maintaining a free society.

Unanimity is, of course, an ideal. In practice, we can afford neither the time nor the effort that would be required to achieve complete unanimity on every issue. We must perforce accept something less. We are thus led to accept majority rule in one form or another as an expedient. That majority rule is an expedient rather than itself a basic principle is clearly shown by the fact that our willingness to resort to majority rule, and the size of the majority we require, themselves depend on the seriousness of the issue involved. If the matter is of little moment and the minority has no strong feelings about being overruled, a bare plurality will suffice. On the other hand, if the minority feels strongly about the issue involved, even a bare majority will not do. Few of us would be willing to have issues of free speech, for example, decided by a bare majority. Our legal structure is full of such distinctions among kinds of issues that require different kinds of majorities. At the extreme are those issues embodied in the Constitution. These are the principles that are so important that we are willing to make minimal concessions to expediency. Something like essential consensus was achieved initially in accepting them, and we require something like essential consensus for a change in them.

The self-denying ordinance to refrain from majority rule on certain kinds of issues that is embodied in our Constitution and in similar written or un-

written constitutions elsewhere, and the specific provisions in these constitutions or their equivalents prohibiting coercion of individuals, are themselves to
be regarded as reached by free discussion and as reflecting essential unanimity
about means.

I turn now to consider more specifically, though still in very broad terms,
what the areas are that cannot be handled through the market at all, or can be
handled only at so great a cost that the use of political channels may be preferable.

### Government as Rule-maker and Umpire

It is important to distinguish the day-to-day activities of people from the general customary and legal framework within which these take place. The day-
to-day activities are like the actions of the participants in a game when they
are playing it; the framework, like the rules of the game they play. And just as
a good game requires acceptance by the players both of the rules and of the
umpire to interpret and enforce them, so a good society requires that its members agree on the general conditions that will govern relations among them, on
some means of arbitrating different interpretations of these conditions, and on
some device for enforcing compliance with the generally accepted rules. As in
games, so also in society, most of the general conditions are the unintended
outcome of custom, accepted unthinkingly. At most, we consider explicitly
only minor modifications in them, though the cumulative effect of a series of
minor modifications may be a drastic alteration in the character of the game or
of the society. In both games and society also, no set of rules can prevail unless
most participants most of the time conform to them without external sanctions; unless, that is, there is a broad underlying social consensus. But we cannot rely on custom or on this consensus alone to interpret and to enforce the
rules; we need an umpire. These then are the basic roles of government in a
free society: to provide a means whereby we can modify the rules, to mediate
differences among us on the meaning of the rules, and to enforce compliance
with the rules on the part of those few who would otherwise not play the
game.

The need for government in these respects arises because absolute freedom is impossible. However attractive anarchy may be as a philosophy, it is
not feasible in a world of imperfect men. Men's freedoms can conflict, and
when they do, one man's freedom must be limited to preserve another's—as a
Supreme Court Justice once put it, "My freedom to move my fist must be limited by the proximity of your chin."

The major problem in deciding the appropriate activities of government
is how to resolve such conflicts among the freedoms of different individuals.
In some cases, the answer is easy. There is little difficulty in attaining near
unanimity to the proposition that one man's freedom to murder his neighbor

must be sacrificed to preserve the freedom of the other man to live. In other cases, the answer is difficult. In the economic area, a major problem arises in respect of the conflict between freedom to combine and freedom to compete. What meaning is to be attributed to "free" as modifying "enterprise"? In the United States, "free" has been understood to mean that anyone is free to set up an enterprise, which means that existing enterprises are not free to keep out competitors except by selling a better product at the same price or the same product at a lower price. In the continental tradition, on the other hand, the meaning has generally been that enterprises are free to do what they want, including the fixing of prices, division of markets, and the adoption of other techniques to keep out potential competitors. Perhaps the most difficult specific problem in this area arises with respect to combinations among laborers, where the problem of freedom to combine and freedom to compete is particularly acute.

A still more basic economic area in which the answer is both difficult and important is the definition of property rights. The notion of property, as it has developed over centuries and as it is embodied in our legal codes, has become so much a part of us that we tend to take it for granted, and fail to recognize the extent to which just what constitutes property and what rights the ownership of property confers are complex social creations rather than self-evident propositions. Does my having title to land, for example, and my freedom to use my property as I wish, permit me to deny to someone else the right to fly over my land in his airplane? Or does his right to use his airplane take precedence? Or does this depend on how high he flies? Or how much noise he makes? Does voluntary exchange require that he pay me for the privilege of flying over my land? Or that I must pay him to refrain from flying over it? The mere mention of royalties, copyrights, patents; shares of stock in corporations; riparian rights, and the like, may perhaps emphasize the role of generally accepted social rules in the very definition of property. It may suggest also that, in many cases, the existence of a well specified and generally accepted definition of property is far more important than just what the definition is.

Another economic area that raises particularly difficult problems is the monetary system. Government responsibility for the monetary system has long been recognized. It is explicitly provided for in the constitutional provision which gives Congress the power "to coin money, regulate the value thereof, and of foreign coin." There is probably no other area of economic activity with respect to which government action has been so uniformly accepted. This habitual and by now almost unthinking acceptance of governmental responsibility makes thorough understanding of the grounds for such responsibility all the more necessary, since it enhances the danger that the scope of government will spread from activities that are, to those that are not, appropriate in a free society, from providing a monetary framework to determining the allocation of resources among individuals. We shall discuss this problem in detail in chapter 3.

In summary, the organization of economic activity through voluntary exchange presumes that we have provided, through government, for the maintenance of law and order to prevent coercion of one individual by another, the enforcement of contracts voluntarily entered into, the definition of the meaning of property rights, the interpretation and enforcement of such rights, and the provision of a monetary framework.

### Action Through Government on Grounds of Technical Monopoly and Neighborhood Effects

The role of government just considered is to do something that the market cannot do for itself, namely, to determine, arbitrate, and enforce the rules of the game. We may also want to do through government some things that might conceivably be done through the market but that technical or similar conditions render it difficult to do in that way. These all reduce to cases in which strictly voluntary exchange is either exceedingly costly or practically impossible. There are two general classes of such cases: monopoly and similar market imperfections, and neighborhood effects. Exchange is truly voluntary only when nearly equivalent alternatives exist. Monopoly implies the absence of alternatives and thereby inhibits effective freedom of exchange. In practice, monopoly frequently, if not generally, arises from government support or from collusive agreements among individuals. With respect to these, the problem is either to avoid governmental fostering of monopoly or to stimulate the effective enforcement of rules such as those embodied in our anti-trust laws. However, monopoly may also arise because it is technically efficient to have a single producer or enterprise. I venture to suggest that such cases are more limited than is supposed but they unquestionably do arise. A simple example is perhaps the provision of telephone services within a community. I shall refer to such cases as "technical" monopoly.

When technical conditions make a monopoly the natural outcome of competitive market forces, there are only three alternatives that seem available: private monopoly, public monopoly, or public regulation. All three are bad so we must choose among evils. Henry Simons, observing public regulation of monopoly in the United States, found the results so distasteful that he concluded public monopoly would be a lesser evil. Walter Eucken, a noted German liberal, observing public monopoly in German railroads, found the results so distasteful that he concluded public regulation would be a lesser evil. Having learned from both, I reluctantly conclude that, if tolerable, private monopoly may be the least of the evils.

If society were static so that the conditions which give rise to a technical monopoly were sure to remain, I would have little confidence in this solution. In a rapidly changing society, however, the conditions making for technical monopoly frequently change and I suspect that both public regulation and public monopoly are likely to be less responsive to such changes in conditions, to be less readily capable of elimination, than private monopoly.

Railroads in the United States are an excellent example. A large degree of monopoly in railroads was perhaps inevitable on technical grounds in the nineteenth century. This was the justification for the Interstate Commerce Commission. But conditions have changed. The emergence of road and air transport has reduced the monopoly element in railroads to negligible proportions. Yet we have not eliminated the ICC. On the contrary, the ICC, which started out as an agency to protect the public from exploitation by the railroads, has become an agency to protect railroads from competition by trucks and other means of transport, and more recently even to protect existing truck companies from competition by new entrants. Similarly, in England, when the railroads were nationalized, trucking was at first brought into the state monopoly. If railroads had never been subjected to regulation in the United States, it is nearly certain that by now transportation, including railroads, would be a highly competitive industry with little or no remaining monopoly elements.

The choice between the evils of private monopoly, public monopoly, and public regulation cannot, however, be made once and for all, independently of the factual circumstances. If the technical monopoly is of a service or commodity that is regarded as essential and if its monopoly power is sizable, even the short-run effects of private unregulated monopoly may not be tolerable, and either public regulation or ownership may be a lesser evil.

Technical monopoly may on occasion justify a *de facto* public monopoly. It cannot by itself justify a public monopoly achieved by making it illegal for anyone else to compete. For example, there is no way to justify our present public monopoly of the post office. It may be argued that the carrying of mail is a technical monopoly and that a government monopoly is the least of evils. Along these lines, one could perhaps justify a government post office but not the present law, which makes it illegal for anybody else to carry mail. If the delivery of mail is a technical monopoly, no one will be able to succeed in competition with the government. If it is not, there is no reason why the government should be engaged in it. The only way to find out is to leave other people free to enter.

The historical reason why we have a post office monopoly is because the Pony Express did such a good job of carrying the mail across the continent that, when the government introduced transcontinental service, it couldn't compete effectively and lost money. The result was a law making it illegal for anybody else to carry the mail. That is why the Adams Express Company is an investment trust today instead of an operating company. I conjecture that if entry into the mail-carrying business were open to all, there would be a large number of firms entering it and this archaic industry would become revolutionized in short order.

A second general class of cases in which strictly voluntary exchange is impossible arises when actions of individuals have effects on other individuals for which it is not feasible to charge or recompense them. This is the problem of "neighborhood effects." An obvious example is the pollution of a stream. The man who pollutes a stream is in effect forcing others to exchange good water for bad. These others might be willing to make the exchange at a price. But it is not feasible for them, acting individually, to avoid the exchange or to enforce appropriate compensation.

A less obvious example is the provision of highways. In this case, it is technically possible to identify and hence charge individuals for their use of the roads and so to have private operation. However, for general access roads, involving many points of entry and exit, the costs of collection would be extremely high if a charge were to be made for the specific services received by each individual, because of the necessity of establishing toll booths or the equivalent at all entrances. The gasoline tax is a much cheaper method of charging individuals roughly in proportion to their use of the roads. This method, however, is one in which the particular payment cannot be identified closely with the particular use. Hence, it is hardly feasible to have private enterprise provide the service and collect the charge without establishing extensive private monopoly.

These considerations do not apply to long-distance turnpikes with high density of traffic and limited access. For these, the costs of collection are small and in many cases are now being paid, and there are often numerous alternatives, so that there is no serious monopoly problem. Hence, there is every reason why these should be privately owned and operated. If so owned and operated, the enterprise running the highway should receive the gasoline taxes paid on account of travel on it.

Parks are an interesting example because they illustrate the difference between cases that can and cases that cannot be justified by neighborhood effects, and because almost everyone at first sight regards the conduct of National Parks as obviously a valid function of government. In fact, however, neighborhood effects may justify a city park; they do not justify a national park, like Yellowstone National Park or the Grand Canyon. What is the fundamental difference between the two? For the city park, it is extremely difficult to identify the people who benefit from it and to charge them for the benefits which they receive. If there is a park in the middle of the city, the houses on all sides get the benefit of the open space, and people who walk through it or by it also benefit. To maintain toll collectors at the gates or to impose annual charges per window overlooking the park would be very expensive and difficult. The entrances to a national park like Yellowstone, on the other hand, are few; most of the people who come stay for a considerable period of time and it is perfectly feasible to set up toll gates and collect admission charges. This is indeed now done, though the charges do not cover the whole costs. If the public wants this kind of an activity enough to pay for it, private enterprises will have every incentive to provide such parks. And, of course, there are many private enterprises of this nature now in existence. I cannot myself conjure up any neighborhood effects or important monopoly effects that would justify governmental activity in this area.

Considerations like those I have treated under the heading of neighborhood effects have been used to rationalize almost every conceivable intervention. In many instances, however, this rationalization is special pleading rather than a legitimate application of the concept of neighborhood effects. Neighborhood effects cut both ways. They can be a reason for limiting the activities of government as well as for expanding them. Neighborhood effects impede voluntary exchange because it is difficult to identify the effects on third parties and to measure their magnitude; but this difficulty is present in governmental activity as well. It is hard to know when neighborhood effects are sufficiently large to justify particular costs in overcoming them and even harder to distribute the costs in an appropriate fashion. Consequently, when government engages in activities to overcome neighborhood effects, it will in part introduce an additional set of neighborhood effects by failing to charge or to compensate individuals properly. Whether the original or the new neighborhood effects are the more serious can only be judged by the facts of the individual case, and even then, only very approximately. Furthermore, the use of government to overcome neighborhood effects itself has an extremely important neighborhood effect which is unrelated to the particular occasion for government action. Every act of government intervention limits the area of individual freedom directly and threatens the preservation of freedom indirectly for reasons elaborated in the first chapter.

Our principles offer no hard and fast line how far it is appropriate to use government to accomplish jointly what it is difficult or impossible for us to accomplish separately through strictly voluntary exchange. In any particular case of proposed intervention, we must make up a balance sheet, listing separately the advantages and disadvantages. Our principles tell us what items to put on the one side and what items on the other and they give us some basis for attaching importance to the different items. In particular, we shall always want to enter on the liability side of any proposed government intervention, its neighborhood effect in threatening freedom, and give this effect considerable weight. Just how much weight to give to it, as to other items, depends upon the circumstances. If, for example, existing government intervention is minor, we shall attach a smaller weight to the negative effects of additional government intervention. This is an important reason why many earlier liberals, like Henry Simons, writing at a time when government was small by today's standards, were willing to have government undertake activities that today's liberals would not accept now that government has become so overgrown.

### Action Through Government on Paternalistic Grounds

Freedom is a tenable objective only for responsible individuals. We do not believe in freedom for madmen or children. The necessity of drawing a line between responsible individuals and others is inescapable, yet it means that there is an essential ambiguity in our ultimate objective of freedom. Paternalism is inescapable for those whom we designate as not responsible.

The clearest case, perhaps, is that of madmen. We are willing neither to permit them freedom nor to shoot them. It would be nice if we could rely on voluntary activities of individuals to house and care for the madmen. But I think we cannot rule out the possibility that such charitable activities will be inadequate, if only because of the neighborhood effect involved in the fact that I benefit if another man contributes to the care of the insane. For this reason, we may be willing to arrange for their care through government.

Children offer a more difficult case. The ultimate operative unit in our society is the family, not the individual. Yet the acceptance of the family as the unit rests in considerable part on expediency rather than principle. We believe that parents are generally best able to protect their children and to provide for their development into responsible individuals for whom freedom is appropriate. But we do not believe in the freedom of parents to do what they will with other people. The children are responsible individuals in embryo, and a believer in freedom believes in protecting their ultimate rights.

To put this in a different and what may seem a more callous way, children are at one and the same time consumer goods and potentially responsible members of society. The freedom of individuals to use their economic resources as they want includes the freedom to use them to have children—to buy, as it were, the services of children as a particular form of consumption. But once this choice is exercised, the children have a value in and of themselves and have a freedom of their own that is not simply an extension of the freedom of the parents.

The paternalistic ground for governmental activity is in many ways the most troublesome to a liberal; for it involves the acceptance of a principle —that some shall decide for others—which he finds objectionable in most applications and which he rightly regards as a hallmark of his chief intellectual opponents, the proponents of collectivism in one or another of its guises, whether it be communism, socialism, or a welfare state. Yet there is no use pretending that problems are simpler than in fact they are. There is no avoiding the need for some measure of paternalism. As Dicey wrote in 1914 about an act for the protection of mental defectives, "The Mental Deficiency Act is the first step along a path on which no sane man can decline to enter, but which, if too far pursued, will bring statesmen across difficulties hard to meet without considerable interference with individual liberty." There is no formula that can tell us where to stop. We must rely on our fallible judgment and, having reached a judgment, on our ability to persuade our fellow men that it is a correct judgment, or their ability to persuade us to modify our views. We must put our faith, here as elsewhere, in a consensus reached by imperfect and biased men through free discussion and trial and error.

## Conclusion

A government which maintained law and order, defined property rights, served as a means whereby we could modify property rights and other rules of the economic game, adjudicated disputes about the interpretation of the rules, enforced contracts, promoted competition, provided a monetary framework, engaged in activities to counter technical monopolies and to overcome neighborhood effects widely regarded as sufficiently important to justify government intervention, and which supplemented private charity and the private family in protecting the irresponsible, whether madman or child—such a government would clearly have important functions to perform. The consistent liberal is not an anarchist.

Yet it is also true that such a government would have clearly limited functions and would refrain from a host of activities that are now undertaken by federal and state governments in the United States, and their counterparts in other Western countries. Succeeding chapters will deal in some detail with some of these activities, and a few have been discussed above, but it may help to give a sense of proportion about the role that a liberal would assign government simply to list, in closing this chapter, some activities currently undertaken by government in the U.S., that cannot, so far as I can see, validly be justified in terms of the principles outlined above:

1. Parity price support programs for agriculture.

2. Tariffs on imports or restrictions on exports, such as current oil import quotas, sugar quotas, etc.

3. Governmental control of output, such as through the farm program, or through prorationing of oil as is done by the Texas Railroad Commission.

4. Rent control, such as is still practiced in New York, or more general price and wage controls such as were imposed during and just after World War II.

5. Legal minimum wage rates, or legal maximum prices, such as the legal maximum of zero on the rate of interest that can be paid on demand deposits by commercial banks, or the legally fixed maximum rates that can be paid on savings and time deposits.

6. Detailed regulation of industries, such as the regulation of transportation by the Interstate Commerce Commission. This had some justification on technical monopoly grounds when initially introduced for railroads; it has none now for any means of transport. Another example is detailed regulation of banking.

7. A similar example, but one which deserves special mention because of

its implicit censorship and violation of free speech, is the control of radio and television by the Federal Communications Commission.

8. Present social security programs, especially the old-age and retirement programs compelling people in effect (a) to spend a specified fraction of their income on the purchase of retirement annuity, (b) to buy the annuity from a publicly operated enterprise.

9. Licensure provisions in various cities and states which restrict particular enterprises or occupations or professions to people who have a license, where the license is more than a receipt for a tax which anyone who wishes to enter the activity may pay.

10. So-called "public-housing" and the host of other subsidy programs directed at fostering residential construction such as FHA and VA guarantee of mortgage, and the like.

11. Conscription to man the military services in peacetime. The appropriate free market arrangement is volunteer military forces; which is to say, hiring men to serve. There is no justification for not paying whatever price is necessary to attract the required number of men. Present arrangements are inequitable and arbitrary, seriously interfere with the freedom of young men to shape their lives, and probably are even more costly than the market alternative. (Universal military training to provide a reserve for war time is a different problem and may be justified on liberal grounds.)

12. National parks, as noted above.

13. The legal prohibition on the carrying of mail for profit.

14. Publicly owned and operated toll roads, as noted above.

This list is far from comprehensive.

ISAAC KRAMNICK

## Equal Opportunity and the Race of Life

Born in 1938, Isaac Kramnick is currently a professor of government at Cornell University in Ithaca, New York. He is the author of numerous articles on American and English liberalism. His books include *Bolingbroke and His Circle* (1970) and *The Rage of Edmund Burke* (1977).

A fair race was what Lyndon Johnson pleaded for in his 1965 commencement address at Howard University that ushered in the era of affirmative action.

> You do not take a person, who for years has been hobbled by chains and liberate him, bring him up to the starting line of a race and then say "you are free to compete with all the others," and still justly believe that you have been completely fair.

Fifteen years later, *Bakke, Weber,* and the politics of affirmative action have stirred up a great public debate. The reasons are obvious. They raise sensitive questions of public policy and have grave implications for how we deal with one another, blacks and whites, men and women, workers and professionals, young and old. The focus of this debate has justifiably been on the here and now. But the doctrine of equal opportunity has occupied a central place in liberal ideology from the seventeenth century to the present, and the metaphor of life as a race was used centuries before Johnson's speech at Howard University.

*Bakke, Weber,* and the debate over affirmative action touch upon the deepest aspects of bourgeois liberalism. They are concerned with the marketplace, open or closed; with access to jobs and high status; with rewards to merit and talent; with privilege and the state. They involve the realization of self through work. They raise to public awareness the insecurity and anxiety inherent in a market society. As these issues are brought into public dialogue today, centuries-old beliefs lurk between every line of the briefs, learned articles, and position papers.

Central and enduring in liberalism is its unique conception of liberty and equality, rooted principally in attitudes toward work and the marketplace, toward achievement and talent. The revolutionary bourgeois attitude is best expressed in two famous cultural documents. The first is Beaumarchais's *Marriage of Figaro*, written in 1783 just before the French Revolution. The play, of course, was the basis of Mozart's opera. The plot, though complicated, is for our purposes, quite simple. It is built around the conflict between the great aristocrat Count Almaviva and commoner, the hardworking, industrious barber, Figaro. The count seems almost to have outwitted Figaro in Act 5, which prompts Figaro to his famous denunciation:

> Just because you're a great Lord, you think you're a genius. Nobility, fortune, rank, position—you're so proud of those things. What have you done to deserve so many rewards? You went to the trouble of being born, and no more.

So subversive were these sentiments that the play was banned and only surfaced again in France after the Revolution had dealt even more definitively with the Almavivas.

The second document is from Thomas Mann, part of whose genius consisted in his ability to describe with meticulous accuracy European bourgeois civilization. In the *Buddenbrooks* Mann gives a much more vivid summary of these basic liberal beliefs than did Beaumarchais: his nineteenth-century liberal revolutionary Morten Schwartzkopf is speaking, criticizing a friend who has just spoken well of an aristocratic acquaintance:

> They need only to be born to be the pick of everything, and look down on all the rest of us. While we, however hard we strive, cannot climb to their level. We, the bourgeoisie—the Third Estate as we have been called—we recognize only that nobility which consists of merit; we refuse to admit any longer the rights of the indolent aristocracy, we repudiate the class distinctions of the present day, we desire that all men should be free and equal. . . . So that all men, without distinction, shall be able to strive together and receive their reward according to their merit.

Writing at the turn of the twentieth century when these values would be assaulted on the left and right (as he so beautifully depicted in his *Magic Mountain*), Mann's sense of liberalism is the same as Beaumarchais's. Basic to both the dreams of Figaro and to Schwartzkopf is a vision of society where the rule or privilege is replaced by equal opportunity and where individuals, now masters of their destiny, are no longer the slaves of history, tradition, or birth.

Figaro's and Schwartzkopf's liberal vision of an ideal society is still with us, especially in America. But it is not some timeless, eternal ideal of humanity found, like so much else of our culture, in the antique world of Greece or Rome of the Judeo-Christian tradition. It emerged at a specific historic moment, for specific reasons, and with specific intellectual justifications. That moment was, of course, the grand transformation wrought in the Europe of the sixteenth, seventeenth, and eighteenth centuries by the rise of Protestantism and capitalism. The traditional hierarchical world was replaced in Western Europe by the modern liberal world as we know it. Central to this transformation were new conceptions of self and work.

Ascription, the assignment to some preordained rank in life, came more and more to be replaced by achievement as the major definer of personal identity. Individuals increasingly came to define themselves as active subjects. They no longer tended to see their place in life as part of some natural, inevitable, and eternal plan. Their own enterprise and ability mattered; they possessed the opportunity (a key word) to determine their place through their own voluntary actions in this life and in this world.

Now, and this is the truly critical step, what one did in this world came soon to be understood primarily as what one did economically, what one did in terms of work. In the world of work one was the author of self. Individuality became an internal subjective quality; work became a concrete test and property a material extension of self. Inherent in this is the birth of the market society, where the allocation and distribution of such valuable things as power, wealth, and fame came to be seen as the result of countless individual decisions, not of some authoritative norms set by custom, God, or ruling class decree. Who has more, who has less, whether some get any, is decided less by a social or moral consensus than by the free action of individual actors seeking their own gain in a context of continuous competition. What one has or gets, and therefore who one is, is no longer the appropriate reward fit to one's prescribed place; it is the product of what one can get and what one does in the competitive market.

The new theory of individuality had profound political implications. To be free, truly self-denying, master of the self, the individual had to eliminate all barriers to that individuality. So war was declared against religious restraint on free thought and against economic restraint on a free market. What I am describing is, of course, the gradual liquidation of the aristocratic world and its replacement by the liberal capitalist order. It is the crusade of Figaro and Schwartzkopf.

In the history of the crusade, we can discern familiar philosophic benchmarks. There is Thomas Hobbes's brilliant model of individualistic society, offered in the 1650s with its vision of human beings as self-moving, self-directing independent machines, constantly competing with one another for power, wealth, and glory. A person's value of worth (a fascinating word if one thinks of it) is determined by the market; people are as the market values them. They are whatever their hard work can get. But competitive individuals, constantly seeking power and wealth, are constantly frightened lest the fruits of their work, their property, be stolen by other competing individuals. Enter then the liberal state with the principal task of protecting the fruits of industry and providing safety and a more commodious living for competitive individuals.

John Locke, in turn, introduces a moral revolution, one absolutely essential for the liberal world of individuality and equal opportunity. The unlimited acquisition of money and wealth, he argues, is neither unjust nor morally wrong. God (a very Protestant God) commanded men to work the earth, and those that were hardworking and industrious had the right to what they worked. While there were limits initially to what one could own in terms of what one could use, and what would not spoil, the invention of money put an end to these restraints. One does not eat money; there are no limits to its use; it never spoils. Since God has given "different degrees of industry" to men, some have more talent, and work harder than others. It is just and ethical, then, for them to have as many possessions as they want (as Locke says, to "heap as much of these durable things as he pleased"). The liberal state, then, as Locke never tires of telling us, is really constructed by property-owning individuals to protect their property.

This, indeed, is the critical point. If individuals are to define their individuality in terms of what they achieve, and if this sense of achievement is seen in terms of work in a market society where God-given talent and industry can have their play, then the barriers to unlimited accumulation have to fall. How else can achievement and sense of self be known if not by economic success?

Adam Smith's great contribution to the liberal theory of equality of opportunity was his conviction that at bottom all men were ambitious. Smith saw in bourgeois man a constant striving. Every individual, Smith wrote, "seeks to better his own condition." This ambition, he wrote in his *Wealth of Nations,* is "a desire which comes with us from the womb and never leaves us till we go into the grave." Smith pulled together the diverse strands of emerging liberal-bourgeois thought and produced the first complete statement of liberal social theory. Life, he wrote, was a "race for wealth and honours and preferements." What a revolution is in this metaphor! Life is no longer a hierarchical ladder or chain of being. It is a race. And this race should be fair; each and every runner in it should have an equal opportunity to win. Each competitor will "run as hard as he can, and strain every move and every muscle, in order to outstrip all his competitors." Interfering with other runners or seizing special advantages is "a violation of fair play." But merit, talent, virtue, and ability are, alas, no sure indicators of success, because government is too involved in the race, according to Smith. By reserving offices, power, and authority for the privileged it tilts the competition in favor of an idle aristocracy devoid of talent and virtue.

Smith has no illusions, however. Even if the unproductive aristocratic social order were eliminated and the race could be run with equal opportunity for all, only some would win. There would remain obvious differences in how each was able to "better his own condition." An unexpected note of pessimism sneaks in with Smith's acknowledgment that the race seldom provides "real satisfaction," and that it is often really "contemptible and trifling." Equally seldom, however, Smith admits, does anyone look at the race in such an "abstract and philosophical light"—and a good thing, too. The race, the competition, the illusion that everyone can win, and the alleged pleasures of victory are all necessary and worthwhile deceptions. "It is this deception which rouses and keeps in continual motion and industry of mankind."

## II

Life as a race becomes the central metaphor in liberal ideology. One group of writers and activists, relatively unknown today, popularized the metaphor and its corollary of equal opportunity more than any other and deserves special mention. In England in the last two decades of the eighteenth century, an amazing group of radical Protestant dissenters (non-Anglicans, that is, Baptists, Presbyterians, Independents, Unitarians, and Quakers) articulated the principles of revolutionary bourgeois ideology in a devastating attack on the aristocracy and the aristocratic world view. The group included the Reverend Joseph Priestley, the eminent scientist, the Reverend Richard Price, Tom Paine, Mary Wollstonecraft, William Godwin, James Burgh, Anna Barbauld, and others. They spoke for a dissenter community very much involved in the creation of a new England. Incredible achievers, the Protestant dissenters, while only 7 percent of the population, were found as leaders in every new and successful enterprise that marked the industrial revolution.

The dissenters operated at the margins of English life in the eighteenth century. For most of the century, it was technically illegal, for example, to carry on a Unitarian service. But much more onerous than this were the dreaded Test and Corporation Acts, which required all holders of offices under the British Crown to receive the sacrament according to the rites of the Anglican Church. The Acts also excluded nonsubscribers to the Anglican creed from any office in an incorporated municipality. Exclusion from public jobs meant that legions of these talented dissenters were denied one of the most important rewards of the successful, prestigious positions in the military or civil establishment.

Priestley warned that if preferment would not come to talented dissenters, than as "citizens of the world" they would get up and go to where their virtuous achievements were rewarded. This was shorthand for America and there, indeed, Priestley went, emigrating to Pennsylvania in 1794. The fiery

Anna Barbauld, another dissenter, did not leave, however, and in making her case for the repeal of the Test and Corporation Acts in 1790 she addressed the social issue straight on. It was no favor she asked, but "a natural and inalienable right," which she claimed. The issue was "power, place and influence."

> To exclude us from jobs is no more reasonable than to exclude all those above five feet high or those whose birthdays are before the summer solstice. These are arbitrary and whimsical distinctions. . . . We want civil offices. And why should citizens not aspire to civil offices? Why should not the fair field of generous competition be freely opened to every one. . . .

Barbauld articulates the very core of liberal-bourgeois social theory. In the competitive scramble of the marketplace, all citizens are equal in their opportunity to win; no one has built-in advantages of birth or status. Freedom involves unrestrained individual competition and equality, an absence of built-in handicaps. No cooperation, no collective good is sought.

These early bourgeois ideologues were extremely sensitive lest their assault on hierarchy and aristocratic privilege be construed as a mere leveling to an absolute equality of conditions. Nothing could be further from their intentions; bourgeois society, they assumed, would still have inequalities. Thomas Walker, a Manchester cotton manufacturer, dissenting layman and political activist summed up the essence of this new radical creed in 1794:

> We do not seek an equality of wealth and possessions, but an equality of rights. What we seek is that all may be equally entitled to the protection and benefit of society, may equally have a voice in elections . . . and may have a fair opportunity of exerting to advantage any talents he may possess. The rule is not "let all mankind be perpetually equal." God and nature have forbidden it. But "let all mankind start fair in the race of life." The inequality derived from labour and successful enterprise, the result of superior industry and good fortune, is an inequality essential to the very existence of society.

What distressed Mary Wollstonecraft, particularly, was not only that in this race the winners were always men, but that women did not even bother to run. She lamented their socially conditioned lack of ambition. "Woman," she wrote in her *Vindication*, was just like the useless aristocrat "in her self complete" possessed of "all those frivolous accomplishments." Unlike bourgeois man she lacked any desire to improve herself.

Women were socialized to avoid the race, to avoid the ambitious individual scramble for rewards to talent and merit. Wollstonecraft's message was that women should become more like the assertive men of the middle class. Instead, "women were always on the watch to please." Instead of "laudable ambitions," they were ruled by "romantic wavering feelings." Only education and political rights could fit them for the race.

These eighteenth-century dissenting radicals reveal a crucial contradiction at the heart of liberal social theory. The ideal of equality of opportunity at its origins was both an effort to reduce inequality and to perpetuate it. It was egalitarian at its birth because it lashed out at the exclusiveness of aristocratic privilege, but it sought to replace an aristocratic elite with a new elite, albeit one more broadly based on talent and merit. Equality of opportunity is not really a theory of equality, but of justified and morally acceptable inequality. What can legitimate some having more than others? Only that all have had an equal opportunity to have more. Equality for liberals really means fairness. Let the race be fair, let all have an equal chance to win.

Equality of opportunity presumes a noncooperative vision of society. There is no ideal of community or quest for the common good. Individuals compete on an equal footing and as in any race, some win, others lose. According to the theory, those that win do so because they are more talented and work harder than the losers. Equality of opportunity presumes that people have different abilities and talents. This basic human inequality in talents will, in a free society, legitimize status differentials. The society is free if the race is fair. The race is not fair; there is no equality of opportunity when freedom to realize oneself through success and achievement is impaired, and this occurs whenever ethical, religious, or social limitations are placed on economic activity, whenever governments interfere in the race by favoring some privileged class, whose members could not win on their own. Equality of opportunity, then, is historically the ideal of the revolutionary middle class, perhaps the most powerful weapon in its battle, ultimately successful, to end the rule of aristocratic privilege.

## III

In the nineteenth century, two important social groups called upon this doctrine of equal opportunity: women, again, and the working class. John Stuart Mill in his essay *The Subjugation of Women* (1860) offers the classic plea that equality of opportunity be extended to women. All the themes discussed here are repeated. Women are ambitious, he writes; they are not totally socialized to be different from men. The problem is that they are barred from market society. They are not allowed to achieve, to compete freely, to have the status they want. They are treated by the modern liberal as if they were living in the feudal, precapitalist world. They were perceived as creatures of status and told to accept their dependent place. They have no opportunity to be or do anything else, no internal subjective mastery and direction of self. In short, the liberal revolution has passed them by. Mill's essay is one long plea for the extension of liberal emancipation to women. He even invokes Figaro. Men rule like aristocrats, regardless of their merit, simply because they have taken the trouble to be born.

The place of the laboring poor in liberal social theory is ambivalent at best. On the one hand, seventeenth- and eighteenth-century theorists saw the competitive society, the race of life, peopled only by middle-class men. Equal opportunity was their subversive weapon against the world of privilege. Workers, like women, lived outside market society. They were expected to accept their place as dependent subordinates barred from the race. This is clearly how Locke and Smith perceived the working class, and why many writers opposed education for the poor lest they become discontented and seek ambitiously to join or even replace their middle-class betters. One of the serious crimes in the ante-bellum South was teaching a slave to read and write; one of the great themes of feminism from Wollstonecraft to this day is equal access to education.

Alongside a conviction that the laboring poor are excluded from the race, that they are naturally dependent, there is in liberal theory another strain insisting that they be treated as if they were free contracting individuals, equal members of market society. This may take the form of ideological myth, rags to riches, Horatio Alger, and so on, or a more commonplace defense of laissez-faire. Workers are surely free individuals, and if they contract for low or subsistence wages or for long hours, it's their own voluntary act. The state ought not to intervene in their behalf. They are free individuals who can raise themselves by talent and hard work, just as their employers have done.

By the latter part of the nineteenth century, more and more European liberals began to have second thoughts and to call upon the state to protect workers with factory legislation, health and education acts, and so on. This came much later (not, indeed, until deep into this century) in America. A principal theorist of this shift in liberal attitudes was T.H. Green, the Oxford philosopher. What Green did in the 1870s was, in fact, to call upon the doctrine of equal opportunity to assist the working-class cause. Workers, he wrote, were not in fact free to act voluntarily in the market. Poorly paid, uneducated, starving, or sick, they could not make the best of themselves; they could not compete on equal terms. He called upon the state, therefore, to establish the conditions that would enable workers to join the race. This meant public schools, factory laws, prohibition, and public health.

But the continuous liberal commitment to individuality and equal opportunity persists in Green's writings. Once that ideal had involved emancipating the individual from feudal restrictions, opening up the market. Now, in the writings of Green, it involved restricting market freedoms to provide conditions that would allow the proletariat to acquire the skills necessary to compete. The state had to augment workers' power and resources, even at the expense of cherished contractual rights. The aim however, is the same as it was earlier: a fair race. The liberal model endures in T.H. Green. He still assumes that life is a scramble for self-realization through achievement and success, and that this is a moral vision of society and of life.

We can readily recognize T.H. Green's vision as the ideology of the American New Deal in the twentieth century. T.H. Green is, in fact, an intellectual ancestor of all those defenders of state action from the New Deal to the present whom Americans describe in their own peculiar way as liberals! They are committed ultimately to individualism, equal opportunity, and a competitive society.

And here we return to the LBJ commencement speech at Howard University. Racial issues were brought to political saliency in this century by these very same liberal descendants of T.H. Green. Their commitment is to that same liberal vision of the race of life. Positive state action is needed, it is argued, to enable blacks to compete on equal terms—which brings us full-circle back to Lyndon Johnson, *Bakke*, and *Weber*.

## IV

One often-noted feature of the contemporary crisis is the pervasive anxiety among whites (and men in general) about the possible loss of status, wealth, and privilege in the wake of an aggressive affirmative action policy. This, too, is nothing new. It has always been a part of the historical legacy of liberal ideology. For all its optimism, assertiveness, and self-confidence, liberalism has another face, a frightened and fearful view of market society and the race of life as fraught with dangers, the most horrible of which, in fact, is the possibility of losing.

A convincing case can be made (as it was twenty years ago by Sheldon Wolin) that liberal social theorists of the seventeenth and eighteenth centuries presumed fear and anxiety to be the basic motive in human nature that first sets men and women running—or, in Smith's words, "rouses and keeps in continual motion the industry of mankind." We are, of course, familiar with the religious interpretation of this linkage from the more recent writings of Max Weber and R.H. Tawney, but less familiar with the explicit claims of the early liberals themselves. Locke, for example, held in his *Essay on Human Understanding* that "the chief, if not the only spur to human industry and action is uneasiness." This feeling of uneasiness, a desire for "some absent good," drives men to enterprise. But men are ever fearful; once driven to the race they never lose their uneasiness. They are permanently cursed, wrote Locke, with "an itch after honour, power, and riches," which in turn unleashes more "fantastical uneasiness."

Anxiety forever haunts bourgeois man. "Fear and anxiety," Smith wrote, are the "two great tormentors of the human breast." They persist because the race of life has winners and losers and, above all else, bourgeois man fears failure. For [Jeremy] Bentham all life was "a universal scramble" for "money, power and prestige," and the "suffering from loss," he wrote, was infinitely greater than "the enjoyment from gain." For Smith the possibility of losing ground was "worse than death."

Runners in the race of life fear losing what they have, or losing simply, because to lose is to become a nonperson. Only success in the marketplace brings the notice and valuation of others. To understand the fear and anxiety of whites and males in the face of affirmative action today one need only re-read these early liberal theorists who knew very well what insecurity lurks in the heart of bourgeois man. To be a loser is to be invisible, according to Smith in his *Theory of Moral Sentiment:*

> What are the advantages which we propose by that great purpose of human life which we call bettering our condition? To be observed, to be attended to, to be taken notice of . . . the poor man, on the contrary, is ashamed of his poverty. He feels that it . . . places him out of the sight of mankind. . . . To feel that we are taken no notice of, necessarily damps the most agreeable hope, and disappoints the most ardent desire, of human nature. The poor man goes out and come in unheeded, and when in the midst of a crowd is in the same obscurity as if shut up in his own house. . . . They turn away their eyes from him.

John Adams repeated this judgement on failure 132 years later in his *Discourses on Davila.* The pain of being a loser consisted not so much in being hated as in being invisible. What motivated men to public and economic activity was a passion for distinction, "the desire to be observed, considered, esteemed, praised, beloved and admired by his fellows." Of those who failed in this quest he wrote:

> Mankind takes no notice of him. He rambles and wanders unheeded. In the midst of a crowd, at church, in the market, at a play, at an execution, or coronation, he is in such obscurity as he would be in a garret or a cellar. He is not disapproved, censured, or reproached, he is only not seen.

Anxiety over failure in the race of life, over becoming invisible, haunts today's marketplace as it did the world of Smith and Adams. And here is the heart of the matter, the grand historical reversal produced by today's crisis of liberal ideology. What whites and men fear in the loss of wealth and status is what the poor, women, and blacks have experienced throughout liberal hegemony. But the age-old invisibility of these latter groups and the fear of invisibility among today's privileged groups follow alike from the inner logic of liberal ideology, where self-esteem and a sense of personality are inextricably tied to degrees of accumulation and success in the race of life.

## V

We can now better appreciate the profound impact of *Bakke*, *Weber*, and affirmative action on our lives. They are much more than political bombshells. They involve an intellectual crisis that goes to the very heart of liberalism. Two important forms of liberal doctrine are being played off against one another. There is the traditional eighteenth-century middle-class meritocratic ideal, and there is the latter-day liberal vision of intervention in the race of life to aid and perhaps award victory to handicapped competitors. A doctrine originally designed to serve the class interests of the talented "have-nots" against the untalented "haves" now pits the talented "haves" against the allegedly untalented "have-nots." Here is the real source of contemporary tension. In historical terms, the talented class has remained the same. What has happened, however, is that it has changed from a revolutionary class to the status quo defender of a new elite, the meritocracy. Its ideology remains the same: that is why certain social policies of recent years, for instance, headstart programs, were not challenged by the meritocrats. Unlike affirmative action, giving children intensive and special preschooling is quite comparable with simply making the race fair. It doesn't definitely give the victory, that is, jobs or medical degrees, to anyone, especially not to anyone seen as untalented and therefore undeserving.

Each of the issues raised in the current debate speaks to a part of the liberal ideological heritage. Are individuals being treated unfairly in the effort to deal equally with groups? Are fundamental beliefs about individual responsibility for achievement and success being violated? Can groups or individuals ever be in a truly competitive position leading to equal opportunity? Can past privations be countered by eliminating present competitive disadvantages? Are governments once again interfering with the race of life and saying who will win? Is this being done not in terms of talent but to meet political considerations? Is past injustice a more solid moral basis of desert than talent? As we grapple with these issues we must realize how the very language of our dilemmas presumes a framework of beliefs centering on individuality, equality of opportunity, and a market society. These are values at the very core of liberal society, and since *Bakke*, *Weber*, and affirmative action involve contradictions and strains within that set of values, the current crisis is bound to be far-reaching and painful.

But we ought also to be clear that certain questions are not confronted by the ideological tradition traced here. What if our talents are in fact ascriptive, given to us by dint not of our worth and intrinsic achievements or merit, but simply, as Figaro and Schwartzkopf noted, by our being born? What if the basic liberal assumptions about the conditioning role of environment, education, and nurturing are wrong? Is it not then possible that the distribution of valuable things to the talented is inherently unjust to those born less privileged?

There are other questions *Bakke* and *Weber* do not confront: Is life truly a race? Is life a marketplace? Is it basic to our humanity to compete with one another? Are winners real people and losers deservedly unnoticed and invisible? Is a race with winners and losers ever fair or moral, no matter how equal the conditions at the starting line? The time has come to go beyond the framework of the current debate and question the very metaphors and assumptions that inform both it and the problems it has created. Difficult as it may be, the time has come to abandon our old and dear friends, Figaro and Schwartzkopf.

What might a new world view look like? It would involve a fundamental abandonment of our sense of life as a competitive race. This means that some appealing suggestions for changing public policy premised on this view would have to be called inadequate. Expanding the number of places in medical schools or the number of medical schools themselves, providing more jobs in the building trades, more jobs for faculty in an expanded system of higher education—all these are no doubt desirable, but in the end they serve merely to enlarge the field of runners. Just as quotas and affirmative action often set blacks to run only with other blacks, whites only with other whites, so a larger pie means simply a larger race. Even more far-reaching alternatives preserve the competitive race. Proposals to broaden the notion of deserving talent and merit beyond successful market skills and to reward the generous, the loving, the kind, the good, the cooperative would again simply provide new races. The same can be said for instituting nonpecuniary rewards for work, effort, and achievement. A society of Stakhanovites is no more congenial, for by definition it assumes the continuation of the race, albeit for lower stakes. Similarly, the lowering of stakes inherent in proposals that would narrow the range of prizes is mere tinkering. It ends the ability of winners to set their own prizes, to be sure, but it keeps the race intact. Like affirmative action itself, all these proposals would promote greater justice and equality. They are but temporary expedients, however, for they assume the context of a competitive race.

One possible way to transcend the world of Figaro and Schwartzkopf is a retreat from meritocracy itself, a tabooed subject for intellectuals whose very place in society may will be owed to that principle. One need not be one of Michael Young's fanciful "prols" to propose a less slavish preoccupation with merit and talent in our society. Imagine the transformation of American life that would come implementing Robert Wolff's suggestion of two decades ago that students be assigned to universities at random by computers. What would America look like if random chance distributed as many valuable things as test scores did? How essential is the expert medical education sought by [Allan] Bakke to the health needs of inner cities of rural America? What are the trade-offs between pushing the advance of America's highly technological medicine for the few or seeking an improved health system for the many provided by a less than expert corps of lay practitioners emphasizing prevention and lacking the talents of an expertly trained medical elite? Might this calculation not be made in other areas of society as well, with greater justice and equality flowing from less obsession with meritocracy?

Abandoning the worship of talent and merit might also introduce new attitudes to work. Capitalists (and even Marxists) are convinced that individuals find fulfillment primarily through productive work. But why should work alone or even principally define one's sense of self? This is not to advocate an updated Consciousness III, but to offer the heretical suggestion that a sense of identity can come just as meaningfully from play, love, spirituality, place or affiliation, as from work. To transcend Figaro and Schwartzkopf may well require a return to some of what they in fact repudiated. Much of the ambience of affirmative action already points to a renaissance of a world where extrinsic affiliation not individual achievement is critical, where ascriptive identity with a geographic place, a race, a sex, or ethnic group helps define one's sense of self, rather than simply the unique talent or merit of that self. This utopian ideal need not revive the entire world that was lost to liberal hegemony. Nor is romantic nostalgia for the stable, ordered, and noncompetitive Middle Ages what I would offer. It is a moral economy, as E.P. Thompson has called it, which flourished before the advent of the free economy of market society, that I want to revive. Drawn from diverse sources, the moral economy assumes that buying and selling is subordinate to the moral purposes of community and social life. It need not be a completely socialist economy with collectivization of the means of production. A moral and natural economy, according to Aristotle, could well blend private ownership of property with public and common use. "Moral goodness," he wrote, "will ensure that the property of each is made to serve the use of all." Public interests and social needs, not individual free choices in the pursuit of private gain, would be the organizing principle of a moral economic life.

In a moral economy individual freedom in the market is subordinate to the constraints of a moral and social consensus insisting that there are natural levels of profit, of income, and of wealth; that the poor have rights to a decent life; that there are moral limits to accumulation. The sense of self in a moral economy comes not from success or failure in the competitive market but from the identification with and the quest to realize the collective moral purpose to which individual economic activity is ultimately subject. A moral economy in the 1980s requires restricting the freedom of economic actors. Just as affirmative action temporarily introduces moral purpose and public good into the market economy while restricting the play of free choice, so the solution to most of our contemporary ills requires public restraint of market freedom. Only in a moral economy can the inevitable bourgeois linkage of work and success with personal identity be broken. And only then can the preoccupation with equal opportunity be transcended, and affirmative action redefined to encompass real equality.

Since metaphors have hovered closely over these reflections, let me end by offering another. Life should be neither a race nor a chain of being; it should be understood as a kind of play. Races begin and end; they must have winners and losers. One runs not only against the others in adjoining lanes, but against the records and achievements of those running in other races or of all those who have ever run. Play need never end, nor need it have winners and losers. In play fulfillment and joy is a product of the common purpose, the shared experience. A market economy is inevitably a race; a moral economy can be play.

There was a time in the West when play not races preoccupied us. [Johan] Huizinga noted in his *Homo Ludens* that the bourgeois era with its utilitarianism, its efficiency, its preoccupation with serious work, has killed off what he called the "play-factor" in social life and ended the imaginative and fanciful sense of self. Another victim has surely been the moral sense of self. Whatever just and progressive purposes the ideal of equal opportunity has served as various historical moments, it still envisages life as a war of all against all with persons of worth as victor. The first great utopian thinker knew already that such an ideal was morally unsatisfactory. Plato wrote:

> Every man and every woman should live life accordingly, and play the noblest games, and be of another mind from what they are at present. For they deem war a serious thing, though in war there is neither play nor culture worthy the name, which are the things we deem most serious. Hence all must live in peace as well as they possibly can. What, then, is the right way of living? Life must be lived as play, playing certain games, making sacrifices, singing and dancing.

*Part Two*

# Conservatism

he liberals must be the conservatives in America today . . . the greatest need is not so much the creation of more liberal institutions as the successful defense of those which already exist."[1] With these words, Samuel Huntington acknowledges the problems facing liberalism and proposes a conservative solution. At first glance, his conservatism seems to fit popular usage. Liberals who attack the welfare state, who would return to a free market, are often labeled conservative. But this label is misleading. Milton Friedman, for example, rejects it. He argues that laissez-faire liberals are radicals because they demand greater freedom and prosperity. Friedman would recapture his liberal label from welfare staters. Yet they too are radicals, though their demands, for greater equality and democracy, differ. The popular liberal/conservative debate takes place between Kramnick's progressive and regressive faces of liberalism. Conservatives, like Huntington, articulate another ideology, in which freedom and prosperity, equality and democracy, play only minor parts.

Why, then, should American liberals become conservatives? Or why is conservatism thriving in America today? To answer these questions, we must examine the peculiar character of conservatism. Huntington discusses three theories of conservative ideology. The first, aristocratic theory, defines it as feudal aristocrats' reaction to the French Revolution. This definition seems too narrow. Nothing limits conservatism to that historical situation. Second, the autonomous theory portrays conservatism as a general system of ideas. This portrayal is too broad. As we see in this section, conservatives attack such abstract ideas. Third, conservatism is defined situationally as "that system of ideas employed to justify any established social order, no matter where or when it exists, against any fundamental challenge to its nature or being, no matter from what quarter."[2] This definition finds a middle ground. It places conservatism in historical context and maintains its theoretical substance. But what is that substance? And does it constitute an ideology? Huntington says yes. He describes conservatism as a nonideational ideology. Its substance is "the articulate, systematic, theoretical resistance to change."[3]

In "On Being Conservative," Michael Oakeshott clarifies the nonideational character of conservatism. He acknowledges the controversy over whether conservatism is an ideology, and he claims that it is one. Yet Oakeshott's "theme is not a creed or a doctrine, but a disposition." He discusses three characteristics of the conservative disposition. First, conservatives "delight in what is present rather than what was or what may be." Second, and closely related, conservatives are "cool and critical in respect of change and innovation." Third, conservatives recognize that change is sometimes necessary, but they ask that it occur gradually and that identity be maintained.

This conservative disposition seems to fit Huntington's situational definition. According to Huntington, conservatism has no inherent affiliation with or opposition to any ideational ideology. Conservatives can love any "familiar present." In particular, Huntington argues, "No necessary dichotomy exists . . . between conservatism and liberalism."[4] American neoconservatives could, then, be resisting fundamental challenges to liberalism. But, even if "no necessary dichotomy" exists, the liberals' progressive spirit does create tensions with a conservative disposition. (It is for this reason that Friedman rejects the conservative label.) Those tensions appear clearly in the selection from Edmund Burke. Huntington notes that Burke defended "Whig institutions in England, democratic institutions in America, autocratic institutions in France, and Hindu institutions in India."[5] But Burke attacked the French Revolution. Conservatives have their doubts about liberal democracy.

Burke has been called the father of conservatism. His *Reflections on the Revolution in France* outlines its fundamental principles.[6] First, for conservatives, society is not merely a contract. It is a moral order: "It is a partnership in all science; a partnership in all art; a partnership in every virtue, and in all perfection." That partnership extends "between those who are living, those who are dead, and those who are to be born." Second, in keeping with this, history, not nature, confers individual rights. They are an "entailed inheritance." "Prescription," Burke says, "is the most solid of all titles." Third, humanity is largely irrational. Our survival and our success depends on the accumulated wisdom of generations. For this reason, tradition and authority, better yet, traditional authorities, should guide politics. Fourth, humanity is also imperfect, marred by original sin. Abstract rights only unleash human passions. Instead, individuals require restraint or an "ordered liberty." Burke puts this well: "Government is a contrivance of human wisdom to provide for human wants. . . . Among these wants is to be reckoned the want, out of civil society, of a sufficient restraint upon their passions." He adds, "Men have no right to what is not reasonable." Fifth, equality (except in an ultimate moral sense) is unreasonable. "In this partnership all men have equal rights, but not to equal things." Equality violates the natural hierarchy of wisdom and virtue. Sixth, politics requires prudence. Society is complex and change has hidden costs. Citizens should moderate their demands; reformers should "conserve and correct." According to Burke, the English and American revolutions, unlike the French, achieved this balance.

Like the conservative disposition, this conservative doctrine creates some tensions with liberalism. This may explain why, until recently, America has not been congenial to conservatism. Still, conservatism has played a part in our history. Working with what they had, American conservatives stressed the cautious side of liberalism. During the nation's founding, the Federalists defended liberalism from democracy. Conservatism appeared in Madison's fear of majority tyranny and Hamilton's call for a strong central government. John Adams defended a natural aristocracy, arguing that "inequalities are part of the natural history of mankind." Despite their best efforts, the Americans and the French cannot make all equally wise, attractive, strong, and/or moral. In fact, "the more you educate . . . the more aristocratic the peoples and the government will be."[7] Adams paralleled Burke: "Real merit should govern the world; men ought to be respected only in proportion to their talents, virtues, and services."[8] The political problem, of course, is how to accomplish this. Fisher Ames, writing after the 1800 election of Thomas Jefferson, doubted Americans could solve that problem: "Our materials for a government were all democratic," and "a democracy cannot last." The American Constitution presumes "the supposed existence of sufficient political virtue and the permanency and authority of the public morals." But American institutions do not encourage this. Ames feared that the revolution would "proceed in exactly the same way, but not with so rapid a pace, as that of France."[9]

For these early American conservatives, democracy threatened liberalism. Is this the threat liberals face today? Is this why they should become conservatives? Yes, according to the remaining authors in this part. In "Capitalism, Socialism, and Nihilism," Irving Kristol traces the rise of neoconservatism to the old inadequacies of liberalism. True, Americans are chastened by recent events—Vietnam, Watergate, the Iran-*Contra* scandal. But America's problems have deeper roots. They reside in liberals' tendency to "think economically," to think that "no superior, authoritative information" exists "about the good life." "Thinking economically" prompts excessive demands for material things, undermines a sense of political obligation, and removes restraints on business activities. Kristol argues that liberalism has been living on "accumulated moral capital" from the past. Now that "capital" is almost gone, and liberalism faces a new danger: nihilism. The nihilists' creed —"nothing means anything and everything is permitted"—is America's current sickness. Kristol asks: "What medicine does one prescribe for a social order that is sick because it has lost its soul?" Neoconservatives' answer is to return to traditional values, decrease demands on government, and increase respect for authority.[10]

The final selection focuses on an American institution that neoconservatives revere: the university. "The Democratization of the University" is an early essay by Allan Bloom. According to Bloom, universities provide an aristocratic influence in democratic societies. They preserve tradition, establish authority, and teach morality. Or this is what they should do. When universities adopt the market mentality and participatory politics of the larger society, however, they undermine their ability to perform these functions. Bloom fears the results. Liberal democracy depends on the university to balance equality with excellence and consent with reason. Bloom warns: "If neither reason nor tradition can bring about consensus, then the force of the first man resourceful and committed enough must needs do so."

Common themes emerge in these conservatives' writings: morality, tradition, authority, irrationality, inequality, and, above all, prudence. Some Americans have become conservatives, as Huntington counseled, to save liberalism from itself. But their conservatism, as disposition and doctrine, fits uneasily with liberalism. Are such tensions unavoidable in a situational ideology? Do they suggest that conservatism is really an autonomous ideology? Or is conservatism not an ideology at all? Is it merely a rationalization of the status quo?

## Notes

1. Samuel Huntington, "Conservatism as an Ideology," *American Political Science Review* 51 (June 1957): 452–73.

2. Ibid., 455.

3. Ibid., 461. According to Huntington, conservatism is nonideational because it lacks a substantive ideal. Instead, "the essence of conservatism is the rationalization of existing institutions in terms of history, God, nature, and man" (p. 457).

4. Ibid., 460.

5. Ibid., 463.

6. As Huntington notes, there are many lists with various numbers of conservative principles. This list, adapted from his summary of Burke, captures the essential ideas.

7. John Adams, "On Natural Aristocracy." In *The Portable Conservative Reader,* ed. Russell Kirk (New York: Penguin Books, 1985), 67.

8. Ibid., 69.

9. Fisher Ames, "The Dangers of American Liberty," ibid., 84–112.

10. Irving Kristol, "What Is a Neo-Conservative?" *Newsweek* 87 (19 January 1976): 17.

# MICHAEL OAKESHOTT

## *On Being Conservative*

Michael Oakeshott's "On Being Conservative" appears in his collection *Rationalism in Politics and Other Essays* (1962). Born in 1901 in Cambridge, England, Oakeshott lectured at Cambridge University and held a chair at the London School of Economics. He is perhaps best known for his moderate conservatism, encapsulated in the phrase "the purpose of government is simply to rule."

### 1

The common belief that it is impossible (or, if not impossible, then so unpromising as to be not worth while attempting) to elicit explanatory general principles from what is recognized to be conservative conduct is not one that I share. It may be true that conservative conduct does not readily provoke articulation in the idiom of general ideas, and that consequently there has been a certain reluctance to undertake this kind of elucidation; but it is not to be presumed that conservative conduct is less eligible than any other for this sort of interpretation, for what it is worth. Nevertheless, this is not the enterprise I propose to engage in here. My theme is not a creed or a doctrine, but a disposition. To be conservative is to be disposed to think and behave in certain manners; it is to prefer certain kinds of conduct and certain conditions of human circumstances to others; it is to be disposed to make certain kinds of choices. And my design here is to construe this disposition as it appears in contemporary character, rather than to transpose it into the idiom of general principles.

The general characteristics of this disposition are not difficult to discern, although they have often been mistaken. They centre upon a propensity to use and to enjoy what is available rather than to wish for or to look for something else; to delight in what is present rather than what was or what may be. Reflection may bring to light an appropriate gratefulness for what is available, and consequently the acknowledgement of a gift or an inheritance from the past; but there is no mere idolizing of what is past and gone. What is esteemed is the present; and it is esteemed not on account of its connections with a remote antiquity, nor because it is recognized to be more admirable than any possible alternative, but on account of its familiarity: not, *Verweile doch, du bist so schön,* but, *Stay with me because I am attached to you.*

If the present is arid, offering little or nothing to be used or enjoyed, then this inclination will be weak or absent; if the present is remarkably unsettled, it will display itself in a search for a firmer foothold and consequently in a recourse to and an exploration of the past; but it asserts itself characteristically when there is much to be enjoyed, and it will be strongest when this is combined with evident risk of loss. In short, it is a disposition appropriate to a man who is acutely aware of having something to lose which he has learned to care for; a man in some degree rich in opportunities for enjoyment, but not so rich that he can afford to be indifferent to loss. It will appear more naturally in the old than in the young, not because the old are more sensitive to loss but because they are apt to be more fully aware of the resources of their world and therefore less likely to find them inadequate. In some people this disposition is weak merely because they are ignorant of what their world has to offer them: the present appears to them only as a residue of inopportunities.

To be conservative, then, is to prefer the familiar to the unknown, to prefer the tried to the untried, fact to mystery, the actual to the possible, the limited to the unbounded, the near to the distant, the sufficient to the superabundant, the convenient to the perfect, present laughter to utopian bliss. Familiar relationships and loyalties will be preferred to the allure of more profitable attachments; to acquire and to enlarge will be less important than to keep, to cultivate and to enjoy; the grief of loss will be more acute than the excitement of novelty or promise. It is to be equal to one's own fortune, to live at the level of one's own means, to be content with the want of greater perfection which belongs alike to oneself and one's circumstances. With some people this is itself a choice; in others it is a disposition which appears, frequently or less frequently, in their preferences and aversions, and is not itself chosen or specifically cultivated.

Now, all this is represented in a certain attitude towards change and innovation; change denoting alterations we have to suffer and innovation those we design and execute.

Changes are circumstances to which we have to accommodate ourselves, and the disposition to be conservative is both the emblem of our difficulty in doing so and our resort in the attempts we make to do so. Changes are without effect only upon those who notice nothing, who are ignorant of what they possess and apathetic to their circumstances; and they can be welcomed indiscriminately only by those who esteem nothing, whose attachments are fleeting and who are strangers to love and affection. The conservative disposition provokes neither of these conditions: the inclination to enjoy what is present and available is the opposite of ignorance and apathy and it breeds attachment and affection. Consequently, it is averse from change, which appears always, in the first place, as deprivation. A storm which sweeps away a copse and transforms a favourite view, the death of friends, the sleep of friendship, the desuetude of customs of behavior, the retirement of a favourite clown, involuntary exile, reversals of fortune, the loss of abilities enjoyed and their replacement by others—these are changes, none perhaps without its compensations, which the man of conservative temperament unavoidably regrets. But he has difficulty in reconciling himself to them, not because what he has lost in them was intrinsically better than any alternative might have been or was incapable of improvement, nor because what takes its place is inherently incapable of being enjoyed, but because what he has lost was something he actually enjoyed and had learned how to enjoy and what takes its place is something to which he has acquired no attachment. Consequently, he will find small and slow changes more tolerable than large and sudden; and he will value highly every appearance of continuity. Some changes, indeed, will present no difficulty; but, again, this is not because they are manifest improvements but merely because they are easily assimilated: the changes of the seasons are mediated by their recurrence and the growing up of children by its continuousness. And, in general, he will accommodate himself more readily to changes which do not offend expectation than to the destruction of what seems to have no ground of dissolution within itself.

Moreover, to be conservative is not merely to be averse from change (which may be an idiosyncrasy); it is also a manner of accommodating ourselves to changes, an activity imposed upon all men. For, change is a threat to identity, and every change is an emblem of extinction. But a man's identity (or that of a community) is nothing more than an unbroken rehearsal of contingencies, each at the mercy of circumstance and each significant in proportion to its familiarity. It is not a fortress into which we may retire, and the only means we have of defending it (that is, ourselves) against the hostile forces of changes is in the open field of our experience; by throwing our weight upon the foot which for the time being is most firmly placed, by cleaving to whatever familiarities are not immediately threatened and thus assimilating what is new without becoming recognizable to ourselves. The Masai, when they were moved from their old country to the present Masai reserve in Kenya, took with them the names of their hills and plains and rivers and gave them to the hills and plains and rivers of the new country. And it is by some such subterfuge of conservatism that every man or people compelled to suffer a notable change avoids the shame of extinction.

Changes, then, have to be suffered; and a man of conservative temperament (that is, one strongly disposed to preserve his identity) cannot be indifferent to them. In the main, he judges them by the disturbance they entail and, like everyone else, deploys his resources to meet them. The idea of innovation, on the other hand, is improvement. Nevertheless, a man of this temperament will not himself be an ardent innovator. In the first place, he is not inclined to think that nothing is happening unless great changes are afoot and therefore he is not worried by the absence of innovation: the use and enjoyment of things as they are occupies most of his attention. Further, he is aware that not all innovation is, in fact, improvement; and he will think that to innovate without improving is either designed or inadvertent folly. Moreover, even when an innovation commends itself as a convincing improvement, he will look twice at its claims before accepting them. From his point of view, because every improvement involves change, the disruption entailed has always to be set against the benefit anticipated. But when he has satisfied himself about this, there will be other considerations to be taken into the account. Innovating is always an equivocal enterprise, in which gain and loss (even excluding the loss of familiarity) are so closely interwoven that it is exceedingly difficult to forecast the final up-shot: there is no such thing as an unqualified improvement. For, innovating is an activity which generates not only the "improvement" sought, but a new and complex situation of which this is only one of the components. The total change is always more extensive than the change designed; and the whole of what is entailed can neither be foreseen nor circumscribed. Thus, whenever there is innovation there is the certainty that the change will be greater than was intended, that there will be loss as well as gain and that the loss and the gain will not be equally distributed among the people affected; there is the chance that the benefits derived will be greater than those which were designed; and there is the risk that they will be off-set by changes for the worse.

From all this the man of conservative temperament draws some appropriate conclusions. First, innovation entails certain loss and possible gain, therefore, the onus of proof, to show that the proposed change may be expected to be on the whole beneficial, rests with the would-be innovator. Secondly, he believes that the more closely an innovation resembles growth (that is, the more clearly it is intimated in and not merely imposed upon the situation), the less likely it is to result in a preponderance of loss. Thirdly, he thinks that an innovation which is a response to some specific defect, one designed to redress some specific disequilibrium, is more desirable than one which springs from a notion of a generally improved condition of human circumstances, and is far more desirable than one generated by a vision of perfection. Consequently, he prefers small and limited innovations to large and indefinite. Fourthly, he favours a slow rather than a rapid pace, and pauses to observe current consequences and make appropriate adjustments. And lastly, he believes the occasion to be important; and, other things being equal, he considers the most favourable occasion for innovation to be when the projected change is most likely to be limited to what is intended and least likely to be corrupted by undesired and unmanageable consequences.

The disposition to be conservative is, then, warm and positive in respect of enjoyment, and correspondingly cool and critical in respect of change and innovation: these two inclinations support and elucidate one another. The man of conservative temperament believes that a known good is not lightly to be surrendered for an unknown better. He is not in love with what is dangerous and difficult; he is unadventurous; he has no impulse to sail uncharted seas; for him there is no magic in being lost, bewildered or shipwrecked. If he is forced to navigate the unknown, he sees virtue in heaving the lead every inch of the way. What others plausibly identify as timidity, he recognizes in himself as rational prudence; what others interpret as inactivity, he recognizes as a disposition to enjoy rather than to exploit. He is cautious, and he is disposed to indicate his assent or dissent, not in absolute, but in graduated terms. He eyes the situation in terms of its propensity to disrupt the familiarity of the features of his world.

## 2

It is commonly believed that this conservative disposition is pretty deeply rooted in what is called "human nature." Change is tiring, innovation calls for effort, and human beings (it is said) are more apt to be lazy than energetic. If they have found a not unsatisfactory way of getting along in the world, they are not disposed to go looking for trouble. They are naturally apprehensive of the unknown and prefer safety to danger. They are reluctant innovators, and they accept change not because they like it but (as Rochefoucauld says, they accept death) because it is inescapable. Change generates sadness rather than exhilaration: heaven is the dream of a changeless no less than of a perfect world. Of course, those who read "human nature" in this way agree that this disposition does not stand alone; they merely contend that it is an exceedingly strong, perhaps the strongest, of human propensities. And, so far as it goes, there is something to be said for this belief: human circumstances would certainly be very different from what they are if there were not a large ingredient of conservatism in human preferences. Primitive peoples are said to cling to what is familiar and to be averse from change; ancient myth is full of warnings against innovation; our folklore and proverbial wisdom about the conduct of life abounds in conservative precepts; and how many tears are shed by children in their unwilling accommodation to change. Indeed, wherever a firm identity has been achieved, and wherever identity is felt to be precariously balanced, a conservative disposition is likely to prevail. On the other hand, the disposition of adolescence is often predominantly adventurous and experimental: when we are young, nothing seems more desirable than to take a chance; *pas de risque, pas de plaisir.* And while some peoples, over long stretches of time, appear successfully to have avoided change, the history of others displays periods of intense and intrepid innovation. There is, indeed, not much profit to be had from general speculation about "human nature," which is no steadier than anything else in our acquaintance. What is more to the point is to consider current human nature, to consider ourselves.

With us, I think, the disposition to be conservative is far from being notably strong. Indeed, if he were to judge by our conduct during the last five centuries or so, an unprejudiced stranger might plausibly suppose us to be in love with change, to have an appetite only for innovation and to be either so out of sympathy with ourselves or so careless of our identity as not to be disposed to give it any consideration. In general, the fascination of what is new is felt far more keenly than the comfort of what is familiar. We are disposed to think that nothing important is happening unless great innovations are afoot, and that what is not being improved must be deteriorating. There is a positive prejudice in favour of the yet untried. We readily presume that all change is, somehow, for the better, and we are easily persuaded that all the consequences of our innovating activity are either themselves improvements or at least a reasonable price to pay for getting what we want. While the conservative, if he were forced to gamble, would bet on the field, we are disposed to back our individual fancies with little calculation and no apprehension of loss. We are acquisitive to the point to greed; ready to drop the bone we have for its reflection magnified in the mirror of the future. Nothing is made to outlast probable improvement in a world where everything is undergoing incessant improvement: the expectation of life of everything except human beings themselves continuously declines. Pieties are fleeting, loyalties evanescent, and the pace of change warns us against too deep attachments. We are willing to try anything once, regardless of the consequences. One activity vies with another in being "up-to-date": discarded motor-cars and television sets have their counterparts in discarded moral and religious beliefs: the eye is ever on the new model. To see is to imagine what might be in the place of what is; to touch is to transform. Whatever the shape or quality of the world, it is not for long as we want it. And those in the van of movement infect those behind with their energy and enterprise. *Omnes eodem cogemur:* when we are no longer light-footed we find a place for ourselves in the band.[1]

Of course, our character has other ingredients besides this lust for change (we are not devoid of the impulse to cherish and preserve), but there can be little doubt about its pre-eminence. And, in these circumstances, it seems appropriate that a conservative disposition should appear, not as an intelligible (or even plausible) alternative to our mainly "progressive" habit of mind, but either as an unfortunate hindrance to the movement afoot, or as the custodian of the museum in which quaint examples of superseded achievement are preserved for children to gape at, and as the guardian of what from time to time is considered not yet ripe for destruction, which we call (ironically enough) the amenities of life.

Here our account of the disposition to be conservative and its current fortunes might be expected to end, with the man in whom this disposition is strong last seen swimming against the tide, disregarded not because what he has to say is necessarily false but because it has become irrelevant; outmanœuvred, not on account of any intrinsic demerit but merely by the flow of circumstance; a faded, timid, nostalgic character, provoking pity as an outcast and contempt as a reactionary. Nevertheless, I think there is something more to be said. Even in these circumstances, when a conservative disposition in respect of things in general is unmistakably at a discount, there are occasions when this disposition remains not only appropriate, but supremely so; and there are connections in which we are unavoidably disposed in a conservative direction.

In the first place, there is a certain kind of activity (not yet extinct) which can be engaged in only in virtue of a disposition to be conservative, namely, activities where what is sought is present enjoyment and not a profit, a reward, a prize or a result in addition to the experience itself. And when these activities are recognized as the emblems of this disposition, to be conservative is disclosed, not as prejudiced hostility to a "progressive" attitude capable of embracing the whole range of human conduct, but as a disposition exclusively appropriate in a large and significant field of human activity. And the man in whom this disposition is pre-eminent appears as one who prefers to engage in activities where to be conservative is uniquely appropriate, and not as a man inclined to impose his conservatism indiscriminately upon all human activity. In short, if we find ourselves (as most of us do) inclined to reject conservatism as a disposition appropriate in respect of human conduct in general, there still remains a certain kind of human conduct for which this disposition is not merely appropriate but a necessary condition.

There are, of course, numerous human relationships in which a disposition to be conservative, a disposition merely to enjoy what they offer for its own sake, is not particularly appropriate: master and servant, owner and bailiff, buyer and seller, principal and agent. In these, each participant seeks some service or some recompense for a service. A customer who finds a shopkeeper unable to supply his wants either persuades him to enlarge his stock or goes elsewhere; and a shopkeeper unable to meet the desires of a customer tries to impose upon him others which he can satisfy. A principal ill-served by his agent, looks for another. A servant ill-recompensed for his service, asks for a rise; and one dissatisfied with his conditions of work, seeks a change. In short, these are all relationships in which some result is sought; each party is concerned with the ability of the other to provide it. If what is sought is lacking, it is to be expected that the relationship will lapse or be terminated. To be conservative in such relationships, to enjoy what is present and available regardless of its failure to satisfy any want and merely because it has struck our fancy and become familiar, is conduct which discloses a *jusqu'aubuiste* conservatism, an irrational inclination to refuse all relationships which call for the exercise of any other disposition. Though even these relationships seem to lack something appropriate to them when they are confined to a nexus of supply and demand and allow no room for the intrusion of the loyalties and attachments which spring from familiarity.

But there are relationships of another kind in which no result is sought and which are engaged in for their own sake and enjoyed for what they are and not for what they provide. This is so of friendship. Here, attachment springs from an intimation of familiarity and subsists in a mutual sharing of personalities. To go on changing one's butcher until one gets the meat one likes, to go on educating one's agent until he does what is required of him, is conduct not inappropriate to the relationship concerned; but to discard friends because they do not behave as we expected and refuse to be educated to our requirements is the conduct of a man who has altogether mistaken the character of friendship. Friends are not concerned with what might be made of one another, but only with the enjoyment of one another; and the condition of this enjoyment is a ready acceptance of what is and the absence of any desire to change or to improve. A friend is not somebody one trusts to behave in a certain manner, who supplies certain wants, who has certain useful abilities, who possesses certain merely agreeable qualities, or who holds certain acceptable opinions; he is somebody who engages the imagination, who excites contemplation, who provokes interest, sympathy, delight and loyalty simply on account of the relationship entered into. One friend cannot replace another; there is all the difference in the world between the death of a friend and the retirement of one's tailor from business. The relationship of friend to friend is dramatic, not utilitarian; the tie is one of familiarity, not usefulness; the disposition engaged is conservative, not "progressive." And what is true of friendship is not less true of other experiences—of patriotism, for example, and of conversation—each of which demands a conservative disposition as a condition of its enjoyment.

But further, there are activities, not involving human relationships, that may be engaged in, not for a prize, but for the enjoyment they generate, and for which the only appropriate disposition is the disposition to be conservative. Consider fishing. If your project is merely to catch fish it would be foolish to be unduly conservative. You will seek out the best tackle, you will discard practices which prove unsuccessful, you will not be bound by unprofitable attachments to particular localities, pieties will be fleeting, loyalties evanescent; you may even be wise to try anything once in the hope of improvement. But fishing is an activity that may be engaged in, not for the profit of a catch, but for its own sake; and the fisherman may return home in the evening not less content for being empty-handed. Where this is so, the activity has become a ritual and a conservative disposition is appropriate. Why worry about the best gear if you do not care whether or not you make a catch? What matters is the enjoyment of exercising skill (or, perhaps, merely passing the time),[2] and this is to be had with any tackle, so long as it is familiar and is not grotesquely inappropriate.

All activities, then, where what is sought is enjoyment springing, not from the success of the enterprise but from the familiarity of the engagement, are emblems of the disposition to be conservative. And there are many of them. Fox placed gambling among them when he said that it gave two supreme pleasures, the pleasure of winning and the pleasure of losing. Indeed, I can think of only one activity of this kind which seems to call for a disposition other than conservative: the love of fashion, that is, wanton delight in change for its own sake no matter what it generates.

But, besides the not inconsiderable class of activities which we can engage in only in virtue of a disposition to be conservative, there are occasions in the conduct of other activities when this is the most appropriate disposition; indeed there are few activities which do not, at some point or other, make a call upon it. Whenever stability is more profitable than improvement, whenever certainty is more valuable than speculation, whenever familiarity is more desirable than perfection, whenever agreed error is superior to controversial truth, whenever the disease is more sufferable than the cure, whenever the satisfaction of expectations is more important than the "justice" of the expectations themselves, whenever a rule of some sort is better than the risk of having no rule at all, a disposition to be conservative will be more appropriate than any other; and on any reading of human conduct these cover a not negligible range of circumstances. Those who see the man of conservative disposition (even in what is vulgarly called a "progressive" society) as a lonely swimmer battling against the overwhelming current of circumstance must be thought to have adjusted their binoculars to exclude a large field of human occasion.

In most activities not engaged in for their own sake a distinction appears, a certain level of observation, between the project undertaken and the means employed, between the enterprise and the tools used for its achievement. This is not, of course, an absolute distinction; projects are often provoked and governed by the tools available, and on rarer occasions the tools are designed to fit a particular project. And what on one occasion is a project, on another is a tool. Moreover there is at least one significant exception: the activity of being a poet. It is, however, a relative distinction of some usefulness because it calls our attention to an appropriate difference of attitude towards the two components of the situation.

In general, it may be said that our disposition in respect of tools is appropriately more conservative than our attitude towards projects; or, in other words, tools are less subject to innovation than projects because, except on rare occasions, tools are not designed to fit a particular project and then thrown aside, they are designed to fit a whole class of projects. And this is intelligible because most tools call for skill in use and skill is inseparable from practice and familiarity: a skilled man, whether he is a sailor, a cook or an accountant, is a man familiar with a certain stock of tools. Indeed, a carpenter is usually more skilful in handling his own tools than in handling other examples of the kind of tools commonly used by carpenters; and the solicitor can use his own (annotated) copy of Pollock on *Partnership* or Jarman on *Wills* more readily than any other. Familiarity is the essence of tool using; and in so far as man is a tool using animal he is disposed to be conservative.

Many of the tools in common use have remained unchanged for generations; the design of others has undergone considerable modification; and our stock of tools is always being enlarged by new inventions and improved by new designs. Kitchens, factories, workshops, building sites and offices disclose a characteristic mixture of long-tried and newly invented equipment. But, be that how it may, when business of any kind is afoot, when a particular project has been engaged in—whether it is baking a pie or shoeing a horse, floating a loan or a company, selling fish or insurance to a customer, building a ship or a suit of clothes, sowing wheat or lifting potatoes, laying down port or putting up a barrage—we recognize it to be an occasion when it is particularly appropriate to be conservative about the tools we employ. If it is a large project, we put it in charge of a man who has the requisite knowledge, and we expect him to engage subordinates who know their own business and are skilled in the use of certain stocks of tools. At some point in this hierarchy of tool-users the suggestion may be made that in order to do this particular job an addition or modification is required in the available stock of tools. Such a suggestion is likely to come from somewhere about the middle of the hierarchy: we do not expect a designer to say "I must go away and do some fundamental research which will take me five years before I can go on with the job" (his bag of tools is a body of knowledge and we expect him to have it handy and to know his way about it); and we do not expect the man at the bottom to have a stock of tools inadequate for the needs of his particular part. But even if such a suggestion is made and is followed up, it will not disrupt the appropriateness of a conservative disposition in respect of the whole stock of tools being used. Indeed, it is clear enough that no job would ever get done, no piece of business could ever be transacted, if, on the occasion, our disposition in respect of our tools were not, generally speaking, conservative. And since doing business of one sort or another occupies most of our time and little can be done without tools of some kind, the disposition to be conservative occupies an unavoidably large place in our character.

The carpenter comes to do a job, perhaps one the exact like of which he has never before tackled; but he comes with his bag of familiar tools and his only chance of doing the job lies in the skill with which he uses what he has at his disposal. When the plumber goes to fetch his tools he would be away even longer than is usually the case if his purpose were to invent new or to improve old ones. Nobody questions the value of money in the market place. No business would ever get done if, before a pound of cheese were weighed or a pint of beer drawn, the relative usefulness of these particular scales of weight and measurement as compared with others were threshed out. The surgeon does not pause in the middle of an operation to redesign his instruments. The MCC does not authorize a new width of bat, a new weight of ball or a new length of wicket in the middle of a Test Match, or even in the middle of a cricket season. When your house is on fire you do not get in touch with a fire-prevention research station to design a new appliance; as Disraeli pointed out, unless you are a lunatic, you send for the parish fire-engine. A musician may improvise music, but he would think himself hardly done-by if, at the same time, he were expected to improvise an instrument. Indeed, when a particularly tricky job is to be done, the workman will often prefer to use a tool that he is thoroughly familiar with rather than another he has in his bag, of new design, but which he has not yet mastered the use of. No doubt there is a time and a place to be radical about such things, for promoting innovation and carrying out improvements in the tools we employ, but these are clearly occasions for the exercise of a conservative disposition.

Now, what is true about tools in general, as distinct from projects, is even more obviously true about a certain kind of tool in common use, namely, general rules of conduct. If the familiarity that springs from relative immunity from change is appropriate to hammers and pincers and to bats and balls, it is supremely appropriate, for example, to an office routine. Routines, no doubt, are susceptible of improvement; but the more familiar they become, the more useful they are. Not to have a conservative disposition in respect of a routine is obvious folly. Of course, exceptional occasions occur which may call for a dispensation; but an inclination to be conservative rather than reformist about a routine is unquestionably appropriate. Consider the conduct of a public meeting, the rules of debate in the House of Commons or the procedure of a court of law. The chief virtue of these arrangements is that they are fixed and familiar; they establish and satisfy certain expectations, they allow to be said in a convenient order whatever is relevant, they prevent extraneous collisions and they conserve human energy. They are typical tools—instruments eligible for use in a variety of different but similar jobs. They are the product of reflection and choice, there is nothing sacrosanct about them, they are susceptible of change and improvement; but if our disposition in respect of them were not, generally speaking, conservative, if we were disposed to argue about them and change them on every occasion, they would rapidly lose their value. And while there may be rare occasions when it is useful to suspend them, it is pre-eminently appropriate that they should not be innovated upon or improved while they are in operation. Or again, consider the rules of a game. These, also, are the product of reflection and choice, and there are occasions when it is appropriate to reconsider them in the light of current experience; but it is inappropriate to have anything but a conservative disposition towards them or to consider putting them all together at one time into the melting-pot; and it is supremely inappropriate to change or improve upon them in the heat and confusion of play. Indeed, the more eager each side is to win, the more valuable is an inflexible set of rules. Players in the course of play may devise new tactics, they may improvise new methods of attack and defence, they may do anything they choose to defeat the expectations of their opponents, except invent new rules. That is an activity to be indulged sparingly and then only in the off-season.

There is much more that might be said about the relevance of the disposition to be conservative and its appropriateness even in a character, such as ours, chiefly disposed in the opposite direction. I have said nothing of morals, nothing of religion; but perhaps I have said enough to show that, even if to be conservative on all occasions and in all connections is so remote from our habit of thought as to be almost unintelligible, there are nevertheless, few of our activities which do not on all occasions call into partnership a disposition to be conservative and on some occasions recognize it as the senior partner; and there are some activities where it is properly master.

## 3

How, then, are we to construe the disposition to be conservative in respect of politics? And in making this inquiry what I am interested in is not merely the intelligibility of this disposition in any set of circumstances, but its intelligibility in our own contemporary circumstances.

Writers who have considered this question commonly direct our attention to beliefs about the world in general, about human beings in general, about associations in general and even about the universe; and they tell us that a conservative disposition in politics can be correctly construed only when we understand it as a reflection of certain beliefs of these kinds. It is said, for example, that conservatism in politics is the appropriate counterpart of a generally conservative disposition in respect of human conduct: to be reformist in business, in morals or in religion and to be conservative in politics is represented as being inconsistent. It is said that the conservative in politics is so by virtue of holding certain religious beliefs; a belief, for example, in a natural law to be gathered from human experience, and in a providential order reflecting a divine purpose in nature and in human history to which it is the duty of mankind to conform its conduct and departure from which spells injustice and calamity. Further, it is said that a disposition to be conservative in politics reflects what is called an "organic" theory of human society; that it is tied up with a belief in the absolute value of human personality, and with a belief in a primordial propensity of human beings to sin. And the "conservatism" of an Englishman has ever been connected with Royalism and Anglicanism.

Now, setting aside the minor complaints one might be moved to make about this account of the situation, it seems to me to suffer from one large defect. It is true that many of these beliefs have been held by people disposed to be conservative in political activity, and it may be true that these people have also believed their disposition to be in some way confirmed by them, or even to be founded upon them; but, as I understand it, a disposition to be conservative in politics does not entail either that we should hold these beliefs to be true or even that we should suppose them to be true. Indeed, I do not think it is necessarily connected with any particular beliefs about the universe, about the world in general or about human conduct in general. What it is tied to is certain beliefs about the activity of governing and the instruments of government, and it is in terms of beliefs on these topics, and not on others, that it can be made to appear intelligible. And, to state my view briefly before elaborating it, what makes a conservative disposition in politics intelligible is nothing to do with a natural law or a providential order, nothing to do with morals or religion; it is the observation of our current manner of living combined with the belief (which from our point of view need be regarded as no more than an hypothesis) that governing is a specific and limited activity, namely the provision and custody of general rules of conduct, which are understood, not as plans for imposing substantive activities, but as instruments enabling people to pursue the activities of their own choice with the minimum frustration, and therefore something which it is appropriate to be conservative about.

Let us begin at what I believe to be the proper starting-place; not in the empyrean, but with ourselves as we have come to be. I and my neighbours, my associates, my compatriots, my friends, my enemies and those who I am indifferent about, are people engaged in a great variety of activities. We are apt to entertain a multiplicity of opinions on every conceivable subject and are disposed to change these beliefs as we grow tired of them or as they prove unserviceable. Each of us is pursuing a course of his own; and there is no project so unlikely that somebody will not be found to engage in it, no enterprise so foolish that somebody will not undertake it. There are those who spend their lives trying to sell copies of the Anglican Catechism to the Jews. And one half of the world is engaged in trying to make the other half want what it has hitherto never felt the lack of. We are all inclined to be passionate about our own concerns, whether it is making things or selling them, whether it is business or sport, religion or learning, poetry, drink or drugs. Each of us has preferences of his own. For some, the opportunities of making choices (which are numerous) are invitations readily accepted; others welcome them less eagerly or even find them burdensome. Some dream dreams of new and better worlds: others are more inclined to move in familiar paths or even to be idle. Some are apt to deplore the rapidity of change, others delight in it; all recognize it. At times we grow tired and fall asleep: it is a blessed relief to gaze in a shop window and see nothing we want; we are grateful for ugliness merely because it repels attention. But, for the most part, we pursue happiness by seeking the satisfaction of desires which spring from one another inexhaustibly. We enter into relationships of interest and of emotion, of competition, partnership, guardianship, love, friendship, jealousy and hatred, some of which are more durable than others. We make agreements with one another; we have expectations about one another's conduct; we approve, we are indifferent and we disapprove. This multiplicity of activity and variety of opinions is apt to produce collisions: we pursue courses which cut across those of others, and we do not all approve the same sort of conduct. But, in the main, we get along with one another, sometimes by giving way, sometimes by standing fast, sometimes in a compromise. Our conduct consists of activity assimilated to that of others in small, and for the most part unconsidered and unobtrusive, adjustments.

Why all this should be so, does not matter. It is not necessarily so. A different condition of human circumstances can easily be imagined, and we know that elsewhere and at other times activity is, or has been, far less multifarious and changeful and opinion far less diverse and far less likely to provoke collision; but, by and large, we recognize this to be our condition. It is an acquired condition, though nobody designed or specifically chose it in preference to all others. It is the product, not of "human nature" let loose, but of human beings impelled by an acquired love of making choices for themselves. And we know as little and as much about where it is leading us as we know about the fashion in hats in twenty years' time or the design of motor-cars.

Surveying the scene, some people are provoked by the absence of order and coherence which appears to them to be its dominant feature; its wastefulness, its frustration, its dissipation of human energy, its lack not merely of a premeditated destination but even of any discernible direction of movement. It provides an excitement similar to that of a stock-car race; but is has none of the satisfaction of a well-conducted business enterprise. Such people are apt to exaggerate the current disorder; the absence of plan is so conspicuous that the small adjustments, and even the more massive arrangements, which restrain the chaos seem to them nugatory; they have no feeling for the warmth of untidiness but only for its inconvenience. But what is significant is not the limitations of their powers of observation, but the turn of their thoughts. They feel that there ought to be something that ought to be done to convert this so-called chaos into order for this is no way for rational human beings to be spending their lives. Like Apollo when he saw Daphne with her hair hung carelessly about her neck, they sigh and say to themselves: "What if it were properly arranged." Moreover, they tell us that they have seen in a dream the glorious, collisionless manner of living proper to all mankind, and this dream they understand as their warrant for seeking to remove the diversities and occasions of conflict which distinguish our current manner of living. Of course, their dreams are not all exactly alike; but they have this in common: each is a vision of a condition of human circumstance from which the occasion of conflict has been removed, a vision of human activity co-ordinated and set going in a single direction and of every resource being used to the full. And such people appropriately understand the office of government to be the imposition upon its subjects of the condition of human circumstances of their dream. To govern is to turn a private dream into a public and compulsory manner of living. Thus, politics becomes an encounter of dreams and the activity in which government is held to this understanding of its office and provided with the appropriate instruments.

I do not propose to criticize this jump to glory style of politics in which governing is understood as a perpetual take-over bid for the purchase of the resources of human energy in order to concentrate them in a single direction; it is not at all unintelligible, and there is much in our circumstances to provoke it. My purpose is merely to point out that there is another quite different understanding of government, and that it is no less intelligible and in some respects perhaps more appropriate to our circumstances.

The spring of this other disposition in respect of governing and the instruments of government—a conservative disposition—is to be found in the acceptance of the current condition of human circumstances as I have described it: the propensity to make our own choices and to find happiness in doing so, the variety of enterprises each pursued with passion, the diversity of beliefs each held with the conviction of its exclusive truth; the inventiveness, the changefulness and the absence of any large design; the excess, the over-activity and the informal compromise. And the office of government is not to impose other beliefs and activities upon its subjects, not to tutor or to educate them, not to make them better or happier in another way, not to direct them, to galvanize them into action, to lead them or to coordinate their activities so that no occasion of conflict shall occur; the office of government is merely to rule. This is a specific and limited activity, easily corrupted when it is combined with any other, and, in the circumstances, indispensable. The image of the ruler is the umpire whose business is to administer the rules of the game, or the chairman who governs the debate according to known rules but does not himself participate in it.

Now people of this disposition commonly defend their belief that proper attitude of government towards the current condition of human circumstance is one of acceptance by appealing to certain general ideas. They contend that there is absolute value in the free play of human choice, that private property (the emblem of choice) is a natural right, that it is only in the enjoyment of diversity of opinion and activity that true belief and good conduct can be expected to disclose themselves. But I do not think that this disposition requires these or any similar beliefs in order to make it intelligible. Something much smaller and less pretentious will do: the observation that this condition of human circumstance is, in fact, current, and that we have learned to enjoy it and how to manage it; that we are not children *in statu pupillari* but adults who do not consider themselves under any obligation to justify their preference for

making their own choices; and that it is beyond human experience to suppose
that those who rule are endowed with a superior wisdom which discloses them
a better range of beliefs and activities and which gives them authority to impose upon their subjects a quite different manner of life. In short, if the man
of this disposition is asked: Why ought governments to accept the current diversity of opinion and activity in preference to imposing upon their subjects a
dream of their own? it is enough for him to reply: Why not? Their dreams are
no different from those of anyone else; and if it is boring to have to listen to
dreams of others being recounted, it is insufferable to be forced to re-enact
them. We tolerate monomaniacs, it is our habit to do so; but why should we
be *ruled* by them? Is it not (the man of conservative disposition asks) an intelligible task for a government to protect its subjects against the nuisance of
those who spend their energy and their wealth in the service of some pet indignation, endeavouring to impose it upon everybody, not by suppressing
their activities in favour of others of a similar kind, but by setting a limit to
the amount of noise anyone may emit?

Nevertheless, if this acceptance is the spring of the conservative's disposition in respect of government, he does not suppose that the office of government is to do nothing. As he understands it, there is work to be done which
can be done only in virtue of a genuine acceptance of current beliefs simply
because they are current and current activities simply because they are afoot.
And, briefly, the office he attributes to government is to resolve some of the
collisions which this variety of beliefs and activities generates; to preserve
peace, not by placing an interdict upon choice and upon the diversity that
springs from the exercise of preference, not by imposing substantive uniformity, but by enforcing general rules of procedure upon all subjects alike.

Government, then, as the conservative in this matter understands it, does
not begin with a vision of another, different and better world, but with the observation of the self-government practised even by men of passion in the conduct of their enterprises; it begins in the informal adjustments of interests to
one another which are designed to release those who are apt to collide from
the mutual frustrations of a collision. Sometimes these adjustments are no
more than agreements between two parties to keep out of each other's way;
sometimes they are of wider application and more durable character, such as
the International Rules for the prevention of collisions at sea. In short, the in-
timations of government are to be found in ritual, not in religion or philosophy; in the enjoyment of orderly and peaceable behaviour, not in the search
for truth or perfection.

But the self-government of men of passionate belief and enterprise is apt
to break down when it is most needed. It often suffices to resolve minor collisions of interest, but beyond these it is not to be relied upon. A more precise
and a less easily corrupted ritual is required to resolve the massive collisions
which our manner of living is apt to generate and to release us from the mas-

sive frustrations in which we are apt to become locked. The custodian of this ritual is "the government," and the rules it imposes are "the law." One may imagine a government engaged in the activity of an arbiter in cases of collisions of interest but doing its business without the aid of laws, just as one may imagine a game without rules and an umpire who was appealed to in cases of dispute and who on each occasion merely used his judgement to devise *ad hoc* a way of releasing the disputants from their mutual frustration. But the diseconomy of such an arrangement is so obvious that it could only be expected to occur to those inclined to believe the ruler to be supernaturally inspired and to those disposed to attribute to him a quite different office—that of leader, or tutor, or manager. At all events the disposition to be conservative in respect of government is rooted in the belief that where government rests upon the acceptance of the current activities and beliefs of its subjects, the only appropriate manner of ruling is by making and enforcing rules of conduct. In short, to be conservative about government is a reflection of the conservatism we have recognized to be appropriate in respect of rules of conduct.

To govern, then, as the conservative understands it, is to provide a *vinculum juris* for those manners of conduct which, in the circumstances, are least likely to result in a frustrating collision of interests; to provide redress and means of compensation for those who suffer from others behaving in a contrary manner; sometimes to provide punishment for those who pursue their own interests regardless of the rules; and, of course, to provide a sufficient force to maintain the authority of an arbiter of this kind. Thus, governing is recognized as a specific and limited activity; not the management of an enterprise, but the rule of those engaged in a great diversity of self-chosen enterprises. It is not concerned with concrete persons, but with activities; and with activities only in respect of their propensity to collide with one another. It is not concerned with moral right and wrong, it is not designed to make men good or even better; it is not indispensable on account of "the natural depravity of mankind" but merely because of their current disposition to be extravagant; its business is to keep its subjects at peace with one another in the activities in which they have chosen to seek their happiness. And if there is any general idea entailed in this view, it is, perhaps, that a government which does not sustain the loyalty of its subjects is worthless; and that while one which (in the old puritan phrase) "commands for truth" is incapable of doing so (because some of its subjects will believe its "truth" to be error), one which is indifferent to "truth" and "error" alike, and merely pursues peace, presents no obstacle to the necessary loyalty.

Now, it is intelligible enough that any man who thinks in this manner about government should be averse from innovation: government is providing rules of conduct, and familiarity is a supremely important virtue in a rule. Nevertheless, he has room for other thoughts. The current condition of human circumstances is one in which new activities (often springing from new inventions) are constantly appearing and rapidly extend themselves, and in which beliefs are perpetually being modified or discarded; and for the rules to be inappropriate to the current activities and beliefs is as unprofitable as for them to be unfamiliar. For example, a variety of inventions and considerable changes in the conduct of business, seem now to have made the current law of copyright inadequate. And it may be thought that neither the newspaper nor the motor-car nor the aeroplane have yet received proper recognition in the law of England; they have all created nuisances that call out to be abated. Or again, at the end of the last century our governments engaged in an extensive codification of large parts of our law and in this manner both brought it into closer relationship with current beliefs and manners of activity and insulated it from the small adjustments to circumstances which are characteristic of the operation of our common law. But many of these Statutes are now hopelessly out of date. And there are older Acts of Parliament (such as the Merchant Shipping Act), governing large and important departments of activity, which are even more inappropriate to current circumstances. Innovation, then, is called for if the rules are to remain appropriate to the activities they govern. But, as the conservative understands it, modification of the rules should always reflect, and never impose, a change in the activities and beliefs of those who are subject to them, and should never on any occasion be so great as to destroy the *ensemble*. Consequently, the conservative will have nothing to do with innovations designed to meet merely hypothetical situations; he will prefer to enforce a rule he has got rather than invent a new one; he will think it appropriate to delay a modification of the rules until it is clear that the change of circumstance it is designed to reflect has come to stay for a while; he will be suspicious of proposals for change in excess of what the situation calls for, of rulers who demand extra-ordinary powers in order to make great changes and whose utterances are tied to generalities like "the public good" or "social justice," and of Saviours of Society who buckle on armour and seek dragons to slay; he will think it proper to consider the occasion of the innovation with care; in short, he will be disposed to regard politics as an activity in which a valuable set of tools is renovated from time to time and kept in trim rather than as an opportunity for perpetual re-equipment.

All this may help to make intelligible the disposition to be conservative in respect of government; and the detail might be elaborated to show, for example, how a man of this disposition understands the other great business of a government, the conduct of a foreign policy; to show why he places so high a value upon the complicated set of arrangements we call "the institution of private property"; to show the appropriateness of his rejection of the view that politics is a shadow thrown by economics; to show why he believes that the main (perhaps the only) specifically economic activity appropriate to government is the maintenance of a stable currency. But, on this occasion, I think there is something else to be said.

To some people, "government" appears as a vast reservoir of power which inspires them to dream of what use might be made of it. They have favourite projects, of various dimensions, which they sincerely believe are for the benefit of mankind, and to capture this source of power, if necessary to increase it, and to use it for imposing their favourite projects upon their fellows is what they understand as the adventure of governing men. They are, thus, disposed to recognize government as an instrument of passion; the art of politics is to inflame and direct desire. In short, governing is understood to be just like any other activity—making and selling a brand of soap, exploiting the resources of a locality, or developing a housing estate—only the power here is (for the most part) already mobilized, and the enterprise is remarkable only because it aims at monopoly and because of its promise of success once the source of power has been captured. Of course a private enterprise politician of this sort would get nowhere in these days unless there were people with wants so vague that they can be prompted to ask for what he has to offer, or with wants so servile that they prefer the promise of a provided abundance to the opportunity of choice and activity on their own account. And it is not all as plain sailing as it might appear: often a politician of this sort misjudges the situation; and then, briefly, even in democratic politics, we become aware of what the camel thinks of the camel driver.

Now, the disposition to be conservative in respect of politics reflects a quite different view of the activity of governing. The man of this disposition understands it to be the business of a government not to inflame passion and give it new objects to feed upon, but to inject into the activities of already too passionate men an ingredient of moderation; to restrain, to deflate, to pacify and to reconcile; not to stoke the fires of desire, but to damp them down. And all this, not because passion is vice and moderation virtue, but because moderation is indispensable if passionate men are to escape being locked in an encounter of mutual frustration. A government of this sort does not need to be regarded as the agent of a benign providence, as the custodian of a moral law, or as the emblem of a divine order. What it provides is something that its subjects (if they are such people as we are) can easily recognize to be valuable; indeed, it is something that, to some extent, they do for themselves in the ordinary course of business or pleasure. They scarcely need to be reminded of its indispensability, as Sextus Empiricus tells us the ancient Persians were accustomed periodically to remind themselves by setting aside all laws for five hair-raising days on the death of a king. Generally speaking, they are not averse from paying the modest cost of this service; and they recognize that the appropriate attitude to a government of this sort is loyalty (sometimes a confident loyalty, at others perhaps the heavy-hearted loyalty of Sidney Godolphin), respect and some suspicion, not love or devotion or affection. Thus, governing is understood to be a secondary activity; but it is recognized also to be a specific activity, not easily to be combined with any other, because all other activities (except the mere contemplation of the scene) entail taking sides and the surrender of the indifference appropriate (on this view of things) not only to the judge but also to the legislator, who is understood to occupy a judicial office. The subjects of such a government require that it shall be strong, alert, resolute, economical and neither capricious nor over-active: they have no use for a referee who does not govern the game according to the rules, who takes sides, who plays a game of his own, or who is always blowing his whistle; after all, the game's the thing, and in playing the game we neither need to be, nor at present are disposed to be, conservative.

But there is something more to be observed in this style of governing than merely the restraint imposed by familiar and appropriate rules. Of course, it will not countenance government by suggestion or cajolery or by any other means than by law; an avuncular Home Secretary or a threatening Chancellor of the Exchequer. But the spectacle of its indifference to the beliefs and substantive activities of its subjects may itself be expected to provoke a habit of restraint. Into the heat of our engagements, into the passionate clash of beliefs, into our enthusiasm for saving the souls of our neighbours or of all mankind, a government of this sort injects an ingredient, not of reason (how should we expect that?) but of the irony that is prepared to counteract one vice by another, of the raillery that deflates extravagance without itself pretending to wisdom, of the mockery that disperses tension, of inertia, and of scepticism: indeed, it might be said that we keep a government of this sort to do for us the scepticism we have neither the time nor the inclination to do for ourselves. It is like the cool touch of the mountain that one feels in the plain even on the hottest summer day. Or, to leave metaphor behind, it is like the "governor" which, by controlling the speed at which its parts move, keeps an engine from racketing itself to pieces.

It is not, then, mere stupid prejudice which disposes a conservative to take this view of the activity of governing; nor are any highfalutin metaphysical beliefs necessary to provoke it or make it intelligible. It is connected merely with the observation that where activity is bent upon enterprise the indispensable counterpart is another order of activity, bent upon restraint, which is unavoidably corrupted (indeed, altogether abrogated) when the power assigned to it is used for advancing favourite projects. An "umpire" who at the same time is one of the players is no umpire; "rules" about which we are not disposed to be conservative are not rules but incitements to disorder; the conjunction of dreaming and ruling generates tyranny.

4

Political conservatism is, then, not at all unintelligible in a people disposed to be adventurous and enterprising, a people in love with change and apt to rationalize their affections in terms of "progress."[3] And one does not need to think that the belief in "progress" is the most cruel and unprofitable of all beliefs, arousing cupidity without satisfying it, in order to think it inappropriate for a government to be conspicuously "progressive." Indeed, a disposition to be conservative in respect of government would seem to be pre-eminently appropriate to men who have something to do and something to think about on their own account, who have a skill to practice or an intellectual fortune to make, to people whose passions do not need to be inflamed, whose desires do not need to be provoked and whose dreams of a better world need no prompting. Such people know the value of a rule which imposes orderliness without directing enterprise, a rule which concentrates duty so that room is left for delight. They might even be prepared to suffer a legally established ecclesiastical order; but it would not be because they believed it to represent some unassailable religious truth, but merely because it restrained the indecent competition of sects and (as Hume said) moderated "the plague of a too diligent clergy".

Now, whether or not these beliefs recommend themselves as reasonable and appropriate to our circumstances and to the abilities we are likely to find in those who rule us, they and their like are in my view what make intelligible a conservative disposition in respect of politics. What would be the appropriateness of this disposition in circumstances other than our own, whether to be conservative in respect of government would have the same relevance in the circumstances of an unadventurous, a slothful or a spiritless people, is a question we need not try to answer: we are concerned with ourselves as we are. I myself think that it would occupy an important place in any set of circumstances. But what I hope I have made clear is that it is not at all inconsistent to be conservative in respect of government and radical in respect of almost every other activity. And, in my opinion, there is more to be learnt about this disposition from Montaigne, Pascal, Hobbes and Hume than from Burke or Bentham.

Of the many entailments of this view of things that might be pointed to, I will notice one, namely, that politics is an activity unsuited to the young, not on account of their vices but on account of what I at least consider to be their virtues.

Nobody pretends that it is easy to acquire or to sustain the mood of indifference which this manner of politics calls for. To rein-in one's own beliefs and desires, to acknowledge the current shape of things, to feel the balance of things in one's hand, to tolerate what is abominable, to distinguish between crime and sin, to respect formality even when it appears to be leading to error, these are difficult achievements; and they are achievements not to be looked for in the young.

Everybody's young days are a dream, a delightful insanity, a sweet solipsism. Nothing in them has a fixed shape, nothing a fixed price; everything is a possibility, and we live happily on credit. There are no obligations to be observed; there are no accounts to be kept. Nothing is specified in advance; everything is what can be made of it. The world is a mirror in which we seek the reflection of our own desires. The allure of violent emotions is irresistible. When we are young we are not disposed to make concessions to the world; we never feel the balance of a thing in our hands—unless it be a cricket bat. We are not apt to distinguish between our liking and our esteem; urgency is our criterion of importance; and we do not easily understand that what is humdrum need not be despicable. We are impatient of restraint; and we readily believe, like Shelley, that to have contracted a habit is to have failed. These, in my opinion, are among our virtues when we are young; but how remote they are from the disposition appropriate for participating in the style of government I have been describing. Since life is a dream, we argue (with plausible but erroneous logic) that politics must be an encounter of dreams, in which we hope to impose our own. Some unfortunate people, like Pitt (laughably called "the Younger"), are born old, and are eligible to engage in politics almost in their cradles; others, perhaps more fortunate, belie the saying that one is young only once, they never grow up. But these are exceptions. For most there is what Conrad called the "shadow line" which, when we pass it, discloses a solid world of things, each with its fixed shape, each with its own point of balance, each with its price; a world of fact, not poetic image, in which what we have spent on one thing we cannot spend on another; a world inhabited by others besides ourselves who cannot be reduced to mere reflections of our own emotions. And coming to be at home in this commonplace world qualifies us (as no knowledge of "political science" can ever qualify us), if we are so inclined and have nothing better to think about, to engage in what the man of conservative disposition understands to be political activity.

## Notes

1. "Which of us," asks a contemporary (not without some equivocation), "would not settle, at whatever cost in nervous anxiety, for a febrile and creative rather than a static society?"

2. When Prince Wen Wang was on a tour of inspection in Tsang, he saw an old man fishing. But his fishing was not real fishing, for he did not fish in order to catch fish, but to amuse himself. So Wen Wang wished to employ him in the administration of government, but he feared his own ministers, uncles and brothers might object. On the other hand, if he let the old man go, he could not bear to think of the people being deprived of his influence. *Chuang Tzu.*

3. I have not forgotten to ask myself the question: Why, then, have we so neglected what is appropriate to our circumstances as to make the activist dreamer the stereotype of the modern politician? And I have tried to answer it elsewhere.

# 8

# EDMUND BURKE

## *Reflections on the Revolution in France*

*Reflections on the Revolution in France* (1790), Edmund Burke's most famous work, greatly influenced British perceptions of and policies toward postrevolutionary France. The British conservatives adopted his philosophy, and today he is rightly called the father of conservatism. Burke was born in Dublin, Ireland, in 1729 and served as a Whig member of Parliament until his death in 1797. In Parliament he worked for the improvement of British colonial relations, especially between England and Ireland.

Dear Sir,

You are pleased to call again, and with some earnestness, for my thoughts on the late proceedings in France. I will not give you reason to imagine, that I think my sentiments of such value as to wish myself to be solicited about them. They are of too little consequence to be very anxiously either communicated or withheld. It was from attention to you, and to you only, that I hesitated at the time, when you first desired to receive them. In the first letter I had the honour to write to you, and which at length I send, I wrote neither for nor from any description of men; nor shall I in this. My errors, if any, are my own. My reputation alone is to answer for them.

You see, Sir, by the long letter I have transmitted to you, that, though I do most heartily wish that France may be animated by a spirit of rational liberty, and that I think you bound, in all honest policy, to provide a permanent body, in which that spirit may reside, and an effectual organ, by which it may act, it is my misfortune to entertain great doubts concerning several material points in your late transactions. . . .

## [Liberty and Order]

I flatter myself that I love a manly, moral, regulated liberty as well as any gentleman of that society, be he who he will; and perhaps I have given as good

proofs of my attachment to that cause, in the whole course of my public conduct. I think I envy liberty as little as they do, to any other nation. But I cannot stand forward, and give praise or blame to any thing which relates to human actions, and human concerns, on a simple view of the object, as it stands
stripped of every relation, in all the nakedness and solitude of metaphysical abstraction. Circumstances (which with some gentlemen pass for nothing) give
in reality to every political principle its distinguishing colour, and discriminat-
ing effect. The circumstances are what render every civil and political scheme
beneficial or noxious to mankind. Abstractedly speaking, government, as well
as liberty, is good; yet could I, in common sense, ten years ago, have felicitated
France on her enjoyment of a government (for she then had a government)
without enquiry what the nature of that government was, or how it was administered? Can I now congratulate the same nation upon its freedom? Is it
because liberty in the abstract may be classed amongst the blessings of mankind, that I am seriously to felicitate a madman, who has escaped from the
protecting restraint and wholesome darkness of his cell, on his restoration to
the enjoyment of light and liberty? Am I to congratulate an highwayman and
murderer, who has broke prison, upon the recovery of his natural rights? This
would be to act over again the scene of the criminals condemned to the gallies,
and their heroic deliverer, the metaphysic Knight of the Sorrowful Countenance.

When I see the spirit of liberty in action, I see a strong principle at work;
and this, for a while, is all I can possibly know of it. The wild *gas*, the fixed air
is plainly broke loose: but we ought to suspend our judgment until the first
effervescence is a little subsided, till the liquor is cleared, and until we see
something deeper than the agitation of a troubled and frothy surface. I must
be tolerably sure, before I venture publicly to congratulate men upon a blessing, that they have really received one. Flattery corrupts both the receiver and
the giver; and adulation is not of more service to the people than to kings. I
should therefore suspend my congratulations on the new liberty of France, until I was informed how it had been combined with government; with public
force; with the discipline and obedience of armies; with the collection of an
effective and well-distributed revenue; with morality and religion; with the solidity of property; with peace and order; with civil and social manners. All
these (in their way) are good things too; and, without them, liberty is not a
benefit whilst it lasts, and is not likely to continue long. The effect of liberty
to individuals is, that they may do what they please: We ought to see what it
will please them to do, before we risque congratulations, which may be soon
turned into complaints. Prudence would dictate this in the case of separate insulated private men; but liberty, when men act in bodies, is *power*. Considerate people, before they declare themselves, will observe the use which is made
of *power*; and particularly of so trying a thing as *new* power in *new* persons, of
whose principles, tempers, and dispositions, they have little or no experience,

and in situations where those who appear the most stirring in the scene may possibly not be the real movers. . . .

## [Continuity and Change]

It is far from impossible to reconcile, if we do not suffer ourselves to be entangled in the mazes of metaphysic sophistry, the use both of a fixed rule and an occasional deviation; the sacredness of an hereditary principle of succession in our government, with a power of change in its application in cases of extreme emergency. Even in that extremity (if we take the measure of our rights by our exercise of them at the Revolution) the change is to be confined to the peccant part only; to the part which produced the necessary deviation; and even then it is to be effected without a decomposition of the whole civil and political mass, for the purpose of originating a new civil order out of the first elements of society.

A state without the means of some change is without the means of its conservation. Without such means it might even risque the loss of that part of the constitution which it wished the most religiously to preserve. The two principles of conservation and correction operated strongly at the two critical periods of the Restoration and Revolution, when England found itself without a king. At both those periods the nation had lost the bond of union in their antient edifice; they did not however, dissolve the whole fabric. On the contrary, in both cases they regenerated the deficient part of the old constitution through the parts which were not impaired. They kept these old parts exactly as they were, that the part recovered might be suited to them. They acted by the ancient organized states in the shape of their old organization, and not by the organic *moleculae* of a disbanded people. At no time, perhaps, did the sovereign legislature manifest a more tender regard to that fundamental principle of British constitutional policy, than at the time of the Revolution, when it deviated from the direct line of hereditary succession. The crown was carried somewhat out of the line in which it had before moved; but the new line was derived from the same stock. It was still a line of hereditary descent; still an hereditary descent in the same blood, though an hereditary descent qualified with protestantism. When the legislature altered the direction, but kept the principle, they shewed that they held it inviolable. . . .

The speculative line of demarcation, where obedience ought to end, and resistance must begin, is faint, obscure, and not easily definable. It is not a single act, or a single event, which determines it. Governments must be abused and deranged indeed, before it can be thought of; and the prospect of the future must be as bad as the experience of the past. When things are in that lamentable condition, the nature of the disease is to indicate the remedy to those whom nature has qualified to administer in extremities this critical, ambiguous, bitter portion to a distempered state. Times and occasions, and provocations, will teach their own lessons. The wise will determine from the gravity of the case; the irritable from sensibility to oppression; the high-minded from disdain and indignation at abusive power in unworthy hands; the brave and bold from the love of honourable danger in a generous cause: but, with or without right, a revolution will be the very last resource of the thinking and the good. . . .

The very idea of the fabrication of a new government, is enough to fill us with disgust and horror. We wished at the period of the Revolution, and do now wish, to derive all we possess as *an inheritance from our forefathers*. Upon that body and stock of inheritance we have taken care not to inoculate any cyon [scion] alien to the nature of the original plant. All the reformations we have hitherto made, have proceeded upon the principle of reference to antiquity; and I hope, nay I am persuaded, that all those which possibly may be made hereafter, will be carefully formed upon analogical precedent, authority, and example. . . .

Our political system is placed in a just correspondence and symmetry with the order of the world, and with the mode of existence decreed to a permanent body composed of transitory parts; wherein, by the disposition of a stupendous wisdom, moulding together the great mysterious incorporation of the human race, the whole, at one time, is never old, or middle-aged, or young, but in a condition of unchangeable constancy, moves on through the varied tenour of perpetual decay, fall, renovation, and progression. Thus, by preserving the method of nature in the conduct of the state, in what we improve we are never wholly new; in what we retain we are never wholly obsolete. By adhering in this manner and on those principles to our forefathers, we are guided not by the superstition of antiquarians, but by the spirit of philosophic analogy. In this choice of inheritance we have given to our frame of polity the image of a relation in blood; binding up the constitution of our country with our dearest domestic ties; adopting our fundamental laws into the bosom of our family affections; keeping inseparable, and cherishing with the warmth of all their combined and mutually reflected charities, our state, our hearths, our sepulchres, and our altars.

Through the same plan of a conformity to nature in our artificial institutions, and by calling in the aid of her unerring and powerful instincts, to fortify the fallible and feeble contrivances of our reason, we have derived several other, and those no small benefits, from considering our liberties in the light of an inheritance. Always acting as if in the presence of canonized forefathers, the spirit of freedom, leading in itself to misrule and excess, is tempered with an awful gravity. This idea of a liberal descent inspires us with a sense of habitual native dignity, which prevents that upstart insolence almost inevitably adhering to and disgracing those who are the first acquirers of any distinction. By this means our liberty becomes a noble freedom. It carries an imposing and majestic aspect. It has a pedigree and illustrating ancestors. It has its bearings and its ensigns armorial. It has its gallery of portraits; its monumental inscriptions; its records, evidences, and titles. We procure reverence to our civil institutions on the principle upon which nature teaches us to revere individual men; on account of their age; and on account of those from whom they are descended. All your sophisters cannot produce any thing better adapted to preserve a rational and manly freedom than the course that we have pursued, who have chosen our nature rather than our speculations, our breasts rather than our inventions, for the great conservatories and magazines of our rights and privileges.

   You might, if you pleased, have profited of our example, and have given to your recovered freedom a correspondent dignity. Your privileges, though discontinued, were not lost to memory. Your constitution, it is true, whilst you were out of possession, suffered waste and dilapidation; but you possessed in some parts the walls, and in all the foundations of a noble and venerable castle. You might have repaired those walls; you might have built on those old foundations. Your constitution was suspended before it was perfected; but you had the elements of a constitution very nearly as good as could be wished. In your old states you possessed that variety of parts corresponding with the various descriptions of which your community was happily composed; you had all that combination, and all that opposition of interests, you had that action and counteraction which, in the natural and in the political world, from the reciprocal struggle of discordant powers, draws out the harmony of the universe. These opposed and conflicting interests, which you considered as so great a blemish in your old and in our present constitution, interpose a salutary check to all precipitate resolutions; they render deliberation a matter not of choice, but of necessity; they make all change a subject of *compromise*, which naturally begets moderation; they produce *temperaments*, preventing the sore evil of harsh, crude, unqualified reformations; and rendering all the headlong exertions of arbitrary power, in the few or in the many, for ever impracticable. Through that diversity of members and interests, general liberty had as many securities as there were separate views in the several orders; whilst by pressing down the whole by the weight of a real monarchy, the separate parts would have been prevented from warping and starting from their allotted places. . . .

## [Real Rights]

They have "the rights of men." Against these there can be no prescription; against these no agreement is binding: these admit no temperament, and no compromise: any thing withheld from their full demand is so much of fraud and injustice. Against these their rights of men let no government look for security in the length of its continuance, or in the justice and lenity of its administration. The objections of these speculatists, if its forms do not quadrate with their theories, are as valid against such an old and beneficent government as against the most violent tyranny, or the greenest usurpation. They are always at issue with governments, not on a question of abuse, but a question of competency, and a question of title. I have nothing to say to the clumsy subtilty of their political metaphysics. Let them be their amusement in the schools—*"Illa se jactet in aula—Aeolus, et clauso ventorum carcere regnet."* But let them not break prison to burst like a *Levanter*, to sweep the earth with their hurricane, and to break up the fountains of the great deep to overwhelm us. . . .

Far am I from denying in theory; full as far is my heart from withholding in practice (if I were of power to give or to withhold) the *real* rights of men. In denying their false claims of right, I do not mean to injure those which are real, and are such as their pretended rights would totally destroy. If civil society be made for the advantage of man, all the advantages for which it is made become his right. It is an institution of beneficence; and law itself is only beneficence acting by a rule. Men have a right to live by that rule; they have a right to justice: as between their fellows, whether their fellows are in politic function or in ordinary occupation. They have a right to the fruits of their industry; and to the means of making their industry fruitful. They have a right to the acquisitions of their parents; to the nourishment and improvement of their offspring; to instruction in life, and to consolation in death. Whatever each man can separately do, without trespassing upon others, he has a right to do for himself; and he has a right to a fair portion of all which society, with all its combinations of skill and force, can do in his favour. In this partnership all men have equal rights; but not to equal things. He that has but five shillings in the partnership, has as good a right to it, as he that has five hundred pounds has to his larger proportion. But he has not a right to an equal dividend in the product of the joint stock; and as to the share of power, authority, and direction which each individual ought to have in the management of the state, that I must deny to be amongst the direct original rights of man in civil society; for I have in my contemplation the civil social man, and no other. It is a thing to be settled by convention. . . .

If civil society be the offspring of convention, that convention must be its law. That convention must limit and modify all the descriptions of constitution which are formed under it. Every sort of legislative, judicial, or executory power are its creatures. They can have no being in any other state of things; and how can any man claim, under the conventions of civil society, rights which do not so much as suppose its existence? Rights which are absolutely repugnant to it? One of the first motives to civil society, and which becomes one of its fundamental rules, is, *that no man should be judge in his own cause.* By this each person has at once divested himself of the first fundamental right of uncovenanted man, that is, to judge for himself, and to assert his own cause.

He abdicates all right to be his own governor. He inclusively, in a great measure, abandons the right of self-defence, the first law of nature. Men cannot enjoy the rights of an uncivil and of a civil state together. That he may obtain justice he gives up his right of determining what it is in points the most essential to him. That he may secure some liberty, he makes a surrender in trust of the whole of it. . . .

Government is not made in virtue of natural rights, which may and do exist in total independence of it; and exist in much greater clearness, and in a much greater degree of abstract perfection: but their abstract perfection is their practical defect. By having a right to every thing they want every thing. Government is a contrivance of human wisdom to provide for human *wants*. Men have a right that these wants should be provided for by this wisdom. Among these wants is to be reckoned the want, out of civil society, of a sufficient restraint upon their passions. Society requires not only that the passions of individuals should be subjected, but that even in the mass and body as well as in the individuals, the inclinations of men should frequently be thwarted, their will controlled, and their passions brought into subjection. This can only be done *by a power out of themselves;* and not, in the exercise of its function, subject to that will and to those passions which it is its office to bridle and subdue. In this sense the restraints on men, as well as their liberties, are to be reckoned among their rights. But as the liberties and the restrictions vary with times and circumstances, and admit of infinite modifications, they cannot be settled upon any abstract rule; and nothing is so foolish as to discuss them upon the principle. . . .


## [Prudence]

The science of government being therefore so practical in itself, and intended for such practical purposes, a matter which requires experience, and even more experience than any person can gain in his whole life, however sagacious and observing he may be, it is with infinite caution that any man ought to venture upon pulling down an edifice which has answered in any tolerable degree for ages the common purposes of society, or on building it up again, without having models and patterns of approved utility before his eyes.

These metaphysic rights entering into common life, like rays of light which pierce into a dense medium, are, by the laws of nature, refracted from their straight line. Indeed in the gross and complicated mass of human passions and concerns, the primitive rights of men undergo such a variety of refractions and reflections, that it becomes absurd to talk of them as if they continued in the simplicity of their original direction. The nature of man is intricate; the objects of society are of the greatest possible complexity; and therefore no simple disposition of direction of power can be suitable either to man's nature, or to the quality of his affairs. When I hear the simplicity of contrivance aimed at and boasted of in any new political constitutions, I am at no loss to decide that the artificers are grossly ignorant of their trade, or totally negligent of their duty. . . .

## [Tradition]

It is now sixteen or seventeen years since I saw the queen of France, then the dauphiness, at Versailles; and surely never lighted on this orb, which she hardly seemed to touch, a more delightful vision. I saw her just above the horizon, decorating and cheering the elevated sphere she just began to move in,—glittering like the morningstar, full of life, and splendor, and joy. Oh! What a revolution! and what an heart must I have, to contemplate without emotion that elevation and that fall! Little did I dream when she added titles of veneration to those of enthusiastic, distant, respectful love, that she should ever be obliged to carry the sharp antidote against disgrace concealed in that bosom; little did I dream that I should have lived to see such disasters fallen upon her in a nation of gallant men, in a nation of men of honour and of cavaliers. I thought ten thousand swords must have leaped from their scabbards to avenge even a look that threatened her with insult.—But the age of chivalry is gone.—That of sophisters, oeconomists, and calculators, has succeeded; and the glory of Europe is extinguished for ever. Never, never more, shall we behold that generous loyalty to rank and sex, that proud submission, that dignified obedience, that subordination of the heart, which kept alive, even in servitude itself, the spirit of an exalted freedom. The unbought grace of life, the cheap defence of nations, the nurse of manly sentiment and heroic enterprize is gone! It is gone, that sensibility of principle, that chastity of honour, which felt a stain like a wound, which inspired courage whilst it mitigated ferocity, which ennobled whatever it touched, and under which vice itself lost half its evil, by losing all its grossness.

This mixed system of opinion and sentiment had its origin in the antient chivalry; and the principle, though varied in its appearance by the varying state of human affairs, subsisted and influenced through a long succession of generations, even to the time we live in. If it should ever be totally extinguished, the loss I fear will be great. It is this which has given its character to modern Europe. It is this which has distinguished it under all its forms of government, and distinguished it to its advantage, from the states of Asia, and possibly from those states which flourished in the most brilliant periods of the antique world. It was this, which, without confounding ranks, had produced a noble equality, and handed it down through all the gradations of social life. It was this opinion which mitigated kings into companions, and raised private men to be fellows with kings. Without force, or opposition, it subdued the fierceness of pride and power; it obliged sovereigns to submit to the soft collar of social esteem, compelled stern authority to submit to elegance, and gave a domination vanquisher of laws, to be subdued by manners.

But now all is to be changed. All the pleasing illusions, which made power gentle, and obedience liberal, which harmonized the different shades of life, and which, by a bland assimilation, incorporated into politics the sentiments which beautify and soften private society, are to be dissolved by this new conquering empire of light and reason. All the decent drapery of life is to be rudely torn off. All the super-added ideas, furnished from the wardrobe of a moral imagination, which the heart owns, and the understanding ratifies, as necessary to cover the defects of our naked shivering nature, and to raise it to dignity in our own estimation, are to be exploded as a ridiculous, absurd, and antiquated fashion.

On this scheme of things, a king is but a man; a queen is but a woman; a woman is but an animal; and an animal not of the highest order. All homage paid to the sex in general as such, and without distinct views, is to be regarded as romance and folly. Regicide, and parricide, and sacrilege, are but fictions of superstition corrupting jurisprudence by destroying its simplicity. The murder of a king, or a queen, or a bishop, or a father, are only common homicide; and if the people are by any chance, or in any way gainers by it, a sort of homicide much the most pardonable, and into which we ought not to make too severe a scrutiny.

On the scheme of this barbarous philosophy, which is the offspring of cold hearts and muddy understandings, and which is as void of solid wisdom, as it is destitute of all taste and elegance, laws are to be supported only by their own terrors, and by the concern, which each individual may find in them, from his own private speculations, or can spare to them from his own private interests. In the groves of *their* academy, at the end of every vista, you see nothing but the gallows. Nothing is left which engages the affections on the part of the commonwealth. On the principles of this mechanic philosophy, our institutions can never be embodied, if I may use the expression, in persons; so as to create in us love, veneration, admiration, or attachment. But that sort of reason which banishes the affections is incapable of filling their place. These public affections, combined with manners, are required sometimes as supplements, sometimes as correctives, always as aids to law. . . .

Thanks to our sullen resistance to innovation, thanks to the cold sluggishness of our national character, we still bear the stamp of our forefathers. We have not (as I conceive) lost the generosity and dignity of thinking of the fourteenth century; nor as yet have we subtilized ourselves into savages. We are not the converts of Rousseau; we are not the disciples of Voltaire; Helvetius has made no progress amongst us. Atheists are not our preachers; madmen are not our lawgivers. We know that *we* have made no discoveries; and we think that no discoveries are to be made, in morality; nor many in the

great principles of government, nor in the ideas of liberty, which were understood long before we were born, altogether as well as they will be after the
grave has heaped its mould upon our presumption, and the silent tomb shall
have imposed its law on our pert loquacity. . . .

You see, Sir, that in this enlightened age I am bold enough to confess,
that we are generally men of untaught feelings; that instead of casting away all
our old prejudices, we cherish them to a very considerable degree, and, to take
more shame to ourselves, we cherish them because they are prejudices; and the
longer they have lasted, and the more generally they have prevailed, the more
we cherish them. We are afraid to put men to live and trade each on his own
private stock of reason; because we suspect that this stock in each man is
small, and that the individuals would do better to avail themselves of the general bank and capital of nations, and of ages. Many of our men of speculation,
instead of exploding general prejudices, employ their sagacity to discover the
latent wisdom which prevails in them. If they find what they seek, and they
seldom fail, they think it more wise to continue the prejudice, with the reason
involved, than to cast away the coat of prejudice, and to leave nothing but the
naked reason; because prejudice, with its reason, has a motive to give action to
that reason, and an affection which will give it permanence. Prejudice is of
ready application in the emergency; it previously engages the mind in a steady
course of wisdom and virtue, and does not leave the man hesitating in the moment of decision, skeptical, puzzled, and unresolved. Prejudice renders a
man's virtue his habit; and not a series of unconnected acts. Through just
prejudice, his duty becomes a part of his nature.

But one of the first and most leading principles on which the commonwealth and the laws are consecrated, is lest the temporary possessors and life-
renters in it, unmindful of what they have received from their ancestors, or of
what is due to their posterity, should act as if they were the entire masters;
that they should not think it amongst their rights to cut off the entail, or commit waste on the inheritance, by destroying at their pleasure the whole original
fabric of their society; hazarding to leave to those who come after them, a ruin
instead of an habitation—and teaching these successors as little to respect
their contrivances, as they had themselves respected the institutions of their
forefathers. By this unprincipled facility of changing the state as often, and as
much, and in as many ways as there are floating fancies or fashions, the whole
chain and continuity of the commonwealth would be broken. No one generation could link with the other. Men would become little better than the flies
of a summer. . . .

## [The Social Contract]

Society is indeed a contract. Subordinate contracts for objects of mere occasional interest may be dissolved at pleasure—but the state ought not to be

considered as nothing better than a partnership agreement in a trade of pepper and coffee, callico or tobacco, or some other such low concern, to be taken up for a little temporary interest, and to be dissolved by the fancy of the parties. It is to be looked on with other reverence; because it is not a partnership in things subservient only to the gross animal existence of a temporary and perishable nature. It is a partnership in all science; a partnership in all art; a partnership in every virtue, and in all perfection. As the ends of such a partnership cannot be obtained in many generations, it becomes a partnership not only between those who are living, but between those who are living, those who are dead, and those who are to be born. Each contract of each particular state is but a clause in the great primaeval contract of eternal society, linking the lower with the higher natures, connecting the visible and invisible world, according to a fixed compact sanctioned by the inviolable oath which holds all physical and all moral natures, each in their appointed place. This law is not subject to the will of those, who by an obligation above them, and infinitely superior, are bound to submit their will to that law. The municipal corporations of that universal kingdom are not morally at liberty at their pleasure, and on their speculations of a contingent improvement, wholly to separate and tear asunder the bands of their subordinate community, and to dissolve it into an unsocial, uncivil, unconnected chaos of elementary principles. It is the first and supreme necessity only, a necessity that is not chosen but chooses, a necessity paramount to deliberation, that admits no discussion, and demands no evidence, which alone can justify a resort to anarchy. This necessity is no exception to the rule; because this necessity itself is a part too of that moral and physical disposition of things to which man must be obedient by consent or force; but if that which is only submission to necessity should be made the object of choice, the law is broken, nature is disobeyed, and the rebellious are outlawed, cast forth, and exiled, from this world of reason, and order, and peace, and virtue, and fruitful penitence, into the antagonist world of madness, discord, vice, confusion, and unavailing sorrow. . . .

## [Prescription]

With the national assembly of France, possession is nothing; law and usage are nothing. I see the national assembly openly reprobate the doctrine of prescription, which one of the greatest of their own lawyers tells us, with great truth, is a part of the law of nature. He tells us, that the positive ascertainment of its limits, and its security from invasion, were among the causes for which civil society itself has been instituted. If prescription be once shaken, no species of property is secure, when it once becomes an object large enough to tempt the cupidity of indigent power. I see a practice perfectly correspondent to their contempt of this great fundamental part of natural law. I see the confiscators begin with bishops, and chapters, and monasteries; but I do not see them end there. I see the princes of the blood, who, by the oldest usages of that kingdom, held large landed estates (hardly with the compliment of a debate), deprived of their possessions, and in lieu of their stable independent property, reduced to the hope of some precarious, charitable pension, at the pleasure of an assembly, which of course will pay little regard to the rights of pensioners at pleasure, when it despises those of legal proprietors. Flushed with the insolence of their first inglorious victories, and pressed by the distresses caused by their lust of unhallowed lucre, disappointed but not discouraged, they have at length ventured completely to subvert all property of all descriptions throughout the extent of a great kingdom. They have compelled all men, in all transactions of commerce, in the disposal of lands, in civil dealing, and through the whole communion of life, to accept as perfect payment and good and lawful tender, the symbols of their speculations on a projected sale of their plunder. What vestiges of liberty or property have they left? The tenant-right of a cabbage-garden, a year's interest in a hovel, the good-will of an alehouse, or a baker's shop, the very shadow of a constructive property, are more ceremoniously treated in our parliament than with you the oldest and most valuable landed possessions, in the hands of the most respectable personages, or than the whole body of the monied and commercial interest of your country. We entertain an high opinion of the legislative authority; but we have never dreamt that parliaments had any right whatever to violate property, to overrule prescription, or to force a currency of their own fiction in the place of that which is real, and recognized by the law of nations. But you, who began with refusing to submit to the most moderate restraints, have ended by establishing an unheard of despotism. I find the ground upon which your confiscators go is this; that indeed their proceedings could not be supported in a court of justice; but that the rules of prescription cannot bind a legislative assembly. So that this legislative assembly of a free nation sits, not for the security, but for the destruction of property, and not of property only, but of every rule and maxim which can give it stability, and of those instruments which can alone give it circulation.

# 9

# IRVING KRISTOL

## Capitalism, Socialism, and Nihilism

Irving Kristol (b. 1920) is a prominent voice in the neoconservative movement in America. Since 1965, he has been the editor, with Nathan Glazer, of *Public Interest*. He is the author of numerous books, among them *Two Cheers for Capitalism* (1978), the source of the essay included here, and *Reflections of a Neoconservative* (1983).

Whenever and wherever defenders of "free enterprise," "individual liberty," and "a free society" assemble these days, one senses a peculiar kind of nostalgia in the air. It is a nostalgia for that time when they were busily engaged in confronting their old and familiar enemies, the avowed proponents of a full-blown "collectivist" economic and social order. In the debate with these traditional enemies, advocates of "a free society" have, indeed, done extraordinarily well. It is therefore a source of considerable puzzlement to them that, though the other side seems to have lost the argument, their side seems somehow not to have won it.

Now, I am aware that within this group itself there are different ideological and philosophical tendencies. Friedrich Hayek is not Milton Friedman, for instance, nor vice versa, and there are interesting differences between the nineteenth-century liberal individualism of the one and the nineteenth-century radical individualism of the other. Still, these twain do meet—and not only in Switzerland. There can be little doubt, for instance, that their thinking has converged into a powerful attack on the traditional socialist notions of central economic planning and a centrally administered economy. And there is absolutely no doubt, in my own mind, that this attack has been enormously successful—far more successful than one would have dreamed possible twenty-five years ago.

This attack, like so many successful attacks, has taken the form of a pincer movement. On the one hand, Professor Hayek has explored, in *The Counterrevolution of Science*, the ideological origins in the nineteenth century of the notion of large-scale "social engineering," and his critical history of what he calls—and of what we now call, after him—"scientism" is a major contribution to the history of ideas. It is in good part because of Professor Hayek's work in this area, and also because of his profound insights—most notably in *The Constitution of Liberty*—into the connection between a free market, the rule of law, and individual liberty, that you don't hear professors saying today, as they used so glibly to say, that "we are all socialists now." They are far more likely to say that the question of socialism is irrelevant and they would prefer not to discuss it.

Milton Friedman, on the other hand, has launched his main attack on "the planned society" through the jungles of social and economic policy, as distinct from the highlands of theory. No other thinker of our time has so brilliantly exposed and publicized the perversities that can be engendered by governmental intervention in the economic life of a nation. Whereas Hayek demonstrated why large-scale, centralized planning does not have the wonderful results it is supposed to, Friedman shows us how governmental rules and regulations so frequently get results that are the opposite of those intended. In addition, Friedman has instructed us all—including most socialists and neo-socialists—in the unsuspected, creative powers of the market as a mechanism for solving social problems. Indeed, we have now reached the stage where planners will solemnly assemble and contemplate ways of using the powers of government to *create markets* in order to reach their goals.

As a result of the efforts of Hayek, Friedman, and the many others who share their general outlook, the idea of a centrally planned and centrally administered economy, so popular in the 1930s and early 1940s, has been discredited. Even in the socialist nations, economists are more interested in reviving the market than in permanently burying it. Whether they can have a market economy without private property is, of course, an issue they will shortly have to face up to.

The question then naturally arises: If the traditional economics of socialism has been discredited, why has not the traditional economics of capitalism been vindicated? I should say that the reasons behind this state of affairs are quite obvious and easily comprehensible—only they are terribly difficult to explain to economists.

## On "Thinking Economically"

The original appeal of the idea of central economic planning—like the traditional appeal of socialism itself—was cast primarily in economic terms. It was felt that such planning was necessary to (a) overcome the recurrent crises —i.e., depressions—of a market economy, and (b) provide for steady economic growth and greater material prosperity for all. This importance which traditional socialism—the Old Left, as we would call it today—ascribed to economics was derived from Marxism, which in turn based itself on the later writings of Marx. But the socialist impulse always had other ideological strands in it, especially a yearning for "fraternity" and "community," and a revulsion against the "alienation" of the individual in liberal-bourgeois society. These ideological strands were prominent among the "utopian socialists," as Engels was to label them, and in the early thought of Karl Marx himself, in which economics received much less attention than religion and political philosophy. They are prominent again today, in the thinking of what is called the "New Left."

The Old Left has been intellectually defeated on its chosen battleground, i.e., economics. But the New Left is now launching an assault on liberal society from quite other directions. One of the most astonishing features of the New Left—astonishing, at least, to a middle-aged observer—is how little interest it really has in economics. I would put it even more strongly: the identifying marks of the New Left are its refusal *to think economically* and its contempt for bourgeois society precisely because this is a society that does think economically.

What do I mean by "thinking economically"? I have found that it is very hard to convey this meaning to economists, who take it for granted that this is the only possible way for a sensible man to think—that, indeed, thinking economically is the same thing as thinking rationally. Economics is the social science *par excellence* of modernity, and economists as a class find it close to impossible to detach themselves from the philosophical presuppositions of modernity. This would not be particularly significant—until recently has not been particularly significant—were it not for the fact that the New Left is in rebellion against these philosophical presuppositions themselves.

Let me give you a simple illustration. One of the keystones of modern economic thought is that it is impossible to have an *a priori* knowledge of what constitutes happiness for other people; that such knowledge is incorporated in an individual's "utility schedules"; and this knowledge, in turn, is revealed by the choices that an individual makes in a free market. This is not merely the keystone of modern economic thought; it is also the keystone of modern, liberal, secular society itself. This belief is so deeply ingrained in us that we are inclined to explain any deviation from it as perverse and pathological. Yet it is a fact that for several millennia, until the advent of modernity, people did not believe any such thing and would, indeed, have found such a belief to be itself shockingly pathological and perverse. For all pre-modern thinkers, *a priori* knowledge of what constituted other people's happiness was not only possible, it was a fact. True, such knowledge was the property of a small elite religious, philosophical, or political. But this was deemed to be altogether proper: such uncommon knowledge could not be expected to be found among common men. So you did not need a free market or a free society to maximize individual happiness; on the contrary, a free market, not being guided by the wisdom of the elite, was bound to be ultimately frustrating, since the common people could not possibly know what they *really* wanted or what would really yield them "true" happiness.

Now, we know from our experience of central economic planning that this pre-modern approach is fallacious—but if, and only if, you define "happiness" and "satisfaction" in terms of the material production and material consumption of commodities. If you do not define "happiness" or "satisfaction" in this way, if you refuse to "think economically," then the pre-modern view is more plausible than not. It is, after all, one thing to say that there is no authentically superior wisdom about people's tastes and preferences in commodities; it is quite another thing to deny that there is a superior wisdom about the spiritual dimensions of a good life. Even today, that last proposition does not sound entirely ridiculous to us. And if you believe that man's spiritual life is infinitely more important than his trivial and transient adventures in the marketplace, then you may tolerate a free market of practical reasons, within narrow limits, but you certainly will have no compunctions about overriding it if you think the free market is interfering with more important things.

## The Shamefaced Counterrevolution

Modern economists are for the most part unaware that their habit of "thinking economically" only makes sense within a certain kind of world, based on certain peculiarly modern presuppositions. They insist that economics is a science, which is certainly true, but only if you accept the premises of modern economics. Thus, one of our most distinguished economists, Ludwig Von Mises, wrote:

> Economics is a theoretical science and as such abstains from any judgment of value. It is not its task to tell people what ends they should aim at. It is a science of the means to be applied for the attainment of ends chosen, not . . . a science of the choosing of ends.

That statement sounds terribly modest and uncontroversial and platitudinous. But is it? Is it really so easy to separate means from ends? What, for example, if we are members of a monastic community and our end is holy poverty—not just poverty but holy poverty, a poverty suffused with a spiritual intention? Can economics help us attain this end? Or, to take a somewhat less extreme instance: What if we are loyal members of the kind of Orthodox Jewish community that even today is to be found in sections of New York City? In such a community, where most people are engaged in business, there unquestionably is some role for an economist—but only within narrow limits. In the end, the superior purpose of such a community is obedience to sacred Law and meditation on the meaning of this Law. For the maximization of such an end, economics is of little use.

Modern liberal, secular society is based on the revolutionary premise that there is no superior, authoritative information available about the good life or the true nature of human happiness, that this information is implicit only in individual preferences, and that therefore the individual has to be free to develop and express these preferences. What we are witnessing in Western society today are the beginnings of a counterrevolution against this conception of man and society. It is a shamefaced counterrevolution, full of bad faith and paltry sophistry, because it feels compelled to define itself as some kind of progressive extension of modernity instead of, what it so clearly is, a reactionary revulsion against modernity. It is this failure in self-definition that gives rise to so much irrelevant controversy.

The debate provoked by the writings of John Kenneth Galbraith is, it seems to me, a case in point. Galbraith thinks he is an economist and, if one takes him at his word, it is easy to demonstrate that he is a bad one. But the truth is that Galbraith is not really an economist at all; he can be more accurately described as a reluctant rabbi. His essential thesis is one familiar to premodern moralists and theologians: consumption *ought not to be* a constant function of relative income. Implicit in this thesis are the corollaries that (1) Galbraith knows better than any common man what "utility schedule" will provide all common men with enduring and meaningful satisfaction, and (2) if common men were uncorrupted by capitalist propaganda, they would permit Galbraith to prescribe "utility schedules" for them. Some of Galbraith's critics think they have refuted him when they make all this explicit. What they have done, I should say, is to enlighten him as to his own true purpose. That he so stubbornly resists such enlightenment is to be explained by his naive conviction that, because he is attacking bourgeois society, he must be a "progressive" thinker.

## The New Left vs. "Economic Man"

A similar confusion, I should say, arises in connection with what we call the "environmentalist" movement. Economists and politicians both—the one with naivety, the other with cunning—have decided to give a literal interpretation to the statements of this movement. And, given this literal interpretation, the thrust of environmentalism is not particularly subversive. If people today are especially concerned about clean air and clean water, then economic analysis can show them different ways—with different costs and benefits

—of getting varying degrees of clean air and clean water. But it turns out that your zealous environmentalists do not want to be shown anything of the sort. They are not really interested in clean air or clean water at all. What *does* interest them is modern industrial society and modern technological civilization, toward which they have profoundly hostile sentiments. When they protest against "the quality of life" in this society and this civilization, they are protesting against nothing so trivial as air or water pollution. Rather they are at bottom rejecting a liberal civilization which is given shape through the interaction of a countless sum of individual preferences. Since they do not like the shape of that civilization, they are moved to challenge—however indirectly or slyly—the process that produces this shape. What environmentalists really want is very simple: they want the authority, the power to create an "environment" which pleases them; and this "environment" will be a society where the rulers will not want to "think economically" and the ruled will not be permitted to do so.

Something similar is going on with the "consumers protection movement," whose true aim is not to "protect" the consumer but rather to circumscribe—and ultimately abolish—his "sovereignty." The objection to such sovereignty is that common people *do* "think economically" when they are liberated from traditional constraints and are encouraged to do whatever they think best for themselves. The "consumers" protection movement, like the "environmentalist" movement, is a revulsion against the kind of civilization that common men create when they are given the power, which a market economy does uniquely give them, to shape the world in which they wish to live.

I think we can summarize our situation as follows: the Old Left accepted the idea of the common good proposed by bourgeois-liberal society. The essential ingredients of this idea were material prosperity and technological progress. Bourgeois liberalism insisted that individual liberty was a precondition of this common good; the Old Left insisted that centralized planning was a precondition but that individual liberty would be an eventual consequence. The experience of the post-World War II decades has revealed that the Old Left simply could not compete with bourgeois liberalism in this ideological debate. The result has been the emergence of a New Left which implicitly rejects both the bourgeois-liberal and the Old Left idea of the common good, and which therefore rejects (again implicitly, for the most part) the ideological presuppositions of modernity itself. This movement, which seeks to end the sovereignty over our civilization of the common man, must begin by seeking the death of "economic man," because it is in the marketplace that this sovereignty is most firmly established. It thinks of itself as a "progressive" movement, whereas its import is regressive. This is one of the reasons why the New Left, every day and in every way, comes more and more to resemble the Old Right, which never did accept the liberal-bourgeois revolutions of the eighteenth and nineteenth centuries.

## The Inadequacies of Liberalism

One is bound to wonder at the inadequacies of bourgeois liberalism that have made it so vulnerable, first to the Old Left and now to the New. These inadequacies do not, in themselves, represent a final judgment upon it; every civilization has its necessary costs and benefits. But it does seem to be the case that, in certain periods, a civilization will have greater difficulty striking an acceptable balance than in others, and that sometimes it arrives at a state of permanent and precarious "tilt" for reasons it cannot quite comprehend. What it is important to realize, and what contemporary social science finds it so hard to perceive, is that such reasons are not necessarily new events or new conditions; they may merely be older inadequacies—long since recognized by some critics—that have achieved so cumulative an effect as to become, suddenly, and seemingly inexplicably, intolerable.

Certainly, one of the key problematic aspects of bourgeois-liberal society has long been known and announced. This is the fact that liberal society is of necessity a secular society, one in which religion is mainly a private affair. Such a disestablishment of religion, it was predicted by Catholic thinkers and others, would gradually lead to a diminution of religious faith and a growing skepticism about the traditional consolations of religion—especially the consolations offered by a life after death. That has unquestionably happened, and with significant consequences. One such consequence is that the demands placed upon liberal society, in the name of temporal "happiness," have become ever more urgent and ever more unreasonable. In every society, the overwhelming majority of the people lead lives of considerable frustration, and if society is to endure, it needs to be able to rely on a goodly measure of stoical resignation. In theory, this could be philosophical rather than religious; in fact, philosophical stoicism has never been found suitable for mass consumption. Philosophical stoicism has always been an aristocratic prerogative; it has never been able to give an acceptable rationale of "one's station and one's duties" to those whose stations are low and whose duties are onerous. So liberal civilization finds itself having spiritually expropriated the masses of its citizenry, whose demands for material compensation gradually become as infinite as the infinity they have lost. All of this was clearly foreseen by many of the anti-modern critics who witnessed the birth of modernity.

Another, and related, consequence of the disestablishment of religion as a publicly sanctioned mythos has been the inability of liberal society ever to come up with a convincing and generally accepted theory of political obligation. Liberal philosophers have proposed many versions of utilitarianism to this end, but these have remained academic exercises and have not had much popular impact. Nor is this surprising: No merely utilitarian definition of civic loyalty is going to convince anyone that it makes sense for him to die for his country. In actual fact, it has been the secular myth of nationalism which, for the past century and a half, has provided this rationale. But this secular myth, though it has evolved hand in hand with bourgeois society, is not intrinsically or necessarily bourgeois. Nationalism ends by establishing "equal sacrifice" as the criterion of justice; and this is no kind of bourgeois criterion. We have seen, in our own day, how the spirit of nationalism can be utterly contemptuous of bourgeois proprieties, and utterly subversive of the bourgeois order itself.

## The Depletion of Moral Capital

Even the very principles of individual opportunity and social mobility, which originally made the bourgeois-liberal idea so attractive, end up—once the spirit of religion is weakened—by creating an enormous problem for bourgeois society. This is the problem of publicly establishing an acceptable set of rules of distributive justice. The problem does not arise so long as the bourgeois ethos is closely linked to what we call the Puritan or Protestant ethos, which prescribes a connection between personal merit—as represented by such bourgeois virtues as honesty, sobriety, diligence, and thrift—and worldly success. But from the very beginnings of modern capitalism there has been a different and equally influential definition of distributive justice. This definition, propagated by [Bernard] Mandeville and [David] Hume, is purely positive and secular rather than philosophical or religious. It says that, under capitalism, whatever is, is just—that all the inequalities of liberal-bourgeois society must be necessary, or else the free market would not have created them, and therefore they must be justified. This point of view makes no distinction between the speculator and the bourgeois-entrepreneur: both are selfish creatures who, in the exercise of their private vices (greed, selfishness, avarice), end up creating public benefits.

Let us leave aside the intellectual deficiencies of this conception of justice—I myself believe these deficiencies are radical—and ask ourselves the question which several contemporaries of Mandeville and Hume asked before us: Will this positive idea of distributive justice commend itself to the people? Will they accept it? Will they revere it? Will they defend it against its enemies? The answer, I submit, is as obvious as it is negative. Only a philosopher could be satisfied with an *ex post facto* theory of justice. Ordinary people will see it merely as a self-serving ideology; they insist on a more "metaphysical" justification of social and economic inequalities. In the absence of such a justification, they will see more sense in simple-minded egalitarianism than in the discourses of Mandeville or Hume. And so it has been: As the connection between the Protestant ethic and liberal-bourgeois society has withered away, the egalitarian temper has grown ever more powerful.

For well over a hundred and fifty years now, social critics have been warning us that bourgeois society was living off the accumulated moral capital of traditional religion and traditional moral philosophy, and that once this capital was depleted, bourgeois society would find its legitimacy ever more questionable. These critics were never, in their lifetime, either popular or persuasive. The educated classes of liberal-bourgeois society simply could not bring themselves to believe that religion or philosophy was that important to a polity. *They* could live with religion or morality as a purely private affair, and they could not see why everyone else—after a proper secular education, of course—could not do likewise. Well, I think it is becoming clear that religion, and a moral philosophy associated with religion, is far more important politically than the philosophy of liberal individualism admits. Indeed, I would go further and say that it is becoming clearer every day that even those who thought they were content with a religion that was a private affair are themselves discovering that such a religion is existentially unsatisfactory.

## Libertarianism and Libertinism

But if the grave problems that secularization would inevitably produce for liberal-bourgeois society were foreseen, if only in general terms, not all the problems that our liberal society faces today were foreseen. While many critics predicted a dissolution of this society under certain stresses and strains, none predicted—none could have predicted—the blithe and mindless self-destruction of bourgeois society which we are witnessing today. *The enemy of liberal capitalism today is not so much socialism as nihilism.* Only liberal capitalism doesn't see nihilism as an enemy, but rather as just another splendid business opportunity.

One of the most extraordinary features of our civilization today is the way in which the "counterculture" of the New Left is being received and sanctioned as a "modern" culture appropriate to "modern" bourgeois society. Large corporations today happily publish books and magazines, or press and sell records, or make and distribute movies, or sponsor television shows which celebrate pornography, denounce the institution of the family, revile the "ethics of acquisitiveness," justify civil insurrection, and generally argue in favor of the expropriation of private industry and the "liquidation" of private industrialists. Some leaders of the New Left are sincerely persuaded that this is part of a nefarious conspiracy to emasculate them through "cooptation." In this, as in almost everything else, they are wrong. There is no such conspiracy—one is almost tempted to add, "alas." Our capitalists promote the ethos of the New Left for only one reason: they cannot think of any reason why they should not. For them, it is "business as usual."

And indeed, why shouldn't they seize this business opportunity? The prevailing philosophy of liberal capitalism gives them no argument against it.

Though Milton Friedman's writings on this matter are not entirely clear —itself an odd and interesting fact, since he is usually the most pellucid of thinkers—one gathers that he is, in the name of "libertarianism," reluctant to impose any prohibition or inhibition on the libertine tendencies of modern bourgeois society. He seems to assume, as I read him, that one must not interfere with the dynamics of "self-realization" in a free society. He further seems to assume that these dynamics cannot, in the nature of things, be self-destructive—that "self-realization" in a free society can only lead to the creation of a self that is compatible with such a society. I don't think it has been sufficiently appreciated that Friedman is the heir, not only to Hume and Mandeville, but to modern romanticism too. In the end, you can maintain the belief that private vices, freely exercised, will lead to public benefits only if you are further persuaded that human nature can never be utterly corrupted by these vices, but rather will always transcend them. The idea of bourgeois virtue has been eliminated from Friedman's conception of bourgeois society, and has been replaced by the idea of individual liberty. The assumption is that, in "the nature of things," the latter will certainly lead to the former. There is much hidden metaphysics here, and of a dubious kind.

And Hayek, too, though obviously hostile in temperament and mood to the new nihilism, has no grounds for opposing it in principle. When Hayek criticizes "scientism," he does indeed write very much like a Burkean Whig, with a great emphasis on the superior wisdom implicit in tradition, and on the need for reverence toward traditional institutions that incorporate this wisdom. But when he turns to a direct contemplation of present-day society, he too has to fall back on a faith in the ultimate benefits of "self-realization"—a phrase he uses as infrequently as possible, but which he nevertheless is forced to use at crucial instances. And what if the "self" that is "realized" under the conditions of liberal capitalism is a self that despises liberal capitalism, and uses its liberty to subvert and abolish a free society? To this question, Hayek—like Friedman—has no answer.

And yet this is *the* question we now confront, as our society relentlessly breeds more and more such selves, whose private vices in no way provide public benefits to a bourgeois order. Perhaps one can say that the secular, "libertarian" tradition of capitalism—as distinct from the Protestant-bourgeois tradition—simply had too limited an imagination when it came to vice. It never really could believe that vice, when unconstrained by religion, morality, and law, might lead to viciousness. It never really could believe that self-destructive nihilism was an authentic and permanent possibility that any society had to guard against. It could refute Marx effectively, but it never thought it would be called upon to refute the Marquis de Sade and Nietzsche. It could demonstrate that the Marxist vision was utopian; but it could not demonstrate that the utopian vision of [Charles] Fourier—the true ancestor of our New Left—was wrong. It was, in its own negligent way, very much a bourgeois tradition in that, while ignoring the bourgeois virtues, it could summon up only a bourgeois vision of vice.

## The Hunger for Legitimacy

Today, the New Left is rushing in to fill the spiritual vacuum at the center of our free and capitalist society. For the most part, it proclaims itself as "socialist," since that is the only tradition available to it. It unquestionably feeds upon the old, socialist yearnings for community—for a pre-individualist society—and is therefore, if not collectivist, at least "communalist" in its economics and politics. But it is also nihilistic in its insistence that, under capitalism, the individual must be free to create his own morality. The New Left is best seen as a socialist heresy, in that it refuses to "think economically" in any serious way. One might say it is a socialist heresy that corresponds to the liberal heresy it is confronting: the heresy of a "free-society" whose individuals are liberated from the bourgeois ethos that used to bind them together in a bourgeois-liberal community. And as the "free-society" produces material affluence, but also moral and political anarchy, so the New Left—even as it pushes individual liberty beyond anarchy itself—longs for a moral and political community in which "thinking economically" will be left to our Helots, the machines. In all their imagined utopian communities, the free individual who contracts for "the good life" has to surrender both his individualism and his freedom.

It is in the nature of heresies to take a part for the whole. Thus, our version of the "free-society" is dedicated to the proposition that to be free is to be good. The New Left, though it echoes this proposition when it is convenient for its purposes, is actually dedicated to the counter-belief—which is the pre-liberal proposition—that to be good is to be free. In the first case, the category of goodness is emptied of any specific meaning; in the second case, it is the category of freedom which is emptied of any specific meaning. In the war between these two heresies, the idea of a free society that is in some specific sense virtuous (the older "bourgeois" ideal) and the idea of a good community that is in some specific sense free (the older "socialist" ideal as represented, say, by European social democracy) are both emasculated; and the very possibility of a society that can be simultaneously virtuous and free, i.e., that organically weds order to liberty, becomes ever more remote.

And yet no society that fails to celebrate the union of order and liberty, in some specific and meaningful way, can ever hope to be accepted as legitimate by its citizenry. The hunger for such legitimacy is, I should say, the dominant political fact in the world today—in the "free" nations and among the "socialist" countries as well. It is instructive, and rather sad, to observe the enormous popularity of the recent TV serial, *The Forsyte Saga*, in both capitalist and socialist societies. Obviously, it evoked a profound nostalgia for an order—a society where virtue and freedom were reconciled, however imperfectly—which some of these nations had lost, and which others had never even known. I should say that something of the sort also explains the international popularity of *Fiddler on the Roof,* which gives us a picture of a different kind of legitimate order—a picture that has obvious appeal even to people who do not know the difference between the Talmud and the Code Napoleon.

I find even more pathetic the efforts of the governments of the "free world" and of the "socialist" nations to achieve some minimum legitimacy by imitating one another. The "free societies" move haltingly toward collectivism, in the hope that this will calm the turbulence that agitates them and threatens to tear them apart. The "socialist" nations take grudging steps toward "liberalization," for the same purpose. The results, in both cases, are perverse. Each such step, so far from pacifying the populace, further provokes them, since each such step appears as a moral justification of the turbulence that caused it.

What medicine does one prescribe for a social order that is sick because it has lost its soul? Our learned doctors, the social scientists, look askance at this kind of "imaginary" illness, which has dramatic physical symptoms but no apparent physical causes. Some, on what we conventionally call the "right," cannot resist the temptation to conclude that the patient is actually in robust health, and that only his symptoms are sick. Others, on what we conventionally call the "left," declare that the patient is indeed sick unto death and assert that it is his symptoms which are the causes of his malady. Such confusion, of course, is exactly what one would expect when both patient and doctors are suffering from the same mysterious disease.

# ALLAN BLOOM

## *The Democratization of the University*

"The Democratization of the University" is an early essay by Allan Bloom, author of the bestselling *The Closing of the American Mind* (1987). This essay introduces the themes Bloom developed there, that is, the threats egalitarianism and relativism pose to the liberal university and a democratic society. The essay is based on Bloom's experiences with student protests in the 1960s at Cornell University. Bloom currently teaches in the Committee on Social Thought at the University of Chicago.

"Do you too believe, as do the many, that certain young men are corrupted by sophists, and that there are certain sophists who in a private capacity corrupt to an extent worth mentioning? Isn't it rather the very men who say this who are the biggest sophists, who educate most perfectly and who turn out young and old, men and women, just the way they want them to be?"

"But when do they do that?" he said.

"When many gathered together sit down in assemblies, courts, theaters, army camps, or any other common meeting of a multitude, and, with a great deal of uproar, blame some of the things said or done, and praise others, both in excess, shouting and clapping; and, besides, the rocks and the very place surrounding them echo and redouble the uproar of blame and praise. Now in such circumstances, as the saying goes, what do you suppose is the state of the young man's heart? Or what kind of private education will hold out for him and not be swept away by such blame and praise and go, borne by the flood, wherever it tends so that he'll say the same things are noble and base as they do, practice what they practice, and be such as they are?"

"The necessity is great, Socrates," he said.

"And yet," I said, "we still haven't mentioned the greatest necessity."

"What?" he said.

"What these educators and sophists inflict in deed when they fail to persuade in speech. Or don't you know that they punish the man who's not persuaded with dishonor, fines and death? . . . So what other sophist or what sort of private speeches do you suppose will go counter to these and prevail? . . . Even the attempt is a great folly."[1]

The modern university was that great folly of an attempt to establish a center for reflection and education independent of the regime and the pervasive influence of its principles, free of the overwhelming effect of public opinion in its crude and subtle forms, devoted to the dispassionate quest for the important and comprehensive truths. It was to be an independent island within civil society, the sovereign Republic of Letters. It tried to disprove the Socratic contention that he who shares bed and board with the rulers, be they kings or peoples, would soon have to share their tastes and way of life, and that thus the thinker must separate himself in heart and mind from the currents of party passion in order to liberate himself from prejudice. The modern university has as its premises that free thought can exist in full view of the community unthreatened by the public passions and that it can be of service while preserving its integrity. Academic freedom was to protect scholars from the most obtrusive violations of their independence and was designed to draw them from private isolation into the public institutions; tenure is the most visible expression of that principle in the modern university.

Previously, it had been understood that democracies were in particular need of the enlightening function of the university, both because democracies necessarily have a large proportion of uneducated rulers and because public opinion reigns supreme in them without the counterpoising effect exercised by an aristocratic class which incorporates different principles and to the protection of which dissenters can repair. The presence of the university was the means of combining excellence with egalitarianism, reason with the consent of the governed. But precisely because it is so necessary to democracies, it is particularly threatened in nations where equality takes on the character of a religion and can call forth all the elements of fanaticism. In the first place this is so because democracy's fundamental beliefs are difficult to question; flattery of the regime and of the people at large is hard to avoid. Democratic sycophancy becomes a great temptation; one not resisted without difficulty and risk. And, in the second place, the university is, willy-nilly, in some sense aristocratic in both the conventional and natural senses of the term. It cannot, within broad limits, avoid being somewhat more accessible to the children of men of means than to the children of the poor, and it forms men of different tastes from those of the people at large who are, it is not to be forgotten, the real rulers. And the university is supposed to educate those who are more intelligent and to set up standards for their achievement which cannot be met by most men. This cannot but be irritating to democratic sensibilities.

Now the most obvious, the most comprehensive, the truest explanation of what is going on in our universities today is the triumph of a radical egalitarian view of democracy over the last remnants of the liberal university. This kind of egalitarianism insists that the goal of a democratic society is not equality of opportunity but factual equality; it comes equipped with all the doctrines which are necessary to persuade its adherents that such an equality is possible and that its not being actual is a result of vicious special interests; it will brook no vestige of differentiation in qualities of men. It would more willingly accept a totalitarian regime than a free one in which the advantages of money, position, education, and even talent are unevenly distributed. The liberal university with its concentration on a humane education and high standards had already been almost engulfed by the multiversity which is directed to the service of the community and responsive to the wishes of its constituency.

Now the universities have become the battleground of a struggle between liberal democracy and radical, or, one might say, totalitarian, egalitarianism. Therefore, it is not only the fact that universities are so much in the news that makes them central to any discussion of how democratic America is, it is also because they educate the best of our young, now more than half of them; because what they teach will ultimately determine the thought of the nation; and because the struggle going on in them concerns the interpretation of the meaning of our institutions and their goodness or badness. All this discussion takes place within the context of democracy, for both the defenders and critics of our regime accept the premise that democracy is the one legitimate regime, the only issue being whether the United States is sufficiently or truly a democracy.

The gradual politicization of the university can be seen partially by the extent of the concern expressed about it in society at large. Political men are constantly talking about universities and what they should or should not do. The universities have lost their neutrality as well as control of their destinies. Previously matters of curricula and student conduct were thought to be properly matters of internal university policy. Now the sense of the university's mission has been lost, and, at the same time, what has been going on within it has succeeded in frightening and arousing the political community. The former secretary of Health, Education and Welfare, Robert Finch, has even gone so far as to make an attack on the tenure system, the vital heart of academic freedom. Following professorial and student radicals, he accurately assessed the fact that it is the faculties which are most likely to be recalcitrant in an attempt to make the universities responsive to immediate concerns and that tenure protects them. He characterized faculties in much the same way as Marxists do the bourgeoisie in a capitalist system. They are, according to him, a privileged class protecting special and private interests. He sees no principle embodied in their unusual status; the issues are so clear, as he sees them, that only private vice could be the source of their unwillingness to change with the times. We are overburdened by the pontifications of journalists as well as politicians, and professors, administrators, and students look to the newspapers and television for publicity and support. All of this indicates the extent to which universities have become a part of the system of public opinion.

But these are only symptoms. One must look within the universities themselves to see the full magnitude of what has happened. The primary fact is the advent of student power, which, if it means anything, means an extreme democratization of the university. It is a democratization in several senses: it extends the range of power to everyone present (things have gone so far that maintenance personnel are to sit in some university legislative bodies); even the usually accepted notions of age and stake in the community as standards for participation are considered discriminatory; and, most important of all, the special claim of competence is ignored or rejected. Professors, as well as students, frequently deny that their learning gives them title to govern the university or to determine what is important for it to represent. Everyone is listening to young people these days, and they are talking.

The most stunning example of this about which I know is what happened at Cornell. When black students carrying guns and thousands of white students supporting them insisted that the faculty abandon the university's judicial system, the minimal condition of civil community within the university, and backed up that insistence with threats, the faculty capitulated. Most of the faculty members who voted for capitulation argued that this was the will of the community, what the students wanted. They had talked to many students, and the students strongly desired that the faculty reverse itself. These professors could satisfy their consciences by turning to public opinion. So democratic had they become that they accepted a mob gathered in an atmosphere of violence as a true public. So weak were their convictions about what a university is that they could find legitimacy only in public approval by their student constituency; their scholarly competence provided no source for independent judgment. Their souls had become democratic and egalitarian to a degree far greater than that demanded by the principles of the regime; the regime requires that every citizen abide by the duly expressed will of the majority, not that the mind of man be determined by the taste of the community at large. In this instance there was a realization of Socrates' comic comparison of a democracy to the solemn deliberations of a group of children who are empowered to choose between the dietary prescriptions of a doctor and those of a pastry chef. Here, though, the doctors accepted the legitimacy of the tribunal.

In order to see the full dimensions of the situation and to recognize that the only real element in the changes occurring and the reforms demanded is radical egalitarianism, one must listen carefully to what is said. The key word is *relevance.* The whole of education must be guided by the standard of relevance. Now, of course, no curriculum was ever intended to be irrelevant; and even if scholars have lost the habit of justifying the importance of their disciplines, there is imbedded in each a serious argument for its study. Relevance is obviously a relative term, implying a standard by which relevant and irrelevant things are judged. Classical liberal education set as its standard the formation of a man possessing intellectual and moral virtue; relevant studies were those that tended to the perfection of the natural faculties, independent of the particular demands of time or place.

This is not the criterion of relevance referred to by today's students. Those students who are doing most of the talking and popularizing the notion of a relevance—that is, the leftist students—mean that education must be directed to the problems of war, poverty, and, particularly, racism as they now present themselves, in other words, to the problems of contemporary democratic society. They not only argue that these are the fundamental issues to which the universities should address themselves, they also insist that certain kinds of solutions are self-evident. When they talk about justice they do not regard knowledge of justice as a problem; it is almost inconceivable to them that there can be a theoretical questioning of the principle of equality, let alone a practical doubt about it. The universities, as they are seen by these students, are meant to preach certain principles and to study their implementation. The movement is anti-intellectual and has the character of a democratic crusade. The theoretical man who stands outside of the movement, who urges that the university's primary function is the pursuit of clarity about such questions, is easily accused of complacency. Such idle lack of commitment can only be tolerated when we have brought peace, prosperity, and equality to the earth. Not even the richest country ever known can afford to devote any of its resources to the useless cultivation of the mind.

The relevant curriculum is to be promoted, watched over, and used by students. Student participation is the catchword in all talk of university reform. The goals to be achieved by student participation are never explicitly defined. It is enough to refer to the democratic view: everyone has the right to a vote. Faculties and administrations everywhere are bustling to "restructure" the universities with a view to greater student participation in everything; it has become an end in itself. To point out that students do not participate in disciplinary procedures, choice of faculty, establishment of curricula, and so forth is sufficient to demonstrate that decisions are illegitimate. There is almost no concern to show that such participation improves the quality of those decisions or contributes in any way to serious educational goals or even that it satisfies the students' wishes, let alone their real needs. I would venture to suggest that none of the moves toward student participation made in the last four or five years has done anything but generate new demands on their part and cause a deterioration of academic standards, an increase of demagogic teaching, and a loss of the sense of a university's purpose. There is a craze for change, but educators have no vision of the purposes of this change; they have nothing to offer but change itself. The direction is given to the drift by the prevailing winds of democratic extremism. Whether an educational institution can be treated as a political community or whether democracy needs any restraints seems never to be a question.

This is a democratic age and democracy is the special place of the young. According to Plato's analysis, the young in their turn exacerbate the weaknesses of democracy and impel it toward anarchy and ultimately tyranny. He describes our situation before the fact:

> As the teacher in such a situation is frightened of the pupils and fawns on them, so the students make light of their teachers, as well as their attendants. And, generally, the young copy their elders and compete with them in speeches and deeds while the old come down to the level of the young; imitating the young, they are overflowing with facility and charm, and that's so that they won't seem to be unpleasant or despotic.[2]

The young are powerful in democracies for many reasons. Estates are not easily transferable within them, so the authority of fathers is diminished. The hierarchies from which the young are excluded and which characterize other regimes are absent in a democracy. The older people lose their special privileges; and, in the atmosphere of liberty, the bodily pleasures, of which the young are more capable, are emancipated and have a higher status. Equality renders most claims to rule over the young illegitimate: age, wisdom, wealth, moral virtue, good family, are all banished, leaving only number, or consent, and force; and it is more difficult to exclude the young from ruling on the basis of these titles. All of this gives ground for believing that when the young become more demanding and the old more compliant, a new stage of democracy has been reached. The young are taking full advantage of their condition, making use of both their special claims to rule, consent and violence, however contradictory the two may appear to be.

In our democracy there is a further reason, of which Plato did not speak, for the dominance of the young. The radical political movements attempt to establish new kinds of societies, to find solutions to what older wisdom said was insoluble, to overcome necessity and master chance or, as Machiavelli put it, fortune.

> I judge that it is better to be impetuous than circumspect, because fortune is a woman; to keep her down it is necessary to beat her and thrash her. One sees that she lets herself be conquered by the impetuous rather than by those who proceed coldly. And, of course, as a woman she is always a friend to the young, because they are less circumspect, more brutal, and command her with greater audacity.[3]

Those who wish to ride the wave of the future know that the young are most skilled at it and do deference to them as such. Only those who have some conviction of the rightness of their principles can stand against the sea of change, and, as we shall see, this conviction is what seems no longer to be generally possessed.

The democratic ruling body constituted by the students establishes, as do all ruling bodies, policies which further its interests. The substantive reforms, as I have said, have no basis other than that they conduce to the equality of all. Open admissions is the new cry. All citizens must go to college; everyone must be allowed into the halls of learning. And this means, in effect, that everyone must graduate from college, for it will soon be found that it is impossible to fail great masses of students in the age of student power. It immediately follows that standards must be lowered or, rather, utterly abandoned, no matter under what shining banner this change is presented. One of the first points of attack is grading; grades are said to degrade, to make students "grinds" rather than independently thoughtful, to make students part of the system, to encourage bad motivations for study. Although these allegations are not without merit, the real reason for the criticism is that grades make distinctions and indicate that some are better, at least as students, than others. Similarly, required courses and traditional majors begin to be abandoned. It would be hard to argue that these courses and programs of study were very well conceived, but they represented the tattered remnants of some thought about the natural articulation of the kinds of knowledge and what a man must know in order to be called minimally educated. A vacuum called freedom takes their place.

Each student is to be permitted to construct his own curriculum and discover his special genius or realize his unique self. The university can no longer provide guidance as to what is important and set standards based on a view of human perfection. It is blithely assumed that the student is capable of doing so for himself and that he has no need of sublimating discipline. In technical studies, of course, fixed courses of study will remain, because, for example, professors of engineering know what they must teach and what a student must know. But the best students in the better universities are no longer interested in a technical education; they are strongly inclined to what are very loosely called the humanities and the social sciences, and here the universities have abandoned their pedagogic function. It is a perfect solution for educators: in the hallowed name of freedom they are relieved of the responsibility of elaborating a curriculum. The true result of all of this is that the most vulgar and philistine things which proliferate in society at large will dominate the university, for the university cannot, as it should, counterpoise them. If the university does not provide alternatives to the prevalent, where else could the student find them?

One thing is certain: the serious study of classic literature will be sacrificed to the reforming spirit. It does not seem relevant to our students, and it is not to be expected that it would. The importance of classic literature, particularly the philosophic literature, could be recognized by young people only after long and exacting discipline. This is particularly true in America where nothing in the students' past or the world outside the university attests to the significance, or even the existence, of these rare and fine things. It was because the university insisted on them that they were preserved and that a university education could be understood to be a transforming experience rather than an exercise in self-expression or "doing one's own thing," no matter what it may happen to be.

The fate of classical languages is the model for what is happening in general. They are less and less studied, for they require an effort which seems pedantic and constraining, and they do not simply relate to the students' untutored, unguided experience. In the absence of knowledge of the languages, there can be no serious study of the texts written in them. In our current atmosphere everything has its place, and no one need feel uncomfortable or left out. At the end, whole new kinds of ephemeral study programs emerge, brought into being by the most popular issues of the day or the inclinations of groups of students.

Finally, the criticism is turned on the professors who not only are the protectors of the old ways but also are charged with being negligent of their students. The professors are understood to be primarily teachers who have lost their taste for teaching. The notion that a professor in a university is, in the first place, a scholar and that this must take most of his time is gradually becoming unintelligible. It used to be considered something of a vice for a man to be too much of a teacher because that would lead him into the temptation of adapting his thought to the demands of the market. He should not have to attract students but should provide a model for them of integrity and independence, of a higher motivation, whether they like it or not. The opportunity to be with a learned man should be considered a privilege and not a right, a privilege reserved for the competent and respectful. This was believed to be for the good not only of science but also of the student. But now it is everywhere deemed appropriate that the professor should teach more, be in closer contact with students, and accept their judgments as to his competence. It is not to be denied that a professor sometimes learns from students, that many professors are bad teachers and also bad scholars, and that often criticism can help him to right his ways in both respects. But to assert that students, as a matter of principle, have a right to judge the value of a professor or what he teaches is to convert the university into a market in which the sellers must please the buyers and the standard of value is determined by demand.

It was precisely to provide a shelter from the suffrages of the economic system and the popular will they represent that universities were founded. Now that the student right to judge has become dogma, the universities have become democracies in which the students are the constituencies to which the professors are responsible; the professors no longer look upward toward the gods but downward toward the people, or, rather, *vox populi* has become *vox dei*. A whole new race of charlatans or pastry chefs has come into being who act as the tribunes of the people. One can expect a wholesale departure from the universities of professors of manly independence.

Thus we have gone very far down the road toward equality. It is somehow now held morally reprehensible to believe that equality is limited by natural differences in men's gifts and that a reasonable understanding of democracy is as a regime which allows men to develop those gifts without conventional or arbitrary hindrances. It is now doctrine that all men are factually equal, and if they do not meet high standards it is due to deprivation or the falseness of the standards. In the theory and practice of our universities we have come to that stage of democratic sentiment at which Tocqueville warned that men prefer equality to freedom, where they are willing to overturn the institutions and laws necessary to freedom in order to gain the sense of equality, where they level rather than raise, indifferent to the deprivations they impose on the superior and on the community at large.

# I

What, then, is the future of liberal education in the face of these powerful tides? By *liberal* education I mean education for freedom, particularly the freedom of the mind, which consists primarily in the awareness of the most important human alternatives. Such an education is largely dedicated to the study of the deepest thinkers of the past, because their works constitute the body of learning which we must preserve in order to remain civilized and because anything new that is serious must be based on, and take account of, them. Without such a study a man's mind is almost necessarily a prisoner of the horizon of his particular time and place, and in a democracy that means of the most fundamental premises or prejudices of public opinion. This study has long had only frail support in the United States, and it is what is most threatened at this moment. It is the sole reason for the being of the university as anything more than an advanced high school for the training and detention of the young.

Addressing myself to this question four years ago, I wrote an article for this series assessing the condition of universities with respect to liberal education.[4] At that time the picture was bleak, but there was some basis for hope that in the interstices of the universities with all their bigness this small vital center might be maintained, not because it had any place guaranteed in the principle of the university but simply out of habit supported by the great wealth and diversity of the American university. That hope has all but disappeared. I saw then that the multiversity had no principle of organization, that it was directed to public usefulness rather than knowledge for its own sake, that the university had lost any sense of the unity of knowledge. It had become a place for specialists without any view of, or longing for, wholeness. The students were beginning to be aroused, and their stirrings seemed to express that longing for wholeness which was absent in the rest of the university. However, they too shared the belief of the specialists that the end of the university is public service, practice not theory. And the intensity of their demands, in sharp contrast to the easygoing, live-and-let-live disposition of the specialists, could easily result in a deterioration of the university's intellectual atmosphere. The liberal arts were likely to be crushed between the aimless diversity of the specialists and the spirit of political reform of the students.

I also saw that administrators were likely to become accomplices of the students for they have almost no education other than that in efficiency; without a clear view of the goals of a university they would, I knew, give in to the greatest pressures. But I based what hopes I had on my belief that the undergraduates did have a *feeling* of what was lacking in the specialist's education; and that their concern for living their lives well might be a wedge for the development of some liberal curricula which would respond to that concern and help to restore some limited sense of the unity of education in a rational and scholarly way. What I did not foresee was, on the one hand, the speed of the collapse of the administrators, and, on the other, the lack of conviction of the professors about the importance of what they were doing. The pieties of the professors about academic freedom and civility have turned out to be largely empty. They are ready to transform the university totally in terms of the untutored wishes of the students. The professors have proved to be so accommodating because they lack clarity, or because they too wish to share the students' idealism, or because they make the interested calculation that their specialties will be spared.

As for the students, I saw in them a potentiality for good or evil. They were freer in some senses than their parents. Necessities of life were better provided to them, and they lived in a world in which most principles of morals, religion, and politics were without great persuasiveness or binding force. This gave them the equipment for a reconsideration of such questions without external constraint. But they were lacking in rootedness, and their almost total lack of education in the tradition gave them no experience of greatness in thought or deed; no books meant much to them. There was that longing for wholeness, partly genuine, partly spurious (in order to have the exhilaration of the sense of depth). Properly controlled and guided, I believed, this longing could be the motor which would drive them to the effort requisite to learn.

But somewhere along the line this dangerous mixture has begun to fall out of balance; perhaps it is, and was always, inevitable, for there is not enough intellectual and moral substance available to discipline their aimless freedom. It was only a small minority of well-endowed students who could have been touched and finally trained, but they required protection and, at the least, an atmosphere of calm in which there is some respect for liberal studies. I suppose that this minority still remains, but all the honors go to a loud group of protestors furnished with easy and appealing ideologies as a substitute for thought; they either attract the really able students, because they appear to represent the only thing that has real force, or they reduce them to a confused silence. At first they seemed to be questing for guidance and leadership of a sort to respond to their sentiments. But, of course, they are easily dupes of movements, political and intellectual, which play to their tastes and are largely sham.

How can they judge, having neither experience nor knowledge? Every year their souls are thinner from want of spiritual nourishment; their openness becomes emptiness, the soil within incapable of sustaining any deep-rooted plant. They test the possible authorities to which they turn and find that none has the power to inspire them or resist them. The adult world makes itself contemptible, seeming to represent nothing itself, and, in what can only appear to the young to be cowardly flattery, praises the idealism and morality of those who have never had the chance to practice either. The great change comes when students no longer quest but teach, confident that they know the answers and are sufficient unto themselves. One of the ugliest spectacles is that of a young person who has no awe, who is shameless, who does not sense his imperfection, for it is the charm of youth to be potentiality striving to perfect itself, to be an essential incompleteness which may one day be truly complete. Adults are almost always imperfect; a youth is surely imperfect, but he at least offers the hope of development. But self-contempt is the basis of self-improvement, and this generation has nothing left in god or man against which to measure itself. Plato's description of the democratic man now seems most appropriate:

> ... he doesn't admit it ... if someone says that there are some pleasures belonging to fine and good desires and some belonging to bad desires. ... He shakes his head at all this and says that all are alike and must be honored on an equal basis. ... He lives along day by day, gratifying the desire that occurs to him, at one time drinking and listening to the flute, at another downing water and reducing; now practicing gymnastics, and again idling and neglecting everything; and sometimes spending his time as though he were occupied with philosophy. Often he engages in politics and jumping up, says and does whatever chances to come to him. ...[5]

To Plato's account must be added a somewhat more sinister element: a rage at the emptiness of this life, and a desire to commit oneself to acts of revolutionary violence. Nonviolence has more or less silently been dropped from the creed of the New Left. College now means to more and more students a place where the young educate the nation and practice self-expression. It should not be surprising that the aristocratic aspiration which democracy frustrates should find its outlet on the radical left. Under the banner of equality these privileged students can lead and, with impunity, express their contempt for the people.

The universities were a fertile field for this development. A survey of the so-called liberal arts segments of the universities reveals that they are unarticulated heaps of departments, each teaching specialized disciplines which have presuppositions that are hardly discussed and are frequently incompatible with those of other disciplines. These disciplines have aggregated to the university at various times over the last one thousand years. There is little coherence to them nor does a view of life and the world evidently emerge from any separately or all together. The most important question has been forgotten, and even the means for a rational discussion of the unity of the university or the unity of life seem to have been lost. We seem to have to make do with tradition or whatever the winds of the day bring along. The state of academic philosophy, which should be the unifying discipline, indicates the severity of the problem. Today it is largely dominated by linguistic analysis which is merely a method for studying discourse rather than itself a source of discourse; it is a universal rule book for playing the game, but it does not tell us what the game is or play it itself. The natural sciences are a world unto themselves, dealing with what are presumably important problems, but they are unable to do anything about conveying their meaning within the total picture. The humanities have also become specialties, and it is rare to find a convincing explanation of their importance; the literatures studied are very rarely understood to be of vital significance for life today, and certainly they are undermined by the notion that science is the domain of reason and cannot understand the world of poetry. And the social sciences are slavishly imitating the natural sciences and are further hampered by their own principle, the fact-value distinction, from speaking about the moral and political good, which is what agitates the students.

Thus when students ask about the good life and the nature of our world, they are met by a deafening silence, for there are no men in the university whose competence enables them to respond to such questions. Many professors are answering the students but not on the basis of their competence; they are biologists or psychologists, or whatever else, speaking about what they have never studied, never adequately reflected on, and what is in no way connected with the things they can claim to know. The questions and pressures of students during these past six years have created a stir among academic men, but it has not caused them to undertake a serious reconsideration of the state of our learning or to look toward a philosophic and scholarly treatment of the issues raised. That just seems impossible; the whole is approached by way of feeling, by identification with popular movements, by "commitment" or "concern." The professors do not try to educate these longings; they try to share them without transforming them. What some social scientists proudly name "post-behavioralism" consists in nothing more than an attempt to keep the "value" hungry wolves from the door.

The university has proved itself incapable of teaching students about the good life because that is not a subject that any part of our universities even knows how to discuss; it belongs to no department nor any group of them added together. The education of our professors has been a specialized, technical one, with more or less old-style humanities mixed in but not really taken seriously or penetrating the special discipline. We have hardly a reminiscence of what was once the central business of universities. During and just after World War II, America was the beneficiary of many generally and humanely educated European scholars. Whatever the difficulties of the teachings many brought with them, these men had roots deep in the best thinkers and had the habit of justifying what they taught by them. One might have thought that the example of their learning and persons would fundamentally affect our universities. But the enormous expansion of higher education and the growth of the multiversity simply drowned their influence. Now, even in the unlikely event that it were to be thought that the philosophic, unifying, synoptic education needed to be reestablished, we would not be in a position to do so, for we no longer have the teachers who sufficiently know or care for the great tradition or are capable of working through the prejudices which seem to have rendered it meaningless and irrelevant.

Until the students became vocal, the university was characterized by easygoing indifference to larger purposes; each discipline followed its own internal development and the administration held the whole together. In the new era, scientists and humanists have come out to meet the students, praise them, agree to reorder "the priorities" and announce that the real purposes of the universities are those proposed by the political movements of the left. Thus a direction and purpose is again given to the university, and a community is established around this purpose. The only problem is whether that purpose is in any way consistent with the premises of science and scholarship.

Some professors become disturbed when they recognize that they must change their teaching in order to fit the movement and that the integrity of their discipline is threatened, that the passionate desires of the indignant are not consonant with the results of dispassionate rational inquiry. But such worried professors are more than counterbalanced by those professors who, excited by their new roles and liberated from what they now recognize to be the fragmented character of their existence, are willing to make their disciplines "relevant." The strength of this group is reenforced by the more or less active support of another group of professors, composed most particularly of natural scientists, who see no threat of a new Lysenkoism in their disciplines and who therefore are of the opinion they can have their cake and eat it. The fact that the interests of the professors can differ so much indicates how little of a real *intellectual* community there was and hence how partial the lives of the professors had become. In these circumstances, the university was an easy conquest for the first movement which exposed its lack of purpose or conviction and which proposed to restore the wholeness of life, the absence of which was even beginning to trouble the complacent professors. This movement usurped the position in the university which by right belonged to liberal education and in the process abolished the throne—occupied by weak and illegitimate pretenders—of the only legitimate ruler, philosophy.

## II

Although the universities have had little to offer in the way of reflection or leadership in recent years, there are those who have jumped into the void created by the absence of philosophy and spoken to the general issues. There is not much thought reflected in what they say but there is the decay of a certain kind of thought here and its language is the only language which appeals to students. Although there have been few political movements which make such modest demands on the minds of their adherents or which have been so profoundly anti-intellectual, this one too is, of course, founded on a comprehensive view of things and is guided by that view. That view was not a product of the founders of the movement, and, because its followers are so unselfconscious, they are unaware of its sources and its implications. They are prisoners of certain European, particularly German, teachings which migrated to the United States and have been so successfully assimilated that they now seem native and part of common sense. We have adopted the language and the consequences of these teachings from the European professors who helped to bring them but have absorbed almost none of the learning which should accompany them. At all events, when thought out, these teachings lead to views and ways of life which are antithetical to this regime, and their dominance would surely undermine it. The German thought reflected in the current language of politics is the thought which is at the roots of both communism and fascism. Although the present political movements are democratic in that they propose to speak for all men, and they are egalitarian, they are based on a critique of liberal democracy and a hostility to it. The egalitarian movement has gathered into its bosom the teachings of men who were, to say the least, not friends of democracy and has used them to the furtherance of equality. The only sacrifice is free society as we know it. Prudent observers who knew something of modern philosophy were not surprised to find that kind of irrationalism which is open to violence, tyranny, and racism emerging in the New Left. This was a necessity of its principles, as I shall try to show.

In the events that have occurred within the universities these past few years, the most sobering fact which has emerged is that neither in the things that are taught in them nor in the actions or reactions of those who are supposed to be responsible for their preservation is there much evidence of a conviction of the truth of the principles on which liberal democracy and the liberal university are founded. When such conviction is lacking, institutions and laws have lost their vitality and maintain themselves only by inertia; their replacement by new modes and orders is only a matter of time. This is not to suggest that by preaching the principles one can give them life; it is only meant as an observation. Somehow our principles are no longer persuasive. Our condition is beautifully characterized by a passage in Dostoyevsky's *Possessed*:

> Do you know that we are tremendously powerful already? Our party does not consist only of those who commit murder and arson, fire off pistols in the traditional way, or bite colonels.... Listen. I've reckoned them all up: a teacher who laughs with children at their God and at their cradle is on our side. The lawyer who defends an educated murderer because he is more cultured than his victims and could not help murdering them to get money is one of us. The schoolboys who murder a peasant for the sake of sensation are ours. The juries who acquit every criminal are ours. The prosecutor who trembles at a trial for fear he should not seem advanced enough is ours, ours. Among officials and literary men we have lots, lots, and they don't know it themselves.... Do you know how many we shall catch by little, ready-made ideas? When I left Russia, Littre's dictum that crime is insanity was all the rage; I came back and find that crime is no longer insanity, but simply common sense, almost a duty; anyway, a gallant protest.

That is a nihilist speaking, looking at the dissolution of the horizon within which his people had lived. The similarity of this situation to our own is no accident. The speaker is not referring essentially to the decay of the Czarist regime but of Western justice and morality and that is what we are experiencing in all liberal society today. Dostoyevsky was one of a small group of clairvoyant men in the last half of the nineteenth century who saw that somehow the old world was sick and dying, not meaning by the "old world" states or regimes, but the Biblical and classical morality which stood behind and made possible all states and regimes as we have known them or can imagine them. Nihilism was a response to the incipient death of all that had gone before, an expression of the meaninglessness of life without a compelling horizon of values, an attempt to destroy the lifeless body which remained after the vital center had died, and, perhaps, a hope of a new world, the outlines of which we cannot yet perceive but to which we must be dedicated for the sake of life. Civil societies are constituted by what they respect, by what men bow their heads before in reverence. When they no longer have anything before which they can bow, their world is near its end, and all the suppressed and lawless monsters within man reemerge. One might suggest that our New Left is a strange mixture of nihilism with respect to past and present and a naive faith in a future of democratic progress.

To put this more compellingly for Americans, the old liberalism is no longer of real concern to today's students. By the old liberalism I mean either the thought of the founding fathers who believed in the natural rights of man, established by reason and applicable to all men, and who constructed a nation dedicated to life, liberty, and the pursuit of happiness, or that of men like John Stuart Mill who believed in the open society dedicated to free speech and the self-determined private life. To the extent that Locke, the Declaration of Independence, *The Federalist,* or Mill are taught in the universities, they are historical matter and hardly anyone supposes that they can be believed or taken as guides for our lives. Without entering into the merits of that older liberal thought, it somehow no longer satisfies the soul for this generation of mankind and seems to be taking its place alongside the teachings which legitimized monarchy and aristocracy in the graveyard of history. Adults still refer to its principles, but when protests against war, poverty, or racism contradict them, those protests carry the day. It is not believed that liberal society insures substantive justice. And anyone whose "life style" is hostile to that of liberal society is considered justified or even heroic in "opting out" of it. What appeals to students now is the language of Marxism and existentialism; it seems to them to describe their situation.

It is a most striking fact that since Mill there has not been a single really influential book supporting liberal democratic society, and Mill cannot be compared in power or depth to men like Marx or Nietzsche, who were his critics. Liberal democracy has come to seem to be negative; it wishes to provide the conditions for freedom or the good life, but it does not give prescriptions for the use of freedom or define the good life. Its neutrality permits the dominance of any one of very many possible ways of life, some of them unattractive. Marx could plausibly assert that it was merely the condition for the existence of bourgeois capitalism, and that freedom meant primarily freedom to be a worker or an owner in this kind of system. And Nietzsche argued that liberal democracy was the home of "the last man," a being without heart or conviction, a shriveled manikin dedicated only to preservation and comfort. All of this criticism has become commonplace in the unremitting attack on white, complacent, middle-class America; it was vulgarized in America by men like [Erich] Fromm and [Herbert] Marcuse. The models for admiration are no longer statesmen but bohemians or revolutionaries.

But in the improbable wedding of Marx and Nietzsche which has recently been arranged, it is clear that Nietzsche is the dominant partner is spite of his rightist inclinations. Marx's egalitarianism, concentration on the poor, hatred of imperialism, and so forth, have been maintained, and leftists would still like to style themselves Marxists. But they no longer read the serious Marx; *Capital* seems both boring and irrelevant; the only Marx which is attractive is found in the early, so-called humanistic, writings, the study of which is of very recent origin. And the attack on reason, the use of terms like self, authenticity, and commitment, which are on everybody's lips, show plainly enough to what extent the Marxist teaching has been adulterated by a newer and more compelling kind of thought and a different understanding of the goals of politics. The New Left is not the Old Left, but is rather a result of the assimilation of the thought of Nietzsche and [Martin] Heidegger to that of the Old Left. However this may be, the prevalent discussion in the highest seats of learning is, to a greater or lesser degree, in the terms of postliberal thought, and this means that soon everyone will think in this way.

But it would perhaps be best to see the changes in our thought by looking to the recent history of the social sciences in America. The social sciences are the disciplines in which one would most expect the political and moral life of man to be discussed and are the sources of our understanding of them. For more than thirty years the social sciences have been dominated by the fact-value distinction. This distinction was made by German sociologists in the 1890s and most influentially propounded by Max Weber. It was imported to this country by sociologists and political scientists in the 1920s. This distinction was based on the assertion that no judgments of good and bad, no moral distinctions, could be grounded on reason, that they were subjective acts of the mind, preferences. The goals by which we guide our lives constitute a horizon by which we orient ourselves, but that horizon is an act of human creativity, not one of reason; no horizon can claim to be authoritative or demonstrable. Weber was persuaded of the truth of this analysis and attempted to salvage some possibility for the existence of science, of the reasonable quest for objective truth. Science was to be the noble endeavor of overcoming one's own values in the name of truth. The consequences of all this for our lives are, as Weber knew, quite far-reaching. Little attention was, however, given by American social scientists to assessing the effect of the distinction or, for that matter, to proving its validity. They accepted it and devoted themselves to the elaboration of an objective social science based on it; they were enchanted by the vision of a value-free social science which would be comparable to the natural sciences.

Although the science itself has not been very impressive, the success of the viewpoint has been breathtaking. Today even school children use the word *value* where another generation would have spoken of good and evil. The new social science had the effect of banishing good and bad, the discussion of the ends, from the domain of the sciences or reason. That was no longer a scholarly theme. The social scientists still had to live as men as well as scholars; but they were almost to a man liberal democrats; they accepted that as their value.

And, unlike Weber, they used the fact-value distinction as a means of sparing themselves the necessity of being concerned about the status of their value. This was just fine until that value was challenged. It had lost its dignity; liberal democracy was just one value among many, and it had eroded from long neglect.

When the students wanted to implement certain policies and found apathy and indifference among adults, they, and their professorial camp followers, launched an attack on value-free social science, insisting that the social sciences should be primarily concerned with values. They accused the social scientists of being easygoing accomplices of the established order. The social scientists were indeed supporters of this order and were also unable to give an account of their reasons for being so. They simply believed that no sane man would question the superiority of liberal democracy to all available alternatives. Indeed, the fact-value distinction had become the last intellectual bastion of liberal democracy: in the absence of any demonstrable superiority of one value over another, that regime which tolerated all values might be understood to be preferable to one which did not. Moreover, since values are equal, they seem to be democratic. Every man has a right to his own values; no one need feel inferior. But the social scientists were utterly unprepared to resist a large group who insisted that its values had to be accepted no matter what others wanted. After all, why not?

It is to be noted that the students, as was to be expected, themselves adopted the fact-value distinction. They made no attempt to return to Marx, who thought that the true goals of human life could be determined by reason. They merely looked at the fact-value distinction and recognized that there was no intrinsic reason why we should concentrate on facts; that choice in itself is a value judgment. Science seems to have demonstrated that the most important thing—the right way of life is the most important thing—is not amenable to scientific, that is rational, treatment. This means men must abandon reason and turn to the establishment of values. This is precisely the analysis made by the profoundest European thinkers in the last century who took the value question seriously. The positing of values is, in this perspective, the most important human activity, and all the specialized activities are guided by the values posited. Thus the social scientists, men so dedicated to reason, were astonished to see their students, even their own children, denying reason, turning to Eastern religions, addicted to drugs, toying with violence, becoming a new breed or species unintelligible to rationalists. But in a sense they were going to the end of roads which their teachers and parents had opened but had themselves not traveled. Phenomena such as the use of drugs cannot be understood on mere sociological and psychological grounds. They are the consequences of the problems in our thought. If reason is superficial, then the irrational must be cultivated for the enrichment of life.

Much of what we recognize to be the most advanced contemporary opinion follows as a consequence from the fact-value distinction. Man is the value-producing being; that is the great discovery implicit in the distinction. If it is values which guide reason, then one must look beneath rational consciousness, the *ego*, to an unconscious, an *id*, a self, in order to find out what man is and discover a source for a meaningful life. This self cannot be understood by reason; it must be creative and hence beyond prediction; it must be listened to as an oracle. One cannot know what it will produce or whether what it produces is good or bad. It is the absolute beginning. With this we see the origin of our concentration on the self and its fulfillment. It is the modern substitute for the soul, which is a rationally ordered structure and is dependent on and subordinate to the order of the *cosmos*. The self has no order and it is dependent on nothing; it makes a *cosmos* out of the chaos that is really outside by imposing an order of values upon it.

In most discussion today one finds little elaboration of what the self is; rather the self is defined by what it is opposed to. The great illness of modern man, according to our critics, is alienation or other-directedness. This means to live according to other people's values, whether they are expressed in laws, schools, work, or whatever. A man who lives in that way is divorced from his self and is hollow. Education must not impose values on the student but let his own values develop and grow. In the absence of any objective standard for judging a man's words or deeds, the only test can be whether they are his own or another's, whether he is a true self or alienated, inner-directed or other-directed, authentic or hypocritical. Authentic is really the word, the replacement for good. Many different ways of life can be authentic; the standard is only in the honesty or sincerity of the expression of that way of life. No matter how criminal or foul you may be, you are cleansed if you are sincere about it; hypocritical obedience to law is the human crime; Jean Genêt is superior by far to the bourgeois father and citizen.

How can one then be sure that one is sincere, that one's values are authentic? Such assurance cannot be achieved by comparison of one man's values with those of another. The only proof is in the intensity of one's *commitment,* in the ultimate case by being willing to die for one's value, in the assertion of one's value against the chaotic outside, bravely facing all risks. It is the strong-willed versus the weak-willed instead of the good versus the bad. We praise men now, not for the rightness of their cause, but because they care; the primary thing is not truth but concern. This, of course, puts a premium on fanaticism, not to speak of fakery.

At all events, man as the value-needing and value-producing animal leads directly to the view that the good society is one which allows selves to commit themselves to authentic values and to grow in terms of them. This is exactly the prescription of the New Left. It is, of course, in the absence of elaboration, empty. One has no idea what such a society would be like; it is utterly unprogrammatic. But it is just such a vision which allows for the most complete rejection and destruction of the present regime and the greatest self-indulgence without guilt; and to be committed to this vision gratifies moralistic vanity at the same time. It is the best of many possible worlds.

Nietzsche, who was the first to present a profound teaching of the self, understood it to be an aristocratic teaching, for true selves are rare. The kind of man who can create a horizon for a whole people and make his values theirs and thus ennoble their lives is extremely rare. This is a natural distinction among men, and democratic society, according to him, effaces this distinction. But, as is easy to see, this teaching, or a corruption of it, easily becomes grist for the mill for radical egalitarianism. Objective standards encourage distinctions of rank among men; each self is a standard unto itself, and there is no rational basis for comparison of one self with another. The self justifies the most extreme freedom, for there is nothing in nature to which the self is subservient; the self is the creator, the Biblical God possessed uniquely by everyone.

In politics, teachings tend to be transformed by what is most powerful in the regime and in turn transform the regime in the direction of its most dangerous tendencies. The corruption of a teaching which was intended to be noble is peculiarly revolting. Not content with understanding democratic citizens as self-regarding but decent men who try to live by laws they themselves set down for the good of the community, we have had to make them into gods to whom nothing can be compared. Every man must be understood to be creative, no matter how much the standards of art and taste have to be debauched in order to do so. Political restraint and moderation must give way to ugly fanaticism in order to give everyone the chance to be committed. The grossest indecencies are permitted in the name of sincerity. And the wisdom of the ages must be forgotten in order to avoid alienating a growing self.

All of this tends to intensify the conformism—the increasingly monolithic quality of life—which it is supposed to overcome; for in the absence of real goals to strive for, men are most likely to fall back into their animal sameness, into the common instincts in the satisfaction of which all men are alike. Real diversity is never the result of the concentration on diversity. And at the same time as we are likely to produce greater conformity, we do not stop to consider whether the *laissez aller* we encourage is consonant with civility or political justice. No one asks whether we have any right to be so hopeful that every healthy self will posit nice civil values for itself which are consonant with everyone else's self-realization. Is there any built-in assurance that the unrestrained growth of each individual will not encroach on the vital space of other individuals? Yet this is all that seems to be talked about; the situation is parallel to that in which Rousseau's rhetoric of compassion was used by every dry, self-serving French bureaucrat in the nineteenth century. One thing at least is certain: in all of this there is no concern for justifying or preserving those restraints which have been necessary to the life of every community ever known to man. If neither reason nor tradition can bring about consensus, then the force of the first man resourceful and committed enough must needs do so.

It cannot be doubted that the status of values is a most perplexed and difficult question. Great men have contributed to the present view of things. They must be studied carefully, and the alternatives to them must be equally considered. Reason can only be abandoned reasonably; without this serious examination the modern view becomes empty and dangerous nonsense. It is precisely in this context that the value of liberal democracy becomes manifest; it is the only regime which permits and encourages such a quest. It should be the university's vocation to carry out this quest. In order for it to restore itself today, its faculties would have to make common cause in defense of free inquiry and at the same time protect and encourage those students who wish to learn. It is highly questionable whether it would any longer be capable of such an effort, for it lacks the awareness, the desire, and the personnel. Instead radical egalitarianism is a dogma within it. Given the increasing and menacing pressures for conformity growing up within the university, it seems reasonable to ask whether it will not be necessary for thinking men to return to the isolation of private life in order to be able to think freely. This is not a happy thought for our universities. However, there is also a larger question: is liberal democracy conceivable in the absence of the liberal university? The liberal university appears to be both the highest expression of liberal democracy and a condition of its perpetuation.

## Appendix

These reflections were set to paper in 1969. The following academic year, 1969–70, only hastened the progress of the disease I have described, culminating in faculties and presidents of major universities, under extreme pressure from students and in their desire to recapture their students' respect, taking political stands on current issues. It was accepted that the business of the university can be interrupted in the name of political activism and that students who abandon their studies to participate will suffer no consequences, that they will receive credit equally with those who do the work of students.

At the moment there appears to be a calm on our campuses, and it may very well endure for a time. But one should not be misled as to the meaning of that calm. The principle of student power has been largely victorious; the students are now at something of a loss as to what to do with that victory. Nothing has been done to reestablish respect for the proper purposes of the university or the rules requisite to the fulfillment of those purposes. The relative quiet results also in part from outside pressure. Hostility to universities has expressed itself in many ways but in particular in the tightening of the purse strings. The highly favorable disposition of the general public toward universities, which was an essential element in the possibility of their success, has been undermined. The public has apparently finally been persuaded of the view of our universities so loudly propounded by students and professors and has come to wonder why it should support such institutions. Economic motivations do indeed seem to have some effect on this generation of idealists.

## Notes

1. Plato, *Republic,* VI 492 a–e.
2. Ibid., VIII 563 a–b.
3. Machiavelli, *The Prince,* chap. 25.
4. Allan Bloom, "The Crisis of Liberal Education" in *Higher Education and Modern Democracy,* ed. Robert A. Goldwin (Chicago: Rand McNally, 1967).
5. Plato, *Republic,* VIII 561 c–d.

# *Part Three*

# Socialism

arl Marx was not the first, though he is the most famous, socialist.[1] Socialist themes are as old as Plato's *Republic* (the ideal city requires communal property, including women and children) and Christ's Sermon on the Mount (the poor in spirit are blessed; the reign of God is theirs). Marx discusses his more immediate predecessors in part 3 of *The Communist Manifesto*. Most important among them are the utopian socialists Charles Fourier (1772–1837), Robert Owen (1771–1858), and Claude-Henri Saint Simon (1760–1828). Like Marx, Saint Simon portrayed history as a conflict between productive and unproductive classes. Owen was an industrialist who founded New Lanark, a model factory based on the principle that better working conditions improve productivity. But it was Charles Fourier, included here, who had the greatest influence upon Marx.

Fourier's central concept is "passionate attraction." According to Fourier, philosophers typically treat human passions as problems. This is true, he argues, only in badly organized societies. Fourier claims that God created the passions and that He rules by attraction. If society suits the passions, then it will be harmonious. Fourier's schemes for a harmonious society are often bizarre. The little hordes who love dirt collect the garbage, and "filth ... be-come[s] their path to glory." The "butterfly principle" rules in the court of love where individuals "flit" from one sexual encounter to another. What most influenced Marx was the idea that work, if properly organized, is desirable. What Marx missed was Fourier's sensuous side. Nothing in Marx's writings even approaches the sexual troubadours![2]

Although Marx learned from the utopian socialists, he also criticized them for neglecting the laws of economics and the necessity for political action. Their naiveté, he feared, would undermine the class struggle.[3] That "the history of all hitherto existing society is the history of class struggle" is the central thesis of Marx and Engels's *Communist Manifesto*.[4] To understand it, an introduction to their theory of history is necessary.

According to Marx, humans are producers. But they do not produce merely to meet physical needs. "Rather it [production] is a definite form of activity ... , a definite form of expressing their life, a definite mode of life on their part."[5] Human productive powers expand historically. As one need is satisfied, another is generated, and then a way of satisfying it. "Their history is ... the history of the evolving productive forces ... and is, therefore, the history of the development of the forces of the individuals themselves."[6] Marx and Engels argue that the productive forces are crucial for understanding a society. They shape its division of labor, class relations, state institutions, and basic values. When productive forces outgrow class relations, social revolution occurs.

Classes themselves are defined by relations of ownership (and with it control) of the productive forces. Marx distinguishes between classes in themselves and classes for themselves. The first is an objective class, defined by shared economic circumstances. The second adds subjective components, consciousness of class interests and collective activity to promote them.[7] The problem for socialist revolutionaries is moving from the first to the second. The *Manifesto* is, in part, an explanation of the development of class consciousness in capitalist society.

The classes in capitalist society are the bourgeoisie (owners of productive forces and buyers of labor power) and the proletariat (sellers of labor power who do not own productive forces). In a sense, both are revolutionary. The bourgeoisie revolutionizes production, centralizing, expanding, internationalizing, and mechanizing it. In the process, it makes work less attractive, less lucrative, and less accessible for the proletariat. This class conflict manifests itself in periodic crises of overproduction and underconsumption. The bourgeoisie produces vast quantities and impoverishes potential consumers. As Marx puts it, the bourgeoisie "forges the weapons which bring death to itself." It also "calls into existence the men who are to wield those weapons." It not only makes work intolerable, but also organizes the proletariat economically and politically, inadvertently preparing it for revolution.

What does that revolution entail? Marx and Engels say only what communism abolishes—the division of labor, private property, nation-states, classes, families, truths. What replaces them remains unclear. Marx and Engels cannot say more because their ideas are also shaped by the productive forces: "They merely express ... actual relations springing from an existing class struggle, from a historical movement going on under our very eyes." To say more would be utopian.

The *Manifesto* emphasizes the inevitability of socialist revolution. The next two selections in this part explain its desirability. "Estranged Labor" is from Marx's early unpublished *Economic and Philosophical Manuscripts*. Most simply, alienation refers to a loss of meaning in life. Marx discusses four aspects of alienation. First, workers are alienated from their products which they produce for the bourgeoisie. Second, they are alienated from their productive activity, which is forced labor. Third, workers' alienation from their species-being manifests itself in attitudes toward nature (as an object to be manipulated and possessed) and society (as a mere means to self-preservation). Fourth, workers experience alienation from their fellow men, with whom they interact through competitive exchanges. According to Marx, alienation pervades capitalist societies and is a necessary result of their mode of production.

Alienation is only one of the problems of capitalism. Another, exploitation, is equally important. Whereas alienation involves a loss of meaning, exploitation involves being used by others.[8] Marx's labor theory of value, outlined in "Value, Price, and Profit," explains the nature of capitalist exploitation. Marx begins by arguing that profit comes from production, not exchange. Some (capitalists) profit from others (proletarians) labor. Is this fair? Yes and no. Capitalists pay workers the full exchange value of their labor power. But labor power is a peculiar commodity: It creates more value than it has. The surplus value it creates is the capitalists' profit. Not surprisingly, capitalists try to increase their surplus value. They gain absolute surplus value by lengthening the working day and relative surplus value by improving productivity. These strategies create the conditions for revolution—the crises of overproduction and underconsumption—described in the *Manifesto*. The labor theory of value also shows why liberation requires revolution. A higher wage and a shorter day are only better conditions for a "slave."

Yet the inevitable revolution has not occurred. Why? Twentieth-century socialists grapple with this question. In *What Is to Be Done?* and *State and Revolution*, Lenin develops the theory of the party vanguard and the proletarian dictatorship. For Marx, capitalist production created the preconditions—economic crisis and class consciousness—for socialist revolution. But Lenin argues that on its own the proletariat develops only trade union consciousness, the desire for "bread and butter" reforms. The party, a small, secret cadre, not subservient to spontaneity, must bring revolutionary consciousness to the proletariat from without. Professional revolutionaries must lead the proletariat, even seizing power in their name. Then, during a transitional dictatorship, the party transforms the proletariat along with the bourgeoisie. As Lenin puts it, "We want the socialist revolution with human nature as it is now, with human nature that cannot do without subordination, control and managers." By emphasizing the party and its rule, Lenin severs Marx's connection between socialist revolution and capitalist development. For Lenin, politics leads economics. Perhaps socialists can even "skip" capitalism. Is this an appropriate adaptation of Marxism to changing circumstances? Lenin does offer an explanation for why European revolutions failed. He also makes Marxism applicable to the Third World. But is Leninism still Marxism? How significant are the differences?

Whereas Lenin adapts Marxism to the Third World, Eduard Bernstein and Sidney Webb apply it to a new Europe. Bernstein was the theorist of the SPD, the largest democratic socialist party in nineteenth-century Europe. Bernstein agreed with Lenin that European workers lacked revolutionary consciousness, but his analysis of the problem and his solution to it differ. According to Bernstein, the economic preconditions for socialist revolution simply do not exist. As he succinctly puts it: "Peasants do not sink; middle class does not disappear; crises do not grow ever larger; misery and serfdom do not increase. There is increase in insecurity, dependence, social distance, social character of production, functional superfluity of property owners."9 Bernstein concludes that a new Marxist theory is required. In *Evolutionary Socialism,* he presents that theory. He argues that current economic and political activities—unions and votes—will eventually lead to socialism. Gradual change is not only possible but also preferable to revolution. "A greater surety of lasting success lies in a steady advance than in a revolutionary cataclysm."10

Sidney Webb, an English Fabian Socialist and author of the 1918 British Labour party platform, articulates similar themes. He also sees socialism as an extension of liberals' principles of liberty and equality. As politics is democratized—Webb wrote after the English Reform Acts, which expanded the suffrage—workers will vote for economic reform. Indeed, writing in 1889, Webb claimed that "the Socialist philosophy of to-day is but the conscious and explicit assertion of principles of social organization which have been already in great part unconsciously adopted." Socialism, "the economic side of the democratic ideal," would come about by legal and peaceful means.

In contrast to Lenin, and perhaps also to Marx, Bernstein and Webb argue that socialists should accept workers as they are. This means listening to their desires, even for "bread and butter" reforms, and working to fulfill them. But what if workers never want socialism? If, as in England, they are content with a welfare state? Of if, as in Germany, they choose fascism? This is the dilemma of democratic socialism.

The final selection in this part, "The Port Huron Statement," was the manifesto of Students for a Democratic Society (SDS) in the 1960s. Marx and

Engels were fascinated by the United States, where "classes . . . have not yet become fixed but, in continual flux, perpetually change and interchange their elements."[11] But they saw social mobility, along with southern slavery, as obstacles to socialism. "Labor," Marx said, "cannot emancipate itself in the white skin when in the black it is branded."[12] Only after the Civil War did Marx expect a "serious workers' party" in the United States.[13] This was not to be. Socialism, like conservatism, has remained marginal in American politics.[14] Still, galvanized by foreign affairs (Vietnam, the Cold War, nuclear weapons) and domestic issues (racism and poverty), the left flourished on campus in the 1960s. Student revolutionaries were privileged, not proletarian. Their concerns—bureaucratization and socialization, apathy and hierarchy—were not explicitly socialist. Authenticity, their goal, is an existentialist theme. Yet what began as a call for freedom on campus became a demand for a democratic society. The student movement ultimately failed; yesterday's hippies are today's yuppies.[15] Again, the question arises, What can socialism be today? Can socialist ends be achieved by democratic means? If not, do those ends justify other means? Or has socialism become a utopian dream?

## Notes

1. I am indebted to Isaac Kramnick for this insight.

2. Feminists have criticized Marx (see Heidi Hartmann in part 6 of this book) for overemphasizing material production and ignoring sexual reproduction.

3. Again, Fourier is instructive. He reportedly advertised for wealthy patrons to "fund a phalanstery." They were to contribute over lunch at a Paris cafe. He waited; none came.

4. Marx and Engels wrote the *Manifesto* for the Communist League on the eve of the 1848 revolutions. This explains its polemical tone and its sense of urgency. Although the failure of the revolutions forced them to revise their claims, they continued to see the *Manifesto* as the best single statement of their views.

5. Karl Marx and Friedrich Engels, *The German Ideology*, tr. C.J. Arthur (London: Lawrence and Wishart, 1970), 42.

6. Ibid., 87.

7. For this distinction, see Karl Marx, *The Eighteenth Brumaire of Louis Bonaparte*, in *The Portable Karl Marx*, ed. Eugene Kamenka (New York: Viking Penguin, 1983), 312.

8. Exploitation and alienation may be related as cause and effect (though workers may be exploited without experiencing alienation, e.g., if they lack class consciousness).

9. Quoted in Peter Gay, *The Dilemma of Democratic Socialism* (New York: Collier, 1962), 250.

10. Eduard Bernstein, *Evolutionary Socialism* (New York: Schocken, 1975), xxviii.

11. Marx, *Eighteenth Brumaire*, 297.

12. Karl Marx, "The American Question in England," *New York Daily Tribune*, 18 September 1861, reprinted in *The American Journalism of Marx and Engels, a Selection from the New York Daily Tribune*, ed. Henry M. Christman (New York: New American Library, 1966), 211–22.

13. Karl Marx, "Preface to the Russian edition of the Communist Manifesto," in Kamenka, *The Portable Karl Marx*, 556.

14. In addition to social mobility and lingering racism, many other explanations have been offered for the marginality of American socialism. Among them are our history of agrarian radicalism, the safety valve provided by the frontier, and the presence of numerous immigrants. The classic on this topic is Werner Sombart, *Why Is There No Socialism in the United States?* ed. C.T. Husbands (White Plains, N.Y.: International Arts and Sciences Press, 1976).

15. See James Miller, *"Democracy Is in the Streets": From Port Huron to the Siege of Chicago* (New York: Simon and Schuster, 1987); Sohnya Sayres et al., eds., *The 60's Without Apology* (Minneapolis: University of Minnesota Press, 1984); Christopher Lasch, *The Agony of the American Left* (New York: Knopf, 1969).

# 11

## CHARLES FOURIER

### *Utopian Socialism*

Charles Fourier, a utopian socialist, lived in Paris from 1772 until 1837. Following the French Revolution, during which he was imprisoned and nearly executed, he began to work for a new social order. His ideal system of social organization was the phalanstery, a group of 1700 to 1800 people whose different psychological traits would be complementary and would produce happiness. The following paragraphs are taken from three major divisions of a topically organized English edition of selections from Fourier's complete works.

## Commerce, Industry, and Work in Civilization

### *True Freedom and Work*

After health and wealth nothing is more precious than freedom. But there are two sorts of freedom: physical freedom and social freedom. The second variety is not the one that the sophists wish to procure for us.

The sophists are used to considering nature in a simplistic manner, and they have allowed their mania for simplification to confuse the debate about freedom. They have not been able to distinguish between the simple, compound and bi-compound varieties of freedom. For more than a thousand years they neglected the first of the freedoms, material or bodily freedom. It was the Christian religion which finally intervened powerfully to emancipate the slaves. But before Christianity the philanthropists of antiquity were used to turning human beings into beasts of burden and to obliging slaves to kill each other in mass combats for the amusement of the virtuous citizens of Rome. When the Romans did not wish to see twenty thousand slaves slaughtered en masse, they had two hundred massacred one by one in gladiatorial combats. These performances repeated with more civic pomp by the virtuous republicans of Sparta. To reduce their slave population the Spartans would gather

185

two thousand of their most faithful slaves, crown them with flowers, parade them around the city, and then slaughter them. The Spartans dispatched their most faithful slaves in this way because they did not want to see them die of slow torture in the galleys. Such were, for a thousand years, the noble ideas of Philosophy about physical freedom. Every good republican applauded these massacres; and if Christianity had not intervened, things might still be at the same point.

If someone had consulted the oracles of wisdom, the Platos and the Aristotles about the emancipation of the slaves, they would have replied with the fine word "impossibility" which France has inherited. The enlightened Aristotle was so sure that slaves were beasts of burden, creatures outside the human race, that he laid down the principle that "there is no virtue proper to a slave." He wished to reduce them to the status of brute beasts, devoid of the rational faculty and of virtue itself. . . .

Under the last Caesars the philosophers saw the granting of bodily freedom, which they had so long regarded as impossible, was in fact quite feasible. They should then have recognized the error of their science with its assumptions about impossibility and its conviction that "nature is limited to known means." But they learned nothing from this lesson, and their secret indifference with regard to freedom is proven by the fact that they made no effort to analyze and spread word of the means by which emancipation had been brought about.

The ideas that people now have about emancipation are superficial and highly impractical. Thus in recent times the attempt to grant bodily freedom to the Negroes was a failure. It was in 1789 that Philosophy undertook the task. Instead of seeking appropriate methods and adopting a policy of judicious philanthropy, Philosophy relied solely on the spirit of partisan politics. It succeeded only in turning Santo Domingo into a bloody battle-ground under the banal pretext of liberty.[1]

Philosophy thus stands convicted of complete incompetence in matters related to bodily or physical freedom and the process of emancipation, whether sudden or gradual. . . . Has Philosophy shown any more skill in the matter of social freedom? This question prompts us to distinguish three kinds of freedom. . . .

1. *Simple or Physical Freedom* without social freedom. This is the condition of a poor man who has a very small fixed income, only enough to provide the barest necessities, a military ration. He enjoys an *active physical* freedom because he is not forced to work like the laborer who has no independent income. Yet his passions are completely unsatisfied. Phebon is quite free to go to the opera. But it costs a crown to get in and Phebon has only enough money to feed himself poorly and to dress himself shabbily. He is free to aspire to the rank of Deputy, but this requires a far greater income than he has. He may take pride in the fine title of Free Man, but his social freedom is a sham. The

doors of the inn and the opera are closed to him, and he has no place among the electorate.[2] He is only a passive member of society. His passions cannot express themselves in an active way, and his opinions are held in contempt.

Such a man is, nonetheless, considerably more free than the laborer who is obliged to work lest he die of starvation and who has just one day a week of *active* physical freedom—Sunday. For the other six days of the week the laborer is in a state of passive physical freedom. He has consented to the form of slavery represented by the workshop. But compared to the idleness and wellbeing which he enjoys on Sunday, this indirect form of slavery is not any less physically constraining than real slavery.

A distinction can also be made between active and passive social freedom. For the time being let us simply point out that the two classes of men just cited do not enjoy social freedom. They only possess simple or physical freedom: it is active for the man with a small fixed income and passive for the laborer. But the laborer is himself much better off than the slave who is denied physical freedom in both its active and its passive forms.

2. *Divergent Compound Freedom.* This includes *active physical* freedom and *active social freedom,* and it permits the complete satisfaction of the passions. Such is the condition of the savages, for they enjoy both these freedoms. A savage deliberates on questions of peace and war just like a cabinet member in civilization. He enjoys, insofar as it is possible in his horde, the complete satisfaction of his soul's passions. Above all, he enjoys freedom from worry, a good almost unknown to civilized men. It is true that he must hunt and fish for his subsistence, but this work is attractive to him and no threat to his active physical freedom. Work which is pleasing is not a form of servitude. While the savage would feel enslaved behind a plow, his hunting is an amusement just as selling is the merchant's amusement. Do you think that a merchant has experienced physical discomfort when he spends his morning setting out a hundred bolts of cloth, lying to his clients and selling many pairs of breeches? The fatigue he may feel is a pleasure, for his work is attractive and he possesses physical freedom. This is proved by the fact that our merchant who is quite content today will be glum and surly tomorrow if the customers don't come and he is unable to lie and to sell.

We have seen that the freedom of the savage is a compound freedom because it is both physically and socially active. But these two *activities* are *divergent* from man's destiny which is attractive labor. If the savage is to enjoy *active, convergent* freedom, he must be offered attractive *productive* work which is carried out in passionate series. Then he will advance to the third type of freedom.

3. *Convergent Compound or Bi-compound Freedom.* This consists of two independent elements, *active physical* freedom and *active social* freedom in alliance with *attractive productive work.* It presupposes unified adherence, the individual consent of every worker—man, woman and child—and their im-

passioned collaboration in the performance of work and in the maintenance of the established order. This third sort of liberty is the destiny of man. (*Œuvres Completes*, 3:152–56. Hereafter cited as *OC*.)

### Work and Compulsion

Freedom from worry is a form of happiness experienced by the animals. But it is also a human right, although it can only be enjoyed in civilization by the very rich. Far from being careless of the morrow, nine-tenths of civilized men are worried about the present day because they are obliged to devote themselves to loathsome work that is forced upon them. And so on Sunday they go to cafes and places of amusement to enjoy a few moments of the sort of carefreeness that is vainly sought by so many rich men who are themselves pursued by anxiety. "*Post equitem sedet atra cura.*"3

Quibblers will say that freedom from worry is a state of mind and not a right. But it becomes a right insofar as it is proscribed in the state of civilization where any sign of carelessness is held in dishonor and resolutely condemned. Let the father of a poor family try to devote himself to his own pleasures without worrying about his workshop and without saving up money for taxes, rent and future needs. Then public opinion through its criticism and the tax collector through his agents will let him know that he does not have the right to be carefree, to enjoy life like the savages and animals. They will tell him that he must master his carefree inclinations. Civilized education, moreover, intervenes systematically to fight against our desire to be carefree, a desire that will be unfettered in Harmony.

As for the Savage, it is obvious that he enjoys his carefree life and does not want to concern himself with the future. Otherwise he would worry that his children and his horde might suffer from hunger. He would then accept the agricultural implements and farming equipment that civilized governments try to offer him. But he doesn't want to give up any of his seven rights. In this he is correct because if he gave up his right to freedom from worry he would lose all his other rights one after the other. Doubtless he does this without calculating, but nature has done his thinking for him. Attraction leads him along the right path. . . .

The only plausible objection that can be raised against the happiness of the Savages is that women do not share it. Although women constitute one-half of the human race, their condition among the Savages is quite servile and very unfortunate. . . .

I have already established that the savage is more advanced than we are in his enjoyment of freedom because he has achieved *compound divergent* freedom. That is, savage males enjoy the seven natural rights. They are thus quite superior to us because we deprive the vast majority of either sex of the advantage. . . .

To indemnify a civilized man for the loss of his seven rights our publicists fobhim off with a few promises and tall stories. They offer him the dignity of possessing the fine title of a free man and the happiness of living under the Charter of 1815. These silly promises don't even deserve to be called illusions. They are incapable of satisfying a wage earner who wants above all to eat to fill, to live happily and free from worry, to hunt, fish, intrigue and steal like the Savage. . . .

When it deprives man of his seven natural rights, Civilization never gives him agreed-upon equivalents. Take an unfortunate worker who has neither work nor bread and is pursued by creditors and tax collector. Ask him if he would not prefer to enjoy the rights of hunting and fishing and to have trees and flocks like the Savage? He will not fail to prefer the life of the Savage. What is he given as an equivalent? The happiness of living under the Charter. But an indigent man cannot satisfy himself by reading the Charter instead of eating dinner. To offer him that sort of compensation is to insult his poverty. He would consider himself happy if he could enjoy the seven natural rights and freedom as does the Savage. But he will not find these in the civilized order. (*OC*, 3:167–70)

The exercise of the industrial faculty which is a delight for the free animals—the beavers, bees, wasps and ants—is a torment for man, who escapes it as soon as he acquires his freedom. Civilized man aspires only to inertia, and the supreme curse which the savage shouts at his enemy is this: "May you be reduced to plowing a field!"

Since we are evidently destined by God for agricultural and manufacturing labor, how has it happened that we have thus far received from him neither a social code regulating our industrial relations nor a natural enticement to work? Why is work, which is said to be our destiny, only a torment for civilized and barbarian wage earners and slaves, who are in constant rebellion against the obligation to work and who would quit working altogether if they were no longer constrained by the fear of punishment?

Work is nonetheless a delight for many creatures such as the beavers, bees, wasps, and ants, who are perfectly free to lapse into a state of inertia. God has provided them with a social mechanism which attracts them to work and makes it a source of happiness for them. Why should he have failed to grant us a benefit which he bestows upon the animals? There is a huge difference between their work and ours! The Russians and the Algerians work out of fear of the whip or the cudgel; the English and the French work from fear of the hunger which besets their poor households. The liberty of the Greeks and Romans is much vaunted, but they had slaves who worked out of fear of being executed just like the Negroes in our colonies today. Such is the happiness of man in the absence of the *attractive industrial code*; such is the result of human laws and of the philosophical constitutions: they make humanity envy the lot of the industrious animals, for whom Attraction turns wearisome tasks into sources of pleasure.

Our happiness would be great indeed if God had treated us like these animals, if he endowed us with *passionate attraction* for the work which we are destined to perform! Our life would be but a succession of delights, and these delights would be a source of great wealth to us. In the absence of the system of attractive labor, however, we are no more than a society of slave-laborers in which a few people manage to avoid the necessity of working and form coalitions in order to remain in a state of idleness. These people are hated by the masses who share their desire to free themselves from work. This is the source of revolutionary ferment. Agitators promise to make the people happy, rich and idle; but once they have gained power, they oppress the multitude and reduce it to a more complete state of servitude in order to consolidate their own position as idlers or as managers of those who work. The latter are no different from the idlers.

In this miserable condition we are reduced to envying the lot of the animals and insects, and bemoaning a providence which appears to have regarded these creatures with a solicitude which it has not had for us. For, if one is to believe the philosophical prejudices, God has not prepared a social code for us, nor a sure industrial mechanism, nor industrial attraction to make our work enjoyable, nor even the guarantee of the work we need for our subsistence. ...

Our philosophers would be vain in claiming that their vague wisdom and their oppressive laws could ever provide us with an attractive *industrial code.* They are vain in promising in their innumerable constitutions to make life enchanting for our wage-earners. All their theories only serve to make work more loathsome and to add to the horror of the seven limbic calamities. (*OC,* 3:249–51)

### The Worker's Misfortunes

The common people have not even reached the level of simple pleasure on the scale of happiness. They do not have enough for subsistence or to satisfy their sense of taste. This is the most imperious of all the senses and its satisfaction is the *sine qua non* of happiness. Rather, the common people are overwhelmed by a host of privations which transform their lives into a permanent hell. These privations constitute all of the degrees of unhappiness: simple, compound, super-compound, bi-compound, and quintessentially subversive or omni-compound, unhappiness.

As many as sixteen causes of despair can be enumerated. They assail the common people of civilization in varying degrees at every moment according to the following scheme.

### Misfortunes of Working People

PRESSING EVIL

1. The burden of taxes: pursuits of fiscal agents who come to extract the

few pennies that a man has painfully amassed to support his unfortunate family.

2. The necessity of endangering his health in excessive and unhealthy work in order to provide for his own subsistence and that of his children.

DIRECT EVIL

3. Repercussion of poverty, shared suffering, or the faculty of feeling the misfortunes of his family whose privations add to his own pain.

4. New misfortunes that redouble his suffering just when he thinks he has endured the worst that fate had in store for him.

5. Unjust stigma of shame: the opprobrium and defamation which plague the poor man because of his destitution and expose him to a disdain which merely increases with his penury.

INDIRECT EVIL

6. The sight of fortune's favorites to whom chance, intrigue or crime brings affluence. This can only increase the despair of the honest worker who is led by his own probity deeper and deeper into the abyss of indigence.

7. Relative regression caused by the progress of luxury which increases the sufferings of the multitude in the same proportion that it creates new means of pleasure for the rich. Deprived of life's necessities, the civilized worker is tormented by a display of increased affluence which the savage does not see.

8. Frustration in seeking legal redress through lawsuits and other claims. He lacks the money and the credit to pay lawyers' fees.

ACCESSORY EVIL

9. Social snare, or the constant danger of being cheated by his fellow citizens, of meeting nothing but a swarm of cheats or disguised enemies in the social world.

10. Poverty anticipated in the present, or the fear of unemployment, which never troubles the savages and the animals.

11. Scientific mockery, or the illusory help of literary charlatans who, while promising the people that they will soften their misfortunes, overwhelm them with new calamities.

12. The trap of morality, or the persecution he attracts when he practices virtue, because virtue shames perverse rivals, excites them to calumny which is always well-received in civilization.

PIVOTS

Y. Loathing for work, and deprivation of the prerogatives enjoyed by animals such as beavers, bees, etc., who are attracted to work and find their happiness in that work which is the civilized man's torture.

YY. Betrayal of nature, or the martyrdom of attraction. The goad of numerous desires which the civilized man cannot satisfy and which lead him to ruin; whereas nature endows animals with only those passions which are suited to guide them and which they have the right to satisfy.

TRANSITIONS

KK. Wearisome reflections on the past, the memory of numerous miseries already endured and yet to be feared.

K. Suffering anticipated in the future, or the awareness that in his old age, in the distant future, he will meet with increased misfortunes and be unable to escape them.

Such is the lot of the common people whom the sophists describe as making great strides toward perfectibility. In fact their condition is worse than that of the wild animals. The lion, for example, is well clothed, well armed, and takes its subsistence where it finds it; it is a hundred times more fortunate than the common people of civilization who are dragged off to the gallows if they ask for any one of their natural rights or for the primordial social right to a *minimum* of subsistence.

Is someone going to object that the common people are so brutish that they are incapable of feeling the enormity of their misfortunes? In that case just what is the significance of the pretension of our sages to spread enlightenment, to give us delicate senses and to refine our minds' perceptions of sensations? Here one might be inclined to praise the obscurantists who want to brutalize the common people. Since all of civilization turns in a vicious circle, the obscurantists may well be right in more than one case. (*OC*, 4:191–93)

## Attractive Work

### Loathsome Work: God's Curse

"We must love work," say our sages. Well! How can we? What is lovable about work in civilization? For nine-tenths of all men work procures nothing but profitless boredom. Rich men, consequently, find work loathsome and do only the easiest and most lucrative kinds of work such as managing companies. How can you make a poor man love work when you are not even able to make work agreeable for the rich? This would require elegant workshops, division of tasks and courteous, loyal, and polished fellow-workers. All of these conditions are impractical in civilization. They can exist only when work is organized in passionate series.

In addition to all the obvious drawbacks of civilized work such as the filthiness of certain workshops, the coarseness of the peasants, theft, complications, isolation, boredom, the risk of loss, etc., there is a still greater drawback. That is the necessity of watching over all phases of a particular kind of work and often of performing all of them oneself. A certain rich man, for example, would very much like to grow flowers and fruits. But he hasn't the courage to order seeds and plants because he is afraid of being cheated by the merchants. (He most certainly will be cheated.) He is discouraged at the prospect that a negligent son or son-in-law may allow his plantings to perish after him. He is surrounded by maladroit, careless, thieving, and hateful workers; by mocking and ignorant neighbors who ridicule his work; by children who come and spitefully lay waste to his flower beds; and by women who devastate his gardens even more stupidly. For women know nothing about flowers and think that they are doing the flower-grower a great honor by cutting and chopping up his flower beds, when they are not able to recognize the different species nor praise the grower intelligently. How can we make work agreeable for the poor man when all kinds of obstacles conspire to disgust even the rich? (*OC,* 4:520–21)

Work, say the Scriptures, is a punishment for man: Adam and his children were condemned to earn their bread by the sweat of their brows. Before the infliction of this punishment, man's primeval happiness consisted in having nothing to do, as in the case now for our populace on Sunday. It is thus well recognized, even by religion, that civilized work is a state of unhappiness for man. Religion admits that man is closer to nature when he indulges in enchanting illusion rather than when he listens to philosophy's promises about the charms of life in a thatched hut. Yet when Scripture told us the truth concerning the unhappiness attached to work today, it did not say that this punishment would not end one day, nor did it claim that man would never be able to return to the happy state he first enjoyed. (*OC,* 4:554–55)

### Drudgery: Work Devoid of Attraction

Drudge duty (40th series) includes all jobs which are isolated and devoid of attraction. These include coach driving, mail delivery, sentry duty at the watchtower, the operation of the telegraph, the guarding of the colors, the playing of the carillon, the night watch at the porter's lodge both at the Phalanstery itself and at the stables, the night patrol, the fire-watch, the tending of the beacon light, etc., etc.

The series of Drudges will receive a substantial dividend in addition to the exemption fees paid by the rich who will be able, as they are today, to purchase exemptions from guard duty. These fees will be allocated to the series as a whole and not to individuals, since individual service for wages would be dishonorable in association.

The Drudges will also be encouraged by various favors such as the right to eat at the second class tables. (Most of them would otherwise eat with the third class.) Our intention is to make the day on which they perform their chores—which recurs about once every two weeks—a day of gaiety for them.

These precautions will seem quite superfluous to the civilized, all of whom are accustomed to regarding oppression as moral wisdom. They tend to forget that every page of this book is concerned with the creation of industrial attraction, the harmonious distribution of wealth, and the fusion of the three classes. It is very important, therefore, to avoid degrading any job or displeas-

ing any class. It is necessary to possess reliable methods capable of infusing repugnant and disdained work with gaiety. (See the section on the Little
Hordes.)[4] (*OC*, 6:136–37)


### The Little Hordes and Disgusting Work

We shall now see that morality has failed to understand the principles governing education and that, according to its habit, it has classed as vices all of the
impulses which nature would employ to create virtues.

Conflict between the instincts and the sexes yields prodigious results in
work and virtue. To create such conflict we will divide children between the
ages of four and fifteen and a half (the four tribes of Cherubs, Seraphs, Pupils
and Students) into two instinctual corps. These are:

The Little Hordes, who perform tasks which are repugnant either to the
senses or to self-esteem.

The Little Bands, who are responsible for the maintenance of collective
luxury.[5]

These two contrasting corporations will usefully employ the instincts
that morality vainly seeks to suppress in both sexes: the taste that little boys
have for filth, and the love that little girls have for finery. By setting these two
tastes off against each other, societary education will lead both sexes to the
same goal by different paths. It will lead the Little Hordes to the beautiful by
way of the good, and the Little Bands to the good by way of the beautiful.

This method gives children a freedom of choice which they do not enjoy
in a society such as ours, which forces them to accept a single system of morals. The societary state will permit them to choose between two contrasting
paths which favor opposite penchants: the penchants for finery and filth.

Two-thirds of all boys have a penchant for filth. They love to wallow in
the mire and play with dirty things. They are unruly, peevish, scurrilous and
overbearing, and they will brave any storm or peril simply for the pleasure of
wreaking havoc. These children will enroll in the Little Hordes whose task is
to perform, dauntlessly and as a point of honor, all those loathsome tasks that
ordinary workers would find debasing. This corporation is a kind of half-sav-
age legion whose wild ways contrast with the refined courtesy of Harmony.
But this contrast is one of style and not of sentiment; for the Little Hordes are
the most ardently patriotic of corporations.

The other third of little boys have a taste for good manners and tranquil
occupations. They will enroll in the Little Bands. By contrasts, a third of all
girls have boyish inclinations and love to horn in on boys' games. They are
called tomboys. Such girls will join the Little Hordes. Thus the Little Hordes
will include ⅔ boys and ⅓ girls, and the Little Bands will include ⅔ girls and
⅓ boys. Each of these two corps will be subdivided into three sections which
must be given names. The Little Hordes will adopt vulgar sobriquets, while

the Little Bands will assume romantic names. This will emphasize the contrast between these two groups which are both vital to the working of industrial attraction.

Let us first analyze the duties and civic virtues of the Little Hordes. . . . The Little Hordes have the rank of *God's Militia* in the service of industrial unity. By virtue of this title, they should be the first to enter the breach whenever unity is threatened. To maintain unity the Little Hordes will be asked to perform a number of tasks which are so disgusting that it would otherwise be necessary to call upon the services of wage-laborers. In performing these tasks they will be divided into three corps: the first is assigned to foul functions such as sewer-cleaning, tending the dung heap, working in the slaughterhouses, etc.; the second is assigned to dangerous functions such as the hunting of reptiles or to jobs requiring dexterity; the third will participate in both these kinds of work. The older members of the Little Hordes will ride on their own dwarf horses.

One of the tasks assigned to the Little Hordes will be the maintenance of roads. They will make it a point of pride to keep the roads of Harmony lined with shrubs and flowers and in more splendid condition than the lanes of our country estates. If a highway is damaged in any way, the alarm will be given at once. The Little Hordes will immediately make temporary repairs and raise a warning flag to make sure that no passer-by might have grounds for accusing the community of having a bad Horde. The same reproach would be made if anyone found a dangerous reptile or a caterpillar's nest or heard the croaking of toads near a highway. The presence of such unclean objects would make people scornful of a Phalanx, and the value of its shares would fall.

Although the Little Hordes perform the most difficult tasks in the Phalanx—tasks which are totally lacking in *direct* attraction—they receive the least retribution. They would accept nothing at all if that were permitted in association. The fact that they receive the smallest share, however, does not prevent any of the members of the Little Hordes from receiving large shares for work performed in other groups and series. But as members of the unitary and philanthropic brotherhood of the Little Hordes, their work is inspired by devotion to the community and not by the hope of remuneration. . . .

Since the Little Hordes are the seedbed of all the civic virtues, they should serve society through the practice of the Christian virtue of *self-abnegation* and the philosophical virtue of *contempt for wealth*. They should exemplify and practice all the virtues that civilization dreams of but only counterfeits. As the guardians of social honor, they should crush evil in all its guises. While ridding the countryside of poisonous reptiles, they will purge society of a poison worse than the viper's, the poison of greed. . . . And in performing their foul tasks, they will eradicate the feelings of pride which make men disdain the laborious class and which tend to promote the spirit of caste, to impair social friendship, and to prevent the fusion of classes. . . .

It might seem that to make children so prodigiously virtuous it would be necessary to resort to supernatural means, as do our monastic orders when they accustom the neophyte to self-abnegation through austere novitiates. We will follow an entirely different course; nothing but the enticement of pleasure will be used with the Little Hordes.

Let us analyze the sources of their virtues. They are four in number, and all of them are condemned by morality. They are the penchant for dirt, and the feelings of pride, impudence and insubordination. It is by abandoning themselves to these so-called vices that the Little Hordes will become virtuous. As we consider this paradox, let us recall that the theory of attraction must restrict itself to utilizing the passions as God made them, without modifying them in any way. In support of this principle I have shown that there are a number of infantile attractions which we are wrong to regard as harmful. *Curiosity* and *flightiness,* for instance, are designed to attract the child to a host of Seristeries where he will discover his industrial vocations. The penchant for *running around with older, tougher children* is also useful; for the example of such children will teach the infant to be enthusiastic about his work in Harmony. *Disobedience toward the father and the teacher* is likewise a perfectly natural impulse. For these are not the persons who should educate the child; his education will be provided by cabalistic rivalries in work groups. Thus all youthful impulses are good in infancy and also in later childhood, provided that they are exercised in passionate series.

The Little Hordes will not be inspired to perform disgusting work from the very outset: they must be gradually introduced to it. First their pride must be aroused by giving them a sense of their own preeminence. All authorities, even monarchs, owe the first salute to the Little Hordes. With their dwarf horses the Little Hordes comprise the globe's foremost regiments of cavalry; no industrial army[6] may begin a campaign without them. They also have the prerogative of initiating all work done in the name of unity. They report to the army on the day set for the beginning of the project. After the engineers have laid out the work, the Little Hordes parade across the battlefield, and in their first charge they are cheered on by the whole army. They spend several days with the army and distinguish themselves in a number of tasks.

During religious ceremonies the Little Hordes are seated in the sanctuary, and on all other festive occasions they are given the place of honor. The purpose of all these distinctions is to utilize their penchant for foul tasks. They must be impassioned for such tasks by the trappings of glory, which cost nothing. Filth must become their path to glory, and it is for this reason that we encourage their pride, impudence and insubordination.

The Little Hordes have their own slang or cabalistic language, as well as their own miniature artillery. They also have their Druids and Druidesses, who are acolytes chosen from those elderly persons who have retained their taste for foul tasks. This service brings the elderly numerous advantages.

The method to follow with the Little Hordes is to utilize their enthusiasm for filth, but not to *use it up* by fatiguing them. In order to avoid exhausting their enthusiasm, they must be made to work gaily, honorifically, and in short sessions. If, for example, there is a particularly filthy job to be done, the Hordes from four or five neighboring Phalanxes are assembled. They arrive to take part in the *delite* or matinal meal which is served at four forty-five. Then after the religious hymn at five and the parade of out-going work groups, the charge of the Little Hordes is sounded in an uproar of bells, chimes, drums and trumpets, a howling of dogs and a bellowing of bulls. Then the Hordes, led by their Khans and Druids, rush forward with a great shout, passing before the priests who sprinkle them with holy water. They run off frenetically to their work, which they perform piously as an act of charity toward the Phalanx, a gesture of devotion to God and to unity.

The job done, they proceed to wash and dress. Then, dispersing into the gardens and workshops until eight, they return triumphantly to breakfast. There each Horde receives a crown of oak leaves which is attached to its banner. After breakfast, they remount their horses and return to their respective Phalanxes.

The Little Hordes should be associated with the priesthood as members of a religious brotherhood. When performing their work they should wear a religious symbol, such as a cross or other emblem, on their clothing. Among their work stimulants we must not forget the religious spirit, which is a very powerful means of inspiring education in children.

After the Little Hordes have developed an enthusiasm for collective work at difficult tasks, it will be easy to accustom them to unattractive day-to-day jobs in the apartments, slaughterhouses, kitchens, stables and laundries. They will always be up at three in the morning, taking the initiative at work on the Phalanx as they do in the industrial army.

The Little Hordes have supreme jurisdiction over the animal kingdom. They watch over the slaughterhouses to prevent unnecessary suffering and to insure every animal the most gentle death. Anyone who mistreats a quadruped, bird, fish or insect by abusing it in any way or by making it suffer at the slaughterhouse will have to answer to the Divan of the Little Hordes. Whatever his age, he will be brought before a tribunal of children because his reason is inferior even to that of children. Since animals are productive only when they are well treated, it is a rule in Harmony that a man who mistreats them is himself more of an animal than the defenseless beasts he persecutes. . . .

I have now said enough to make it clear that this corps of children, who indulge all the inclinations that morality forbids, is a device which will realize all the virtuous fancies with which the moralists feed their imaginations:

1. *Sweet Fraternity.* If a particular task is disdained because it is filthy, the men who perform it will become a class of pariahs, degraded beings with whom the rich will not wish to associate. In Harmony all of the tasks which

might lead to such bad consequences are performed by the Little Hordes. The Little Hordes ennoble loathsome work and thereby promote unity and social harmony, the fusion of the rich, middle and poor classes.

2. *Contempt for Wealth*. The Little Hordes do not disdain wealth as such, but rather its egotistical use. They will sacrifice a portion of their own wealth to increase that of the whole Phalanx and to maintain the true source of wealth: industrial attraction. When all three classes—rich, middle and poor —become subject to industrial attraction, they will work together affectionately on all sorts of tasks, even including the dirty work which is reserved for children. For children of rich parents will be as eager as those of the poor to join the ranks of the Little Hordes. It is personality that determines which corporation a child will choose. . . .

If our moralists had studied human nature, they would have recognized that most male children like filth and they would have sought to employ this inclination usefully. This is what the societary order does; it makes use of the taste for filth to form a corporation of industrial Deciuses. It encourages the dirty inclinations which are repressed with heavy-handed whippings by a tender morality that makes no effort to utilize the passions as God gave them to us. (*OC*, 6:206–14)

### Work, Love, and the Industrial Armies

Love, which is a source of disorder, idleness and expense in civilization, will become a source of profit and industrial miracles in the combined order. I am going to demonstrate this through a discussion of one of the most difficult administrative problems of civilization: the recruitment of armies. In the combined order this task will be accomplished by means of amorous strategy.

In each Phalanx there are two major series devoted to love, the *half-type* and the *whole type*. The latter is divided into nine groups beginning with the Vestalate which I shall now discuss.[7]

In each Phalanx the virginal members of the choir of Striplings[8] elect a quadrille of Vestals consisting of two parading couples and two meritorious couples. The former are chosen for their beauty and the latter for their accomplishments in the sciences and the arts or for their dedication to work.

The Vestals hold the rank of Magnates. When the poorest girl is elected a Vestal, she travels in a carriage which is studded with jewels and drawn by six white horses. . . . This youthful elite has the privilege of voyaging with the industrial armies. It is during their magnificent campaigns that the Vestals have their first love affairs.

Every day after their work is done the industrial armies hold magnificent festivities. These festivities are all the more splendid in that they bring together young people who have been chosen for their great beauty and talent. They also offer an excellent occasion for displays of courtliness. For each of the Vestals has numerous suitors and he or she must choose between them during the course of the campaign. Those who wish to form bonds with a single love join the ranks of the Damsels who are constant lovers representing the second of the nine amorous types. Others who have penchants for inconstancy take their places in the seven remaining categories. The principal result of these diversions is that immense industrial armies are formed without any constraint. The only ruse employed is that of showing off and honoring those virgins whom the philosophers would like to keep hidden and surrounded by chaperons and prejudices.

## Scenes and Episodes from the New Amorous World

### A Session of the Court of Love

The band of adventurers moves forward through a cloud of perfume and a rain of flowers. The choral groups and musicians of the Phalanx welcome them with hymns of joy. As soon as the visitors have reached the colonnades of the Phalanstery, bowls of flaming punch are brought in and a hundred different nectars spurt from the opened fountains. All the knights and ladies are wearing their most seductive clothing. Two hundred priests and priestesses, who are dressed no less elegantly, greet their guests and perform the introductions. After refreshments have been served, the whole group mounts to the throne room where the pontiff Isis is seated. The welcoming ceremonies are concluded there and, after washing, all the visitors proceed to the confessional.

The high priests begin to examine the adventurers and to read their written declarations. A few adventurers, who have been examined at their last stop, give the priests the commentaries written by their previous confessors. Everyone hands over a written summary of his or her most recent confession together with whatever observations may have been added by the consistory of the last Phalanx visited.

While the visitors are eating a light snack, the work of analyzing and classifying their confessions goes on in the consistory. A list of five or six sympathetic relationships is drawn up for each knight and lady on the basis of the examinations conducted by the young priests and priestesses who wish to become sympathetic with the adventurers. Before the snack is over the fairies and genies have completed their task of match-making. Their recommendations are delivered to the office of the High Matron along with a summary of each confession. Sympathetic matching takes everything into account, and the final choices made are those which seem most likely to complement previous encounters either through contrast or identity.

I am only speaking here about young adventurers. The amorous affairs of the older adventurers are handled by the fakirs who use other methods. . . .

The first moments of the visit are taken up by ceremonial activities which should always include an informal meal. This meal will give everyone a chance to satisfy his curiosity, to move about from one person to another and to form some general impression of the visitors. Of course they too need to see how the land lies. People should get a brief look at one another before amorous affairs get underway. This interlude also allows time for the theoretical determination of sympathies; it enables everyone to have his own list of partners in time for the opening of the court of love. It should be added that up until the opening of the court of love the Vestals and the children are free to mingle with the visitors and to satisfy their curiosity about them. This is a most important precaution since the children might otherwise wish to enter the court of love, which they are not allowed to do. Thus the session does not begin until they have seen all they want of the visitors and are quite ready for bed. Only then do the adventurers go to the office of the High Matron to get back their papers and to look at the portraits of their designated sympathetic partners.

When the preludes are over the adventurers and their hosts gather in the salon. A salvo is fired to announce the opening of the session. On one side of the salon stands the whole band of adventurers. On the other side the priesthood is gathered along with other people who have been designated as sympathetic partners or who have come to take part in the amorous activities. The priests are placed opposite the adventuresses and the priestesses opposite the adventurers.

When the Head Fairy waves her wand a semi-bacchanalia gets underway. The members of both groups rush into each other's arms, and in the ensuing scramble caresses are liberally given and received. Everyone strokes and investigates whatever comes to hand and surrenders himself or herself to the unfettered impulses of simple nature. Each participant flits from one person to another, bestowing kisses everywhere with as much eagerness as rapidity. Everyone also makes a special point of encountering those individuals who caught his or her eye earlier. This brief bacchanalia allows people to verify the physical attributes of those to whom they are attracted, and it can lay the ground work for the establishment of sympathetic relationships between people who are more inclined to physical than spiritual pleasure.

It would be wrong, however, to suppose that this first confused skirmish exercises a decisive influence on the match-making that is to follow. Indeed, it would be bad form for anyone to make a binding commitment at the outset before formally encountering his designated sympathetic partners. People who have gotten together in the scramble will be able to renew their acquaintance later, and they will only love each other all the more if it turns out that their calculated sympathies, of which they are as yet unaware, are consistent with the preferences revealed in the bacchanalia.

Some of our civilized materialists might wish to conclude their investigations at this point. They would claim that this opening skirmish is all they need to make their choice. It will, in fact, be enough for monogynies dominated by the passion of touch; and they will not be prevented from forming sensual relationships with like-minded partners encountered during the bacchanalia. But such relationships, which are no more than simple amorous ties, deriving from purely physical affinities, will satisfy no more than a twentieth of the lovers in Harmony. . . . For the goal of Harmony is to establish compound amorous relationships based on both physical and spiritual affinities. Thus while the opening sensual skirmish is indispensable, it is only a prelude. It is the first phase in a process which moves, according to the law of progression, from the simple to the compound. Since nature's first thrust is always towards the physical, it would be contrary to the natural order of things to begin by occupying lovers with transcendent and spiritual illusions. The natural impulse should first be reinforced by a little opening bacchanalia, and then the sentiments should be brought into play with the help of the fairies. When sentimental inclinations are linked to the physical ties already established, pleasure will be compounded.

Let us return to our narrative. The opening caresses and exploratory activities should last no more than a few minutes, barely a quarter of an hour. To break up the skirmish, use should be made of a divisive agent. Since everything is done by attraction in Harmony, mixed or homosexual attractions should be employed. Groups of Sapphists and Spartites[9] should therefore be thrown into the fray to attack people of their own kind. Such people are easy to recognize in Harmony since everyone wears plumes or epaulettes designating his passions. These two new groups will create a general distraction and disunite a number of couples. At that point the senior confessors will have no difficulty in calling a halt to the skirmish, and everyone will proceed to the reconnoitering-room.

The reconnoitering-room contains two tiered and elevated stands. These stands face each other in such a way that anyone on one stand can get a good look at everyone on the other. All of the adventurers are placed on one side and all the sympathetic candidates on the other.

The actual matching is done by the matrons each of whom takes charge of five or six lovers. . . . The matrons point out the various partners who have been designated for each individual. The individual has been given a list with precise information concerning the spiritual affinities and temporary inclinations of each of his potential partners. He is also able to determine their physical attraction since they are right before his eyes and since he has perhaps already gotten acquainted with them during the introductory bacchanalia. . . .

When the inspection is over, everyone proceeds to the festival hall where the encounter takes place. The encounter is supervised by the fairies and genies whose tasks are much more delicate than those of the matrons. First of all there will be certain problems to resolve. A number of people may desire the same lover. A given priest may be desired by ten adventuresses and a given priestess by ten adventurers. Such conflicting claims would be very troublesome in civilized gatherings. . . . But anyone who has been in love several times knows that people often develop passionate spiritual sympathies for individuals who did not seem at all attractive to them at first. The whole point of the operations of the court of love is to determine these spiritual sympathies at the very outset in order to minimize competition for the most physically attractive individuals. Such competition leaves some people with throngs of admirers and leaves a great many other people in a state of abandonment.

In Harmony sheer physical attractiveness will not have the colossal influence that it has in civilization where everyone is transfixed by the sight of a beautiful woman. Of course the Harmonians will not fail to appreciate physical beauty; in fact their judgment will be considerably more discerning than ours. But when it comes to the selection of sympathetic partners their choices will not be determined by physical charm. For their desire for sensual gratification will be satisfied in several different ways.

First of all the adventurers will never fail to ask for an exhibition of simple nature, a session in which the amorous notabilities of the area, and of their own band, show off their most remarkable attributes. A woman who has only a beautiful bosom exhibits only the bosom and leaves the rest of her body covered. Another who has only an attractive waist bares it and leaves the rest covered. Another who wishes to exhibit everything she has appears completely naked. Men do the same. No one can say after this session that he has been denied a chance to admire all the physical attractions of the region.

In addition to this exhibition of simple nature, the visitors will be able to organize orgies to be held the following day. At these orgies, which will be appropriately harmonized, everyone will have ample opportunity to derive satisfaction from the beauties displayed at the exhibition.[10]

The physical needs of the adventurers are satisfied in this way at every Phalanx they visit. Given the human need for variety and contrast, the most pressing desire of the adventurers when they arrive at a new Phalanx will therefore be for spiritual sympathy rather than for mere physical gratification.

It should also be pointed out that if, at the end of a visit, an adventuress takes a fancy to a handsome priest with whom she has not made love, it will be possible for her to obtain satisfaction during the farewell session. Such gestures of traditional courtesy should not be refused to any member of a departing band.

As a result of these measures, no one will suffer from a lack of physical gratification. Thus the important problems to be dealt with at the court of love will concern the establishment of spiritual sympathies. . . . The encounters which take place in the festival hall will be run in an alternating pattern. First of all the adventurers and adventuresses will be taken by their fairies to meet the priests and priestesses whom they have chosen as their most desirable sympathetic partners. Then the priests and priestesses will go to meet the adventurers whom they have selected. No final decisions will be made until everyone has had a chance to converse with all his or her candidates. Everyone must have a chance to present himself to those he desires and to inspect the information recorded on their escutcheons concerning their personalities, their habits, current caprices, most recent passions, and their need of alternating and contrasting pleasures.

Little by little, as alliances are established, the group will grow smaller. The first and most rapid matchings will be dictated by romantic inspiration or by pure sensuality. But these sudden alliances may well be compound sympathies since everyone has already had the opportunity to study his list and to scrutinize his potential partners. . . . All those who are definitively matched up withdraw in order to permit the others to proceed with their encounters. Although it may be necessary for repeated enquiries to be made, this should be done without undue haste. Some alliances take a long time to form: preliminary discussions may go awry and a couple may only come to terms in the ballroom or even at supper. Such delays are commonplace among the more refined individuals.

Those who are the last to make up their minds do not run the risk of being left out or badly matched, for the fakirs may always intervene to satisfy them. But in general the tardy couples . . . get along particularly well because they have spent a long time flirting with each other. Moreover, if the sympathies which bind the tardy couples are somewhat lacking in intensity, their pleasures are always compound and never simple.

In all of these encounters great care is taken to avoid wounding anyone's pride. This is the particular responsibility of the fairies. Even when they are serving as protectors to just two individuals, they can make sure that no one's feelings are hurt. For if after a conversation one person wishes to refuse his or her suitor, the reason for the refusal is told only to the fairy who explains things to the rejected suitor with the utmost delicacy. The fairies abandon their proteges only when they are no longer needed, when two potential partners have established a sufficiently intimate relationship to reach an agreement of their own accord.

I have only described a single phase in the workings of the court of love. But it is already clear that in just two or three hours' time it can cement a host of happy alliances or compound sympathetic relationships of a sort that it takes months to establish in civilization. For it takes an extremely long time to understand the character of any civilized individual, and especially of a civilized woman.

The sympathetic intrigue which take place on the morning after the arrival of a group of visitors will be even more lively than those of the night before. For affairs which miscarried or failed to ripen will be renewed, and there will also be cases of infidelity to lend a touch of variety. The sympathetic relationships which endure will be particularly noteworthy in view of the fact that there will be many temptations to overcome. During a visit of three days almost all the adventurers and adventuresses will waver in their sympathies, finally returning to partners whom they barely got to know in the opening session. All this of course is quite independent of their participation in the orgies, the exposition of simple nature, the bacchanalias, etc. These material distractions are interludes in which both partners in a sympathetic relationship generally participate by mutual consent. They are moments of respite which do not destroy a relationship and which are not even considered to be acts of infidelity when they have been mutually agreed upon. Momentary respites of this sort are widely practiced in Harmony not only by sympathetic partners but also by the most faithful lovers. For on special occasions such as the visit of a band of adventurers . . . there are so many temptations that even the most faithful are likely to succumb. In order to avoid losing the privileges of fidelity they agree to break off their relationship for a stipulated period in accordance with the provision of the code of love. . . .

It is evident that the task of arranging sympathetic relationships cannot be assumed by young people. . . . Decisions must be made which can only be entrusted to elderly and experienced individuals. Without their cooperation a band of visitors would be reduced to forming brutish relationships like the dirty and dangerous orgies of civilization in which partners are chosen uniquely on the basis of simple love and physical attraction. . . .

Let us consider the benefits that the elderly will derive from their services as amorous intermediaries. The task will not be at all wearisome for them. A skilled and knowledgeable pontiff will take pride in his or her abilities as a match-maker. . . . It will also be common for a traveler to become passionately attached to his confessors. For apart from the fact that many individuals have an innate penchant for elderly people when they are agreeable, there will also be times when this penchant will be aroused by the methodical progression of sympathies. A skillful confessoress will manage to discern this need in the soul of her client and she will even try to call it forth. No one will be taken by surprise in such cases since, according to the custom of the court of love, the confessoress herself will be wearing medals or epaulettes indicating her own spiritual situation, her character, and her most recent impressions. Whenever the need for a sympathetic union between persons of divergent ages arises, it will be very much to the advantage of the confessors and confessoresses.

They say that no one does anything for nothing in this world; and if it is right for the elderly to assist the young in amorous affairs, it is just as right for them to be repaid for their services. . . . I cannot repeat too often, however, that customs so alien to ours cannot be established during the first years of Harmony. It will first be necessary to purge the globe of syphilis and other skin diseases. Until this is accomplished, Harmony will be more circumspect about love than civilization now is. (*OC*, 7:209–20)

# Notes

1. Fourier refers to the decade of fighting which followed the Negro rebellion led by Toussaint L'Ouverture at Haiti during the French Revolution.

2. According to the French electoral laws which prevailed in 1822, when this text was published, the right to vote was contingent upon the payment of at least 300 francs a year in direct taxes. To run for elective office a man had to pay at least 1000 francs in taxes. In all of France only 110,000 "electors" and 16,000 eligible office holders met these qualifications.

3. "Black care rides behind the horseman." Horace, *Odes* bk. III, i. 40.

4. Elsewhere (*OC,* 4:37) Fourier notes that drudge duty "will be assigned to a few individuals whose temperaments are appropriate to such tasks, which they will transform into games."

5. The Little Bands, most of whom were girls, were to provide material adornment and moral uplift in Harmony. Although their contribution was less essential than that of the Little Hordes, it should not be neglected. The following account of their functions is drawn from OC, 6:214–16:

"The Little Bands are the guardians of *social charm.* Their job is less spectacular than that of the Little Hordes, who are entrusted with the defense of *social harmony.* However, great importance is attached to finery and to collective luxury in the societary system, and the Little Bands make a valuable contribution in this domain. Their main function is the *physical and spiritual* adornment of the whole community. . . .

"Completely different in style from the Little Hordes, they are devotees of Attic restraint and purity. They are very polite; it is the girls rather than the boys who set the tone among them. . . . Only a third of the members of the Little Bands are boys, and they are the studious ones, the precocious scholars like Pascal, as well as those effeminate young lads who show early tendencies to indolence.

"Less active than the Little Hordes, the Little Bands are slower to rise and they do not get to the workshops until four o'clock in the morning. They wouldn't be needed earlier since they have little to do with the care of the larger animals. But they are devoted to those species which are difficult to raise and tame, such as passenger pigeons and other birds, beavers and zebras.

"The Little Bands have jurisdiction over the vegetable kingdom. Anyone who breaks a tree-branch, picks a forbidden flower or an unripe fruit, or accidentally steps on a plant is brought before the Senate of the Little Bands. This Senate renders judgment by virtue of a special penal code similar to the code of animal care which is enforced by the Divan of the Little Hordes.

"Entrusted with the spiritual and physical adornment of the community, the Little Bands perform academic functions similar to those of the French Academy. They censor bad language and faulty pronunciation. . . . The Senate of the Little Bands even has the right to censor literary works produced by adults. It draws up a list of the mistakes in grammar and pronunciation made by every member of the community and forwards the list to the guilty parties, advising them not to repeat the same mistakes. . . .

"Just as the Little Hordes have their Druids and Druidesses, the Little Bands have their own adult associates, who are known as Corybants. They also have their own allies among the groups of voyagers who travel about Harmony. Whereas the Little Hordes are allied to the big hordes of Adventurers and Adventuresses who belong to the industrial armies, the Little Bands are affiliated with the big bands of Knights and Ladies Errant who are dedicated to the fine arts."

6. On the industrial armies see below . . . .

7. On the Vestals see below . . . .

8. Young men and women between the ages of 15½ and 20.

9. Female and male homosexuals.

10. Elsewhere in *Le Nouveau monde amoureux* (*OC*, 7:329–32) Fourier discusses a variation on these proceedings: a type of "museum orgy" offering no more than visual gratification and designed to encourage the development of the aesthetic faculties of the Harmonians. His discussion concludes: "In civilization such meetings would be no more than bawdy gatherings because artistic taste and knowledge are not widespread. Our generation lacks the means to ennoble the amorous orgy, and especially the museum orgy. We are even more lacking in the general goodwill which will prevail among the Harmonians. Thus it is not surprising that the expression 'amorous orgy' evokes ideas of secret debauchery" (*OC*, 7:331).

# KARL MARX

## *Estranged Labor*[1]

Karl Marx (1818–83) is the foremost socialist thinker. The three selections from his writings included in this section span his so-called early humanistic and later scientific periods. "Estranged Labor," from *The Economic and Philosophical Manuscripts of 1844,* describes his theory of alienation under capitalism. *The Communist Manifesto* was written with his friend and collaborator Friedrich Engels for the Communist League on the eve of the revolutions of 1848. Although the failure of the revolutions forced them to revise some of its claims, Marx and Engels continued to regard it as the best single statement of their views. "Value, Price, and Profit" is a popular summary of the labor theory of value Marx develops in the three volumes of *Capital.* In his eulogy at Marx's funeral, Engels identified "the law of development of human history" and "the theory of surplus value" as Marx's great discoveries. These selections introduce you to both of them. Engels also correctly predicted that Marx's "name will endure through the ages, and so also will his work!"

We have proceeded from the premises of political economy. We have accepted its language and its laws. We presupposed private property, the separation of labor, capital and land, and of wages, profit of capital and rent of land—likewise division of labor, competition, the concept of exchange-value, etc. On the basis of political economy itself, in its own words, we have shown that the worker sinks to the level of a commodity and becomes indeed the most wretched of commodities; that the wretchedness of the worker is in inverse proportion to the power and magnitude of his production; that the necessary result of competition is the accumulation of capital in a few hands, and thus the restoration of monopoly in a more terrible form; and that finally the distinction between capitalist and land rentier, like that between the tiller of the soil and the factory worker, disappears and that the whole of society must fall apart into the two classes—the property *owners* and the propertyless *workers.*

Political economy starts with the fact of private property, but it does not explain it to us. It expresses in general, abstract formulas the *material* process through which private property actually passes, and these formulas it then takes for *laws*. It does not *comprehend* these laws, i.e., it does not demonstrate how they arise from the very nature of private property. Political economy does not disclose the source of the division between labor and capital, and between capital and land. When, for example, it defines the relationship of wages to profit, it takes the interest of the capitalists to be the ultimate cause, i.e., it takes for granted what it is supposed to explain. Similarly, competition comes in everywhere. It is explained from external circumstances. As to how far these external and apparently accidental circumstances are but the expression of a necessary course of development, political economy teaches us nothing. We have seen how exchange itself appears to it as an accidental fact. The only wheels which political economy sets in motion are *greed* and the war *amongst the greedy—competition.*

Precisely because political economy does not grasp the way the movement is connected, it was possible to oppose, for instance, the doctrine of competition to the doctrine of monopoly, the doctrine of the freedom of the crafts to the doctrine of the guild, the doctrine of the division of landed property to the doctrine of the big estate—for competition, freedom of the crafts and the division of landed property were explained and comprehended only as accidental, premeditated and violent consequences of monopoly, of the guild system, and of feudal property, not as their necessary, inevitable and natural consequences.

Now, therefore, we have to grasp the essential connection between private property, greed, and the separation of labor, capital and landed property; between exchange and competition, value and the devaluation of men, monopoly and competition, etc.—the connection between this whole estrangement and the *money* system.

Do not let us go back to a fictitious primordial condition as the political economist does, when he tries to explain. Such a primordial condition explains nothing; it merely pushes the question away into a gray nebulous distance. It assumes in the form of a fact, of an event, what the economist is supposed to deduce—namely, the necessary relationship between two things —between, for example, division of labor and exchange. Theology in the same way explains the origin of evil by the fall of man; that is, it assumes as a fact, in historical form, what has to be explained.

We proceed from an economic fact *of the present.*

The worker becomes all the poorer the more wealth he produces, the more his production increases in power and size. The worker becomes an ever cheaper commodity the more commodities he creates. With the *increasing value* of the world of things proceeds in direct proportion the *devaluation* of the world of men. Labor produces not only commodities: it produces itself and the worker as a *commodity*—and this in the same general proportion in which it produces commodities.

This fact expresses merely that the object which labor produces—labor's product—confronts it as *something alien*, as a *power independent* of the producer. The product of labor is labor which has been embodied in an object, which has become material: it is the *objectification*[2] of labor. Labor's realization is its objectification. In the sphere of political economy this realization of labor appears as *loss of realization*[3] for the workers; objectification as *loss of the object* and *bondage to it*; appropriation as *estrangement*, as *alienation*.[4]

So much does labor's realization appear as loss of realization that the worker loses realization to the point of starving to death. So much does objectification appear as loss of the object that the worker is robbed of the objects most necessary not only for his life but for his work. Indeed, labor itself becomes an object which he can obtain only with the greatest effort and with the most irregular interruptions. So much does the appropriation of the object appear as estrangement that the more objects the worker produces the less he can possess and the more he falls under the sway of his product, capital.

All these consequences result from the fact that the worker is related to the *product of his labor* as to an *alien* object. For on this premise it is clear that the more the worker spends himself, the more powerful becomes the alien world of objects which he creates over and against himself, the poorer he himself—his inner world—becomes, the less belongs to him as his own. It is the same in religion. The more man puts into God, the less he retains in himself. The worker puts his life into the object; but now his life no longer belongs to him but to the object. Hence, the greater this activity, the greater is the worker's lack of objects. Whatever the product of his labor is, he is not. Therefore the greater this product, the less is he himself. The *alienation* of the worker in his product means not only that his labor becomes an object, an *external* existence, but that it exists *outside him*, independently, as something alien to him, and that it becomes a power on its own confronting him. It means that the life which he has conferred on the object confronts him as something hostile and alien.

Let us now look more closely at the *objectification*, at the production of the worker; and in it at the *estrangement*, the *loss* of the object, of his product.

The worker can create nothing without *nature*, without the *sensuous external world*.[5] It is the material on which his labor is realized, in which it is active, from which and by means of which it produces.

But just as nature provides labor with the *means of life* in the sense that labor cannot *live* without objects on which to operate, on the other hand, it also provides the *means of life* in the more restricted sense, i.e., the means for the physical subsistence of the *worker* himself.

Thus the more the worker by his labor *appropriates* the external world, hence sensuous nature, the more he deprives himself of *means of life* in a double manner: first, in that the sensuous external world more and more ceases to be an object belonging to his labor—to be his labor's *means of life;* and secondly, in that it more and more ceases to be *means of life* in the immediate sense, means for the physical subsistence of the worker.

In both respects, therefore, the worker becomes a slave of his object, first, in that he receives an *object of labor,* i.e., in that he receives *work;* and secondly, in that he receives *means of subsistence.* Therefore, it enables him to exist, first, as a *worker;* and, second, as a *physical subject.* The height of this bondage is that it is only as a worker that he continues to maintain himself as a *physical subject,* and that it is only as a physical subject that he is a *worker.*

(The laws of political economy express the estrangement of the worker in his object thus: the more the worker produces, the less he has to consume; the more values he creates, the more valueless, the more unworthy he becomes; the better formed his product, the more deformed becomes the worker; the more civilized his object, the more barbarous becomes the worker; the more powerful labor becomes, the more powerless becomes the worker; the more ingenious labor becomes, the less ingenious becomes the worker and the more he becomes nature's bondsman.)

*Political economy conceals the estrangement inherent in the nature of labor by not considering the direct relationship between the worker* (labor) *and production.* It is true that labor produces for the rich wonderful things—but for the worker it produces privation. It produces palaces—but for the worker, hovels. It produces beauty but for the worker, deformity. It replaces labor by machines, but it throws a section of the workers back to a barbarous type of labor, and it turns the other workers into machines. It produces intelligence —but for the worker stupidity, cretinism.

*The direct relationship of labor to its products is the relationship of the worker to the objects of his production.* The relationship of the man of means to the objects of production and to production itself is only a *consequence* of this first relationship—and confirms it. We shall consider this other aspect later.

When we ask, then, what is the essential relationship of labor we are asking about the relationship of the *worker* to production.

Till now we have been considering the estrangement, the alienation of the worker only in one of its aspects, i.e., the worker's *relationship to the products of his labor.* But the estrangement is manifested not only in the result but in the *act of production,* within the *producing activity,* itself. How could the worker come to face the product of his activity as a stranger, were it not that in the very act of production he was estranging himself from himself? The product is after all but the summary of the activity, of production. If then the product of labor is alienation, production itself must be active alienation, the alienation of activity, the activity of alienation. In the estrangement of the object of labor is merely summarized the estrangement, the alienation, in the activity of labor itself.

What, then, constitutes the alienation of labor?

First, the fact that labor is *external* to the worker, i.e., it does not belong to his essential being; that in his work, therefore, he does not affirm himself but denies himself, does not feel content but unhappy, does not develop freely his physical and mental energy but mortifies his body and ruins his mind. The worker therefore only feels himself outside his work, and in his work feels outside himself. He is at home when he is not working, and when he is working he is not at home. His labor is therefore not voluntary, but coerced; it is *forced labor*. It is therefore not the satisfaction of a need; it is merely a *means* to satisfy needs external to it. Its alien character emerges clearly in the fact that as soon as no physical or other compulsion exists, labor is shunned like the plague. External labor, labor in which man alienates himself, is a labor of self-sacrifice, of mortification. Lastly, the external character of labor for the worker appears in the fact that it is not his own, but someone else's, that it does not belong to him, that in it he belongs, not to himself, but to another. Just as in religion the spontaneous activity of the human imagination, of the human brain and the human heart, operates independently of the individual—that is, operates on him as an alien, divine or diabolical activity—so is the worker's activity not his spontaneous activity. It belongs to another; it is the loss of his self.

As a result, therefore, man (the worker) only feels himself freely active in his animal functions—eating, drinking, procreating, or at most in his dwelling and in dressing-up, etc.; and in his human functions he no longer feels himself to be anything but an animal. What is animal becomes human and what is human becomes animal.

Certainly eating, drinking, procreating, etc., are also genuinely human functions. But abstractly taken, separated from the sphere of all other human activity and turned into sole and ultimate ends, they are animal functions.

We have considered the act of estranging practical human activity, labor, in two of its aspects.

1. The relation of the worker to the *product of labor* as an alien object exercising power over him. This relation is at the same time the relation to the sensuous external world, to the objects of nature, as an alien world inimically opposed to him.

2. The relation of labor to the *act of production* within the *labor* process. This relation is the relation of the worker to his own activity as an alien activity not belonging to him; it is activity as suffering, strength as weakness, begetting as emasculating, the worker's *own* physical and mental energy, his personal life indeed, what is life but activity?—as an activity which is turned against him, independent of him and not belonging to him. Here we have *self-estrangement*, as previously we had the estrangement of the *thing*.

We have still a third aspect of *estranged labor* to deduce from the two already considered.

Man is a species being,[6] not only because in practice and in theory he adopts the species as his object (his own as well as those of other things), but—and this is only another way of expressing it—also because he treats himself as the actual, living species; because he treats himself as a *universal* and therefore a free being.

The life of the species, both in man and in animals, consists physically in the fact that man (like the animal) lives on inorganic nature; and the more universal man is compared with an animal, the more universal is the sphere of inorganic nature on which he lives. Just as plants, animals, stones, air, light, etc., constitute theoretically a part of human consciousness, partly as objects of natural science, partly as objects of art—his spiritual inorganic nature, spiritual nourishment which he must first prepare to make palatable and digestible—so also in the realm of practice they constitute a part of human life and human activity. Physically man lives only on these products of nature, whether they appear in the form of food, heating, clothes, a dwelling, etc. The universality of man appears in practice precisely in the universality which makes all nature his *inorganic* body—both inasmuch as nature is (1) his direct means of life, and (2) the material, the object, and the instrument of his life activity. Nature is man's *inorganic body*—nature, that is, in so far as it is not itself the human body. Man *lives* on nature—means that nature is his *body*, with which he must remain in continuous interchange if he is not to die. That man's physical and spiritual life is linked to nature means simply that nature is linked to itself, for man is a part of nature.

In estranging from man (1) nature, and (2) himself, his own active functions, his life activity, estranged labor estranges the *species* from man. It changes for him the *life of the species* into a means of individual life. First it estranges the life of the species and individual life, and secondly it makes individual life in its abstract form the purpose of the life of the species, likewise in its abstract and estranged form.

Indeed, labor, *life-activity, productive life* itself, appears in the first place merely as a *means* of satisfying a need—the need to maintain physical existence. Yet the productive life is the life of the species. It is life-engendering life. The whole character of a species—its species character—is contained in the character of its life activity; and free, conscious activity is man's species character. Life itself appears only as a *means to life.*

The animal is immediately one with its life activity. It does not distinguish itself from it. It is *its life activity.* Man makes his life activity itself the object of his will and of his consciousness. He has conscious life activity. It is not a determination with which he directly merges. Conscious life activity distinguishes man immediately from animal life activity. It is just because of this that he is a species being. Or rather, it is only because he is a species being that he is a conscious being, i.e., that his own life is an  object for him. Only be cause of that is his activity free activity. Estranged labor reverses this relationship, so that it is just because man is a conscious being that he makes his life activity, his *essential* being, a mere means to his *existence.*

In creating a *world of objects*[7] by his practical activity, in *his work upon* inorganic nature, man proves himself a conscious species being, i.e., as a being that treats the species as its own essential being, or that treats itself as a species being. Admittedly animals also produce. They build themselves nests, dwellings, like the bees, beavers, ants, etc. But an animal only produces what it immediately needs for itself or its young. It produces one-sidedly, whilst man produces universally. It produces only under the dominion of immediate physical need, whilst man produces even when he is free from physical need and only truly produces in freedom therefrom. An animal produces only itself, whilst man reproduces the whole of nature. An animal's product belongs immediately to its physical body, whilst man freely confronts his product. An animal forms things in accordance with the standard and the need of the species to which it belongs, whilst man knows how to produce in accordance with the standard of every species, and knows how to apply everywhere the inherent standard to the object. Man therefore also forms things in accordance with the laws of beauty.

It is just in his work upon the objective world, therefore, that man first really proves himself to be a *species being.* This production is his active species life. Through and because of this production, nature appears as *his* work and his reality. The object of labor is, therefore, the *objectification of man's species life:* for he duplicates himself not only, as in consciousness, intellectually, but also actively, in reality, and therefore he contemplates himself in a world that he has created. In tearing away from man the object of his production, therefore, estranged labor tears from him his *species life,* his real objectivity as a member of the species and transforms his advantage over animals into the disadvantage that his inorganic body, nature, is taken away from him.

Similarly, in degrading spontaneous, free, activity, to a means, estranged labor makes man's species life a means to his physical existence.

The consciousness which man has of his species is thus transformed by estrangement in such a way that species life becomes for him a means.

Estranged labor turns thus:

3. *Man's species being,* both nature and his spiritual species property, into a being *alien* to him, into a *means* to his *individual existence.* It estranges from man his own body, as well as external nature and his spiritual essence, his *human* being.

4. An immediate consequence of the fact that man is estranged from the product of his labor, from his life activity, from his species being is the *estrangement of man* from *man.* When man confronts himself, he confronts the *other* man. What applies to a man's relation to his work, to the product of his

labor and to himself, also holds of a man's relation to the other man, and to the other man's labor and object of labor.

In fact, the proposition that man's species nature is estranged from him means that one man is estranged from the other, as each of them is from man's essential nature.

The estrangement of man, and in fact every relationship in which man stands to himself, is first realized and expressed in the relationship in which a man stands to other men.

Hence within the relationship of estranged labor each man views the other in accordance with the standard and the relationship in which he finds himself as a worker.

We took our departure from a fact of political economy—the estrangement of the worker and his production. We have formulated this fact in conceptual terms as *estranged, alienated* labor. We have analyzed this concept —hence analyzing merely a fact of political economy.

Let us now see, further, how the concept of estranged, alienated labor must express and present itself in real life.

If the product of labor is alien to me, if it confronts me as an alien power, to whom, then, does it belong?

If my own activity does not belong to me, if it is an alien, a coerced activity, to whom, then, does it belong?

To a being *other* than myself.

Who is this being?

The *gods*? To be sure, in the earliest times the principal production (for example, the building of temples, etc., in Egypt, India and Mexico) appears to be in the service of the gods, and the product belongs to the gods. However, the gods on their own were never the lords of labor. No more was *nature*. And what a contradiction it would be if, the more man subjugated nature by his labor and the more the miracles of the gods were rendered superfluous by the miracles of industry, the more man were to renounce the joy of production and the enjoyment of the product in favor of these powers.

The *alien* being, to whom labor and the product of labor belongs, in whose service labor is done and for whose benefit the product of labor is provided, can only be *man* himself.

If the product of labor does not belong to the worker, if it confronts him as an alien power, then this can only be because it belongs to some *other man than the worker*. If the worker's activity is a torment to him, to another it must be *delight* and his life's joy. Not the gods, not nature, but only man himself can be this alien power over man.

We must bear in mind the previous proposition that man's relation to himself only becomes for him *objective* and *actual*[8] through his relation to the other man. Thus, if the product of his labor, his labor *objectified*, is for him an *alien*, hostile, powerful object independent of him, then his position towards it is such that someone else is master of this object, someone who is alien, hostile, powerful, and independent of him. If his own activity is to him related as an unfree activity, then he is related to it as an activity performed in the service, under the dominion, the coercion, and the yoke of another man.

Every self-estrangement of man, from himself and from nature, appears in the relation in which he places himself and nature to men other than and differentiated from himself. For this reason religious self-estrangement necessarily appears in the relationship of the layman to the priest, or again to a mediator, etc., since we are here dealing with the intellectual world. In the real practical world self-estrangement can only become manifest through the real practical relationship to other men. The medium through which estrangement takes place is itself *practical*. Thus through estranged labor man not only creates his relationship to the object and to the act of production as to men that are alien and hostile to him; he also creates the relationship in which other men stand to his production and to his product, and the relationship in which he stands to these other men. Just as he creates his own production as the loss of his reality, as his punishment; his own product as a loss, as a product not belonging to him; so he creates the domination of the person who does not produce over production and over the product. Just as he estranges his own activity from himself, so he confers to the stranger an activity which is not his own.

We have until now only considered this relationship from the standpoint of the worker and later we shall be considering it also from the standpoint of the non-worker.

Through *estranged, alienated labor,* then, the worker produces the relationship to this labor of a man alien to labor and standing outside it. The relationship of the worker to labor created the relation to it of the capitalist (or whatever one chooses to call the master of labor). *Private property* is thus the product, the result, the necessary consequence, of *alienated labor,* of the external relation of the worker to nature and to himself.

*Private property* thus results by analysis from the concept of *alienated labor,* i.e., of *alienated man,* of estranged labor, of estranged life, of *estranged* man.

True, it is as a result of the *movement of private property* that we have obtained the concept of *alienated labor (of alienated life)* from political economy. But on analysis of this concept it becomes clear that though private property appears to be the source, the cause of alienated labor, it is rather its consequence, just as the gods are *originally* not the cause but the effect of man's intellectual confusion. Later this relationship becomes reciprocal.

Only at the last culmination of the development of private property does this, its secret, appear again, namely, that on the one hand it is the *product* of alienated labor, and that on the other it is the *means* by which labor alienates itself, the *realization of this alienation.*

This exposition immediately sheds light on various hitherto unsolved conflicts.

1. Political economy starts from labor as the real soul of production; yet to labor it gives nothing, and to private property everything. Confronting this contradiction, [Pierre-Joseph] Proudhon has decided in favor of labor against private property. We understand, however, that this apparent contradiction is the contradiction of *estranged labor* with itself, and that political economy has merely formulated the laws of estranged labor.

We also understand, therefore, that *wages* and *private property* are identical: since the product, as the object of labor pays for labor itself, therefore the wage is but a necessary consequence of labor's estrangement. After all, in the wage of labor, labor does not appear as an end in itself but as the servant of the wage. We shall develop this point later, and meanwhile will only derive some conclusions.[9]

*An enforced increase of wages* (disregarding all other difficulties, including the fact that it would only be by force, too, that higher wages, being an anomaly, could be maintained) would therefore be nothing but *better payment for the slave*, and would not win either for the worker or for labor their human status and dignity.

Indeed, even the *equality of wages* demanded by Proudhon only transforms the relationship of the present-day worker to his labor into the relationship of all men to labor. Society is then conceived as an abstract capitalist.

Wages are a direct consequence of estranged labor, and estranged labor is the direct cause of private property. The downfall of the one must involve the downfall of the other.

2. From the relationship of estranged labor to private property it follows further that the emancipation of society from private property, etc., from servitude, is expressed in the *political* form of the *emancipation of the workers;* not that *their* emancipation alone is at stake, but because the emancipation of the workers contains universal human emancipation—and it contains this, because the whole of human servitude is involved in the relation of the worker to production, and every relation of servitude is but a modification and consequence of this relation.

Just as we have derived the concept of *private property* from the concept of *estranged, alienated labor* by *analysis,* so we can develop every *category* of political economy with the help of these two factors; and we shall find again in each category, e.g., trade, competition, capital, money, only a *definite* and *developed expression* of these first elements.

Before considering this aspect, however, let us try to solve two problems.

1. To define the general *nature of private property,* as it has arisen as a result of estranged labor, in its relation to truly *human* and *social property.*

2. We have accepted the *estrangement of labor,* its *alienation,* as a fact, and we have analyzed this fact. How, we now ask, does *man* come to *alienate,* to

estrange, *his labor*? How is this estrangement rooted in the nature of human development? We have already gone a long way to the solution of this problem by *transforming* the question of the *origin of private property* into the question of the relation of *alienated labor* to the course of humanity's development. For when one speaks of *private property*, one thinks of dealing with something external to man. When one speaks of labor, one is directly dealing with man himself. This new formulation of the question already contains its solution.

*As to (1): The general nature of private property and its relation to truly human property.*

Alienated labor has resolved itself for us into two elements which mutually condition one another, or which are but different expressions of one and the same relationship. *Appropriation* appears as *estrangement, as alienation;* and *alienation* appears as *appropriation, estrangement* as true introduction into society.[10]

We have considered the one side—*alienated* labor in relation to the *worker* himself, i.e., the *relation of alienated labor to itself.* The *property relation of the non-worker to the worker and to labor* we have found as the product, the necessary outcome of this relationship. *Private property,* as the material, summary expression of alienated labor, embraces both relations—the *relation of the worker to work and to the product of his labor and to the non-worker,* and the relation of the *non-worker to the worker and to the product of his labor.*

Having seen that in relation to the worker who *appropriates* nature by means of his labor, this appropriation appears as estrangement, his own spontaneous activity as activity for another and as activity of another, vitality as a sacrifice of life, production of the object as loss of the object to an alien power, to an *alien* person—we shall now consider the relation to the worker, to labor and its object of this person who is *alien* to labor and the worker.

First it has to be noted that everything which appears in the worker as an *activity of alienation, of estrangement,* appears in the non-worker as a *state of alienation, of estrangement.*

Secondly, that the worker's *real, practical attitude* in production and to the product (as a state of mind) appears in the non-worker confronting him as a *theoretical* attitude.

*Thirdly,* the non-worker does everything against the worker which the worker does against himself; but he does not do against himself what he does against the worker.

Let us look more closely at these three relations.

[*At this point the first manuscript breaks off unfinished.*]

# Notes

1. Estranged Labor—*Die Entfremdete Arbeit.*

2. Objectification, *Vergegenständlichung:* the process of becoming an object.

3. Loss of realization, *Entwirklichung.* A better translation might be "devaluation." Marx, in true Hegel fashion, opposes *Verwirklichung,* here translated as *realization,* to *Entwirklichung,* the taking away of reality. Here *realization* is meant as accomplishment, performance, making something real. Marx states that the accomplishment of labor turns into its opposite.

4. Alienation, *Entäusserung.*

5. Sensuous, *sinnlich:* what can be observed by means of the senses.

6. Species being, *Gattungswesen,* a term used by Feuerbach, who takes as the *Gattung* mankind as a whole, hence the human species.

Species nature (just like species being), *Gattungswesen:* man's essential nature, *menschliches Wesen.*

The following passages from Feuerbach's *Essence of Christianity* may help readers to understand the ideological background to this part of Marx's thought, and, incidentally, to see how Marx accepted but infused with new content concepts made current by Feuerbach as well as by Hegel and the political economists:

"What is this essential difference between man and the brute? . . . Consciousness—but consciousness in the strict sense; for the consciousness implied in the feeling of self as an individual, in discrimination by the senses, in the perception and even judgment of outward things according to definite sensible signs, cannot be denied to the brutes. Consciousness in the strictest sense is present only in a being to whom his species, his essential nature, is an object of thought. The brute is indeed conscious of himself as an individual—and he has accordingly the feeling of self as the common center of successive sensations—but not as a species. . . . In practical life we have to do with individuals; in science, with species. . . . But only a being to whom his own species, his own nature, is an object of thought, can make the essential nature of other things or beings an object of thought. . . . The brute has only a simple, man a twofold life; in the brute, the inner life is one with the outer. Man has both an inner and an outer life. The inner life of man is the life which has relation to his species—to his general, as distinguished from his individual nature. . . . The brute can exercise no function which has relation to its species without another individual external to itself; but man can perform the functions of thought and speech, which strictly imply such a relation, apart from another individual. . . . Man is in fact at once I and Thou; he can put himself in the place of another, for his reason, that to him his species, his essential nature, and not merely his individuality, is an object of thought. . . . An object to which a subject essentially, necessarily relates, is nothing else than this subject's own, but objective nature. . . ."

"The relation of the sun to the earth is, therefore, at the same time a relation of the earth to itself, or to its own nature, for the measure of the size and of the intensity of light which the sun possesses as the object of the earth, is the measure of the distance, which determines the peculiar nature of the earth. . . . In the object which he contemplates, therefore, man becomes acquainted with himself. . . . The power of the object over him is therefore the power of his own nature." (*The Essence of Christianity,* by Ludwig Feuerbach, translated from the second German edition by Marian Evans, London, 1854, pp. 1–5.)

7. Marx's term *gegenständlich* can be translated by "objective," but what is meant is an adjective belonging to *Gegenstand,* object. We believe that *gegenständliche Welt* may be rendered best by "world of objects."

8. *Gegenständlich, wirklich,* in Marx, see previous note. Just as *gegenständlich* belongs

to *Gegenstand,* so does *wirklich* belong to *Wirken,* to work. A better translation might be: "man's relation to himself only becomes for him a relation of objects and of work."

9. This obscure sentence becomes somewhat more intelligible, if we remember that in Hegelian terminology "identity" often stands for "unity." There is, Marx seems to say, a unity of opposites between wages and private property, since wages result in private property, and private property is the result of the wage system. Labor, in this process, plays only a mediating role: wages and property are the real poles.

10. Marx calls estrangement *die wahre Einbürgerung.* This means "truly becoming a part of society." The sentence seems to mean that alienation is the key to society.

# KARL MARX AND FRIEDRICH ENGELS

## *The Communist Manifesto*

A spectre is haunting Europe—the spectre of Communism. All the Powers of old Europe have entered into a holy alliance to exorcize this spectre: Pope and Czar, Metternich and Guizot, French Radicals and German policy spies.

Where is the party in opposition that has not been decried as Communistic by its opponents in power? Where the Opposition that has not hurled back the branding reproach of Communism, against the more advanced opposition parties as well as against its reactionary adversaries?

Two things result from this fact:

I. Communism is already acknowledged by all European Powers to be itself a Power.

II. It is high time that Communists should openly, in the face of the whole world, publish their views, their aims, their tendencies, and meet this nursery tale of the Spectre of Communism with a Manifesto of the party itself.

To this end, Communists of various nationalities have assembled in London, and sketched the following Manifesto, to be published in the English, French, German, Italian, Flemish and Danish languages.

## Bourgeois and Proletarians*

The history of all hitherto existing society† is the history of class struggles.

Freeman and slave, patrician and plebeian, lord and serf, guild-master

---

\* By bourgeoisie is meant the class of modern Capitalists, owners of the means of social production and employers of wage labor. By proletariat, the class of modern wage-laborers who, having no means of production of their own, are reduced to selling their labor power in order to live. [Note by Engels to the English edition of 1888.]

† That is, all *written* history. In 1847, the pre-history of society, the social organi-

and journeyman, in a word, oppressor and oppressed, stood in constant opposition to one another, carried on an uninterrupted, now hidden, now open fight, a fight that each time ended, either in a revolutionary reconstitution of society at large, or in the common ruin of the contending classes.

In the earlier epochs of history, we find almost everywhere a complicated arrangement of society into various orders, a manifold gradation of social rank. In ancient Rome we have patricians, knights, plebeians, slaves; in the Middle Ages, feudal lords, vassals, guild-masters, journeymen, apprentices, serfs; in almost all of these classes, again, subordinate gradations.

The modern bourgeois society that has sprouted from the ruins of feudal society has not done away with class antagonisms. It has but established new classes, new conditions of oppression, new forms of struggle in place of the old ones.

Our epoch, the epoch of the bourgeoisie, possesses, however, this distinctive feature: it has simplified the class antagonisms. Society as a whole is more and more splitting up into two great hostile camps, into two great classes directly facing each other: Bourgeoisie and Proletariat.

From the serfs of the Middle Ages sprang the chartered burghers of the earliest towns. From these burgesses the first elements of the bourgeoisie were developed.

The discovery of America, the rounding of the Cape, opened up fresh ground for the rising bourgeoisie. The East-Indian and Chinese markets, the colonization of America, trade with the colonies, the increase in the means of exchange and in commodities generally, gave to commerce, to navigation, to industry, an impulse never before known, and thereby, to the revolutionary element in the tottering feudal society, a rapid development.

The feudal system of industry, under which industrial production was monopolized by closed guilds, now no longer sufficed for the growing wants of the new markets. The manufacturing system took its place. The guild-masters were pushed on one side by the manufacturing middle class; division of labour between the different corporate guilds vanished in the face of division of labour in each single workshop.

Meantime the markets kept ever growing, the demand ever rising. Even

zation existing previous to recorded history, was all but unknown. Since then, Haxthausen discovered common ownership of land in Russia, Maurer proved it to be the social foundation from which all Teutonic races started in history, and by and by village communities were found to be, or to have been the primitive form of society everywhere from India to Ireland. The inner organization of this primitive Communistic society was laid bare, in its typical form, by Morgan's crowning discovery of the true nature of the *gens* and its relation to the tribe. With the dissolution of these primeval communities society begins to be differentiated into separate and finally antagonistic classes. I have attempted to retrace this process of dissolution in: *Der Ursprung der Familie, des Privateigenthums und des Staats* (*The Origin of the Family, Private Property and the State*), 2d edition, Stuttgart 1886. [Note by Engels to the English edition of 1888.]

manufacture no longer sufficed. Thereupon, steam and machinery revolution-ized industrial production. The place of manufacture was taken by the giant, Modern Industry, the place of the industrial middle class, by industrial mil-lionaires, the leaders of whole industrial armies, the modern bourgeois.

Modern industry has established the world market, for which the discovery of America paved the way. This market has given an immense development to commerce, to navigation, to communication by land. This development has, in its turn, reacted on the extension of industry; and in proportion as indus-try, commerce, navigation, railways extended, in the same proportion the bourgeoisie developed, increased its capital, and pushed into the background every class handed down from the Middle Ages.

We see, therefore, how the modern bourgeoisie is itself the product of a long course of development, of a series of revolutions in the modes of produc-tion and of exchange.

Each step in the development of the bourgeoisie was accompanied by a corresponding political advance of that class. An oppressed class under the sway of the feudal nobility, an armed and self-governing association in the me-dieval commune; here independent urban republic (as in Italy and Germany), there taxable "third estate" of the monarchy (as in France), afterwards, in the period of manufacture proper, serving either the semi-feudal or the absolute monarchy as a counterpoise against the nobility, and, in fact, corner-stone of the great monarchies in general, the bourgeoisie has at last, since the establish-ment of Modern Industry and of the world market, conquered for itself, in the modern representative State, exclusive political sway. The executive of the modern State is but a committee for managing the common affairs of the whole bourgeoisie.

The bourgeoisie, historically, has played a most revolutionary part.

The bourgeoisie, wherever it has got the upper hand, has put an end to all feudal, patriarchal, idyllic relations. It has pitilessly torn asunder the motley feudal ties that bound man to his "natural superiors," and has left remaining no other nexus between man and man than naked self-interest, than callous "cash payment." It has drowned the most heavenly ecstasies of religious fervour, of chivalrous enthusiasm, of philistine sentimentalism, in the icy wa-ter of egotistical calculation. It has resolved personal worth into exchange value, and in place of the numberless indefeasible chartered freedoms, has set up that single, unconscionable freedom—Free Trade. In one word, for exploi-tation, veiled by religious and political illusions, it has substituted naked, shameless, direct, brutal exploitation.

The bourgeoisie has stripped of its halo every occupation hitherto hon-oured and looked up to with reverent awe. It has converted the physician, the lawyer, the priest, the poet, the man of science, into its paid wage-labourers.

The bourgeoisie has torn away from the family its sentimental veil, and has reduced the family relation to a mere money relation.

The bourgeoisie has disclosed how it came to pass that the brutal display of vigour in the Middle Ages, which Reactionists so much admire, found its fitting complement in the most slothful indolence. It has been the first to show what man's activity can bring about. It has accomplished wonders far surpassing Egyptian pyramids, Roman aqueducts, and Gothic cathedrals; it has conducted expeditions that put in the shade all former Exoduses of nations and crusades.

The bourgeoisie cannot exist without constantly revolutionizing the instruments of production, and thereby the relations of production, and with them the whole relations of society. Conservation of the old modes of production in unaltered form, was, on the contrary, the first condition of existence for all earlier industrial classes. Constant revolutionizing of production, uninterrupted disturbance of all social conditions, everlasting uncertainty and agitation distinguish the bourgeois epoch from all earlier ones. All fixed, fast-frozen relations, with their train of ancient and venerable prejudices and opinions are swept away, all new-formed ones become antiquated before they can ossify. All that is solid melts into air, all that is holy is profaned, and man is at last compelled to face with sober senses, his real conditions of life, and his relations with his kind.

The need of a constantly expanding market of its products chases the bourgeoisie over the whole surface of the globe. It must nestle everywhere, settle everywhere, establish connexions everywhere.

The bourgeoisie has through its exploitation of the world market given a cosmopolitan character to production and consumption in every country. To the great chagrin of Reactionists, it has drawn from under the feet of industry the national ground on which it stood. All old-established national industries have been destroyed or are daily being destroyed. They are dislodged by new industries, whose introduction becomes a life and death question for all civilized nations, by industries that no longer work up indigenous raw material, but raw material drawn from the remotest zones; industries whose products are consumed, not only at home, but in every quarter of the globe. In place of the old wants, satisfied by the productions of the country, we find new wants, requiring for their satisfaction the products of distant lands and climes. In place of the old local and national seclusion and self-sufficiency, we have intercourse in every direction, universal inter-dependence of nations. And as in material, so also in intellectual production. The intellectual creations of individual nations become common property. National one-sidedness and narrow-mindedness become more and more impossible, and from the numerous national and local literatures, there arises a world literature.

The bourgeoisie, by the rapid improvement of all instruments of production, by the immensely facilitated means of communication, draws all, even the most barbarian, nations into civilization. The cheap prices of its commodities are the heavy artillery with which it batters down all Chinese walls, with which it forces the barbarians' intensely obstinate hatred of foreigners to capitulate. It compels all nations, on pain of extinction, to adopt the bourgeois mode of production; it compels them to introduce what it calls civilization into their midst, i.e., to become bourgeois themselves. In one word, it creates a world after its own image.

The bourgeoisie has subjected the country to the rule of the towns. It has created enormous cities, has greatly increased the urban population as compared with the rural, and has thus rescued a considerable part of the population from the idiocy of rural life. Just as it has made the country dependent on the towns, so it has made barbarian and semi-barbarian countries dependent on the civilized ones, nations of peasants on nations of bourgeois, the East on the West.

The bourgeoisie keeps more and more doing away with the scattered state of the population, of the means of production, and of property. It has agglomerated population, centralized means of production, and has concentrated property in a few hands. The necessary consequence of this was political centralization. Independent, or but loosely connected, provinces with separate interests, laws, governments and systems of taxation, became lumped together into one nation, with one government, one code of laws, one national class-interest, one frontier and one customs-tariff.

The bourgeoisie, during its rule of scarce one hundred years, has created more massive and more colossal productive forces than have all preceding generations together. Subjection of Nature's forces to man, machinery, application of chemistry to industry and agriculture, steam-navigation, railways, electric telegraphs, clearing of whole continents for cultivation, canalization of rivers, whole populations conjured out of the ground—what earlier century had even a presentiment that such productive forces slumbered in the lap of social labour?

We see then: the means of production and of exchange, on whose foundation the bourgeoisie built itself up, were generated in feudal society. At a certain stage in the development of these means of production and of exchange, the conditions under which feudal society produced and exchanged, the feudal organization of agriculture and manufacturing industry, in one word, the feudal relations of property became no longer compatible with the already developed productive forces; they became so many fetters. They had to be burst asunder; they were burst asunder.

Into their place stepped free competition, accompanied by a social and political constitution adapted to it, and by the economical and political sway of the bourgeois class.

A similar movement is going on before our own eyes. Modern bourgeois society with its relations of production, of exchange and of property, a society that has conjured up such gigantic means of production and of exchange, is like the sorcerer, who is no longer able to control the powers of the nether world whom he has called up by his spells. For many a decade past the history of industry and commerce is but the history of the revolt of modern productive forces against modern conditions of production, against the property relations that are the conditions for the existence of the bourgeoisie and of its rule. It is enough to mention the commercial crises that by their periodical return put on its trial, each time more threateningly, the existence of the entire bourgeois society. In these crises a great part not only of the existing products, but also of the previously created productive forces, are periodically destroyed. In these crises there breaks out an epidemic that, in all earlier epochs, would have seemed an absurdity—the epidemic of overproduction. Society suddenly finds itself put back into a state of momentary barbarism; it appears as if a famine, a universal war of devastation had cut off the supply of every means of subsistence; industry and commerce seem to be destroyed; and why? Because there is too much civilization, too much means of subsistence, too much industry, too much commerce. The productive forces at the disposal of society no longer tend to further the development of the conditions of bourgeois property; on the contrary, they have become too powerful for these conditions, by which they are fettered, and so soon as they overcome these fetters, they bring disorder into the whole of bourgeois society, endanger the existence of bourgeois property. The conditions of bourgeois society are too narrow to comprise the wealth created by them. And how does the bourgeoisie get over these crises? On the one hand by enforced destruction of a mass of productive forces; on the other, by the conquest of new markets, and by the more thorough exploitation of the old ones. That is to say, by paving the way for more extensive and more destructive crises, and by diminishing the means whereby crises are prevented.

The weapons with which the bourgeoisie felled feudalism to the ground are now turned against the bourgeoisie itself.

But not only has the bourgeoisie forged the weapons that bring death to itself; it has also called into existence the men who are to wield those weapons —the modern working class—the proletarians.

In proportion as the bourgeoisie, i.e., capital, is developed, in the same proportion is the proletariat, the modern working class, developed—a class of labourers, who live only so long as they find work, and who find work only so long as their labour increases capital. These labourers, who must sell themselves piecemeal, are a commodity, like every other article of commerce, and are consequently exposed to all the vicissitudes of competition, to all the fluctuations of the market.

Owing to the extensive use of machinery and to division of labour, the work of the proletarians has lost all individual character, and, consequently, all charm for the workman. He becomes an appendage of the machine, and it is only the most simple, most monotonous, and most easily acquired knack, that is required of him. Hence, the cost of production of a workman is restricted,

almost entirely, to the means of subsistence that he requires for his maintenance, and for the propagation of his race. But the price of a commodity, and
therefore also of labour, is equal to its cost of production. In proportion,
therefore, as the repulsiveness of the work increases, the wage decreases. Nay
more, in proportion as the use of machinery and division of labour increases,
in the same proportion the burden of toil also increases, whether by prolongation of the working hours, by increase of the work exacted in a given time or
by increased speed of the machinery, etc.

Modern industry has converted the little workshop of the patriarchal
master into the great factory of the industrial capitalist. Masses of labourers,
crowded into the factory, are organized like soldiers. As privates of the industrial army they are placed under the command of a perfect hierarchy of officers
and sergeants. Not only are they slaves of the bourgeois class, and of the bourgeois State; they are daily and hourly enslaved by the machine, by the
overlooker, and, above all, by the individual bourgeois manufacturer himself.
The more openly this despotism proclaims gain to be its end and aim, the
more petty, the more hateful and the more embittering it is.

The less the skill and exertion of strength implied in manual labour, in
other words, the more modern industry becomes developed, the more is the
labour of men superseded by that of women. Differences of age and sex have
no longer any distinctive social validity for the working class. All are instruments of labour, more or less expensive to use, according to their age and sex.

No sooner is the exploitation of the labourer by the manufacturer, so far,
at an end, that he receives his wages in cash, than he is set upon by the other
portions of the bourgeoisie, the landlord, the shopkeeper, the pawnbroker, etc.

The lower strata of the middle class—the small trades people, shopkeepers, and retired tradesmen generally, the handicraftsmen and peasants—
all these sink gradually into the proletariat, partly because their diminutive
capital does not suffice for the scale on which Modern Industry is carried on,
and is swamped in the competition with the large capitalists, partly because
their specialized skill is rendered worthless by new methods of production.
Thus the proletariat is recruited from all classes of the population.

The proletariat goes through various stages of development. With its
birth begins its struggle with the bourgeoisie. At first the contest is carried on
by individual labourers, then by the work-people of a factory, then by the
operatives of one trade, in one locality, against the individual bourgeois who
directly exploits them. They direct their attacks not against the bourgeois conditions of production, but against the instruments of production themselves;
they destroy imported wares that compete with their labour, they smash to
pieces machinery, they set factories ablaze, they seek to restore by force the
vanished status of the workman of the Middle Ages.

At this stage the labourers still form an incoherent mass scattered over
the whole country, and broken up by their mutual competition. If anywhere

they unite to form more compact bodies, this is not yet the consequence of their own active union, but of the union of the bourgeoisie, which class, in order to attain its own political ends, is compelled to set the whole proletariat in motion, and is moreover yet, for a time, able to do so. At this stage, therefore, the proletarians do not fight their enemies, but the enemies of their enemies, the remnants of absolute monarchy, the landowners, the non-industrial bourgeois, the petty bourgeoisie. Thus the whole historical movement is concentrated in the hands of the bourgeoisie; every victory so obtained is a victory for the bourgeoisie.

But with the development of industry the proletariat not only increases in number; it becomes concentrated in greater masses, its strength grows, and it feels that strength more. The various interests and conditions of life within the ranks of the proletariat are more and more equalized, in proportion as machinery obliterates all distinctions of labour, and nearly everywhere reduces wages to the same low level. The growing competition among the bourgeois, and the resulting commercial crises, make the wages of the workers ever more fluctuating. The unceasing improvement of machinery, ever more rapidly developing, makes their livelihood more and more precarious; the collision between individual workmen and individual bourgeois take more and more the character of collision between two classes. Thereupon the workers begin to form combinations (Trades Unions) against the bourgeois; they club together in order to keep up the rate of wages; they found permanent associations in order to make provision beforehand for these occasional revolts. Here and there the contest breaks out into riots.

Now and then the workers are victorious, but only for a time. The real fruit of their battles lies, not in the immediate result, but in the ever-expanding union of the workers. This union is helped on by the improved means of communication that are created by modern industry and that place the workers of different localities in contact with one another. It was just this contact that was needed to centralize the numerous local struggles, all of the same character, into one national struggle between classes. But every class struggle is a political struggle. And that union, to attain which the burghers of the Middle Ages, with their miserable highways, required centuries, the modern proletarians, thanks to railways, achieve in a few years.

This organization of the proletarians into a class, and consequently into a political party, is continually being upset again by the competition between the workers themselves. But it ever rises up again, stronger, firmer, mightier. It compels legislative recognition of particular interests of the workers, by taking advantage of the divisions among the bourgeoisie itself. Thus the Ten Hours bill in England was carried.

Altogether collisions between the classes of the old society further, in many ways, the course of development of the proletariat. The bourgeoisie finds itself involved in a constant battle. At first with the aristocracy; later on, with those portions of the bourgeoisie itself, whose interests have become antagonistic to the progress of industry; at all times, with the bourgeoisie of foreign countries. In all these battles it sees itself compelled to appeal to the proletariat, to ask for its help, and thus, to drag it into the political arena. The bourgeoisie itself, therefore, supplies the proletariat with its own elements of political and general education, in other words, it furnishes the proletariat with weapons for fighting the bourgeoisie.

Further, as we have already seen, entire sections of the ruling classes are, by the advance of industry, precipitated into the proletariat, or are at least threatened in their conditions of existence. These also supply the proletariat with fresh elements of enlightenment and progress.

Finally, in times when the class struggle nears the decisive hour, the process of dissolution going on within the ruling class, in fact within the whole range of old society, assumes such a violent, glaring character, that a small section of the ruling class cuts itself adrift, and joins the revolutionary class, the class that holds the future in its hands. Just as, therefore, at an earlier period, a section of the nobility went over to the bourgeoisie, so now a portion of the bourgeoisie goes over to the proletariat, and in particular, a portion of the bourgeois ideologists, who have raised themselves to the level of comprehending theoretically the historical movement as a whole.

Of all the classes that stand face to face with the bourgeoisie today, the proletariat alone is a really revolutionary class. The other classes decay and finally disappear in the face of modern industry; the proletariat is its special and essential product.

The lower middle class, the small manufacturer, the shopkeeper, the artisan, the peasant, all these fight against the bourgeoisie, to save from extinction their existence as fractions of the middle class. They are therefore not revolutionary, but conservative. Nay more, they are reactionary, for they try to roll back the wheel of history. If by chance they are revolutionary, they are so only in view of their impending transfer into the proletariat, they thus defend not their present, but their future interests, they desert their own standpoint to place themselves at that of the proletariat.

The "dangerous class," the social scum, that passively rotting mass thrown off by the lowest layers of old society, may, here and there, be swept into the movement by a proletarian revolution; its conditions of life, however, prepare it far more for the part of a bribed tool of reactionary intrigue.

In the conditions of the proletariat, those of old society at large are already virtually swamped. The proletarian is without property; his relation to his wife and children has no longer anything in common with the bourgeois family relations; modern industrial labour, modern subjection to capital, the same in England as in France, in America as in Germany, has stripped him of every trace of national character. Law, morality, religion, are to him so many bourgeois prejudices, behind which lurk in ambush just as many bourgeois interests.

All the preceding classes that got the upper hand sought to fortify their already acquired status by subjecting society at large to their conditions of appropriation. The proletarians cannot become masters of the productive forces of society, except by abolishing their own previous mode of appropriation, and thereby also every other previous mode of appropriation. They have nothing of their own to secure and to fortify; their mission is to destroy all previous securities for, and insurances of, individual property.

All previous historical movements were movements of minorities, or in the interest of minorities. The proletarian movement is the self-conscious, independent movement of the immense majority, in the interest of the immense majority. The proletariat, the lowest stratum of our present society, cannot stir, cannot raise itself up, without the whole superincumbent strata of official society being sprung into the air.

Though not in substance, yet in form, the struggle of the proletariat with the bourgeoisie is at first a national struggle. The proletariat of each country must, of course, first of all settle matters with its own bourgeoisie.

In depicting the most general phases of the development of the proletariat, we traced the more or less veiled civil war, raging within existing society, up to the point where that war breaks out into open revolution, and where the violent overthrow of the bourgeoisie lays the foundation for the sway of the proletariat.

Hitherto, every form of society has been based, as we have already seen, on the antagonism of oppressing and oppressed classes. But in order to oppress a class, certain conditions must be assured to it under which it can, at least, continue its slavish existence. The serf, in the period of serfdom, raised himself to membership in the commune, just as the petty bourgeois, under the yoke of feudal absolutism, managed to develop into a bourgeois. The modern labourer, on the contrary, instead of rising with the progress of industry, sinks deeper and deeper below the conditions of existence of his own class. He becomes a pauper, and pauperism develops more rapidly than population and wealth. And here it becomes evident, that the bourgeoisie is unfit any longer to be the ruling class in society, and to impose its condition of existence upon society as an overriding law. It is unfit to rule because it is incompetent to assure an existence to its slave within his slavery, because it cannot help letting him sink into such a state, that it has to feed him, instead of being fed by him. Society can no longer live under this bourgeoisie, in other words, its existence is no longer compatible with society.

The essential condition for the existence, and for the sway of the bourgeois class, is the formation and augmentation of capital; the condition for capital is wage labour. Wage labour rests exclusively on competition between the labourers. The advance of industry, whose involuntary promoter is the bourgeoisie, replaces the isolation of the labourers, due to competition, by their revolutionary combination, due to association. The development of

Modern Industry, therefore, cuts from under its feet the very foundation on which the bourgeoisie produces and appropriates products. What the bourgeoisie, therefore, produces, above all, is its own grave-diggers. Its fall and the victory of the proletariat are equally inevitable.

## 2. Proletarians and Communists

In what relation do the Communists stand to the proletarians as a whole?

The Communists do not form a separate party opposed to other working-class parties.

They have no interests separate and apart from those of the proletariat as a whole.

They do not set up any sectarian principles of their own, by which to shape and mould the proletarian movement.

The Communists are distinguished from the other working-class parties by this only:

1. In the national struggles of the proletarians of the different countries, they point out and bring to the front the common interests of the entire proletariat, independently of all nationality.

2. In the various stages of development which the struggle of the working class against the bourgeoisie has to pass through, they always and everywhere represent the interests of the movement as a whole.

The Communists, therefore, are on the one hand, practically, the most advanced and resolute section of the working-class parties of every country, that section which pushes forward all others; on the other hand, theoretically, they have over the great mass of the proletariat the advantage of clearly understanding the line of march, the conditions, and the ultimate general results of the proletarian movement.

The immediate aim of the Communists is the same as that of all the other proletarian parties: formation of the proletariat into a class, overthrow of the bourgeois supremacy, conquest of political power by the proletariat.

The theoretical conclusions of the Communists are in no way based on ideas or principles that have been invented, or discovered, by this or that would-be universal reformer.

They merely express, in general terms, actual relations springing from an existing class struggle, from a historical movement going on under our very eyes. The abolition of existing property relations is not at all a distinctive feature of Communism.

All property relations in the past have continually been subject to historical change consequent upon the change in historical conditions.

The French Revolution, for example, abolished feudal property in favour of bourgeois property.

The distinguishing feature of Communism is not the abolition of property generally, but the abolition of bourgeois property. But modern bourgeois private property is the final and most complete expression of the system of producing and appropriating products, that is based on class antagonisms, on the exploitation of the many by the few.

In this sense, the theory of the Communists may be summed up in the single sentence: Abolition of private property.

We Communists have been reproached with the desire of abolishing the right of personally acquiring property as the fruit of a man's own labour, which property is alleged to be the ground work of all personal freedom, activity and independence.

Hard-won, self-acquired, self-earned property! Do you mean the property of the petty artisan and of the small peasant, a form of property that preceded the bourgeois form? There is no need to abolish that; the development of industry has to a great extent already destroyed it, and is still destroying it daily.

Or do you mean modern bourgeois private property?

But does wage labour create any property for the labourer? Not a bit. It creates capital, i.e., that kind of property which exploits wage labour, and which cannot increase except upon condition of begetting a new supply of wage labour for fresh exploitation. Property, in its present form, is based on the antagonism of capital and wage labour. Let us examine both sides of this antagonism.

To be a capitalist is to have not only a purely personal but a social *status* in production. Capital is a collective product, and only by the united action of many members, nay, in the last resort, only by the united action of all members of society, can it be set in motion.

Capital is, therefore, not a personal, it is a social power.

When, therefore, capital is converted into common property, into the property of all members of society, personal property is not thereby transformed into social property. It is only the social character of the property that is changed. It loses its class character.

Let us now take wage labour.

The average price of wage labour is the minimum wage, i.e., that quantum of the means of subsistence which is absolutely requisite to keep the labourer in bare existence as a labourer. What, therefore, the wage-labourer appropriates by means of his labour, merely suffices to prolong and reproduce a bare existence. We by no means intend to abolish this personal appropriation of the products of labour, an appropriation that is made for the maintenance and reproduction of human life, and that leaves no surplus wherewith to command the labour of others. All that we want to do away with is the miserable character of this appropriation, under which the labourer lives merely to increase capital, and is allowed to live only in so far as the interest of the ruling class requires it.

In bourgeois society, living labour is but a means to increase accumulated labour. In Communist society, accumulated labour is but a means to widen, to enrich, to promote the existence of the labourer.

In bourgeois society, therefore, the past dominates the present; in Communist society, the present dominates the past. In bourgeois society capital is independent and has individuality, while the living person is dependent and has no individuality.

And the abolition of this state of things is called by the bourgeois, abolition of individuality and freedom! And rightly so. The abolition of bourgeois individuality, bourgeois independence, and bourgeois freedom is undoubtedly aimed at.

By freedom is meant, under the present bourgeois conditions of production, free trade, free selling and buying.

But if selling and buying disappears, free selling and buying disappears also. This talk about free selling and buying, and all the other "brave words" of our bourgeoisie about freedom in general, have a meaning, if any, only in contrast with restricted selling and buying, with the fettered traders of the Middle Ages, but have no meaning when opposed to the Communistic abolition of buying and selling, of the bourgeois conditions of production, and of the bourgeoisie itself.

You are horrified at our intending to do away with private property. But in your existing society, private property is already done away with for nine-tenths of the population; its existence for the few is solely due to its non-existence in the hands of those nine-tenths. You reproach us, therefore, with intending to do away with a form of property the necessary condition for whose existence is the non-existence of any property for the immense majority of society.

In one word, you reproach us with intending to do away with your property. Precisely so; that is just what we intend.

From the moment when labour can no longer be converted into capital, money, or rent, into a social power capable of being monopolized, i.e., from the moment when individual property can no longer be transformed into bourgeois property, into capital, from that moment, you say, individuality vanishes.

You must, therefore, confess that by "individual" you mean no other person than the bourgeois, than the middle-class owner of property. This person must, indeed, be swept out of the way, and made impossible.

Communism deprives no man of the power to appropriate the products of society; all that it does is to deprive him of the power to subjugate the labour of others by means of such appropriation.

It has been objected that upon the abolition of private property all work will cease, and universal laziness will overtake us.

According to this, bourgeois society ought long ago to have gone to the dogs through sheer idleness; for those of its members who work, acquire nothing, and those who acquire anything, do not work. The whole of this objection is but another expression of the tautology: that there can no longer be any wage labour when there is no longer any capital.

All objections urged against the Communistic mode of producing and appropriating material products, have, in the same way, been urged against the Communistic modes of producing and appropriating intellectual products. Just as, to the bourgeois, the disappearance of class property is the disappearance of production itself, so the disappearance of class culture is to him identical with the disappearance of all culture.

That culture, the loss of which he laments, is, for the enormous majority, a mere training to act as a machine.

But don't wrangle with us so long as you apply, to our intended abolition of bourgeois property, the standard of your bourgeois notions of freedom, culture, law, etc. Your very ideas are but the outgrowth of the conditions of your bourgeois production and bourgeois property, just as your jurisprudence is but the will of your class made into a law for all, a will, whose essential character and direction are determined by the economical conditions of existence of your class.

The selfish misconception that induces you to transform into eternal laws of nature and of reason, the social forms springing from your present mode of production and form or property—historical relations that rise and disappear in the progress of production—this misconception you share with every ruling class that has preceded you. What you see clearly in the case of ancient property, what you admit in the case of feudal property, you are of course forbidden to admit in the case of your own bourgeois form of property.

Abolition of the family! Even the most radical flare up at this infamous proposal of the Communists.

On what foundation is the present family, the bourgeois family, based? On capital, on private gain. In its completely developed form this family exists only among the bourgeoisie. But this state of things finds its complement in the practical absence of the family among the proletarians, and in public prostitution.

The bourgeois family will vanish as a matter of course when its complement vanishes, and both will vanish with the vanishing of capital.

Do you charge us with wanting to stop the exploitation of children by their parents? To this crime we plead guilty.

But, you will say, we destroy the most hallowed of relations, when we replace home education by social.

And your education! Is not that also social, and determined by the social conditions under which you educate, by the intervention, direct or indirect, of society, by means of schools, etc.? The Communists have not invented the intervention of society in education; they do but seek to alter the character of that intervention, and to rescue education from the influence of the ruling class.

The bourgeois clap-trap about the family and education, about the hallowed co-relation of parent and child, becomes all the more disgusting, the more, by the action of Modern Industry, all family ties among the proletarians are torn asunder, and their children transformed into simple articles of commerce and instruments of labour.

But you Communists would introduce community of women, screams the whole bourgeoisie in chorus.

The bourgeois sees in his wife a mere instrument of production. He hears that the instruments of production are to be exploited in common, and, naturally, can come to no other conclusion than that the lot of being common to all will likewise fall to the women.

He has not even a suspicion that the real point aimed at is to do away with the status of women as mere instruments of production.

For the rest, nothing is more ridiculous than the virtuous indignation of our bourgeois at the community of women which, they pretend, is to be openly and officially established by the Communists. The Communists have no need to introduce community of women; it has existed almost from time immemorial.

Our bourgeois, not content with having the wives and daughters of their proletarians at their disposal, not to speak of common prostitutes, take the greatest pleasure in seducing each other's wives.

Bourgeois marriage is in reality a system of wives in common and thus, at the most, what the Communists might possibly be reproached with, is that they desire to introduce, in substitution for a hypocritically concealed, an openly legalized community of women. For the rest, it is self-evident that the abolition of the present system of production must bring with it the abolition of the community of women springing from that system, i.e., of prostitution both public and private.

The Communists are further reproached with desiring to abolish countries and nationality.

The working men have no country. We cannot take from them what they have not got. Since the proletariat must first of all acquire political supremacy, must rise to be the leading class of the nation, must constitute itself *the* nation, it is, so far, itself national, though not in the bourgeois sense of the word.

National differences and antagonism between peoples are daily more and more vanishing, owing to the development of the bourgeoisie, to freedom of commerce, to the world market, to uniformity in the mode of production and in the conditions of life corresponding thereto.

The supremacy of the proletariat will cause them to vanish still faster. United action, of the leading civilized countries at least, is one of the first conditions for the emancipation of the proletariat.

In proportion as the exploitation of one individual by another is put an end to, the exploitation of one nation by another will also be put an end to. In proportion as the antagonism between classes within the nation vanishes, the hostility of one nation to another will come to an end.

The charges against Communism made from a religious, a philosophical, and, generally, from an ideological standpoint, are not deserving of serious examination.

Does it require deep intuition to comprehend that man's ideas, views and conceptions, in one word, man's consciousness, changes with every change in the conditions of his material existence, in his social relations and in his social life?

What else does the history of ideas prove, than that intellectual production changes in character in proportion as material production is changed? The ruling ideas of each age have ever been the ideas of its ruling class.

When people speak of ideas that revolutionize society, they do but express the fact, that within the old society, the elements of a new one have been created, and that the dissolution of the old ideas keeps even pace with the dissolution of the old conditions of existence.

When the ancient world was in its last throes, the ancient religions were overcome by Christianity. When Christian ideas succumbed in the eighteenth century to rationalist ideas, feudal society fought its death battle with the then revolutionary bourgeoisie. The ideas of religious liberty and freedom of conscience, merely gave expression to the sway of free competition within the domain of knowledge.

"Undoubtedly," it will be said, "religious, moral, philosophical and juridical ideas have been modified in the course of historical development. But religion, morality, philosophy, political science, and law, constantly survived this change.

"There are, besides, eternal truths, such as Freedom, Justice, etc., that are common to all states of society. But Communism abolishes eternal truths, it abolishes all religion, and all morality, instead of constituting them on a new basis; it therefore acts in contradiction to all past historical experience."

What does this accusation reduce itself to? The history of all past society has consisted in the development of class antagonisms, antagonisms that assumed different forms at different epochs.

But whatever form they may have taken, one fact is common to all past ages, viz., the exploitation of one part of society by the other. No wonder, then, that the social consciousness of past ages, despite all the multiplicity and variety it displays, moves within certain common forms, or general ideas, which cannot completely vanish except with the total disappearance of class antagonisms.

The Communist revolution is the most radical rupture with traditional property relations; no wonder that its development involves the most radical rupture with traditional ideas.

But let us have done with the bourgeois objections to Communism.

We have seen above, that the first step in the revolution by the working class, is to raise the proletariat to the position of ruling class, to win the battle of democracy.

The proletariat will use its political supremacy to wrest, by degrees, all capital from the bourgeoisie, to centralize all instruments of production in the hands of the State, i.e., of the proletariat organized as the ruling class; and to increase the total of productive forces as rapidly as possible.

Of course, in the beginning, this cannot be effected except by means of despotic inroads on the rights of property, and on the conditions of bourgeois production; by means of measures, therefore, which appear economically insufficient and untenable, but which, in the course of the movement, outstrip themselves, necessitate further inroads upon the old social order, and are unavoidable as a means of entirely revolutionizing the mode of production.

The measures will of course be different in different countries.

Nevertheless, in the most advanced countries, the following will be pretty generally applicable:

1. Abolition of property in land and application of all rents of land to public purposes.

2. A heavy progressive or graduated income tax.

3. Abolition of all right of inheritance.

4. Confiscation of the property of all emigrants and rebels.

5. Centralization of credit in the hands of the State, by means of a national bank with State capital and an exclusive monopoly.

6. Centralization of the means of communication and transport in the hands of the State.

7. Extension of factories and instruments of production owned by the State; the bringing into cultivation of wastelands, and the improvement of the soil generally in accordance with a common plan.

8. Equal liability of all to labour. Establishment of industrial armies, especially for agriculture.

9. Combination of agriculture with manufacturing industries; gradual abolition of the distinction between town and country, by a more equable distribution of the population over the country.

10. Free education for all children in public schools. Abolition of children's factory labour in its present form. Combination of education with industrial production, etc., etc.

When, in the course of development, class distinctions have disappeared, and all production has been concentrated in the whole nation, the public power will lose its political character. Political power, properly so called, is merely the organized power of one class for oppressing another. If the proletariat during its contest with the bourgeoisie is compelled, by the force of circumstances, to organize itself as a class, if, by means of a revolution, it makes itself the ruling class, and, as such, sweeps away by force the old conditions of production, then it will, along with these conditions, have swept away the conditions for the existence of class antagonisms and of classes generally, and will thereby have abolished its own supremacy as a class.

In place of the old bourgeois society, with its classes and class antagonisms, we shall have an association, in which the free development of each is the condition for the free development of all.

## 3. Socialist and Communist Literature

### *I. Reactionary Socialism*

*a. Feudal Socialism.*—Owing to their historical position, it became the vocation of the aristocracies of France and England to write pamphlets against modern bourgeois society. In the French revolution of July 1830, and in the English reform agitation, these aristocracies again succumbed to the hateful upstart. Thenceforth, a serious political contest was altogether out of question. A literary battle alone remained possible. But even in the domain of literature the old cries of the restoration period had become impossible.

In order to arouse sympathy, the aristocracy were obliged to lose sight, apparently, of their own interests, and to formulate their indictment against the bourgeoisie in the interest of the exploited working class alone. Thus the aristocracy took their revenge by singing lampoons on their new master, and whispering in his ears sinister prophecies of coming catastrophe.

In this way arose feudal Socialism: half lamentation, half lampoon; half echo of the past, half menace of the future; at times, by its bitter, witty and incisive criticism, striking the bourgeoisie to the very heart's core; but always ludicrous in its effect, through total incapacity to comprehend the march of modern history.

The aristocracy, in order to rally the people to them, waved the proletarian alms-bag in front for a banner. But the people, so often as it joined them, saw on their hindquarters the old feudal coats of arms, and deserted with loud and irreverent laughter.

One section of the French Legitimist and 'Young England' exhibited this spectacle.

In pointing out that their mode of exploitation was different to that of the bourgeoisie, the feudalists forget that they exploited under circumstances and conditions that were quite different, and that are now antiquated. In showing that, under their rule, the modern proletariat never existed, they forget that the modern bourgeoisie is the necessary offspring of their own form of society.

For the rest, so little do they conceal the reactionary character of their criticism that their chief accusation against the bourgeoisie amount to this, that under the bourgeois *regime* a class is being developed, which is destined to cut up root and branch the old order of society.

What they upbraid the bourgeoisie with is not so much that it creates a proletariat, as that it creates a *revolutionary* proletariat.

In political practice, therefore, they join in all coercive measures against the working class; and in ordinary life, despite their high-falutin phrases, they stoop to pick up the golden apples dropped from the tree of industry, and to barter truth, love, and honour for traffic in wool, beetroot-sugar, and potato spirits.

As the parson has ever gone hand in hand with the landlord, so has Clerical Socialism with Feudal Socialism.

Nothing is easier than to give Christian asceticism a Socialist tinge. Has not Christianity declaimed against private property, against marriage, against the State? Has it not preached in the place of these, charity and poverty, celibacy and mortification of the flesh, monastic life and Mother Church? Christian Socialism is but the holy water with which the priest consecrates the heart-burnings of the aristocrat.

*b. Petty-Bourgeois Socialism.*—The feudal aristocracy was not the only class that was ruined by the bourgeoisie, not the only class whose conditions of existence pined and perished in the atmosphere of modern bourgeois society. The medieval burgesses and the small peasant proprietors were the precursors of the modern bourgeoisie. In those countries which are but little developed, industrially and commercially, these two classes still vegetate side by side with the rising bourgeoisie.

In countries where modern civilization has become fully developed, a new class of petty bourgeois has been formed, fluctuating between proletariat and bourgeoisie and ever renewing itself as a supplementary part of bourgeois society. The individual members of this class, however, are being constantly hurled down into the proletariat by the action of competition, and, as modern industry develops, they even see the moment approaching when they will completely disappear as an independent section of modern society, to be replaced, in manufacture, agriculture and commerce, by overlookers, bailiffs and shopmen.

In countries like France, where the peasants constitute far more than half of the population, it was natural that writers who sided with the proletariat against the bourgeoisie, should use, in their criticism of the bourgeois *regime*, the standard of the peasant and petty bourgeois, and from the standpoint of these intermediate classes should take up the cudgels for the working class. Thus arose petty-bourgeois Socialism. [Jean Charles] Sismondi was the head of this school, not only in France but also in England.

This school of Socialism dissected with great acuteness the contradictions in the conditions of modern production. It laid bare the hypocritical apologies of economists. It proved, incontrovertibly, the disastrous effects of machinery and division of labour; the concentration of capital and land in a few hands; over-production and crises; it pointed out the inevitable ruin of the petty bourgeois and peasant, the misery of the proletariat, the anarchy in production, the crying inequalities in the distribution of wealth, the industrial war of extermination between nations, the dissolution of old moral bonds, of the old family relations, of the old nationalities.

In its positive aims, however, this form of Socialism aspires either to restoring the old means of production and of exchange, and with them the old property relations, and the old society, or to cramping the modern means of production and of exchange, within the framework of the old property relations that have been, and were bound to be, exploded by those means. In either case, it is both reactionary and Utopian.

Its last words are: corporate guilds for manufacture; patriarchal relations in agriculture.

Ultimately, when stubborn historical facts had dispersed all intoxicating effects of self-deception, this form of Socialism ended in a miserable fit of the blues.

*c. German, or "True," Socialism.*—The Socialist and Communist literature of France, a literature that originated under the pressure of a bourgeoisie in power, and that was the expression of the struggle against this power, was introduced into Germany at a time when the bourgeoisie, in that country, had just begun its contest with feudal absolutism.

German philosophers, would-be philosophers, and *beaux esprits,* eagerly seized on this literature, only forgetting, that when these writings immigrated from France into Germany, French social conditions had not immigrated along with them. In contact with German social conditions, this French literature lost all its immediate practical significance, and assumed a purely literary aspect. Thus, to the German philosophers of the Eighteenth Century, the demands of the first French Revolution were nothing more than the demands of "Practical Reason" in general, and the utterance of the will of the revolutionary French bourgeoisie signified in their eyes the laws of pure Will, of Will as it was bound to be, of true human Will generally.

The work of the German *literati* consisted solely in bringing the new French ideas into harmony with their ancient philosophical conscience, or rather, in annexing the French ideas without deserting their own philosophic point of view.

This annexation took place in the same way in which a foreign language is appropriated, namely, by translation.

It is well known how the monks wrote silly lives of Catholic Saints *over* the manuscripts on which the classical works of ancient heathendom had been written. The German *literati* reversed this process with the profane French literature. They wrote their philosophical nonsense beneath the French original. For instance, beneath the French criticism of the economic functions of money, they wrote "Alienation of Humanity," and beneath the French criticism of the bourgeois State they wrote, "Dethronement of the Category of the General," and so forth.

The introduction of these philosophical phrases at the back of the French historical criticisms they dubbed "Philosophy of Action," "True Socialism," "German Science of Socialism," "Philosophical Foundation of Socialism," and so on.

The French Socialist and Communist literature was thus completely emasculated. And, since it ceased in the hands of the German to express the struggle of one class with the other, he felt conscious of having overcome "French one-sidedness" and of representing, not true requirements, but the requirements of Truth; not the interests of the proletariat, but the interests of Human Nature, of Man in general, who belongs to no class, has no reality, who exists only in the misty realm of philosophical fantasy.

This German Socialism, which took its schoolboy task so seriously and solemnly, and extolled its poor stock-in-trade in such mountebank fashion, meanwhile gradually lost its pedantic innocence.

The fight of the German, and, especially of the Prussian bourgeoisie, against feudal aristocracy and absolute monarchy, in other words, the liberal movement, became more earnest.

By this, the long wished-for opportunity was offered to "True" Socialism of confronting the political movement with the Socialist demands, of hurling the traditional anathemas against liberalism, against representative government, against bourgeois competition, bourgeois freedom of the press, bourgeois legislation, bourgeois liberty and equality, and of preaching to the masses that they had nothing to gain, and everything to lose, by this bourgeois movement. German Socialism forgot, in the nick of time, that the French criticism, whose silly echo it was, presupposed the existence of modern bourgeois society, with its corresponding economic conditions of existence, and the political constitution adapted thereto, the very things whose attainment was the object of the pending struggle in Germany.

To the absolute governments, with their following of parsons, professors, country squires and officials, it served as a welcome scarecrow against the threatening bourgeoisie.

It was a sweet finish after the bitter pills of floggings and bullets with which these same governments, just at that time, dosed the German working-class risings.

While this "True" Socialism thus served the governments as a weapon for fighting the German bourgeoisie, it, at the same time, directly represented a reactionary interest, the interest of the German Philistines. In Germany the *petty-bourgeois* class, a relic of the sixteenth century, and since then constantly cropping up again under various forms, is the real social basis of the existing state of things.

To preserve this class is to preserve the existing state of things in Germany. The industrial and political supremacy of the bourgeoisie threatens it with certain destruction; on the one hand, from the concentration of capital; on the other, from the rise of a revolutionary proletariat. "True" Socialism appeared to kill these two birds with one stone. It spread like an epidemic.

The robe of speculative cobwebs, embroidered with flowers of rhetoric, steeped in the dew of sickly sentiment, this transcendental robe in which the German Socialists wrapped their sorry "eternal truths," all skin and bone, served to wonderfully increase the sale of their goods amongst such a public.

And on its part, German Socialism recognized, more and more, its own calling as the bombastic representative of the petty-bourgeois Philistine.

It proclaimed the German nation to be the model nation, and the German petty Philistine to be the typical man. To every villainous meanness of this model man it gave a hidden, higher, Socialistic interpretation, the exact contrary of its real character. It went to the extreme length of directly opposing the "brutally destructive" tendency of Communism, and of proclaiming its supreme and impartial contempt of all class struggles. With very few exceptions, all the so-called Socialist and Communist publications that now (1847) circulate in Germany belong to the domain of this foul and enervating literature.

## II. Conservative, or Bourgeois, Socialism

A part of the bourgeoisie is desirous of redressing social grievances, in order to secure the continued existence of bourgeois society.

To this section belong economists, philanthropists, humanitarians, improvers of the condition of the working class, organizers of charity, members of societies for the prevention of cruelty to animals, temperance fanatics, hole-and-corner reformers of every imaginable kind. This form of Socialism has, moreover, been worked out into complete systems.

We may cite Proudhon's *Philosophie de la Misère* as an example of this form.

The Socialistic bourgeois want all the advantages of modern social conditions without the struggles and dangers necessarily resulting therefrom. They desire the existing state of society minus its revolutionary and disintegrating elements. They wish for a bourgeoisie without a proletariat. The bourgeoisie naturally conceives the world in which it is supreme to be the best; and bourgeois Socialism develops this comfortable conception into various more or less complete systems. In requiring the proletariat to carry out such a system, and thereby to march straightway into the social New Jerusalem, it but requires in reality, that the proletariat should remain within the bounds of existing society, but should cast away all its hateful ideas concerning the bourgeoisie.

A second and more practical, but less systematic, form of this Socialism sought to depreciate every revolutionary movement in the eyes of the working class, by showing that no mere political reform, but only a change in the material conditions of existence, in economical relations, could be of any advantage to them. By changes in the material conditions of existence, this form of Socialism, however, by no means understands abolition of the bourgeois relations of production, an abolition that can be effected only by a revolution, but administrative reforms, based on the continued existence of these relations; reforms, therefore, that in no respect affect the relations between capital and labour, but, at the best, lessen the cost, and simplify the administrative work, of bourgeois government.

Bourgeois Socialism attains adequate expression, when, and only when, it becomes a mere figure of speech.

Free trade: for the benefit of the working class. Protective duties: for the benefit of the working class. Prison Reform: for the benefit of the working class. This is the last word and the only seriously meant word of bourgeois Socialism.

It is summed up in the phrase: the bourgeois is a bourgeois—for the benefit of the working class.

### III. Critical-Utopian Socialism and Communism

We do not here refer to that literature which, in every great modern revolution, has always given voice to the demands of the proletariat, such as the writings of Babeuf and other.

The first direct attempts of the proletariat to attain its own ends, made in times of universal excitement, when feudal society was being overthrown, these attempts necessarily failed, owing to the then undeveloped state of the proletariat, as well as to the absence of the economic conditions for its emancipation, conditions that had yet to be produced, and could be produced by the impending bourgeois epoch alone. The revolutionary literature that accompanied these first movements of the proletariat had necessarily a reactionary character. It inculcated universal asceticism and social levelling in its crudest form.

The Socialist and Communist systems properly so called, those of Saint-Simon, Fourier, Owen and others, spring into existence in the early undeveloped period, described above, of the struggle between proletariat and bourgeoisie (see Section 1, Bourgeois and Proletarians).

The founders of these systems see, indeed, the class antagonisms, as well as the action of the decomposing elements in the prevailing form of society. But the proletariat, as yet in its infancy, offers to them the spectacle of a class without any historical initiative or any independent political movement.

Since the development of class antagonism keeps even pace with the development of industry, the economic situation, as they find it, does not as yet offer to them the material conditions for the emancipation of the proletariat. They therefore search after a new social science, after new social laws, that are to create these conditions.

Historical action is to yield to their personal inventive action, historically created conditions of emancipation to fantastic ones, and the gradual, spontaneous class organization of the proletariat to an organization of society specially contrived by these inventors. Future history resolves itself, in their eyes, into the propaganda and the practical carrying out of their social plans.

In the formation of their plans they are conscious of caring chiefly for the interests of the working class, as being the most suffering class. Only from the point of view of being the most suffering class does the proletariat exist for them.

The undeveloped state of the class struggle, as well as their own surroundings, causes Socialists of this kind to consider themselves far superior to all class antagonisms. They want to improve the condition of every member of society, even that of the most favoured. Hence, they habitually appeal to society at large, without distinction of class; nay, by preference, to the ruling class. For how can people, when once they understand their system, fail to see in it the best possible plan of the best possible state of society?

Hence, they reject all political, and especially all revolutionary, action; they wish to attain their ends by peaceful means, and endeavour, by small experiments, necessarily doomed to failure, and by the force of example, to pave the way for the new social Gospel.

Such fantastic pictures of future society, painted at a time when the proletariat is still in a very undeveloped state and has but a fantastic conception of its own position correspond with the first instinctive yearnings of that class for a general reconstruction of society.

But these Socialist and Communist publications contain also a critical element. They attack every principle of existing society. Hence they are full of the most valuable materials for the enlightenment of the working class. The practical measures proposed in them—such as the abolition of the distinction between town and country, of the family, of the carrying on of industries for the account of private individuals, and of the wage system, the proclamation of social harmony, the conversion of the functions of the State into a mere superintendence of production, all these proposals point solely to the disappearance of class antagonisms which were, at that time, only just cropping up, and which, in these publications, are recognized in their earliest indistinct and undefined forms only. These proposals, therefore, are of a purely Utopian character.

The significance of Critical-Utopian Socialism and Communism bears an inverse relation to historical development. In proportion as the modern class struggle develops and takes definite shape, this fantastic standing apart from the contest, these fantastic attacks on it, lose all practical value and all theoretical justification. Therefore, although the originators of these systems were, in many respects, revolutionary, their disciples have, in every case, formed mere reactionary sects. They hold fast by the original views of their masters, in opposition to the progressive historical development of the proletariat. They, therefore, endeavour, and that consistently, to deaden the class struggle and to reconcile the class antagonisms. They still dream of experimental realization of their social Utopias, of founding isolated *'phalanstères,'* of establishing 'Home Colonies,' of setting up a 'Little Icaria'—duodecimo editions of the New Jerusalem—and to realize all these castles in the air, they are compelled to appeal to the feelings and purses of the bourgeois. By degrees they sink into the category of the reactionary conservative Socialists depicted above, differing from these only by more systematic pedantry, and by their fanatical and superstitious belief in the miraculous effects of their social science.

They, therefore, violently oppose all political action on the part of the working class; such action, according to them, can only result from blind unbelief in the new Gospel.

The Owenites in England, and the Fourierists in France, respectively oppose the Chartists and the *Réformistes*.

## 4. Position of the Communists in Relation to the Various Existing Opposition Parties

Section 2 has made clear the relations of the Communists to the existing working-class parties, such as the Chartists in England and the Agrarian Reformers in America.

The Communists fight for the attainment of the immediate aims, for the enforcement of the momentary interests of the working class; but in the movement of the present, they also represent and take care of the future of that movement. In France the Communists ally themselves with the Social- Democrats, against the conservative and radical bourgeoisie, reserving, however, the right to take up a critical position in regard to phrases and illusions traditionally handed down from the great Revolution.

In Switzerland they support the Radicals, without losing sight of the fact that this party consists of antagonistic elements, partly of Democratic Socialists, in the French sense, partly of radical bourgeois.

In Poland they support the party that insists on an agrarian revolution as the prime condition for national emancipation, that party which fomented the insurrection of Cracow in 1846.

In Germany they fight with the bourgeoisie whenever it acts in a revolutionary way, against the absolute monarchy, the feudal squirearchy, and the petty bourgeoisie.

But they never cease, for a single instant, to instil into the working class the clearest possible recognition of the hostile antagonism between bourgeoisie and proletariat, in order that the German workers may straightway use, as so many weapons against the bourgeoisie, the social and political conditions that the bourgeoisie must necessarily introduce along with its supremacy, and in order that, after the fall of the reactionary classes in Germany, the fight against the bourgeoisie itself may immediately begin.

The Communists turn their attention chiefly to Germany, because that country is on the eve of a bourgeois revolution that is bound to be carried out under more advanced conditions of European civilization, and with a much more developed proletariat, than that of England was in the seventeenth, and of France in the eighteenth century, and because the bourgeois revolution in Germany will be but the prelude to an immediately following proletarian revolution.

In short, the Communists everywhere support every revolutionary movement against the existing social and political order of things.

In all these movements they bring to the front, as the leading question in each, the property question, no matter what its degree of development at the time.

Finally, they labour everywhere for the union and agreement of the democratic parties of all countries.

The Communists disdain to conceal their views and aims. They openly declare that their ends can be attained only by the forcible overthrow of all existing social conditions. Let the ruling classes tremble at a Communistic revolution. The proletarians have nothing to lose but their chains. They have a world to win.

WORKING MEN OF ALL COUNTRIES, UNITE!

# KARL MARX

## *Value, Price, and Profit*

### VI.
### Value and Labour

Citizens, I have now arrived at a point where I must enter upon the real development of the question. I cannot promise to do this in a very satisfactory way, because to do so I should be obliged to go over the whole field of political economy. I can, as the French would say, but *effleurer la question,* touch upon the main points.

The first question we have to put is: what is the *value* of a commodity? How is it determined?

At first sight it would seem that the value of a commodity is a thing quite *relative,* and not to be settled without considering one commodity in its relations to all other commodities. In fact, in speaking of the value, the value in exchange of a commodity, we mean the proportional quantities in which it exchanges with all other commodities. But then arises the question: How are the proportions in which commodities exchange with each other regulated?

We know from experience that these proportions vary infinitely. Taking one single commodity, wheat, for instance, we shall find that a quarter of wheat exchanges in almost countless variations of proportion with different commodities. Yet, *its value remaining always the same,* whether expressed in silk, gold, or any other commodity, it must be something distinct from, and independent of, these *different rates of exchange* with different articles. It must be possible to express, in a very different form, these various equations with various commodities.

Besides, if I say a quarter of wheat exchanges with iron in a certain proportion, or the value of a quarter of wheat is expressed in a certain amount of iron, I say that the value of wheat and its equivalent in iron are equal *to some third thing,* which is neither wheat nor iron, because I suppose them to express the same magnitude in two different shapes. Either of them, the wheat or the iron, must, therefore, independently of the other, be reducible to this third thing which is their common measure.

To elucidate this point I shall recur to a very simple geometrical illustration. In comparing the areas of triangles of all possible forms and magnitudes, or comparing triangles with rectangles, or any other rectilinear figure, how do we proceed? We reduce the area of any triangle whatever to an expression quite different from its visible form. Having found from the nature of the triangle that its area is equal to half the product of its base by its height, we can then compare the different values of all sorts of triangles, and of all rectilinear figures whatever, because all of them may be resolved into a certain number of triangles.

The same mode of procedure must obtain with the values of commodities. We must be able to reduce all of them to an expression common to all, and distinguishing them only by the proportions in which they contain that same and identical measure.

As the *exchangeable values* of commodities are only *social functions* of those things, and have nothing at all to do with the *natural* qualities, we must first ask: What is the common *social substance* of all commodities? It is *labour*. To produce a commodity a certain amount of labour must be bestowed upon it, or worked up in it. And I say not only *labour*, but *social labour*. A man who produces an article for his own immediate use, to consume it himself, creates a *product*, but not a *commodity*. As a self-sustaining producer he has nothing to do with society. But to produce a *commodity*, a man must not only produce an article satisfying some *social* want, but his labour itself must form part and parcel of the total sum of labour expended by society. It must be subordinate to the *division of labour within society*. It is nothing without the other division of labour, and on its part is required to *integrate* them.

If we consider *commodities as values*, we consider them exclusively under the single aspect of *realised, fixed*, or, if you like, *crystallised social labour*. In this respect they can *differ* only by representing greater or smaller quantities of labour, as, for example, a greater amount of labour may be worked up in a silken handkerchief than in a brick. But how does one measure *quantities of labour?* By the *time the labour lasts,* in measuring the labour by the hour, the day, etc. Of course, to apply this measure, all sorts of labour are reduced to average or simple labour as their unit.

We arrive, therefore, at this conclusion. A commodity has a *value*, because it is a *crystallisation of social labour*. The *greatness* of its value, or its *relative* value, depends upon the greater or less amount of that social substance contained in it; that is to say, on the relative mass of labour necessary for its production. The *relative values of commodities* are, therefore, determined by the *respective quantities or amounts of labour, worked up, realised, fixed in them*. The *correlative* quantities of commodities which can be produced in the *same time of labour* are *equal*. Or the value of one commodity is to the value of another commodity as the quantity of labour fixed in the one is to the quantity of labour fixed in the other.

I suspect that many of you will ask: Does then, indeed, there exist such a vast, or any difference whatever, between determining of values of commodities by *wages,* and determining them by the *relative quantities of labour* necessary for their production? You must, however, be aware that the *reward* for labour, and *quantity* of labour, are quite disparate things. Suppose, for example, *equal quantities of labour* to be fixed in one quarter of wheat and one ounce of gold. I resort to the example because it was used by Benjamin Franklin in his first essay published in 1721, and entitled: *A Modest Enquiry into the Nature and Necessity of a Paper Currency,* where he, one of the first, hit upon the true nature of value. Well. We suppose, then, that one quarter of wheat and one ounce of gold are *equal values* or *equivalents,* because they are *crystallisations of equal amounts of average labour,* of so many days' or so many weeks' labour respectively fixed in them. In thus determining the relative values of gold and corn, do we refer in any way whatever to the *wages* of the agricultural labourer and the miner? Not a bit. We leave it quite *indeterminate how* their day's or week's labour was paid, or even whether wages labour was employed at all. If it was, wages may have been very unequal. The labourer whose labour is realised in the quarter of wheat may receive two bushels only, and the labourer employed in mining may receive one-half of the ounce of gold. Or, supposing their wages to be equal, they may deviate in all possible proportions from the values of the commodities produced by them. They may amount to one-half, one-third, one-fourth, one-fifth, or any other proportional part of the one-quarter of corn or the one ounce of gold. Their *wages* can, of course, not *exceed,* not be more than the values of the commodities they produced, but they can be *less* in every possible degree. Their *wages* will be *limited* by the *values* of the products, but the *values of their products* will not be limited by the wages. And above all, the values, the relative values of corn and gold, for example, will have been settled without any regard whatever to the value of the labour employed, that is to say, to *wages.* To determine the values of commodities by the *relative quantities of labour fixed in them,* is, therefore, a thing quite different from the tautological method of determining the values of commodities by the value of labour, or by wages. This point, however, will be further elucidated in the progress of our inquiry.

In calculating the exchangeable value of a commodity we must add to the quantity of labour *last* employed the quantity of labour *previously* worked up in the raw material of the commodity, and the labour bestowed on the implements, tools, machinery, and buildings, with which such labour is assisted. For example, the value of a certain amount of cotton yarn is the crystallisation of the quantity of labour added to the cotton during the spinning process, the quantity of labour previously realised in the cotton itself, the quantity of labour realised in the coal, oil, and other auxiliary matter used, the quantity of labour fixed in the steam-engine, the spindles, the factory building, and so forth. Instruments of production properly so-called, such as tools, machinery, buildings, serve again and again for a longer or shorter period during repeated processes of production. If they were used up at once, like the raw material, their whole value would at once be transferred to the commodities they assist in producing. But as a spindle, for example, is but gradually used up, an average calculation is made, based upon the average time it lasts, and its average waste or wear and tear during a certain period, say a day. In this way we calculate how much of the value of the spindle is transferred to the yarn daily spun, and how much, therefore, of the total amount of labour realised in a pound of yarn, for example, is due to the quantity of labour previously realised in the spindle. For our present purpose it is not necessary to dwell any longer upon this point.

It might seem that if the value of a commodity is determined by the *quantity of labour bestowed upon its production,* the lazier a man, or the clumsier a man, the more valuable his commodity, because the greater the time of labour required for finishing the commodity. This, however, would be a sad mistake. You will recollect that I used the word "*social* labour," and many points are involved in this qualification of "social." In saying that the value of a commodity is determined by the *quantity of labour* worked up or crystallised in it, we mean the *quantity of labour necessary* for its production in a given state of society, under certain social average conditions of production, with a given social average intensity, and average skill of the labour employed. When, in England, the power-loom came to compete with the hand-loom, only one-half the former time of labour was wanted to convert a given amount of yarn into a yard of cotton or cloth. The poor hand-loom weaver now worked seventeen and eighteen hours daily, instead of the nine or ten hours he had worked before. Still the product of twenty hours of his labour represented now only ten social hours of labour, or ten hours of labour socially necessary for the conversion of a certain amount of yarn into textile stuffs. His product of twenty hours had, therefore, no more value than his former product of ten hours.

If then the quantity of socially necessary labour realised in commodities regulates their exchangeable values, every increase in the quantity of labour wanted for the production of a commodity must augment its value, as every diminution must lower it.

If the respective quantities of labour necessary for the production of the respective commodities remained constant, their relative values also would be constant. But such is not the case. The quantity of labour necessary for the production of a commodity changes continuously with the changes in the productive powers of the labour employed. The greater the productive powers of labour, the more produce is finished in a given time of labour; and the smaller the productive powers of labour, the less produce is finished in the same time. If, for example, in the progress of population it should become necessary to cultivate less fertile soils, the same amount of produce would be only attainable by a greater amount of labour spent, and the value of agricultural produce would consequently rise. On the other hand, if with the modern means of production, a single spinner converts into yarn, during one working day, many thousand times the amount of cotton which he could have spun during the same time with the spinning wheel, it is evident that every single pound of cotton will absorb many thousand times less of spinning labour than it did before, and, consequently, the value added by spinning to every single pound of cotton will be a thousand times less than before. The value of yarn will sink accordingly.

Apart from the different natural energies and acquired working abilities of different peoples, the productive powers of labour must principally depend:

Firstly. Upon the *natural* conditions of labour, such as fertility of soil, mines, and so forth.

Secondly. Upon the progressive improvement of the *social powers of labour,* such as are derived from production on a grand scale, concentration of capital and combination of labour, subdivision of labour, machinery, improved methods, appliance of chemical and other natural agencies, shortening of time and space by means of communication and transport, and every other contrivance by which science presses natural agencies into the service of labour, and by which the social or co-operative character of labour is developed. The greater the productive powers of labour, the less labour is bestowed upon a given amount of produce; hence the smaller the value of this produce. The smaller the productive powers of labour, the more labour is bestowed upon the same amount of produce; hence the greater its value. As a general law we may, therefore, set it down that:

*The values of commodities are directly as the times of labour employed in their production, and are inversely as the productive powers of the labour employed.*

Having till now only spoken of *value,* I shall add a few words about *price,* which is a peculiar form assumed by value.

Price, taken by itself, is nothing but the *monetary expression of value.* The values of all commodities of this country, for example, are expressed in gold prices, while on the Continent they are mainly expressed in silver prices. The value of gold or silver, like that of all other commodities, is regulated by the quantity of labour necessary for getting them. You exchange a certain amount of your national products, in which a certain amount of your national labour is crystallised, for the produce of the gold and silver producing countries, in which a certain quantity of *their* labour is crystallised. It is in this way, in fact by barter, that you learn to express in gold and silver the values of all commodities, that is the respective quantities of labour bestowed upon them. Looking somewhat closer into *the monetary expression of value,* or, what comes to the same, the *conversion of value into price,* you will find that it is a process by which you give to the *values* of all commodities an *independent* and *homogeneous form,* or by which you express them as quantities of *equal* social labour. So far as it is but the monetary expression of value, price has been called *natural price* by Adam Smith, *prix nécessaire* by the French physiocrats.

What then is the relation between *value* and *market prices*, or between *natural prices* and *market prices?* You all know that the *market price* is the *same* for all commodities of the same kind, however the conditions of production may differ for the individual producers. The market price expresses only the *average amount of social labour* necessary, under the average conditions of production, to supply the market with a certain mass of a certain article. It is calculated upon the whole lot of a commodity of a certain description.

So far the *market price* of a commodity coincides with its *value.* On the other hand, the oscillations of market prices, rising now over, sinking now under the value or natural price, depend upon the fluctuations of supply and demand. The deviations of market prices from values are continual, but as Adam Smith says: "The natural price is the central price to which the prices of commodities are continually gravitating. Different accidents may sometimes keep them suspended a good deal above it, and sometimes force them down even somewhat below it. But whatever may be the obstacles which hinder them from settling in this center of repose and continuance, they are constantly tending towards it."

I cannot now sift this matter. It suffices to say that *if* supply and demand equilibrate each other, the market prices of commodities will correspond with their natural prices, that is to say with their values, as determined by the respective quantities of labour required for their production. But supply and demand *must* constantly tend to equilibrate each other, although they do so only by compensating one fluctuation by another, a rise by a fall, and *vice versa*. If instead of considering only the daily fluctuations you analyse the movement of market prices for longer periods, as Mr. [Thomas] Tooke, for example, has done in his *History of Prices,* you will find that the fluctuations of market prices, their deviations from values, their ups and downs, paralyse and compensate each other; so that apart from the effect of monopolies and some other modifications I must now pass by, all descriptions of commodities are, on the average, sold at their respective *values* or natural prices. The average periods during which the fluctuations of market prices compensate each other are different for different kinds of commodities, because with one kind it is easier to adapt supply to demand than with the other.

If then, speaking broadly, and embracing somewhat longer periods, all descriptions of commodities sell at their respective values, it is nonsense to suppose that profit, not in individual cases, but that the constant and usual profits of different trades spring from surcharging the prices of commodities or selling them at a price over and above their *value*. The absurdity of this notion becomes evident if it is generalised. What a man would constantly win as a seller he would as constantly lose as a purchaser. It would not do to say that there are men who are buyers without being sellers, or consumers without being producers. What these people pay to the producers, they must first get from them for nothing. If a man first takes your money and afterwards returns that money in buying your commodities, you will never enrich yourselves by selling your commodities too dear to that same man. This sort of transaction might diminish a loss, but would never help in realising a profit.

To explain, therefore, the *general nature of profits*, you must start from the theorem that, on an average, commodities are *sold at their real values*, and that *profits are derived from selling them at their values*, that is, in proportion to the quantity of labour realised in them. If you cannot explain profit upon this supposition, you cannot explain it at all. This seems paradox and contrary to everyday observation. It is also paradox that the earth moves round the sun, and that water consists of two highly inflammable gases. Scientific truth is always paradox, if judged by everyday experience, which catches only the delusive appearance of things.

## VII.
### Labouring Power[1]

Having now, as far as it could be done in such a cursory manner, analysed the nature of *Value*, of the *Value of any commodity whatever*, we must turn our attention to the specific *Value of Labour*. And here, again, I must startle you by a seeming paradox. All of you feel sure that what they daily sell is their Labour; that, therefore, Labour has a Price, and that, the price of a commodity being only the monetary expression of its value, there must certainly exist such a thing as the *Value of Labour*. However, there exists no such thing as the *Value of Labour* in the common acceptance of the word. We have seen that the amount of necessary labour crystallised in a commodity constitutes its value. Now, applying this notion of value, how could we define, say, the value of a ten hours' working day? How much labour is contained in that day? Ten hours' labour. To say that the value of a ten hours' working day is equal to ten hours labour, or the quantity of labour contained in it, would be a tautological and, moreover, a nonsensical expression. Of course, having once found out the true but hidden sense of the expression "*Value of Labour*," we shall be able to interpret this irrational, and seemingly impossible application of value, in the same way that, having once made sure of the real movement of the celestial bodies, we shall be able to explain their apparent or merely phenomenal movements.

What the working man sells is not directly his *Labour*, but his *Labouring Power*, the temporary disposal of which he makes over to the capitalist. This is so much the case that I do not know whether by the English laws, but certainly by some Continental laws, the *maximum time* is fixed for which a man is allowed to sell his labouring power. If allowed to do so for any indefinite period whatever, slavery would be immediately restored. Such a sale, if it comprised his lifetime, for example, would make him at once the lifelong slave of his employer.

One of the oldest economists and most original philosophers of England —Thomas Hobbes—has already, in his *Leviathan*, instinctively hit upon this point overlooked by all his successors. He says: "The *value or worth of a man* is, as in all other things, his *price:* that is so much as would be given for the *Use of his Power.*"

Proceeding from this basis, we shall be able to determine the *Value of Labour* as that of all other commodities.

But before doing so, we might ask, how does this strange phenomenon arise, that we find on the market a set of buyers, possessed of land, machinery, raw material, and the means of life, all of them, save land in its crude state, the *products of labour,* and on the other hand, a set of sellers who have nothing to sell except their labouring power, their working arms and brains? That the one set buys continually in order to make a profit and enrich themselves, while the other set continually sells in other to earn their livelihood? The inquiry into this question would be an inquiry into what the economists call *"Previous, or Original Accumulation,"* but which ought to be called *Original Expropriation.* We should find that this so-called *Original Accumulation* means nothing but a series of historical processes, resulting in a *Decomposition of the Original Union* existing between the Labouring Man and his Means of Labour. Such an inquiry, however, lies beyond the pale of my present subject. The *Separation* between the Man of Labour and the Means of Labour once established, such a state of things will maintain itself and reproduce itself upon a constantly increasing scale, until a new and fundamental revolution in the mode of production should again overturn it, and restore the original union in a new historical form.

What, then, is the *Value of Labouring Power?*

Like that of every other commodity, its value is determined by the quantity of labour necessary to produce it. The labouring power of a man exists only in his living individuality. A certain mass of necessaries must be consumed by a man to grow up and maintain his life. But the man, like the machine, will wear out, and must be replaced by another man. Beside the mass of necessaries required for *his own* maintenance, he wants another amount of necessaries to bring up a certain quota of children that are to replace him on the labour market and to perpetuate the race of labourers. Moreover, to develop his labouring power, and acquire a given skill, another amount of values must be spent. For our purpose it suffices to consider only average labour, the costs of whose education and development are vanishing magnitudes. Still I must seize upon this occasion to state that, as the costs of producing labouring powers of different quality do differ, so must differ the values of the labouring powers employed in different trades. The cry for an *equality of wages* rests, therefore, upon a mistake, is an inane wish never to be fulfilled. It is an

offspring of that false and superficial radicalism that accepts premises and tries
to evade conclusions. Upon the basis of the wages system the value of labouring power is settled like that of every other commodity; and as different kinds
of labouring power have different values, or require different quantities of labour for their production, they *must* fetch different prices in the labour market. To clamour for *equal or even equitable retribution* on the basis of the
wages system is the same as to clamour for *freedom* on the basis of the slavery
system. What you think just or equitable is out of the question. The question
is: What is necessary and unavoidable with a given system of production?

   After what has been said, the *value of labouring power* is determined by
the *value of the necessaries* required to produce, develop, maintain, and perpetuate the labouring power.

## VIII.
### Production of Surplus Value

Now suppose that the average amount of the daily necessaries of a labouring
man require *six hours of average labour* for their production. Suppose, moreover, six hours of average labour to be also realised in a quantity of gold equal
to 3s. [shillings]. Then 3s. would be the *Price,* or the monetary expression of
the *Daily Value* of that man's *Labouring Power.* If he worked daily six hours he
would daily produce a value sufficient to buy the average amount of his daily
necessaries, or to maintain himself as a labouring man.

   But our man is a wages labourer. He must, therefore, sell his labouring
power to a capitalist. If he sells it at 3s. daily, or 18s. weekly, he sells it at its
value. Suppose him to be a spinner. If he works six hours daily he will add to
the cotton a value of 3s. daily. This value, daily added by him, would be an exact equivalent for the wages, or the price of his labouring power, received
daily. But in that case no *surplus value* or *surplus produce* whatever would to go
the capitalist. Here, then, we come to the rub.

   In buying the labouring power of the workman, and paying its value, the
capitalist, life every other purchaser, has acquired the right to consume or use
the commodity bought. You consume or use the labouring power of a man by
making him work, as you consume or use a machine by making it run. By
paying the daily or weekly value of the labouring power of the workman, the
capitalist has, therefore, acquired the right to use or make that labouring
power work during the *whole day or week*. The working day or the working
week has, of course, certain limits, but those we shall afterwards look more
closely at.

   For the present I want to turn your attention to one decisive point.

   The *value* of the labouring power is determined by the quantity of labour
necessary to maintain or reproduce it, but the *use* of that labouring power is
only limited by the active energies and physical strength of the labourer. The

daily or weekly *value* of the labouring power is quite distinct from the daily or weekly exercise of that power, the same as the food a horse wants and the time it can carry the horseman are quite distinct. The quantity of labour by which the *value* of the workman's labouring power is limited forms by no means a limit to the quantity of labour which his labouring power is apt to perform. Take the example of our spinner. We have seen that, to daily reproduce his labouring power, he must daily reproduce a value of 3s., which he will do by working six hours daily. But this does not disable him from working ten or twelve or more hours a day. But by paying the daily or weekly *value* of the spinner's labouring power the capitalist has acquired the right of using that labouring power during *the whole day or week.* He will, therefore, make him work daily, say, *twelve* hours. *Over and above* the six hours required to replace his wages, or the value of his labouring power, he will, therefore, have to work *six other hours,* which I shall call hours of *surplus labour,* which surplus labour will realise itself in a *surplus value* and a *surplus produce.* If our spinner, for example, by his daily labour of six hours, added 3s. value to the cotton, a value forming an exact equivalent to his wages, he will, in twelve hours, add 6s. worth to the cotton, and produce *a proportional surplus of yarn.* As he has sold his labouring power to the capitalist, the whole value or produce created by him belongs to the capitalist, the owner *pro tem.* of his labouring power. By advancing 3s., the capitalist will, therefore, realise a value of 6s., because, advancing a value in which six hours of labour are crystallised, he will receive in return a value in which twelve hours of labour are crystallised. By repeating this same process daily, the capitalist will daily advance 3s. and daily pocket 6s., one half of which will go to pay wages anew, and the other half of which will form the *surplus value,* for which the capitalist pays no equivalent. It is this *sort of exchange between capital and labour* upon which capitalistic production, or the wages system, is founded, and which must constantly result in reproducing the working man as a working man, and the capitalist as a capitalist.

*The rate of surplus value,* all other circumstances remaining the same, will depend on the proportion between that part of the working day necessary to reproduce the value of the labouring power and the *surplus time* or *surplus labour* performed for the capitalist. It will, therefore, depend on the *ratio in which the working day is prolonged over and above that extent,* by working which the working man would only reproduce the value of his labouring power, or replace his wages.

## IX.
## Value of Labour

We must now return to the expression, "*Value, or Price of Labour.*"

We have seen that, in fact, it is only the value of the labouring power, measured by the values of commodities necessary for its maintenance. But since the workman receives his wages *after* his labour is performed, and knows, moreover, that what he actually gives to the capitalist is his labour, the value or price of his labouring power necessarily appears to him as the *price* or *value of his labour itself.* If the price of his labouring power is 3s., in which six hours of labour are realised, and if he works twelve hours, he necessarily considers these 3s. as the value or price of twelve hours of labour, although these twelve hours of labour realise themselves in a value of 6s. A double consequence flows from this.

Firstly. *The value or price of the labouring power* takes the semblance of the *price or value of labour itself,* although, strictly speaking, value and price of labour are senseless terms.

Secondly. Although one part only of the workman's daily labour is *paid,* while the other part is *unpaid,* and while that unpaid or surplus labour constitutes exactly the fund out of which *surplus value* or *profit* is formed, it seems as if the aggregate labour was paid labour.

This false appearance distinguishes *wages labour* from other *historical* forms of labour. On the basis of the wages system even the *unpaid* labour seems to be *paid* labour. With the *slave,* on the contrary, even that part of his labour which is paid appears to be unpaid. Of course, in order to work the slave must live, and one part of his working day goes to replace the value of his own maintenance. But since no bargain is struck between him and his master, and no acts of selling and buying are going on between the two parties, all his labour seems to be given away for nothing.

Take, on the other hand, the peasant serf, such as he, I might say, until yesterday existed in the whole east of Europe. This peasant worked, for example, three days for himself on his own field or the field allotted to him, and the three subsequent days he performed compulsory and gratuitous labour on the estate of his lord. Here, then, the paid and unpaid parts of labour were visibly separated, separated in time and space; and our Liberals overflowed with moral indignation at the preposterous notion of making a man work for nothing.

In point of fact, however, whether a man works three days of the week for himself on his own field and three days for nothing on the estate of his lord, or whether he works in the factory or the workshop six hours daily for himself and six for his employer, comes to the same, although in the latter case the paid and unpaid portions of labour are inseparably mixed up with each other, and the nature of the whole transaction is completely masked by the *intervention of a contract* and the *pay* received at the end of the week. The gratuitous labour appears to be voluntarily given in the one instance, and to be compulsory in the other. That makes all the difference.

In using the work "*value of labour,*" I shall only use it as a popular slang term for "*value of labouring power.*"

## X.
## Profit Is Made by Selling a Commodity at Its Value

Suppose an average hour of labour to be realised in a value equal to sixpence, or twelve average hours of labour to be realised in 6s. Suppose, further, the value of labour to be 3s. or the produce of six hours' labour. If, then, in the raw material, machinery, and so forth, used up in a commodity, twenty-four average hours of labour were realised, its value would amount to 12s. If, moreover, the workman employed by the capitalist added twelve hours of labour to those means of production, these twelve hours would be realised in an additional value of 6s. The *total value of the product* would, therefore, amount to thirty-six hours of realised labour, and be equal to 18s. But as the value of labour, or the wages paid to the workman, would be 3s. only, no equivalent would have been paid by the capitalist for the six hours of surplus labour worked by the workman, and realised in the value of the commodity. By selling this commodity at its value for 18s., the capitalist would, therefore, realise a value of 3s., for which he had paid no equivalent. These 3s. would constitute the surplus value or profit pocketed by him. The capitalist would consequently realise the profit of 3s., not by selling his commodity at a price *over and above* its value, but by selling it *at its real value.*

The value of a commodity is determined by the *total quantity of labour* contained in it. But part of that quantity of labour is realised in a value, for which an equivalent has been paid in the form of wages; part of it is realised in a value for which *no* equivalent has been paid. Part of the labour contained in the commodity is *paid* labour; part is *unpaid* labour. By selling, therefore, the commodity *at its value,* that is, as the crystallisation of the *total quantity of labour* bestowed upon it, the capitalist must necessarily sell it at a profit. He sells not only what has cost him an equivalent, but he sells also what has cost him nothing, although it has cost the labour of his workman. The cost of the commodity to the capitalist and its real cost are different things. I repeat, therefore, that normal and average profits are made by selling commodities not *above,* but *at their real values.*

## XI.
## The Different Parts into Which Surplus Value
## Is Decomposed

The *surplus value,* or that part of the total value of the commodity in which the *surplus labour* or *unpaid labour* of the working man is realised, I call *Profit.* The whole of that profit is not pocketed by the employing capitalist. The monopoly of land enables the landlord to take one part of that *surplus value,* under the name of *rent,* whether the land is used for agriculture or buildings or railways, or for any other productive purpose. On the other hand, the very fact that the possession of the *means of labour* enables the employing capitalist to produce a *surplus value,* or, what comes to the same, to *appropriate to himself a certain amount of unpaid labour,* enables the owner of the means of labour, which he lends wholly or partly to the employing capitalist— enables, in one word, the *money-lending capitalist* to claim for himself under the name of *interest* another part of that surplus value, so that there remains to the employing capitalist *as such* only what is called *industrial* or *commercial profit.*

By what laws this division of the total amount of surplus value amongst the three categories of people is regulated is a question quite foreign to our subject. This much, however, results from what has been stated.

*Rent, Interest, and Industrial Profit* are only *different names for different parts* of the *surplus value* of the commodity, or the *unpaid labour realised in it,* and they are *equally derived from this source, and from this source alone.* They are not derived from *land* as such nor from *capital* as such, but land and capital enable their owners to get their respective shares out of the surplus value extracted by the employing capitalist from the labourer. For the labourer himself it is a matter of subordinate importance whether that surplus value, the result of his surplus labour, or unpaid labour, is altogether pocketed by the employing capitalist, or whether the latter is obliged to pay portions of it, under the names of rent and interest, away to third parties. Suppose the employing capitalist to use only his own capital and to be his own landlord, then the whole surplus value would go into his pocket.

It is the employing capitalist who immediately extracts from the labourer this surplus value, whatever part of it he may ultimately be able to keep for himself. Upon this relation, therefore, between the employing capitalist and the wages labourer the whole wages system and the whole present system of production hinge. Some of the citizens who took part in our debate were, therefore, wrong in trying to mince matters, and to treat this fundamental relation between the employing capitalist and the working man as a secondary question, although they were right in stating that, under given circumstances, a rise of prices might affect in very unequal degrees the employing capitalist, the landlord, the moneyed capitalist, and, if you please, the taxgatherer.

Another consequence follows from what has been stated.

That part of the value of the commodity which represents only the value of the raw materials, the machinery, in one word, the value of the means of production used up, forms *no revenue* at all, but replaces *only capital.* But, apart from this, it is false that the other part of the value of the commodity *which forms revenue,* or may be spent in the form of wages, profits, rent, interest, is *constituted* by the value of wages, the value of rent, the value of profit, and so forth. We shall, in the first instance, discard wages, and only treat industrial profits, interest, and rent. We have just seen that the *surplus value* contained in the commodity, or that part of its value in which *unpaid labour* is realised, resolves itself into different fractions, bearing three different names. But it would be quite the reverse of the truth to say that its value is *composed* of, or *formed* by, the *addition* of the *independent values of these three constituents*.

If one hour of labour realises itself in a value of sixpence, if the working day of the labourer comprises twelve hours, if half of this time is unpaid labour, that surplus labour will add to the commodity a *surplus value* of 3s., that is of value for which no equivalent has been paid. This surplus value of 3s. constitutes the *whole fund* which the employing capitalist may divide, in whatever proportions, with the landlord and the money-lender. The value of these 3s. constitutes the limit of the value they have to divide amongst them. But it is not the employing capitalist who adds to the value of the commodity an arbitrary value for his profit, to which another value is added for the landlord, and so forth, so that the addition of these arbitrarily fixed values would constitute the total value. You see, therefore, the fallacy of the popular notion, which confounds the *decomposition* of a *given value* into three parts, with the *formation* of that value by the addition of three *independent* values, thus converting the aggregate value, from which rent, profit, and interest are derived, into an arbitrary magnitude.

If the total profit realised by a capitalist be equal to 100, we call this sum, considered as absolute magnitude, the *amount of profit*. But if we calculate the ratio which those 100 bear to the capital advanced, we call this *relative* magnitude, the *rate of profit*. It is evident that this rate of profit may be expressed in a double way.

Suppose 100 to be the capital *advanced in wages*. If the surplus value created is also 100—and this would show us that half the working day of the labourer consists of *unpaid* labour—and if we measured this profit by the value of the capital advanced in wages, we should say that the *rate of profit* amounted to 100 percent, because the value advanced would be 100 and the value realised would be 200.

If, on the other hand, we should not only consider the *capital advanced in wages*, but the *total capital* advanced, say, for example, 500, of which 400 represented the value of raw materials, machinery, and so forth, we should say that the *rate of profit* amounted only to 20 percent, because the profit of 100 would be but the fifth part of the *total* capital advanced.

The first mode of expressing the rate of profit is the only one which shows you the real ratio between paid and unpaid labour, the real degree of the *exploitation* (you must allow me this French word) *of labour*. The other mode of expression is that in common use, and is, indeed, appropriate for certain purposes. At all events, it is very useful for concealing the degree in which the capitalist extracts gratuitous labour from the workman.

In the remarks I have still to make I shall use the word *Profit* for the whole amount of the surplus value extracted by the capitalist without any regard to the division of that surplus value between different parties, and in using the words *Rate of Profit*, I shall always measure profits by the value of the capital advanced in wages.

# XII.
## General Relation of Profits, Wages and Prices

Deduct from the value of a commodity the value replacing the value of the raw materials, and other means of production used upon it, that is to say, deduct the value representing the *past* labour contained in it, and the remainder of its value will resolve into the quantity of labour added by the working man *last* employed. If that working man works twelve hours daily, if twelve hours of average labour crystallise themselves in an amount of gold equal to 6s., this additional value of 6s. is the *only* value his labour will have created. This given value, determined by the time of his labour, is the only fund from which both he and the capitalist have to draw their respective shares or dividends, the only value to be divided into wages and profits. It is evident that this value itself will not be altered by the variable proportions in which it may be divided amongst the two parties. There will also be nothing changed if in the place of one working man you put the whole working population, twelve million working days, for example, instead of one.

Since the capitalist and workman have only to divide this limited value, that is, the value measured by the total labour of the working man, the more the one gets the less will the other get, and *vice versa*. Whenever a quantity is given, one part of it will increase inversely as the other decreases. If the wages change, profits will change in an opposite direction. If wages fall, profits will rise; and if wages rise, profits will fall. If the working man, on our former supposition gets 3s., equal to one-half of the value he has created, or if his whole working day consists half of paid, half of unpaid labour, the *rate of profit* will be 100 percent because the capitalist would also get 3s. If the working man receives only 2s. or works only one-third of the whole day for himself, the capitalist will get 4s., and the rate of profit will be 200 percent. If the working man receives 4s., the capitalist will only receive 2s., and the rate of profit would sink to 50 percent, but all these variations will not affect the value of the commodity. A general rise of wages would, therefore, result in a fall of the general rate of profit, but not affect values. But although the values of commodities, which must ultimately regulate their market prices, are exclusively determined by the total quantities of labour fixed in them, and not by the division of that quantity into paid and unpaid labour, it by no means follows that the values of the single commodities, or lots of commodities, produced during twelve hours, for example, will remain constant. The *number* or mass of commodities produced in a given time of labour, or by a given quantity of labour, depends upon the *productive power* of the labour employed, and not upon its *extent* or length. With one degree of the productive power of spinning labour, for example, a working day of twelve hours may produce twelve pounds of yarn, with a lesser degree of productive power only two pounds. If then twelve hours' average labour were realised in the value of 6s. in the one case, the twelve pounds of yarn would cost 6s., in the other case the two pounds of yarn would also cost 6s. One pound of yarn would, therefore, cost sixpence in the one case, and 3s. in the other. This difference of price would result from the difference in the productive powers of labour employed. One hour of labour would be realised in one pound of yarn with the greater productive power, while with the smaller productive power, six hours of labour would be realised in one pound of yarn. The price of a pound of yarn would, in the one instance, be only sixpence, although wages were relatively high and the rate of profit low; it would be 3s. in the other instance, although wages were low and the rate of profit high. This would be so because the price of the pound of yarn is regulated by the *total amount of labour worked up in it*, and not by the *proportional division of that total amount into paid and unpaid labour*. The fact I have before mentioned that high-priced labour may produce cheap, and low-priced labour may produce dear commodities, loses, therefore, its paradoxical appearance. It is only the expression of the general law that the value of a commodity is regulated by the quantity of labour worked up in it, but that quantity of labour worked up in it depends altogether upon the productive powers of the labour employed, and will, therefore, vary with every variation in the productivity of labour.

## XIII.
### Main Cases of Attempts at Raising Wages or Resisting Their Fall

Let us now seriously consider the main cases in which a rise of wages is attempted or a reduction of wages resisted.

1. We have seen that the *value of the labouring power,* or in more popular parlance, the *value of labour,* is determined by the value of necessaries, or the quantity of labour required to produce them. If, then, in a given country the value of the daily average necessaries of the labourer represented six hours of labour expressed in 3s., the labourer would have to work six hours daily to produce an equivalent for his daily maintenance. If the whole working day was twelve hours, the capitalist would pay him the value of his labour by paying him 3s. Half the working day would be unpaid labour, and the rate of profit would amount to 100 percent. But now suppose that, consequent upon a decrease of productivity, more labour should be wanted to produce, say, the same amount of agricultural produce, so that the price of the average daily

necessaries should rise from 3 to 4s. In that case the *value* of labour would rise by one-third, or 33$^1$/$_3$ percent. Eight hours of the working day would be required to produce an equivalent for the daily maintenance of the labourer, according to his old standard of living. The surplus labour would therefore sink from six hours to four, and the rate of profit from 100 to 50 percent. But in insisting upon a rise of wages, the labourer would only insist upon getting the *increased value of his labour*, like every other seller of a commodity, who, the costs of his commodities having increased, tries to get its increased value paid. If wages did not rise, or not sufficiently rise, to compensate for the increased values of necessaries, the *price* of labour would sink *below the value of labour*, and the labourer's standard of life would deteriorate.

But a change might also take place in an opposite direction. By virtue of the increased productivity of labour, the same amount of the average daily necessaries might sink from 3 to 2s., or only four hours out of the working day, instead of six, be wanted to reproduce an equivalent for the value of the daily necessaries. The working man would now be able to buy with 2s. as many necessaries as he did before with 3s. Indeed, the *value of labour* would have sunk, but that diminished value would command the same amount of commodities as before. Then profits would rise from 3 to 4s., and the rate of profit from 100 to 200 percent. Although the labourer's absolute standard of life would have remained the same, his *relative* wages, and therewith his *relative social position*, as compared with that of the capitalist, would have been lowered. If the working man should resist that reduction of relative wages, he would only try to get some share in the increased productive powers of his own labour, and to maintain his former relative position in the social scale. Thus, after the abolition of the Corn Laws, and in flagrant violation of the most solemn pledges given during the anti–Corn Law agitation, the English factory lords generally reduced wages 10 percent. The resistance of the workmen was at first baffled, but, consequent upon circumstances I cannot now enter upon, the 10 percent lost were afterwards regained.

2. The *values* of necessaries, and consequently the *value of labour*, might remain the same, but a change might occur in their *money prices*, consequent upon a previous *change* in the *value of money*.

By the discovery of more fertile mines and so forth, two ounces of gold might, for example, cost no more labour to produce than one ounce did before. The *value* of gold would then be depreciated by one-half, or 50 percent. As the *values* of all other commodities would then be expressed in twice their former *money prices*, so also the same with the *value of labour*. Twelve hours of labour, formerly expressed in 6s., would now be expressed in 12s. If the working man's wages should remain 3s., instead of rising to 6s., the *money price of his labour* would only be equal to *half the value of his labour*, and his standard of life would fearfully deteriorate. This would also happen in a greater or lesser degree if his wages should rise, but not proportionately to the fall in the value of gold. In such a case nothing would have been changed, either in the productive powers of labour, or in supply and demand, or in values. Nothing would have been changed except the money *names* of those values. To say that in such a case the workman ought not to insist upon a proportionate rise of wages, is to say that he must be content to be paid with names, instead of with things. All past history proves that whenever such a depreciation of money occurs, the capitalists are on the alert to seize this opportunity for defrauding the workman. A very large school of political economists assert that, consequent upon the new discoveries of gold lands, the better working of silver mines, and the cheaper supply of quicksilver, the value of precious metals has been again depreciated. This would explain the general and simultaneous attempts on the Continent at a rise of wages.

3. We have till now supposed that the *working day* has given limits. The working day, however, has, by itself, no constant limits. It is the constant tendency of capital to stretch it to its utmost physically possible length, because in the same degree surplus labour, and consequently the profit resulting therefrom, will be increased. The more capital succeeds in prolonging the working day, the greater the amount of other people's labour it will appropriate. During the seventeenth and even the first two-thirds of the eighteenth century a ten hours' working day was the normal working day all over England. During the anti-Jacobin war, which was in fact a war waged by the British barons against the British working masses, capital celebrated its bacchanalia, and prolonged the working day from ten to twelve, fourteen, eighteen hours. [Thomas] Malthus, by no means a man whom you would suspect of a maudlin sentimentalism, declared in a pamphlet, published about 1815, that if this sort of thing was to go on, the life of the nation would be attacked at its very source. A few years before the general introduction of the newly-invented machinery, about 1765, a pamphlet appeared in England under the title: *An Essay on Trade.* The anonymous author, an avowed enemy of the working classes, declaims on the necessity of expanding the limits of the working day. Amongst other means to this end, he proposes *working houses,* which, he says, ought to be "*Houses of Terror.*" And what is the length of the working day he prescribes for these "Houses of Terror"? *Twelve hours,* the very same time which in 1832 was declared by capitalists, political economists, and ministers to be not only the existing but the necessary time of labour for a child under twelve years.

By selling his labouring power, and he must do so under the present system, the working man makes over to the capitalist the consumption of that power, but within certain rational limits. He sells his labouring power in order to maintain it, apart from its natural wear and tear, but not to destroy it. In selling his labouring power at its daily or weekly value, it is understood that in one day or one week that labouring power shall not be submitted to two days' or two weeks' waste or wear and tear. Take a machine worth 1000. If it is used up in ten years it will add to the value of the commodities in whose production it assists 100 yearly. If it be used up in five years it would add 200 yearly, or the value of its annual wear and tear is in inverse ratio to the quickness with which it is consumed. But this distinguishes the working man from the machine. Machinery does not wear out exactly in the same ratio in which it is used. Man, on the contrary, decays in a greater ratio than would be visible from the mere numerical addition of work.

In their attempts at reducing the working day to its former rational dimensions, or, where they cannot enforce a legal fixation of a normal working day, at checking overwork by a rise of wages, a rise not only in proportion to the surplus time exacted, but in a greater proportion, working men fulfil only a duty to themselves and their race. They only set limits to the tyrannical usurpations of capital. Time is the room of human development. A man who has no free time to dispose of, whose whole lifetime, apart from the mere physical interruptions by sleep, meals, and so forth, is absorbed by his labour for the capitalist, is less than a beast of burden. He is a mere machine for producing foreign wealth, broken in body and brutalised in mind. Yet the whole history of modern industry shows that capital, if not checked, will recklessly and ruthlessly work to cast down the whole working class to this utmost state of degradation.

In prolonging the working day the capitalist may pay *higher wages* and still lower the *value of labour*, if the rise of wages does not correspond to the greater amount of labour extracted, and the quicker decay of the labouring power thus caused. This may be done in another way. Your middle-class statisticians will tell you, for instance, that the average wages of factory families in Lancashire has risen. They forget that instead of the labour of the man, the head of the family, his wife and perhaps three or four children are now thrown under the Juggernaut wheels of capital, and that the rise of the aggregate wages does not correspond to the aggregate surplus labour extracted from the family.

Even with given limits of the working day, such as they now exist in all branches of industry subjected to the factory laws, a rise of wages may become necessary, if only to keep up the old standard *value of labour*. By increasing the *intensity* of labour, a man may be made to expend as much vital force in one hour as he formerly did in two. This has, to a certain degree, been effected in the trades, placed under the Factory Acts, by the acceleration of machinery, and the greater number of working machines which a single individual has now to superintend. If the increase in the intensity of labour or the mass of labour spent in an hour keeps some fair proportion to the decrease in the extent of the working day, the working man will still be the winner. If this limit is overshot, he loses in one form what he has gained in another, and ten hours of labour may then become as ruinous as twelve hours were before. In checking this tendency of capital, by struggling for a rise of wages corresponding to the rising intensity of labour, the working man only resists the depreciation of his labour and the deterioration of his race.

4. All of you know that, from reasons I have not now to explain, capital-istic production moves through certain periodical cycles. It moves through a state of quiescence, growing animation, prosperity, overtrade, crisis, and stag-nation. The market prices of commodities, and the market rates of profit, fol-low these phases, now sinking below their averages, now rising above them. Considering the whole cycle, you will find that one deviation of the market price is being compensated by the other, and that, taking the average of the cycle, the market prices of commodities are regulated by their values. Well! During the phase of sinking market prices and the phases of crisis and stagna-tion, the working man, if not thrown out of employment altogether, is sure to have his wages lowered. Not to be defrauded, he must, even with such a fall of market prices, debate with the capitalist in what proportional degree a fall of wages has become necessary. If, during the phases of prosperity, when extra profits are made, he did not battle for a rise of wages, he would, taking the av-erage of one industrial cycle, not even receive his *average wages,* or the *value* of his labour. It is the utmost height of folly to demand that while his wages are necessarily affected by the adverse phases of the cycle, he should exclude him-self from compensation during the prosperous phases of the cycle. Generally, the *values* of all commodities are only realised by the compensation of the con-tinuously changing market prices, springing from the continuous fluctuations of demand and supply. On the basis of the present system labour is only a commodity like others. It must, therefore, pass through the same fluctuations to fetch an average price corresponding to its value. It would be absurd to treat it on the one hand as a commodity, and to want on the other hand to exempt it from the laws which regulate the prices of commodities. The slave receives a permanent and fixed amount of maintenance; the wages labourer does not. He must try to get a rise of wages in the one instance, if only to compensate for a fall of wages in the other. If he resigned himself to accept the will, the dictates of the capitalist as a permanent economic law, he would share in all the miser-ies of the slave, without the security of the slave.

5. In all the cases I have considered, and they form ninety-nine out of a hundred, you have seen that a struggle for a rise of wages follows only in the track of *previous* changes, and is the necessary offspring of previous changes in the amount of production, the productive powers of labour, the value of la-bour, the value of money, the extent or the intensity of labour extracted, the fluctuations of market prices, dependent upon the fluctuations of demand and supply, and co-existent with the different phases of the industrial cycle; in one word, as reactions of labour against the previous action of capital. By treating the struggle for a rise of wages independently of all these circumstances, by looking only upon the change of wages, and overlooking all the other changes from which they emanate, you proceed from a false premise in order to arrive at false conclusions.

## XIV.
## The Struggle between Capital and Labour
## and Its Results

1. Having shown that the periodical resistance on the part of the working men against a reduction of wages, and their periodical attempts at getting a rise of wages, are inseparable from the wages system, and dictated by the very fact of labour being assimilated to commodities, and therefore subject to the laws regulating the general movement of prices; having, furthermore, shown that a general rise of wages would result in a fall in the general rate of profit, but not affect the average prices of commodities, or their values, the question now ultimately arises, how far, in this incessant struggle between capital and labour, the latter is likely to prove successful.

I might answer by a generalisation, and say that, as with all other commodities, so with labour, its *market price* will, in the long run, adapt itself to its *value;* that, therefore, despite all the ups and downs, and do what he may, the working man will, on an average, only receive the value of his labour, which resolves into the value of his labouring power, which is determined by the value of the necessaries required for its maintenance and reproduction, which value of necessaries finally is regulated by the quantity of labour wanted to produce them.

But there are some peculiar features which distinguish the *value of the labouring power,* or the *value of labour,* from the values of all other commodities. The value of the labouring power is formed by two elements—the one merely physical, the other historical or social. Its *ultimate limit* is determined by the *physical* element, that is to say, to maintain and reproduce itself, to perpetuate its physical existence, the working class must receive the necessaries absolutely indispensable for living and multiplying. The *value* of those indispensable necessaries forms, therefore, the ultimate limit of the *value of labour.* On the other hand, the length of the working day is also limited by ultimate, although very elastic boundaries. Its ultimate limit is given by the physical force of the labouring man. If the daily exhaustion of his vital forces exceeds a certain degree, it cannot be exerted anew, day by day. However, as I said, this limit is very elastic. A quick succession of unhealthy and short-lived generations will keep the labour market as well supplied as a series of vigorous and long-lived generations.

Besides this mere physical element, the value of labour is in every country determined by a *traditional standard of life.* It is not mere physical life, but it is the satisfaction of certain wants springing from the social conditions in which people are placed and reared up. The English standard of life may be reduced to the *Irish* standard; the standard of life of a German peasant to that of a Livonian peasant. The important part which historical tradition and social habitude play in this respect, you may learn from Mr. Thornton's work on *Overpopulation,* where he shows that the average wages in different agricultural districts of England still nowadays differ more or less according to the more or less favourable circumstances under which the districts have emerged from the state of serfdom.

This historical or social element, entering into the value of labour, may be expanded, or contracted, or altogether extinguished, so that nothing remains but the *physical limit*. During the time of the *anti-Jacobin war,* undertaken, as the incorrigible tax-eater and sinecurist, old George Rose, used to say, to save the comforts of our holy religion from the inroads of the French infidels, the honest English farmers, so tenderly handled in a former session of ours, depressed the wages of the agricultural labourers even beneath that *mere physical minimum,* but made up by *Poor Laws* the remainder necessary for the physical perpetuation of the race. This was a glorious way to convert the wages labourer into a slave, and Shakespeare's proud yeoman into a pauper.

By comparing the standard wages or values of labour in different countries, and by comparing them in different historical epochs of the same country, you will find that the *value of labour* itself is not a fixed but a variable magnitude, even supposing the values of all other commodities to remain constant.

A similar comparison would prove that not only the *market rates of profit* change, but its *average* rates.

But as to *profits,* there exists no law which determines their *minimum*. We cannot say what is the ultimate limit of their decrease. And why cannot we fix that limit? Because, although we can fix the *minimum* of wages, we cannot fix their *maximum*. We can only say that, the limits of the working day being given, the *maximum of profit* corresponds to the *physical minimum of wages;* and that wages being given, the *maximum of profit* corresponds to such a prolongation of the working day as is compatible with the physical forces of the labourer. The maximum of profit is therefore limited by the physical minimum of wages and the physical maximum of the working day. It is evident that between the two limits of this *maximum rate of profit* an immense scale of variations is possible. The fixation of its actual degree is only settled by the continuous struggle between capital and labour, the capitalist constantly tending to reduce wages to their physical minimum, and to extend the working day to its physical maximum, while the working man constantly presses in the opposite direction.

The question resolves itself into a question of the respective powers of the combatants.

2. As to the *limitation of the working day*, in England, as in all their countries, it has never been settled except by *legislative interference*. Without the working men's continuous pressure from without that interference would never have taken place. But at all events, the result was not to be attained by private settlement between the working men and the capitalists. This very necessity of *general political action* affords the proof that in its merely economic action capital is the stronger side.

As to the *limits* of the *value of labour*, its actual settlement always depends upon supply and demand, I mean the demand for labour on the part of capital, and the supply of labour by the working men. In colonial countries the law of supply and demand favours the working man. Hence the relatively high standard of wages in the United States. Capital may there try its utmost. It cannot prevent the labour market from being continuously emptied by the continuous conversion of wage labourers into dependent, self-sustaining peasants. The function of a wage labourer is for a very large part of the American people but a probational state, which they are sure to leave within a longer or shorter term. To mend this colonial state of things, the paternal British government accepted for sometime what is called the modern colonisation theory, which consists in putting an artificial high price upon colonial land, in order to prevent the too quick conversion of the wage labourer into the independent peasant.

But let us now come to old civilised countries, in which capital domineers over the whole process of production. Take, for example, the rise in England of agricultural wages from 1849 to 1859. What was its consequence? The farmers could not, as our friend [John] Weston would have advised them, raise the value of wheat, nor even its market prices. They had, on the contrary, to submit to their fall. But during these eleven years they introduced machinery of all sorts, adopted more scientific methods, converted part of arable land into pasture, increased the size of farms, and with this the scale of production, and by these and other processes diminishing the demand for labour by increasing its productive power, made the agricultural population again relatively redundant. This is the general method in which a reaction, quicker or slower, of capital against a rise of wages takes place in old, settled countries. [David] Ricardo has justly remarked that machinery is in constant competition with labour, and can often be only introduced when the price of labour has reached a certain height, but the appliance of machinery is but one of the many methods for increasing the productive powers of labour. This very same development which makes common labour relatively redundant simplifies on the other hand skilled labour, and thus depreciates it.

The same law obtains in another form. With the development of the productive powers of labour the accumulation of capital will be accelerated, even despite a relatively high rate of wages. Hence, one might infer, as Adam Smith, in whose days modern industry was still in its infancy, did infer, that the accelerated accumulation of capital must turn this balance in favour of the working man, by securing a growing demand for his labour. From this same standpoint many contemporary writers have wondered that English capital having grown in the last twenty years so much quicker than English population, wages should not have been more enhanced. But simultaneously with the progress of accumulation there takes place a *progressive change in the composition of capital.* That part of the aggregate capital which consists of fixed capital, machinery, raw materials, means of production in all possible forms, progressively increases as compared with the other part of capital, which is laid out in wages or in the purchase of labour. This law has been stated in a more or less accurate manner by Mr. Barton, Ricardo, Sismondi, Professor Richard Jones, Professor Ramsay, Cherbulliez, and others.

If the proportion of these two elements of capital was originally one to one, it will, in the progress of industry, become five to one, and so forth. If of a total capital of 600, 300 is laid out in instruments, raw materials, and so forth, and 300 in wages, the total capital wants only to be doubled to create a demand for 600 working men instead of for 300. But if of a capital of 600, 500 is laid out in machinery, materials, and so forth, and 100 only in wages, the same capital must increase from 600 to 3600 in order to create a demand for 600 workmen instead of for 300. In the progress of industry the demand for labour keeps, therefore, no pace with the accumulation of capital. It will still increase, but increase in a constantly diminishing ratio as compared with the increase of capital.

These few hints will suffice to show that the very development of modern industry must progressively turn the scale in favour of the capitalist against the working man, and that consequently the general tendency of capitalistic production is not to raise, but to sink the average standard of wages, or to push the *value of labour* more or less to its *minimum limit*. Such being the tendency of *things* in this system, is this to say that the working class ought to renounce their resistance against the encroachments of capital and abandon their attempt at making the best of the occasional chances for their temporary improvement? If they did, they would be degraded to one level mass of broken down wretches past salvation. I think I have shown that their struggles for the standard of wages are incidents inseparable from the whole wages system, that in 99 cases out of 100 their efforts at raising wages are only efforts at maintaining the given value of labour and that the necessity of debating their price with the capitalist is inherent to their condition of having to sell themselves as commodities. By cowardly giving way in their everyday conflict with capital, they would certainly disqualify themselves for the initiating of any larger movement.

At the same time, and quite apart from the general servitude involved in the wages system, the working class ought not to exaggerate to themselves the ultimate working of these everyday struggles. They ought not to forget that they are fighting with effects, but not with the causes of those effects; that they are retarding the downward movement, but not changing its direction; that they are applying palliatives, not curing the malady. They ought, therefore, not to be exclusively absorbed in these unavoidable guerrilla fights incessantly springing up from the never-ceasing encroachments of capital or changes of the market. They ought to understand that, with all the miseries it imposes upon them, the present system simultaneously engenders the *material condi-*

*tions* and the *social forms* necessary for an economic reconstruction of society. Instead of the *conservative* motto: *"A fair day's wages for a fair day's work!"* they ought to inscribe on their banner the *revolutionary* watchword: *"Abolition of the wages system!"*

After this very long and, I fear, tedious exposition, which I was obliged to enter into to do some justice to the subject matter, I shall conclude by proposing the following resolutions:

Firstly. A general rise in the rate of wages would result in a fall of the general rate of profit, but, broadly speaking, not affect the prices of commodities.

Secondly. The general tendency of capitalist production is not to raise, but to sink the average standard of wages.

Thirdly. Trades Unions work well as centres of resistance against the encroachments of capital. They fail partially from an injudicious use of their power. They fail generally from limiting themselves to a guerrilla war against the effects of the existing system, instead of simultaneously trying to change it, instead of using their organised forces as a lever for the final emancipation of the working class, that is to say, the ultimate abolition of the wages system.

## Note

1. "Labour Power" in the English translation of *Capital.*

# 15

## V.I. LENIN

## *What Is to Be Done?*

In his pamphlet *What Is to Be Done?* published in 1902, Lenin anticipated the circumstances that led to the failure of the Russian Revolution of 1905: a bourgeoisie too ready to sell out to the autocracy and
a proletariat too disorganized to resist it. He argued that, on their
own, the masses could only riot. Genuine revolutions require the
leadership of a party of professional revolutionaries. Only late in life
did Lenin begin to weigh the costs of party vanguards and proletarian dictatorships. He died apprehensive about the growth of Soviet
bureaucracy and the loss of worker control.

### 3A. Political Agitation and Its Restriction
### by the Economists

Everyone knows that the economic[1] struggle of the Russian workers under-
went widespread development and consolidation simultaneously with the
production of "literature" exposing economic (factory and occupational) conditions. The "leaflets" were devoted mainly to the exposure of the factory system, and very soon a veritable passion for exposures was roused among the
workers. As soon as the workers realised that the Social-Democratic study
circles desired to, and could, supply them with a new kind of leaflet that told
the whole truth about their miserable existence, about their unbearably hard
toil, and their lack of rights, they began to send in, actually flood us with, correspondence from the factories and workshops. This "exposure literature" created a tremendous sensation, not only in the particular factory exposed in the
given leaflet, but in all the factories to which news of the revealed facts spread.
And since the poverty and want among the workers in the various enterprises
and in the various trades are much the same, the "truth about the life of the
workers" stirred *everyone*. Even among the most backward workers, a veritable
passion arose to "get into print"—a noble passion for this rudimentary form
of war against the whole of the present social system which is based upon rob-

271

bery and oppression. And in the overwhelming majority of cases these "leaflets" were in truth a declaration of war, because the exposures served greatly to agitate the workers; they evoked among them common demands for the removal of the most glaring outrages and roused in them a readiness to support the demands with strikes. Finally, the employers themselves were compelled to recognise the significance of these leaflets as a declaration of war, so much so that in a large number of cases they did not even wait for the outbreak of hostilities. As is always the case, the mere publication of these exposures made them effective, and they acquired the significance of a strong moral influence. On more than one occasion, the mere appearance of a leaflet proved sufficient to secure the satisfaction of all or part of the demands put forward. In a word, economic (factory) exposures were and remain an important lever in the economic struggle. And they will continue to retain this significance as long as there is capitalism, which makes it necessary for the workers to defend themselves. Even in the most advanced countries of Europe it can still be seen that the exposure of abuses in some backward trade, or in some forgotten branch of domestic industry, serves as a starting-point for the awakening of class-consciousness, for the beginning of a trade-union struggle, and for the spread of socialism.[2]

The overwhelming majority of Russian Social-Democrats have of late been almost entirely absorbed by this work of organising the exposure of factory conditions. Suffice it to recall *Rabochaya Mysl* to see the extent to which they have been absorbed by it—so much so, indeed, that they have lost sight of the fact that this, *taken by itself,* is in essence still not Social-Democratic work, but merely trade-union work. As a matter of fact, the exposures merely dealt with the relations between the workers *in a given trade* and their employers, and all they achieved was that the sellers of labour-power learned to sell their "commodity" on better terms and to fight the purchasers over a purely commercial deal. These exposures could have served (if properly utilised by an organisation of revolutionaries) as a beginning and a component part of Social-Democratic activity; but they could also have led (and, given a worshipful attitude towards spontaneity, were bound to lead) to a "purely trade-union" struggle and to a non-Social-Democratic working-class movement. Social-Democracy leads the struggle of the working class, not only for better terms for the sale of labour-power, but for the abolition of the social system that compels the propertyless to sell themselves to the rich. Social-Democracy represents the working class, not in its relation to a given group of employers alone, but in its relation to all classes of modern society and to the state as an organised political force. Hence, it follows that not only must Social-Democrats not confine themselves exclusively to the economic struggle, but that they must not allow the organisation of economic exposures to become the predominant part of their activities. We must take up actively the political education of the working class and the development of its political consciousness. *Now* that

*Zarya* and *Iskra* have made the first attack upon Economism, "all are agreed" on this (although some agree only in words, as we shall soon see).

The question arises, what should political education consist in? Can it be confined to the propaganda of working-class hostility to the autocracy? Of course not. It is not enough to *explain* to the workers that they are politically oppressed (any more than it is to *explain* to them that their interests are antagonistic to the interests of the employers). Agitation must be conducted with regard to every concrete example of this oppression (as we have begun to carry on agitation round concrete examples of economic oppression). Inasmuch as *this* oppression affects the most diverse classes of society, inasmuch as it manifests itself in the most varied spheres of life and activity—vocational, civic, personal, family, religious, scientific, etc., etc.—is it not evident that *we shall not be fulfilling our task* of developing the political consciousness of the workers if we do not *undertake* the organisation of the *political exposure* of the autocracy in *all its aspects*? In order to carry on agitation round concrete instances of oppression, these instances must be exposed (as it is necessary to expose factory abuses in order to carry on economic agitation).

One might think this to be clear enough. It turns out, however, that it is only in words that "all" are agreed on the need to develop political consciousness, *in all its aspects*. It turns out that *Rabocheye Dyelo*, for example, far from tackling the task of organising (or making a start in organising) comprehensive political exposure, is even trying *to drag Iskra*, which has undertaken this task, *away from it*. Listen to the following: "The political struggle of the working class is merely [it is certainly not "merely"] the most developed, wide, and effective form of the economic struggle" (programme of *Rabocheye Dyelo*, published in issue no. 1, p. 3). "The Social-Democrats are now confronted with the task of lending the economic struggle itself, as far as possible, a political character" ([A.] Martynov, *Rabocheye Dyelo*, no. 10, p. 42). "The economic struggle is the most widely applicable means of drawing the masses into active political struggle" (resolution adopted by the Conference of the Union Abroad and "amendments" thereto, *Two Conferences*, pp. 11 and 17). As the reader will observe, all these theses permeate *Rabocheye Dyelo* from its very first number to the latest "Instructions to the Editors," and all of them evidently express a single view regarding political agitation and struggle. Let us examine this view from the standpoint of the opinion prevailing among all Economists, that political agitation must *follow* economic agitation. Is it true that, in general,[3] the economic struggle "is the most widely applicable means" of drawing the masses into the political struggle? It is entirely untrue. *Any and every* manifestation of police tyranny and autocratic outrage, not only in connection with the economic struggle, is not one whit less "widely applicable" as a means of "drawing in" the masses. The rural superintendents and the flogging of peasants, the corruption of the officials and the police treatment of the "common people" in the cities, the fight against the famine-stricken and the suppression of the popular striving towards enlightenment and knowledge, the extortion of taxes and the persecution of the religious sects, the humiliating treatment of soldiers and the barrack methods in the treatment of the students and liberal intellectuals—do all these and a thousand other similar manifestations of tyranny, though not directly connected with the "economic" struggle, represent in general, *less* "widely applicable" means and occasions for political agitation and for drawing the masses into the political struggle? The very opposite is true. Of the sum total of cases in which the workers suffer (either on their own account or on account of those closely connected with them) from tyranny, violence, and the lack of rights, undoubtedly only a small minority represent cases of police tyranny in the trade-union struggle as such. Why then should we, beforehand, *restrict* the scope of political agitation by declaring only *one* of the means to be "the most widely applicable," when Social-Democrats must have, in addition, other, generally speaking, no less "widely applicable" means?

In the dim and distant past (a full year ago! . . . ) *Rabocheye Dyelo* wrote: "The masses begin to understand immediate political demands after one strike, or at all events, after several", "as soon as the government sets the police and gendarmerie against them" (*August,* 1900, no. 7, p. 15). This opportunist theory of stages has now been rejected by the Union Abroad, which makes a concession to us by declaring: "There is no need whatever to conduct political agitation right from the beginning, exclusively on an economic basis" (*Two Conferences,* p. 11). The Union's repudiation of part of its former errors will show the future historian of Russian Social-Democracy better than any number of lengthy arguments the depths to which our Economists have degraded socialism! But the Union Abroad must be very naïve indeed to imagine that the abandonment of one form of restricting politics will induce us to agree to another form. Would it not be more logical to say, in this case too, that the economic struggle should be conducted on the widest possible basis, that it should always be utilised for political agitation, but that "there is no need whatever" to regard the economic struggle as the *most* widely applicable means of drawing the masses into active political struggle?

The Union Abroad attaches significance to the fact that it has substituted the phrase "most widely applicable means" for the phrase "the best means" contained in one of the resolutions of the Fourth Congress of the Jewish Workers' Union (Bund). We confess that we find it difficult to say which of these resolutions is the better one. In our opinion they are *both worse.* Both the Union Abroad and the Bund fall into the error (partly, perhaps, unconsciously, under the influence of tradition) of giving an Economist, trade-unionist interpretation to politics. Whether this is done by employing the word "best" or the words "most widely applicable" makes no essential difference whatever. Had the Union Abroad said that "political agitation on an economic basis" is the most widely applied (not "applicable") means, it would have been right in regard to a certain period in the development of our Social-Democratic movement. It would have been right in regard to the *Economists* and to many (if not the majority) of the practical workers of 1898–1901; for these practical Economists *applied* political agitation (to the extent that they applied it at all) *almost exclusively on an economic basis.* Political agitation on *such* lines was recognised and, as we have seen, even recommended by *Rabochaya Mysl* and the Self-Emancipation Group. *Rabocheye Dyelo* should have *strongly condemned* the fact that the useful work of economic agitation was accompanied by the harmful restriction of the political struggle; instead, it declares the means most widely *applied (by the Economists)* to be the most widely *applicable!* It is not surprising that when we call these people Economists, they can do nothing but pour every manner of abuse upon us; call us "mystifiers," "disrupters," "papal nuncio," and "slanderers";[4] go complaining to the whole world that we have mortally offended them; and declare almost on oath that "not a single Social-Democratic organisation is now tinged with Economism."[5] Oh, those evil, slanderous politicians! They must have deliberately invented this Economism, out of sheer hatred of mankind, in order mortally to offend other people.

What concrete, real meaning attaches to Martynov's words when he sets before Social-Democracy the task of "lending the economic struggle itself a political character"? The economic struggle is the collective struggle of the workers against their employers for better terms *in the sale of their labour-power,* for better living and working conditions. This struggle is necessarily a trade-union struggle, because working conditions differ greatly in different trades, and, consequently, the struggle *to improve* them can only be conducted on the basis of trade organisations (in the Western countries, through trade unions; in Russia, through temporary trade associations and through leaflets, etc.). Lending "the economic struggle itself a political character" means, therefore, striving to secure satisfaction of these trade demands, the improvement of working conditions in each separate trade by means of "legislative and administrative measures" (as Martynov puts it on the ensuing page of his article, p. 43). This is precisely what all workers' trade unions do and always have done. Read the works of the soundly scientific (and "soundly" opportunist) Mr. [Sidney] and Mrs. [Beatrice] Webb and you will see that the British trade unions long ago recognised, and have long been carrying out, the task of "lending the economic struggle itself a political character"; they have long been fighting for the right to strike, for the removal of all legal hindrances to the co-operative and trade-union movements, for laws to protect women and children, for the improvement of labour conditions by means of health and factory legislation, etc.

Thus, the pompous phrase about "lending the economic struggle *itself* a political character," which sounds so "terrifically" profound and revolutionary, serves as a screen to conceal what is in fact the traditional striving *to degrade*

Social-Democratic politics to the level of trade-union politics. Under the guise of rectifying the one-sidedness of *Iskra,* which, it is alleged, places "the revolutionising of dogma higher than the revolutionising of life,"[6] we are presented with the *struggle for economic reforms* as if it were something entirely new. In point of fact, the phrase "lending the economic struggle itself a political character" means nothing more than the struggle for economic reforms. Martynov himself might have come to this simple conclusion, had he pondered over the significance of his own words. "Our Party," he says, training his heaviest guns on *Iskra,* "could and should have presented concrete demands to the government for legislative and administrative measures against economic exploitation, unemployment, famine, etc." (*Rabocheye Dyelo,* no. 10, pp. 42–43). Concrete demands for measures—does not this mean demands for social reforms? Again we ask the impartial reader: Are we slandering the *Rabocheye Dyelo*ites (may I be forgiven for this awkward, currently used designation!) by calling them concealed Bernsteinians when, as their point of *disagreement* with *Iskra,* they advance their thesis on the necessity of struggling for economic reforms?

Revolutionary Social-Democracy has always included the struggle for reforms as part of its activities. But it utilises "economic" agitation for the purpose of presenting to the government, not only demands for all sorts of measures, but also (and primarily) the demand that it cease to be an autocratic government. Moreover, it considers it its duty to present this demand to the government on the basis, not of the economic struggle *alone,* but of all manifestations in general of public and political life. In a word, it subordinates the struggle for reforms, as the part to the whole, to the revolutionary struggle for freedom and for socialism. Martynov, however, resuscitates the theory of stages in new form and strives to prescribe, as it were, an exclusively economic path of development for the political struggle. By advancing at this moment, when the revolutionary movement is on the upgrade, an alleged special "task" of struggling for reforms, he is dragging the party backwards and is playing into the hands of both "Economist" and liberal opportunism.

To proceed. Shamefacedly hiding the struggle for reforms behind the pompous thesis of "lending the economic struggle itself a political character," Martynov advanced, as if it were a special point, *exclusively economic* (indeed, exclusively factory) *reforms.* As to the reason for his doing that, we do not know it. Carelessness, perhaps? Yet if he had in mind something else besides "factory" reforms, then the whole of his thesis, which we have cited, loses all sense. Perhaps he did it because he considers it possible and probable that the government will make "concessions" only in the economic sphere?[7] If so, then it is a strange delusion. Concessions are also possible and are made in the sphere of legislation concerning flogging, passports, land redemption payments, religious sects, the censorship, etc., etc. "Economic" concessions (or pseudo-concessions) are, of course, the cheapest and most advantageous from the government's point of view, because by these means it hopes to win the confidence of the working masses. For this very reason, we Social-Democrats *must not* under any circumstances or in any way whatever create grounds for the belief (or the misunderstanding) that we attach greater value to economic reforms, or that we regard them as being particularly important, etc. "Such demands," writes Martynov, speaking of the concrete demands for legislative and administrative measures referred to above, "would not be merely a hollow sound, because, promising certain palpable results, they might be actively supported by the working masses. . . ." We are not Economists, oh no! We only cringe as slavishly before the "palpableness" of concrete results as do the Bernsteins, the Prokoviches, the Struves, the R.M.'s, and *tutti quanti*! We only wish to make it understood (together with Nartsis Tuporylov) that all which "does not promise palpable results" is merely a "hollow sound"! We are only trying to argue as if the working masses were incapable (and had not already proved their capabilities, notwithstanding those who ascribe their own philistinism to them) of actively supporting *every* protest against the autocracy, even if it *promises absolutely no palpable results whatever*!

Let us take, for example, the very "measures" for the relief of unemployment and the famine that Martynov himself advances. *Rabocheye Dyelo* is enaged, judging by what it has promised, in drawing up and elaborating a programme of "concrete [in the form of bills?] demands for legislative and administrative measures," "promising palpable results," while *Iskra*, which "constantly places the revolutionising of dogma higher than the revolutionising of life," has tried to explain the inseparable connection between unemployment and the whole capitalist system, has given warning that "famine is coming," has exposed the police "fight against the famine-stricken," and the outrageous "provisional penal servitude regulations"; and *Zarya* has published a special reprint, in the form of an agitational pamphlet, of a section of its "Review of Home Affairs," dealing with the famine.[8] But good God! How "one-sided" were these incorrigibly narrow and orthodox doctrinaires, how deaf to the calls of "life itself"! Their articles contained—oh horror!—*not a single*, can you imagine it?—not a single "concrete demand" "promising palpable results"! Poor doctrinaires! They ought to be sent to Krichevsky and Martynov to be taught that tactics are a process of growth, of that which grows, etc., and that the economic struggle *itself* should be given a political character!

"In addition to its immediate revolutionary significance, the economic struggle of the workers against the employers and the government (*'economic struggle against the government'*!) has also this significance: it constantly brings home to the workers the fact that they have no political rights" (Martynov, p. 44). We quote this passage, not in order to repeat for the hundredth and thousandth time what has been said above, but in order to express particular thanks to Martynov for this excellent new formula: "the economic struggle of the workers against the employers and the government." What a pearl! With what inimitable skill and mastery in eliminating all partial disagreements and shades of differences among Economists this clear and concise proposition expresses the *quintessence of Economism,* from summoning the workers "to the political struggle, which they carry on in the general interest, for the improvement of the conditions of all the workers,"9 continuing through the theory of stages, and ending in the resolution of the Conference on the "most widely applicable," etc. "Economic struggle against the government" is precisely trade-unionist politics, which is still very far from being Social-Democratic politics.

### 4E. "Conspiratorial" Organisation and "Democratism"

Yet there are many people among us who are so sensitive to the "voice of life" that they fear it more than anything in the world and charge the adherents of the views here expounded with following a Narodnaya Volya line, with failing to understand "democratism," etc. These accusations, which, of course, have been echoed by *Rabocheye Dyelo,* need to be dealt with.

The writer of these lines knows very well that the St. Petersburg Economists levelled the charge of Narodnaya Volya tendencies also against *Rabochaya Gazeta* (which is quite understandable when one compares it with *Rabochaya Mysl*). We were not in the least surprised, therefore, when, soon after the appearance of *Iskra,* a comrade informed us that the Social-Democrats in the town of X describe *Iskra* as a Narodnaya Volya organ. We, of course, were flattered by this accusation; for what decent Social-Democrat has not been accused by the Economists of being a Narodnaya Volya sympathiser?

These accusations are the result of a twofold misunderstanding. First, the history of the revolutionary movement is so little known among us that the name "Narodnaya Volya" is used to denote any idea of a militant centralised organisation which declares determined war upon tsarism. But the magnificent organisation that the revolutionaries had in the seventies, and that should serve us as a model, was not established by the Narodnaya Volya, but by the *Zemlya i Volya,* which split up into the Chorny Peredel and the Narodnaya Volya. Consequently, to regard a militant revolutionary organisation as something specifically Narodnaya Volya in character is absurd both historically and logically; for *no* revolutionary trend, if it seriously thinks of struggle, can dispense with such an organisation. The mistake the Narodnaya Volya committed was not in striving to enlist *all* the discontented in the organisation and to direct this organisation to resolute struggle against the autocracy; on the contrary, that was its great historical merit. The mistake was in relying on a theory which in substance was not a revolutionary theory at all, and the Narodnaya Volya members either did not know how, or were unable, to link their movement inseparably with the class struggle in the developing capitalist society. Only a gross failure to understand Marxism (or an "understanding" of it in the spirit of "Struveism") could prompt the opinion that the rise of a mass, spontaneous working-class movement *relieves* us of the duty of creating as good as an organisation of revolutionaries as the Zemlya i Volya had, or, indeed, an incomparably better one. On the contrary, this movement *imposes* the duty upon us; for the spontaneous struggle of the proletariat will not become its genuine "class struggle" until this struggle is led by a strong organisation of revolutionaries.

Secondly, many people, including apparently B. Krichevsky (*Rabocheye Dyelo*, no. 10, p. 18), misunderstand the polemics that Social-Democrats have always waged against the "conspiratorial" view of the political struggle. We have always protested, and will, of course, continue to protest against *confining* the political struggle to conspiracy.[10] But this does not, of course, mean that we deny the need for a strong revolutionary organisation. Thus, in the pamphlet mentioned in the preceding footnote, after the polemics against reducing the political struggle to a conspiracy, a description is given (as a Social-Democratic ideal) of an organisation so strong as to be able to "resort to . . . rebellion" and to every "other form of attack," in order to "deliver a smashing blow against absolutism."[11] In *form* such a strong revolutionary organisation in an autocratic country may also be described as a "conspiratorial" organisation, because the French word "conspiration" is the equivalent of the Russian word "*zagovor*" ("conspiracy"), and such an organisation must have the utmost secrecy. Secrecy is such a necessary condition for this kind of organisation that all the other conditions (number and selection of members, functions, etc.) must be made to conform to it. It would be extremely naïve indeed, therefore, to fear the charge that we Social-Democrats desire to create a conspiratorial organisation. Such a charge should be as flattering to every opponent of Economism as the charge of following a Narodnaya Volya line.

The objection may be raised that such a powerful and strictly secret organisation, which concentrates in its hands all the threads of secret activities, an organisation which of necessity is centralised, may too easily rush into a premature attack, may thoughtlessly intensify the movement before the growth of political discontent, the intensity of the ferment and anger of the working class, etc., have made such an attack possible and necessary. Our reply to this is: Speaking abstractly, it cannot be denied, of course, that a militant organisation *may* thoughtlessly engage in battle, which *may* end in a defeat entirely avoidable under other conditions. But we cannot confine ourselves to abstract reasoning on such a question, because every battle bears within itself the abstract possibility of defeat, and there is no way of *reducing* this possibility except by organised preparation for battle. If, however, we proceed from the concrete conditions at present obtaining in Russia, we must come to the positive conclusion that a strong revolutionary organisation is absolutely necessary precisely for the purpose of giving stability to the movement and of *safeguarding* it against the possibility of making thoughtless attacks. Precisely at the

present time, when no such organisation yet exists, and when the revolutionary movement is rapidly and spontaneously growing, we *already observe* two
opposite extremes (which, as is to be expected, "meet"). These are: the utterly
unsound Economism and the preaching of moderation, and the equally unsound "excitative terror", which strives "artificially to call forth symptoms of
the end of the movement, which is developing and strengthening itself, when
this movement is as yet nearer to the start than to the end" (V. Zasulich, in
*Zarya*, no. 2-3, p. 353). And the instance of *Rabocheye Dyelo* shows that *there
exist* Social-Democrats who give way to both these extremes. This is not surprising, for, apart from other reasons, the "economic struggle against the employers and the government" can *never* satisfy revolutionaries, and opposite
extremes will therefore always appear here and there. Only a centralised, militant organisation that consistently carries out a Social-Democratic policy, that
satisfies, so to speak, all revolutionary instincts and strivings, can safeguard the
movement against making thoughtless attacks and prepare attacks that hold
out the promise of success.

A further objection may be raised, that the views on organisation here expounded contradict the "democratic principle." Now, while the earlier accusation was specifically Russian in origin, this one is *specifically foreign* in
character. And only an organisation abroad (the Union of Russian Social-
Democrats Abroad) was capable of giving its Editorial Board instructions like
the following:

> "*Organisational Principle.* In order to secure the successful development and
> unification of Social-Democracy, the broad democratic principle of Party orga-
> nisation must be emphasised, developed, and fought for; this is particularly
> necessary in view of the anti-democratic tendencies that have revealed them-
> selves in the ranks of our Party (*Two Conferences*, p. 18)"

We shall see in the next chapter how *Rabocheye Dyelo* combats *Iskra's*
"anti-democratic tendencies." For the present, we shall examine more closely
the "principle" that the Economists advance. Everyone will probably agree
that "the broad democratic principle" presupposes the two following conditions: first, full publicity, and secondly, election to all offices. It would be absurd to speak of democracy without publicity, moreover, without a publicity
that is not limited to the membership of the organisation. We call the German
Socialist Party a democratic organisation because all its activities are carried
out publicly; even its party congresses are held in public. But no one would
call an organisation democratic that is hidden from every one but its members
by a veil of secrecy. What is the use, then, of advancing "the *broad* democratic
principle" when the fundamental condition for this principle *cannot be fulfilled* by a secret organisation? "The broad principle" proves itself simply to be
a resounding but hollow phrase. Moreover, it reveals a total lack of under-

standing of the urgent tasks of the moment in regard to organisation. Everyone knows how great the lack of secrecy is among the "broad" masses of our revolutionaries. We have heard the bitter complaints of B—v on this score and his absolutely just demand for a "strict selection of members" (*Rabocheye Dyelo*, no. 6, p. 42). Yet, persons who boast a keen "sense of realities" *urge*, in a situation like this, not the strictest secrecy and the strictest (consequently, more restricted) selection of members, but "the *broad* democratic principle"! This is what you call being wide off the mark.

Nor is the situation any better with regard to the second attribute of democracy, the principle of election. In politically free countries, this condition is taken for granted. "They are members of the Party who accept the principles of the Party programme and render the Party all possible support," reads Clause 1 of the Rules of the German Social-Democratic Party. Since the entire political arena is as open to the public view as is a theatre stage to the audience, this acceptance or non-acceptance, support or opposition, is known to all from the press and from public meetings. Everyone knows that a certain political figure began in such and such a way, passed through such and such an evolution, behaved in a trying moment in such and such a manner, and possesses such and such qualities; consequently, *all* party members, knowing all the facts, can elect or refuse to elect this person to a particular party office. The general control (in the literal sense of the term) exercised over every act of a party man in the political field brings into existence an automatically operating mechanism which produces what in biology is called the "survival of the fittest." "Natural selection" by full publicity, election, and general control provides the assurance that, in the last analysis, every political figure will be "in his proper place," do the work for which he is best fitted by his powers and abilities, feel the effects of his mistakes on himself, and prove before all the world his ability to recognise mistakes and to avoid them.

Try to fit this picture into the frame of our autocracy! Is it conceivable in Russia for all "who accept the principles of the Party programme and render the Party all possible support" to control every action of the revolutionary working in secret? Is it possible for all to elect one of these revolutionaries to any particular office, when, in the very interests of the work, the revolutionary *must* conceal his identity from nine out of ten of these "all"? Reflect somewhat over the real meaning of the high-sounding phrases to which *Rabocheye Dyelo* gives utterance, and you will realise that "broad democracy" in Party organisation, amidst the gloom of the autocracy and the domination of gendarmerie, is nothing more than a *useless and harmful toy*. It is a useless toy because, in point of fact, no revolutionary organisation has ever practised, or could practise, *broad* democracy, however much it may have desired to do so. It is a harmful toy because any attempt to practice "the broad democratic principle" will simply facilitate the work of the police in carrying out large-scale raids, will perpetuate the prevailing primitiveness, and will divert the thoughts of the practical workers from the serious and pressing task of training themselves to become professional revolutionaries to that of drawing up detailed "paper" rules for election systems. Only abroad, where very often people with no opportunity for conducting really active work gather, could this "playing at democracy" develop here and there, especially in small groups.

To show the unseemliness of *Rabocheye Dyelo's* favorite trick of advancing the plausible "principle" of democracy in revolutionary affairs, we shall again summon a witness. This witness, Y. Serebryakov, editor of the London magazine, *Nakanune,* has a soft spot for *Rabocheye Dyelo* and is filled with a great hatred for Plekhanov and the "Plekhanovites." In its articles on the split in the Union of Russian Social-Democrats Abroad, *Nakanune* definitely sided with *Rabocheye Dyelo* and poured a stream of petty abuse upon Plekhanov. All the more valuable, therefore, is this witness in the question at issue. In *Nakanune* for July (no. 7) 1899, in an article entitled "Concerning the Manifesto of the Self-Emancipation of the Workers Group," Serebryakov argued that it was "indecent" to talk about such things as "self-deception, leadership, and the so-called Areopagus in a serious revolutionary movement" and, *inter alia,* wrote:

"Myshkin, Rogachov, Zhelyabov, Mikhailov, Perovskaya, Figner, and others never regarded themselves as leaders, and no one ever elected or appointed them as such, although in actuality, they were leaders, because, in the propaganda period, as well as in the period of the struggle against the government, they took the brunt of the work upon themselves, they went into the most dangerous places, and their activities were the most fruitful. They became leaders, not because they wished it, but because the comrades surrounding them had confidence in their wisdom, in their energy, in their loyalty. To be afraid of some kind of Areopagus (if it is not feared, why write about it?) that would arbitrarily govern the movement is far too naïve. Who would pay heed to it?"

We ask the reader, in what way does the "Areopagus" differ from "anti-democratic tendencies"? And is it not evident that *Rabocheye Dyelo's* "plausible" organisational principle is equally naïve and indecent; naïve, because no one would pay heed to the "Areopagus," or people with "anti-democratic tendencies," if "the comrades surrounding them had" no "confidence in their wisdom, energy, and loyalty"; indecent, because it is a demagogic sally calculated to play on the conceit of some, on the ignorance of others regarding the actual state of our movement, and on the lack of training and the ignorance of the history of the revolutionary movement on the part of still others. The only serious organisational principle for the active workers of our movement should be the strictest secrecy, the strictest selection of members, and the training of professional revolutionaries. Given these qualities, something even more than "democratism" would be guaranteed to us, namely, complete, comradely, mutual confidence among revolutionaries. This is absolutely essential for us, because there can be no question of replacing it by general democratic control in Russia. It would be a great mistake to believe that the impossibility of establishing real "democratic" control renders the members of the revolutionary organisation beyond control altogether. They have not the time to think about toy forms of democratism (democratism within a close and compact body of comrades in which complete, mutual confidence prevails), but they have a lively sense of their *responsibility*, knowing as they do from experience that an organisation of real revolutionaries will stop at nothing to rid itself of an unworthy member. Moreover, there is a fairly well-developed public opinion in Russian (and international) revolutionary circles which has a long history behind it, and which sternly and ruthlessly punishes every departure from the duties of comradeship (and "democratism," real and not toy democratism, certainly forms a component part of the conception of comradeship). Take all this into consideration and you will realise that this talk and these resolutions about "anti-democratic tendencies" have the musty odour of the playing at generals which is indulged in abroad.

It must be observed also that the other source of this talk, viz., naïveté, is likewise fostered by the confusion of ideas concerning the meaning of democracy. In Mr. and Mrs. Webb's book on the English trade unions there is an interesting chapter entitled "Primitive Democracy." In it the authors relate how the English workers, in the first period of existence of their unions, considered it an indispensable sign of democracy for all the members to do all the work of managing the unions; not only were all questions decided by the vote of all the members, but all official duties were fulfilled by all the members in turn. A long period of historical experience was required for workers to realise the absurdity of such a conception of democracy and to make them understand the necessity for representative institutions, on the one hand, and for full-time officials, on the other. Only after a number of cases of financial bankruptcy of trade-union treasuries occurred did the workers realise that the rates of contributions and benefits cannot be decided merely by a democratic vote, but that this requires also the advice of insurance experts. Let us take also [Karl] Kautsky's book on parliamentarism and legislation by the people. There we find that the conclusions drawn by the Marxist theoretician coincide with the lessons learned from many years of practical experience by the workers who organised "spontaneously." Kautsky strongly protests against Rittinghausen's primitive conception of democracy; he ridicules those who in the name of democracy demand that "popular newspapers shall be edited directly by the people"; he shows the need for *professional* journalists, parliamentarians, etc., for the Social-Democratic leadership of the proletarian class struggle; he attacks the "socialism of anarchists and *littérateurs*," who in their "striving for effect" extol direct legislation by the whole people, completely failing to understand that this idea can be applied only relatively in modern society.

Those who have performed practical work in our movement know how widespread the "primitive" conception of democracy is among the masses of the students and workers. It is not surprising that this conception penetrates also into rules of organisations and into literature. The Economists of the Bernsteinian persuasion included in their rules the following: "§10. All affairs affecting the interests of the whole of the union organisation shall be decided by a majority vote of all its members." The Economists of the terrorist persuasion repeat after them: "The decisions of the committee shall become effective only after they have been referred to all the circles" (*Svoboda,* no. 1, p. 67). Observe that this proposal for a widely applied referendum is advanced *in addition* to the demand that *the whole of* the organisation be built on an elective basis! We would not, of course, on this account condemn practical workers who have had too few opportunities for studying the theory and practice of real democratic organisations. But when *Rabocheye Dyelo,* which lays claim to leadership, confines itself, under such conditions, to a resolution on broad democratic principles, can this be described as anything but a mere "striving for effect"?

## Notes

1. To avoid misunderstanding, we must point out that here, and throughout this pamphlet, by economic struggle, we imply (in keeping with the accepted usage among us) the "practical economic struggle", which Engels, in the passage quoted above, described as "resistance to the capitalists", and which in free countries is known as the organised-labour, syndical, or trade-union struggle.

2. In the present chapter we deal only with the *political* struggle, in its broader or narrower meaning. Therefore, we note only in passing, merely as a curiosity, *Rabocheye Dyelo's* charge that *Iskra* is "too restrained" in regard to the economic struggle (*Two Conferences,* p. 27, rehashed by Martynov in his pamphlet, *Social-Democracy and the Working Class*). If the accusers computed by the hundredweights or reams (as they are so fond of doing) any given year's discussion of the economic struggle in the industrial section of *Iskra,* in comparison with the corresponding sections of *Rabocheye Dyelo* and *Rabochaya Mysl* combined, they would easily see that the latter lag behind even in this respect. Apparently, the realisation of this simple truth compels them to resort to arguments that clearly reveal their confusion. "*Iskra,*", they write, "willy-nilly [!] is compelled [!] to reckon with the imperative demands of life and to publish at least [!!] correspondence about the working-class movement" (*Two Conferences,* p. 27). Now this is really a crushing argument!

3. We say "in general", because *Rabocheye Dyelo* speaks of general principles and of the general tasks of the Party as a whole. Undoubtedly, cases occur in practice when politics really *must* follow economics, but only Economists can speak of this in a resolution intended to apply to the whole of Russia. Cases do occur when *it is possible* "right from the beginning" to carry on political agitation "exclusively on an economic basis"; yet *Rabocheye Dyelo* came in the end to the conclusion that "there is no need for this whatever" (*Two Conferences,* p. 11). In the following chapter, we shall show that the tactics of the "politicians" and revolutionaries not only do not ignore the trade-union tasks of Social-Democracy, but that, on the contrary, they alone *can secure* their consistent fulfillment.

4. These are the precise expressions used in *Two Conferences,* pp. 31, 32, 28, and 30.

5. *Two Conferences,* p. 32.

6. *Rabocheye Dyelo,* no. 10, p. 60. This is the Martynov variation of the application, which we have characterised above, of the thesis "Every step of real movement is more important than a dozen programmes" to the present chaotic state of our movement. In fact, this is merely a translation into Russian of the notorious Bernsteinian sentence: "The movement is everything, the final aim is nothing."

7. P.43. "Of course, when we advise the workers to present certain economic demands to the government, we do so because in the *economic* sphere the autocratic government is, of necessity, prepared to make certain concessions."

8. See *Collected Works,* vol. 5, pp. 253–74.—Ed.

9. *Rabochaya Mysl,* "*Separate Supplement,*" p. 14.

10. Cf. *The Tasks of the Russian Social-Democrats,* p. 21, polemics against P. L. Lavrov. (See *Collected Works,* vol. 2 pp. 340–41.—Ed.)

11. *The Tasks of the Russian Social-Democrats,* p. 23 (See *Collected Works,* vol. 2, p. 342—*Ed.*) Apropos, we shall give another illustration of the fact that *Rabocheye Dyelo* either does not understand what it is talking about or changes its views "with the wind". In no. 1 of *Rabocheye Dyelo,* we find the following passage in italics: "*The substance set forth in the pamphlet accords entirely with the editorial programme of Rabocheye Dyelo*" (p. 142). Really? Does the view that the overthrow of the autocracy must not be set as the first task of the mass movement accord with the views expressed in *The Tasks of the Russian Social-Democrats?* Do the theory of "the economic struggle against the employers and the government" and the stages theory accord with the views expressed in that pamphlet? We leave it to the reader to judge whether a periodical that understands the meaning of "accordance in opinion" in this peculiar manner can have firm principles.

## V.I. LENIN

## *The Economic Base of the Withering Away*
## *of the State*

In 1917 Lenin returned from Europe to lead the Bolsheviks in the Russian Revolution. In the following selections from *The State and Revolution,* written in that year, Lenin explains how to continue the revolution and consolidate its gains. In greater detail than Marx, he outlines the transition from bourgeois democracy to proletarian dictatorship to higher communism.

A most detailed elucidation of this question is given by Marx in his *Critique of the Gotha Programme* (letter to Bracke, 15 May 1875, printed only in 1891 in the *Neue Zeit,* IX-1, and in a special Russian edition).[1] The polemical part of this remarkable work, consisting of a criticism of Lassalleanism, has, so to speak, overshadowed its positive part, namely, the analysis of the connection between the development of Communism and the withering away of the state.

### 1. Formulation of the Question by Marx

From a superficial comparison of the letter of Marx to Bracke (15 May 1875) with Engels's letter to [August] Bebel (28 March 1875), analysed above, it might appear that Marx was much more "pro-state" than Engels, and that the difference of opinion between the two writers on the question of the state is very considerable.

Engels suggests to Bebel that all the chatter about the state should be thrown overboard; that the word "state" should be eliminated from the programme and replaced by "community"; Engels even declares that the Commune was really no longer a state in the proper sense of the word. And Marx even speaks of the "future state in Communist society," i.e., he is apparently recognising the necessity of a state even under Communism.

But such a view would be fundamentally incorrect. A closer examination shows that Marx's and Engels's views on the state and its withering away were completely identical, and that Marx's expression quoted above refers merely to this withering away of the state.

It is clear that there can be no question of defining the exact moment of the *future* withering away—the more so as it must obviously be a rather lengthy process. The apparent difference between Marx and Engels is due to the different subjects they dealt with, the different aims they were pursuing. Engels set out to show to Bebel, in plain, bold and broad outline, all the absurdity of the current superstitions concerning the state, shared to no small degree by [Ferdinand] Lassalle himself. Marx, on the other hand, only touches upon *this* question in passing, being interested mainly in another subject—the *evolution* of Communist society.

The whole theory of Marx is an application of the theory of evolution —in its most consistent, complete, well considered and fruitful form—to modern capitalism. It was natural for Marx to raise the question of applying this theory both to the *coming* collapse of capitalism and to the *future* evolution of *future* Communism.

On the basis of what *data* can the future evolution of future Communism be considered?

On the basis of the fact that *it has its origin* in capitalism, that it develops historically from capitalism, that it is the result of the action of a social force to which capitalism *has given birth*. There is no shadow of an attempt on Marx's part to conjure up a Utopia, to make idle guesses about that which cannot be known. Marx treats the question of Communism in the same way as a naturalist would treat the question of the evolution of, say, a new biological species, if he knew that such and such was its origin, and such and such the direction in which it changed.

Marx, first of all, brushes aside the confusion the Gotha Programme brings into the question of the interrelation between state and society.

> "Contemporary society" is the capitalist society—he writes—which exists in all civilised countries, more or less free of medieval admixture, more or less modified by each country's particular historical development, more or less developed. In contrast with this, the "contemporary state" varies with every state boundary. It is different in the Prusso-German Empire from what it is in Switzerland, and different in England from what it is in the United States. The "contemporary state" is therefore a fiction.

Nevertheless, in spite of the motley variety of their forms, the different states of the various civilised countries all have  this in common: they are all

based on modern bourgeois society, only a little more or less capitalistically developed. Consequently, they also have certain essential characteristics in common. In this sense, it is possible to speak of the "contemporary state" in contrast to the future, when its present root, bourgeois society, will have perished.

Then the question arises: what transformation will the state undergo in a
Communist society? In other words, what social functions analogous to the
present functions of the state will then still survive? This question can only be
answered scientifically, and however many thousand times the word people is
combined with the word state, we get not a flea-jump closer to the problem. . . .[2]

Having thus ridiculed all talk about a "people's state," Marx formulates
the question and warns us, as it were, that to arrive at a scientific answer one
must rely only on firmly established scientific data.

The first fact that has been established with complete exactness by the
whole theory of evolution, by science as a whole—a fact which the Utopians
forgot, and which is forgotten by the present-day opportunists who are afraid
of the Socialist revolution—is that, historically, there must undoubtedly be a
special stage or epoch of *transition* from capitalism to Communism.

## 2. Transition from Capitalism to Communism

Between capitalist and Communist society—Marx continues—lies the
period of the revolutionary transformation of the former into the latter. To this
also corresponds a political transition period, in which the state can be no other
than *the revolutionary dictatorship of the proletariat.*[3]

This conclusion Marx bases on an analysis of the role played by the proletariat in modern capitalist society, on the data concerning the evolution of
this society, and on the irreconcilability of the opposing interests of the proletariat and the bourgeoisie.

Earlier the question was put thus: to attain its emancipation, the proletariat must overthrow the bourgeoisie, conquer political power and establish
its own revolutionary dictatorship.

Now the question is put somewhat differently: the transition from capitalist society, developing towards Communism, towards a Communist society,
is impossible without a "political transition period," and the state in this period can only be the revolutionary dictatorship of the proletariat.

What, then, is the relation of this dictatorship to democracy?

We have seen that the *Communist Manifesto* simply places side by side
the two ideas: the "transformation of the proletariat into the ruling class," and

the "establishment of democracy." On the basis of all that has been said above, one can define more exactly how democracy changes in the transition from capitalism to Communism.

In capitalist society, under the conditions most favourable to its development, we have more or less complete democracy in the democratic republic. But this democracy is always bound by the narrow framework of capitalist exploitation, and consequently always remains, in reality, a democracy for the minority, only for the possessing classes, only for the rich. Freedom in capitalist society always remains just about the same as it was in the ancient Greek republics: freedom for the slave-owners. The modern wage-slaves, owing to the conditions of capitalist exploitation, are so much crushed by want and poverty that "democracy is nothing to them," "politics is nothing to them"; that, in the ordinary peaceful course of events, the majority of the population is debarred from participating in social and political life.

The correctness of this statement is perhaps most clearly proved by Germany, just because in this state constitutional legality lasted and remained stable for a remarkably long time—for nearly half a century (1871–1914)—and because Social-Democracy in Germany during that time was able to achieve far more than in other countries in "utilising legality," and was able to organise into a political party a larger proportion of the working class than anywhere else in the world.

What, then, is this largest proportion of politically conscious and active wage-slaves that has so far been observed in capitalist society? One million members of the Social-Democratic Party—out of fifteen million wage-workers! Three million organised in trade unions—out of fifteen million!

Democracy for an insignificant minority, democracy for the rich—that is the democracy of capitalist society. If we look more closely into the mechanism of capitalist democracy, everywhere, both in the "petty"—so-called petty—details of the suffrage (residential qualification, exclusion of women, etc.), and in the technique of the representative institutions, in the actual obstacles to the right of assembly (public buildings are not for "beggars"!), in the purely capitalist organisation of the daily press, etc., etc.—on all sides we see restriction after restriction upon democracy. These restrictions, exceptions, exclusions, obstacles for the poor, seem slight, especially in the eyes of one who has himself never known want and has never been in close contact with the oppressed classes in their mass life (and nine-tenths, if not ninety-nine hundredths, of the bourgeois publicists and politicians are of this class), but in their sum total these restrictions exclude and squeeze out the poor from politics and from an active share in democracy.

Marx splendidly grasped this *essence* of capitalist democracy, when, in analysing the experience of the Commune, he said that the oppressed were allowed, once every few years, to decide which particular representatives of the oppressing class should be in parliament to represent and repress them!

But from this capitalist democracy—inevitably narrow, subtly rejecting the poor, and therefore hypocritical and false to the core—progress does not march onward, simply, smoothly and directly, to "greater and greater democracy," as the liberal professors and petty-bourgeois opportunists would have us believe. No, progress marches onward, i.e., towards Communism, through the dictatorship of the proletariat; it cannot do otherwise, for there is no one else and no other way to *break the resistance* of the capitalist exploiters.

But the dictatorship of the proletariat—i.e., the organisation of the vanguard of the oppressed as the ruling class for the purpose of crushing the oppressors—cannot produce merely an expansion of democracy. *Together* with an immense expansion of democracy which *for the first time* becomes democracy for the poor, democracy for the people, and not democracy for the rich folk, the dictatorship of the proletariat produces a series of restrictions of liberty in the case of the oppressors, the exploiters, the capitalists. We must crush them in order to free humanity from wage-slavery; their resistance must be broken by force; it is clear that where there is suppression there is also violence, there is no liberty, no democracy.

Engels expressed this splendidly in his letter to Bebel when he said, as the reader will remember, that "as long as the proletariat still *needs* the state, it needs it not in the interests of freedom, but for the purpose of crushing its antagonists; and as soon as it becomes possible to speak of freedom, then the state, as such, ceases to exist."

Democracy for the vast majority of the people, and suppression by force, i.e., exclusion from democracy, of the exploiters and oppressors of the people —this is the modification of democracy during the *transition* from capitalism to Communism.

Only in Communist society, when the resistance of the capitalists has been completely broken, when the capitalists have disappeared, when there are no classes (i.e., there is no difference between the members of society in their relation to the social means of production), *only then* "the state ceases to exist," and "*it becomes possible to speak of freedom*." Only then a really full democracy, a democracy without any exceptions, will be possible and will be realised. And only then will democracy itself begin to *wither away* due to the simple fact that, freed from capitalist slavery, from the untold horrors, savagery, absurdities and infamies of capitalist exploitation, people will gradually *become accustomed* to the observance of the elementary rules of social life that have been known for centuries and repeated for thousands of years in all school books; they will become accustomed to observing them without force, without compulsion, without subordination, without the *special apparatus* for compulsion which is called the state.

The expression "the state *withers away*," is very well chosen, for it indicates both the gradual and the elemental nature of the process. Only habit can, and undoubtedly will, have such an effect; for we see around us millions of times how readily people get accustomed to observe the necessary rules of life in common, if there is no exploitation, if there is nothing that causes indignation, that calls forth protest and revolt and has to be *suppressed.*

Thus, in capitalist society, we have a democracy that is curtailed, poor, false; a democracy only for the rich, for the minority. The dictatorship of the proletariat, the period of transition to Communism, will, for the first time, produce democracy for the people, for the majority, side by side with the necessary suppression of the minority—the exploiters. Communism alone is capable of giving a really complete democracy, and the more complete it is the more quickly will it become unnecessary and wither away of itself.

In other words: under capitalism we have a state in the proper sense of the word, that is, special machinery for the suppression of one class by another, and of the majority by the minority at that. Naturally, for the successful discharge of such a task as the systematic suppression by the exploiting minority of the exploited majority, the greatest ferocity and savagery of suppression are required, seas of blood are required, through which mankind is marching in slavery, serfdom, and wage-labour.

Again, during the *transition* from capitalism to Communism, suppression is *still* necessary; but it is the suppression of the minority of exploiters by the majority of exploited. A special apparatus, special machinery for suppression, the "state," is *still* necessary, but this is now a transitional state, no longer a state in the usual sense, for the suppression of the minority of exploiters, by the majority of the wage slaves of *yesterday,* is a matter comparatively so easy, simple and natural that it will cost far less bloodshed than the suppression of the risings of slaves, serfs or wage labourers, and will cost mankind far less. This is compatible with the diffusion of democracy among such an overwhelming majority of the population, that the need for *special machinery* of suppression will begin to disappear. The exploiters are, naturally, unable to suppress the people without a most complex machinery for performing this task; but *the people* can suppress the exploiters even with very simple "machinery," almost without any "machinery," without any special apparatus, by the simple *organisation of the armed masses* (such as the Soviets of Workers' and Soldiers' Deputies, we may remark, anticipating a little).

Finally, only Communism renders the state absolutely unnecessary, for there is *no one* to be suppressed—"no one" in the sense of a *class,* in the sense of a systematic struggle with a definite section of the population. We are not Utopians, and we do not in the least deny the possibility and inevitability of excesses on the part of *individual persons,* nor the need to suppress *such* excesses. But, in the first place, no special machinery, no special apparatus of repression is needed for this; this will be done by the armed people itself, as simply and as readily as any crowd of civilised people, even in modern society, parts a pair of combatants or does not allow a woman to be outraged. And, secondly, we know that the fundamental social cause of excesses which consist in violating the rules of social life is the exploitation of the masses, their want and their poverty. With the removal of this chief cause, excesses will inevitably begin to "*wither away*." We do not know how quickly and in what succession, but we know that they will wither away. With their withering away, the state will also *wither away.*

Without going into Utopias, Marx defined more fully what can *now* be defined regarding this future, namely, the difference between the lower and the higher phases (degrees, stages) of Communist society.

### 3. First Phase of Communist Society

In the *Critique of the Gotha Programme,* Marx goes into some detail to disprove the Lassallean idea of the workers' receiving under Socialism the "undiminished" or the "full product of their labour." Marx shows that out of the whole of the social labour of society, it is necessary to deduct a reserve fund, a fund for the expansion of production, for the replacement of worn-out machinery, and so on; then, also, out of the means of consumption must be deducted a fund for the expenses of management, for schools, hospitals, homes for the aged, and so on.

Instead of the hazy, obscure, general phrase of Lassalle's—"the full product of his labour for the worker"—Marx gives a sober estimate of exactly how a Socialist society will have to manage its affairs. Marx undertakes a *concrete* analysis of the conditions of life of a society in which there is no capitalism, and says:

> What we are dealing with here [analysing the programme of the party] is not a Communist society which has *developed* on its own foundations, but, on the contrary, one which is just *emerging* from capitalist society, and which therefore in all respects—economic, moral and intellectual—still bears the birthmarks of the old society from whose womb it sprung.[4]

And it is this Communist society—a society which has just come into the world out of the womb of capitalism, and which, in all respects, bears the stamp of the old society—that Marx terms the "first," or lower, phase of Communist society.

The means of production are no longer the private property of individuals. The means of production belong to the whole of society. Every member of society, performing a certain part of socially necessary work, receives a certificate from society to the effect that he has done such and such a quantity of work. According to this certificate, he receives from the public warehouses, where articles of consumption are stored, a corresponding quantity of products. Deducting that proportion of labour which goes to the public fund, every worker, therefore, receives from society as much as he has given it.

"Equality" seems to reign supreme.

But when Lassalle, having in view such a social order (generally called Socialism, but termed by Marx the first phase of Communism), speaks of this as "just distribution," and says that this is "the equal right of each to an equal product of labour," Lassalle is mistaken, and Marx exposes his error.

"Equal right," says Marx, we indeed have here; but it is *still* a "bourgeois right," which, like every right, *presupposes inequality.* Every right is an application of the *same* measure to *different* people who, in fact, are not the same and are not equal to one another; this is why "equal right" is really a violation of equality, and an injustice. In effect, every man having done as much social labour as every other, receives an equal share of the social products (with the above-mentioned deductions).

But different people are not alike: one is strong, another is weak; one is married, the other is not; one has more children, another has less, and so on.

> . . . With equal labour—Marx concludes—and therefore an equal share in the social consumption fund, one man in fact receives more than the other, one is richer than the other, and so forth. In order to avoid all these defects, rights, instead of being equal, must be unequal.[5]

The first phase of Communism, therefore, still cannot produce justice and equality; differences, and unjust differences, in wealth will still exist, but the *exploitation* of man by man will have become impossible, because it will be impossible to seize as private property the *means of production,* the factories, machines, land, and so on. In tearing down Lassalle's petty-bourgeois, confused phrase about "equality" and "justice" *in general,* Marx shows the *course of development* of Communist society, which is forced at first to destroy *only* the "injustice" that consists in the means of production having been seized by private individuals, and which *is not capable* of destroying at once the further injustice consisting in the distribution of the articles of consumption "according to work performed" (and not according to need).

The vulgar economists, including the bourgeois professors and also "our" Tugan-Baranovsky, constantly reproach the Socialists with forgetting the inequality of people and with "dreaming" of destroying this inequality. Such a reproach, as we see, only proves the extreme ignorance of the gentlemen propounding bourgeois ideology.

Marx not only takes into account with the greatest accuracy the inevitable inequality of men; he also takes into account the fact that the mere conversion of the means of production into the common property of the whole of society ("Socialism" in the generally accepted sense of the word) *does not remove* the defects of distribution and the inequality of "bourgeois right" which *continue to rule* as long as the products are divided "according to work performed."

　　But these defects—Marx continues—are unavoidable in the first phase of Communist society, when, after long travail, it first emerges from capitalist society. Justice can never rise superior to the economic conditions of society and the cultural development conditioned by them.[6]

And so, in the first phase of Communist society (generally called Socialism) "bourgeois right" is *not* abolished in its entirety, but only in part, only in proportion to the economic transformation so far attained, i.e., only in respect of the means of production. "Bourgeois right" recognises them as the private property of separate individuals. Socialism converts them into common property. *To that extent,* and to that extent alone, does "bourgeois right" disappear.

However, it continues to exist as far as its other part is concerned; it remains in the capacity of regulator (determining factor) distributing the products and allotting labour among the members of society. "He who does not work, shall not eat"—this Socialist principle is *already* realised; "for an equal quantity of labour, an equal quantity of products"—this Socialist principle is also *already* realised. However, this is not yet Communism, and this does not abolish "bourgeois right," which gives to unequal individuals, in return for an unequal (in reality unequal) amount of work, an equal quantity of products.

This is a "defect," says Marx, but it is unavoidable during the first phase of Communism; for, if we are not to fall into Utopianism, we cannot imagine that, having overthrown capitalism, people will at once learn to work for society *without any standards of right*; indeed, the abolition of capitalism *does not immediately lay* the economic foundations for *such* a change.

And there is no other standard yet than that of "bourgeois right." To this extent, therefore, a form of state is still necessary, which, while maintaining public ownership of the means of production, would preserve the equality of labour and equality in the distribution of products.

The state is withering away in so far as there are no longer any capitalists, any classes, and, consequently, no *class* can be suppressed.

But the state has not yet altogether withered away, since there still remains the protection of "bourgeois right" which sanctifies actual inequality. For the complete extinction of the state, complete Communism is necessary.

## 4. Higher Phase of Communist Society

Marx continues:

In a higher phase of Communist society, when the enslaving subordination of individuals in the division of labour has disappeared, and with it also the antagonism between mental and physical labour; when labour has become not only a means of living, but itself the first necessity of life; when, along with the all-round development of individuals, the productive forces too have grown, and all the springs of social wealth are flowing more freely—it is only at that stage that it will be possible to pass completely beyond the narrow horizon of bourgeois rights, and for society to inscribe on its banners: from each according to his ability; to each according to his needs![7]

Only now can we appreciate the full correctness of Engels's remarks in which he mercilessly ridiculed all the absurdity of combining the words "freedom" and "state." While the state exists there is no freedom. When there is freedom, there will be no state.

The economic basis for the complete withering away of the state is that high stage of development of Communism when the antagonism between mental and physical labour disappears, that is to say, when one of the principal sources of modern *social* inequality disappears—a source, moreover, which it is impossible to remove immediately by the mere conversion of the means of production into public property, by the mere expropriation of the capitalists.

This expropriation will make a gigantic development of the productive forces *possible.* And seeing how incredibly, even now, capitalism *retards* this development, how much progress could be made even on the basis of modern technique at the level it has reached, we have a right to say, with the fullest confidence, that the expropriation of the capitalists will inevitably result in a gigantic development of the productive forces of human society. But how rapidly this development will go forward, how soon it will reach the point of breaking away from the division of labour, of removing the antagonism between mental and physical labour, of transforming work into the "first necessity of life"—this we do not and *cannot* know.

Consequently, we have a right to speak solely of the inevitable withering away of the state, emphasising the protracted nature of this process and its dependence upon the rapidity of development of the *higher phase* of Communism; leaving quite open the question of lengths of time, or the concrete forms of withering away, since material for the solution of such questions is *not available.*

The state will be able to wither away completely when society has realised the rule: "From each according to his ability; to each according to his needs," i.e., when people have become accustomed to observe the fundamental rules of social life, and their labour is so productive, that they voluntarily work *according to their ability.* "The narrow horizon of bourgeois rights," which compels one to calculate, with the hard-heartedness of a Shylock, whether he has not worked half an hour more than another, whether he is not getting less pay than another—this narrow horizon will then be left behind. There will then be no need for any exact calculation by society of the quantity of products to be distributed to each of its members; each will take freely "according to his needs."

From the bourgeois point of view, it is easy to declare such a social order "a pure Utopia," and to sneer at the Socialists for promising each the right to receive from society, without any control of the labour of the individual citizen, any quantity of truffles, automobiles, pianos, etc. Even now, most bourgeois "savants" deliver themselves of such sneers, thereby displaying at once their ignorance and their self-seeking defense of capitalism.

Ignorance—for it has never entered the head of any Socialist to "promise" that the highest phase of Communism will arrive; while the great Socialists, in *foreseeing* its arrival, presupposed both a productivity of labour unlike the present and a person not like the present man in the street, capable of spoiling, without reflection, like the seminary students in Pomyalovsky's book,[8] the stores of social wealth, and of demanding the impossible.

Until the "higher" phase of Communism arrives, the Socialists demand the *strictest* control, *by society and by the state,* of the quantity of labour and the quantity of consumption; only this control must *start* with the expropriation of the capitalists, with the control of the workers over the capitalists, and must be carried out, not by a state of bureaucrats, but by a state of *armed workers*.

Self-seeking defence of capitalism by the bourgeois ideologists (and their hangers-on like Tsereteli, Chernov and Co.) consists in that they *substitute* disputes and discussions about the distant future for the essential imperative questions of present-day policy: the expropriation of the capitalists, the conversion of *all* citizens into workers and employees of *one* huge "syndicate" —the whole state—and the complete subordination of the whole of the work of this syndicate to the really democratic state of the *Soviets of Workers' and Soldiers' Deputies.*

In reality, when a learned professor, and following him some philistine, and following the latter Messrs. Tsereteli and Chernov, talk of the unreasonable Utopias, of the demagogic promises of the Bolsheviks, of the impossibility of "introducing" Socialism, it is the higher stage or phase of Communism which they have in mind, and which no one has ever promised, or even thought of "introducing," for the reason that, generally speaking, it cannot be "introduced."

And here we come to that question of the scientific difference between Socialism and Communism, upon which Engels touched in his above-quoted discussion on the incorrectness of the name "Social-Democrat." The political difference between the first, or lower, and the higher phase of Communism will in time, no doubt, be tremendous; but it would be ridiculous to emphasise it now, under capitalism, and only, perhaps, some isolated Anarchist could invest it with primary importance (if there are still some people among the Anarchists who have learned nothing from the Plekhanov-like conversion of the Kropotkins, the Graveses, the Cornelissens, and other "leading lights" of Anarchism to social-chauvinism or Anarcho-*Jusquaubout*-ism,[9] as Ge, one of the few Anarchists still preserving honour and conscience, has expressed it).

But the scientific difference between Socialism and Communism is clear. What is generally called Socialism was termed by Marx the "first" or lower phase of Communist society. In so far as the means of production become *public* property, the word "Communism" is also applicable here, providing we do not forget that it is *not* full Communism. The great significance of Marx's elucidations consists in this: that here, too, he consistently applies materialist dialectics, the doctrine of evolution, looking upon Communism as something which evolves *out* of capitalism. Instead of artificial, "elaborate," scholastic definitions and profitless disquisitions on the meaning of words (what Socialism is, what Communism is), Marx gives an analysis of what may be called stages in the economic ripeness of Communism.

In its first phase or first stage Communism *cannot* as yet be economically ripe and entirely free of all tradition and of all taint of capitalism. Hence the interesting phenomenon of Communism retaining, in its first phase, "the narrow horizon of bourgeois rights." Bourgeois rights, with respect to distribution of articles of *consumption,* inevitably presupposes, of course, the existence of the *bourgeois state,* for rights are nothing without an apparatus capable of *enforcing* the observance of the rights.

Consequently, for a certain time not only bourgeois rights, but even the bourgeois state remains under Communism, without the bourgeoisie!

This may look like a paradox, or simply a dialectical puzzle for which Marxism is often blamed by people who would not make the least effort to study its extraordinarily profound content.

But, as a matter of fact, the old surviving in the new confronts us in life at every step, in nature as well as in society. Marx did not smuggle a scrap of "bourgeois" rights into Communism of his own accord; he indicated what is economically and politically inevitable in a society issuing *from the womb* of capitalism.

Democracy is of great importance for the working class in its struggle for freedom against the capitalists. But democracy is by no means a limit one may not overstep; it is only one of the stages in the course of development from feudalism to capitalism, and from capitalism to Communism.

Democracy means equality. The great significance of the struggle of the proletariat for equality, and the significance of equality as a slogan, are apparent, if we correctly interpret it as meaning the abolition of *classes.* But democracy means only *formal* equality. Immediately after the attainment of equality for all members of society *in respect of* the ownership of the means of production, that is, of equality of labour and equality of wages, there will inevitably arise before humanity the question of going further from formal equality to real equality, i.e., to realising the rule, "From each according to his ability; to each according to his needs." By what stages, by means of what practical measures humanity will proceed to this higher aim—this we do not and cannot know. But it is important to realise how infinitely mendacious is the usual bourgeois presentation of Socialism as something lifeless, petrified, fixed once for all, whereas in reality, it is *only* with Socialism that there will commence a rapid, genuine, real mass advance, in which first the *majority* and then the whole of the population will take part—an advance in all domains of social and individual life.

Democracy is a form of the state—one of its varieties. Consequently, like every state, it consists in organised, systematic application of force against human beings. This on the one hand. On the other hand, however, it signifies the formal recognition of the equality of all citizens, the equal right of all to determine the structure and administration of the state. This, in turn, is connected with the fact that, at a certain stage in the development of democracy, it first rallies the proletariat as a revolutionary class against capitalism, and gives it an opportunity to crush, to smash to bits, to wipe off the face of the earth the bourgeois state machinery—even its republican variety: the standing army, the police, and bureaucracy; then it substitutes for all this a *more* democratic, but still a state machinery in the shape of armed masses of workers, which becomes transformed into universal participation of the people in the militia.

Here "quantity turns into quality": *such* a degree of democracy is bound up with the abandonment of the framework of bourgeois society, and the beginning of its Socialiste reconstruction. If *every one* really takes part in the administration of the state, capitalism cannot retain its hold. In its turn, capitalism, as it develops, itself creates *prerequisites* for "every one" *to be able* really to take part in the administration of the state. Among such prerequisites are: universal literacy, already realised in most of the advanced capitalist countries, then the "training and disciplining" of millions of workers by the huge, complex, and socialised apparatus of the post-office, the railways, the big factories, large-scale commerce, banking, etc., etc.

With such *economic* prerequisites it is perfectly possible, immediately, within twenty-four hours after the overthrow of the capitalists and bureaucrats, to replace them, in the control of production and distribution, in the business of *control* of labour and products, by the armed workers, by the whole people in arms. (The question of control and accounting must not be confused with the question of the scientifically educated staff of engineers, agronomists and so on. These gentlemen work today, obeying the capitalists; they will work even better tomorrow, obeying the armed workers.)

Accounting and control—these are the *chief* things necessary for the organising and correct functioning of the *first phase* of Communist society. *All* citizens are here transformed into hired employees of the state, which is made up of the armed workers. *All* citizens become employees and workers of *one* national state "syndicate." All that is required is that they should work equally, should regularly do their share of work, and should receive equal pay. The accounting and control necessary for this have been *simplified* by capitalism to the utmost, till they have become the extraordinarily simple operations of watching, recording and issuing receipts, within the reach of anybody who can read and write and knows the first four rules of arithmetic.[10]

When the *majority* of the people begin everywhere to keep such accounts and maintain such control over the capitalists (now converted into employees) and over the intellectual gentry, who still retain capitalist habits, this control will really become universal, general, national; and there will be no way of getting away from it, there will be "nowhere to go."

The whole of society will have become one office and one factory, with equal work and equal pay.

But this "factory" discipline, which the proletariat will extend to the whole of society after the defeat of the capitalists and the overthrow of the exploiters, is by no means our ideal, or our final aim. It is but a *foothold* necessary for the radical cleansing of society of all the hideousness and foulness of capitalist exploitation, *in order to advance further.*

From the moment when all members of society, or even only the overwhelming majority, have learned how to govern the state *themselves*, have taken this business into their own hands, have "established" control over the insignificant minority of capitalists, over the gentry with capitalist leanings, and the workers thoroughly demoralised by capitalism—from this moment the need for any government begins to disappear. The more complete the democracy, the nearer the moment when it begins to be unnecessary. The more democratic the "state" consisting of armed workers, which is "no longer a state in the proper sense of the word," the more rapidly does *every* state begin to wither away.

For when *all* have learned to manage, and independently are actually managing by themselves social production, keeping accounts, controlling the idlers, the gentlefolk, the swindlers and similar "guardians of capitalist traditions," then the escape from this national accounting and control will inevitably become so increasingly difficult, such a rare exception, and will probably be accompanied by such swift and severe punishment (for the armed workers are men of practical life, not sentimental intellectuals, and they will scarcely allow any one to trifle with them), that very soon the *necessity* of observing the simple, fundamental rules of every-day social life in common will have become a *habit.*

The door will then be wide open for the transition from the first phase of Communist society to its higher phase, and along with it to the complete withering away of the state.

## Notes

1. English translation in *Critique of the Social-Democratic Programmes.*—Ed.

2. Ibid.—Ed.

3. Ibid.—Ed.

4. Ibid.—Ed.

5. Ibid.—Ed.

6. Ibid.—Ed.

7. Ibid.—Ed.

8. Pomyalovsky's *Seminary Sketches* depicted a group of student ruffians who engaged in destroying things for the pleasure it gave them.—Ed.

9. *Jusquaubout*—combination of French words meaning "until the end." Thus, Anarcho-*Jusquaubout*-ism—Anarcho-until-the-End-ism.—Ed.

10. When most of the functions of the state are reduced to this accounting and control by the workers themselves, then it ceases to be a "political state," and the "public functions will lose their political character and be transformed into simple administrative functions" (cf. Chap. IV, 2 on Engels's polemic against the Anarchists).

# EDUARD BERNSTEIN

# *Evolutionary Socialism*

In 1906, Lenin said of his *What Is to Be Done?*: "The Economists have gone to one extreme. To straighten matters out somebody had to pull in the opposite direction—that is what I have done." The democratic socialist Eduard Bernstein (1850–1932) was among the economists to whom Lenin referred. Bernstein's life spanned the rise and fall of German social democracy, from defeat in the 1848 revolution to dominance in the Reichstag to co-optation in the Weimar Republic. *Evolutionary Socialism* (1899), his statement of social democratic principles, adapts Marxism to a new Europe in which the proletariat has greater economic prosperity and increased political power.

## Chapter 2
## The Economic Development of Modern Society

### d. *The Crises and Possibilities of Adjustment in Modern Economy*

The contradictions inherent in the movement of capitalist society impress themselves upon the practical bourgeoisie most strikingly in the changes of the periodic cycle through which modern industry runs, and whose crowning point is the universal crisis. —Marx, Preface to the second edition of *Capital.*

... The time that has elapsed since this was written has left the question unanswered. Signs of an economic world-wide crash of unheard-of violence have not been established, nor can one describe the improvement of trade in the intervals between the crises as particularly short-lived. Much more does a third question arise which after all is partly contained already in the second —namely: (1) whether the enormous extension of the world market, in conjunction with the extraordinary shortening of time necessary for the transmission of news and for the transport trade, has so increased the possibilities of adjustment of disturbances; and (2) whether the enormously increased wealth of the European states, in conjunction with the elasticity of the modern credit system and the rise of industrial Kartels, has so limited the reacting force of local or individual disturbances that, at least for some time, general commercial crises similar to the earlier ones are to be regarded as improbable.

This question, raised by me in an essay on the "Socialist Theory of a Catastrophic Development of Society," has experienced all kinds of opposition.[1] Among others it has caused Rosa Luxemburg to lecture me in a series of articles published in the *Leipzig Volkszeitung* of September, 1898, on the nature of credit and the possibilities of capitalism in regard to adaptation. As these articles, which have also passed into other socialist papers, are true examples of false dialectics, but handled at the same time with great skill, it appears to me to be opportune to examine them here.

Rosa Luxemburg maintains that the credit system, far from working against crises, is the means of pushing them to an extremity. It first made possible the unmeasured extension of capitalistic production, the acceleration of the exchange of goods and of the cyclic course of the process of production, and in this way it is the means of bringing into active conflict as often as possible the differences between production and consumption. It puts into the hand of the capitalist the disposal of the capital of others, and with it the means of foolhardy speculation, and if depression sets in it intensifies the crisis. Its function is to banish the residue of stability from all capitalist conditions, to make all capitalist forces in the highest degree elastic, relative, and sensitive.

Now all that is not exactly new to anyone who knows a little of the literature of socialism in general and of Marxist socialism in particular. The only question is whether it rightly represents the real facts of the case to-day, or whether the picture has not another side. According to the laws of dialectic evolution to which Rosa Luxemburg so much likes to give play, it ought certainly to be the case; but even without falling back upon these, one should realise that a thing like credit, capable of so many forms, must under different conditions work in different ways. Marx treats credit by no means from the point of view that it is only a destructive agent in the capitalist system. He assigns to it, amongst other things,[2] the function of "creating the form of transition to a new modus of production," and with regard to it he expressly brings into prominence "the double-sided characteristics of the credit system." Frau Luxemburg knows the passage referred to very well; she even reprints the sentence from it where Marx speaks of the mixed character, "half swindler, half prophet," of the chief promulgators of credit (John Law, Isaac Pereire, etc.). But she refers exclusively to the destructive side of the credit system, and mentions not a word of its capacity for establishing and creating, which Marx expressly includes. Why this amputation, why this noteworthy silence with respect to the "double-sided characteristics"? The brilliant dialectical fireworks by means of which the power of the credit system is represented as a means of adaptation in the light of a "one-day fly," end in smoke and mist as soon as one looks more closely at this other side which Frau Luxemburg passes by so shyly.

That the credit system makes speculation easier is an experience centuries old; and very old, too, is the experience that speculation does not stop production when industrial circumstances are far enough developed to suit it. Meanwhile, speculation is conditioned by the relation of the knowable to the unknown circumstances. The more the latter predominate the more will speculation flourish; the more it is restrained by the former, the more the ground is cut from under its feet. Therefore the maddest outbursts of commercial speculation come to pass at the dawn of the capitalistic era, and speculation celebrates its wildest orgies usually in the countries where the capitalistic development is youngest. In the domain of industry speculation flourished most luxuriantly in new branches of production. The older a branch of production is under modern forms—with the exception of the manufacture of mere articles of fashion—the more does the speculative momentum cease to play a decisive part in it. The conditions and movements of the market are then more exactly foreseen and are taken into consideration with greater certainty.

Nevertheless, this certainty is only relative, because competition and technical development exclude an absolute control of the market. Over-production is to a certain extent unavoidable. But over-production in single industries does not mean general crises. If it leads to such a one, either the industries concerned must be of such importance as consumers of the manufactures of other industries, as that their stagnation also stops these industries, or indeed they must take from them, through the medium of the money market—that is, through the paralysis of general credit—the means of carrying on production. But it is evident that there is always a lessening probability of this latter result. The richer a country is, the more developed its credit organisation—which is not to be confused with a more widely spread habit to produce with a borrowed capital. For here the possibilities of adjustment multiply in an increasing measure. In some passage, which I cannot find at the moment, Marx said once—and the correctness of the sentence can be proved by the most abundant evidence—that the contractions in the centre of the money market are much more quickly overcome than in the different points of the circumference. But the change of the means of communication brought about in the meantime has more than neutralized the consequences of great distances in this respect.[3]

If the crises of the money market are not quite banished from the world yet, as far as concerns us here, the tightenings of that market by vast commercial undertakings controlled with difficulty are very much reduced.

The relations of financial crises to trade and business crises are not yet so fully explained that one can say with any certainty when both happen together that it was the trade crisis—*i.e.,* over-production—which directly caused the money crisis. In most cases it was quite clear that it was not actual over-production, but over-speculation, which paralysed the money market, and by this depressed the whole business. That is proved from the isolated facts which Marx mentions in the third volume of *Capital,* taken from the official inquiries into the crises of 1847 and 1857, as well as from the facts which Professor Herkner adduces on these and other crises in his sketch of the history of trade crises in his *Handwörterbuch der Staatswissenschaften.* Frau Luxemburg deduces on the basis of the facts adduced by Herkner that the crises hitherto have not at all been the right crises, but that they were only infantile illnesses of the capitalistic economy, the accompanying phenomena not of narrowing but of widening the domain of the capitalistic economy—that we "have not yet entered upon that phase of perfect capitalistic maturity which is presumed in the Marxist scheme of the periodicity of crises." According to her, we find ourselves "in a phase where crises no longer accompany the rise of capital nor yet its decline." This time will only come when the world market is fully developed and can be enlarged by no sudden extensions. Then the struggle between the productive powers and the limits of exchange will become continually sharper and more stormy.

To that one must observe that the formula of the crises in and for Marx was no picture of the future, but a picture of the present day which it was expected would recur in the future in always sharper forms and in greater acuteness. As soon as Frau Luxemburg denies to it the significance which Marx imputed to it for the whole epoch lying behind us, and sets it up as a deduction which did not yet correspond with reality, but was only a logical forecast based on the existence of certain elements in an embryonic state, she immediately questions the whole Marxist prediction of the coming social evolution, so far as this is based on the theory of crises. For if this was not based on experience at the time when it was set up, and has not become manifest in the interval between then and now, in what more distant future can one place its formula as coming true? Its relegation to the time when the world market has been fully developed is a flight into the next world.

No one knows when the world market will be fully developed. Frau Luxemburg is not ignorant of the fact that there is an intensive as well as an extensive broadening of the world market, and that the former is to-day of much greater importance than the latter.

In the trade statistics of the great industrial countries exports play by far the greatest part in regard to the countries longest occupied. England exports to the whole of Australia (all the Australian colonies, New Zealand, etc.) values less in amount than to a single country, France; to the whole of British North America (Canada, British Columbia, etc.) not so much as to Russia only; to both colonial territories together, which are indeed of a respectable age, not so much as to Germany. Its trade with all its colonies, including the whole of the immense Indian Empire, is not a third of its trade with the rest of the world; and as regards the colonial acquisitions of the last twenty years, the exports thither have been ridiculously small. The extensive widenings of the world market are accomplished much too slowly to allow sufficient outlet for the actual increase of production, if the countries already drawn into it did not offer it an increasing market. A limit to this increasing and intensive amplifying of the world market, along with the extension of its area, cannot be set up *a priori*. If the universal crisis is the inherent law of capitalistic production, it must prove its reality now or in the near future. Otherwise the proof of its inevitableness hovers in the air of abstract speculation.

We have seen that the credit system to-day undergoes less, not more, contractions, leading to the general paralysis of production, and so far, therefore, takes a minor place as a factor in forming crises. But so far as it is a means of a hothouse forcing of over-production, the associations of manufacturers meet this inflation of production in separate countries, and even internationally here and there, ever more frequently, by trying to regulate production as a Kartel, a syndicate, or a trust. Without embarking in prophecies as to its final power of life and work, I have recognised its capacity to influence the relation of productive activity to the condition of the market so far as to diminish the danger of crises. Frau Luxemburg refutes this also.

First she denies that the association of manufactures can be general. She says the final aim and effect of such associations are, by excluding competition within a branch, to increase their share of the total amount of profit gained in the market of commodities. But, she adds, one branch of industry could only attain this at the cost of another, and the organisation could not possibly, therefore, be general. "Extended into all branches of production it would itself put an end to its effect."

This proof does not differ by a hair's-breadth from the proof, long ago abandoned, of the uselessness of trades unions. Its support is even immeasurably more fragile than the wages fund theory of blessed memory. It is the presumption unproven, unprovable, or, rather, proved to be false, that in the commodity market only a fixed amount of profit is to be divided. It presumes, amongst other things, a fixing of prices independently of the movements in the cost of production. But even given a fixed price, and, moreover, a fixed technological basis of production, the amount of profit in a branch of industry can be raised without thereby lessening the profits of another—namely, by the lessening of unproductive expenses, the ceasing of cutting competition, better organisation of production, and the like. That the association of manufactures is an effective means towards this is self-evident. The problem of the division of profits is the last obstacle of all which stands in the way of a general union of associations of employers.

It stands somewhat better with the last objection of Frau Luxemburg. According to it, the Kartels are unsuitable for preventing the anarchy of produc-

tion because the Kartels of manufacturers as a rule obtain their higher profit
rate on the home market, because they use the portion of capital that cannot
be applied to this for manufacturing products for foreign countries at a much
less profit rate. The consequence is, increased anarchy on the world market
—the opposite to the object aimed at.

"As a rule" this manoeuvre can only be upheld where a protective duty
affords the Kartel protection, so as to make it impossible for the foreign country to repay it in like coin. Meanwhile we are concerned here neither with denying the harmful effects of the present simple and high protectionist system,
nor with an apology for the syndicates of manufacturers. It has not occurred
to me to maintain that Kartels, etc., are the last word of economic development, and are suited to remove for ever the contradictions of modern industrial life. I am, on the contrary, convinced that where in modern industrial
countries Kartels and trusts are supported and strengthened by protective duties, they must, in fact, become factors of the crises in the industry concerned—also, if not at first, in any case finally, for the "protected" land itself.
The question only arises how long the people concerned will be content with
this arrangement. Protective tariffs are in themselves no product of economy,
but an encroachment on economy by the political power seeking to secure
economic results. It is otherwise with the industrial Kartel. It has—although
favoured by protective tariffs—grown out of the economic soil, and is a national means of adapting production to the movements of the market. That it
is, or can be, at the same time the means of monopolist exploitation is another
matter. But it is just as much beside the question that in the former capacity it
means an increase of all earlier remedial measures for overproduction. With
much less risk than the individual undertaking, it can, in times of a glut on
the market, temporarily limit production. Better than this, it is also in a position to meet foreign cutting competition abroad. To deny this is to deny the
superiority of organisation over anarchic competition. But we do so, if we
deny on principle that Kartels can work as a modifying influence on the nature and frequency of crises. How *far* they can do so is for the present a matter
for conjecture, for we have not sufficient experience to allow of a conclusive
judgment in this respect. But still fewer conclusive facts can be given under
these circumstances for anticipating future general crises as they hovered before Marx and Engels, repetitions on a larger scale of the crises of 1825, 1836,
1847, 1857, 1873. The mere fact that whilst for a long time socialists generally
believed in an increasing contraction of the industrial cycle as the natural consequence of the increasing concentration of capital—a development in the
form of a spiral—Friedrich Engels in 1894 found himself driven to question
whether a new enlarging of the cycle was not in front of us, and thus to suggest the exact contrary of the former assumption, and he warned us against the
abstract deduction that these crises must repeat themselves in the old form.[4]

The history of individual industries shows that their crises by no means always coincide with the so-called general crises. Marx, as we have seen, believed he could establish on the need of an accelerated renewal of fixed capital (implements of production, etc.) a material foundation for periodic crises,[5] and it is undoubtedly true that an important reason for crises is to be found here. But it is not accurate, or not more accurate, that these periods of renewal coincide as to time in the various industries. And therewith a further factor of the great general crisis is done away with.

There remains then only so much, that the capacity for production in modern society is much greater than the actual demand for products determined by the buying capacity; that millions live insufficiently housed, insufficiently clad, and insufficiently nourished, in spite of abundant means at hand for sufficient housing, nourishment, and clothing; that out of this incongruity, over-production appears again and again in different branches of production, so that either actually certain articles are produced in greater amounts than can be used—for example, more yarn than the present weaving mills can work—or that certain articles are produced not indeed in a greater quantity than can be used, but in greater quantity than can be bought; that in consequence of this, great irregularity occurs in the employment of the workers, which makes their situation extremely insecure, weighs them down in unworthy dependence, brings forth over-work here and want of work there; and that of the means employed to-day to counteract the most visible part of this evil, the Kartels represent monopolist unions—on the one side against the workers, and on the other against the great public—which have a tendency to carry on warfare over the heads of these and at their cost with the same kind of monopolist unions in other industries or other lands, or, by international or inter-industrial agreements, arbitrarily to adapt production and prices to their need of profit. The capitalistic means of defence against crises virtually bear within themselves the possibilities of a new and more hopeless serfdom for the working classes, as well as of privileges of production which revive in acute form the old guild privileges. It appears to me to be much more important at present, from the standpoint of the workers, to keep before our eyes the possibilities of Kartels and trusts than to prophesy their "impotence." It is for the working class a subordinate question whether these combinations will be able, in the course of time, to attain their first-mentioned object—the warding off of crises. But it becomes a question full of importance as soon as expectations of any kind as regards the movement for the emancipation of the working classes are made dependent upon the question of the general crisis. For then the belief that Kartels are of no effect against crises may be the cause of very disastrous neglect.

The short sketch which we gave in the introduction to this chapter of the Marx-Engels explanations of economic crises will suffice, in conjunction with the corresponding facts adduced, to show that the problem of crises cannot be solved by a few well-preserved catch-words. We can only investigate what elements of modern economy work in favour of crises and what work against them. It is impossible to pre-judge *a priori* the ultimate relation of these forces to one another, or their development. Unless unforeseen external events bring about a general crisis—and as we have said, that can happen any day—there is no urgent reason for concluding that such a crisis will come to pass for purely economic reasons. Local and partial depressions are unavoidable; general stagnation is not unavoidable with the present organisation and extension of the world market, and particularly with the great extension of the production of articles of food. The latter phenomenon is of peculiar importance for our problem. Perhaps nothing has contributed so much to the mitigation of commercial crises or to the stopping of their increase as the fall of rent and of the price of food.[6]

## Chapter 3
## The Tasks and Possibilities of Social Democracy

### c. *Democracy and Socialism*

On February 24th, 1848, broke the first dawn of a new period of history. Who speaks of universal suffrage utters a cry of reconciliation.
— Lasalle, *Workers' Programme*

. . . The trade unions are the democratic element in industry. Their tendency is to destroy the absolutism of capital, and to procure for the worker a direct influence in the management of an industry. It is only natural that great differences of opinion should exist on the degree of influence to be desired. To a certain mode of thought it may appear a breach of principle to claim less for the union than an unconditional right of decision in the trade. The knowledge that such a right under present circumstances is just as Utopian as it would be contrary to the nature of a socialist community, has led others to deny trade unions any lasting part in economic life, and to recognise them only temporarily as the lesser of various unavoidable evils. There are socialists in whose eyes the union is only an object lesson to prove the uselessness of any other than political revolutionary action. As a matter of fact, the union to-day—and in the near future—has very important social tasks to fulfil for the trades, which, however, do not demand, nor are even consistent with, its omnipotence in any way.

The merit of having first grasped the fact that trade unions are indispensable organs of the democracy, and not only passing coalitions, belongs to a group of English writers. This is not wonderful if one considers that trade unions attained importance in England earlier than anywhere else, and that

England in the last third of the nineteenth century passed through a change from an oligarchic to an almost democratic state of government. The latest and most thorough work on this subject, the book on the theory and the practice of the British Trade Unions, by Sydney and Beatrice Webb, has been rightly described by the authors as a treatment of *Industrial Democracy*. Before them the late Thorold Rogers, in his lectures on the *Economic Interpretation of History* (which, in the passing, has little in common with the materialist conception of history, but only touches it in single points), called the trade union, Labour Partnership—which comes to the same thing in principle, but at the same time points out the limits to which the function of a trade union can extend in a democracy, and beyond which it has no place in a democratic community. Independently of whether the state, the community, or capitalists are employers, the trade union as an organisation of all persons occupied in certain trades can only further simultaneously the interests of its members and the general good as long as it is content to remain a partner. Beyond that it would run into danger of degenerating into a close corporation with all the worst qualities of a monopoly. It is the same as with the co-operative society. The trade union, as mistress of a whole branch of production, the ideal of various older socialists, would really be only a monopolist productive association, and as soon as it relied on its monopoly or worked upon it, it would be antagonistic to socialism and democracy, let its inner constitution be what it may. Why it is contrary to socialism needs no further explanation. Associations against the community are as little socialism as is the oligarchic government of the state. But why should such a trade union not be in keeping with the principles of a democracy?

This question necessitates another. What is the principle of democracy?

The answer to this appears very simple. At first one would think it settled by the definition "government by the people." But even a little consideration tells us that by that only quite a superficial, purely formal definition is given, whilst nearly all who use the word democracy to-day understand by it more than a mere form of government. We shall come much nearer to the definition if we express ourselves negatively, and define democracy as an absence of class government, as the indication of a social condition where a political privilege belongs to no one class as opposed to the whole community. By that the explanation is already given as to why a monopolist corporation is in principle anti-democratic. This negative definition has, besides, the advantage that it gives less room than the phrase "government by the people" to the idea of the oppression of the individual by the majority which is absolutely repugnant to the modern mind. To-day we find the oppression of the minority by the majority "undemocratic," although it was originally held to be quite consistent with government by the people.[7] The idea of democracy includes, in the conception of the present day, a notion of justice—an equality of rights for all members of the community, and in that principle the rule of the majority, to which in every concrete case the rule of the people extends, finds its limits. The more it is adopted and governs the general consciousness, the more will democracy be equal in meaning to the highest possible degree of freedom for all.

Democracy is in principle the suppression of class government, though it is not yet the actual suppression of classes. They speak of the conservative character of the democracy, and to a certain degree rightly. Absolutism, or semi-absolutism, deceives its supporters as well as its opponents as to the extent of their power. Therefore in countries where it obtains, or where its traditions still exist, we have flitting plans, exaggerated language, zigzag politics, fear of revolution, hope in oppression. In a democracy the parties, and the classes standing behind them, soon learn to know the limits of their power, and to undertake each time only as much as they can reasonably hope to carry through under the existing circumstances. Even if they make their demands rather higher than they seriously mean in order to give way in the unavoidable compromise—and democracy is the high school of compromise—they must still be moderate. The right to vote in a democracy makes its members virtually partners in the community, and this virtual partnership must in the end lead to real partnership. With a working class undeveloped in numbers and culture the general right vote may long appear as the right to choose "the butcher"; with the growing number and knowledge of the workers it is changed, however, into the implement by which to transform the representatives of the people from masters into real servants of the people.

Universal suffrage in Germany could serve Bismarck temporarily as a tool, but finally it compelled Bismarck to serve it as a tool. It could be of use for a time to the squires of the East Elbe district, but it has long been the terror of these same squires. In 1878 it could bring Bismarck into a position to forge the weapon of socialistic law, but through it this weapon became blunt and broken, until by the help of it Bismarck was thoroughly beaten. Had Bismarck in 1878, with his then majority, created a politically exceptional law, instead of a police one, a law which would have placed the worker outside the franchise, he would for a time have hit social democracy more sharply than with the former. It is true, he would then have hit other people also. Universal franchise is, from two sides, the alternative to a violent revolution. But universal suffrage is only a part of democracy, although a part which in time must draw the other parts after it as the magnet attracts to itself the scattered portions of iron. It certainly proceeds more slowly than many would wish, but in spite of that it is at work. And social democracy can not further this work better than by taking its stand unreservedly on the theory of democracy—on the ground of universal suffrage with all the consequences resulting therefrom to its tactics.

In practice—that is, in its actions—it has in Germany always done so. But in their explanations its literary advocates have often acted otherwise, and still often do so to-day. Phrases which were composed in a time when the political privilege of property ruled all over Europe, and which under these circumstances were explanatory, and to a certain degree also justified, but which to-day are only a dead weight, are treated with such reverence as though the progress of the movement depended on them and not on the understanding of what can be done, and what should be done. Is there any sense, for example, in maintaining the phrase of the "dictatorship of the proletariat" at a time when in all possible places representatives of social democracy have placed themselves practically in the arena of Parliamentary work, have declared for the proportional representation of the people, and for direct legislation—all of which is inconsistent with a dictatorship.

The phrase is to-day so antiquated that it is only to be reconciled with reality by stripping the word dictatorship of its actual meaning and attaching to it some kind of weakened interpretation. The whole practical activity of social democracy is directed towards creating circumstances and conditions which shall render possible and secure a transition (free from convulsive outbursts) of the modern social order into a higher one. From the consciousness of being the pioneers of a higher civilisation, its adherents are ever creating fresh inspiration and zeal. In this rests also, finally, the moral justification of the socialist expropriation towards which they aspire. But the "dictatorship of the classes" belongs to a lower civilisation, and apart from the question of the expediency and practicability of the thing, it is only to be looked upon as a reversion, as political atavism. If the thought is aroused that the transition from a capitalist to a socialist society must necessarily be accomplished by means of the development of forms of an age which did not know at all, or only in quite an imperfect form, the present method of the initiating and carrying of laws, and which was without the organs fit for the purpose, reaction will set in.

I say expressly transition from a capitalist to a socialist society, and not from a "civic society," as is so frequently the expression used to-day. This application of the word "civic" is also much more an atavism, or in any case an ambiguous way of speaking, which must be considered an inconvenience in the phraseology of German social democracy, and which forms an excellent bridge for mistakes with friend and foe. The fault lies partly in the German language, which has no special word for the idea of the citizen with equal civic rights separate from the idea of privileged citizens.

What is the struggle against, or the abolition of, a civic society? What does it mean specially in Germany, in whose greatest and leading state, Prussia, we are still constantly concerned with first getting rid of a great part of feudalism which stands in the path of civic development? No man thinks of destroying civic society as a civilised ordered system of society. On the contrary, social democracy does not wish to break up this society and make all its members proletarians together; it labours rather incessantly at raising the worker from the social position of a proletarian to that of a citizen, and thus to make citizenship universal. It does not want to set up a proletarian society instead of a civic society, but a socialist order of society instead of a capitalist one. It would be well if one, instead of availing himself of the former ambiguous expression, kept to the latter quite clear declaration. Then one would be quite free of a good portion of other contradictions which opponents, not quite without reason, assert do exist between the phraseology and the practice of social democracy. A few socialist newspapers find a pleasure to-day in forced anti-civic language, which at the most would be in place if we lived in a sectarian fashion as anchorites, but which is absurd in an age which declares it to be no offence to the socialist sentiment to order one's private life throughout in a "bourgeois fashion."[8]

Finally, it is to be recommended that some moderation should be kept in the declaration of war against "liberalism." It is true that the great liberal movement of modern times arose for the advantage of the capitalist bourgeoisie first of all, and the parties which assumed the names of liberals were, or became in due course, simple guardians of capitalism. Naturally, only opposition can reign between these parties and social democracy. But with respect to liberalism as a great historical movement, socialism is its legitimate heir, not only in chronological sequence, but also in its spiritual qualities, as is shown moreover in every question of principle in which social democracy has had to take up an attitude.

Wherever an economic advance of the socialist programme had to be carried out in a manner, or under circumstances, that appeared seriously to imperil the development of freedom, social democracy has never shunned taking up a position against it. The security of civil freedom has always seemed to it to stand higher than the fulfillment of some economic progress.

The aim of all socialist measures, even of those which appear outwardly as coercive measures, is the development and the securing of a free personality. Their more exact examination always shows that the coercion included will raise the sum total of liberty in society, and will give more freedom over a more extended area than it takes away. The legal day of a maximum number of hours' work, for example, is actually a fixing of a minimum of freedom, a prohibition to sell freedom longer than for a certain number of hours daily, and, in principle, therefore, stands on the same ground as the prohibition agreed to by all liberals against selling oneself into personal slavery. It is thus no accident that the first country where a maximum hours' day was carried out was Switzerland, the most democratically progressive country in Europe, and democracy is only the political form of liberalism. Being in its origin a counter-movement to the oppression of nations under institutions imposed from without or having a justification only in tradition, liberalism first sought its realisation as the principle of the sovereignty of the age and of the people, both of which principles formed the everlasting discussion of the philosophers of the rights of the state in the seventeenth and eighteenth centuries, until

Rousseau set them up in his *Contrat Social* as the fundamental conditions of the legitimacy of every constitution, and the French Revolution proclaimed them—in the Democratic Constitution of 1793 permeated with Rousseau's spirit—as inalienable rights of men.[9]

The Constitution of 1793 was the logical expression of the liberal ideas of the epoch, and a cursory glance over its contents shows how little it was, or is, an obstacle to socialism. Baboeuf, and the believers in absolute equality, saw in it an excellent starting point for the realisation of their communistic strivings, and accordingly wrote "The Restoration of the Constitution of 1793" at the head of their demands.

There is actually no really liberal thought which does not also belong to the elements of the ideas of socialism. Even the principle of economic personal responsibility which belongs apparently so entirely to the Manchester School cannot, in my judgment, be denied in theory by socialism nor be made inoperative under any conceivable circumstances. Without responsibility there is no freedom; we may think as we like theoretically about man's freedom of action, we must practically start from it as the foundation of the moral law, for only under this condition is social morality possible. And similarly, in our states which reckon with millions, a healthy social life is, in the age of traffic, impossible if the economic personal responsibility of all those capable of work is not assumed. The recognition of individual responsibility is the return of the individual to society for services rendered or offered him by society. . . .

Socialism will create no new bondage of any kind whatever. The individual is to be free, not in the metaphysical sense, as the anarchists dreamed—*i.e.,* free from all duties towards the community—but free from every economic compulsion in his action and choice of a calling. Such freedom is only possible for all by means of organisation. In this sense one might call socialism "organising liberalism," for when one examines more closely the organisations that socialism wants and how it wants them, he will find that what distinguishes them above all from the feudalistic organisations, outwardly like them, is just their liberalism, their democratic constitution, their accessibility. Therefore the trade union, striving after an arrangement similar to a guild, is in the eyes of the socialist, the product of self-defence against the tendency of capitalism to overstock the labour market; but, at the same time, just on account of its tendency towards a guild, and to the degree in which that obtains, is it an unsocialistic corporate body.

The work here indicated is no very simple problem; it rather conceals within itself a whole series of dangers. Political equality alone has never hitherto sufficed to secure the healthy development of communities whose centre of gravity was in the giant towns. It is, as France and the United States show, no unfailing remedy against the rank growth of all kinds of social parasitism and corruption. If solidity did not reach so far down in the constitution of the French nation, and if the country were not so well favoured geographically,

France would have long since been ruined by the land plague of the official class which has gained a footing there. In any case this plague forms one of the causes why, in spite of the great keenness of the French mind, the industrial development of France remains more backward than that of the neighbouring countries. If democracy is not to excel centralised absolutism in the breeding of bureaucracies, it must be built up on an elaborately organised self-government with a corresponding economic, personal responsibility of all the units of administration as well as of the adult citizens of the state. Nothing is more injurious to its healthy development than enforced uniformity and a too abundant amount of protectionism or subventionism.

To create the organisations described—or, so far as they are already begun, to develop them further—is the indispensable preliminary to what we call socialism of production. Without them the so-called social appropriation of the means of production would only result presumably in reckless devastation of productive forces, insane experimentalising and aimless violence, and the political sovereignty of the working class would, in fact, only be carried out in the form of a dictatorial, revolutionary, central power, supported by the terrorist dictatorship of revolutionary clubs. . . .

There is not the least doubt (and it has since then been proved many times practically) that the general development of modern society is along the line of a constant increase of the duties of municipalities and the extension of municipal freedom, that the municipality will be an ever more important lever of social emancipation. It appears to me doubtful if it was necessary for the first work of democracy to be such a dissolution of the modern state system and complete transformation of its organisation as Marx and Proudhon pictured (the formation of the national assembly out of delegates from provincial or district assemblies, which in their turn were composed of delegates from municipalities) so that the form the national assemblies had hitherto taken had to be abolished. Evolution has given life to too many institutions and bodies corporate, whose sphere has outgrown the control of municipalities and even of provinces and districts for it to be able to do without the control of the central governments unless or before their organisation is transformed. The absolute sovereignty of the municipality, etc., is besides no ideal for me. The parish or commune is a component part of the nation, and hence has duties towards it and rights in it. We can as little grant the district, for example, an unconditional and exclusive right to soil as we can to the individual. Valuable royalties, rights of forest and river, etc., belong, in the last instance, not to the parishes or the districts, which indeed only are their usufructuaries, but to the nation. Hence an assembly in which the national, and not the provincial or local, interest stands in the forefront or is the first duty of the representatives, appears to be indispensable, especially in an epoch of transition. But beside it, those other assemblies and representative bodies will attain an ever greater importance, so that Revolution or not, the functions of the central assemblies become constantly narrowed, and therewith the danger of these assemblies or authorities to the democracy is also narrowed. It is already very little in advanced countries to-day.

But we are less concerned here with a criticism of separate items in the quoted programme than with bringing into prominence the energy with which it emphasises autonomy as the preliminary condition of social emancipation, and with showing how the democratic organisation from the bottom upwards is depicted as the way to the realisation of socialism, and how the antagonists Proudhon and Marx meet again in—liberalism.

The future itself will reveal how far the municipalities and other self-governing bodies will discharge their duties under a complete democracy, and how far they will make use of these duties. But so much is clear: the more suddenly they come in possession of their freedom, the more experiments they will make in number and in violence and therefore be liable to greater mistakes, and the more experience the working class democracy has had in the school of self-government, the more cautiously and practically will it proceed.

Simple as democracy appears to be at the first glance, its problems in such a complicated society as ours are in no way easy to solve. Read only in the volumes of *Industrial Democracy* by Mr. and Mrs. Webb how many experiments the English trade unions had to make and are still making in order to find out the most serviceable forms of government and administration, and of what importance this question of constitution is to trade unions. The English trade unions have been able to develop in this respect for over seventy years in perfect freedom. They began with the most elementary form of self-government and have been forced to convince themselves that this form is only suited to the most elementary organisms, for quite small, local unions. As they grew they gradually learned to renounce as injurious to their successful development certain cherished ideas of doctrinaire democracy (the imperative mandate, the unpaid official, the powerless central representation), and to form instead of it a democracy capable of governing with representative assemblies, paid officials, and central government with full powers. This section of the history of the development of "trade union democracy" is extremely instructive. If all that concerns trade unions does not quite fit the units of national administration, yet much of it does. The chapter referred to in *Industrial Democracy* belongs to the theory of democratic government. In the history of the development of trade unions is shown how the executive central management—their state government—can arise simply from division of labour which becomes necessary through the extension in area of the society and through the number of its members. It is possible that with the socialist development of society this centralisation may also later on become superfluous. But for the present it cannot be dispensed with in democracy. As was demonstrated at the end of the first division of this chapter it is an impossibility for the municipalities of great towns or industrial centres to take over under their own management all local productive and commercial undertakings. It is also, on practical grounds, improbable—not to mention grounds of equity which are against it—that they should "expropriate" those undertakings each and all offhand in revolutionary upheaval. But even if they did (whereby in the majority of cases would only empty husks come into their hands) they would be obliged to lease the mass of the businesses to associations, whether individual or trade union, for associated management.[10]

In every one of these cases, as also in the municipal and national undertakings, certain interests of the different trades would have to be protected, and so there would always remain a need for active supervision on the part of trade unions. In the transition period particularly, the multiplicity of organs will be of great value.

Meantime we are not yet so far on, and it is not my intention to unfold pictures of the future. I am not concerned with what will happen in the more distant future, but with what can and ought to happen in the present, for the present and the nearest future. And so the conclusion of this exposition is the very banal statement that the conquest of the democracy, the formation of political and social organs of the democracy, is the indispensable preliminary condition to the realisation of socialism.

Feudalism, with its unbending organisations and corporations, had to be destroyed nearly everywhere by violence. The liberal organisations of modern society are distinguished from those exactly because they are flexible, and capable of change and development. They do not need to be destroyed, but only to be further developed. For that we need organisation and energetic action, but not necessarily a revolutionary dictatorship. "As the object of the class war is especially to destroy distinctions of class," wrote some time since (October, 1897) a social democratic Swiss organ, the *Vorwärts* of Basle, "a period must logically be agreed upon in which the realisation of this object, of this ideal, must be begun. This beginning, these periods following on one another, are already founded in our democratic development; they come to our help, to serve gradually as a substitute for the class war, to absorb it into themselves by the building up of the social democracy." "The bourgeoisie, of whatever shade of opinion it may be," declared lately the Spanish socialist, Pablo Iglesias, "must be convinced of this, that we do not wish to take possession of the Government by the same means that were once employed, by violence and bloodshed, but by lawful means which are suited to civilisation" (*Vorwärts*, October 16, 1898). From a similar point of view the *Labour Leader,* the leading organ of the English Independent Labour Party, agreed unreservedly with the remarks of Vollmar on the Paris Commune. But no one will accuse this paper of timidity in fighting capitalism and the capitalist parties. And another organ of the English socialist working class democracy the *Clarion,* accompanied an extract from my article on the theory of catastrophic evolution with the following commentary:

"The formation of a true democracy—I am quite convinced that that is the most pressing and most important duty which lies before us. This is the lesson which the socialist campaign of the last ten years has taught us. That is the doctrine which emerges out of all my knowledge and experiences of politics. We must build up a nation of democrats before socialism is possible."

## Notes

1. The essay criticised the opinion laid down in a resolution of the International Socialist Congress of 1896 that we were on the eve of a great catastrophic crisis that would produce a total revolution of social conditions. The said resolution ran thus: "The economic and industrial development is going on with such rapidity that a crisis may occur within a comparatively short time. The Congress, therefore, impresses upon the proletariat of all countries the imperative necessity of learning, as class-conscious citizens, how to administer the business of their respective countries for the common good." I gladly recognised the usefulness of the final recommendation, but I boldly disputed the truth of the premise. This occasioned some violent attacks, to which I replied in the letter reprinted in the preface of this book.

2. vol. 3, i., p. 429.

3. Engels calculates that America and India have been brought nearer to the industrial countries of Europe, by means of the Suez Canal, steamer transport, etc., by 70 to 90 per cent., and adds "that owing to this the two great incubators of crises from 1825 to 1857 lost a great part of their destructive power" (*Capital*, vol. 3, Part I, p. 45). On p. 395, of the same volume, Engels maintains that certain speculative business formed on risky schemes of credit, which Marx pictures as factors of crises in the money market, have been brought to an end through the oceanic cable. The correcting parenthesis of Engels on p. 56 of the second part of vol. 3 is also worthy of notice for its criticism of the development of the credit system.

4. We are, of course, only speaking here of the purely economic foundation of crises. Crises as results of political events (wars and serious threatenings of war) or of very widespread failures of crops—local failures no longer exercise any effect in this respect—are of course always possible.

5. The use of the word "material" in the passage mentioned (vol. 2, p. 164) is not without interest in judging how Marx understood this word. According to the present usual definition of the word the explanation of crises from under-consumption would be quite as materialistic as founding it on changes in the process of production, or in implements.

6. *Note to the English edition.*—This was written in the winter of 1898–1899 before the South African War had produced new conditions on the money market and a great increase in armaments. In spite of these facts the crisis that broke out in 1901 was of shorter life than a good many of the earlier crises, and was followed by a longer period of prosperity.

7. The consistent advocates of Blanquism also always conceived of democracy as at first an oppressive force. Thus Hippolyte Castille publishes a preliminary introduction to his *History of the Second Republic* which culminates in a veritable glorification of the Reign of Terror. "The most perfect community," he says, "would be where tyranny was an affair

of the whole community. That proves fundamentally that the most perfect society would be one where there is least freedom in the satanic (*i.e.,* individualistic) meaning of this word. . . . What is called political freedom is only a beautiful name to adorn the justifiable tyranny of the many. Political freedom is only the sacrifice of the freedom of a number of individuals to the despotic God of human societies, to social reason, to the social contract." "From this epoch (the time from October, 1793, to April, 1794, when Girondists, Hebertists, Dantonists, were beheaded one after the other) dates in truth the re-incarnation of the principle of authority, of this eternal defensive warfare of human societies. Freed from the moderates and the ultras, secured against every conflict of authority, the committee of public safety acquires the form of government necessitated by the given circumstances, the necessary force and unity to maintain its position and to protect France from a threatening anarchy. . . . No, it is not the government that killed the first French Republic, but the Parliamentarians, the traitors of Thermidor. The anarchist and liberal republicans whose swarming hordes covered France, continue in vain the old calumny. Robespierre remains a remarkable man, not on account of his talents and virtues, which are here incidental, but on account of his genius for authority, on account of his strong political instinct."

This worship of Robespierre was not to outlast the second Empire. To the younger generation of the Blanquist socialist revolutionaries who stepped on the stage in the middle of the 'sixties and who were above all anti-clerical, Robespierre was too philistine on account of his Deism. They swore by Hebert and Anacharsis Cloots. But for the rest they reasoned like Castille—*i.e.,* they carried out to extremes, like him, the just idea of the subordination of individual interests to the general interests of the community.

8. In this point Lassalle was much more logical than we are to-day, granted that it was one-sidedness to derive the ideal of the bourgeois simply from political privilege instead of at least from his economic position of power also. But for the rest he was sufficient realist to blunt beforehand the point of the above contradiction when he declared in the *Workers' Programme:* "In the German language the word 'bourgeoisie' had to be translated by 'Bürgerthum' (citizendom). But it has not this meaning with me. We are all citizens ('Bürger')—the workman, the poor citizen, the rich citizen, and so forth. In the course of history the word 'bourgeoisie' has rather acquired a meaning by which to denote a well defined, political line of thought" (*Collected Works,* 2, p. 27). What Lassalle further says there of the distorted logic of Sansculottism is especially to be recommended to writers in the *belles lettres* style who study the middle class "naturalistically" in the *café* and then judge the whole class according to their dried fruits, as the philistine thinks he sees the type of the modern workman in his fellow tippler. I feel no hesitation in declaring that I consider the middle class—not excepting the German—in their bulk to be still fairly healthy, not only economically, but also morally.

9. Sovereignty "rests with the people. It is indivisible, imprescriptible, inalienable" (Article 25). "A people has at any time the right to revise, reform and alter its constitution. No generation can bind the next to its laws" (Article 28).

10. This would certainly bring about complicated problems. Think of the many joint undertakings of modern times which employ members of all possible trades.

# SIDNEY WEBB

## *Historic*

Along with Bernard Shaw, Graham Wallas, and Beatrice Potter
Webb, Sidney James Webb (1859–1947) was a member of the Fabian
Society. The Fabians' philosophy had many sources, both liberal and
socialist. They supported the Liberal and Labour parties—indeed all
parties dedicated to economic and political reform. This essay was
delivered as a public lecture as part of the Fabians' educational program and published in *Fabian Essays in Socialism,* edited by George
Bernard Shaw.

### The Development of the Democratic Ideal

In discussing the historic groundwork of Socialism, it is worth remembering
that no special claim is made for Socialism in the assertion that it possesses a
basis in history. Just as every human being has an ancestry, unknown to him
though it may be; so every idea, every incident, every movement has in the
past its own long chain of causes, without which it could not have been. Formerly we were glad to let the dead bury their dead: nowadays we turn lovingly
to the records, whether of persons or things; and we busy ourselves willingly
among origins, even without conscious utilitarian end. We are no longer
proud of having ancestors, since everyone has them; but we are more than ever
interested in our ancestors, now that we find in them the fragments which
compose our very selves. The historic ancestry of the English social organization during the present century stands witness to the irresistible momentum
of the ideas which Socialism denotes. The record of the century in English social history begins with the trial and hopeless failure of an almost complete industrial individualism, in which, however, unrestrained private ownership of
land and capital was accompanied by subjection to a political oligarchy. So
little element of permanence was there in this individualistic order that, with
the progress of political emancipation, private ownership of the means of pro-

duction has been, in one direction or another, successively regulated, limited and superseded, until it may now fairly be claimed that the Socialist philosophy of to-day is but the conscious and explicit assertion of principles of social organization which have been already in great part unconsciously adopted. The economic history of the century is an almost continuous record of the progress of Socialism.[1]

Socialism, too, has in the record of its internal development a history of its own. Down to the present generation, the aspirant after social regeneration naturally vindicated the practicability of his ideas by offering an elaborate plan with specifications of a new social order from which all contemporary evils were eliminated. Just as Plato had his Republic and Sir Thomas More his Utopia, so Baboeuf had his Charter of Equality, Cabet his Icaria, St. Simon his Industrial System, and Fourier his ideal Phalanstery. Robert Owen spent a fortune in pressing upon an unbelieving generation his New Moral World and even August Comte, superior as he was to many of the weaknesses of his time, must needs add a detailed Polity to his Philosophy of Positivism.

The leading feature of all these proposals was what may be called their statical character. The ideal society was represented as in perfectly balanced equilibrium, without need or possibility of future organic alteration. Since their day we have learned that social reconstruction must not be gone at in this fashion. Owing mainly to the efforts of Comte, Darwin, and Herbert Spencer, we can no longer think of the ideal society as an unchanging State. The social ideal from being static has become dynamic. The necessity of the constant growth and development of the social organism has become axiomatic. No philosopher now looks for anything but the gradual evolution of the new order from the old, without breach of continuity or abrupt change of the entire social tissue at any point during the process. The new becomes itself old, often before it is consciously recognized as new; and history shews us no example of the sudden substitution of Utopian and revolutionary romance.

Though Socialists have learnt this lesson[2] better than most of their opponents, the common criticism of Socialism has not yet noted the change, and still deals mainly with the obsolete Utopias of the pre-evolutionary age. Parodies of the domestic details of an imaginary Phalanstery, and homilies on the failure of Brook Farm or Icaria, may be passed over as belated and irrelevant now that Socialists are only advocating the conscious adoption of a principle of social organization which the world has already found to be the inevitable outcome of Democracy and the Industrial Revolution. For Socialism is by this time a wave surging throughout all Europe; and for want of a grasp of the series of apparently unconnected events by which and with which it has been for two generations rapidly coming upon us—for want, in short, of knowledge of its intellectual history—we in England to-day see our political leaders in a general attitude of astonishment at the changing face of current politics; both great parties drifting vaguely before a nameless undercurrent which they fail utterly to recognize or understand.[3] With some dim impression that Socialism is one of the Utopian dreams they remember to have heard comfortably disposed of in their academic youth as the impossible ideal of Humanity-intoxicated Frenchmen, they go their ways through the nineteenth century as a countryman blunders through Cheapside. One or two are history fanciers, learned in curious details of the past: the present eludes these no less than the others. They are so near to the individual events that they are blind to the onward sweep of the column. They cannot see the forest for the trees.

History not only gives the clue to the significance of contemporary events; it also enables us to understand those who have not yet found that clue. We learn to class men and ideas in a kind of geological order in time. The Comte de Paris gives us excellent proofs that in absolute monarchy lies the only safety of social order. He is a survival: the type flourished in the sixteenth century; and the splendid fossils of that age can be studied in any historic museum. Lord Bramwell will give cogent reasons for the belief that absolute freedom of contract, subject to the trifling exception of a drastic criminal law, will ensure a perfect State. His lordship is a survival from a nearer epoch: about 1840 this was as far as social science had got; and there are still persons who have learnt nothing of later date. When I see the Hipparion at South Kensington I do not take his unfamiliar points to be those of a horse of a superior kind: I know that he is an obsolete and superseded pattern, from which the horse has developed. Historic fossils are more dangerous; for they are left at large, and are not even excluded from Downing Street or Westminster. But against the stream of tendencies they are ultimately powerless. Though they sometimes appear victorious, each successive struggle takes place further down the current which they believe themselves to be resisting.

The main stream which has borne European society towards Socialism during the past 100 years is the irresistible progress of Democracy. [Alexis de] Tocqueville drove and hammered this truth into the reluctant ears of the Old World two generations ago; and we have all pretended to carry it about as part of our mental furniture ever since. But like most epigrammatic commonplaces, it is not generally realized; and Tocqueville's book has, in due course, become a classic which everyone quotes and nobody reads. The progress of Democracy is, in fact, often imagined, as by Sir Henry Maine, to be merely the substitution of one kind of political machinery for another; and there are many political Democrats to-day who cannot understand why social or economic matters should be mixed up with politics at all. It was not for this that they broke the power of the aristocracy: they were touched not so much with love of the many as with hatred of the few;[4] and, as has been acutely said —though usually by foolish persons—they are Radicals merely because they are not themselves lords. But it will not long be possible for any man to persist in believing that the political organization of society can be completely altered without corresponding changes in economic and social relations. Tocqueville expressly pointed out that the progress of Democracy meant nothing less than a complete dissolution of the nexus by which society was held together under the old *régime*. This dissolution is followed by a period of anarchic spiritual isolation of the individual from his fellows, and to that extent by a general denial of the very idea of society. But man is a social animal; and after more or less interval there necessarily comes into existence a new nexus, differing so entirely from the old-fashioned organization that the historic fossil goes about denying that it is a nexus at all, or that any new nexus is possible or desirable. To him, mostly through lack of economics, the progress of Democracy is nothing more than the destruction of old political privileges; and, naturally enough, few can see any beauty in mere dissolution and destruction. Those few are the purely political Radical abhorred of Comte and [Thomas] Carlyle: they are in social matters the empiricist survivals from a pre-scientific age.

The mere Utopians, on the other hand, who wove the baseless fabric of their visions of reconstructed society on their own private looms, equally failed, as a rule, to comprehend the problem of the age. They were, in imagination, resuscitated Joseph the Seconds, benevolent despots who would have poured the old world, had it only been fluid, into their new moulds. Against their crude plans the Statesman, the Radical, and the Political Economist were united; for they took no account of the blind social forces which they could not control, and which went on inexorably working out social salvation in ways unsuspected by the Utopian.

In the present Socialist movement these two streams are united: advocates of social reconstruction have learnt the lesson of Democracy, and know that it is through the slow and gradual turning of the popular mind to new principles that social reorganization bit by bit comes. All students of society who are abreast of their time, Socialists as well as Individualists, realize that important organic changes can only be (1) democratic, and thus acceptable to a majority of the people, and prepared for in the minds of all; (2) gradual, and thus causing no dislocation, however rapid may be the rate of progress; (3) not regarded as immoral by the mass of the people, and thus not subjectively demoralizing to them; and (4) in this country at any rate, constitutional and peaceful. Socialists may therefore be quite at one with Radicals in their political methods. Radicals, on the other hand, are perforce realizing that mere political levelling is insufficient to save a State from anarchy and despair. Both sections have been driven to recognize that the root of the difficulty is economic; and there is every day a wider consensus that the inevitable outcome of Democracy is the control by the people themselves, not only of their own political organization, but, through that, also of the main instruments of wealth production; the gradual substitution of organized co-operation for the anarchy of the competitive struggle; and the consequent recovery, in the only possible way, of what John Stuart Mill calls "the enormous share which the possessors of the instruments of industry are able to take from the produce."[5] The economic side of the democratic ideal is, in fact, Socialism itself. . . .

## The Intellectual and Moral Revolt; and Its Political Outlook

. . . The whole of the immediately practicable demands of the most exacting Socialist are, indeed, now often embodied in the current Radical programme; and the following exposition of it, from the pages of the State newspaper, 8 August 1888, may serve as a statement of the current Socialist demands for further legislation.[6]

### Revision of Taxation

*Object:* Complete shifting of burden from the workers, of whatever grade, to the recipients of rent and interest, with a view to the ultimate and gradual extinction of the latter class.

*Means:* 1. Abolition of all customs and excise duties, except those on spirits. 2. Increase of income tax, differentiating in favor of earned as against unearned incomes, and graduating cumulatively by system of successive levels of abatement. 3. Equalization and increase of death duties and the use of the proceeds as capital, not income. 4. Shifting of local rates and house duty from occupier to owner, any contract to the contrary notwithstanding. 5. Compulsory redemption of existing land tax and reimposition on all ground rents and increased values. 6. Abolition of fees on licenses for employment. 7. Abolition of police-court fees.

### Extension of Factory Acts

*Object:* To raise, universally, the standard of comfort by obtaining the general recognition of a minimum wage and a maximum working day.

*Means:* 1. Extension of the general provisions of the Factory and Workshops Acts (or the Mines Regulation Acts, as the case may be) to all employers of labor. 2. Compulsory registration of all employers of more than three (?) workers. 3. Largely increased number of inspectors, and these to include women, and to be mainly chosen from the wage-earning class. 4. Immediate reduction of maximum hours to eight per day in all Government and municipal employment, in all mines, and in all licensed monopolies such as railways, tramways, gasworks, waterworks, docks, harbors, etc.; and in any trade in which a majority of the workers desire it. 5. The compulsory insertion of clauses in all contracts for Government or municipal supplies, providing that (*a*) there shall be no sub-contracting, (*b*) that no worker shall be employed more than eight hours per day, and (*c*) that no wages less than a prescribed minimum shall be paid.

## Educational Reform

*Object:* To enable all, even the poorest, children to obtain not merely some, but the best education they are capable of.

*Means:* 1. The immediate abolition of all fees in public elementary schools, Board or voluntary, with a corresponding increase in the Government grant. 2. Creation of a Minister for Education, with control over the whole educational system, from the elementary school to the University, and over all educational endowments. 3. Provision of public technical and secondary schools wherever needed, and creation of abundant public secondary scholarships. 4. Continuation, in all cases, of elementary education at evening schools. 5. Registration and inspection of all private educational establishments.

## Re-organization of Poor Law Administration

*Object:* To provide generously, and without stigma, for the aged, the sick, and those destitute through temporary want of employment, without relaxing the "tests" against the endowment of able-bodied idleness.

*Means:* 1. The separation of the relief of the aged and the sick from the workhouse system, by a universal system of aged pensions, and public infirmaries. 2. The industrial organization and technical education of all able-bodied paupers. 3. The provision of temporary relief works for the unemployed. 4. The supersession of the Boards of Guardians by the local municipal authorities.

## Extension of Municipal Activity

*Object:* The gradual public organization of labor for all public purposes, and the elimination of the private capitalist and middleman.

*Means:* 1. The provision of increased facilities for the acquisition of land, the destruction without compensation of all dwellings found unfit for habitation, and the provision of artisan dwellings by the municipality. 2. The facilitation of every extension of municipal administration, in London and all other towns, of gas, water, markets, tramways, hospitals, cemeteries, parks, muse-

ums, art galleries, libraries, reading-rooms, schools, docks, harbors, rivers, etc.
3. The provision of abundant facilities for the acquisition of land by local rural
authorities, for allotments, common pastures, public halls, reading rooms, etc.

## Amendment of Political Machinery

*Object:* To obtain the most accurate representation and expression of the
desires of the majority of the people at every moment.

*Means:* 1. Reform of registration so as to give a vote, both Parliamentary
and municipal, to every adult. 2. Abolition of any period of residence as a
qualification for registration. 3. Biannual registration of special public officer.
4. Annual Parliaments. 5. Payment of election expenses, including postage of
election addresses and polling cards. 6. Payment of all public representatives,
parliamentary, county, or municipal. 7. Second ballot. 8. Abolition or painless
extinction of the House of Lords.[7]

This is the programme to which a century of industrial revolution has
brought the Radical working man. Like John Stuart Mill,[8] though less explicitly, he has turned from mere political Democracy to a complete, though unconscious, Socialism.[9]

## The New Synthesis

It need hardly be said that the social philosophy of the time did not remain unaffected by the political evolution and the industrial development.
Slowly sinking into men's minds all this while was the conception of a new social nexus, and a new end of social life. It was discovered (or rediscovered) that
a society is something more than an aggregate of so many individual units
—that it possesses existence distinguishable from those of any of its components. A perfect city became recognized as something more than any number
of good citizens—something to be tried by other tests, and weighed in other
balances than the individual man. The community must necessarily aim, consciously or not, at its continuance as a community: its life transcends that of
any of its members; and the interests of the individual unit must often clash
with those of the whole. Though the social organism has itself evolved from
the union of individual men, the individual is now created by the social organism of which he forms a part: his life is born of the larger life; his attributes are
moulded by the social pressure; his activities, inextricably interwoven with
others, belong to the activity of the whole. Without the continuance and
sound health of the social organism, no man can now live or thrive; and its
persistence is accordingly his paramount end. His conscious motive for action
may be, nay always must be, individual to himself; but where such action

proves inimical to the social welfare, it must sooner or later be checked by the whole, lest the whole perish through the error of its member. The conditions of social health are accordingly a matter for scientific investigation. There is, at any moment, one particular arrangement of social relations which involves the minimum of human misery then and there possible amid the "niggardliness of nature." Fifty years ago it would have been assumed that absolute freedom in the sense of individual or "manly" independence, plus a criminal code, would spontaneously result in such an arrangement for each particular nation; and the effect was the philosophic apotheosis of *Laisser Faire*. To-day every student is aware that no such optimistic assumption is warranted by the facts of life.[10] We know now that in natural selection at the stage of development where the existence of civilized mankind is at stake, the units selected from are not individuals, but societies. Its action at earlier stages, though analogous, is quite dissimilar. Among the lower animals physical strength or agility is the favored quality: if some heaven-sent genius among the cuttle-fish developed a delicate poetic faculty, this high excellence would not delay his succumbing to his hulking neighbor. When, higher up in the scale, mental cunning became the favored attribute, an extra brain convolution, leading primitive man to the invention of fire or tools, enabled a comparatively puny savage to become the conqueror and survivor of his fellows.

Brain culture accordingly developed apace; but we do not yet thoroughly realize that this has itself been superseded as the "selected" attribute, by social organization. The cultivated Athenians, Saracens, and Provençals went down in the struggle for existence before their respective competitors, who, individually inferior, were in possession of a, at that time, more valuable social organization. The French nation was beaten in the last war, not because the average German was an inch and a half taller than the average Frenchman, or because he had read five more books, but because the German social organism was, for the purposes of the time, superior in efficiency to the French. If we desire to hand on to the afterworld our direct influence, and not merely the memory of our excellence, we must take even more care to improve the social organism of which we form part, than to perfect our own individual developments. Or rather, the perfect fitting development of each individual is not necessarily the utmost and highest cultivation of his own personality, but the filling, in the best possible way, of his humble function in the great social machine. We must abandon the self-conceit of imagining that we are independent units, and bend our jealous minds, absorbed in their own cultivation, to this subjection to the higher end, the Common Weal. Accordingly, conscious "direct adaptation" steadily supplants the unconscious and wasteful "indirect adaptation" of the earlier form of the struggle for existence; and with every advance in sociological knowledge Man is seen to assume more and more, not only the master of "things," but also a conscious control over social destiny itself.

This new scientific conception of the Social Organism has put completely out of countenance the cherished principles of the Political Economist and the Philosophic Radical. We left them sailing into Anarchy on the stream of *Laisser Faire.* Since then the tide has turned. The publication of John Stuart Mill's *Political Economy* in 1848 marks conveniently the boundary of the old individualist Economics. Every edition of Mill's book became more and more Socialistic. After his death the world learnt the personal history, penned by his own hand,[11] of his development from a mere political democrat to a convinced Socialist.

The change in tone since then has been such that one competent economist, professedly anti-Socialist,[12] publishes regretfully to the world that all the younger men are now Socialists, as well as many of the older Professors. It is, indeed, mainly from these that the world has learnt how faulty were the earlier economic generalizations, and above all, how incomplete as guides for social or political action. These generalizations are accordingly now to be met with only in leading articles, sermons, or the speeches of Ministers or Bishops.[13] The Economist himself knows them no more.

The result of this development of Sociology is to compel a revision of the relative importance of liberty and equality as principles to be kept in view in social administration. In Bentham's celebrated "ends" to be aimed at in a civil code, liberty stands predominant over equality, on the ground that full equality can be maintained only by the loss of security for the fruits of labor. That exposition remains as true as ever; but the question for decision remains, how much liberty? Economic analysis has destroyed the value of the old criterion of respect for the equal liberty of others. Bentham, whose economics were weak, paid no attention to the perpetual tribute on the fruits of others' labor which full private property in land inevitably creates. In his view liberty and security to property meant that every worker should be free to obtain the full result of his own labor; and there appeared no inconsistency between them. The political economist now knows that with free competition and private property in land and capital, no individual can possibly obtain the full result of his own labor. The student of industrial development, moreover, finds it steadily more and more impossible to trace what is precisely the result of each separate man's toil. Complete rights of liberty and property necessarily involve, for example, the spoliation of the Irish cottier tenant for the benefit of Lord Clanricarde. What then becomes of the Benthamic principle of the greatest happiness of the greatest number? When the Benthamite comes to understand the Law of Rent, which of the two will he abandon? For he cannot escape the lesson of the century, taught alike by the economists, the statesmen, and the "practical men," that complete individual liberty, with unrestrained private ownership of the instruments of wealth production, is irreconcilable with the common weal. The free struggle for existence among ourselves menaces our survival as a healthy and permanent social organism. Evolution, Professor Huxley[14] declares, is the substitution of consciously regulated co-ordination among the units of each organism, for blind anarchic competition. Thirty years ago Herbert Spencer demonstrated the incompatibility of full private property in land with the modern democratic State;[15] and almost every economist now preaches the same doctrine. The Radical is rapidly arriving, from practical experience, at similar conclusions; and the steady increase of the government regulation of private enterprise, the growth of municipal administration, and the rapid shifting of the burden of taxation directly to rent and interest, mark in treble lines the statesman's unconscious abandonment of the old Individualism, and our irresistible glide into collectivist Socialism.

It was inevitable that the Democracy should learn this lesson. With the masses painfully conscious of the failure of Individualism to create a decent social life for four-fifths of the people,[16] it might have been foreseen that Individualism could not survive their advent to political power. If private property in land and capital necessarily keeps the many workers permanently poor (through no fault of their own) in order to make the few idlers rich (from no merit of their own), private property in land and capital will inevitably go the way of the feudalism which it superseded. The economic analysis confirms the rough generalization of the suffering people. The history of industrial evolution points to the same result; and for two generations the world's chief ethical teachers have been urging the same lesson. No wonder the heavens of Individualism are rolling up before our eyes like a scroll and even the Bishops believe and tremble.[17]

It is, of course, possible, as Sir Henry Maine and others have suggested, that the whole experience of the century is a mistake, and that political power will once more swing back into the hands of a monarch or an aristocratic oligarchy. It is, indeed, want of faith in Democracy which holds back most educated sympathisers with Socialism from frankly accepting its principles. What the economic side of such political atavism would be is not easy to forecast. The machine industry and steam power could hardly be dismissed with the caucus and the ballot-box. So long, however, as Democracy in political administration continues to be the dominant principle, Socialism may be quite safely predicted as its economic obverse, in spite of those freaks or aberrations of Democracy which have already here and there thrown up a short-lived monarchy or a romantic dictatorship. Every increase in the political power of the proletariat will most surely be used by them for their economic and social protection. In England, at any rate, the history of the century serves at once as their guide and their justification.

## Notes

1. See *Socialism in England*, American Economic Association, vol. 4, pt. 2, May 1889, in which a portion of this has been embodied.

2. "I am aware that there are some who suppose that our present bourgeois arrangements must be totally destroyed and others substituted almost at a blow. But however successful a revolution might be, it is certain that mankind cannot change its whole nature all at once. Break the old shell, certainly; but never forget the fact that the new forms must grow out of the old." H.M. Hyndman, *Historical Basis of Socialism* (1883), 305.

3. See the article on "Socialism in English Politics" by William Clarke in the *Political Science Quarterly*, December 1888.

4. Even Bentham said this of James Mill (Bain's *Life of James Mill*, p. 461), of whom it was hardly true.

5. *Principles of Political Economy*, last ed. (1865), 477 (quoting from Feugueray).

6. It is interesting to compare this programme, with its primary insistence on economic and social reform, with the bare political character of the "Five Points" of the Chartists, viz., Manhood Suffrage, Vote by Ballot, Annual Parliaments, Payment of Members relieved from the property qualification, and Equal Electoral Districts.

7. It need hardly be said that schemes of "free land," peasant proprietorship, or leasehold enfranchisement, find no place in the modern programme of the Socialist Radical, or Social Democrat. They are survivals of the Individualistic Radicalism which is passing away. Candidates seeking a popular "cry" more and more avoid these reactionary proposals.

8. *Autobiography*, 231-32. See also book 4 of the *Principles of Political Economy*, popular ed., (1865).

9. For a forecast of the difficulties which this programme will have to encounter as its full scope and intention become more clearly realized, see the eighth essay in this volume, by Hubert Bland.

10. See D.G. Ritchie, Fellow and Tutor of Jesus College, Oxford, *Darwinism and Politics* (London: Swan Sonnenschein, 1889).

11. *Autobiography*, 231-32.

12. Rev. F.W. Aveling, Principal of Taunton Independent College, in leaflet *Down with the Socialist*, August 1888. See also Professor H. Sidgwich on "Economic Socialism," *Contemporary Review*, November 1886.

13. That is to say, unfortunately, in nearly all the utterances which profess to guide our social and political action.

14. *Contemporary Review*, February 1888.

15. "Social Statics," passim.

16. See Professor Leone Levi's letter to the *Times*, 13 August 1886, and Mr. Frederic Harrison's speech at the Industrial Remuneration Conference held in January 1885 (*Report*, 429).

17. See *Report of the Lambeth Episcopal Conference*, 1888; subject, "Socialism": also the Proceedings of the Central Conference of Diocesan Councils, June 1889 (paper on Socialism by Canon Furst).

# 19

## STUDENTS FOR A DEMOCRATIC SOCIETY

## *The Port Huron Statement*

"The Port Huron Statement" was adopted by the Students for a Democratic Society (SDS) at their convention in Port Huron, Michigan, 11–15 June 1962. The author of the original draft was Tom Hayden, a leader of the student movement at that time, who was elected to the California Assembly in 1982. The statement is widely regarded as "one of the best pronouncements of New Left democratic theorizing."

### Introduction: Agenda for a Generation

We are people of this generation, bred in at least modest comfort, housed now in universities, looking uncomfortably to the world we inherit.

When we were kids the United States was the wealthiest and strongest country in the world; the only one with the atom bomb, the least scarred by modern war, and initiator of the United Nations that we thought would distribute Western influence throughout the world. Freedom and equality for each individual, government of, by, and for the people—these American values we found good, principles by which we could live as men. Many of us began maturing in complacency.

As we grew, however, our comfort was penetrated by events too troubling to dismiss. First, the permeating and victimizing fact of human degradation, symbolized by the Southern struggle against racial bigotry, compelled most of us from silence to activism. Second, the enclosing fact of the Cold War, symbolized by the presence of the Bomb, brought awareness that we ourselves, and our friends, and millions of abstract "others" we knew more directly because of our common peril, might die at any time. We might deliberately ignore, or avoid, or fail to feel all other human problems, but not these two, for these were too immediate and crushing in their impact, too challenging in the demand that we as individuals take the responsibility for encounter and resolution.

While these and other problems either directly oppressed us or rankled our consciences and became our own subjective concerns, we began to see complicated and disturbing paradoxes in our surrounding America. The declaration "all men are created equal" rang hollow before the facts of Negro life in the South and the big cities of the North. The proclaimed peaceful intentions of the United States contradicted its economic and military investments in the Cold War status quo.

We witnessed, and continue to witness, other paradoxes. With nuclear energy whole cities can easily be powered, yet the dominant nation-states seem more likely to unleash destruction greater than that incurred in all wars of human history. Although our own technology is destroying old and creating new forms of social organization, men still tolerate meaningless work and idleness. While two-thirds of mankind suffers undernourishment, our own upper classes revel amidst superfluous abundance. Although world population is expected to double in forty years, the nations still tolerate anarchy as a major principle of international conduct and uncontrolled exploitation governs the sapping of the earth's physical resources. Although mankind desperately needs revolutionary leadership, America rests in national stalemate, its goals ambiguous and tradition-bound instead of informed and clear, its democratic system apathetic and manipulated rather than "of, by, and for the people."

Not only did tarnish appear on our image of American virtue, not only did disillusion occur when the hypocrisy of American ideals was discovered, but we began to sense that what we had originally seen as the American Golden Age was actually the decline of an era. The worldwide outbreak or revolution against colonialism and imperialism, the entrenchment of totalitarian states, the menace of war, overpopulation, international disorder, supertechnology—these trends were testing the tenacity of our own commitment to democracy and freedom and our abilities to visualize their application to a world in upheaval.

Our work is guided by the sense that we may be the last generation in the experiment with living. But we are a minority—the vast majority of our people regard the temporary equilibriums of our society and world as eternally functional parts. In this is perhaps the outstanding paradox: we ourselves are imbued with urgency, yet the message of our society is that there is no viable alternative to the present. Beneath the reassuring tones of the politicians, beneath the common opinion that America will "muddle through," beneath the stagnation of those who have closed their minds to the future, is the pervading feeling that there simply are no alternatives, that our times have witnessed the exhaustion not only of Utopias, but of any new departures as well. Feeling the press of complexity upon the emptiness of life, people are fearful of the thought that at any moment things might be thrust out of control. They fear change itself, since change might smash whatever invisible framework seems to hold back chaos for them now. For most Americans, all crusades are suspect, threatening. The fact that each individual sees apathy in his fellows perpetuates the common reluctance to organize for change. The dominant institutions are complex enough to blunt the minds of their potential critics, and entrenched enough to swiftly dissipate or entirely repel the energies of protest and reform, thus limiting human expectancies. Then, too, we are a materially improved society, and by our own improvements we seem to have weakened the case for further change.

Some would have us believe that Americans feel contentment amidst prosperity—but might it not better be called a glaze above deeply felt anxieties about their role in the new world? And if these anxieties produce a developed indifference to human affairs, do they not as well produce a yearning to believe there *is* an alternative to the present, that something *can* be done to change circumstances in the school, the workplaces, the bureaucracies, the government? It is to this latter yearning, at once the spark and engine of change, that we direct our present appeal. The search for truly democratic alternatives to the present, and a commitment to social experimentation with them, is a worthy and fulfilling human enterprise, one which moves us and, we hope, others today. On such a basis do we offer this document of our convictions and analysis: as an effort in understanding and changing the conditions of humanity in the late twentieth century, an effort rooted in the ancient, still unfulfilled conception of man attaining determining influence over his circumstances of life.

## Values

Making values explicit—an initial task in establishing alternatives—is an activity that has been devalued and corrupted. The conventional moral terms of the age, the politician moralities—"free world," "people's democracies" —reflect realities poorly, if at all, and seem to function more as ruling myths than as descriptive principles. But neither has our experience in the universities brought us moral enlightenment. Our professors and administrators sacrifice controversy to public relations; their curriculums change more slowly than the living events of the world; their skills and silence are purchased by investors in the arms race; passion is called unscholastic. The questions we might want raised—what is really important? can we live in a different and better way? if we wanted to change society, how would we do it?—are not thought to be questions of a "fruitful, empirical nature," and thus are brushed aside.

Unlike youth in other countries, we are used to moral leadership being exercised and moral dimensions being clarified by our elders. But today, for us, not even the liberal and socialist preachments of the past seem adequate to the forms of the present. Consider the old slogans: Capitalism Cannot Reform

Itself, United Front Against Fascism, General Strike, All Out on May Day. Or, more recently, No Cooperation with Commies and Fellow Travellers, Ideologies Are Exhausted, Bipartisanship, No Utopias. These are incomplete, and there are few new prophets. It has been said that our liberal and socialist predecessors were plagued by vision without program, while our own generation is plagued by program without vision. All around us there is astute grasp of method, technique—the committee, the ad hoc group, the lobbyist, the hard and soft sell, the make, the projected image—but, if pressed critically, such expertise is incompetent to explain its implicit ideals. It is highly fashionable to identify oneself by old categories, or by naming a respected political figure, or by explaining "how we would vote" on various issues.

Theoretic chaos has replaced the idealistic thinking of old—and, unable to reconstitute theoretic order, men have condemned idealism itself. Doubt has replaced hopefulness—and men act out a defeatism that is labelled realistic. The decline of utopia and hope is in fact one of the defining features of social life today. The reasons are various: the dreams of the older left were perverted by Stalinism and never re-created; the congressional stalemate makes men narrow their view of the possible; the specialization of human activity leaves little room for sweeping thought; the horrors of the twentieth century, symbolized in the gas ovens and concentration camps and atom bombs, have blasted hopefulness. To be idealistic is to be considered apocalyptic, deluded. To have no serious aspirations, on the contrary, is to be "tough-minded."

In suggesting social goals and values, therefore, we are aware of entering a sphere of some disrepute. Perhaps matured by the past, we have no sure formulas, no closed theories—but that does not mean values are beyond discussion and tentative determination. A first task of any social movement is to convince people that the search for orienting theories and the creation of human values is complex but worthwhile. We are aware that to avoid platitudes we must analyze the concrete conditions of social order. But to direct such an analysis we must use the guideposts of basic principles. Our own social values involve conceptions of human beings, human relationships, and social systems.

We regard *men* as infinitely precious and possessed of unfulfilled capacities for reason, freedom, and love. In affirming these principles we are aware of countering perhaps the dominant conceptions of man in the twentieth century: that he is a thing to be manipulated, and that he is inherently incapable of directing his own affairs. We oppose the depersonalization that reduces human beings to the status of things—if anything, the brutalities of the twentieth century teach that means and ends are intimately related, that vague appeals to "posterity" cannot justify the mutilations of the present. We oppose, too, the doctrine of human incompetence because it rests essentially on the modern fact that men have been "competently" manipulated into incompetence—we see little reason why men cannot meet with increasing skill the complexities and responsibilities of their situation, if society is organized not for minority, but for majority, participation in decision-making.

Men have unrealized potential for self-cultivation, self-direction, self-understanding, and creativity. It is this potential that we regard as crucial and to which we appeal, not to the human potentiality for violence, unreason, and submission to authority. The goal of man and society should be human independence: a concern not with image of popularity but with finding a meaning in life that is personally authentic; a quality of mind not compulsively driven by a sense of powerlessness, nor one which unthinkingly adopts status values, nor one which represses all threats to its habits, but one which has full, spontaneous access to present and past experiences, one which easily unites the fragmented parts of personal history, one which openly faces problems which are troubling and unresolved; one with an intuitive awareness of possibilities, an active sense of curiosity, an ability and willingness to learn.

This kind of independence does not mean egotistic individualism—the object is not to have one's way so much as it is to have a way that is one's own. Nor do we deify man—we merely have faith in his potential.

*Human relationships* should involve fraternity and honesty. Human interdependence is contemporary fact; human brotherhood must be willed, however, as a condition of future survival and as the most appropriate form of social relations. Personal links between man and man are needed, especially to go beyond the partial and fragmentary bonds of function that bind men only as worker to worker, employer to employee, teacher to student, American to Russian.

Loneliness, estrangement, isolation describe the vast distance between man and man today. These dominant tendencies cannot be overcome by better personnel management, nor by improved gadgets, but only when a love of man overcomes the idolatrous worship of things by man. As the individualism we affirm is not egoism, the selflessness we affirm is not self-elimination. On the contrary, we believe in generosity of a kind that imprints one's unique individual qualities in the relation to other men, and to all human activity. Further, to dislike isolation is not to favor the abolition of privacy; the latter differs from isolation in that it occurs or is abolished according to individual will.

We would replace power rooted in possession, privilege, or circumstance by power and uniqueness rooted in love, reflectiveness, reason, and creativity. As a *social system* we seek the establishment of a democracy of individual participation, governed by two central aims: that the individual share in those social decisions determining the quality and direction of his life; that society be organized to encourage independence in men and provide the media for their common participation.

In a participatory democracy, the political life would be based in several root principles:

> that decision-making of basic social consequence be carried on by public groupings;
>
> that politics be seen positively, as the art of collectively creating an acceptable pattern of social relations;
>
> that politics has the function of bringing people out of isolation and into community, thus being a necessary, though not sufficient, means of finding meaning in personal life;
>
> that the political order should serve to clarify problems in a way instrumental to their solution; it should provide outlets for the expression of personal grievance and aspiration; opposing views should be organized so as to illuminate choices and facilitate the attainment of goals; channels should be commonly available to relate men to knowledge and to power so that private problems—from bad recreation facilities to personal alienation—are formulated as general issues.

The economic sphere would have as its basis the principles:

> that work should involve incentives worthier than money or survival. It should be educative, not stultifying; creative, not mechanical; self-directed, not manipulated, encouraging independence, a respect for others, a sense of dignity, and a willingness to accept social responsibility, since it is this experience that has crucial influence on habits, perceptions, and individual ethics;
>
> that the economic experience is so personally decisive that the individual must share in its full determination;
>
> that the economy itself is of such social importance that its major resources and means of production should be open to democratic participation and subject to democratic social regulation.

Like the political and economic ones, major social institutions—cultural, educational, rehabilitative, and others—should be generally organized with the well-being and dignity of man as the essential measure of success.

In social change or interchange, we find violence to be abhorrent because it requires generally the transformation of the target, be it a human being or a community of people, into a depersonalized object of hate. It is imperative that the means of violence be abolished and the institutions—local, national, international—that encourage non-violence as a condition of conflict be developed.

These are our central values, in skeletal form. It remains vital to understand their denial or attainment in the context of the modern world.

## The Students

In the last few years, thousands of American students demonstrated that they at least felt the urgency of the times. They moved actively and directly against racial injustices, the threat of war, violations of individual rights of conscience, and, less frequently, against economic manipulation. They succeeded in restoring a small measure of controversy to the campuses after the stillness of the McCarthy period. They succeeded, too, in gaining some concessions from the people and institutions they opposed, especially in the fight against racial bigotry.

The significance of these scattered movements lies not in their success or failure in gaining objectives—at least, not yet. Nor does the significance lie in the intellectual "competence" or "maturity" of the students involved—as some pedantic elders allege. The significance is in the fact that students are breaking the crust of apathy and overcoming the inner alienation that remain the defining characteristics of American college life.

If student movements for change are still rarities on the campus scene, what is commonplace there? The real campus, the familiar campus, is a place of private people, engaged in their notorious "inner emigration." It is a place of commitment to business-as-usual, getting ahead, playing it cool. It is a place of mass affirmation of the Twist, but mass reluctance toward the controversial public stance. Rules are accepted as "inevitable," bureaucracy as "just circumstances," irrelevance as "scholarship," selflessness as "martyrdom," politics as "just another way to make people, and an unprofitable one, too."

Almost no students value activity as citizens. Passive in public, they are hardly more idealistic in arranging their private lives: Gallup concludes they will settle for "low success, and won't risk high failure." There is not much willingness to take risks (not even in business), no setting of dangerous goals, no real conception of personal identity except one manufactured in the image of others, no real urge for personal fulfillment except to be almost as successful as the very successful people. Attention is being paid to social status (the quality of shirt collars, meeting people, getting wives or husbands, making solid contacts for later on); much, too, is paid to academic status (grades, honors, the med school rat race). But neglected generally is real intellectual status, the personal cultivation of the mind.

"Students don't even give a damn about the apathy," one has said. Apathy toward apathy begets a privately constructed universe, a place of systematic study schedules, two nights each week for beer, a girl or two, and early marriage; a framework infused with personality, warmth, and under control, no matter how unsatisfying otherwise.

Under these conditions university life loses all relevance to some. Four hundred thousand of our classmates leave college every year.

But apathy is not simply an attitude; it is a product of social institutions, and of the structure and organization of higher education itself. The extracurricular life is ordered according to *in loco parentis* theory, which ratifies the Administration as the moral guardian of the young.

The accompanying "let's pretend" theory of student extracurricular affairs validates student government as a training center for those who want to spend their lives in political pretense, and discourages initiative from the more articulate, honest, and sensitive students. The bounds and style of controversy are delimited before controversy begins. The university "prepares" the student for "citizenship" through perpetual rehearsals and, usually, through emasculation of what creative spirit there is in the individual.

The academic life contains reinforcing counterparts to the way in which extracurricular life is organized. The academic world is founded on a teacher-student relation analogous to the parent-child relation which characterizes *in loco parentis*. Further, academia includes a radical separation of the student from the material of study. That which is studied, the social reality, is "objectified" to sterility, dividing the student from life—just as he is restrained in active involvement by the deans controlling student government. The specialization of function and knowledge, admittedly necessary to our complex technological and social structure, has produced an exaggerated compartmentalization of study and understanding. This has contributed to an overly parochial view, by faculty, of the role of its research and scholarship; to a discontinuous and truncated understanding, by students, of the surrounding social order; and to a loss of personal attachment, by nearly all, to the worth of study as a humanistic enterprise.

There is, finally, the cumbersome academic bureaucracy extending throughout the academic as well as the extracurricular structures, contributing to the sense of outer complexity and inner powerlessness that transforms the honest searching of many students to a ratification of convention and, worse, to a numbness to present and future catastrophes. The size and financing systems of the university enhance the permanent trusteeship of the administrative bureaucracy, their power leading to a shift within the university toward the value standards of business and the administrative mentality. Huge foundations and other private financial interests shape the under-financed colleges and universities, making them not only more commercial, but less disposed to diagnose society critically, less open to dissent. Many social and physical scientists, neglecting the liberating heritage of higher learning, develop "human relations" or "moral-producing" techniques for the corporate economy, while others exercise their intellectual skills to accelerate the arms race.

Tragically, the university could serve as a significant source of social criticism and an initiator of new modes and molders of attitudes. But the actual intellectual effect of the college experience is hardly distinguishable from that of any other communications channel—say, a television set—passing on the stock truths of the day. Students leave college somewhat more "tolerant" than when they arrived, but basically unchallenged in their values and political orientations. With administrators ordering the institution, and faculty the curriculum, the student learns by his isolation to accept elite rule within the university, which prepares him to accept later forms of minority control. The real function of the educational system—as opposed to its more rhetorical function of "searching for truth"—is to impart the key information and styles that will help the student get by, modestly but comfortably, in the big society beyond.

## The Society Beyond

Look beyond the campus, to America itself. That student life is more intellectual, and perhaps more comfortable, does not obscure the fact that the fundamental qualities of life on the campus reflect the habits of society at large. The fraternity president is seen at the junior manager levels; the sorority queen has gone to Grosse Pointe; the serious poet burns for a place, any place, to work; the once-serious and never-serious poets work at the advertising agencies. The desperation of people threatened by forces about which they know little and of which they can say less; the cheerful emptiness of people "giving up" all hope of changing things; the faceless ones polled by Gallup who listed "international affairs" fourteenth on their list of "problems" but who also expected thermonuclear war in the next few years; in these and other forms, Americans are in withdrawal from public life, from any collective effort at directing their own affairs.

Some regard these national doldrums as a sign of healthy approval of the established order—but is it approval by consent or manipulated acquiescence? Others declare that the people are withdrawn because compelling issues are fast disappearing—perhaps there are fewer breadlines in America, but is Jim Crow gone, is there enough work and work more fulfilling, is world war a diminishing threat, and what of the revolutionary new peoples? Still others think the national quietude is a necessary consequence of the need for elites to resolve complex and specialized problems of modern industrial society—but, then, why should *business* elites help decide foreign policy, and who controls the elites anyway, and are they solving mankind's problems? Others, finally, shrug knowingly and announce that full democracy never worked anywhere in the past—but why lump qualitatively different civilizations together, and how can a social order work well if its best thinkers are skeptics, and is man really doomed forever to the domination of today?

There are no convincing apologies for the contemporary malaise. While the world tumbles toward the final war, while men in other nations are trying desperately to alter events, while the very future qua future is uncertain —America is without community impulse, without the inner momentum necessary for an age when societies cannot successfully perpetuate themselves by their military weapons, when democracy must be viable because of its quality of life, not its quantity of rockets.

The apathy here is, first, *subjective*—the felt powerlessness of ordinary people, the resignation before the enormity of events. But subjective apathy is encouraged by the *objective* American situation—the actual structural separation of people from power, from relevant knowledge, from pinnacles of decision-making. Just as the university influences the student way of life, so do major social institutions create the circumstances in which the isolated citizen will try hopelessly to understand his world and himself.

The very isolation of the individual—from power and community and ability to aspire—means the rise of a democracy without publics. With the great mass of people structurally remote and psychologically hesitant with respect to democratic institutions, those institutions themselves attenuate and become, in the fashion of the vicious circle, progressively less accessible to those few who aspire to serious participation in social affairs. The vital democratic connection between community and leadership, between the mass and the several elites, has been so wrenched and perverted that disastrous policies go unchallenged time and again. . . .

## The University and Social Change

There is perhaps little reason to be optimistic about the above analysis. True, the Dixiecrat-GOP coalition is the weakest point in the dominating complex of corporate, military, and political power. But the civil rights, peace, and student movements are too poor and socially slighted, and the labor movement too quiescent, to be counted with enthusiasm. From where else can power and vision be summoned? We believe that the universities are an overlooked seat of influence.

First, the university is located in a permanent position of social influence. Its educational function makes it indispensable and automatically makes it a crucial institution in the formation of social attitudes. Second, in an unbelievably complicated world, it is the central institution for organizing, evaluating, and transmitting knowledge. Third, the extent to which academic resources presently are used to buttress immoral social practice is revealed, first, by the extent to which defense contracts make the universities engineers of the arms race. Too, the use of modern social science as a manipulative tool reveals itself in the "human relations" consultants to the modern corporations, who introduce trivial sops to give laborers feelings of "participation" or "belonging," while actually deluding them in order to further exploit their labor. And, of course, the use of motivational research is already infamous as a manipulative aspect of American politics. But these social uses of the universities' resources also demonstrate the unchangeable reliance by men of power on the men and storehouses of knowledge: this makes the university functionally tied to society in new ways, revealing new potentialities, new levers for change. Fourth, the university is the only mainstream institution that is open to participation by individuals of nearly any viewpoint.

These, at least, are facts, no matter how dull the teaching, how paternalistic the rules, how irrelevant the research that goes on. Social relevance, the accessibility to knowledge, and internal openness—these together make the university a potential base and agency in a movement of social change.

1. Any new left in America must be, in large measure, a left with real intellectual skills, committed to deliberativeness, honesty, reflection as working tools. The university permits the political life to be an adjunct to the academic one, and action to be informed by reason.

2. A new left must be distributed in significant social roles throughout the country. The universities are distributed in such a manner.

3. A new left must consist of younger people who matured in the postwar world, and partially be directed to the recruitment of younger people. The university is an obvious beginning point.

4. A new left must include liberals and socialists, the former for their relevance, the latter for their sense of thoroughgoing reforms in the system. The university is a more sensible place than a political party for these two traditions to begin to discuss their differences and look for political synthesis.

5. A new left must start controversy across the land, if national policies and national apathy are to be reversed. The ideal university is a community of controversy, within itself and in its effects on communities beyond.

6. A new left must transform modern complexity into issues that can be understood and felt close-up by every human being. It must give form to the feelings of helplessness and indifference, so that people may see the political, social, and economic sources of their private troubles and organize to change society. In a time of supposed prosperity, moral complacency, and political manipulation, a new left cannot rely on only aching stomachs to be the engine force of social reform. The case for change, for alternatives that will involve uncomfortable personal efforts, must be argued as never before. The university is a relevant place for all of these activities.

But we need not indulge in illusions: the university system cannot complete a movement of ordinary people making demands for a better life. From its schools and colleges across the nation, a militant left might awaken its allies, and by beginning the process towards peace, civil rights, and labor struggles, reinsert theory and idealism where too often reign confusion and political barter. The power of students and faculty united is not only potential; it has shown its actuality in the South, and in the reform movements of the North.

The bridge to political power, though, will be built through genuine cooperation, locally, nationally, and internationally, between a new left of young people and an awakening community of allies. In each community we must look within the university and act with confidence that we can be powerful, but we must look outwards to the less exotic but more lasting struggles for justice.

To turn these possibilities into realities will involve national efforts at university reform by an alliance of students and faculty. They must wrest control of the educational process from the administrative bureaucracy. They must make fraternal and functional contact with allies in labor, civil rights, and other liberal forces outside the campus. They must import major public issues into the curriculum—research and teaching on problems of war and peace is an outstanding example. They must make debate and controversy, not dull pedantic cant, the common style for educational life. They must consciously build a base for their assault upon the loci of power.

As students for a democratic society, we are committed to stimulating this kind of social movement, this kind of vision and program in campus and community across the country. If we appear to seek the unattainable, as it has been said, then let it be known that we do so to avoid the unimaginable.

# Part Four

# Anarchism

mma Goldman introduces her essay, "Anarchism: What It Really Stands For," with the words of John Henry McKay: "I am an Anarchist! Wherefore I will/Not rule, and also ruled I will not be!" Most simply, anarchism means without government. Its popular meaning—chaos or disorder—has been inferred from that. But anarchists resist the association of government with order and freedom with chaos. Anarchists maintain that anarchism involves a natural, not an artificial, order. It is the order of "organized, living society." Goldman's complete definition of anarchism reads: "The philosophy of a new social order based on liberty unrestricted by man-made law; the theory that all forms of government rest on violence, and are therefore wrong and harmful, as well as unnecessary." Anarchists destroy all forms of government in order to create a new social order.

In her essay, Goldman attacks four standard defenses of government. First, she questions claims that the state rests upon natural law. Nature works freely and spontaneously, for example, human needs for food, sex, light, air, and exercise are natural laws. By requiring coercion to maintain themselves, states reveal their opposition to nature. Second, Goldman argues that states do not manage to maintain order, their supposed purpose. She says, "Order derived through submission and maintained by terror is not much of a safe guaranty; yet that is the only 'order' that governments have ever maintained." Third, the state not only fails to prevent crime but also creates criminals by misdirecting human energies. The state itself is the greatest criminal. It breaks written and natural laws, stealing through taxes and killing with wars. Fourth, states neither increase productivity nor promote prosperity. Instead, they protect the property of the nonproductive, who make labor unbearable for others. To arguments that human nature nonetheless requires states, Goldman responds: "Poor human nature, what horrible crimes have been committed in thy name! Every fool ... presumes to speak authoritatively of human nature. ... Yet, how can any one speak of it today, with every soul in a prison, with every heart fettered, wounded, and maimed?" In short, humanity has yet to see what it is capable of without government.

Nevertheless, Goldman's essay leaves the constructive side of anarchism vague. She only says that "it is the philosophy of the sovereignty of the individual. It is the theory of social harmony." Her positive vision includes two themes—individual sovereignty and social harmony—that are not easily combined. Since anarchists usually emphasize one or the other, their proposals can be divided into two categories: individualist anarchism and socialist anarchism.[1]

In his defense of limited government, Milton Friedman said, "The consistent liberal is not an anarchist." Yet individualist anarchists claim to be just that—consistent liberals. They see even limited government as a violation of individual freedom. As Max Stirner puts it, "There is no freedom but that which the individual conquers for himself. Freedom given or conceded [by the state] is not freedom but 'stolen goods.'"[2] That liberal government is also popular government does not help. Votes only mask power; liberal democracy is constitutional tyranny. Coupled with freedom, individualist anarchists stress responsibility. According to William Godwin, "A virtuous disposition is principally generated by the uncontrolled exercise of private judgment and the rigid conformity of every man to the dictates of his conscience."[3]

In Henry David Thoreau's essay "On Civil Disobedience" this combination of freedom and responsibility emerges clearly. Thoreau begins with a seemingly liberal argument: That government is best which governs least. But he quickly states that no government would be better still. Government saps human vitality; individuals serve it as machines, not men. It also undermines integrity. In innumerable acts of daily life, individuals sanction state policies with which they might on reflection disagree. Thoreau asks us to consult our consciences and not to "lend [ourselves] to the wrong which [we] condemn." He maintains, "The only obligation which I have a right to assume is to do at any time what I think right." This means that the majority cannot bind me: "Any man more right than his neighbors constitutes a majority of one."

What kind of society results when individuals act from principle? Individualist anarchists generally say little about this. Like Goldman, they are clearer about what they attack than what they defend. It is socialist anarchists who outline a new social order. Like individualist anarchists, they claim to be consistent, in this case, consistent socialists.

Pierre-Joseph Proudhon provides a suitable transition between individualist and socialist anarchism. He was the first to use the word *anarchism*, commonly a term of abuse, to characterize an ideal society. But he based that society on individual rights to equality, liberty, and security. According to Proudhon, "No one is obliged to do more than comply with this injunction: In the exercise of your own rights do not encroach upon the rights of another." In society, these rights are absolute, that is, "each associate receives as much as he gives—liberty for liberty, equality for equality, security for security. . . ." Another fallacious right—to property—is the source of sorrow and misery in society. The French Revolution sought to overcome these ills by legalizing and extending property, by placing it among the inalienable rights of man. But Proudhon says that although the poor are proprietors, "instead of inferring therefrom that property should be shared by all, I demand, in the name of general security, its entire abolition. . . ." This is necessary because, unlike the other rights, property divides society by pitting rich against poor. Proudhon concludes that "if we are associated for the sake of liberty, equality, and security, we are not associated for the sake of property." Indeed, property and society are utterly irreconcilable: "Either society must perish, or it must destroy property."

Petyr Kropotkin and Mikhail Bakunin, the other socialist anarchists included in this part, provide a more complete picture of the ideal society. Kropotkin, a Russian aristocrat, wrote in the late nineteenth and early twentieth centuries. His *Mutual Aid* responds to charges that anarchists overestimate human nature, specifically, our capacity to cooperate. Unlike Darwin, Kropotkin finds that mutual aid better guarantees species survival than mutual struggle. He does not romanticize humanity, however. An instinct of human solidarity, not love or even sympathy, prompts mutual aid: "It is the conscience—be it only at the stage of an instinct—of human solidarity. It is the unconscious recognition of the force that is borrowed by each man from the practice of mutual aid; of the close dependency of every one's happiness upon the happiness of all."

Historically, however, the state has superseded mutual aid institutions. It has absorbed social functions, undermined social responsibility, and fostered "the development of an unbridled, narrow-minded individualism." According to Kropotkin, "The result is, that the theory which maintains that men can, and must seek their own happiness in a disregard of other people's wants is now triumphant all round—in law, in science, in religion." Still, some mutual aid survives: "In our mutual relations every one of us has his moments of revolt against the fashionable individualist creed of the day."

Although Kropotkin's concept of mutual aid is fundamental for social anarchists, Mikhail Bakunin is better known. This is largely because of his conflict with Karl Marx, which destroyed the First International.[4] That conflict was, in part, personal. Although Bakunin claimed to be Marx's disciple, Marx called him "an ass" and his work "an assembled rubbish mishmash." Their more important doctrinal differences center on the relationship between economics and politics. For Marx, politics is ultimately determined by economics. This economic determinism diminishes the importance and the dangers of political power. Hence, Marx advises the revolutionary proletariat to seize the state and remains confident that the state will eventually wither away.

Bakunin disagrees. He warns that all men—even "sincere socialist revolutionaries"—possess a natural instinct for power. "A government that does not abuse its power," he says, "is, like squaring the circle, an unattainable ideal because it runs counter to human nature. . . . Take the most radical revolutionist and place him upon the all-Russian throne or give him dictatorial power . . . and within a year he will have become worse than the Emperor himself."[5] Struggle against the state is, then, as important as struggle against capital: "In order to humanize society as a whole, it is necessary ruthlessly to destroy all the causes and all the economic, political, and social conditions which produce within individuals a tradition of evil."[6]

Bakunin's and Marx's revolutionary strategies differ accordingly. Bakunin argues that economic and political revolution must occur simultaneously. Otherwise, the revolution will stop halfway; the transitional proletarian dictatorship will become a permanent proletarian state. Bakunin asks: "What does it mean for the proletariat to be organized as the ruling class? Can it really be that the entire proletariat will stand at the head of the new socialist administration?"[7] He answers: "It will. be the reign of the scientific mind, the most aristocratic, despotic, arrogant, and contemptuous of all regimes. There will be a new class, a new hierarchy of real and bogus learning. . . . Let the masses Beware."[8] Revolutions, this suggests, must occur spontaneously, arising "from the very depths of the soul of the people." They come like "thiefs in the night," prompted by the "force of events." The people need to be educated and organized, but not by a party vanguard. Bakunin's revolutionary leaders are "midwives" to the masses' "self-liberation." They direct, not by "ostensible power," but by "a dictatorship without insignia, title, or official rights, all the more powerful because it will have none of the marks of power."[9]

Throughout their debate, Marx and Bakunin had different fears. As Engels shows in his "On Authority," Marx feared proletarian disorganization and capitalist opposition. Revolutions are authoritarian and must remain so, at least temporarily, to consolidate their power. Engels asks of the anarchists: "Have these gentlemen ever seen a revolution? A revolution is the most authoritarian thing there is . . . and if the victorious party does not want to have fought in vain, it must maintain this rule by means of . . . terror." In contrast,

Bakunin feared corruption of revolutionaries and continuation of state power. History suggests that Bakunin was right. The antistatist Marx inspired a massive state; his means betrayed his ends. Was Marx also right, that nonauthoritarian revolution is a utopian dream? To answer this question you might want to explore anarchist movements.[10]

Whatever one concludes, it is important to remember that anarchism survives. Today, individualist strains appear among libertarians or anarcho-capitalists. They would create free markets by eliminating states. This, they claim, better protects property. According to Murray Rothbard, "The state provides a legal, orderly, systematic channel for the predation of private property."[11] Private corporations could assume public services, for example, police, roads, schools. Since national security problems would decrease—it is states that make wars—even armies could be privately funded. Socialist anarchism also persists, most prominently, among radical or anarcho-feminists. Since Monique Wittig's "One Is Not Born a Woman" represents them later, I do not discuss their views here.

Anarchists stress the dangers of the state, the importance of individual responsibility, and the possibility of social harmony. While other ideologies debate the nature of government, anarchists ask the fundamental question: Is government necessary at all?

## Notes

1. Daniel Guerin suggests this categorization in *Anarchism: From Theory to Practice* (New York: Monthly Review Press, 1970), pt. 1.

2. Quoted in ibid., 28.

3. William Godwin, "The Rights of Man and the Principles of Society," in *The Anarchists*, ed. Irving L. Horowitz (New York: Dell, 1964), 118.

4. The First International, or International Workingmen's Association, was organized by Marx and Engels in 1864 to unite trade unions across nations. For a discussion of Marx's and Bakunin's differences, see Alvin Gouldner, "Marx's Last Battle; Bakunin and the First International," *Theory and Society* 11 (1982): 853–84. Also see Paul Thomas, *Karl Marx and the Anarchists* (London: Routledge and Kegan Paul, 1980).

5. Mikhail Bakunin, "The Social and Economic Bases of Anarchism" in Horowitz, *Anarchists*, 128.

6. G.P. Maximoff, *The Political Philosophy of Bakunin: Scientific Anarchism* (New York: Free Press, 1953), 369.

7. "After the Revolution: Mar Debates Bakunin," quoted in Alvin W. Gouldner, "Bakunin and the First International," *Theory and Society* 11 (1982): 865.

8. Ibid., 866.

9. Quoted in Guerin, *Anarchism*, 33–34.

10. For a discussion of anarchism in the Russian Revolution, the Italian Factory Councils, and the Spanish Civil War, see Guerin, *Anarchism*, pt. 3. Specifically on the

Spanish Civil War, see George Orwell, *Homage to Catalonia* (New York: Harcourt, Brace, 1952), and Franz Borkenau, *The Spanish Cockpit* (Ann Arbor: University of Michigan Press, 1963).

11. Murray Newton Rothbard, *For a New Liberty: The Libertarian Manifesto* (New York: University Press of America, 1978), 46.

# 20

## EMMA GOLDMAN

# *Anarchism: What It Really Stands For*

Emma Goldman (1869–1940) was born in Russia and emigrated to New York in 1885. There she began her lifelong association with anarchist politics. She was often imprisoned for her protest activities, and was deported to Russia in 1919. In 1921, she fled Soviet Russia. Like many anarchists, she was disillusioned with the Bolshevik revolution. She lived in Canada until her death. Goldman is also known for her feminist writings, published in *The Traffic in Women and Other Essays on Feminism.*


Anarchy

Ever reviled, accursed, ne'er understood,
   Thou art the grisly terror of our age.
"Wreck of all order," cry the multitude,
   "Art thou, and war and murder's endless rage."
O, let them cry. To them that ne'er have striven
   The truth that lies behind a word to find,
To them the word's right meaning was not given.
   They shall continue blind among the blind.
But thou, O word, so clear, so strong, so pure,
   Thou sayest all which I for goal have taken.
I give thee to the future! Thine secure
   When each at least unto himself shall waken.
Comes it in sunshine? In the tempest's thrill?
   I cannot tell—but it the earth shall see!
I am an Anarchist! Wherefore I will
   Not rule, and also ruled I will not be!
               —John Henry Mackay

The history of human growth and development is at the same time the history of the terrible struggle of every new idea heralding the approach of a brighter dawn. In its tenacious hold on tradition, the Old has never hesitated to make use of the foulest and cruelest means to stay the advent of the New, in whatever form or period the latter may have asserted itself. Nor need we retrace our steps into the distant past to realize the enormity of opposition, difficulties, and hardships placed in the path of every progressive idea. The rack, the thumbscrew, and the knout are still with us; so are the convict's garb and the social wrath, all conspiring against the spirit that is serenely marching on.

Anarchism could not hope to escape the fate of all other ideas of innovation. Indeed, as the most revolutionary and uncompromising innovator, Anarchism must needs meet with the combined ignorance and venom of the world it aims to reconstruct.

To deal even remotely with all that is being said and done against Anarchism would necessitate the writing of a whole volume. I shall therefore meet only two of the principal objections. In so doing, I shall attempt to elucidate what Anarchism really stands for.

The strange phenomenon of the opposition to Anarchism is that it brings to light the relation between so-called intelligence and ignorance. And yet this is not so very strange when we consider the relativity of all things. The ignorant mass has in its favor that it makes no pretense of knowledge or tolerance. Acting, as it always does, by mere impulse, its reasons are like those of a child. "Why?" "Because." Yet the opposition of the uneducated to Anarchism deserves the same consideration as that of the intelligent man.

What, then, are the objections? First, Anarchism is impractical, though a beautiful ideal. Second, anarchism stands for violence and destruction, hence it must be repudiated as vile and dangerous. Both the intelligent man and the ignorant mass judge not from a thorough knowledge of the subject, but either from hearsay or false interpretation.

A practical scheme, says Oscar Wilde, is either one already in existence or a scheme that could be carried out under the existing conditions; but it is exactly the existing conditions that one objects to, and any scheme that could accept these conditions is wrong and foolish. The true criterion of the practical, therefore, is not whether the latter can keep intact the wrong or foolish; rather is it whether the scheme has vitality enough to leave the stagnant waters of the old, and build, as well as sustain, new life. In the light of this conception, Anarchism is indeed practical. More than any other idea, it is helping to do away with the wrong and foolish; more than any other idea, it is building and sustaining new life.

The emotions of the ignorant man are continuiously kept at a pitch by the most blood-curdling stories about Anarchism. Not a thing too outrageous to be employed against this philosophy and its exponents. Therefore Anarchism represents to the unthinking what the proverbial bad man does to the child—a black monster bent on swallowing everything; in short, destruction and violence.

Destruction and violence! How is the ordinary man to know that the most violent element in society is ignorance; that its power of destruction is the very thing Anarchism is combating? Nor is he aware that Anarchism, whose roots, as it were, are part of nature's forces, destroys, not healthful tissue, but parasitic growths that feed on the life's essence of society. It is merely clearing the soil from weeds and sagebrush, that it may eventually bear healthy fruit.

Someone has said that it requires less mental effort to condemn than to think. The widespread mental indolence, so prevalent in society, proves this to be only too true. Rather than to go to the bottom of any given idea, to examine into its origin and meaning, most people will either condemn it altogether, or rely on some superficial or prejudicial definition of non-essentials.

Anarchism urges man to think, to investigate, to analyze every proposition; but that the brain capacity of the average reader be not taxed too much, I also shall begin with a definition, and then elaborate on the latter.

> ANARCHISM: The philosophy of a new social order based on liberty unrestricted by man-made law; the theory that all forms of government rest on violence, and are therefore wrong and harmful, as well as unnecessary.

The new social order rests, of course, on the materialistic basis of life; but while all Anarchists agree that the main evil today is an economic one, they maintain that the solution of that evil can be brought about only through the consideration of *every phase* of life—individual, as well as the collective; the internal, as well as the external phases.

A thorough perusal of the history of human development will disclose two elements in bitter conflict with each other; elements that are only now beginning to be understood, not as foreign to each other, but as closely related and truly harmonious, if only placed in proper environment: the individual and social instincts. The individual and society have waged a relentless and bloody battle for ages, each striving for supremacy, because each was blind to the value and importance of the other. The individual and social instincts —the one a most potent factor for individual endeavor, for growth, aspiration, self-realization; the other an equally potent factor for mutual helpfulness and social well-being.

The explanation of the storm raging within the individual, and between him and his surroundings, is not far to seek. The primitive man, unable to understand his being, much less the unity of all life, felt himself absolutely dependent on blind, hidden forces ever ready to mock and taunt him. Out of that attitude grew the religious concepts of man as a mere speck of dust dependent on superior powers on high, who can only be appeased by complete surrender. All the early sagas rest on that idea, which continues to be the *Leit-motiv* of the biblical tales dealing with the relation of man to God, to the State, to society. Again and again the same motif, *man is nothing, the powers are everything.* Thus Jehovah would only endure man on condition of complete surrender. Man can have all the glories of the earth, but he must not become conscious of himself. The State, society, and moral laws all sing the same refrain: Man can have all the glories of the earth, but he must not become conscious of himself.

Anarchism is the only philosophy which brings to man the consciousness of himself; which maintains that God, the State, and society are non-existent, that their promises are null and void, since they can be fulfilled only through man's subordination. Anarchism is therefore the teacher of the unity of life; not merely in nature, but in man. There is no conflict between the individual and the social instincts, any more than there is between the heart and the lungs: the one the receptacle of a precious life essence, the other the repository of the element that keeps the essence pure and strong. The individual is the heart of society, conserving the essence of social life; society is the lungs which are distributing the element to keep the life essence—that is, the individual—pure and strong.

"The one thing of value in the world," says Emerson, "is the active soul; this every man contains within him. The soul active sees absolute truth and utters truth and creates." In other words, the individual instinct is the thing of value in the world. It is the true soul that sees and creates the truth alive, out of which is to come a still greater truth, the re-born social soul.

Anarchism is the great liberator of man from the phantoms that have held him captive; it is the arbiter and pacifier of the two forces for individual and social harmony. To accomplish that unity, Anarchism has declared war on the pernicious influences which have so far prevented the harmonious blending of individual and social instincts, the individual and society.

Religion, the dominion of the human mind; Property, the dominion of human needs; and Government, the dominion of human conduct, represent the stronghold of man's enslavement and all the horrors it entails. Religion! How it dominates man's mind, how it humiliates and degrades his soul. God is everything, man is nothing, says religion. But out of that nothing God has created a kingdom so despotic, so tyrannical, so cruel, so terribly exacting that naught but gloom and tears and blood have ruled the world since gods began. Anarchism rouses man to rebellion against this black monster. Break your mental fetters, says Anarchism to man, for not until you think and judge for yourself will you get rid of the dominion of darkness, the greatest obstacle to all progress.

Property, the dominion of man's needs, the denial of the right to satisfy his needs. Time was when property claimed a divine right, when it came to man with the same refrain, even as religion, "Sacrifice! Abnegate! Submit!" The spirit of Anarchism has lifted man from his prostrate position. He now stands erect, with his face toward the light. He has learned to see the insatiable, devouring, devastating nature of property, and he is preparing to strike the monster dead.

"Property is robbery," said the great French Anarchist Proudhon. Yes, but without risk and danger to the robber. Monopolizing the accumulated efforts of man, property has robbed him of his birthright, and has turned him loose a pauper and an outcast. Property has not even the time-worn excuse that man does not create enough to satisfy all needs. The A B C student of economics knows that the productivity of labor within the last few decades far exceeds normal demand. But what are normal demands to an abnormal institution? The only demand that property recognizes is its own gluttonous appetite for greater wealth, because wealth means power; the power to subdue, to crush, to exploit, the power to enslave, to outrage, to degrade. America is particularly boastful of her great power, her enormous national wealth. Poor America, of what avail is all her wealth, if the individuals comprising the nation are wretchedly poor? If they live in squalor, in filth, in crime, with hope and joy gone, a homeless, soilless army of human prey.

It is generally conceded that unless the returns of any business venture exceed the cost, bankruptcy is inevitable. But those engaged in the business of producing wealth have not yet learned even this simple lesson. Every year the cost of production in human life is growing larger (50,000 killed, 100,000 wounded in America last year); the returns to the masses, who help to create wealth, are ever getting smaller. Yet America continues to be blind to the inevitable bankruptcy of our business of production. Nor is this the only crime of the latter. Still more fatal is the crime of turning the producer into a mere particle of a machine, with less will and decision than his master of steel and iron. Man is being robbed not merely of the products of his labor, but of the power of free initiative, of originality, and the interest in, or desire for, the things he is making.

Real wealth consists in things of utility and beauty, in things that help to create strong, beautiful bodies and surroundings inspiring to live in. But if man is doomed to wind cotton around a spool, or dig coal, or build roads for thirty years of his life, there can be no talk of wealth. What he gives to the world is only gray and hideous things, reflecting a dull and hideous existence—too weak to live, too cowardly to die. Strange to say, there are people who extol this deadening method of centralized production as the proudest achievement of our age. They fail utterly to realize that if we are to continue in machine subserviency, our slavery is more complete than was our bondage to the King. They do not want to know that centralization is not only the deathknell of liberty, but also of health and beauty, of art and science, all these being impossible in a clocklike, mechanical atmosphere.

Anarchism cannot but repudiate such a method of production: its goal is the freest possible expression of all the latent powers of the individual. Oscar Wilde defines a perfect personality as "one who develops under perfect conditions, who is not wounded, maimed, or in danger." A perfect personality, then, is only possible in a state of society where man is free to choose the mode of work, the conditions of work, and the freedom to work. One to whom the making of a table, the building of a house, or the tilling of the soil, is what the painting is to the artist and the discovery to the scientist—the result of inspiration, of intense longing, and deep interest in work as a creative force. That being the ideal of Anarchism, its economic arrangements must consist of voluntary productive and distributive associations, gradually developing into free communism, as the best means of producing with the least waste of human energy. Anarchism, however, also recognizes the right of the individual, or numbers of individuals, to arrange at all times for other forms of work, in harmony with their tastes and desires.

Such free display of human energy being possible only under complete individual and social freedom, Anarchism directs its forces against the third and greatest foe of all social equality; namely, the State, organized authority, or statutory law—the dominion of human conduct.

Just as religion has fettered the human mind, and as property, or the monopoly of things, has subdued and stifled man's needs, so has the State enslaved his spirit, dictating every phase of conduct. "All government in essence," says Emerson, "is tyranny." It matters not whether it is government by divine right or majority rule. In every instance its aim is the absolute subordination of the individual.

Referring to the American government, the greatest American Anarchist, David Thoreau, said: "Government, what is it but a tradition, though a recent one, endeavoring to transmit itself unimpaired to posterity, but each instance losing its integrity; it has not the vitality and force of a single living man. Law never made man a whit more just; and by means of their respect for it, even the well disposed are daily made agents of injustice."

Indeed, the keynote of government is injustice. With the arrogance and self-sufficiency of the King who could do no wrong, governments ordain, judge, condemn, and punish the most insignificant offenses, while maintaining themselves by the greatest of all offenses, the annihilation of individual liberty. Thus Ouida is right when she maintains that "the State only aims at instilling those qualities in its public by which its demands are obeyed, and its exchequer is filled. Its highest attainment is the reduction of mankind to clockwork. In its atmosphere all those finer and more delicate liberties, which require treatment and spacious expansion, inevitably dry up and perish. The State requires a taxpaying machine in which there is no hitch, an exchequer in which there is never a deficit, and a public, monotonous, obedient, colorless, spiritless, moving humbly like a flock of sheep along a straight high road between two walls."

Yet even a flock of sheep would resist the chicanery of the State, if it were not for the corruptive, tyrannical, and oppressive methods it employs to serve its purposes. Therefore Bakunin repudiates the State as synonymous with the surrender of the liberty of the individual or small minorities—the destruction of social relationship, the curtailment, or complete denial even, of life itself, for its own aggrandizement. The State is the altar of political freedom and, like the religious altar, it is maintained for the purpose of human sacrifice.

In fact, there is hardly a modern thinker who does not agree that government, organized authority, or the State, is necessary *only* to maintain or protect property and monopoly. It has proven efficient in that function only.

Even George Bernard Shaw, who hopes for the miraculous from the State under Fabianism, nevertheless admits that "it is at present a huge machine for robbing and slave-driving of the poor by brute force." This being the case, it is hard to see why the clever prefacer wishes to uphold the State after poverty shall have ceased to exist.

Unfortunately there are still a number of people who continue in the fatal belief that government rests on natural laws, that it maintains social order and harmony, that it diminishes crime, and that it prevents the lazy man from fleecing his fellows. I shall therefore examine these contentions.

A natural law is that factor in man which asserts itself freely and spontaneously without any external force, in harmony with the requirements of nature. For instance, the demand for nutrition, for sex gratification, for light, air, and exercise, is a natural law. But its expression needs not the machinery of government, needs not the club, the gun, the handcuff, or the prison. To obey such laws, if we may call it obedience, requires only spontaneity and free opportunity. That governments do not maintain themselves through such harmonious factors is proven by the terrible array of violence, force, and coercion all governments use in order to live. Thus Blackstone is right when he says, "Human laws are invalid, because they are contrary to the laws of nature."

Unless it be the order of Warsaw after the slaughter of thousands of people, it is difficult to ascribe to governments any capacity for order or social harmony. Order derived through submission and maintained by terror is not much of a safe guaranty; yet that is the only "order" that governments have ever maintained. True social harmony grows naturally out of solidarity of interests. In a society where those who always work never have anything, while those who never work enjoy everything, solidarity of interests is non-existent; hence social harmony is but a myth. The only way organized authority meets this grave situation is by extending still greater privileges to those who have already monopolized the earth, and by still further enslaving the disinherited masses. Thus the entire arsenal of government—laws, police, soldiers, the courts, legislatures, prisons—is strenuously engaged in "harmonizing" the most antagonistic elements in society.

The most absurd apology for authority and law is that they serve to diminish crime. Aside from the fact that the State is itself the greatest criminal, breaking every written and natural law, stealing in the form of taxes, killing in the form of war and capital punishment, it has come to an absolute standstill in coping with crime. It has failed utterly to destroy or even minimize the horrible scourge of its own creation.

Crime is naught but misdirected energy. So long as every institution of today, economic, political, social, and moral, conspires to misdirect human energy into wrong channels; so long as most people are out of place doing the things they hate to do, living a life they loathe to live, crime will be inevitable, and all the laws on the statutes can only increase, but never do away with, crime. What does society, as it exists today, know of the process of despair, the poverty, the horrors, the fearful struggle the human soul must pass on its way to crime and degradation. Who that knows this terrible process can fail to see the truth in these words of Peter Kropotkin:

> Those who will hold the balance between the benefits thus attributed to law and punishment and the degrading effect of the latter on humanity; those who will estimate the torrent of depravity poured abroad in human society by the informer, favored by the Judge even, and paid for in clinking cash by governments, under the pretext of aiding to unmask crime; those who will go within prison walls and there see what human beings become when deprived of liberty, when subjected to the care of brutal keepers, to coarse, cruel words, to a thousand stinging, piercing humiliations, will agree with us that the entire apparatus of prison and punishment is an abomination which ought to be brought to an end.

The deterrent influence of law on the lazy man is too absurd to merit consideration. If society were only relieved of the waste and expense of keeping a lazy class, and the equally great expense of the paraphernalia of protection this lazy class requires, the social tables would contain an abundance for all, including even the occasional lazy individual. Besides, it is well to consider that laziness results either from special privileges, or physical and mental abnormalities. Our present insane system of production fosters both, and the most astounding phenomenon is that people should want to work at all now. Anarchism aims to strip labor of its deadening, dulling aspect, of its gloom and compulsion. It aims to make work an instrument of joy, of strength, of color, of real harmony, so that the poorest sort of a man should find in work both recreation and hope.

To achieve such an arrangement of life, government, with its unjust, arbitrary, repressive measures, must be done away with. At best it has but imposed one single mode of life upon all, without regard to individual and social variations and needs. In destroying government and statutory laws, Anarchism proposes to rescue the self-respect and independence of the individual from all restraint and invasion by authority. Only in freedom can man grow to his full stature. Only in freedom will he learn to think and move, and give the very best in him. Only in freedom will he realize the true force of the social bonds which knit men together, and which are the true foundation of a normal social life.

But what about human nature? Can it be changed? And if not, will it endure under Anarchism?

Poor human nature, what horrible crimes have been committed in thy name! Every fool, from king to policeman, from the flatheaded parson to the visionless dabbler in science, presumes to speak authoritatively of human nature. The greater the mental charlatan, the more definite his insistence on the wickedness and weaknesses of human nature. Yet, how can any one speak of it today, with every soul in a prison, with every heart fettered, wounded, and maimed?

John Burroughs has stated that experimental study of animals in captivity is absolutely useless. Their character, their habits, their appetites undergo a complete transformation when torn from their soil in field and forest. With human nature caged in a narrow space, whipped daily into submission, how can we speak of its potentialities?

Freedom, expansion, opportunity, and, above all, peace and repose, alone can teach us the real dominant factors of human nature and all its wonderful possibilities.

Anarchism, then, really stands for the liberation of the human mind from the dominion of religion; the liberation of the human body from the dominion of property; liberation from the shackles and restraint of government. Anarchism stands for a social order based on the free grouping of individuals for the purpose of producing real social wealth; an order that will guarantee to every human being free access to the earth and full enjoyment of the necessities of life, according to individual desires, tastes, and inclinations.

This is not a wild fancy or an aberration of the mind. It is the conclusion arrived at by hosts of intellectual men and women the world over; a conclusion resulting from the close and studious observation of the tendencies of modern society: individual liberty and economic equality, the twin forces for the birth of what is fine and true in man.

As to methods. Anarchism is not, as some may suppose, a theory of the future to be realized through divine inspiration. It is a living force in the affairs of our life, constantly creating new conditions. The methods of Anarchism therefore do not comprise an iron-clad program to be carried out under all circumstances. Methods must grow out of the economic needs of each place and clime, and of the intellectual and temperamental requirements of the individual. The serene, calm character of a Tolstoy will wish different methods for social reconstruction than the intense, overflowing personality of a Michael Bakunin or a Peter Kropotkin. Equally so it must be apparent that the economic and political needs of Russia will dictate more drastic measures than would England or America. Anarchism does not stand for military drill and uniformity; it does, however, stand for the spirit of revolt, in whatever form, against everything that hinders human growth. All Anarchists agree in that, as they also agree in their opposition to the political machinery as a means of bringing about the great social change.

"All voting," says Thoreau, "is a sort of gaming, like checkers, or backgammon, a playing with right and wrong; its obligation never exceeds that of expediency. Even voting for the right thing is doing nothing for it. A wise man will not leave the right to the mercy of chance, nor wish it to prevail through the power of the majority." A close examination of the machinery of politics and its achievements will bear out the logic of Thoreau.

What does the history of parliamentarism show? Nothing but failure and defeat, not even a single reform to ameliorate the economic and social stress of the people. Laws have been passed and enactments made for the improvement and protection of labor. Thus it was proven only last year that Illinois, with the most rigid laws for mine protection, had the greatest mine disasters. In States where child labor laws prevail, child exploitation is at its highest, and though with us the workers enjoy full political opportunities, capitalism has reached the most brazen zenith.

Even were the workers able to have their own representatives, for which our good Socialist politicians are clamoring, what chances are there for their honesty and good faith? One has but to bear in mind the process of politics to realize that its path of good intentions is full of pitfalls: wirepulling, intriguing, flattering, lying, cheating; in fact, chicanery of every description, whereby the political aspirant can achieve success. Added to that is a complete demoralization of character and conviction, until nothing is left that would make one hope for anything from such a human derelict. Time and time again the people were foolish enough to trust, believe, and support with their last farthing aspiring politicians, only to find themselves betrayed and cheated.

It may be claimed that men of integrity would not become corrupt in the political grinding mill. Perhaps not; but such men would be absolutely helpless to exert the slightest influence in behalf of labor, as indeed has been shown in numerous instances. The State is the economic master of its servants. Good men, if such there be, would either remain true to their political faith and lose their economic support, or they would cling to their economic master and be utterly unable to do the slightest good. The political arena leaves one no alternative, one must either be a dunce or a rogue.

The political superstition is still holding sway over the hearts and minds of the masses, but the true lovers of liberty will have no more to do with it. Instead, they believe with [Max] Stirner that man has as much liberty as he is willing to take. Anarchism therefore stands for direct action, the open defiance of, and resistance to, all laws and restrictions, economic, social, and moral.

But defiance and resistance are illegal. Therein lies the salvation of man. Everything illegal necessitates integrity, self-reliance, and courage. In short, it calls for free, independent spirits, for "men who are men, and who have a bone in their backs which you cannot pass your hand through."

Universal suffrage itself owes its existence to direct action. If not for the spirit of rebellion, of the defiance on the part of the American revolutionary fathers, their posterity would still wear the King's coat. If not for the direct action of a John Brown and his comrades, America would still trade in the flesh of the black man. True, the trade in white flesh is still going on; but that, too, will have to be abolished by direct action. Trade-unionism, the economic arena of the modern gladiator, owes its existence to direct action. It is but recently that law and government have attempted to crush the trade-union movement, and condemned the exponents of man's right to organize to prison as conspirators. Had they sought to assert their cause through begging, pleading, and compromise, trade-unionism would today be a negligible quantity. In France, in Spain, in Italy, in Russia, nay even in England (witness the growing rebellion of English labor unions), direct, revolutionary, economic action has become so strong a force in the battle for industrial liberty as to make the world realize the tremendous importance of labor's power. The General Strike, the supreme expression of the economic consciousness of the workers, was ridiculed in America but a short time ago. Today every great strike, in order to win, must realize the importance of the solidaric general protest.

Direct action, having proven effective along economic lines, is equally potent in the environment of the individual. There a hundred forces encroach upon his being, and only persistent resistance to them will finally set him free. Direct action against the authority in the shop, direct action against the invasive, meddlesome authority of our moral code, is the logical, consistent method of Anarchism.

Will it not lead to a revolution? Indeed, it will. No real social change has ever come about without a revolution. People are either not familiar with their history, or they have not yet learned that revolution is but thought carried into action.

Anarchism, the great leaven of thought, is today permeating every phase of human endeavor. Science, art, literature, the drama, the effort of economic betterment, in fact every individual and social opposition to the existing disorder of things, is illumined by the spiritual light of Anarchism. It is the philosophy of the sovereignty of the individual. It is the theory of social harmony. It is the great, surging, living truth that is reconstructing the world, and that will usher in the Dawn.

# 21

# HENRY DAVID THOREAU

## *Essay on Civil Disobedience*

Henry David Thoreau (1817–62) is best known for his account of his tranquil experiences at Walden Pond. But in 1846 he was arrested for failing to pay his taxes. That prompted him to write the "Essay on Civil Disobedience," which justifies disobeying the laws of a government whose policies one cannot support. Thoreau's concern was the Mexican-American War, but his essay continues to inspire protests on issues ranging from civil rights to nuclear energy.

I heartily accept the motto, "That government is best which governs least"; and I should like to see it acted up to more rapidly and systematically. Carried out, it finally amounts to this, which also I believe—"That government is best which governs not at all"; and when men are prepared for it, that will be the kind of government which they will have. Government is at best but an expedient; but most governments are usually, and all governments are sometimes, inexpedient. The objections which have been brought against a standing army, and they are many and weighty, and deserve to prevail, may also at last be brought against a standing government. The standing army is only an arm of the standing government. The government itself, which is only the mode which the people have chosen to execute their will, is equally liable to be abused and perverted before the people can act through it. Witness the present Mexican war, the work of comparatively a few individuals using the standing government as their tool; for, in the outset, the people would not have consented to this measure.

This American government—what is it but a tradition, though a recent one, endeavoring to transmit itself unimpaired to posterity, but each instant losing some of its integrity? It has not the vitality and force of a single living man; for a single man can bend it to his will. It is a sort of wooden gun to the people themselves. But it is not the less necessary for this; for the people must have some complicated machinery or other, and hear its din, to satisfy that idea of government which they have. Governments show thus how success-fully men can be imposed on, even impose on themselves, for their own ad-vantage. It is excellent, we must all allow. Yet this government never of itself furthered any enterprise, but by the alacrity with which it got out of its way. *It* does not keep the country free. *It* does not settle the West. *It* does not edu-cate. The character inherent in the American people has done all that has been accomplished; and it would have done somewhat more, if the government had not sometimes got in its way. For government is an expedient by which men would fain succeed in letting one another alone; and, as has been said, when it is most expedient, the governed are most let alone by it. Trade and commerce, if they were not made of India-rubber, would never manage to bounce over the obstacles which legislators are continually putting in their way; and, if one were to judge these men wholly by the effects of their actions and not partly by their intentions, they would deserve to be classed and punished with those mischievous persons who put obstructions on the railroads.

But, to speak practically and as a citizen, unlike those who call them-selves no-government men, I ask for, not at once no government, but *at once* a better government. Let every man make known what kind of government would command his respect, and that will be one step toward obtaining it.

After all, the practical reason why, when the power is once in the hands of the people, a majority are permitted, and for a long period continue, to rule is not because they are most likely to be in the right, nor because this seems fairest to the minority, but because they are physically the strongest. But a government in which the majority rule in all cases cannot be based on justice, even as far as men understand it. Can there not be a government in which ma-jorities do not virtually decide right and wrong, but conscience?—in which majorities decide only those questions to which the rule of expediency is appli-cable? Must the citizen ever for a moment, or in the least degree, resign his conscience to the legislator? Why has every man a conscience, then? I think that we should be men first, and subjects afterward. It is not desirable to culti-vate a respect for the law, so much as for the right. The only obligation which I have a right to assume is to do at any time what I think right. It is truly enough said, that a corporation has no conscience; but a corporation of con-scientious men is a corporation *with* a conscience. Law never made men a whit more just; and, by means of their respect for it, even the well-disposed are daily made the agents of injustice. A common and natural result of an un-due respect for law is, that you may see a file of soldiers, colonel, captain, cor-poral, privates, powder-monkeys, and all, marching in admirable order over hill and dale to the wars, against their wills, ay, against their common sense and consciences, which makes it very steep marching indeed, and produces a palpitation of the heart. They have no doubt that it is a damnable business in which they are concerned; they are all peaceably inclined. Now, what are they? Men at all? or small movable forts and magazines, at the service of some unscrupulous man in power? Visit the Navy-Yard, and behold a marine, such a man as an American government can make, or such as it can make a man with its black arts—a mere shadow and reminiscence of humanity, a man laid out alive and standing, and already, as one may say, buried under arms with funeral accompaniments, though it may be—

> "Not a drum was heard, not a funeral note,
> As his corse to the rampart we hurried;
> Not a soldier discharged his farewell shot
> O'er the grave where our hero we buried."

The mass of men serve the state thus, not as men mainly, but as machines, with their bodies. They are the standing army, and the militia, jailers, constables, posse comitatus, etc. In most cases there is no free exercise whatever of the judgment or of the moral sense; but they put themselves on a level with wood and earth and stones; and wooden men can perhaps be manufactured that will serve the purpose as well. Such command no more respect than men of straw or a lump of dirt. They have the same sort of worth only as horses and dogs. Yet such as these even are commonly esteemed good citizens. Others—as most legislators, politicians, lawyers, ministers, and office-holders —serve the state chiefly with their heads; and, as they rarely make any moral distinctions, they are as likely to serve the Devil, without *intending* it, as God. A very few, as heroes, patriots, martyrs, reformers in the great sense, and *men*, serve the state with their consciences also, and so necessarily resist it for the most part; and they are commonly treated as enemies by it. A wise man will only be useful as a man, and will not submit to be "clay," and "stop a hole to keep the wind away," but leave that office to his dust at least:

> "I am too high-born to be propertied,
> To be a secondary at control,
> Or useful serving-man and instrument
> To any sovereign state throughout the world."

He who gives himself entirely to his fellowmen appears to them useless and selfish; but he who gives himself partially to them is pronounced a benefactor and philanthropist.

How does it become a man to behave toward this American government today? I answer, that he cannot without disgrace be associated with it. I cannot for an instant recognize that political organization as *my* government which is the *slave's* government also.

All men recognize the right of revolution; that is, the right to refuse allegiance to, and to resist, the government, when its tyranny or its inefficiency are great and unendurable. But almost all say that such is not the case now.

But such was the case, they think, in the Revolution of '75. If one were to tell me that this was a bad government because it taxed certain foreign commodities brought to its ports, it is most probable that I should not make an ado about it, for I can do without them. All machines have their friction; and possibly this does enough good to counterbalance the evil. At any rate, it is a great evil to make a stir about it. But when the friction comes to have its machine, and oppression and robbery are organized, I say, let us not have such a machine any longer. In other words, when a sixth of the population of a nation which has undertaken to be the refuge of liberty are slaves, and a whole country is unjustly overrun and conquered by a foreign army, and subjected to military law, I think that it is not too soon for honest men to rebel and revolutionize. What makes this duty the more urgent is the fact that the country so overrun is not our own, but ours is the invading army.

[William] Paley, a common authority with many on moral questions, in his chapter on the "Duty of Submission to Civil Government," resolves all civil obligation into expediency; and he proceeds to say, "that so long as the interest of the whole society requires it, that is, so long as the established government cannot be resisted or changed without public inconveniency, it is the will of God that the established government be obeyed, and no longer. . . . This principle being admitted, the justice of every particular case of resistance is reduced to a computation of the quantity of the danger and grievance on the one side, and of the probability and expense of redressing it on the other." Of this, he says, every man shall judge for himself. But Paley appears never to have contemplated those cases to which the rule of expediency does not apply, in which a people, as well as an individual, must do justice, cost what it may. If I have unjustly wrested a plank from a drowning man, I must restore it to him though I drown myself. This, according to Paley, would be inconvenient. But he that would save his life, in such a case, shall lose it. This people must cease to hold slaves, and to make war on Mexico, though it cost them their existence as a people.

In their practice, nations agree with Paley; but does any one think that Massachusetts does exactly what is right at the present crisis?

> *"A drab of state, a cloth-o'-silver slut,*
> *To have her train borne up, and her soul*
> *trail in the dirt."*

Practically speaking, the opponents to a reform in Massachusetts are not a hundred thousand politicians at the South, but a hundred thousand merchants and farmers here, who are more interested in commerce and agriculture than they are in humanity, and are not prepared to do justice to the slave and to Mexico, *cost what it may.* I quarrel not with far-off foes, but with those who, near at home, cooperate with, and do the bidding of, those far away, and without whom the latter would be harmless. We are accustomed to say, that the mass of men are unprepared; but improvement is slow, because the few are not materially wiser or better than the many. It is not so important that many should be as good as you, as that there be some absolute goodness somewhere; for that will leaven the whole lump. There are thousands who are *in opinion* opposed to slavery and to the war, who yet in effect do nothing to put an end to them; who, esteeming themselves children of Washington and Franklin, sit down with their hands in their pockets, and say that they know not what to do, and do nothing; who even postpone the question of freedom to the question of free trade, and quietly read the prices-current along with the latest advices from Mexico, after dinner, and, it may be, fall asleep over them both. What is the price-current of an honest man and patriot today? They hesitate, and they regret, and sometimes they petition; but they do nothing in earnest and with effect. They will wait, well disposed, for others to remedy the evil, that they may no longer have it to regret. At most, they give only a cheap vote, and a feeble countenance and Godspeed, to the right, as it goes by them. There are nine hundred and ninety-nine patrons of virtue to one virtuous man. But it is easier to deal with the real possessor of a thing than with the temporary guardian of it.

All voting is a sort of gaming, like checkers or backgammon, with a slight moral tinge to it, a playing with right and wrong, with moral questions; and betting naturally accompanies it. The character of the voters is not staked. I cast my vote, perchance, as I think right; but I am not vitally concerned that that right should prevail. I am willing to leave it to the majority. Its obligation, therefore, never exceeds that of expediency. Even voting *for the right* is *doing* nothing for it. It is only expressing to men feebly your desire that it should prevail. A wise man will not leave the right to the mercy of chance, nor wish it to prevail through the power of the majority. There is but little virtue in the action of masses of men. When the majority shall at length vote for the abolition of slavery, it will be because they are indifferent to slavery, or because there is but little slavery left to be abolished by their vote. *They* will then be the only slaves. Only *his* vote can hasten the abolition of slavery who asserts his own freedom by his vote.

I hear of a convention to be held at Baltimore, or elsewhere, for the selection of a candidate for the Presidency, made up chiefly of editors, and men who are politicians by profession; but I think, what is it to any independent, intelligent, and respectable man what decision they may come to? Shall we not have the advantage of his wisdom and honesty, nevertheless? Can we not count upon some independent votes? Are there not many individuals in the country who do not attend conventions? But no: I find that the respectable man, so called, has immediately drifted from his position, and despairs of his country, when his country has more reason to despair of him. He forthwith adopts one of the candidates thus selected as the only *available* one, thus proving that he is himself *available* for any purposes of the demagogue. His vote is of no more worth than that of any unprincipled foreigner or hireling native, who may have been bought. O for a man who is a *man*, and, as my neighbor says, has a bone in his back which you cannot pass your hand through! Our statistics are at fault: the population has been returned too large. How many *men* are there to a square thousand miles in this country? Hardly one. Does not America offer any inducement for men to settle here? The American has dwindled into an Odd Fellow—one who may be known by the development of his organ of gregariousness, and a manifest lack of intellect and cheerful self-reliance; whose first and chief concern, on coming into the world, is to see that the almshouses are in good repair; and, before yet he has lawfully donned the virile garb, to collect a fund for the support of the widows and orphans that may be; who, in short, ventures to live only by the aid of the Mutual Insurance company, which has promised to bury him decently.

It is not a man's duty, as a matter of course, to devote himself to the eradication of any, even the most enormous wrong; he may still properly have other concerns to engage him; but it is his duty, at least, to wash his hands of it, and, if he gives it no thought longer, not to give it practically his support. If I devote myself to other pursuits and contemplations, I must first see, at least, that I do not pursue them sitting upon another man's shoulders. I must get off him first, that he may pursue his contemplations too. See what gross inconsistency is tolerated. I have heard some of my townsmen say, "I should like to have them order me out to help put down an insurrection of the slaves, or to march to Mexico; see if I would go"; and yet these very men have each, directly by their allegiance, and so indirectly, at least, by their money, furnished a substitute. The soldier is applauded who refuses to serve in an unjust war by those who do not refuse to sustain the unjust government which makes the war; is applauded by those whose own act and authority he disregards and sets at naught; as if the state were penitent to that degree that it hired one to scourge it while it sinned, but not to that degree that it left off sinning for a moment. Thus, under the name of Order and Civil Government, we are all made at last to pay homage to and support our own meanness. After the first blush of sin comes its indifference; and from immoral it becomes, as it were, *un*moral, and not quite unnecessary to that life which we have made.

The broadest and most prevalent error requires the most disinterested virtue to sustain it. The slight reproach to which the virtue of patriotism is commonly liable, the noble are most likely to incur. Those who, while they disapprove of the character and measures of a government, yield to it their allegiance and support are undoubtedly its most conscientious supporters, and so frequently the most serious obstacles to reform. Some are petitioning the state to dissolve the Union, to disregard the requisitions of the President. Why do they not dissolve it themselves—the union between themselves and the state—and refuse to pay their quota into its treasury? Do not they stand in the same relation to the state that the state does to the Union? And have not the same reasons prevented the state from resisting the Union which have prevented them from resisting the state?

How can a man be satisfied to entertain an opinion merely, and enjoy *it?* Is there any enjoyment in it, if his opinion is that he is aggrieved? If you are cheated out of a single dollar by your neighbor, you do not rest satisfied with knowing that you are cheated, or with saying that you are cheated, or even with petitioning him to pay you your due; but you take effectual steps at once to obtain the full amount, and see that you are never cheated again. Action from principle, the perception and the performance of right, changes things and relations; it is essentially revolutionary, and does not consist wholly with anything which was. It not only divides states and churches, it divides families; ay, it divides the *individual,* separating the diabolical in him from the divine.

Unjust laws exist: shall we be content to obey them, or shall we endeavor to amend them, and obey them until we have succeeded, or shall we transgress them at once? Men generally, under such a government as this, think that they ought to wait until they have persuaded the majority to alter them. They think that, if they should resist, the remedy would be worse than the evil. But it is the fault of the government itself that the remedy is worse than the evil. *It* makes it worse. Why is it not more apt to anticipate and provide for reform? Why does it not cherish its wise minority? Why does it cry and resist before it is hurt? Why does it not encourage its citizens to be on the alert to point out its faults, and do better than it would have them? Why does it always crucify Christ, and excommunicate Copernicus and Luther, and pronounce Washington and Franklin rebels?

One would think, that a deliberate and practical denial of its authority was the only offense never contemplated by government; else, why has it not assigned its definite, its suitable and proportionate penalty? If a man who has no property refuses but once to earn nine shillings for the state, he is put in prison for a period unlimited by any law that I know, and determined only by the discretion of those who placed him there; but if he should steal ninety times nine shillings from the state, he is soon permitted to go at large again.

If the injustice is part of the necessary friction of the machine of government, let it go, let it go: perchance it will wear smooth—certainly the machine will wear out. If the injustice has a spring, or a pulley, or a rope, or a crank, exclusively for itself, then perhaps you may consider whether the remedy will not be worse than the evil; but if it is of such a nature that it requires you to be the agent of injustice to another, then, I say, break the law. Let your life be a counter friction to stop the machine. What I have to do is to see, at any rate, that I do not lend myself to the wrong which I condemn.

As for adopting the ways which the state has provided for remedying the evil, I know not of such ways. They take too much time, and a man's life will be gone. I have other affairs to attend to. I came into this world, not chiefly to make this a good place to live in, but to live in it, be it good or bad. A man has not everything to do, but something; and because he cannot do *everything*, it is not necessary that he should do *something* wrong. It is not my business to be petitioning the Governor or the Legislature any more than it is theirs to petition me; and if they should not hear my petition, what should I do then? But in this case the state has provided no way: its very constitution is the evil. This may seem to be harsh and stubborn and unconciliatory; but it is to treat with the utmost kindness and consideration the only spirit that can appreciate or deserves it. So is all change for the better, like birth and death, which convulse the body.

I do not hesitate to say, that those who call themselves Abolitionists should at once effectually withdraw their support, both in person and property, from the government of Massachusetts, and not wait till they constitute a majority of one, before they suffer the right to prevail through them. I think that it is enough if they have God on their side, without waiting for that other one. Moreover, any man more right than his neighbors constitutes a majority of one already.

# 22

## PIERRE-JOSEPH PROUDHON

## *What Is Property? or, An Inquiry into the Principle of Right and of Government*

Pierre-Joseph Proudhon (1809–65) was the first to use the word *anarchism,* once a term of abuse, to characterize an ideal society. He was a French peasant by birth, a printer by training, and an activist in the French revolution of 1848. His ideas influenced many later anarchists, among them Kropotkin, Bakunin, Herzen, and Sorel. As Bakunin put it: "Proudhon is the master of us all." *What Is Property?* is his most famous work. Despite their later disagreements, Marx hailed it as the "first decisive, vigorous, and scientific examination" of the subject.

### I.
### Method Pursued in This Work.
### The Idea of a Revolution

If I were asked to answer the following question: *What is slavery?* and I should answer in one word, *It is murder,* my meaning would be understood at once. No extended argument would be required to show that the power to take from a man his thought, his will, his personality, is a power of life and death; and that to enslave a man is to kill him. Why, then, to this other question: *What is property?* may I not likewise answer, *It is robbery,* without the certainty of being misunderstood; the second proposition being no other than a transformation of the first?

I undertake to discuss the vital principle of our government and our institutions, property: I am in my right. I may be mistaken in the conclusion which shall result from my investigations: I am in my right. I think best to place the last thought of my book first: still am I in my right.

Such an author teaches that property is a civil right, born of occupation and sanctioned by law; another maintains that it is a natural right, originating

368

in labor—and both of these doctrines, totally opposed as they may seem, are encouraged and applauded. I contend that neither labor, nor occupation, nor law, can create property; that it is an effect without a cause: am I censurable?

But murmurs arise!

*Property is robbery!* That is the war-cry of '93! That is the signal of revolutions!

Reader, calm yourself: I am no agent of discord, no firebrand of sedition. I anticipate history by a few days; I disclose a truth whose development we may try in vain to arrest; I write the preamble of our future constitution. This proposition which seems to you blasphemous—*property is robbery*—would, if our prejudices allowed us to consider it, be recognized as the lightning-rod to shield us from the coming thunderbolt; but too many interests stand in the way! . . . Alas! philosophy will not change the course of events: destiny will fulfill itself regardless of prophecy. Besides, must not justice be done and our education be finished?

*Property is robbery!* . . . What a revolution in human ideas! *Proprietor* and *robber* have been at all times expressions as contradictory as the beings whom they designate are hostile; all languages have perpetuated this opposition. On what authority, then, do you venture to attack universal consent, and give the lie to the human race? Who are you, that you should question the judgment of the nations and the ages?

Of what consequence to you, reader, is my obscure individuality? I live, like you, in a century in which reason submits only to fact and to evidence. My name, like yours, is TRUTHSEEKER.[1] My mission is written in these words of the law: *Speak without hatred and without fear; tell that which thou knowest!* The work of our race is to build the temple of science, and this science includes man and Nature. Now, truth reveals itself to all; today to Newton and Pascal, tomorrow to the herdsman in the valley and the journeyman in the shop. Each one contributes his stone to the edifice; and, his task accomplished, disappears. Eternity precedes us, eternity follows us: between two infinities, of what account is one poor mortal that the century should inquire about him?

Disregard then, reader, my title and my character, and attend only to my arguments. It is in accordance with universal consent that I undertake to correct universal error; from the *opinion* of the human race I appeal to its *faith*. Have the courage to follow me; and, if your will is untrammelled, if your conscience is free, if your mind can unite two propositions and deduce a third therefrom, my ideas will inevitably become yours. In beginning by giving you my last word, it was my purpose to warn you, not to defy you; for I am certain that, if you read me, you will be compelled to assent. The things of which I am to speak are so simple and clear that you will be astonished at not having perceived them before, and you will say: "I have neglected to think." Others offer you the spectacle of genius wresting Nature's secrets from her, and unfolding before you her sublime messages; you will find here only a series of experiments upon *justice* and *right*, a sort of verification of the weights and measures of your conscience. The operations shall be conducted under your very eyes; and you shall weigh the result.

Nevertheless, I build no system. I ask an end to privilege, the abolition of slavery, equality of rights, and the reign of law. Justice, nothing else; that is the alpha and omega of my argument: to others I leave the business of governing the world.

One day I asked myself: Why is there so much sorrow and misery in society? Must man always be wretched? And not satisfied with the explanations given by the reformers—these attributing the general distress to governmental cowardice and incapacity, those to conspirators and *émuetes,* still others to ignorance and general corruption—and weary of the interminable quarrels of the tribune and the press, I sought to fathom the matter myself. I have consulted the masters of science; I have read a hundred volumes of philosophy, law, political economy, and history: would to God that I had lived in a century in which so much reading had been useless! I have made every effort to obtain exact information, comparing doctrines, replying to objections, continually constructing equations and reductions from arguments, and weighing thousands of syllogisms in the scales of the most rigorous logic. In this laborious work, I have collected many interesting facts which I shall share with my friends and the public as soon as I have leisure. But I must say that I recognized at once that we had never understood the meaning of these words, so common and yet so sacred: *Justice, equity, liberty;* that concerning each of these principles our ideas have been utterly obscure; and, in fact, that this ignorance was the sole cause, both of the poverty that devours us, and of all the calamities that have ever afflicted the human race.

My mind was frightened by this strange result: I doubted my reason. What! said I, that which eye has not seen, nor ear heard, nor insight penetrated, you have discovered! Wretch, mistake not the visions of your diseased brain for the truths of science! Do you not know (great philosophers have said so) that in point of practical morality universal error is a contradiction?

I resolved then to test my arguments; and in entering upon this new labor I sought an answer to the following questions: Is it possible that humanity can have been so long and so universally mistaken in the application of moral principles? How and why could it be mistaken? How can its error, being universal, be capable of correction?

These questions, on the solution of which depended the certainty of my conclusions, offered no lengthy resistance to analysis. It will be seen, in chapter 5 of this work, that in morals, as in all other branches of knowledge, the gravest errors are the dogmas of science; that, even in works of justice, to be mistaken is a privilege which ennobles man; and that whatever philosophical merit may attach to me is infinitely small. To name a thing is easy: the difficulty is to discern it before its appearance. In giving expression to the last stage of an idea—an idea which permeates all minds, which tomorrow will be proclaimed by another if I fail to announce it today—I can claim no merit save that of priority of utterance. Do we eulogize the man who first perceives the dawn?

Yes: all men believe and repeat that equality of conditions is identical with equality of rights; that *property* and *robbery* are synonymous terms; that every social advantage accorded, or rather usurped, in the name of superior talent or service, is iniquity and extortion. All men in their hearts, I say, bear witness to these truths; they need only to be made to understand it. . . .

Now, of what do the lawyers and the publicists treat? Of *justice, equity, liberty, natural law, civil laws, etc.* But what is justice? What is its principle, its character, its formula? To this question our doctors evidently have no reply; for otherwise their science, starting with a principle clear and well defined, would quit the region of probabilities, and all disputes would end.

What is justice? The theologians answer: "All justice comes from God." That is true; but we know no more than before.

The philosophers ought to be better informed: they have argued so much about justice and injustice! Unhappily, an examination proves that their knowledge amounts to nothing, and that with them—as with the savages whose every prayer to the sun is simply *O! O!* —it is a cry of admiration, love, and enthusiasm; but who does not know that the sun attaches little meaning to the interjection *O!* That is exactly our position toward the philosophers in regard to justice. Justice, they say, is a *daughter of Heaven; a light which illumines every man that comes into the world; the most beautiful prerogative of our nature; that which distinguishes us from the beasts, and likens us to God*—and a thousand other similar things. What, I ask, does this pious litany amount to? To the prayer of the savages: *O!*

All the most reasonable teachings of human wisdom concerning justice are summed up in that famous adage: *Do unto others that which you would that others should do unto you; Do not unto others that which you would not that others should do unto you.* But this rule of moral practice is unscientific: what have I a right to wish that others should do or not do to me? It is of no use to tell me that my duty is equal to my right, unless I am told at the same time what my right is.

Let us try to arrive at something more precise and positive.

Justice is the central star which governs societies, the pole around which the political world revolves, the principle and the regulator of all transactions. Nothing takes place between men save in the name of *right*; nothing without the invocation of justice. Justice is not the work of the law: on the contrary, the law is only a declaration and application of *justice* in all circumstances where men are liable to come in contact. If, then, the idea that we form of justice and right were ill-defined, if it were imperfect or even false, it is clear that all our legislative applications would be wrong, our institutions vicious, our politics erroneous: consequently there would be disorder and social chaos.

This hypothesis of the perversion of justice in our minds, and, as a necessary result, in our acts, becomes a demonstrated fact when it is shown that the opinions of men have not borne a constant relation to the notion of justice and its applications; that at different periods they have undergone modifications: in a word, that there has been progress in ideas. Now, that is what history proves by the most overwhelming testimony.

. . . When our ideas on any subject, material, intellectual, or social, undergo a thorough change in consequence of new observations, I call that movement of the mind *revolution*. If the ideas are simply extended or modified, there is only *progress*. Thus the system of Ptolemy was a step in astronomical progress, that of Copernicus was a revolution. So, in 1789, there was struggle and progress; revolution there was none. An examination of the reforms which were attempted proves this.

The nation, so long a victim of monarchical selfishness, thought to deliver itself for ever by declaring that it alone was sovereign. But what was monarchy? The sovereignty of one man. What is democracy? The sovereignty of the nation, or, rather, of the national majority. But it is, in both cases, the sovereignty of man instead of the sovereignty of the law, the sovereignty of the will instead of the sovereignty of the reason; in one word, the passions instead of justice. Undoubtedly, when a nation passes from the monarchical to the democratic state, there is progress, because in multiplying the sovereigns we increase the opportunities of the reason to substitute itself for the will; but in reality there is no revolution in the government, since the principle remains the same. Now, we have the proof today that, with the most perfect democracy, we cannot be free.[2]

Nor is that all. The nation-king cannot exercise its sovereignty itself; it is obliged to delegate it to agents: this is constantly reiterated by those who seek to win its favor. Be these against five, ten, one hundred, or a thousand, of what consequence is the number; and what matters the name? It is always the government of man, the rule of will and caprice. I ask what this pretended revolution has revolutionized?

We know, too, how this sovereignty was exercised; first by the Convention, then by the Directory, afterwards confiscated by the Consul. As for the Emperor, the strong man so much adored and mourned by the nation, he never wanted to be dependent on it; but, as if intending to set its sovereignty at defiance, he dared to demand its suffrage: that is, its abdication, the abdication of this inalienable sovereignty; and he obtained it.

But what is sovereignty? It is, they say, the *power to make laws*.[3] Another absurdity, a relic of despotism. The nation had long seen kings issuing their commands in this form: *for such is our pleasure;* it wished to taste in its turn the pleasure of making laws. For fifty years it has brought them forth by myriads; always, be it understood, through the agency of representatives. The play is far from ended.

The definition of sovereignty was derived from the definition of the law. The law, they said, is *the expression of the will of the sovereign:* then, under a monarchy, the law is the expression of the will of the king; in a republic, the law is the expression of the will of the people. Aside from the difference in the number of wills, the two systems are exactly identical: both share the same error, namely, that the law is the expression of a will; it ought to be the expression of a fact. Moreover they followed good leaders: they took the citizen of Geneva for their prophet, and the *contrat social* for their Koran.

Bias and prejudice are apparent in all the phrases of the new legislators. The nation had suffered from a multitude of exclusions and privileges; its representatives issued the following declaration: *All men are equal by nature and before the law;* an ambiguous and redundant declaration. *Men are equal by nature:* does that mean that they are equal in size, beauty, talents, and virtue? No; they meant, then, political and civil equality. Then it would have been sufficient to have said: *All men are equal before the law.*

But what is equality before the law? Neither the constitution of 1790, nor that of '93, nor the granted charter, nor the accepted charter, have defined it accurately. All imply an inequality in fortune and station incompatible with even a shadow of equality in rights. In this respect it may be said that all our constitutions have been faithful expressions of the popular will: I am going to prove it.

Formerly the people were excluded from civil and military offices; it was considered a wonder when the following high sounding article was inserted in the Declaration of Rights: "All citizens are equally eligible to office; free nations know no qualifications in their choice of officers save virtues and talents."

They certainly ought to have admired so beautiful an idea: they admired a piece of nonsense. Why! the sovereign people, legislators, and reformers, see in public offices, to speak plainly, only opportunities for pecuniary advancement. And, because it regards them as a source of profit, it decrees the eligibility of citizens. For of what use would this precaution be, if there were nothing to gain by it? No one would think of ordaining that none but astronomers and geographers should be pilots, nor of prohibiting stutterers from acting at the theatre and the opera. The nation was still aping the kings: like them it wished to award the lucrative positions to its friends and flatterers. Unfortunately, and this last feature completes the resemblance, the nation did not control the list of livings; that was in the hands of its agents and representatives. They, on the other hand, took care not to thwart the will of their gracious sovereign.

This edifying article of the Declaration of Rights, retained in the charters of 1814 and 1830, implies several kinds of civil inequality; that is, of inequality before the law, inequality of station, since the public functions are sought only for the consideration and emoluments which they bring; inequality of wealth, since, if it had been desired to equalize fortunes, public service would have been regarded as a duty, not as a reward; inequality of privilege, the law not stating what it means by *talents* and *virtues*. Under the empire, virtue and talent consisted simply in military bravery and devotion to the emperor; that was shown when Napoleon created his nobility, and attempted to connect it with the ancients. To-day, the man who pays taxes to the amount of two hundred francs is virtuous; the talented man is the honest pickpocket: such truths as these are accounted trivial.

The people finally legalized property. God forgive them, for they knew not what they did! For fifty years they have suffered for their miserable folly. But how came the people, whose voice, they tell us, is the voice of God, and whose conscience is infallible—how came the people to err? How happens it that, when seeking liberty and equality, they fell back into privilege and slavery? Always through copying the ancient *régime*.

Formerly, the nobility and the clergy contributed towards the expenses of the State only by voluntary aid and gratuitous gift; their property could not be seized even for debt—while the plebeian, overwhelmed by taxes and statute-labor, was continually tormented, now by the king's tax-gatherers, now by those of the nobles and clergy. He whose possessions were subject to mortmain could neither bequeath nor inherit property; he was treated like the animals, whose services and offspring belong to their master by right of accession. The people wanted the conditions of *ownership* to be alike for all; they thought that every one should *enjoy and freely dispose of his possessions, his income, and the fruit of his labor and industry*. The people did not invent property; but as they had not the same privileges in regard to it, which the nobles and clergy possessed, they decreed that the right should be exercised by all under the same conditions. The more obnoxious forms of property—statute-labor, mortmain, *maîtrise*, and exclusion from public office—have disappeared; the conditions of its enjoyment have been modified: the principle still remains the same. There has been progress in the regulation of the right; there has been no revolution.

These, then, are the three fundamental principles of modern society, established one after another by the movements of 1789 and 1830: (1) *Sovereignty of the human will;* in short, *despotism.* (2) *Inequality of wealth and rank.* (3) *Property*—above JUSTICE, always invoked as the guardian angel of sovereigns, nobles, and proprietors: JUSTICE, the general, primitive, categorical law of all society.

We must ascertain whether the ideas of *despotism, civil inequality,* and *property,* are in harmony with the primitive notion of *justice,* and necessarily follow from it—assuming various forms according to the condition, position, and relation of persons; or whether they are not rather the illegitimate result of a confusion of different things, a fatal association of ideas. And since justice deals especially with the questions of government, the condition of persons, and the possession of things, we must ascertain under what conditions, judging by universal opinion and the progress of the human mind, government is just, the condition of citizens is just, and the possession of things is just; then, striking out every thing which fails to meet these conditions, the result will at once tell us what legitimate government is, what the legitimate condition of citizens is, and what the legitimate possession of things is; and finally, as the last result of the analysis, what *justice* is.

Is the authority of man over man just?

Everybody answers, "No; the authority of man is only the authority of the law, which ought to be justice and truth." The private will counts for nothing in government, which consists, first, in discovering truth and justice in order to make the law; and, second, in superintending the execution of this law. I do not now inquire whether our constitutional form of government satisfies these conditions; whether, for example, the will of the ministry never influences the declaration and interpretation of the law; or whether our deputies, in their debates are more intent on conquering by argument than by force of numbers: it is enough for me that my definition of a good government is allowed to be correct. This idea is exact. Yet we see that nothing seems more just to the Oriental nations than the despotism of their sovereigns; that, with the ancients and in the opinion of the philosophers themselves, slavery was just; that in the middle ages the nobles, the priests, and the bishops felt justified in holding slaves; that Louis XIV thought that he was right when he said, "The State! I am the State"; and that Napoleon deemed it a crime for the State to oppose his will. The idea of justice, then, applied to sovereignty and government, has not always been what it is today; it has gone on developing and shaping itself by degrees, until it has arrived at its present state. But has it reached its last phase? I think not: only, as the last obstacle to be overcome arises from the institution of property which we have kept intact, in order to finish the reform in government and consummate the revolution, this very institution we must attack.

Is political and civil inequality just?

Some say yes; others no. To the first I would reply that, when the people abolished all privileges of birth and caste, they did it, in all probability, because it was for their advantage; why then do they favor the privileges of fortune more than those of rank and race? Because, say they, political inequality is a result of property; and without property society is impossible: thus the question just raised becomes a question of property. To the second I content myself with this remark: If you wish to enjoy political equality, abolish property; otherwise, why do you complain?

Is property just?

Everybody answers without hesitation, "Yes, property is just." I say everybody, for up to the present time no one who thoroughly understood the meaning of his words has answered no. For it is no easy thing to reply understandingly to such a question; only time and experience can furnish an answer. Now, this answer is given; it is for us to understand it. I undertake to prove it. . . .

## 2.
## Property Considered as a Natural Right. Occupation and Civil Law as Efficient Bases of Property

### Definitions

The Roman law defined property as the right to use and abuse one's own within the limits of the law. . . . A justification of the word *abuse* has been attempted, on the ground that it signifies not senseless and immoral abuse, but only absolute domain. Vain distinction! invented as an excuse for property, and powerless against the frenzy of possession, which it neither prevents nor represses. The proprietor may, if he chooses, allow his crops to rot under foot; sow his field with salt; milk his cows on the sand; change his vineyard into a desert, and use his vegetable-garden as a park: do these things constitute abuse, or not? In the matter of property, use and abuse are necessarily indistinguishable.

According to the Declaration of Rights, published as a preface to the Constitution of '93, property is "the right to enjoy and dispose at will of one's goods, one's income, and the fruit of one's labor and industry."

Code Napoléon, article 544: "Property is the right to enjoy and dispose of things in the most absolute manner, provided we do not overstep the limits prescribed by the laws and regulations."

These two definitions do not differ from that of the Roman law: all give the proprietor an absolute right over a thing; and as for the restriction imposed by the code—*provided we do not overstep the limits prescribed by the laws and regulations*—its object is not to limit property, but to prevent the domain of one proprietor from interfering with that of another. That is a confirmation of the principle, not a limitation of it.

There are different kinds of property: (1) Property pure and simple, the dominant and seignorial power over a thing; or, as they term it, *naked property*. (2) *Possession*. "Possession," says Duranton, "is a matter of fact, not of right." Toullier: "Property is a right, a legal power; possession is a fact." The tenant, the farmer, the *commandité*, the usufructuary, are possessors; the owner who lets and lends for use, the heir who is to come into possession on the death of a usufructuary, are proprietors. If I may venture the comparison: a lover is a possessor, a husband is a proprietor.

This double definition of property—domain and possession—is of the highest importance; and it must be clearly understood, in order to comprehend what is to follow.

From the distinction between possession and property arise two sorts of rights: the *jus in re*, the right *in* a thing, the right by which I may reclaim the property which I have acquired, in whatever hands I find it; and the *jus ad rem*, the right *to* a thing, which gives me a claim to become a proprietor. Thus the right of the partners to a marriage over each other's person is the *jus in re;* that of two who are betrothed is only the *jus ad rem*. In the first, possession and property are united; the second includes only naked property. With me who, as a laborer, have a right to the possession of the products of Nature and my own industry—and who, as a proletaire, enjoy none of them—it is by virtue of the *jus ad rem* that I demand admittance to the *jus in re*.

This distinction between the *jus in re* and the *jus ad rem* is the basis of the famous distinction between *possessoire* and *petitoire*—actual categories of jurisprudence, the whole of which is included within their vast boundaries. *Petitoire* refers to every thing relating to property; *possessoire* to that relating to possession. In writing this memoir against property, I bring against universal society an *action petitoire:* I prove that those who do not possess today are proprietors by the same title as those who do possess; but, instead of inferring therefrom that property should be shared by all, I demand, in the name of general security, its entire abolition. . . .

*1. Property as a Natural Right.*—The Declaration of Rights has placed property in its list of the natural and inalienable rights of man, four in all: *liberty, equality, property, security.* What rule did the legislators of '93 follow in compiling this list? None. They laid down principles, just as they discussed sovereignty and the laws; from a general point of view, and according to their own opinion. They did every thing in their own blind way.

If we can believe Toullier: "The absolute rights can be reduced to three: *security, liberty,* and *property.* " Equality is eliminated by the Rennes professor; why? Is it because *liberty* implies it, or because property prohibits it? On this point the author of "Droit Civil Expliqué" is silent: it has not even occurred to him that the matter is under discussion.

Nevertheless, if we compare these three or four rights with each other, we find that property bears no resemblance whatever to the others; that for the majority of citizens it exists only potentially, and as a dormant faculty without exercise; that for the others, who do enjoy it, it is susceptible of certain transactions and modifications which do not harmonize with the idea of a natural right; that, in practice, governments, tribunals, and laws do not respect it; and finally that everybody, spontaneously and with one voice, regards it as chimerical.

Liberty is inviolable. I can neither sell nor alienate my liberty; every contract, every condition of a contract, which has in view the alienation or suspension of liberty, is null: the slave, when he plants his foot upon the soil of liberty, at that moment becomes a free man. When society seizes a malefactor and deprives him of his liberty, it is a case of legitimate defence: whoever violates the social compact by the commission of a crime declares himself a public enemy; in attacking the liberty of others, he compels them to take away his own. Liberty is the original condition of man; to renounce liberty is to renounce the nature of man: after that, how could we perform the acts of man?

Likewise, equality before the law suffers neither restriction nor exception. All Frenchmen are equally eligible to office: consequently, in the presence of this equality, condition and family have, in many cases, no influence upon choice. The poorest citizen can obtain judgment in the courts against one occupying the most exalted station. Let the millionaire, Ahab, build a château upon the vineyard of Naboth: the court will have the power, according to the circumstances, to order the destruction of the château, though it has cost millions; and to force the trespasser to restore the vineyard to its original state, and pay the damages. The law wishes all property, that has been legitimately acquired, to be kept inviolate without regard to value, and without respect for persons.

The charter demands, it is true, for the exercise of certain political rights, certain conditions of fortune and capacity; but all publicists know that the legislator's intention was not to establish a privilege, but to take security. Provided the conditions fixed by law are complied with, every citizen may be an elector, and every elector eligible. The right, once acquired, is the same for all; the law compares neither persons nor votes. I do not ask now whether this system is the best; it is enough that, in the opinion of the charter and in the eyes of every one, equality before the law is absolute, and, like liberty, admits of no compromise.

It is the same with the right of security. Society promises its members no half-way protection, no sham defence; it binds itself to them as they bind themselves to it. It does not say to them, "I will shield you, provided it costs me nothing; I will protect you, if I run no risks thereby." It says, "I will defend you against everybody; I will save and avenge you, or perish myself." The whole strength of the State is at the service of each citizen; the obligation which binds them together is absolute.

How different with property! Worshipped by all, it is acknowledged by none: laws, morals, customs, public and private conscience, all plot its death and ruin.

To meet the expenses of government, which has armies to support, tasks to perform, and officers to pay, taxes are needed. Let all contribute to these expenses: nothing more just. But why should the rich pay more than the poor? That is just, they say, because they possess more. I confess that such justice is beyond my comprehension.

Why are taxes paid? To protect all in the exercise of their natural rights—liberty, equality, security, and property; to maintain order in the State; to furnish the public with useful and pleasant conveniences.

Now, does it cost more to defend the rich man's life and liberty than the poor man's? Who, in time of invasion, famine, or plague, causes more trouble—the large proprietor who escapes the evil without the assistance of the State, or the laborer who sits in his cottage unprotected from danger?

Is public order endangered more by the worthy citizen, or by the artisan and journeyman? Why, the police have more to fear from a few hundred laborers, out of work, than from two hundred thousand electors!

Does the man of large income appreciate more keenly than the poor man national festivities, clean streets, and beautiful monuments? Why, he prefers his country-seat to all the popular pleasures; and when he wants to enjoy himself, he does not wait for the greased pole!

One of two things is true; either the proportional tax affords greater security to the larger tax-payers, or else it is a wrong. Because, if property is a natural right, as the Declaration of '93 declares, all that belongs to me by virtue of this right is a sacred as my person; it is my blood, my life, myself: whoever touches it offends the apple of my eye. My income of one hundred thousand francs is as inviolable as the grisette's daily wage of seventy-five centimes; her attic is no more sacred than my suite of apartments. The tax is not levied in proportion to strength, size, or skill: no more should it be levied in proportion to property.

If, then, the State takes more from me, let it give me more in return, or cease to talk of equality of rights; for otherwise, society is established, not to defend property, but to destroy it. The State, through the proportional tax, becomes the chief of robbers; the State sets the example of systematic pillage: the State should be brought to the bar of justice at the head of those hideous brigands, that execrable mob which it now kills from motives of professional jealousy.

But, they say, the courts and the police force are established to restrain this mob; government is a company, not exactly for insurance, for it does not insure, but for vengeance and repression. The premium which this company exacts, the tax, is divided in proportion to property; that is, in proportion to the trouble which each piece of property occasions the avengers and repressers paid by the government.

This is any thing but the absolute and inalienable right of property. Under this system the poor and the rich distrust, and make war upon, each other. But what is the object of the war? Property. So that property is necessarily accompanied by war upon property. The liberty and security of the rich do not suffer from the liberty and security of the poor; far from that, they mutually strengthen and sustain each other. The rich man's right of property, on the contrary, has to be continually defended against the poor man's desire for property. What a contradiction!

In England they have a poor-rate: they wish me to pay this tax. But what relation exists between my natural and inalienable right of property and the hunger from which ten million wretched people are suffering? When religion commands us to assist our fellows, it speaks in the name of charity, not in the name of law. The obligation of benevolence, imposed upon me by Christian morality, cannot be imposed upon me as a political tax for the benefit of any person or poor-house. I will give alms when I see fit to do so, when the sufferings of others excite in me that sympathy of which philosophers talk, and in which I do not believe: I will not be forced to bestow them. No one is obliged to do more than comply with this injunction: *In the exercise of your own rights do not encroach upon the rights of another;* an injunction which is the exact definition of liberty. Now, my possessions are my own; no one has a claim upon them: I object to the placing of the third theological virtue in the order of the day. . . .

To sum up: liberty is an absolute right, because it is to man what impenetrability is to matter—a *sine qua non* of existence; equality is an absolute right, because without equality there is no society; security is an absolute right, because in the eyes of every man his own liberty and life are as precious as another's. These three rights are absolute; that is, susceptible of neither increase nor diminution; because in society each associate receives as much as he gives—liberty for liberty, equality for equality, security for security, body for body, soul for soul, in life and in death.

But property, in its derivative sense, and by the definitions of law, is a right outside of society; for it is clear that, if the wealth of each was social wealth, the conditions would be equal for all, and it would be a contradiction to say: *Property is a man's right to dispose at will of social property.* Then if we are associated for the sake of liberty, equality, and security, we are not associated for the sake of property; then if property is a *natural* right, this natural right is not *social,* but *anti-social.* Property and society are utterly irreconcilable institutions. It is as impossible to associate two proprietors as to join two magnets by their opposite poles. Either society must perish, or it must destroy property.

## Notes

1. In Greek, σκεπτικος, examiner: a philosopher whose business is to seek the truth.

2. See De Tocqueville, *Democracy in the United States;* and Michel Chevalier, *Letters on North America.* Plutarch tells us, Life of Pericles, that in Athens honest people were obliged to conceal themselves while studying, fearing they would be regarded as aspirants for office.

3. "Sovereignty," according to Toullier, "is human omnipotence." A materialistic definition: if sovereignty is any thing, it is a *right,* not a *force* or *faculty.* And what is human omnipotence?

# PETYR KROPOTKIN

## *Mutual Aid*

Petyr Kropotkin (1842–1921) was the son of a prince, an aide to Tsar Alexander II, an officer in the Russian army, and a prominent scientist. In the 1870s he became an anarchist and began to organize Russian workers. He was imprisoned for his activities, escaped, and fled to western Europe. He remained there until the revolution when, shortly before his death, he returned to Russia. In *Mutual Aid* (1902), Kropotkin's best-known book, he argues that cooperation is the chief factor in the evolution of species.

## Introduction

Two aspects of animal life impressed me most during the journeys which I made in my youth in Eastern Siberia and Northern Manchuria. One of them was the extreme severity of the struggle for existence which most species of animals have to carry on against an inclement Nature; the enormous destruction of life which periodically results from natural agencies; and the consequent paucity of life over the vast territory which fell under my observation. And the other was, that even in those few spots where animal life teemed in abundance, I failed to find—although I was eagerly looking for it—that bitter struggle for the means of existence, *among animals belonging to the same species,* which was considered by most Darwinists (though not always by Darwin himself) as the dominant characteristic of struggle for life, and the main factor of evolution.

The terrible snow-storms which sweep over the northern portion of Eurasia in the later part of the winter, and the glazed frost that often follows them; the frosts and the snow-storms which return every year in the second half of May, when the trees are already in full blossom and insect life swarms everywhere; the early frosts and, occasionally, the heavy snowfalls in July and August, which suddenly destroy myriads of insects, as well as the second broods of the birds in the prairies; the torrential rains, due to the monsoons, which fall in more temperate regions in August and September—resulting in inundations on a scale which is only known in America and in Eastern Asia, and swamping, on the plateaus, areas as wide as European States; and finally, the heavy snowfalls, early in October, which eventually render a territory as large as France and Germany, absolutely impracticable for ruminants, and destroy them by the thousand—these were the conditions under which I saw animal life struggling in Northern Asia. They made me realize at an early date the overwhelming importance in Nature of what Darwin described as "the natural checks to over-multiplication," in comparison to the struggle between individuals of the same species for the means of subsistence, which may go on here and there, to some limited extent, but never attains the importance of the former. Paucity of life, underpopulation—not over-population—being the distinctive feature of that immense part of the globe which we name Northern Asia, I conceived since then serious doubts—which subsequent study has only confirmed—as to the reality of that fearful competition for food and life within each species, which was an article of faith with most Darwinists, and, consequently, as to the dominant part which this sort of competition was supposed to play in the evolution of new species.

On the other hand, wherever I saw animal life in abundance, as, for instance, on the lakes where scores of species and millions of individuals came together to rear their progeny; in the colonies of rodents; in the migrations of birds which took place at that time on a truly American scale along the Usuri; and especially in a migration of fallow-deer which I witnessed on the Amur, and during which scores of thousands of these intelligent animals came together from an immense territory, flying before the coming deep snow, in order to cross the Amur where it is narrowest—in all these scenes of animal life which passed before my eyes, I saw Mutual Aid and Mutual Support carried on to an extent which made me suspect in it a feature of the greatest importance for the maintenance of life, the preservation of each species, and its further evolution.

And finally, I saw among the semi-wild cattle and horses in Transbaikalia, among the wild ruminants everywhere, the squirrels, and so on, that when animals have to struggle against scarcity of food, in consequence of one of the above-mentioned causes, the whole of that portion of the species which is affected by the calamity, comes out of the ordeal so much impoverished in vigour and health, that *no progressive evolution of the species can be based upon such periods of keen competition.*

Consequently, when my attention was drawn, later on, to the relations between Darwinism and Sociology, I could agree with none of the works and pamphlets that had been written upon this important subject. They all endeavoured to prove that Man, owing to his higher intelligence and knowledge, *may* mitigate the harshness of the struggle for life between men; but they all recognized at the same time that the struggle for the means of existence, of every animal against all its congeners, and of every man against all other men, was "a law of Nature." This view, however, I could not accept, because I was persuaded that to admit a pitiless inner war for life within each species, and to see in that war a condition of progress, was to admit something which not only had not yet been proved, but also lacked confirmation from direct observation. . . .

It may be objected to this book that both animals and men are represented in it under too favourable an aspect; that their sociable qualities are insisted upon, while their anti-social and self-asserting instincts are hardly touched upon. This was, however, unavoidable. We have heard so much lately of the "harsh, pitiless struggle for life," which was said to be carried on by every animal against all other animals, every "savage" against all other "savages," and every civilized man against all his co-citizens—and these assertions have so much become an article of faith—that it was necessary, first of all, to oppose to them a wide series of facts showing animal and human life under a quite different aspect. It was necessary to indicate the overwhelming importance which sociable habits play in Nature and in the progressive evolution of both the animal species and human beings: to prove that they secure to animals a better protection from their enemies, very often facilities for getting food (winter provisions, migrations, etc.), longevity, and therefore a greater facility for the development of intellectual faculties; and that they have given to men, in addition to the same advantages, the possibility of working out those institutions which have enabled mankind to survive in its hard struggle against Nature, and to progress, notwithstanding all the vicissitudes of its history. It is a book on the law of Mutual Aid, viewed at as one of the chief factors of evolution—not on *all* factors of evolution and their respective values; and this first book had to be written, before the latter could become possible.

I should certainly be the last to underrate the part which the self-assertion of the individual has played in the evolution of mankind. However, this subject requires, I believe, a much deeper treatment than the one it has hitherto received. In the history of mankind, individual self-assertion has often been, and continually is, something quite different from, and far larger and deeper than, the petty, unintelligent narrowmindedness, which, with a large class of writers, goes for "individualism" and "self-assertion." Nor have history-making individuals been limited to those whom historians have represented as heroes. My intention, consequently, is, if circumstances permit it, to discuss separately the part taken by the self-assertion of the individual in the progressive evolution of mankind. I can only make in this place the following general remark: When the Mutual Aid institutions—the tribe, the village community, the guilds, the mediaeval city—began, in the course of history, to lose their primitive character, to be invaded by parasitic growths, and thus to become hindrances to progress, the revolt of individuals against these institutions took always two different aspects. Part of those who rose up strove to purify the old institutions, or to work out a higher form of commonwealth, based upon the same Mutual Aid principles; they tried, for instance, to introduce the principle of "compensation," instead of the *lex talionis,* and later on, the pardon of offenses, or a still higher ideal of equality before the human conscience, *in lieu* of "compensation,"according to class-value. But at the very same time, another portion of the same individual rebels endeavoured to break down the protective institutions of mutual support, with no other intention but to increase their own wealth and their own powers. In this three-cornered contest, between the two classes of revolted individuals and the supporters of what existed, lies the real tragedy of history. But to delineate that contest, and honestly to study the part played in the evolution of mankind by each one of these three forces, would require at least as many years as it took me to write this book. . . .

## Chapter 7
## Mutual Aid amongst Ourselves

Popular revolts at the beginning of the State-period. Mutual Aid institutions of the present time. The village community: its struggles for resisting its abolition by the State. Habits derived from the village-community life, retained in our modern villages. Switzerland, France, Germany, Russia.

The mutual-aid tendency in man has so remote an origin, and is so deeply interwoven with all the past evolution of the human race, that it has been maintained by mankind up to the present time, notwithstanding all vicissitudes of history. It was chiefly evolved during periods of peace and prosperity; but when even the greatest calamities befell men—when whole countries were laid waste by wars, and whole populations were decimated by misery, or groaned under the yoke of tyranny—the same tendency continued to live in the villages and among the poorer classes in the towns; it still kept them together, and in the long run it reacted even upon those ruling, fighting, and devastating minorities which dismissed it as sentimental nonsense. And whenever mankind had to work out a new social organization, adapted to a new phasis of development, its constructive genius always drew the elements and the inspiration for the new departure from that same ever-living tendency. New economical and social institutions, in so far as they were a creation of the masses, new ethical systems, and new religions, all have originated from the same source, and the ethical progress of our race, viewed in its broad lines, appears as a gradual extension of the mutual-aid principles from the tribe to always larger and larger agglomerations, so as to finally embrace one day the whole of mankind, without respect to its divers creeds, languages, and races.

After having passed through the savage tribe, and next through the village community, the Europeans came to work out in mediaeval times a new form of organization, which had the advantage of allowing great latitude for individual initiative, while it largely responded at the same time to man's need of mutual support. A federation of village communities, covered by a network of guilds and fraternities, was called into existence in the mediaeval cities. The immense results achieved under this new form of union—in well-being for all, in industries, art, science, and commerce—were discussed at some length in two preceding chapters, and an attempt was also made to show why, towards the end of the fifteenth century, the mediaeval republics—surrounded by domains of hostile feudal lords, unable to free the peasants from servitude, and gradually corrupted by ideas of Roman Caesarism—were doomed to become a prey to the growing military States.

However, before submitting for three centuries to come, to the all-absorbing authority of the State, the masses of the people made a formidable attempt at reconstructing society on the old basis of mutual aid and support. It is well known by this time that the great movement of the reform was not a mere revolt against the abuses of the Catholic Church. It had its constructive ideal as well, and that ideal was life in free, brotherly communities. Those of the early writings and sermons of the period which found most response with the masses were imbued with ideas of the economical and social brotherhood of mankind. The "Twelve Articles" and similar professions of faith, which were circulated among the German and Swiss peasants and artisans, maintained not only every one's right to interpret the Bible according to his own understanding, but also included the demand of communal lands being restored to the village communities and feudal servitudes being abolished, and they always alluded to the "true" faith—a faith of brotherhood. At the same time scores of thousands of men and women joined the communist fraternities of Moravia, giving them all their fortune and living in numerous and prosperous settlements constructed upon the principles of communism.[1] Only wholesale massacres by the thousand could put a stop to this widely spread popular movement, and it was by the sword, the fire, and the rack that the young States secured their first and decisive victory over the masses of the people.[2]

For the next three centuries the States, both on the Continent and in these islands, systematically weeded out all institutions in which the mutual-aid tendency had formerly found its expression. The village communities were bereft of their folkmotes, their courts and independent administration; their lands were confiscated. The guilds were spoliated of their possessions and liberties, and placed under the control, the fancy, and the bribery of the State's official. The cities were divested of their sovereignty, and the very springs of their inner life—the folkmote, the elected justices and administration, the sovereign parish and the sovereign guild—were annihilated; the State's functionary took possession of every link of what formerly was an organic whole. Under that fatal policy and the wars it engendered, whole regions, once populous and wealthy, were laid bare; rich cities became insignificant boroughs; the very roads which connected them with other cities became impracticable. Industry, art, and knowledge fell into decay. Political education, science, and law were rendered subservient to the idea of State centralization. It was taught in the Universities and from the pulpit that the institutions in which men formerly used to embody their needs of mutual support could not be tolerated in a properly organized State; that the State alone could represent the bonds of union between its subjects; that federalism and "particularism" were the enemies of progress, and the State was the only proper initiator of further development. By the end of the last century the kings on the Continent, the Parliament in these isles, and the revolutionary Convention in France, although they were at war with each other, agreed in asserting that no separate unions between citizens must exist within the State; that hard labour and death were the only suitable punishments to workers who dared to enter into "coalitions." "No state within the State!" The State alone, and the State's Church, must take care of matters of general interest, while the subjects must represent loose aggregations of individuals, connected by no particular bonds, bound to appeal to the Government each time that they feel a common need. Up to the middle of this century this was the theory and practice in Europe. Even commercial and industrial societies were looked at with suspicion. As to the workers, their unions were treated as unlawful almost within our own lifetime in this country and within the last twenty years on the Continent. The whole system of our State education was such that up to the present time, even in this country, a notable portion of society would treat as a revolutionary measure the concession of such rights as every one, freeman or serf, exercised five hundred years ago in the village folkmote, the guild, the parish, and the city.

The absorption of all social functions by the State necessarily favoured the development of an unbridled, narrow-minded individualism. In proportion as the obligations towards the State grew in numbers the citizens were evidently relieved from their obligations towards each other. In the guild—and in mediaeval times every man belonged to some guild or fraternity—two "brothers" were bound to watch in turns a brother who had fallen ill; it would be sufficient now to give one's neighbour the address of the next paupers' hospital. In barbarian society, to assist at a fight between two men, arisen from a quarrel, and not to prevent it from taking a fatal issue, meant to be oneself treated as a murderer; but under the theory of the all-protecting State the bystander need not intrude: it is the policeman's business to interfere, or not. And while in a savage land, among the Hottentots, it would be scandalous to eat without having loudly called out thrice whether there is not somebody wanting to share the food, all that a respectable citizen has to do now is to pay the poor tax and to let the starving starve. The result is, that the theory which maintains that men can, and must, seek their own happiness in a disregard of other people's wants is now triumphant all round—in law, in science, in religion. It is the religion of the day, and to doubt of its efficacy is to be a dangerous Utopian. Science loudly proclaims that the struggle of each against all is the leading principle of nature, and of human societies as well. To that struggle Biology ascribes the progressive evolution of the animal world. History takes the same line of argument; and political economists, in their naïve ignorance, trace all progress of modern industry and machinery to the "wonderful" effects of the same principle. The very religion of the pulpit is a religion of individualism, slightly mitigated by more or less charitable relations to one's neighbours, chiefly on Sundays. "Practical" men and theorists, men of science and religious preachers, lawyers and politicians, all agree upon one thing—that individualism may be more or less softened in its harshest effects by charity, but that it is the only secure basis for the maintenance of society and its ulterior progress.

It seems, therefore, hopeless to look for mutual-aid institutions and practices in modern society. What could remain of them? And yet, as soon as we try to ascertain how the millions of human beings live, and begin to study their everyday relations, we are struck with the immense part which the mutual-aid and mutual-support principles play even now-a-days in human life. Although the destruction of mutual-aid institutions has been going on in practice and theory, for full three or four hundred years, hundreds of millions of men continue to live under such institutions; they piously maintain them and endeavour to reconstitute them where they have ceased to exist. In our mutual relations every one of us has his moments of revolt against the fashionable individualistic creed of the day, and actions in which men are guided by their mutual-aid inclinations constitute so great a part of our daily intercourse that if a stop to such actions could be put all further ethical progress would be stopped at once. Human society itself could not be maintained for even so much as the lifetime of one single generation. These facts, mostly neglected by sociologists and yet of the first importance for the life and further elevation of mankind, we are now going to analyze, beginning with the standing institutions of mutual support, and passing next to those acts of mutual aid which have their origin in personal or social sympathies. . . .

## Conclusion

If we take now the teachings which can be borrowed from the analysis of modern society, in connection with the body of evidence relative to the importance of mutual aid in the evolution of the animal world and of mankind, we may sum up our inquiry as follows.

In the animal world we have seen that the vast majority of species live in societies, and that they find in association the best arms for the struggle for life: understood, of course, in its wide Darwinian sense—not as a struggle for the sheer means of existence, but as a struggle against all natural conditions unfavourable to the species. The animal species, in which individual struggle has been reduced to its narrowest limits, and the practice of mutual aid has attained the greatest development, are invariably the most numerous, the most prosperous, and the most open to further progress. The mutual protection which is obtained in this case, the possibility of attaining old age and of accumulating experience, the higher intellectual development, and the further growth of sociable habits, secure the maintenance of the species, its extension, and its further progressive evolution. The unsociable species, on the contrary, are doomed to decay.

Going next over to man, we found him living in clans and tribes at the very dawn of the stone age; we saw a wide series of social institutions developed already in the lower savage stage, in the clan and the tribe; and we found that the earliest tribal customs and habits gave to mankind the embryo of all the institutions which made later on the leading aspects of further progress. Out of the savage tribe grew up the barbarian village community; and a new, still wider, circle of social customs, habits, and institutions, numbers of which are still alive among ourselves, was developed under the principles of common possession of a given territory and common defence of it, under the jurisdiction of the village folkmote, and in the federation of villages belonging, or supposed to belong, to one stem. And when new requirements induced men to make a new start, they made it in the city, which represented a double network of territorial units (village communities), connected with guilds— these latter arising out of the common prosecution of a given art or craft, or for mutual support and defence.

And finally, in the last two chapters facts were produced to show that although the growth of the State on the pattern of Imperial Rome had put a violent end to all mediaeval institutions for mutual support, this new aspect of civilization could not last. The State, based upon loose aggregations of individuals and undertaking to be their only bond of union, did not answer its purpose. The mutual-aid tendency finally broke down its iron rules; it reappeared and reasserted itself in an infinity of associations which now tend to embrace all aspects of life and to take possession of all that is required by man for life and for reproducing the waste occasioned by life.

It will probably be remarked that mutual aid, even though it may represent one of the factors of evolution, covers nevertheless one aspect only of human relations; that by the side of this current, powerful though it may be, there is, and always has been, the other current—the self-assertion of the individual, not only in its efforts to attain personal or caste superiority, economical, political, and spiritual, but also in its much more important although less evident function of breaking through the bonds, always prone to become crystallized, which the tribe, the village community, the city, and the State impose upon the individual. In other words, there is the self-assertion of the individual taken as progressive element.

It is evident that no review of evolution can be complete, unless these two dominant currents are analyzed. However, the self-assertion of the individual or of groups of individuals, their struggles for superiority, and the conflicts which resulted therefrom, have already been analyzed, described, and glorified from time immemorial. In fact, up to the present time, this current alone has received attention from the epical poet, the annalist, the historian, and the sociologist. History, such as it has hitherto been written, is almost entirely a description of the ways and means by which theocracy, military power, autocracy, and, later on, the richer classes' rule have been promoted, established, and maintained. The struggles between these forces make, in fact, the substance of history. We may thus take the knowledge of the individual factor in human history as granted—even though there is full room for a new study of the subject on the lines just alluded to; while, on the other side, the mutual-aid factor has been hitherto totally lost sight of; it was simply denied, or even scoffed at, by the writers of the present and past generation. It was therefore necessary to show, first of all, the immense part which this factor plays in the evolution of both the animal world and human societies. Only after this has been fully recognized will it be possible to proceed to a comparison between the two factors.

To make even a rough estimate of their relative importance by any method more or less statistical, is evidently impossible. One single war—we all know —may be productive of more evil, immediate and subsequent, than hundreds of years of the unchecked action of the mutual-aid principle may be productive of good. But when we see that in the animal world, progressive development and mutual aid go hand in hand, while the inner struggle within the species is concomitant with retrogressive development; when we notice that with man, even success in struggle and war is proportionate to the development of mutual aid in each of the two conflicting nations, cities, parties, or tribes, and that in the process of evolution war itself (so far as it can go this way) has been made subservient to the ends of progress in mutual aid within the nation, the city or the clan—we already obtain a perception of the dominating influence of the mutual-aid factor as an element of progress. But we see also that the practice of mutual aid and its successive developments have created the very conditions of society life in which man was enabled to develop his arts, knowledge, and intelligence; and that the periods when institutions based on the mutual-aid tendency took their greatest development were also the periods of the greatest progress in arts, industry, and science. In fact, the study of the inner life of the mediaeval city and of the ancient Greek cities reveals the fact that the combination of mutual aid, as it was practised within the guild and the Greek clan, with a large initiative which was left to the individual and the group by means of the federative principle, gave to mankind the two greatest periods of its history—the ancient Greek city and the mediaeval city periods; while the ruin of the above institutions during the State periods of history, which followed, corresponded in both cases to a rapid decay.

As to the sudden industrial progress which has been achieved during our own century, and which is usually ascribed to the triumph of individualism and competition, it certainly has a much deeper origin than that. Once the great discoveries of the fifteenth century were made, especially that of the pressure of the atmosphere, supported by a series of advances in natural philosophy—and they were made under the mediaeval city organization —once these discoveries were made, the invention of the steam-motor, and all the revolution which the conquest of a new power implied, had necessarily to follow. If the mediaeval cities had lived to bring their discoveries to that point, the ethical consequences of the revolution effected by steam might have been different; but the same revolution in technics and science would have inevitably taken place. It remains, indeed, an open question whether the general decay of industries which followed the ruin of the free cities, and was especially noticeable in the first part of the eighteenth century, did not considerably retard the appearance of the steam-engine as well as the consequent revolution in arts. When we consider the astounding rapidity of industrial progress from the twelfth to the fifteenth centuries—in weaving, working of metals, architecture and navigation, and ponder over the scientific discoveries which that industrial progress led to at the end of the fifteenth century—we must ask ourselves whether mankind was not delayed in its taking full advantage of these conquests when a general depression of arts and industries took place in Europe after the decay of mediaeval civilization. Surely it was not the disappearance of the artist-artisan, nor the ruin of large cities and the extinction of intercourse between them, which could favour the industrial revolution; and we know indeed that James Watt spent twenty or more years of his life in order to render his invention serviceable, because he could not find in the last century what he would have readily found in mediaeval Florence or Brügge, that is, the artisans capable of realizing his devices in metal, and of giving them the artistic finish and precision which the steam-engine requires.

To attribute, therefore, the industrial progress of our century to the war of each against all which it has proclaimed, is to reason like the man who, knowing not the causes of rain, attributes it to the victim he has immolated before his clay idol. For industrial progress, as for each other conquest over nature, mutual aid and close intercourse certainly are, as they have been, much more advantageous than mutual struggle.

However, it is especially in the domain of ethics that the dominating importance of the mutual-aid principle appears in full. That mutual aid is the real foundation of our ethical conceptions seems evident enough. But whatever the opinions as to the first origin of the mutual-aid feeling or instinct may be—whether a biological or a supernatural cause is ascribed to it—we must trace its existence as far back as to the lowest stages of the animal world; and from these stages we can follow its uninterrupted evolution, in opposition to a number of contrary agencies, through all degrees of human development, up to the present times. Even the new religions which were born from time to time—always at epochs when the mutual-aid principle was falling into decay in the theocracies and despotic States of the East, or at the decline of the Roman Empire—even the new religions have only reaffirmed that same principle. They found their first supporters among the humble, in the lowest, down-trodden layers of society, where the mutual-aid principle is the necessary foundation of every-day life; and the new forms of union which were introduced in the earliest Buddhist and Christian communities, in the Moravian brotherhoods and so on, took the character of a return to the best aspects of mutual aid in early tribal life.

Each time, however, that an attempt to return to this old principle was made, its fundamental idea itself was widened. From the clan it was extended to the stem, to the federation of stems, to the nation, and finally—in ideal, at least—to the whole of mankind. It was also refined at the same time. In primitive Buddhism, in primitive Christianity, in the writings of some of the Mussulman teachers, in the early movements of the Reform, and especially in the ethical and philosophical movements of the last century and of our own times, the total abandonment of the idea of revenge, or of "due reward"—of good for good and evil for evil—is affirmed more and more vigorously. The higher conception of "no revenge for wrongs," and of freely giving more than one expects to receive from his neighbours, is proclaimed as being the real principle of morality—a principle superior to mere equivalence, equity, or justice, and more conducive to happiness. And man is appealed to be guided in his acts, not merely by love, which is always personal, or at the best tribal, but by the perception of his oneness with each human being. In the practice of mutual aid, which we can retrace to the earliest beginnings of evolution, we thus find the positive and undoubted origin of our ethical conceptions; and we can affirm that in the ethical progress of man, mutual support—not mutual struggle—has had the leading part. In its wide extension, even at the present time, we also see the best guarantee of a still loftier evolution of our race.

## Notes

1. A bulky literature, dealing with this formerly much neglected subject, is now growing in Germany. Keller's works, *Ein Apostel der Wiedertaüfer* and *Geschichte der Wiedertaüfer,* Cornelius's *Geschichte des münsterischen Aufruhrs,* and Jannsen's *Geschichte des deutschen Volkes* may be named as the leading sources. The first attempt at familiarizing English readers with the results of the wide researches made in German in this direction has been made in an excellent little work by Richard Heath—

"Anabaptism from Its Rise at Zwickau to Its Fall at Munster, 1521–1536," London, 1895 (*Baptist Manuals,* vol. 1.)—where the leading features of the movement are well indicated, and full bibliographical information is given. Also K. Kautsky's *Communism in Central Europe in the Time of the Reformation,* London, 1897.

2. Few of our contemporaries realize both the extent of this movement and the means by which it was suppressed. But those who wrote immediately after the great peasant war estimated at from 100,000 to 150,000 men the number of peasants slaughtered after their defeat in Germany. See Zimmermann's *Allgemeine Geschichte des grossen Bauernkrieges.* For the measures taken to suppress the movement in the Netherlands see Richard Heath's *Anabaptism.*

# MIKHAIL BAKUNIN

## *Scientific Anarchism*

Mikhail Bakunin (1814–76) is best known for his conflict with Karl Marx, which ended in the disintegration of the First International Workingmen's Association. That conflict was personal and political. Beneath their genuine dislike, which resulted in petty accusations (e.g., Marx claimed Bakunin embezzled a 300-ruble advance for a Russian translation of *Capital*), were serious doctrinal differences. Bakunin supported peasant revolution and stressed the dangers of proletarian dictatorship. Engels's response to Bakunin's critique of Marxism is included in chapter 25.

### Ethics: Truly Human or
### Anarchist Morality

*The Instinct for Individual Self-Preservation and for Preservation of Species.* The elements of what we call morality are already found in the animal world. In all the animal species, with no exception, but with a great difference in development, we find two opposed instincts: the instinct for preservation of the individual and the instinct for preservation of the species; or, speaking in human terms, *the egoistic and the social instincts.* From the point of view of science, as well as from the point of view of Nature itself, those two instincts are equally natural and hence equally legitimate, and, what is even more important, they are equally necessary in the natural economy of beings. The individual instinct is in itself the basic condition for the preservation of the species, for if the individuals did not defend themselves with all their power against all the privations and against all the external pressures constantly menacing their existence, the species itself, which only lives in and through the individuals, would not be able to maintain its existence. But if those two drives are to be judged only from the absolute point of view of the exclusive interest of the species, one may say that social instinct is good, and individual instinct, inasmuch as it is opposed to it, is bad.

*The Unbalanced Development of Those Instincts in the Animal World and Among Higher Insects.* With the ants and bees it is virtue that predominates, for in both of them social instinct appears to over-ride individual instinct. It is altogether different among wild beasts, and in general one may say that in the animal world egoism is the predominant instinct. Here the instinct of the species, on the contrary, awakens only during short intervals and lasts only so long as it is necessary for the procreation and education of the family.

*Egoism and Sociability Are Paramount in Man.* It is altogether different with man. It seems, and this has provided one of the pillars of his great superiority over other animal species, that both these opposed instincts—egoism and sociability—are much more powerful and much less distinct from each other in man than among all the other animals. He is more ferocious in his egoism than the wildest beasts and at the same time he is more sociable than ants and bees.

*Humanity Is Present Even in the Lowest Character.* All human morality, every collective and individual morality, rests basically upon *human respect.* What do we mean by human respect? It is recognition of humanity, of human right and of human dignity in every man of whatever race, color, and degree of intellectual and even moral development he may be. But if a man is stupid, wicked, contemptible, can I respect him? If that were the case, no doubt I would find it impossible to respect his villainy, his stupidity, and brutality; they would make me feel disgusted and indignant; and if necessary I would take most energetic measures against them, not even stopping at killing such a man if no other means were left to defend my life against him, my rights, or whatever I respect or is dear to me. But in the midst of the most energetic and fierce—and if necessary even mortal—struggle against him, I would have to respect his human nature.

*Regeneration of Character Possible with Change of Social Conditions.* Only at the price of showing such respect can I retain my own human dignity. But if he himself does not recognize this dignity in others, can we recognize the same in himself? If he is a kind of ferocious animal, or even worse, as it sometimes happens, would it not be to indulge in fictions if we acknowledged human nature in him? Not at all! For whatever depths his intellectual and moral degradation may reach at any particular moment, unless he is congenitally insane or an idiot—in which case he should be treated not as a criminal but as a sick person—and if he is in full possession of the sense and intelligence allotted to him by Nature, then his human character, amid the most monstrous deviations, still exists in him, in a very real manner, *as a possibility, always present with him so long as he lives, that somehow he may become aware of his humanity if only a radical change is effected in the social conditions which made him what he is.*

*Social Environment the Determining Factor.* Take the most intelligent ape possessing the finest character, put it under the best, most humane conditions—and you will never succeed in making a man out of it. Take the most hardened criminal or a man of the poorest mind, and, provided neither one of them suffers from some organic *lesion* which may bring about either idiocy or incurable madness of the other—you will soon come to recognize that if one has become a criminal and the other has not yet developed to the conscious awareness of his humanity and human duties, *the fault lies not with them nor with their nature, but with the social environment in which they were born and have been developing.* . . .

*Socialism Is Based on Determinism.* Socialism, being founded upon positive science, absolutely rejects the doctrine of *"free will."* It recognizes that whatever is called human vice and virtue is absolutely the product of the combined action of Nature and society. Nature, through its ethnographical, physiological, and pathological action, creates faculties and dispositions which are called natural, and the organization of society develops them, or on the other hand halts or falsifies their development. All individuals, with no exception, are at every moment of their lives what Nature and society have made them.

*Improvement of Man's Morality Is Conditioned by Moralization of Social Environment.* Hence it clearly follows that to make men moral it is necessary to make their social environment moral. And that can be done in only one way: by assuring the triumph of justice, that is, the complete liberty of everyone in the most perfect equality for all. Inequality of conditions and rights, and the resulting lack of liberty for all, is the great collective iniquity begetting all individual iniquities. Suppress this source of iniquities and all the rest will vanish along with it.

*A Moral Environment Will Be Created by Revolution.* In view of the lack of enthusiasm shown by men of privilege for moral improvement—or what is the same thing, for equalizing their rights with others—we fear that the triumph of justice can be effected only through a social revolution.

Three things are necessary for men to become moral, that is, complete men in the full meaning of the word: birth under hygienic conditions; a rational and integral education accompanied by an upbringing based upon respect for work, reason, equality, and liberty: and a social environment wherein the human individual, enjoying full liberty, will be equal, in fact and by right, to all others.

Does such an environment exist? It does not. It follows then that it has to be created. . . .

*Freedom Is Not the Negation of Solidarity.* Social solidarity is the first human law; freedom is the second law. Both laws interpenetrate each other and, being inseparable, constitute the essence of humanity. Thus freedom is not the negation of solidarity; on the contrary, it represents the development and, so to speak, the humanizing of it.

Thus respect for the freedom of someone else constitutes the highest duty of men. The only virtue is to love this freedom and serve it. This is the basis of all morality, and there is no other basis.

Since freedom is the result and the clearest expression of solidarity, that is, of mutuality of interests, it can be realized only under conditions of equality. Political equality can be based only upon economic and social equality. And justice is precisely the realization of freedom through such equality. . . .

## Society and the Individual

*Society Is the Basis of Human Existence.* Society, preceding in time any development of humanity and fully partaking of the almighty power of natural laws, actions, and manifestations, constitutes the very essence of human existence. Man is born into society, just as an ant is born into an ant-hill or a bee into its hive; man is born into society from the very moment that he becomes a human being, that is, a being possessing to a greater or lesser extent the power of speech and thought. Man does not choose society; on the contrary, he is the product of the latter, and he is just as inevitably subjected to natural laws governing his necessary development as to all other natural laws which he must obey. Society antedates and at the same time survives every human individual, being in this respect like Nature itself; it is eternal like Nature, or rather, having been born upon this earth, it will last as long as our earth itself.

*Revolt Against Society Is Inconceivable.* A radical revolt by man against society would therefore be just as impossible as a revolt against Nature, human society being nothing else but the last great manifestation or creation of Nature upon this earth. And an individual who would want to rebel against society, that is, against Nature in general and his own nature in particular, would place himself beyond the pale of real existence, would plunge into nothingness, into an absolute void, into lifeless abstraction, into God. It follows that it is just as impossible to ask whether society is good or evil as it is to ask whether Nature—the universal, material, real, absolute, sole, and supreme being—is good or evil. It is much more than that: it is an immense, overwhelming fact, a positive and primitive fact, having existence prior to all consciousness, to all ideas, to all intellectual and moral discernment. It is the very basis, it is the world in which inevitably, and at a much later stage, there begins to develop what we call good and evil.

*There Is No Humanity Outside of Society.* During a very long period, lasting thousands of years, our species roamed the earth in isolated herds. That was before, together with the first emergence of speech and the first gleam of thought, there awakened within the social and animal environment of one of those human herds, the first self-conscious or free individuality. Apart from society, man would never cease to be a speechless and an unreasoning animal, a thousand times poorer and more dependent upon external Nature than most of the quadrupeds, above which he now towers so proudly.

Even the most wretched individual of our present society could not exist and develop without the cumulative social efforts of countless generations. Thus the individual, his freedom and reason, are the products of society, and not *vice versa:* society is not the product of individuals comprising it; and the higher, the more fully the individual is developed, the greater his freedom —and the more he is the product of society, the more does he receive from society and the greater his debt to it. . . .

## Property Could Arise Only in the State

The doctrinaire philosophers, as well as the jurists and economists, always assume that property came into existence before the rise of the State, whereas it is clear that the juridical idea of property, as well as family law, could arise historically only in the State, the first inevitable act of which was the establishment of this law and of property.

Property is a god. This god already has its theology (which is called State politics and juridical right) and also its morality, the most adequate expression of which is summed up in the phrase: "This man is worth so much."

*The Theology and Metaphysics of Property.* The property god also has its metaphysics. It is the science of the bourgeois economists. Like any metaphysics it is a sort of twilight, a compromise between truth and falsehood, with the latter benefiting by it. It seeks to give falsehood the appearance of truth and leads truth to falsehood. Political economy seeks to sanctify property through labor and to represent it as the realization, the fruit, of labor. If it succeeds in doing this, it will save property and the bourgeois world. For labor is sacred, and whatever is based upon labor, is good, just, moral, human, legitimate. One's faith, however, must be of the sturdy kind to enable him to swallow this doctrine, for we see the vast majority of workers deprived of all property; and what is more, we have the avowed statements of the economists and their own scientific proofs to the effect that under the present economic organization, which they defend so passionately, the masses *will never come to own property;* that, consequently, their labor does not emancipate and ennoble them, for, all their labor notwithstanding, they are condemned to remain eternally without property—that is, outside of morality and humanity.

*Only Non-Productive Labor Yields Property.* On the other hand, we see that the richest property owners, and consequently the most worthy, humane, moral, and respectable citizens, are precisely those who work the least or who do not work at all. To that the answer is made that nowadays it is impossible to remain rich—to preserve, and even less so, to increase one's wealth—without working. Well, let us then agree upon the proper use of the term *work:*

there is work and work. There is productive labor and there is the labor of exploitation.

The first is the labor of the proletariat; the second that of property owners. He who turns to good account lands cultivated by someone else, simply exploits someone else's labor. And he who increases the value of his capital, whether in industry or in commerce, exploits the labor of others. The banks which grow rich as a result of thousands of credit transactions, the Stock Exchange speculators, the shareholders who get large dividends without raising a finger; Napoleon III, who became so rich that he was able to raise to wealth all his protégés; King William I, who, proud of his victories, is preparing to levy billions upon poor unfortunate France, and who already has become rich and is enriching his soldiers with this plunder—all those people are workers, but what kind of workers! Highway robbers! Thieves and plain ordinary robbers are "workers" to a much greater extent, for in order to get rich in their own way they have to "work" with their own hands.

It is evident to anyone who is not blind about this matter that productive work creates wealth and yields the producers only misery, and that it is only non-productive, exploiting labor that yields property. But since property is morality, it follows that *morality, as the bourgeois understands it, consists in exploiting someone else's labor.* . . .

## Criticism of Marxism

. . . *The Fallacious Premise of the Doctrinaire Revolutionists.* Idealists of all sorts, metaphysicians, positivists, those who uphold the priority of science over life, the doctrinaire revolutionists—all of them champion, with equal zeal although differing in their argumentation, the idea of the State and State power, seeing in them, quite logically from their point of view, the only salvation of society. *Quite logically,* I say, having taken as their basis the tenet—a fallacious tenet in our opinion—that thought is prior to life, and abstract theory is prior to social practice, and that therefore sociological science must become the starting point for social upheavals and social reconstruction—they necessarily arrived at the conclusion that since thought, theory, and science are, for the present at least, the property of only a very few people, those few should direct social life, and not only foment and stimulate but rule all movements of the people; and that on the morrow of the Revolution the new social organization should be set up not by the free integration of workers' associations, villages, communes, and regions from below upward, conforming to the needs and instincts of the people, but solely by the dictatorial power of this learned minority, allegedly expressing the general will of the people.

*The Common Ground of the Theory of Revolutionary Dictatorship and the Theory of the State.* It is upon this fiction of people's representation and upon the actual fact of the masses of people being ruled by a small handful of privileged individuals elected, or for that matter not even elected, by throngs herded together on election day and ever ignorant of why and whom they elect; it is upon this fictitious and abstract expression of the fancied general will and thought of the people, of which the living and real people have not the slightest conception—that the theory of the State and that of revolutionary dictatorship are based in equal measure.

Between revolutionary dictatorship and the State principle the difference is only in the external situation. In substance both are one and the same: the ruling of the majority by the minority in the name of the alleged stupidity of the first and the alleged superior intelligence of the second. Therefore both are equally reactionary, both having as their result the invariable consolidation of the political and economic privileges of the ruling minority and the political and economic enslavement of the masses of people.

*Doctrinaire Socialists Are the Friends of the State.* Now it is clear why the doctrinaire Socialists who have for their aim the overthrow of the existing authorities and regimes in order to build upon the ruins of the latter a dictatorship of their own, never were and never will be enemies of the State, but on the contrary that they were and ever will be its zealous champions. They are enemies of the powers-that-be only because they cannot take their places. They are enemies of the existing political institutions because such institutions preclude the possibility of carrying out their own dictatorship, but they are at the same time the most ardent friends of State power, without which the Revolution, by freeing the toiling masses, would deprive this would-be revolutionary minority of all hope of putting the people into a new harness and heap upon them the blessings of their governmental measures. . . .

*Socialism via Peaceful Reform.* How is the proletariat to capture the State? There are but two means available for that purpose: a political revolution or a lawful agitation on behalf of a peaceful reform. [Ferdinand] Lassalle chose the second course.

In this sense, and for that purpose, he formed a political party of German workers possessing considerable strength, having organized it along hierarchical lines and submitted it to rigorous discipline and to a sort of personal dictatorship; in other words, he did what M. Marx had tried to do to the International during the last three years. Marx's attempt proved to be a failure, while Lassalle was wholly successful. As his direct aim Lassalle set himself the task of impelling a popular movement and agitation for the winning of universal suffrage, for the right of the people to elect State representatives and authorities.

Having won this right, the people would send their own representatives to the Parliament, which in turn, by various decrees and enactments, would transform the given State into a People's State (*Volks-Staat*). And the first task of this People's State would be to open unlimited credit to the producers' and consumers' associations, which only then will be able to combat bourgeois capital, finally succeeding in conquering and assimilating it. When this process of absorption has been completed, then the period of the radical change of society will dawn upon mankind.

*The Fiction of the People's State.* Such is the program of Lassalle, such is the program of the Social-Democratic Party. Properly speaking, it belongs not to Lassalle but to Marx, who fully expressed it in the well-known *Manifesto of the Communist Party* published by Marx and Engels in 1848. This program is likewise alluded to in the first *Manifesto of the International Association* written by Marx in 1864, in the words: "The first duty of the working class should be to conquer for itself political power," or as the *Manifesto of the Communist Party* says in that respect: "The first step in the revolution by the working class, is to raise the proletariat to the position of a ruling class. . . . The proletariat will centralize the instruments of production in the hands of the State, that is, the proletariat raised to the position of a ruling class."

We already have expressed our abhorrence for the theories of Lassalle and Marx, theories which counseled the workers—if not as their ultimate ideal, at least as their next chief aim—*to form a People's State,* which, according to their interpretation, will only be "the proletariat raised to the position of a ruling class."

. . . But the State connotes domination, and domination connotes exploitation, which proves that the term *the People's State (Volks-Staat),* which unfortunately still remains the watchword of the German Social-Democratic Party, is a ridiculous contradiction, a fiction, a falsehood—doubtless an unconscious falsehood—and for the proletariat a very dangerous pitfall. The State, however popular it be made in form, will always be an institution of domination and exploitation, and it will therefore ever remain a permanent source of slavery and misery. Consequently there is no other means of emancipating the people economically and politically, of providing them with wellbeing and freedom, but to abolish the State, all States, and once and for all do away with that which until now has been called *politics.*

*The Implication of the Dictatorship of the Proletariat.* One may ask then: if the proletariat is to be the ruling class, over whom will it rule? The answer is that there will remain another proletariat which will be subjected to this new domination, this new State. It may be, for example, the peasant "rabble," which, as we know, does not stand in great favor with the Marxists, and who, finding themselves on a lower level of culture, probably will be ruled by the city and factory proletariat; or considered from the national point of view, the Slavs, for instance, will assume, for precisely the same reason, the same position of slavish subjection to the victorious German proletariat which the latter now holds with respect to its own bourgeoisie.

If there is a State, there must necessarily be domination, and therefore slavery; a State without slavery, overt or concealed, is unthinkable—and that is why we are enemies of the State.

What does it mean: "the proletariat raised into a ruling class?" Will the proletariat as a whole be at the head of the government? There are about forty million Germans. Will all the forty million be members of the government? The whole people will govern and there will be no one to be governed. It means that there will be no government, no State, but if there is a State in existence there will be people who are governed, and there will be slaves.

This dilemma is solved very simply in the Marxist theory. By a people's government they mean the governing of people by means of a small number of representatives elected by the people. Universal suffrage—the right of the whole people to elect its so-called representatives and rulers of the State—this is the last word of the Marxists as well as of the democratic school. And this is a falsehood behind which lurks the despotism of a governing minority, a falsehood which is all the more dangerous in that it appears as the ostensible expression of a people's will.

Thus, from whatever angle we approach the problem, we arrive at the same sorry result: the rule of great masses of people by a small privileged minority. But, the Marxists say, this minority will consist of workers. Yes, indeed, of *ex-workers*, who, once they become rulers or representatives of the people, cease to be workers and begin to look down upon the toiling people. From that time on they represent not the people but themselves and their own claims to govern the people. Those who doubt this know precious little about human nature.

*Dictatorship Cannot Beget Freedom.* But these elected representatives will be convinced Socialists, and learned Socialists at that. The words "learned Socialist" and "scientific Socialism" which are met with constantly in the works and speeches of the Lassalleans and Marxists, prove only that this would-be people's State will be nothing else but despotic rule over the toiling masses by a new, numerically small aristocracy of genuine or sham scientists. The people lack learning and so they will be freed from the cares of government, will be wholly regimented into one common herd of governed people. Emancipation indeed!

The Marxists are aware of this contradiction, and, realizing that government by scientists (the most distressing, offensive, and despicable type of government in the world) will be, notwithstanding its democratic form, a veritable dictatorship—console themselves with the thought that this dictatorship will be only temporary and of brief duration. They say that the only care and aim of this government will be to educate and uplift the people—economically and politically—to such an extent that no government will be necessary, and that the State, having lost its political character, that is, its character of rule and domination, will turn all by itself into an altogether free organization of economic interests and communes.

Here we have an obvious contradiction. If their State is going to be a genuine people's State, why should it then dissolve itself—and if its rule is necessary for the real emancipation of the people, how dare they call it a people's State? Our polemic had the effect of making them realize that freedom or Anarchism, that is, the free organization of workers from below upward, is the ultimate aim of social development, and that every State, their own people's State included, is a yoke, which means that it begets despotism on one hand and slavery on the other.

They say that this State yoke—the dictatorship—is a necessary transitional means in order to attain the emancipation of the people: Anarchism or freedom is the goal, the State or dictatorship is the means. Thus to free the working masses, it is first necessary to enslave them.

That is as far as our polemic went. They maintain that only a dictatorship—their dictatorship, of course—can create the will of the people, while our answer to this is: No dictatorship can have any other aim but that of self-perpetuation, and it can beget only slavery in the people tolerating it; freedom can be created only by freedom, that is, by a universal rebellion on the part of the people and free organization of the toiling masses from the bottom up.

*Powerfully Centralized State the Goal of the Marxists.* While the political and social theory of the anti-State Socialists or Anarchists leads them steadily toward a full break with all governments, and with all varieties of bourgeois policy, leaving no other way out but a social revolution, the opposite theory of the State Communists and scientific authority also inevitably draws and enmeshes its partisans, under the pretext of political tactics, into ceaseless compromises with governments and political parties; that is, it pushes them toward downright reaction.

The basic point of Lassalle's politico-social program and the Communist theory of Marx is *the (imaginary) emancipation of the proletariat by means of the State.* But for that it is necessary that the State consent to take upon itself the task of emancipating the proletariat from the yoke of bourgeois capital. How can the State be imbued with such a will? There are only two means whereby that can be done.

The proletariat ought to wage a revolution in order to capture the State—a rather heroic undertaking. And in our opinion, once the proletariat captures the State, it should immediately proceed with its destruction as the everlasting prison for the toiling masses. Yet according to the theory of M. Marx, the people not only should not destroy the State but should strengthen and reinforce it, and transfer it in this form into the hands of its benefactors, guardians, and teachers, the chiefs of the Communist Party—in a word, to M. Marx and his friends, who will begin to emancipate it in their own fashion.

They will concentrate all the powers of government in strong hands, because the very fact that the people are ignorant necessitates strong, solicitous care by the government. They will create a single State bank, concentrating in its hands all the commercial, industrial, agricultural, and even scientific production; and they will divide the mass of people into two armies—industrial and agricultural armies under the direct command of the State engineers who will constitute the new privileged scientific-political class.

One can see then what a shining goal the German Communist school has set up before the people.

## Social-Democratic Program Examined

... *Political and Social Revolution Must Go Together.* We should ruthlessly eliminate the politics of bourgeois democrats or bourgeois Socialists who, in declaring that "political liberty is the *preliminary* condition of economic emancipation," understand by those words only the following: "Political reforms, or a political revolution, must precede economic reforms or an economic revolution; therefore the workers must ally themselves with the more or less radical bourgeois in order to carry out a political revolution together with the bourgeoisie, and then wage an economic revolution against the latter."

We loudly protest against this baneful theory, which can end only with the workers being used once more as an instrument against themselves and being turned over again to bourgeois exploitation.

To win political freedom first can signify no other thing but to win this freedom only, leaving for the first days at least economic and social relations in the same old state—that is, leaving the proprietors and capitalists with their insolent wealth, and the workers with their poverty.

But, it is argued, this freedom, once won, shall serve the workers later as an instrument with which to win *equality* or *economic justice.*

Freedom is indeed a magnificent and powerful instrument. The question, however, is whether workers really can make use of it, whether it will actually be in their possession, or whether, as has been the case until now, their *political liberty* will prove to be only a deceitful appearance, a mere fiction. ...

## Stateless Socialism: Anarchism

... *Organization of Productive Forces in Place of Political Power.* It is necessary to abolish completely, both in principle and in fact, all that which is called political power; for, so long as political power exists, there will be ruler and ruled, masters and slaves, exploiters and exploited. Once abolished, political power should be replaced by an organization of productive forces and economic service.

Notwithstanding the enormous development of modern states—a development which in its ultimate phase is quite logically reducing the State to an absurdity—it is becoming evident that the days of the State and the State principle are numbered. Already we can see approaching the full emancipation of the toiling masses and their free social organization, free from governmental intervention, formed by economic associations of the people and brushing aside all the old State frontiers and national distinctions, and having as its basis only productive labor, humanized labor, having one common interest in spite of its diversity.

*The Ideal of the People.* This ideal of course appears to the people as signifying first of all the end of want, the end of poverty, and the full satisfaction of all material needs by means of collective labor, equal and obligatory for all, and then, as the end of domination and the free organization of the people's lives in accordance with their needs—not from the top down, as we have it in the State, but from the bottom up, an organization formed by the people themselves, apart from all governments and parliaments, a free union of associations of agricultural and factory workers, of communes, regions, and nations, and finally, in the more remote future, the universal human brotherhood, triumphing above the ruins of all States.

*The Program of a Free Society.* Outside of the Mazzinian system, which is the system of the republic in the form of a State, there is no other system but that of the republic as a commune, the republic as a federation, a Socialist and a genuine people's republic—the system of Anarchism. It is the politics of the Social Revolution, which aims at the abolition of the State, and the economic, altogether free organization of the people, an organization from below upward, by means of a federation.

. . . There will be no possibility of the existence of a political government, for this government will be transformed into a simple administration of common affairs.

Our program can be summed up in a few words:

Peace, emancipation, and the happiness of the oppressed.

War upon all oppressors and all despoilers.

Full restitution to workers: all the capital, the factories, and all the instruments of work and raw materials to go to the associations, and the land to those who cultivate it with their own hands.

Liberty, justice, and fraternity in regard to all human beings born upon the earth.

Equality for all.

To all, with no distinction whatever, all the means of development, education, and upbringing, and the equal possibility of living while working.

Organizing of a society by means of a free federation from below upward, of workers' associations, industrial as well as agricultural, scientific as well as literary associations—first into a commune, then a federation of communes into regions, of regions into nations, and of nations into an international fraternal association.

*Correct Tactics During a Revolution.* In a social revolution, which in everything is diametrically opposed to a political revolution, the actions of individuals hardly count at all, whereas the spontaneous action of the masses is everything. All that individuals can do is to clarify, propagate, and work out ideas corresponding to the popular instinct, and, what is more, to contribute their incessant efforts to revolutionary organization of the natural power of the masses—but nothing else beyond that; the rest can and should be done by the people themselves. Any other method would lead to political dictatorship, to the re-emergence of the State, of privileges, of inequalities, of all the oppressions of the State—that is, it would lead in a roundabout but logical way toward re-establishment of political, social, and economic slavery of the masses of people.

Varlin and all his friends, like all sincere Socialists, and in general like all workers born and brought up among the people, shared to a high degree this perfectly legitimate bias against the initiative coming from isolated individuals, against the domination exercised by superior individuals, and being above all consistent, they extended the same prejudice and distrust to their own persons. . . .

*Freedom Must Go Hand-in-Hand with Equality.* I am a convinced partisan of *economic and social equality,* for I know that outside of this equality, freedom, justice, human dignity, morality, and the well-being of individuals as well as the prosperity of nations are all nothing but so many falsehoods. But being at the same time a partisan of freedom—the first condition of humanity—I believe that equality should be established in the world by a spontaneous organization of labor and collective property, by the free organization of producers' associations into communes, and the free federation of communes —but nowise by means of the supreme and tutelary action of the State.

*The Difference Between Authoritarian and Libertarian Revolutionists.* It is this point which mainly divides the Socialists or revolutionary collectivists from the authoritarian Communists, the partisans of the absolute initiative of the State. The goal of both is the same: both parties want the creation of a new social order based exclusively upon collective labor, under economic conditions that are equal for all—that is, under conditions of collective ownership of the tools of production.

Only the Communists imagine that they can attain through development and organization of the political power of the working classes, and chiefly of the city proletariat, aided by bourgeois radicalism—whereas the revolutionary Socialists, the enemies of all ambiguous alliances, believe, on the contrary, that this common goal can be attained not through the political but through the social (and therefore anti-political) organization and power of the working masses of the cities and villages, including all those who, though belonging by birth to the higher classes, have broken with their past of their own free will, and have openly joined the proletariat and accepted its program.

*The Methods of the Communists and the Anarchists.* Hence the two different methods. The Communists believe that it is necessary to organize the forces of the workers in order to take possession of the political might of the State. The revolutionary Socialists organize with the view of destroying, or if you prefer a more refined expression, of liquidating the State. The Communists are the partisans of the principle and practice of authority, while revolutionary Socialists place their faith only in freedom. Both are equally the partisans of science, which is to destroy superstition and take the place of faith; but the first want to impose science upon the people, while the revolutionary collectivists try to diffuse science and knowledge among the people, so that the various groups of human society, when convinced by propaganda, may organize and spontaneously combine into federations, in accordance with their natural tendencies and their real interests, but never according to a plan traced in advance and *imposed upon the ignorant masses*by a few "superior" minds.

Revolutionary Socialists believe that there is much more of practical reason and intelligence in the instinctive aspirations and real needs of the masses of people than in the profound minds of all these learned doctors and self-appointed tutors of humanity, who, having before them the sorry examples of so many abortive attempts to make humanity happy, still intend to keep on working in the same direction. But revolutionary Socialists believe, on the contrary, that humanity has permitted itself to be ruled for a long time, much too long, and that the source of its misfortune lies not in this nor in any other form of government but in the principle and the very existence of the government, whatever its nature may be.

It is this difference of opinion, which already has become historic, that now exists between the scientific Communism, developed by the German school and partly accepted by American and English Socialists, and Proudhonism, extensively developed and pushed to its ultimate conclusions, and by now accepted by the proletariat of the Latin countries. Revolutionary Socialism has made its first brilliant and practical appearance in the Paris Commune.

# FRIEDRICH ENGELS

## *On Authority*

## *and*

## *Versus the Anarchists*

Friedrich Engels (1820–95) was Karl Marx's colleague and co-author. In the following selections, Engels outlines the disagreements between Marx and the anarchists, especially Mikhail Bakunin, which split the First International. The first piece, "On Authority," is taken from an article Engels wrote in October 1872 and published in the 1874 collection *Almanacco Repubblicano*. In it he argues that the "principle of authority" is unavoidable during *and* after the revolution. The second piece, "Versus the Anarchists," comes from a letter of January 24, 1872, to Theodor Cuno. It focuses on revolutionary tactics regarding the state.

### "On Authority"

A number of Socialists have latterly launched a regular crusade against what they call the *principle of authority*. It suffices to tell them that this or that act is *authoritarian* for it to be condemned. This summary mode of procedure is being abused to such an extent that it has become necessary to look into the matter somewhat more closely. Authority, in the sense in which the word is used here, means: the imposition of the will of another upon ours; on the other hand, authority presupposes subordination. Now, since these two words sound bad and the relationship which they represent is disagreeable to the subordinated party, the question is to ascertain whether there is any way of dispensing with it, whether—given the conditions of present-day society—we could not create another social system, in which this authority would be given no scope any longer and would consequently have to disappear. On examining the economic, industrial and agricultural conditions which form the basis of present-day bourgeois society, we find that they tend more and more to replace isolated action by combined action of individuals. Modern industry with its big factories and mills, where hundreds of workers supervise complicated machines driven by steam, has superseded the small workshops of the separate producers; the carriages and wagons of the highways have been substituted by railway trains, just as the small schooners and sailing feluccas have been by steam-boats. Even agriculture falls increasingly under the dominion of the machine and of steam, which slowly but relentlessly put in the place of the small proprietors big capitalists, who with the aid of hired workers cultivate vast stretches of land. Everywhere combined action, the complication of processes dependent upon each other, displaces independent action by individuals. But whoever mentions combined action speaks of organisation; now, is it possible to have organisation without authority?

Supposing a social revolution dethroned the capitalists, who now exercise their authority over the production and circulation of wealth. Supposing, to adopt entirely the point of view of the anti-authoritarians, that the land and the instruments of labour had become the collective property of the workers who use them. Will authority have disappeared or will it only have changed its form? Let us see.

Let us take by way of example a cotton spinning mill. The cotton must pass through at least six successive operations before it is reduced to the state of thread, and these operations take place for the most part in different rooms. Furthermore, keeping the machines going requires an engineer to look after the steam engine, mechanics to make the current repairs, and many other labourers whose business it is to transfer the products from one room to another, and so forth. All these workers, men, women and children, are obliged to begin and finish their work at the hours fixed by the authority of the steam, which cares nothing for individual autonomy. The workers must, therefore, first come to an understanding on the hours of work; and these hours, once they are fixed, must be observed by all, without any exception. Thereafter particular questions arise in each room and at every moment concerning the mode of production, distribution of materials, etc., which must be settled at once on pain of seeing all production immediately stopped; whether they are settled by decision of a delegate placed at the head of each branch of labour or, if possible, by a majority vote, the will of the single individual will always have to subordinate itself, which means that questions are settled in an authoritarian way. The automatic machinery of a big factory is much more despotic than the small capitalists who employ workers ever have been. At least with regard to the hours of work one may write upon the portals of these factories: *Lasciate ogni autonomia, voi che entrate!* [Abandon all autonomy, you who enter!] If man, by dint of his knowledge and inventive genius, has subdued the forces of nature, the latter avenge themselves upon him by subjecting him, in so far as he employs them, to a veritable despotism independent of all social organisation. Wanting to abolish authority in large-scale industry is tantamount to wanting to abolish industry itself, to destroy the power loom in order to return to the spinning wheel.

Let us take another example—the railway. Here too the co-operation of an infinite number of individuals is absolutely necessary, and this co-operation must be practised during precisely fixed hours so that no accidents may happen. Here, too, the first condition of the job is a dominant will that settles all subordinate questions, whether this will is represented by a single delegate or a committee charged with the execution of the resolutions of the majority of persons interested. In either case there is very pronounced authority. Moreover, what would happen to the first train dispatched if the authority of the railway employees over the Honorable passengers were abolished?

But the necessity of authority, and of imperious authority at that, will nowhere be found more evident than on board a ship on the high seas. There, in time of danger, the lives of all depend on the instantaneous and absolute obedience of all to the will of one.

When I submitted arguments like these to the most rabid anti-authoritarians the only answer they were able to give me was the following: Yes, that's true, but here it is not a case of authority which we confer on our delegates, *but of a commission entrusted!* These gentlemen think that when they have changed the names of things they have changed the things themselves. This is how these profound thinkers mock at the whole world.

We have thus seen that, on the one hand, a certain authority, no matter how delegated, and, on the other hand, a certain subordination, are things which, independently of all social organisation, are imposed upon us together with the material conditions under which we produce and make products circulate.

We have seen besides, that the material conditions of production and circulation inevitably develop with large-scale industry and large-scale agriculture, and increasingly tend to enlarge the scope of this authority. Hence it is absurd to speak of the principle of authority as being absolutely evil, and of the principle of autonomy as being absolutely good. Authority and autonomy are relative things whose spheres vary with the various phases of the development of society. If the autonomists confined themselves to saying that the social organisation of the future would restrict authority solely to the limits within which the conditions of production render it inevitable, we could understand each other; but they are blind to all facts that make the thing necessary and they passionately fight the word.

Why do the anti-authoritarians not confine themselves to crying out against political authority, the state? All Socialists are agreed that the political state, and with it political authority, will disappear as a result of the coming social revolution, that is, that public functions will lose their political character and be transformed into the simple administrative functions of watching over the true interests of society. But the anti-authoritarians demand that the authoritarian political state be abolished at one stroke, even before the social conditions that gave birth to it have been destroyed. They demand that the first act of the social revolution shall be the abolition of authority. Have these gentlemen ever seen a revolution? A revolution is certainly the most authoritarian thing there is; it is the act whereby one part of the population imposes its will upon the other part by means of rifles, bayonets and cannon—authoritarian means, if such there be at all; and if the victorious party does not want to have fought in vain, it must maintain this rule by means of the terror which its arms inspire in the reactionaries. Would the Paris Commune have lasted a single day if it had not made use of this authority of the armed people against the bourgeois? Should we not, on the contrary, reproach it for not having used it freely enough?

Therefore, either one of two things: either the anti-authoritarians don't know what they are talking about, in which case they are creating nothing but confusion; or they do know, and in that case they are betraying the movement of the proletariat. In either case they serve the reaction.

### "Versus the Anarchists"

Bakunin, who up to 1868 had intrigued against the International, joined it after he had suffered a fiasco at the Berne Peace Congress and at once began to conspire *within it* against the General Council. Bakunin has a peculiar theory of his own, a medley of Proudhonism and communism, the chief point of which is, in the first place, that he does not regard capital—and therefore the class antagonism between capitalists and wage-workers which has arisen through social development—but the *state* as the main evil to be abolished. While the great mass of the Social-Democratic workers hold our view that the state power is nothing more than the organisation with which the ruling classes —landlords and capitalists—have provided themselves in order to protect their social privileges, Bakunin maintains that it is the *state* which has created capital, that the capitalist has his capital *only by the grace of the state.* As, therefore, the state is the chief evil, it is above all the state which must be done away with and then capitalism will go to blazes of itself. We, on the contrary, say: do away with capital, the concentration of all means of production in the hands of the few, and the state will fall of itself. The difference is an essential one: Without a previous social revolution the abolition of the state is nonsense; the abolition of capital *is* precisely the social revolution and involves a change in the whole mode of production. Now then, inasmuch as to Bakunin the state is the main evil, nothing must be done which can maintain the existence of the state, that is, of any state, whether it be a republic, a monarchy or anything else. Hence *complete abstention from all politics.* To commit a political act, and especially to take part in an election, would be a betrayal of principle. The thing to do is to carry on propaganda, heap abuse upon the state; organise, and when *ALL* the workers are won over, that is, the majority, depose all the authorities, abolish the state and replace it by the organisation of the International. This great act, with which the millennium begins, is called *social liquidation*.

All this sounds extremely radical, and is so simple that it can be learnt by heart in five minutes; that is why this theory of Bakunin's has speedily found favour in Italy and Spain among young lawyers, doctors and other doctrinaires. But the mass of the workers will never allow itself to be persuaded that the public affairs of their countries are not also their own affairs, they are by nature *political* and whoever tries to make out to them that they should leave politics alone will in the end be left alone. To preach to the workers that they should in all circumstances abstain from politics is to drive them into the arms of the priests of the bourgeois republicans.

Now, as the International, according to Bakunin, was not formed for political struggle but in order that it may at once replace the old state organisation as soon as social liquidation takes place, it follows that it must come as near as possible to the Bakuninist ideal of the society of the future. In this society there will above all be no *authority*, for authority = state = an absolute evil. (Indeed, how these people propose to run a factory, operate a railway or steer a ship without having in the last resort one deciding will, without single management, they of course do not tell us.) The authority of the majority over the minority also ceases. Every individual and every community is autonomous; but as to how a society, even of only two people, is possible unless each gives up some of his autonomy, Bakunin again maintains silence.

# Part Five

# Fascism

*I*s fascism possible in America today? A growing number of scholars fear that it is. David Calleo concludes *The German Problem Reconsidered* with these words: "For it is not to Germany that we would go today to find the most egregious examples of ambitions outrunning resources, nor, it might be argued, is it the Germans whose arrogant failure to adjust to a new world strains the international system beyond endurance."[1] In their *American Ideologies*, Kenneth and Patricia Dolbeare agree, insisting that "it is of the utmost importance that we free ourselves of both 'It can't happen here' mentality and the rigidly time-specific or exclusively ideological understanding of fascism."[2] According to Bertram Gross, America's future is "friendly fascism," that is, social management by a benevolent bureaucracy.[3] Neo-Nazi movements call its "friendliness" into question.

Clearly, fascism can no longer be portrayed as an isolated event, limited to France, Germany, and Italy in the interwar years. Specific factors, among them the Versailles Treaty, economic instability, authoritarian psychology, and charismatic leadership, may have contributed to those fascist outbreaks. But fascism is not a "German (French or Italian) problem." It is a human problem. To whom, then, does it appeal? What is its appeal? To answer these questions, we must examine its essential ideas.

One of those ideas is nationalism. Its roots reach back into the nineteenth century, to the writings of Joseph Mazzini and the struggle for Italian unification. Mazzini describes a nation as more than a mere territory: "It is the sentiment of love, the sense of fellowship which binds together all the sons of that territory." It is an organic whole, a moral and political unity, greater than the sum of its parts, to which individuals owe a sacred duty. For Mazzini, to be worthy of the name a nation must represent all its people; it must be a republic—"the Country of all and for all." Votes, education, and work are its common foundation.

Twentieth-century fascist dictatorships repudiated these republican principles. They also rejected Mazzini's synthesis of independence and interdependence, national and internationalism. Mazzini argued that "the universal recognition of the right of national self-determination would bring universal peace."4 Still, fascism is an extension, as well as a perversion, of Mazzini's nationalist vision. The relationship is perhaps best captured by his own words: "Men fight to lose the battle, and the thing they fought for comes about in spite of their defeat, and when it comes it turns out not to be what they meant, and other men have to fight for what they meant under another name."5

Mussolini clearly articulates fascists' relationship to nationalism; the nation fulfills the people's longing for unity. He says, "Never before have the peoples thirsted for authority, direction, order, as they do now. If each age has its doctrine, then innumerable symptoms indicate that the doctrine of our age is the Fascist." Mussolini argues that fascism replaces the now obsolete liberal and socialist ideologies. He criticizes both, focusing on their shared "theory of economic man." Mussolini argues that "the economic man does not exist. Man is integral, he is political, he is economic, he is religious, he is saint, he is warrior." This theme, "economic" versus "integral" man, informs fascist politics and economics.

Fascists argue that the economic emphasis of liberalism and socialism undermines the state. The liberal state is subordinate to individual rights, especially property rights, which it exists to protect. Socialists treat states as superstructures, instruments of the ruling class, and argue that eventually they will wither away, leaving freely organized producers. In contrast, the state is the "keystone" of fascist doctrine. Fascists glorify, even spiritualize, the state. It is man's "conscience," his "living, ethical will." Mussolini says, "Thus understood, fascism, is totalitarian, and the Fascist State—a synthesis and a unit inclusive of all values—interprets, develops, and potentiates the whole life of a people." As this suggests, fascism is anti-individualistic. It "accepts the individual only in so far as his interests coincide with those of the state." But fascists maintain that the "rights of the state" express "the real essence of the individual." Individuals find meaning through the state, especially through sacrifice for it. Positive liberty (freedom for) supersedes negative liberty (freedom from). Or, as Mussolini puts it, "Fascism stands for liberty, and for the only liberty worth having, the liberty of the State and of the individual within the State."

Fascists are also antimajoritarian. Majority rule divides states, reducing them to sums of individual interests. Hitler speaks contemptuously of representative government. Note his description of Parliament, of delegates absent or asleep, of endless, meaningless debates. Representatives, he says, are "butterflies." Each election brings on a metamorphosis: They pander to their constituents and deny responsibility for their actions. According to Hitler, great men cannot win popular elections. "The revulsion of the masses for every outstanding genius is positively instinctive. Sooner will a camel pass through a needle's eye than a great man be 'discovered' by an election." Yet only great men can embody the collective will. They rule not because of who they represent, but because of who they are: "The Führer is no 'representative' of a particular group whose wishes he must carry out. . . . He is rather the bearer of the collective will of the people. In his will the will of the people is realized. He transforms the mere feelings of the people into a conscious will." The Führer also takes responsibility for his actions, answering "with his fortune and his life for his choice."

This glorification of the state leads easily to imperialist politics. A personified state—a "living, ethical will"—grows or dies. Mussolini puts it well: "Fascism sees in the imperialistic spirit—i.e., in the tendency of nations to expand—a manifestation of their vitality. In the opposite tendency, which would limit their interests to the home country, it sees a symptom of decadence. Peoples who rise or re-arise are imperialistic; renunciation is characteristic of dying peoples." He insists, however, that this imperialism is not only territorial but also spiritual.

Fascists' attack on "economic man" also involves a critique of capitalist and socialist economies. Capitalists' free market and socialists' class war undermine national prosperity. Hitler explains: "Just as surely as a worker sins against the spirit of a real national community when, without regard for the common welfare and the survival of a national economy, he uses his power to raise extortionate demands, an employer breaks this community to the same extent when he conducts his business in an inhuman, exploiting way, misuses the national labor force and makes millions out of its sweat." He concludes that workers and employers should moderate their demands. The "class compromise" he proposes is called *corporatism*.

Corporatism involves state supervision of production and distribution through functional economic groups. Philippe Schmitter provides the classic definition: "A system of interest and/or attitude representation, a particular model or ideal-typical institutional arrangement for linking the associationally

organized interests of civil society with the decisional structures of the state."6
Schmitter distinguishes corporatism from pluralism. Pluralist interest groups
are spontaneous, competitive, voluntary, and independent; corporatist ones
are functional, cooperative, compulsory, and state sanctioned. This distinction, he admits, is difficult to draw. Although hardly parallel to Nazi super-
agencies, many advanced industrialized democracies today have industrial policies and/or planned economies. These also require integrating government,
business, and labor. Is this neoliberalism really fascism, albeit a "friendly" variety? Schmitter avoids this conclusion by distinguishing societal (bottom-up)
from state (top-down) corporatism. Others argue, however, that these arrangements differ only in degree and not in kind.7 A continuum is more appropriate than a typology. This suggests that origins matter less than outcomes, that
state and societal versions of corporatism could converge. If so, fears of a fascist America as government intervenes to stabilize the economy may be
justified. The Dolbeares' words echo Hitler's and Mussolini's: "Modern fascism is the only way capitalism as we know it will survive."8

So far, I have neglected the most often emphasized aspect of fascism: anti-
Semitism. This is because anti-Semitism is not essential to fascism, though its
functional equivalent is. To explain, I must delve brifl y into the intellectual
origins of fascism.9 Those origins are vast, ranging from the Comte de
Gobineau's racism to G.W.F. Hegel's *Staatsraison* to Joseph Mazzini's nationalism. But a more immediate influence, Friedrich Nietzsche, is relevant
here. Interpreters often try to show a direct historical connection between
Nietzsche and Nazism. This is difficult, because Nietzsche's politics are not
overtly Nazi. (He did condemn nationalism and anti-Semitism.) A more satisfactory interpretation is that Nietzsche diagnosed a crisis in Western values
and then proposed a cure that only intensified it. Nietzsche speaks of man's
need for horizons: "This is a universal law: a living thing can only be healthy,
strong, and productive within a certain horizon."10 Yet science has demystified
the modern world, destroying successive horizons. "God," Nietzsche tells us,
"is dead." Echoes of conservatism appear here, but for Nietzsche there is no
going back. His *Übermensch*, an extraordinary individual, will consciously create new horizons.

Hitler and Mussolini are such self-proclaimed creators. Hitler describes
propaganda as an "art." That art "lies in understanding the emotional ideas of
the great masses and finding, through a psychologically correct form, the way
to the attention and thence to the heart of the broad masses." To unite the
masses, leaders must give them a "scapegoat," a "common enemy." Hitler's
history of the struggle between a culture-bearing Aryan and a culture-destroy-
ing Jewish race does this. Mussolini adds the obvious: Such myths need not be
true. "We have created our myth. The myth is a faith, it is passion. It is not
necessary that it be a reality. It is reality by the fact that it is a goal, a hope, a
faith."11

A modern fascism requires new horizons, functional equivalents for Aryan anti-Semitism. Does the United States have them? Certainly racism persists in America today. Are communists also our scapegoats? Is national superiority our myth? Or, perhaps ours is a softer nihilism, a rampant relativism, a pervasive despair?[12] To the extent that Americans crave meaning and expect leaders to provide it, we are vulnerable to fascism. That vulnerability manifests itself in contemporary neo-Nazi movements. The final selection here describes the Ku Klux Klan's recent alliance with the Nazis, their new underground strategy (the fifth era), and their new political commitment (racial genocide). The Klan's radicalization does not surprise *Klanwatch* reporters. Fascism, they argue, is a logical extension of racism. They also warn that the stigma of Nazism has worn off with a new generation.

Can fascism succeed in the United States today? How deep is our liberal tradition? How strong are our psyches? Milton Mayer's *They Thought They Were Free* is among the most disturbing studies of German fascism. Mayer visited a German village in the 1940s to learn what fascism meant to its inhabitants. He listened to the villagers describe how good life was under the Nazis. The villagers belonged to the party or, at least, the nation. They had summer camps and job security. None "knew" Nazism as evil, and none opposed it. Mayer concludes, "What we call freedom is not, even if they had all the freedom we have, an adequate substitute, in my friends' view, for all that they had and have lost." The danger is that "men who did not know that they were slaves do not know that they have been freed."[13]

## Notes

1. David Calleo, *The German Problem Reconsidered: Germany and the World Order, 1870 to the Present* (Cambridge and New York: Cambridge University Press, 1978), 209.

2. Kenneth Dolbeare and Patricia Dolbeare, *American Ideologies* (Prospect Heights, Ill.: Waveland Press, 1988), 225.

3. Bertram Myron Gross, *Friendly Fascism, the New Face of Power in America* (New York: M. Evans, 1980).

4. Joseph Mazzini, *The Duties of Man*, intro. Thomas Jones (New York: Dutton, 1969), xxxiii.

5. Ibid., xxxi.

6. Philippe C. Schmitter, "Still the Century of Corporatism," *Review of Politics* 36 (January 1974): 86.

7. Michael Ranis, "On the Centralization of Interest Group Systems: Corporatist Theory in the Western Democratic Context," ms.

8. Dolbeare and Dolbeare, *American Ideologies*, 223.

9. For a brief discussion, see F.L. Carsten, *The Rise of Fascism* (Berkeley: University of California Press, 1967), chap. 1, "Nationalism and Anti-Semitism before 1914."

10. Friedrich Nietzsche, *The Use and Abuse of History*, trans. Adrian Collins (New York: Bobbs-Merrill, 1957), 7.

11. Leon P. Baradat quoted Mussolini in *Political Ideologies, Their Origins and Impact* (Englewood Cliffs, N.J.: Prentice Hall, 1984), 258.

12. The Dolbeares identify this as the "second-line defense of capitalist-liberal ideology." See Dolbeare and Dolbeare, *American Ideologies*, 229.

13. Milton Mayer, *They Thought They Were Free, The Germans*, 1933–45 (Chicago: University of Chicago Press, 1955), 62.

# JOSEPH MAZZINI

## *The Duties of Man*

Joseph Mazzini (1805–72) was an ardent Italian nationalist and republican. He founded Young Italy, an organization dedicated to liberating and uniting the Italian city-states. His life is a tale of insurrection, imprisonment, and exile. Though he lived to see Italian unification, it occurred under a monarchical, not a republican, government. He continued to work to educate his countrymen, especially the working class, until his death. *The Duties of Man,* describes man's desire for unity expressed in love of country.

### 5
### Duties to Country

Your first Duties—first, at least, in importance—are, as I have told you, to Humanity. You are *men* before you are *citizens* or *fathers.* If you do not embrace the whole human family in your love, if you do not confess your faith in its unity—consequent on the unity of God—and in the brotherhood of the Peoples who are appointed to reduce that unity to fact—if wherever one of your fellow men groans, wherever the dignity of human nature is violated by falsehood or tyranny, you are not prompt, being able, to succour that wretched one, or do not feel yourself called, being able, to fight for the purpose of relieving the deceived or oppressed—you disobey your law of life, or do not comprehend the religion which will bless the future.

But what can *each* of you, with his isolated powers, *do* for the moral improvement, for the progress of Humanity? You can, from time to time, give sterile expression to your belief; you may, on some rare occasion, perform an act of *charity* to a brother not belonging to your own land, no more. Now, *charity* is not the watchword of the future faith. The watchword of the future faith is *association,* fraternal cooperation towards a common aim, and this is as much superior to *charity* as the work of many uniting to raise with one accord a building for the habitation of all together would be superior to that which you would accomplish by raising a separate hut each for himself, and only helping one another by exchanging stones and bricks and mortar. But divided as you are in language tendencies, habits, and capacities, you cannot attempt this common work. The *individual* is too weak, and Humanity too vast. *My God,* prays the Breton mariner as he puts out to sea, *protect me, my ship is so little, and Thy ocean so great!* And this prayer sums up the condition of each of you, if no means is found of multiplying your forces and your powers of action indefinitely. But God gave you this means when he gave you a Country, when, like a wise overseer of labour, who distributes the different parts of the work according to the capacity of the workmen, he divided Humanity into distinct groups upon the face of our globe, and thus planted the seeds of nations. Bad governments have disfigured the design of God, which you may see clearly marked out, as far, at least, as regards Europe, by the courses of the great rivers, by the lines of the lofty mountains, and by other geographical conditions; they have disfigured it by conquest, by greed, by jealousy of the just sovereignty of others; disfigured it so much that to-day there is perhaps no nation except England and France whose confines correspond to this design. They did not, and they do not, recognise any country except their own families and dynasties, the egoism of caste. But the divine design will infallibly be fulfilled. Natural divisions, the innate spontaneous tendencies of the peoples will replace the arbitrary divisions sanctioned by bad governments. The map of Europe will be remade. The Countries of the People will rise, defined by the voice of the free, upon the ruins of the Countries of Kings and privileged castes. Between these Countries there will be harmony and brotherhood. And then the work of Humanity for the general amelioration, for the discovery and application of the real law of life, carried on in association and distributed according to local capacities, will be accomplished by peaceful and progressive development; then each of you, strong in the affections and in the aid of many millions of men speaking the same language, endowed with the same tendencies, and educated by the same historic tradition, may hope by your personal effort to benefit the whole of Humanity.

To you, who have been born in Italy, God has allotted, as if favouring you specially, the best-defined country in Europe. In other lands, marked by more uncertain or more interrupted limits, questions may arise which the pacific vote of all will one day solve, but which have cost, and will yet perhaps cost, tears and blood; in yours, no. God has stretched round you sublime and indisputable boundaries; on one side the highest mountains of Europe, the Alps; on the other the sea, the immeasurable sea. Take a map of Europe and place one point of a pair of compasses in the north of Italy on Parma; point the other to the mouth of the Var, and describe a semicircle with it in the direction of the Alps; this point, which will fall, when the semicircle is completed, upon the mouth of the Isonzo, will have marked the frontier which God has given you. As far as this frontier your language is spoken and understood; beyond this you have no rights. Sicily, Sardinia, Corsica, and the smaller islands between them and the mainland of Italy belong undeniably to you. Brute force may for a little while contest these frontiers with you, but they have been recognised from of old by the tacit general consent of the peoples; and the day when, rising with one accord for the final trial, you plant your tricoloured flag upon that frontier, the whole of Europe will acclaim re-risen Italy, and receive her into the community of the nations. To this final trial all your efforts must be directed.

Without Country you have neither name, token, voice, nor rights, no admission as brothers into the fellowship of the Peoples. You are the bastards of Humanity. Soldiers without a banner, Israelites among the nations, you will find neither faith nor protection; none will be sureties for you. Do not beguile yourselves with the hope of emancipation from unjust social conditions if you do not first conquer a Country for yourselves; where there is no Country there is no common agreement to which you can appeal; the egoism of self-interest rules alone, and he who has the upper hand keeps it, since there is no common safeguard for the interests of all. Do not be led away by the idea of improving your material conditions without first solving the national question. You cannot do it. Your industrial associations and mutual help societies are useful as a means of educating and disciplining yourselves; as an economic fact they will remain barren until you have an Italy. The economic problem demands, first and foremost, an increase of capital and production; and while your Country is dismembered into separate fragments—while shut off by the barrier of customs and artificial difficulties of every sort, you have only restricted markets open to you—you cannot hope for this increase. To-day —do not delude yourselves—you are not the working-class of Italy; you are only fractions of that class; powerless, unequal to the great task which you propose to yourselves. Your emancipation can have no practical beginning until a National Government, understanding the signs of the times, shall, seated in Rome, formulate a Declaration of Principles to be the guide for Italian progress, and shall insert into it these words, *Labour is sacred, and is the source of the wealth of Italy.*

Do not be led astray, then, by hopes of material progress which in your present conditions can only be illusions. Your Country alone, the vast and rich Italian Country, which stretches from the Alps to the farthest limit of Sicily, can fulfil these hopes. You cannot obtain your *rights* except by obeying the commands of *Duty*. Be worthy of them, and you will have them. O my Brothers! love your Country. Our Country is our home, the home which God has given us, placing therein a numerous family which we love and are loved by, and with which we have a more intimate and quicker communion of feeling and thought than with others; a family which by its concentration upon a given spot, and by the homogeneous nature of its elements, is destined for a special kind of activity. Our Country is our field of labour; the products of our activity must go forth from it for the benefit of the whole earth; but the instruments of labour which we can use best and most effectively exist in it, and we may not reject them without being unfaithful to God's purpose and diminishing our own strength. In labouring according to true principles for our Country we are labouring for Humanity; our Country is the fulcrum of the lever which we have to wield for the common good. If we give up this fulcrum we run the risk of becoming useless to our Country and to Humanity. Before *associating* ourselves with the Nations which compose Humanity we must exist as a Nation. There can be no association except among equals; and you have no recognised collective existence.

Humanity is a great army moving to the conquest of unknown lands, against powerful and wary enemies. The Peoples are the different corps and divisions of that army. Each has a post entrusted to it; each a special operation to perform; and the common victory depends on the exactness with which the different operations are carried out. Do not disturb the order of the battle. Do not abandon the banner which God has given you. Wherever you may be, into the midst of whatever people circumstances may have driven you, fight for the liberty of that people if the moment calls for it; but fight as Italians, so that the blood which you shed may win honour and love, not for you only, but for your Country. And may the constant thought of your soul be for Italy, may all the acts of your life be worthy of her, and may the standard beneath which you range yourselves to work for Humanity be Italy's. Do not say *I;* say *we.* Be every one of you an incarnation of your Country, and feel himself and make himself responsible for his fellow-countrymen; let each one of you learn to act in such a way that in him men shall respect and love his Country.

Your Country is one and indivisible. As the members of a family cannot rejoice at the common table if one of their number is far away, snatched from the affection of his brothers, so you should have no joy or repose as long as a portion of the territory upon which your language is spoken is separated from the Nation.

Your Country is the token of the mission which God has given you to fulfil in Humanity. The faculties, the strength of *all* its sons should be united for the accomplishment of this mission. A certain number of common duties and rights belong to every man who answers to the *Who are you?* or the other peoples, *I am an Italian.* Those duties and those rights cannot be represented except by one *single* authority resulting from your votes. A Country must have, then, a single government. The politicians who call themselves federalists, and who would make Italy into a brotherhood of different states, would dismember the Country, not understanding the idea of Unity. The States into which Italy is divided to-day are not the creation of our own people; they are the result of the ambitions and calculations of princes or of foreign conquerors, and serve no purpose but to flatter the vanity of local aristocracies for which a narrower sphere than a great Country is necessary. What you, the people, have created, beautified, and consecrated with your affections, with your joys, with your sorrows, and with your blood, is the City and the Commune, not the Province or the State. In the City, in the Commune, where your fathers sleep and where your children will live, where you exercise your faculties and your personal rights, you live out your lives as *individuals.* It is of your City that each of you can say what the Venetians say of theirs: *Venezia la xe nostra: l'avemo fatta nu* (Venice is our own: we have made her). In your City you have need of *liberty* as in your Country you have need of *association.* The Liberty of the Commune and the Unity of the Country—let that, then, be your faith. Do not say Rome and Tuscany, Rome and Lombardy, Rome and Sicily; say Rome and Florence, Rome and Siena, Rome and Leghorn, and so through all the Communes of Italy. Rome for all that represents Italian life; your commune for whatever represents the *individual* life. All the other divisions are artificial, and are not confirmed by your national tradition.

A Country is a fellowship of free and equal men bound together in a brotherly concord of labour towards a single end. You must make it and maintain it such. A Country is not an aggregation, it is an *association.* There is no true Country without a uniform right. There is no true Country where the uniformity of that right is violated by the existence of caste, privilege, and inequality—where the powers and faculties of a large number of individuals are suppressed or dormant—where there is no common principle accepted, recognised, and developed by all. In such a state of things there can be no Nation, no People, but only a multitude, a fortuitous agglomeration of men whom circumstances have brought together and different circumstances will separate. In the name of your love for your Country you must combat without truce the existence of every privilege, every inequality, upon the soil which has given you birth. One privilege only is lawful—the privilege of Genius when Genius reveals itself in brotherhood with Virtue; but it is a privilege conceded by God and not by men, and when you acknowledge it and follow its inspirations, you acknowledge it freely by the exercise of your own reason and your own choice. Whatever privilege claims your submission in virtue of force or heredity, or any right which is not a common right, is a usurpation and a tyranny, and you ought to combat it and annihilate it. Your Country should be your Temple. God at the summit, a People of equals at the base. Do not accept any other formula, any other moral law, if you do not want to dishonour your Country and yourselves. Let the secondary laws for the gradual regulation of your existence be the progressive application of this supreme law.

And in order that they should be so, it is necessary that *all* should contribute to the making of them. The laws made by one fraction of the citizens only can never by the nature of things and men do otherwise than reflect the thoughts and aspirations and desires of that fraction; they represent, not the whole country, but a third, a fourth part, a class, a zone of the country. The law must express the general aspiration, promote the good of all, respond to a beat of the nation's heart. The whole nation therefore should be, directly or indirectly, the legislator. By yielding this mission to a few men, you put the egoism of one class in the place of the Country, which is the union of *all* the classes.

A Country is not a mere territory; the particular territory is only its foundation. The Country is the idea which rises upon that foundation; it is the sentiment of love, the sense of fellowship which binds together all the sons of that territory. So long as a single one of your brothers is not represented by his own vote in the development of the national life—so long as a single one vegetates uneducated among the educated—so long as a single one able and willing to work languishes in poverty for want of work—you have not got a Country such as it ought to be, the Country of all and for all. *Votes, education, work* are the three main pillars of the nation; do not rest until your hands have solidly erected them.

And when they have been erected—when you have secured for every one of you food for both body and soul—when freely united, entwining your right hands like brothers round a beloved mother, you advance in beautiful and holy concord towards the development of your faculties and the fulfilment of the Italian mission—remember that that mission is the moral unity of Europe; remember the immense duties which it imposes upon you. Italy is the only land that has twice uttered the great word of unification to the disjoined nations. Twice Rome has been the metropolis, the temple, of the European world; the first time when our conquering eagles traversed the known world from end to end and prepared it for union by introducing civilised institutions; the second time when, after the Northern conquerors had themselves been subdued by the potency of Nature, of great memories and of religious inspiration, the genius of Italy incarnated itself in the Papacy and undertook the solemn mission—abandoned four centuries ago—of preaching the union of souls to the peoples of the Christian world. To-day a third mission is dawning for our Italy; as much vaster than those of old as the Italian People, the free and united Country which you are going to found, will be greater and more powerful than Caesars or Popes. The presentiment of this mission agitates Europe and keeps the eye and the thought of the nations chained to Italy.

Your duties to your Country are proportioned to the loftiness of this mission. You have to keep it pure from egoism, uncontaminated by falsehood and by the arts of that political Jesuitism which they call diplomacy.

The government of the country will be based through your labours upon the worship of principles, not upon the idolatrous worship of interests and of opportunity. There are countries in Europe where Liberty is sacred within, but is systematically violated without; peoples who say, *Truth is one thing, utility another: theory is one thing, practice another.* Those countries will have inevitably to expiate their guilt in long isolation, oppression, and anarchy. But you know the mission of our Country, and will pursue another path. Through you Italy will have, with one only God in the heavens, one only truth, one only faith, one only rule of political life upon earth. Upon the edifice, sublimer than Capitol or Vatican, which the people of Italy will raise, you will plant the banner of Liberty and of Association, so that it shines in the sight of all the nations, nor will you lower it ever for terror of despots or lust for the gains of a day. You will have boldness as you have faith. You will speak out aloud to the world, and to those who call themselves the lords of the world, the thought which thrills in the heart of Italy. You will never deny the sister nations. The life of the Country shall grow through you in beauty and in strength, free from servile fears and the hesitations of doubt, keeping as its *foundation* the people, as its *rule* the consequences of its principles logically deduced and energetically applied, as its *strength* the strength of all, as its *outcome* the amelioration of all, as its *end* the fulfilment of the mission which God has given it. And because you will be ready to die for Humanity, the life of your Country will be immortal.

# BENITO MUSSOLINI

## *Fascism: Doctrine and Institutions*

Benito Mussolini (1883–1945) led the Fascist movement to power in
Italy. In 1925, he declared himself head of state, ended parliamentary
government, and outlawed opposing political parties. In 1940, he
joined the Axis powers in declaring war on the Allies. But his poor
leadership during the war led the Fascist Grand Council to dismiss,
arrest, and imprison him in 1943. He was later rescued by the Germans, only to be recaptured and executed by the Italians after the
defeat of Germany. Although many of his works were ghost-written,
he authored such slogans as "Feel don't think"; "Believe, obey,
fight"; and "Fascism is Mussolinism; Mussolini is always right."

### Fundamental Ideas

Like all sound political conceptions, Fascism is action and it is thought; action
in which doctrine is immanent, and doctrine arising from a given system of
historical forces in which it is inserted, and working on them from within (1).
It has therefore a form correlated to contingencies of time and space; but it has
also an ideal content which makes it an expression of truth in the higher region of the history of thought (2). There is no way of exercising a spiritual
influence in the world as a human will dominating the will of others, unless
one has a conception both of the transient and the specific reality on which
that action is to be exercised, and of the permanent and universal reality in
which the transient dwells and has its being. To know men one must know
man; and to know man one must be acquainted with reality and its laws.
There can be no conception of the State which is not fundamentally a conception of life: philosophy or intuition, system of ideas evolving within the framework of logic or concentrated in a vision or a faith, but always, at least potentially, an organic conception of the world.

Thus many of the practical expressions of Fascism—such as party organisation, system of education, discipline—can only be understood when
considered in relation to its general attitude toward life. A spiritual attitude

(3). Fascism sees in the world not only those superficial, material aspects in which man appears as an individual, standing by himself, self-centered, subject to natural law which instinctively urges him toward a life of selfish momentary pleasure; it sees not only the individual but the nation and the country; individuals and generations bound together by a moral law, with common traditions and a mission which suppressing the instinct for life closed in a brief circle of pleasure, builds up a higher life, founded on duty, a life free from the limitations of time and space, in which the individual, by self-sacrifice, the renunciation of self-interest, by death itself, can achieve that purely spiritual existence in which his value as a man consists.

The conception is therefore a spiritual one, arising from the general reaction of the century against the fla[c]cid materialistic positivism of the nineteenth century. Anti-positivistic but positive; neither sceptical nor agnostic; neither pessimistic nor supinely optimistic as are, generally speaking, the doctrines (all negative) which place the centre of life outside man; whereas, by the exercise of his free will, man can and must create his own world.

Fascism wants man to be active and to engage in action with all his energies; it wants him to be manfully aware of the difficulties besetting him and ready to face them. It conceives of life as a struggle in which it behoves a man to win for himself a really worthy place, first of all by fitting himself (physically, morally, intellectually) to become the implement required for winning it. As for the individual, so for the nation, and so for mankind (4). Hence the high value of culture in all its forms (artistic, religious, scientific) (5), and the outstanding importance of education. Hence also the essential value of work, by which man subjugates nature and creates the human world (economic, political, ethical, intellectual).

This positive conception of life is obviously an ethical one. It invests the whole field of reality as well as the human activities which master it. No action is exempt from moral judgement; no activity can be despoiled of the value which a moral purpose confers on all things. Therefore life, as conceived of by the Fascist, is serious, austere, religious; all its manifestations are poised in a world sustained by moral forces and subject to spiritual responsibilities. The Fascist disdains an "easy" life (6).

The Fascist conception of life is a religious one (7), in which man is viewed in his immanent relation to a higher law, endowed with an objective will transcending the individual and raising him to conscious membership of a spiritual society. Those who perceive nothing beyond opportunistic considerations in the religious policy of the Fascist regime fail to realize that Fascism is not only a system of government but also and above all a system of thought.

In the Fascist conception of history, man is man only by virtue of the spiritual process to which he contributes as a member of the family, the social group, the nation, and in function of history to which all nations bring their contribution. Hence the great value of tradition in records, in language, in customs, in the rules of social life (8). Outside history man is a nonentity. Fascism is therefore opposed to all individualistic abstractions based on eighteenth century materialism; and it is opposed to all Jacobinistic utopias and innovations. It does not believe in the possibility of "happiness" on earth as conceived by the economistic literature of the eighteenth century, and it therefore rejects the teleological notion that at some future time the human family will secure a final settlement of all its difficulties. This notion runs counter to experience which teaches that life is in continual flux and in process of evolution. In politics Fascism aims at realism; in practice it desires to deal only with those problems which are the spontaneous product of historic conditions and which find or suggest their own solutions (9). Only by entering in to the process of reality and taking possession of the forces at work within it, can man act on man and on nature (10).

Anti-individualistic, the Fascist conception of life stresses the importance of the State and accepts the individual only in so far as his interests coincide with those of the State, which stands for the conscience and the universal will of man as a historic entity (11). It is opposed to classical liberalism which arose as a reaction to absolutism and exhausted its historical function when the State became the expression of the conscience and will of the people. Liberalism denied the State in the name of the individual; Fascism reasserts the rights of the State as expressing the real essence of the individual (12). And if liberty is to be the attribute of living men and not of abstract dummies invented by individualistic liberalism, then Fascism stands for liberty, and for the only liberty worth having, the liberty of the State and of the individual within the State (13). The Fascist conception of the State is all-embracing; outside of it no human or spiritual values can exist, much less have value. Thus understood, Fascism is totalitarian, and the Fascist State—a synthesis and a unit inclusive of all values—interprets, develops, and potentiates the whole life of a people (14).

No individuals or groups (political parties, cultural associations, economic unions, social classes) outside the State (15). Fascism is therefore opposed to Socialism to which unity within the State (which amalgamates classes into a single economic and ethical reality) is unknown, and which sees in history nothing but the class struggle. Fascism is likewise opposed to tradeunionism as a class weapon. But when brought within the orbit of the State, Fascism recognises the real needs which gave rise to socialism and tradeunionism, giving them due weight in the guild or corporative system in which divergent interests are coordinated and harmonised in the unity of the State (16).

Grouped according to their several interests, individuals form classes; they form trade-unions when organised according to their several economic activities; but first and foremost they form the State, which is no mere matter of numbers, the sum of the individuals forming the majority. Fascism is therefore opposed to that form of democracy which equates a nation to the majority, lowering it to the level of the largest number (17); but it is the purest form of democracy if the nation be considered—as it should be—from the point of view of quality rather than quantity, as an idea, the mightiest because the most ethical, the most coherent, the truest, expressing itself in a people as the conscience and will of the few, if not, indeed, of one, and ending to express itself in the conscience and the will of the mass, of the whole group ethnically moulded by natural and historical conditions into a nation, advancing, as one conscience and one will, along the self-same line of development and spiritual formation (18). Not a race, nor a geographically defined region, but a people, historically perpetuating itself; a multitude unified by an idea and imbued with the will to live, the will to power, self-consciousness, personality (19).

In so far as it is embodied in a State, this higher personality becomes a nation. It is not the nation which generates the State; that is an antiquated naturalistic concept which afforded a basis for nineteenth-century publicity in favor of national governments. Rather is it the State which creates the nation, conferring volition and therefore real life on a people made aware of their moral unity.

The right to national independence does not arise from any merely literary and idealistic form of self-consciousness; still less from a more or less passive and unconscious *de facto* situation, but from an active, self-conscious, political will expressing itself in action and ready to prove its rights. It arises, in short, from the existence, at least *in fieri*, of a State. Indeed, it is the State which, as the expression of a universal ethical will, creates the right to national independence (20).

A nation, as expressed in the State, is a living, ethical entity only in so far as it is progressive. Inactivity is death. Therefore the State is not only Authority which governs and confers legal form and spiritual value on individual wills, but it is also Power which makes its will felt and respected beyond its own frontiers, thus affording practical proof of the universal character of the decisions necessary to ensure its development. This implies organisation and expansion, potential it not actual. Thus the State equates itself to the will of man, whose development cannot be checked by obstacles and which, by achieving self-expression, demonstrates its own infinity (21).

The Fascist State, as a higher and more powerful expression of personality, is a force, but a spiritual one. It sums up all the manifestations of the moral and intellectual life of man. Its functions cannot therefore be limited to those of enforcing order and keeping the peace, as the liberal doctrine had it. It is no mere mechanical device for defining the sphere within which the individual may duly exercise his supposed rights. The Fascist State is an inwardly accepted standard and rule of conduct, a discipline of the whole person; it permeates the will no less than the intellect. It stands for a principle which becomes the central motive of man as a member of civilised society, sinking deep down into his personality; it dwells in the heart of the man of action and of the thinker, of the artist and of the man of science: soul of the soul (22).

Fascism, in short, is not only a law-giver and a founder of institutions, but an educator and a promoter of spiritual life. It aims at refashioning not only the forms of life but their content—man, his character, and his faith. To achieve this purpose it enforces discipline and uses authority, entering into the soul and ruling with undisputed sway. Therefore it has chosen as its emblem the Lictor's rods, the symbol of unity, strength, and justice.

## Political and Social Doctrine

... The Fascist negation of socialism, democracy, liberalism, should not, however, be interpreted as implying a desire to drive the world backwards to positions occupied prior to 1789, a year commonly referred to as that which opened the demo-liberal century. History does not travel backwards. The Fascist doctrine has not taken [Joseph] De Maistre as its prophet. Monarchical absolutism is of the past, and so is ecclesiolatry. Dead and done for are feudal privileges and the division of society into closed, uncommunicating castes. Neither has the Fascist conception of authority anything in common with that of a police-ridden State.

A party governing a nation "totalitarianly" is a new departure in history. There are no points of reference nor of comparison. From beneath the ruins of liberal, socialist, and democratic doctrines, Fascism extracts those elements which are still vital. It preserves what may be described as "the acquired facts" of history; it rejects all else. That is to say, it rejects the idea of a doctrine suited to all times and to all people. Granted that the nineteenth century was the century of socialism, liberalism, democracy, this does not mean that the twentieth century must also be the century of socialism, liberalism, democracy. Political doctrines pass; nations remain. We are free to believe that this is the century of authority, a century tending to the "right," a Fascist century. If the nineteenth century was the century of the individual (liberalism implies individualism), we are free to believe that this is the "collective" century, and therefore the century of the State. It is quite logical for a new doctrine to make use of the still vital elements of other doctrines. No doctrine was ever born quite new and bright and unheard of. No doctrine can boast absolute originality. It is always connected, if only historically, with those which preceded it and those which will follow it. Thus the scientific socialism of Marx links up to the utopian socialism of the Fouriers, the Owens, the Saint-Simons; thus the liberalism of the nineteenth century traces its origin back to the illuministic movement of the eighteenth, and the doctrines of democracy to those of the Encyclopaedists. All doctrines aim at directing the activities of men towards a given objective; but these activities in their turn react on the doctrine, modifying and adjusting it to new needs, or outstripping it. A doctrine must therefore be a vital act and not a verbal display. Hence the pragmatic strain in Fascism, its will to power, its will to live, its attitude toward violence, and its value.

The key-stone of the Fascist doctrine is its conception of the State, of its essence, its functions, and its aims. For Fascism the State is absolute, individuals and groups relative. Individuals and groups are admissable in so far as they come within the State. Instead of directing the game and guiding the material and moral progress of the community, the liberal State restricts its activities to recording results. The Fascist State is wide awake and has a will of its own. For this reason it can be described as "ethical." At the first quinquennial assembly of the regime, in 1929, I said:

> The Fascist State is not a night-watchman, solicitous only of the personal safety of the citizens; nor is it organised exclusively for the purpose of guarantying a certain degree of material prosperity and relatively peaceful conditions of life, a board of directors would do as much. Neither is it exclusively political, divorced from practical realities and holding itself aloof from the multifarious activities of the citizens and the nation. The State, as conceived and realised by Fascism, is a spiritual and ethical entity for securing the political, juridical, and economic organisation of the nation, an organisation which in its origin and growth is a manifestation of the spirit. The State guarantees the internal and external safety of the country, but it also safeguards and transmits the spirit of the people, elaborated down the ages in its language, its customs, its faith. The State is not only the present, it is also the past and above all the future. Transcending the individual's brief spell of life, the State stands for the immanent conscience of the nation. The forms in which it finds expression change, but the need for it remains. The State educates the citizens to civism, makes them aware of their mission, urges them to unity; its justice harmonises their divergent interests; it transmits to future generations the conquests of the mind in the fields of science, art, law, human solidarity; it leads men up from primitive tribal life to that highest manifestation of human power, imperial rule. The State hands down to future generations the memory of those who laid down their lives to ensure its safety or to obey its laws; it sets up as examples and records for future ages the names of the captains who enlarged its territory and of the men of genius who have made it famous. Whenever respect for the State declines and the disintegrating and centrifugal tendencies of individuals and groups prevail, nations are headed for decay.

Since 1929 economic and political development have everywhere emphasised these truths. The importance of the State is rapidly growing. The so-called crisis can only be settled by State action and within the orbit of the State. Where are the shades of the Jules Simons who, in the early days of liberalism proclaimed that the "State should endeavor to render itself useless and prepare to hand in its resignation"? Or of the MacCullochs who in the second half of last century urged that the State should desist from governing too much? And what of the English Bentham who considered that all industry asked of government was to be left alone, and of the German Humbolt who expressed the opinion that the best government was a "lazy" one? What would they say now to the unceasing, inevitable, and urgently requested interventions of government in business? It is true that the second generation of economists was less uncompromising in this respect than the first, and that even Adam Smith left the door ajar—however cautiously—for government intervention in business.

If liberalism spells individualism, Fascism spells government. The Fascist State is, however, a unique and original creation. It is not reactionary but revolutionary, for it anticipates the solution of certain universal problems which have been raised elsewhere, in the political field by the splitting-up of parties, the usurpation of power by parliaments, the irresponsibility of assemblies; in the economic field by the increasingly numerous and important functions discharged by trade-unions and trade associations with their disputes and ententes, affecting both capital and labor; in the ethical field by the need felt for order, discipline, obedience to the moral dictates of patriotism.

Fascism desires the State to be strong and organic, based on broad foundations of popular support. The Fascist State lays claim to rule in the economic field no less than in others; it makes its action felt throughout the length and breadth of the country by means of its corporative, social, and educational institutions, and all the political, economic, and spiritual forces of the nation, organised in their respective associations, circulate within the State.

A State based on millions of individuals who recognise its authority, feel its action, and are ready to serve its ends is not the tyrannical state of a mediaeval lordling. It has nothing in common with the despotic States existing prior to or subsequent to 1789. Far from crushing the individual, the Fascist State multiplies his energies, just as in a regiment a soldier is not diminished but multiplied by the number of his fellow soldiers.

The Fascist State organises the nation, but it leaves the individual adequate elbow room. It has curtailed useless or harmful liberties while preserving those which are essential. In such matters the individual cannot be the judge, but the State only.

The Fascist State is not indifferent to religious phenomena in general nor does it maintain an attitude of indifference to Roman Catholicism, the special, positive religion of Italians. The State has not got a theology but it has a moral code. The Fascist State sees in religion one of the deepest of spiritual manifestations and for this reason it not only respects religion but defends and protects it. The Fascist State does not attempt, as did Robespierre at the height of the revolutionary delirium of the convention, to set up a "god" of its own; nor does it vainly seek, as does Bolschevism, to efface God from the soul of man. Fascism respects the God of ascetics, saints, and heroes, and it also respects God as conceived by the ingenuous and primitive heart of the people, the God to whom their prayers are raised.

The Fascist State expresses the will to exercise power and to command. Here the Roman tradition is embodied in a conception of strength. Imperial power, as understood by the Fascist doctrine, is not only territorial, or military, or commercial; it is also spiritual and ethical. An imperial nation, that is to say a nation which directly or indirectly is a leader of others, can exist without the need of conquering a single square mile of territory. Fascism sees in the imperialistic spirit—i.e. in the tendency of nations to expand—a manifestation of their vitality. In the opposite tendency, which would limit their interests to the home country, it sees a symptom of decadence. Peoples who rise or rearise are imperialistic; renunciation is characteristic of dying peoples. The Fascist doctrine is that best suited to the tendencies and feelings of a people which, like the Italian, after lying fallow during centuries of foreign servitude, is now reasserting itself in the world.

But imperialism implies discipline, the coordination of efforts, a deep sense of duty and a spirit of self-sacrifice. This explains many aspects of the practical activity of the regime, and the direction taken by many of the forces of the State, as also the severity which has to be exercised towards those who would oppose this spontaneous and inevitable movement of twentieth-century Italy by agitating outgrown ideologies of the nineteenth century, ideologies rejected wherever great experiments in political and social transformations are being dared.

Never before have the peoples thirsted for authority, direction order, as they do now. If each age has its doctrine, then innumerable symptoms indicate that the doctrine of our age is the Fascist. That it is vital is shown by the fact that it has aroused a faith; that this faith has conquered souls is shown by the fact that Fascism can point to its fallen heroes and its martyrs.

Fascism has now acquired throughout the world that universality which belongs to all doctrines which by achieving self-expression represent a moment in the history of human thought.

### The Corporations

The statement I submitted yesterday evening defined the guild as we intend and wish to create it, and it also defined its objectives. The corporation, it says, is formed to expand the wealth, the political power, and the well-being of the Italian people. These three objectives are conditional each on the other.

Political strength creates wealth, and wealth in its turn invigorates political action.

I should like to call your attention to the objective stated: the well-being of the Italian people. It is essential that these institutions we have set up should at a given moment be felt and perceived by the masses themselves as instruments through which those masses improve their standard of life.

At a given moment the worker, the tiller of the soil, must be able to say to himself and to his family: if I am really better off to-day, it is due to the institutions which the Fascist Revolution has created.

In all national societies there is an inevitable residuum of poverty. A certain number of people live on the margin of society; special institutions deal with them. Viceversa, that which distresses our spirit is the poverty of strong, capable men, feverishly and vainly seeking work.

We wish that the Italian workers, who interest us as Italians, as workers, and as Fascists, should feel that we are setting up institutions not only to give expression to our doctrinal views but that we are setting up institutions which at a given moment are to yield positive results; concrete, practical, and tangible.

I will not dwell on the conciliatory functions which the corporations can exercise and I see no drawback to the practice of conciliation.

Whenever the Government has to take measures of some importance it already consults the parties concerned. If to-morrow this consultation on certain specified matters becomes obligatory I see no harm in it, for everything that brings the citizen into closer contact with the State, everything that makes the citizen part of the machinery of the State, is advantageous to the social and national aims of Fascism.

### A Step Forward on the Path of the Revolution

We have rejected the theory of the economic man, the liberal theory, and we have risen in indignation every time we have heard labor spoken of as a commodity.

The economic man does not exist. Man is integral, he is political, he is economic, he is religious, he is saint, he is warrior.

To-day we are taking a further step forward on the path of the revolution. . . .

In conclusion, let us ask ourselves: can the guild system be applied to other countries? We should ask this question because it is being asked in all other countries; everywhere the matter is being studied and efforts are being made to understand. There is no doubt that in view of the general crisis of capitalism the guild solution will force itself to the front everywhere, but if the guild system is to be carried out fully, completely, integrally, revolutionarily, three conditions are required:

A single party, so that economic discipline may be accompanied by political discipline and so that rising above contrasting interests all may be bound together by a common faith.

Nor is this enough. After the single party there must be the totalitarian

State, that is to say the State which absorbs all the energies, all the interests, all the hopes of a people in order to transform and potentiate them.

And this is not yet enough. The third and last and most important condition is to live a period of high ideal tension.

That is why, step by step, we shall strengthen and consolidate all our achievements, why we shall translate into action our whole doctrine. Who can deny that our Fascist period is a period of high ideal tension? No one can deny it. This is the time in which arms have been crowned with victory; institutions renewed; the land redeemed; new cities founded.

# ADOLF HITLER

## *Mein Kampf*

The son of a minor customs official, Adolf Hitler (1889–1945) rose to become the leader of the Third Reich. His magnum opus, *Mein Kampf,* was published in 1925. Early sales were small, but by the late 1920s the book had become a bestseller. The success of Hitler and his party, the National Socialists (NSDAP), was closely linked to the Great Depression. As Germany's economy collapsed, Hitler offered explanations for its problems and solutions to them. Imperialism, part of his solution, led to his demise. He died in 1945, in a Berlin bunker encircled by Allied troops.

### [Representative Government]

At the head of those institutions which could most clearly have revealed the erosion of the Austrian monarchy, even to a shopkeeper not otherwise gifted with sharp eyes, was one which ought to have had the greatest strength—parliament, or, as it was called in Austria, the Reichsrat.

Obviously the example of this body had been taken from England, the land of classical "democracy." From there the whole blissful institution was taken and transferred as unchanged as possible to Vienna.

The English two-chamber system was solemnly resurrected in the *Abgeordnetenhaus* and the *Herrenhaus.* Except that the "houses" themselves were somewhat different. When Barry raised his parliament buildings from the waters of the Thames, he thrust into the history of the British Empire and from it took the decorations for the twelve hundred niches, consoles, and pillars of his magnificent edifice. Thus, in their sculpture and painting, the House of Lords and the House of Commons became the nation's Hall of Fame.

This was where the first difficulty came in for Vienna. For when Hansen, the Danish builder, had completed the last pinnacle on the marble building of the new parliament, there was nothing he could use as decoration except borrowings from antiquity. Roman and Greek statesmen and philosophers now embellish this opera house of Western democracy, and in symbolic irony the *quadrigae* fly from one another in all four directions above the two houses, in this way giving the best external expression of the activities that went on inside the building.

The "nationalities" had vetoed the glorification of Austrian history in this work as an insult and provocation, just as in the Reich itself it was only beneath the thunder of World War battles that they dared to dedicate Wallot's Reichstag Building to the German people by an inscription.

When, not yet twenty years old, I set foot for the first time in the magnificent building on the Franzensring to attend a session of the House of Deputies as a spectator and listener, I was seized with the most conflicting sentiments.

I had always hated parliament, but not as an institution in itself. On the contrary, as a freedom-loving man I could not even conceive of any other possibility of government, for the idea of any sort of dictatorship would, in view of my attitude toward the House of Habsburg, have seemed to me a crime against freedom and all reason.

What contributed no little to this was that as a young man, in consequence of my extensive newspaper reading, I had, without myself realizing it, been inoculated with a certain admiration for the British Parliament, of which I was not easily able to rid myself. The dignity with which the Lower House there fulfilled its tasks (as was so touchingly described in our press) impressed me immensely. Could a people have any more exalted form of self-government?

But for this very reason I was an enemy of the Austrian parliament. I considered its whole mode of conduct unworthy of the great example. To this the following was now added:

The fate of the Germans in the Austrian state was dependent on their position in the Reichsrat. Up to the introduction of universal and secret suffrage, the Germans had had a majority, though an insignificant one, in parliament. Even this condition was precarious, for the Social Democrats, with their unreliable attitude in national questions, always turned against German interests in critical matters affecting the Germans—in order not to alienate the members of the various foreign nationalities. Even in those days the Social Democracy could not be regarded as a German party. And with the introduction of universal suffrage the German superiority ceased even in a purely numerical sense. There was no longer any obstacle in the path of the further de-Germanization of the state.

For this reason my instinct of national self-preservation caused me even in those days to have little love for a representative body in which the Germans were always misrepresented rather than represented. Yet these were deficiencies which, like so many others, were attributable, not to the thing in itself, but to the Austrian state. I still believed that if a German majority were restored in the representative bodies, there would no longer be any reason for a principled op-position to them, that is, as long as the old state continued to exist at all.

These were my inner sentiments when for the first time I set foot in these halls as hallowed as they were disputed. For me, to be sure, they were hallowed only by the lofty beauty of the magnificent building. A Hellenic miracle on German soil!

How soon was I to grow indignant when I saw the lamentable comedy that unfolded beneath my eyes!

Present were a few hundred of these popular representatives who had to take a position on a question of most vital economic importance.

The very first day was enough to stimulate me to thought for weeks on end.

The intellectual content of what these men said was on a really depress-ing level, in so far as you could understand their babbling at all; for several of the gentlemen did not speak German, but their native Slavic languages or rather dialects. I now had occasion to hear with my own ears what previously I had known only from reading the newspapers. A wild gesticulating mass screaming all at once in every different key, presided over by a good-natured old uncle who was striving in the sweat of his brow to revive the dignity of the House by violently ringing his bell and alternating gentle reproofs with grave admonitions.

I couldn't help laughing.

A few weeks later I was in the House again. The picture was changed be-yond recognition. The hall was absolutely empty. Down below everybody was asleep. A few deputies were in their places, yawning at one another; one was "speaking." A vice-president of the House was present, looking into the hall with obvious boredom.

The first misgivings arose in me. From now on, whenever time offered me the slightest opportunity, I went back and, with silence and attention, viewed whatever picture presented itself, listened to the speeches in so far as they were intelligible, studied the more or less intelligent faces of the elect of the peoples of this woe-begone state—and little by little formed my own ideas.

A year of this tranquil observation sufficed totally to change or eliminate my former view of the nature of this institution. My innermost position was no longer against the misshapen form which this idea assumed in Austria; no, by now I could no longer accept the parliament as such. Up till then I had seen the misfortune of the Austrian parliament in the absence of a German majority; now I saw that its ruination lay in the whole nature and essence of the institution as such.

A whole series of questions rose up in me.

I began to make myself familiar with the democratic principle of majority rule as the foundation of this whole institution, but devoted no less attention to the intellectual and moral values of these gentlemen, supposedly the elect of the nations, who were expected to serve this purpose.

Thus I came to know the institution and its representatives at once.

In the course of a few years, my knowledge and insight shaped a plastic model of that most dignified phenomenon of modern times: the parliamentarian. He began to impress himself upon me in a form which has never since been subjected to any essential change.

Here again the visual instruction of practical reality had prevented me from being stifled by a theory which at first sight seemed seductive to so many, but which none the less must be counted among the symptoms of human degeneration.

The Western democracy of today is the forerunner of Marxism which without it would not be thinkable. It provides this world plague with the culture in which its germs can spread. In its most extreme form, parliamentarianism created a "monstrosity of excrement and fire,"[1] in which, however, sad to say, the "fire" seems to me at the moment to be burned out.

I must be more than thankful to Fate for laying this question before me while I was in Vienna, for I fear that in Germany at that time I would have found the answer too easily. For if I had first encountered this absurd institution known as "parliament" in Berlin, I might have fallen into the opposite fallacy, and not without seemingly good cause have sided with those who saw the salvation of the people and the Reich exclusively in furthering the power of the imperial idea, and who nevertheless were alien and blind at once to the times and the people involved.

In Austria this was impossible.

Here it was not so easy to go from one mistake to the other. If parliament was worthless, the Habsburgs were even more worthless—in no event, less so. To reject "parliamentarianism" was not enough, for the question still remained open: what then? The rejection and abolition of the Reichsrat would have left the House of Habsburg the sole governing force, a thought which, especially for me, was utterly intolerable.

The difficulty of this special case led me to a more thorough contemplation of the problem as such than would otherwise have been likely at such tender years.

What gave me most food for thought was the obvious absence of any responsibility in a single person.

The parliament arrives at some decision whose consequences may be ever so ruinous—nobody bears any responsibility for this, no one can be taken to account. For can it be called an acceptance of responsibility if, after an unparalleled catastrophe, the guilty government resigns? Or if the coalition changes, or even if parliament is itself dissolved?

Can a fluctuating majority of people ever be made responsible in any case?

Isn't the very idea of responsibility bound up with the individual?

But can an individual directing a government be made practically responsible for actions whose preparation and execution must be set exclusively to the account of the will and inclination of a multitude of men?

Or will not the task of a leading statesman be seen, not in the birth of a creative idea or plan as such, but rather in the art of making the brilliance of his projects intelligible to a herd of sheep and blockheads, and subsequently begging for their kind approval?

Is it the criterion of the statesman that he should possess the art of persuasion in as high degree as that of political intelligence in formulating great policies or decisions? Is the incapacity of a leader shown by the fact that he does not succeed in winning for a certain idea the majority of a mob thrown together by more or less savory accidents?

Indeed, has this mob ever understood an idea before success proclaimed its greatness?

Isn't every deed of genius in this world a visible protest of genius against the inertia of the mass?

And what should the statesman do, who does not succeed in gaining the favor of this mob for his plans by flattery?

Should he buy it?

Or, in view of the stupidity of his fellow citizens, should he renounce the execution of the tasks which he has recognized to be vital necessities? Should he resign or should he remain at his post?

In such a case, doesn't a man of true character find himself in a hopeless conflict between knowledge and decency, or rather honest conviction?

Where is the dividing line between his duty toward the general public and his duty toward his personal honor?

Mustn't every true leader refuse to be thus degraded to the level of a political gangster?

And, conversely, mustn't every gangster feel that he is cut out for politics, since it is never he, but some intangible mob, which has to bear the ultimate responsibility?

Mustn't our principle of parliamentary majorities lead to the demolition of any idea of leadership?

Does anyone believe that the progress of this world springs from the mind of majorities and not from the brains of individuals?

Or does anyone expect that the future will be able to dispense with this premise of human culture?

Does it not, on the contrary, today seem more indispensable than ever?

By rejecting the authority of the individual and replacing it by the numbers of some momentary mob, the parliamentary principle of majority rule sins against the basic aristocratic principle of Nature, though it must be said that this view is not necessarily embodied in the present-day decadence of our upper ten thousand.

The devastation caused by this institution of modern parliamentary rule is hard for the reader of Jewish newspapers to imagine, unless he has learned to think and examine independently. It is, first and foremost, the cause of the incredible inundation of all political life with the most inferior, and I mean the most inferior, characters of our time. Just as the true leader will withdraw from all political activity which does not consist primarily in creative achievement and work, but in bargaining and haggling for the favor of the majority, in the same measure this activity will suit the small mind and consequently attract it.

The more dwarfish one of these present-day leather-merchants is in spirit and ability, the more clearly his own insight makes him aware of the lamentable figure he actually cuts—that much more will he sing the praises of a system which does not demand of him the power and genius of a giant, but is satisfied with the craftiness of a village mayor, preferring in fact this kind of wisdom to that of a Pericles. And this kind doesn't have to torment himself with responsibility for his actions. He is entirely removed from such worry, for he well knows that, regardless what the result of his "statesmanlike" bungling may be, his end has long been written in the stars: one day he will have to cede his place to another equally great mind, for it is one of the characteristics of this decadent system that the number of great statesmen increases in proportion as the stature of the individual decreases. With increasing dependence on parliamentary majorities it will inevitably continue to shrink, since on the one hand great minds will refuse to be the stooges of idiotic incompetents and big-mouths, and on the other, conversely, the representatives of the majority, hence of stupidity, hate nothing more passionately than a superior mind.

For such an assembly of wise men of Gotham, it is always a consolation to know that they are headed by a leader whose intelligence is at the level of those present: this will give each one the pleasure of shining from time to time—and, above all, if Tom can be master, what is to prevent Dick and Harry from having their turn too?

This invention of democracy is most intimately related to a quality which in recent times has grown to be a real disgrace, to wit, the cowardice of a great part of our so-called "leadership." What luck to be able to hide behind the skirts of a so-called majority in all decisions of any real importance!

Take a look at one of these political bandits. How anxiously he begs the approval of the majority for every measure, to assure himself of the necessary accomplices, so he can unload the responsibility at any time. And this is one of the main reasons why this type of political activity is always repulsive and hateful to any man who is decent at heart and hence courageous, while it attracts all low characters—and anyone who is unwilling to take personal responsibility for his acts, but seeks a shield, is a cowardly scoundrel. When the leaders of a nation consist of such vile creatures, the results will soon be deplorable. Such a nation will be unable to muster the courage for any determined act; it will prefer to accept any dishonor, even the most shameful, rather than rise to a decision; for there is no one who is prepared of his own accord to pledge his person and his head for the execution of a dauntless resolve.

For there is one thing which we must never forget: in this, too, the majority can never replace the man. It is not only a representative of stupidity, but of cowardice as well. And no more than a hundred empty heads make one wise man will an heroic decision arise from a hundred cowards.

The less the responsibility of the individual leader, the more numerous will be those who, despite their most insignificant stature, feel called upon to put their immortal forces in the service of the nation. Indeed, they will be unable to await their turn; they stand in a long line, and with pain and regret count the number of those waiting ahead of them, calculating almost the precise hour at which, in all probability, their turn will come. Consequently, they long for any change in the office hovering before their eyes, and are thankful for any scandal which thins out the ranks ahead of them. And if some man is unwilling to move from the post he holds, this in their eyes is practically a breach of a holy pact of solidarity. They grow vindictive, and they do not rest until the impudent fellow is at last overthrown, thus turning his warm place back to the public. And, rest assured, he won't recover the position so easily. For as soon as one of these creatures is forced to give up a position, he will try at once to wedge his way into the "waiting-line" unless the hue and cry raised by the others prevents him.

The consequence of all this is a terrifying turn-over in the most important offices and positions of such a state, a result which is always harmful, but sometimes positively catastrophic. For it is not only the simpleton and incompetent who will fall victim to this custom, but to an even greater extent the real leader, if Fate somehow manages to put one in this place. As soon as this fact has been recognized, a solid front will form against him, especially if such a mind has not arisen from their own ranks, but none the less dares to enter into this exalted society. For on principle these gentry like to be among themselves and they hate as a common enemy any brain which stands even slightly above the zeros. And in this respect their instinct is as much sharper as it is deficient in everything else.

The result will be a steadily expanding intellectual impoverishment of the leading circles. The result for the nation and the state, everyone can judge for himself, excepting in so far as he himself is one of these kind of "leaders."

Old Austria possessed the parliamentary regime in its purest form.

To be sure, the prime ministers were always appointed by the Emperor and King, but this very appointment was nothing but the execution of the parliamentary will. The haggling and bargaining for the individual portfolios represented Western democracy of the first water. And the results corresponded to the principles applied. Particularly the change of individual personalities occurred in shorter and shorter terms, ultimately becoming a veritable chase. In the same measure, the stature of the "statesmen" steadily diminished until finally no one remained but that type of parliamentary gangster whose statesmanship could only be measured and recognized by their ability in pasting together the coalitions of the moment; in other words, concluding those pettiest of political bargains which alone demonstrate the fitness of these representatives of the people for practical work.

Thus the Viennese school transmitted the best impressions in this field.

But what attracted me no less was to compare the ability and knowledge of these representatives of the people and the tasks which awaited them. In this case, whether I liked it or not, I was impelled to examine more closely the intellectual horizon of these elect of the nations themselves, and in so doing, I could not avoid giving the necessary attention to the processes which lead to the discovery of these ornaments of our public life.

The way in which the real ability of these gentlemen was applied and placed in the service of the fatherland—in other words the technical process of their activity—was also worthy of thorough study and investigation.

The more determined I was to penetrate these inner conditions, to study the personalities and material foundations with dauntless and penetrating objectivity, the more deplorable became my total picture of parliamentary life. Indeed, this is an advisable procedure in dealing with an institution which, in the person of its representatives, feels obliged to bring up "objectivity" in every second sentence as the only proper basis for every investigation and opinion. Investigate these gentlemen themselves and the laws of their sordid existence, and you will be amazed at the result.

There is no principle which, objectively considered, is as false as that of parliamentarianism.

Here we may totally disregard the manner in which our fine representatives of the people are chosen, how they arrive at their office and their new dignity. That only the tiniest fraction of them rise in fulfillment of a general desire, let alone a need, will at once be apparent to anyone who realizes that the political understanding of the broad masses is far from being highly enough developed to arrive at definite general political views of their own accord and seek out the suitable personalities.

The thing we designate by the word "public opinion" rests only in the smallest part on experience or knowledge which the individual has acquired by himself, but rather on an idea which is inspired by so-called "enlightenment," often of a highly persistent and obtrusive type.

Just as a man's denominational orientation is the result of upbringing and only the religious need as such slumbers in his soul, the political opinion of the masses represents nothing but the final result of an incredibly tenacious and thorough manipulation of their mind and soul.

By far the greatest share in their political "education," which in this case is most aptly designated by the word "propaganda," falls to the account of the press. It is foremost in performing this "work of enlightenment" and thus represents a sort of school for grown-ups. This instruction, however, is not in the hands of the state, but in the claws of forces which are in part very inferior. In Vienna as a very young man I had the best opportunity to become acquainted with the owners and spiritual manufacturers of this machine for educating the masses. At first I could not help but be amazed at how short a time it took this great evil power within the state to create a certain opinion even where it meant totally falsifying profound desires and views which surely existed among the public. In a few days a ridiculous episode had become a significant state action, while, conversely, at the same time, vital problems fell a prey to public oblivion, or rather were simply filched from the memory and consciousness of the masses.

Thus, in the course of a few weeks it was possible to conjure up names out of the void, to associate them with incredible hopes on the part of the broad public, even to give them a popularity which the really great man often does not obtain his whole life long; names which a month before no one had even seen or heard of, while at the same time old and proved figures of political or other public life, though in the best of health, simply died as far as their fellow men were concerned, or were heaped with such vile insults that their names soon threatened to become the symbol of some definite act of infamy or villainy. We must study this vile Jewish technique of emptying garbage pails full of the vilest slanders and defamations from hundreds and hundreds of sources at once, suddenly and as if by magic, on the clean garments of honorable men, if we are fully to appreciate the entire menace represented by these scoundrels of the press.

There is absolutely nothing one of these spiritual robber-barons will not do to achieve his savory aims.

He will poke into the most secret family affairs and not rest until his truffle-searching instinct digs up some miserable incident which is calculated to finish off the unfortunate victim. But if, after the most careful sniffing, absolutely nothing is found, either in the man's public or private life, one of these scoundrels simply seizes on slander, in the firm conviction that despite a thousand refutations something always sticks and, moreover, through the immediate and hundredfold repetition of his defamations by all his accomplices, any resistance on the part of the victim is in most cases utterly impossible; and it must be borne in mind that this rabble never acts out of motives which might seem credible or even understandable to the rest of humanity. God forbid! While one of these scum is attacking his beloved fellow men in the most contemptible fashion, the octopus covers himself with a veritable cloud of respectability and unctuous phrases, prates about "journalistic duty" and suchlike lies, and even goes so far as to shoot off his mouth at committee meetings and congresses—that is, occasions where these pests are present in large numbers—about a very special variety of "honor," to wit, the journalistic variety, which the assembled rabble gravely and mutually confirm.

These scum manufacture more than three-quarters of the so-called "public opinion," from whose foam the parliamentarian Aphrodite arises. To give an accurate description of this process and depict it in all its falsehood and improbability, one would have to write volumes. But even if we disregard all this and examine only the given product along with its activity, this seems to me enough to make the objective lunacy of this institution dawn on even the naïvest mind.

This human error, as senseless as it is dangerous, will most readily be understood as soon as we compare democratic parliamentarianism with a truly Germanic democracy.

The distinguishing feature of the former is that a body of, let us say five hundred men, or in recent times even women, is chosen and entrusted with making the ultimate decision in any and all matters. And so for practical purposes they alone are the government; for even if they do choose a cabinet which undertakes the external direction of the affairs of state, this is a mere sham. In reality this so-called government cannot take a step without first obtaining the approval of the general assembly. Consequently, it cannot be made responsible for anything, since the ultimate decision never lies with it, but with the majority of parliament. In every case it does nothing but carry out the momentary will of the majority. Its political ability can only be judged according to the skill with which it understands how either to adapt itself of the will of the majority or to pull the majority over to its side. Thereby it sinks from the heights of real government to the level of a beggar confronting the momentary majority. Indeed, its most urgent task becomes nothing more than either to secure the favor of the existing majority, as the need arises, or to form a majority with more friendly inclinations. If this succeeds, it may "govern" a little while longer; if it doesn't succeed, it can resign. The soundness of its purposes as such is beside the point.

For practical purposes, this excludes all responsibility.

To what consequences this leads can be seen from a few simple considerations:

The internal composition of the five hundred chosen representatives of the people, with regard to profession or even individual abilities, gives a picture as incoherent as it is usually deplorable. For no one can believe that these men elected by the nation are elect of spirit or even of intelligence! It is to be hoped that no one will suppose that the ballots of an electorate which is anything else than brilliant will give rise to statesmen by the hundreds. Altogether we cannot be too sharp in condemning the absurd notion that geniuses can be born from general elections. In the first place, a nation only produces a real statesman once in a blue moon and not a hundred or more at once; and in the second place, the revulsion of the masses for every outstanding genius is positively instinctive. Sooner will a camel pass through a needle's eye than a great man be "discovered" by an election.

In world history the man who really rises above the norm of the broad average usually announces himself personally.

As it is, however, five hundred men, whose stature is to say the least modest, vote on the most important affairs of the nation, appoint governments which in every single case and in every special question have to get the approval of the exalted assembly, so that policy is really made by five hundred.

And that is just what it usually looks like.

But even leaving the genius of these representatives of the people aside, bear in mind how varied are the problems awaiting attention, in what widely removed fields solutions and decisions must be made, and you will realize how inadequate a governing institution must be which transfers the ultimate right of decision to a mass assembly of people, only a tiny fraction of which possess knowledge and experience of the matter to be treated. The most important economic measures are thus submitted to a forum, only a tenth of whose members have any economic education to show. This is nothing more nor less than placing the ultimate decision in a matter in the hands of men totally lacking in every prerequisite for the task.

The same is true of every other question. The decision is always made by a majority of ignoramuses and incompetents, since the composition of this institution remains unchanged while the problems under treatment extend to nearly every province of public life and would thereby presuppose a constant turn-over in the deputies who are to judge and decide on them, since it is impossible to let the same persons decide matters of transportation as, let us say, a question of high foreign policy. Otherwise these men would all have to be universal geniuses such as we actually seldom encounter once in centuries. Unfortunately we are here confronted, for the most part, not with "thinkers," but with dilettantes as limited as they are conceited and inflated, intellectual *demi-monde* of the worst sort. And this is the source of the often incomprehensible frivolity with which these gentry speak and decide on things which would require careful meditation even in the greatest minds. Measures of the gravest significance for the future of a whole state, yes, of a nation, are passed as though a game of *Schafkopf* or *Tarock*,[2] which would certainly be better suited to their abilities, lay on the table before them and not the fate of a race.

Yet it would surely be unjust to believe that all of the deputies in such a parliament were personally endowed with so little sense of responsibility.

No, by no means.

But by forcing the individual to take a position on such questions completely ill-suited to him, this system gradually ruins his character. No one will summon up the courage to declare: "Gentlemen, I believe we understand nothing about this matter. I personally certainly do not." (Besides, this would change matters little, for surely this kind of honesty would remain totally unappreciated, and what is more, our friends would scarcely allow one honorable jackass to spoil their whole game.) Anyone with a knowledge of people will realize that in such an illustrious company no one is eager to be the stupidest, and in certain circles honesty is almost synonymous with stupidity.

Thus, even the representative who at first was honest is thrown into this track of general falsehood and deceit. The very conviction that the non-participation of an individual in the business would in itself change nothing kills every honorable impulse which may rise up in this or that deputy. And finally, moreover, he may tell himself that he personally is far from being the worst among the others,[3] and that the sole effect of his collaboration is perhaps to prevent worse things from happening.

It will be objected, to be sure, that though the individual deputy possesses no special understanding in this or that matter, his position has been discussed by the fraction which directs the policy of the gentleman in question, and that the fraction has its special committees which are more than adequately enlightened by experts anyway.

At first glance this seems to be true. But then the question arises: Why are five hundred chosen when only a few possess the necessary wisdom to take a position in the most important matters?

And this is the worm in the apple!

It is not the aim of our present-day parliamentarianism to constitute an assembly of wise men, but rather to compose a band of mentally dependent nonentities who are the more easily led in certain directions, the greater is the personal limitation of the individual. That is the only way of carrying on party politics in the malodorous present-day sense. And only in this way is it possible for the real wirepuller to remain carefully in the background and never personally be called to responsibility. For then every decision, regardless how harmful to the nation, will not be set to the account of a scoundrel visible to all, but will be unloaded on the shoulders of a whole fraction.

And thereby every practical responsibility vanishes. For responsibility can lie only in the obligation of an individual and not in a parliamentary bull session.

Such an institution can only please the biggest liars and sneaks of the sort that shun the light of day, because it is inevitably hateful to an honorable, straightforward man who welcomes personal responsibility.

And that is why this type of democracy has become the instrument of that race which in its inner goals must shun the light of day, now and in all ages of the future. Only the Jew can praise an institution which is as dirty and false as he himself.

Juxtaposed to this is the truly Germanic democracy characterized by the free election of a leader and his obligation fully to assume all responsibility for his actions and omissions. In it there is no majority vote on individual questions, but only the decision of an individual who must answer with his fortune and his life for his choice.

If it be objected that under such conditions scarcely anyone would be prepared to dedicate his person to so risky a task, there is but one possible answer:

Thank the Lord, Germanic democracy means just this: that any old climber or moral slacker cannot rise by devious paths to govern his national comrades,[4] but that, by the very greatness of the responsibility to be assumed, incompetents and weaklings are frightened off.

But if, nevertheless, one of these scoundrels should attempt to sneak in, we can find him more easily, and mercilessly challenge him: Out, cowardly scoundrel! Remove your foot, you are besmirching the steps; the front steps of the Pantheon of history are not for sneak-thieves, but for heroes!


## [The State]

With the victorious march of German technology and industry, the rising successes of German commerce, the realization was increasingly lost that all this was only possible on the basis of a strong state. On the contrary, many circles went so far as to put forward the conviction that the state owed its very existence to these phenomena, that the state itself primarily represented an economic institution, that it could be governed according to economic requirements, and that its very existence depended on economics, a state of affairs which was regarded and glorified as by far the healthiest and most natural.

But the state has nothing at all to do with any definite economic conception or development.

It is not a collection of economic contracting parties in a definite delimited living space for the fulfillment of economic tasks, but the organization of a community of physically and psychologically similar living beings for the better facilitation of the maintenance of their species and the achievement of the aim which has been allotted to this species by Providence. This and nothing else is the aim and meaning of a state. Economics is only one of the many instruments required for the achievement of this aim. It is never the cause or the aim of a state unless this state is based on a false, because unnatural, foundation to begin with. Only in this way can it be explained that the state as such does not necessarily presuppose territorial limitation. This will be necessary only among the peoples who want to secure the maintenance of their national comrades by their own resources; in other words, are prepared to fight the struggle for existence by their own labor. Peoples who can sneak their way into the rest of mankind like drones, to make other men work for them under all sorts of pretexts, can form states even without any definitely delimited living space of their own. This applies first and foremost to a people under whose parasitism the whole of honest humanity is suffering, today more than ever: the Jews.

The Jewish state was never spatially limited in itself, but universally unlimited as to space, though restricted in the sense of embracing but one race. Consequently, this people has always formed a state within states. It is one of the most ingenious tricks that was ever devised, to make this state sail under the flag of "religion," thus assuring it of the tolerance which the Aryan is always ready to accord a religious creed. For actually the Mosaic religion is nothing other than a doctrine for the preservation of the Jewish race. It therefore embraces almost all sociological, political, and economic fields of knowledge which can have any bearing on this function.

The urge to preserve the species is the first cause for the formation of human communities; thus the state is a national organism and not an economic organization. A difference which is just as large as it is incomprehensible, particularly to our so-called "statesmen" of today. That is why they think they can build up the state through economics while in reality it results and always will result solely from the action of those qualities which lie in line with the will to preserve the species and race. And these are always heroic virtues and never the egoism of shopkeepers, since the preservation of the existence of a species presupposes a spirit of sacrifice in the individual. The sense of the poet's words, "If you will not stake your life, you will win no life," is that the sacrifice of personal existence is necessary to secure the preservation of the species. Thus, the most sensible prerequisite for the formation and preservation of a state is the presence of a certain feeling of cohesion based on similarity of nature and species, and a willingness to stake everything on it with all possible means, something which in peoples with soil of their own will create heroic virtues, but in parasites will create lying hypocrisy and malignant cruelty, or else these qualities must already be present as the necessary and demonstrable basis for their existence as a state so different in form. The formation of a state, originally at least, will occur through the exercise of these qualities, and in the subsequent struggle for self-preservation those nations will be defeated—this is, will fall a prey to subjugation and thus sooner or later die out—which in the mutual struggle possess the smallest share of heroic virtues, or are not equal to the lies and trickery of the hostile parasite. But in this case, too, this must almost always be attributed less to a lack of astuteness than to a lack of determination and courage, which only tries to conceal itself beneath a cloak of humane convictions.

How little the state-forming and state-preserving qualities are connected with economics is most clearly shown by the fact that the inner strength of a state only in the rarest cases coincides with so-called economic prosperity, but that the latter, in innumerable cases, seems to indicate the state's approaching decline. If the formation of human societies were primarily attributable to economic forces or even impulses, the highest economic development would have to mean the greatest strength of the state and not the opposite.

Belief in the state-forming and state-preserving power of economics seems especially incomprehensible when it obtains in a country which in all things clearly and penetratingly shows the historic reverse. Prussia, in particular, demonstrates with marvelous sharpness that not material qualities but ideal virtues alone make possible the formation of a state. Only under their protection can economic life flourish, until with the collapse of the pure state-forming faculties the economy collapses too; a process which we can observe in so terrible and tragic a form right now. The material interests of man can always thrive best as long as they remain in the shadow of heroic virtues; but as soon as they attempt to enter the primary sphere of existence, they destroy the basis for their own existence.

Always when in Germany there was an upsurge of political power, the economic conditions began to improve; but always when economics became the sole content of our people's life, stifling the ideal virtues, the state collapsed and in a short time drew economic life along with it.

If, however, we consider the question, what, in reality, are the state-forming or even state-preserving forces, we can sum them up under one single head: the ability and will of the individual to sacrifice himself for the totality. That these virtues have nothing at all to do with economics can be seen from the simple realization that man never sacrifices himself for the latter, or, in other words: a man does not die for business, but only for ideals. Nothing proved the Englishman's superior psychological knowledge of the popular soul better than the motivation which he gave to his struggle. While we fought for bread, England fought for "freedom"; and not even for her own, no, for that of the small nations. In our country we laughed at this effrontery, or were enraged at it, and thus only demonstrated how empty-headed and stupid the so-called statesmen of Germany had become even before the War. We no longer had the slightest idea concerning the essence of the force which can lead men to their death of their own free will and decision.

In 1914, as long as the German people thought they were fighting for ideals, they stood firm; but as soon as they were told to fight for their daily bread, they preferred to give up the game.

And our brilliant "statesmen" were astonished at this change in attitude. It never became clear to them that from the moment when a man begins to fight for an economic interest, he avoids death as much as possible, since death would forever deprive him of his reward for fighting. Anxiety for the rescue of her own child makes a heroine of even the feeblest mother, and only the struggle for the preservation of the species and the hearth, or the state that protects it, has at all times driven men against the spears of their enemies.

The following theorem may be established as an eternally valid truth:

Never yet has a state been founded by peaceful economic means, but always and exclusively by the instincts of preservation of the species regardless whether these are found in the province of heroic virtue or of cunning craftiness; the one results in Aryan states based on work and culture, the other in Jewish colonies of parasites. As soon as economics as such begins to choke out these instincts in a people or in a state, it becomes the seductive cause of subjugation and oppression.

The belief of pre-war days that the world could be peacefully opened up to, let alone conquered for, the German people by a commercial and colonial policy was a classic sign of the loss of real state-forming and state-preserving virtues and of all the insight, will power, and active determination which follow from them; the penalty for this, inevitable as the law of nature, was the World War with its consequences.

For those who do not look more deeply into the matter, this attitude of the German nation—for it was really as good as general—could only represent an insoluble riddle: for was not Germany above all other countries a marvelous example of an empire which had risen from foundations of pure political power? Prussia, the germ-cell of the Empire, came into being through resplendent heroism and not through financial operations or commercial deals, and the Reich itself in turn was only the glorious reward of aggressive political leadership and the death-defying courage of its soldiers. How could this very German people have succumbed to such a sickening of its political instinct? For here we face, not an isolated phenomenon, but forces of decay which in truly terrifying number soon began to flare up like will-o'-the-wisps, brushing up and down the body politic, or eating like poisonous abscesses into the nation, now here and now there. It seemed as though a continuous stream of poison was being driven into the outermost blood-vessels of this once heroic body by a mysterious power, and was inducing progressively greater paralysis of sound reason and the simple instinct of self-preservation.

As innumerable times I passed in review all these questions, arising through my position on the German alliance policy and the economic policy of the Reich in the years 1912 to 1914—the only remaining solution to the riddle became to an ever-increasing degree that power which, from an entirely different viewpoint, I had come to know earlier in Vienna: the Marxist doctrine and philosophy, and their organizational results.

For the second time I dug into this doctrine of destruction—this time no longer led by the impressions and effects of my daily associations, but directed by the observation of general processes of political life. I again immersed myself in the theoretical literature of this new world, attempting to achieve clarity concerning its possible effects, and then compared it with the actual phenomena and events it brings about in political, cultural, and economic life.

Now for the first time I turned my attention to the attempts to master this world plague.

I studied Bismarck's Socialist legislation[5] in its intention, struggle, and success. Gradually I obtained a positively granite foundation for my own conviction, so that since that time I have never been forced to undertake a shift in my own inner view on this question. Likewise the relation of Marxism to the Jews was submitted to further thorough examination.

Though previously in Vienna, Germany above all had seemed to me an unshakable colossus, now anxious misgivings sometimes entered my mind. In silent solitude and in the small circles of my acquaintance, I was filled with wrath at German foreign policy and likewise with what seemed to me the incredibly frivolous way in which the most important problem then existing for Germany, Marxism, was treated. It was really beyond me how people could rush so blindly into a danger whose effects, pursuant to the Marxists' own intention, were bound some day to be monstrous. Even then, among my acquaintance, just as today on a large scale, I warned against the phrase with which all wretched cowards comfort themselves: "Nothing can happen to us!" This pestilential attitude had once been the downfall of a gigantic empire. Could anyone believe that Germany alone was not subject to exactly the same laws as all other human organisms?

In the years 1913 and 1914, I, for the first time in various circles which today in part faithfully support the National Socialist movement, expressed the conviction that the question of the future of the German nation was the question of destroying Marxism.

In the catastrophic German alliance policy I saw only one of the consequences called forth by the disruptive work of this doctrine; for the terrible part of it was that this poison almost invisibly destroyed all the foundations of a healthy conception of economy and state, and that often those affected by it did not themselves realize to what an extent their activities and desires emanated from this philosophy which they otherwise sharply rejected.

The internal decline of the German nation had long since begun, yet, as so often in life, people had not achieved clarity concerning the force that was destroying their existence. Sometimes they tinkered around with the disease, but confused the forms of the phenomenon with the virus that had caused it. Since they did not know or want to know the cause, the struggle against Marxism was no better than bungling quackery.

## [The Spiritualization of Violence]

For me, as for every German, there now began the greatest and most unforgettable time of my earthly existence. Compared to the events of this gigantic struggle, everything past receded to shallow nothingness. Precisely in these days, with the tenth anniversary of the mighty event approaching, I think back with proud sadness on those first weeks of our people's heroic struggle, in which Fate graciously allowed me to take part.

As though it were yesterday, image after image passes before my eyes. I see myself donning the uniform in the circle of my dear comrades, turning out for the first time, drilling, etc., until the day came for us to march off.

A single worry tormented me at that time, me, as so many others: would we not reach the front too late? Time and time again this alone banished all my calm. Thus, in every cause for rejoicing at a new, heroic victory, a slight drop of bitterness was hidden, for every new victory seemed to increase the danger of our coming too late.

At last the day came when we left Munich to begin the fulfillment of our duty. For the first time I saw the Rhine as we rode westward along its quiet waters to defend it, the German stream of streams, from the greed of the old enemy. When through the tender veil of the early morning mist the Niederwald Monument gleamed down upon us in the gentle first rays of the sun, the old *Watch on the Rhine* roared out of the endless transport train into the morning sky, and I felt as though my heart would burst.

And then came a damp, cold night in Flanders, through which we marched in silence, and when the day began to emerge from the mists, suddenly an iron greeting came whizzing at us over our heads, and with a sharp report sent the little pellets flying between our ranks, ripping up the wet ground; but even before the little cloud had passed, from two hundred throats the first hurrah rose to meet the first messenger of death. Then a crackling and a roaring, a singing and a howling began, and with feverish eyes each one of us was drawn forward, faster and faster, until suddenly past turnip fields and hedges the fight began, the fight of man against man. And from the distance the strains of a song reached our ears, coming closer and closer, leaping from company to company, and just as Death plunged a busy hand into our ranks, the song reached us too and we passed it along: "*Deutschland, Deutschland über Alles, Über Alles in der Welt!*"

Four days later we came back. Even our step had changed. Seventeen-year-old boys now looked like men.

The volunteers of the List Regiment may not have learned to fight properly, but they knew how to die like old soldiers.

This was the beginning.

Thus it went on year after year; but the romance of battle had been replaced by horror. The enthusiasm gradually cooled and the exuberant joy was stifled by mortal fear. The time came when every man had to struggle between the instinct of self-preservation and the admonitions of duty. I, too, was not spared by this struggle. Always when Death was on the hunt, a vague something tried to revolt, strove to represent itself to the weak body as reason, yet it was only cowardice, which in such disguises tried to ensnare the individual. A grave tugging and warning set in, and often it was only the last remnant of

conscience which decided the issue. Yet the more this voice admonished one
to caution, the louder and more insistent its lures, the sharper resistance grew
until at last, after a long inner struggle, consciousness of duty emerged victorious. By the winter of 1915–16, this struggle had for me been decided. At last
my will was undisputed master. If in the first days I went over the top with rejoicing and laughter, I was now calm and determined. And this was enduring.
Now Fate could bring on the ultimate tests without my nerves shattering or
my reason failing.

The young volunteer had become an old soldier.

And this transformation had occurred in the whole army. It had issued
old and hard from the eternal battles, and as for those who could not stand up
under the storm—well, they were broken.

Now was the time to judge this army. Now, after two or three years, during which it was hurled from one battle into another, forever fighting against
superiority in numbers and weapons, suffering hunger and bearing privations,
now was the time to test the quality of this unique army.

Thousands of years may pass, but never will it be possible to speak of
heroism without mentioning the German army and the World War. Then
from the veil of the past the iron front of the gray steel helmet will emerge, un-
wavering and unflinching, an immortal monument. As long as there are Germans alive, they will remember that these men were sons of their nation. . . .

The application of force alone, without the impetus of a basic spiritual
idea as a starting point, can never lead to the destruction of an idea and its
dissemination, except in the form of a complete extermination of even the
very last exponent of the idea and the destruction of the last tradition. This,
however, usually means the disappearance of such a state from the sphere of
political importance, often for an indefinite time and sometimes forever; for
experience shows that such a blood sacrifice strikes the best part of the people,
since every persecution which occurs without a spiritual basis seems morally
unjustified and whips up precisely the more valuable parts of a people in protest, which results in an adoption of the spiritual content of the unjustly persecuted movement. In many this occurs simply through a feeling of opposition
against the attempt to bludgeon down an idea by brute force.

As a result, the number of inward supporters grows in proportion as the
persecution increases. Consequently, the complete annihilation of the new
doctrine can be carried out only through a process of extermination so great
and constantly increasing that in the end all the truly valuable blood is drawn
out of the people or state in question. The consequence is that, though so-
called "inner" purge can now take place, it will only be at the cost of total impotence. Such a method will always prove vain in advance if the doctrine to be
combated has overstepped a certain small circle.

Consequently, here, too, as in all growth, the first period of childhood is
most readily susceptible to the possibility of extermination, while with the

mounting years the power of resistance increases and only with the weakness of approaching old age cedes again to new youth, though in another form and for different reasons.

Indeed, nearly all attempts to exterminate a doctrine and its organizational expression, by force without spiritual foundation, are doomed to failure, and not seldom end with the exact opposite of the desired result for the following reason:

The very first requirement for a mode of struggle with the weapons of naked force is and remains persistence. In other words: only the continuous and steady application of the methods for repressing a doctrine, etc., makes it possible for a plan to succeed. But as soon as force wavers and alternates with forbearance, not only will the doctrine to be repressed recover again and again, but it will also be in a position to draw new benefit from every persecution, since, after such a wave of pressure has ebbed away, indignation over the suffering induced leads new supporters to the old doctrine, while the old ones will cling to it with greater defiance and deeper hatred than before, and even schismatic heretics, once the danger has subsided, will attempt to return to their old viewpoint. Only in the steady and constant application of force lies the very first prerequisite for success. This persistence, however, can always and only arise from a definite spiritual conviction. Any violence which does not spring from a firm, spiritual base, will be wavering and uncertain. It lacks the stability which can only rest in a fanatical outlook. It emanates from the momentary energy and brutal determination of an individual, and is therefore subject to the change of personalities and to their nature and strength.

## [The Use of Propaganda]

There seems to have been no clarity on the very first question: Is propaganda a means or an end?

It is a means and must therefore be judged with regard to its end. It must consequently take a form calculated to support the aim which it serves. It is also obvious that its aim can vary in importance from the standpoint of general need, and that the inner value of the propaganda will vary accordingly. The aim for which we were fighting the War was the loftiest, the most overpowering, that man can conceive: it was the freedom and independence of our nation, the security of our future food supply, and—our national honor; a thing which, despite all contrary opinions prevailing today, nevertheless exists, or rather should exist, since peoples without honor have sooner or later lost their freedom and independence, which in turn is only the result of a higher justice, since generations of rabble without honor deserve no freedom. Any man who wants to be a cowardly slave can have no honor, or honor itself would soon fall into general contempt.

The German nation was engaged in a struggle for a human existence, and the purpose of war propaganda should have been to support this struggle; its aim to help bring about victory.

When the nations on this planet fight for existence—when the question of destiny, "to be or not to be," cries out for a solution—then all considerations of humanitarianism or aesthetics crumble into nothingness; for all these concepts do not float about in the ether, they arise from man's imagination and are bound up with man. When he departs from this world, these concepts are again dissolved into nothingness, for Nature does not know them. And even among mankind, they belong only to a few nations or rather races, and this in proportion as they emanate from the feeling of the nation or race in question. Humanitarianism and aesthetics would vanish even from a world inhabited by man if this world were to lose the races that have created and upheld these concepts.

But all such concepts become secondary when a nation is fighting for its existence; in fact, they become totally irrelevant to the forms of the struggle as soon as a situation arises where they might paralyze a struggling nation's power of self-preservation. And that has always been their only visible result.

As for humanitarianism, Moltke[6] said years ago that in war it lies in the brevity of the operation, and that means that the most aggressive fighting technique is the most humane.

But when people try to approach these questions with drivel about aesthetics, etc., really only one answer is possible: where the destiny and existence of a people are at stake, all obligation toward beauty ceases. The most unbeautiful thing there can be in human life is and remains the yoke of slavery. Or do these Schwabing[7] decadents view the present lot of the German people as "aesthetic"? Certainly we don't have to discuss these matters with the Jews, the most modern inventors of this cultural perfume. Their whole existence is an embodied protest against the aesthetics of the Lord's image.

And since these criteria of humanitarianism and beauty must be eliminated from the struggle, they are also inapplicable to propaganda.

Propaganda in the War was a means to an end, and the end was the struggle for the existence of the German people; consequently, propaganda could only be considered in accordance with the principles that were valid for this struggle. In this case the most cruel weapons were humane if they brought about a quicker victory; and only those methods were beautiful which helped the nation to safeguard the dignity of its freedom.

This was the only possible attitude toward war propaganda in a life-and-death struggle like ours.

If the so-called responsible authorities had been clear on this point, they would never have fallen into such uncertainty over the form and application of this weapon: for even propaganda is no more than a weapon, though a frightful one in the hand of an expert.

The second really decisive question was this: To whom should propaganda be addressed? To the scientifically trained intelligentsia or to the less educated masses?

It must be addressed always and exclusively to the masses.

What the intelligentsia—or those who today unfortunately often go by that name—what they need is not propaganda but scientific instruction. The content of propaganda is not science any more than the object represented in a poster is art. The art of the poster lies in the designer's ability to attract the attention of the crowd by form and color. A poster advertising an art exhibit must direct the attention of the public to the art being exhibited; the better it succeeds in this, the greater is the art of the poster itself. The poster should give the masses an idea of the significance of the exhibition, it should not be a substitute for the art on display. Anyone who wants to concern himself with the art itself must do more than study the poster; and it will not be enough for him just to saunter through the exhibition. We may expect him to examine and immerse himself in the individual works, and thus little by little form a fair opinion.

A similar situation prevails with what we today call propaganda.

The function of propaganda does not lie in the scientific training of the individual, but in calling the masses' attention to certain facts, processes, necessities, etc., whose significance is thus for the first time placed within their field of vision.

The whole art consists in doing this so skillfully that everyone will be convinced that the fact is real, the process necessary, the necessity correct, etc. But since propaganda is not and cannot be the necessity in itself, since its function, like the poster, consists in attracting the attention of the crowd, and not in educating those who are already educated or who are striving after education and knowledge, its effect for the most part must be aimed at the emotions and only to a very limited degree at the so-called intellect.

All propaganda must be popular and its intellectual level must be adjusted to the most limited intelligence among those it is addressed to. Consequently, the greater the mass it is intended to reach, the lower its purely intellectual level will have to be. But if, as in propaganda for sticking out a war, the aim is to influence a whole people, we must avoid excessive intellectual demands on our public, and too much caution cannot be exerted in this direction.

The more modest its intellectual ballast, the more exclusively it takes into consideration the emotions of the masses, the more effective it will be. And this is the best proof of the soundness or unsoundness of a propaganda campaign, and not success in pleasing a few scholars or young aesthetes.

The art of propaganda lies in understanding the emotional ideas of the great masses and finding, through a psychologically correct form, the way to the attention and thence to the heart of the broad masses. The fact that our bright boys do not understand this merely shows how mentally lazy and conceited they are.

Once we understand how necessary it is for propaganda to be adjusted to the broad mass, the following rule results:

It is a mistake to make propaganda many-sided, like scientific instruction, for instance.

The receptivity of the great masses is very limited, their intelligence is small, but their power of forgetting is enormous. In consequence of these facts, all effective propaganda must be limited to a very few points and must harp on these in slogans until the last member of the public understands what you want him to understand by your slogan. As soon as you sacrifice this slogan and try to be many-sided, the effect will piddle away, for the crowd can neither digest nor retain the material offered. In this way the result is weakened and in the end entirely cancelled out.

Thus we see that propaganda must follow a simple line and correspondingly the basic tactics must be psychologically sound.

## [The Purification of Culture]

A further example of the half-heartedness and weakness of the leaders of pre-War Germany in meeting the most important vital questions of the nation is the following: running parallel to the political, ethical, and moral contamination of the people, there had been for many years a no less terrible poisoning of the health of the national body. Especially in the big cities, syphilis was beginning to spread more and more, while tuberculosis steadily reaped its harvest of death throughout nearly the whole country.

Though in both cases the consequences were terrible for the nation, the authorities could not summon up the energy to take decisive measures.

Particularly with regard to syphilis, the attitude of the leadership of the nation and the state can only be designated as total capitulation. To fight it seriously, they would have had to take somewhat broader measures than was actually the case. The invention of a remedy of questionable character and its commercial exploitation can no longer help much against this plague. Here again it was only the fight against causes that mattered and not the elimination of the symptoms. The cause lies, primarily, in our prostitution of love. Even if its result were not this frightful plague, it would nevertheless be profoundly injurious to man, since the moral devastations which accompany this degeneracy suffice to destroy a people slowly but surely. This Jewification of our spiritual life and mammonization of our mating instinct will sooner or later destroy our entire offspring, for the powerful children of a natural emotion will be replaced by the miserable creatures of financial expediency which is becoming more and more the basis and sole prerequisite of our marriages. Love finds its outlet elsewhere.

Here, too, of course, Nature can be scorned for a certain time, but her vengeance will not fail to appear, only it takes a time to manifest itself, or rather: it is often recognized too late by man.

But the devastating consequences of a lasting disregard of the natural requirements for marriage can be seen in our nobility. Here we have before us the results of procreation based partly on purely social compulsion and partly on financial grounds. The one leads to a general weakening, the other to a poisoning of the blood, since every department store Jewess is considered fit to augment the offspring of His Highness—and, indeed, the offspring look it. In both cases complete degeneration is the consequence.

Today our bourgeoisie strive to go the same road, and they will end up at the same goal.

Hastily and indifferently, people tried to pass by the unpleasant truths, as though by such an attitude events could be undone. No, the fact that our big city population is growing more and more prostituted in its love life cannot just be denied out of existence; it simply is so. The most visible results of this mass contamination can, on the one hand, be found in the insane asylums, and on the other, unfortunately, in our—children. They in particular are the sad product of the irresistibly spreading contamination of our sexual life; the vices of the parents are revealed in the sicknesses of the children. . . .

How truly wretched was the attitude of pre-War Germany on this one very question! What was done to check the contamination of our youth in the big cities? What was done to attack the infection and mammonization of our love life? What was done to combat the resulting syphilization of our people?

This can be answered most easily by stating what should have been done. . . .

The very first prerequisite needed for attacking such a difficult stretch of the human road is for the leadership to succeed in representing to the masses of the people the partial goal which now has to be achieved, or rather conquered, as the one which is solely and alone worthy of attention, on whose conquest everything depends. The great mass of the people cannot see the whole road ahead of them without growing weary and despairing of the task. A certain number of them will keep the goal in mind, but will only be able to see the road in small, partial stretches, like the wanderer, who likewise knows and recognizes the end of his journey, but is better able to conquer the endless highway if he divides it into sections and boldly attacks each one as though it represented the desired goal itself. Only in this way does he advance without losing heart.

Thus, by the use of all propagandist means, the question of combating syphilis should have been made to appear as *the* task of the nation. Not just *one more* task. To this end, its injurious effects should have been thoroughly hammered into people as the most terrible misfortune, and this by the use of all available means, until the entire nation arrived at the conviction that every-thing—future or ruin—depended upon the solution of this question.

Only after such a preparation, if necessary over a period of years, will the attention, and consequently the determination, of the entire nation be aroused to such an extent that we can take exceedingly hard measures exacting the greatest sacrifices without running the risk of not being understood or of sud-denly being left in the lurch by the will of the masses.

For, seriously to attack this plague, tremendous sacrifices and equally great labors are necessary.

The fight against syphilis demands a fight against prostitution, against prejudices, old habits, against previous conceptions, general views among them not least the false prudery of certain circles.

The first prerequisite for even the moral right to combat these things is the facilitation of earlier marriage for the coming generation. In late marriage alone lies the compulsion to retain an institution which, twist and turn as you like, is and remains a disgrace to humanity, an institution which is damned ill-suited to a being who with his usual modesty likes to regard himself as the "image" of God.

Prostitution is a disgrace to humanity, but it cannot be eliminated by moral lectures, pious intentions, etc.; its limitation and final abolition presup-pose the elimination of innumerable preconditions. The first is and remains the creation of an opportunity for early marriage as compatible with human nature—particularly for the man, as the woman in any case is only the passive part.

How lost, how incomprehensible a part of humanity has become today can be seen from the fact that mothers in so-called "good" society can not sel-dom be heard to say that they are glad to have found their child a husband who has sown his wild oats, etc. Since there is hardly any lack of these, but rather the contrary, the poor girl will be happy to find one of these worn-out Siegfrieds,[8] and the children will be the visible result of this "sensible" mar-riage. If we bear in mind that, aside from this, propagation as such is limited as much as possible, so that Nature is prevented from making any choice, since naturally every creature, regardless how miserable, must be preserved, the only question that remains is why such an institution exists at all any more and what purpose it is supposed to serve? Isn't it exactly the same as prostitution itself? Hasn't duty toward posterity passed completely out of the picture? Or do people fail to realize what a curse on the part of their children and children's children they are heaping on themselves by such criminal frivolity in observing the ulti-mate natural law as well as our ultimate natural obligation?[9]

Thus, the civilized peoples degenerate and gradually perish.

And marriage cannot be an end in itself, but must serve the one higher goal, the increase and preservation of the species and the race. This alone is its meaning and its task. . . .

In the second place, education and training must eradicate a number of evils about which today no one bothers at all. Above all, in our present education a balance must be created between mental instruction and physical training. The institution that is called a *Gymnasium* today is a mockery of the Greek model. In our educational system it has been utterly forgotten that in the long run a healthy mind can dwell only in a healthy body. Especially if we bear in mind the mass of the people, aside from a few exceptions, this statement becomes absolutely valid. . . .

The excessive emphasis on purely intellectual instruction and the neglect of physical training also encourage the emergence of sexual ideas at a much too early age. The youth who achieves the hardness of iron by sports and gymnastics succumbs to the need of sexual satisfaction less than the stay-at-home fed exclusively on intellectual fare. And a sensible system of education must bear this in mind. It must, moreover, not fail to consider that the healthy young man will expect different things from the woman than a prematurely corrupted weakling.

Thus, the whole system of education must be so organized as to use the boy's free time for the useful training of his body. He has no right to hang about in idleness during these years, to make the streets and movie-houses unsafe; after his day's work he should steel and harden his young body, so that later life will not find him too soft. To begin this and also carry it out, to direct and guide it, is the task of education, and not just the pumping of so-called wisdom. We must also do away with the conception that the treatment of the body is the affair of every individual. There is no freedom to sin at the cost of posterity and hence of the race.

Parallel to the training of the body, a struggle against the poisoning of the soul must begin. Our whole public life today is like a hothouse for sexual ideas and stimulations. Just look at the bill of fare served up in our movies, vaudeville and theaters, and you will hardly be able to deny that this is not the right kind of food, particularly for the youth. In shop windows and billboards the vilest means are used to attract the attention of the crowd. Anyone who has not lost the ability to think himself into their soul must realize that this must cause great damage in the youth. This sensual, sultry atmosphere leads to ideas and stimulations at a time when the boy should have no understanding of such things. The result of this kind of education can be studied in present-day youth, and it is not exactly gratifying. They mature too early and consequently grow old before their time. Sometimes the public learns of court proceedings which permit shattering insights into the emotional life of our fourteen- and fifteen-year-olds. Who will be surprised that even in these age-groups syphilis begins to seek its victims? And is it not deplorable to see a good number of these physically weak, spiritually corrupted young men obtaining their introduction to marriage through big-city whores?

No, anyone who wants to attack prostitution must first of all help to eliminate its spiritual basis. He must clear away the filth of the moral plague of big-city "civilization" and he must do this ruthlessly and without wavering in the face of all the shouting and screaming that will naturally be let loose. If we do not lift the youth out of the morass of their present-day environment, they will drown in it. Anyone who refuses to see these things supports them, and thereby makes himself an accomplice in the slow prostitution of our future which, whether we like it or not, lies in the coming generation. This cleansing of our culture must be extended to nearly all fields. Theater, art, literature, cinema, press, posters, and window displays must be cleansed of all manifestations of our rotting world and placed in the service of a moral, political, and cultural idea. Public life must be freed from the stifling perfume of our modern eroticism, just as it must be freed from all unmanly, prudish hypocrisy. In all these things the goal and the road must be determined by concern for the preservation of the health of our people in body and soul. The right of personal freedom recedes before the duty to preserve the race.

Only after these measures are carried out can the medical struggle against the plague itself be carried through with any prospect of success. But here, too, there must be no half-measures; the gravest and most ruthless decisions will have to be made. It is a half-measure to let incurably sick people steadily contaminate the remaining healthy ones. This is in keeping with the humanitarianism which, to avoid hurting one individual, lets a hundred others perish. The demand that defective people be prevented from propagating equally defective offspring is a demand of the clearest reason and if systematically executed represents the most humane act of mankind. It will spare millions of unfortunates undeserved sufferings, and consequently will lead to a rising improvement of health as a whole. The determination to proceed in this direction will oppose a dam to the further spread of venereal diseases. For, if necessary, the incurably sick will be pitilessly segregated—a barbaric measure for the unfortunate who is struck by it, but a blessing for his fellow men and posterity. The passing pain of a century can and will redeem millenniums from sufferings.

The struggle against syphilis and the prostitution which prepares the way for it is one of the most gigantic tasks of humanity, gigantic because we are facing, not the solution of a single question, but the elimination of a large number of evils which bring about this plague as a resultant manifestation. For in this case the sickening of the body is only the consequence of a sickening of the moral, social, and racial instincts.

## [Nation and Race]

There are some truths which are so obvious that for this very reason they are not seen or at least not recognized by ordinary people. They sometimes pass by such truisms as though blind and are most astonished when someone suddenly discovers what everyone really ought to know. Columbus's eggs lie around by the hundreds of thousands, but Columbuses are met with less frequently.

Thus men without exception wander about in the garden of Nature; they imagine that they know practically everything and yet with few exceptions pass blindly by one of the most patent principles of Nature's rule: the inner segregation of the species of all living beings on this earth.

Even the most superficial observation shows that Nature's restricted form of propagation and increase is an almost rigid basic law of all the innumerable forms of expression of her vital urge. Every animal mates only with a member of the same species. The titmouse seeks the titmouse, the finch the finch, the stork the stork, the field mouse the field mouse, the dormouse the dormouse, the wolf the she-wolf, etc.

Only unusual circumstances can change this, primarily the compulsion of captivity or any other cause that makes it impossible to mate within the same species. But then Nature begins to resist this with all possible means, and her most visible protest consists either in refusing further capacity for propagation to bastards or in limiting the fertility of later offspring; in most cases, however, she takes away the power of resistance to disease or hostile attacks.

This is only too natural.

Any crossing of two beings not at exactly the same level produces a medium between the level of the two parents. This means: the offspring will probably stand higher than the racially lower parent, but not as high as the higher one. Consequently, it will later succumb in the struggle against the higher level. Such mating is contrary to the will of Nature for a higher breeding of all life. The precondition for this does not lie in associating superior and inferior, but in the total victory of the former. The stronger must dominate and not blend with the weaker, thus sacrificing his own greatness. Only the born weakling can view this as cruel, but he after all is only a weak and limited man; for if this law did not prevail, any conceivable higher development of organic living beings would be unthinkable.

The consequence of this racial purity,[10] universally valid in Nature, is not only the sharp outward delimitation of the various races, but their uniform character in themselves. The fox is always a fox, the goose a goose, the tiger a tiger, etc., and the difference can lie at most in the varying measure of force, strength, intelligence, dexterity, endurance, etc., of the individual specimens. But you will never find a fox who in his inner attitude might, for example, show humanitarian tendencies toward geese, as similarly there is no cat with a friendly inclination toward mice.

Therefore, here, too, the struggle among themselves arises less from inner aversion than from hunger and love. In both cases, Nature looks on calmly, with satisfaction, in fact. In the struggle for daily bread all those who are weak and sickly or less determined succumb, while the struggle of the males for the female grants the right or opportunity to propagate only to the healthiest. And struggle is always a means for improving a species' health and power of resistance and, therefore, a cause of its higher development.

If the process were different, all further and higher development would cease and the opposite would occur. For, since the inferior always predominates numerically over the best, if both had the same possibility of preserving life and propagating, the inferior would multiply so much more rapidly that in the end the best would inevitably be driven into the background, unless a correction of this state of affairs were undertaken. Nature does just this by subjecting the weaker part to such severe living conditions that by them alone the number is limited, and by not permitting the remainder to increase promiscuously, but making a new and ruthless choice according to strength and health.

No more than Nature desires the mating of weaker with stronger individuals, even less does she desire the blending of a higher with a lower race, since, if she did, her whole work of higher breeding, over perhaps hundreds of thousands of years, might be ruined with one blow.

Historical experience offers countless proofs of this. It shows with terrifying clarity that in every mingling of Aryan blood with that of lower peoples the result was the end of the cultured people. North America, whose population consists in by far the largest part of Germanic elements who mixed but little with the lower colored peoples, shows a different humanity and culture from Central and South America, where the predominantly Latin immigrants often mixed with the aborigines on a large scale. By this one example, we can clearly and distinctly recognize the effect of racial mixture. The Germanic inhabitant of the American continent, who has remained racially pure and unmixed, rose to be master of the continent; he will remain the master as long as he does not fall a victim to defilement of the blood.

The result of all racial crossing is therefore in brief always the following:

*a.* Lowering of the level of the higher race;

*b.* Physical and intellectual regression and hence the beginning of a slowly but surely progressing sickness.

To bring about such a development is, then, nothing else but to sin against the will of the eternal creator.

And as a sin this act is rewarded.

When man attempts to rebel against the iron logic of Nature, he comes into struggle with the principles to which he himself owes his existence as a man. And this attack[11] must lead to his own doom. . . .

Everything we admire on this earth today—science and art, technology and inventions—is only the creative product of a few peoples and originally perhaps of *one* race. On them depends the existence of this whole culture. If they perish, the beauty of this earth will sink into the grave with them.

However much the soil, for example, can influence men, the result of the influence will always be different depending on the races in question. The low fertility of a living space may spur the one race to the highest achievements; in others it will only be the cause of bitterest poverty and final undernourishment with all its consequences. The inner nature of peoples is always determining for the manner in which outward influences will be effective. What leads the one to starvation trains the other to hard work.

All great cultures of the past perished only because the originally creative race died out from blood poisoning.

The ultimate cause of such a decline was their forgetting that all culture depends on men and not conversely; hence that to preserve a certain culture the man who creates it must be preserved. This preservation is bound up with the rigid law of necessity and the right to victory of the best and stronger in this world.[12]

Those who want to live, let them fight, and those who do not want to fight in this world of eternal struggle do not deserve to live.

Even if this were hard—that is how it is! Assuredly, however, by far the harder fate is that which strikes the man who thinks he can overcome Nature, but in the last analysis only mocks her. Distress, misfortune, and diseases are her answer.

The man who misjudges and disregards the racial laws actually forfeits the happiness that seems destined to be his. He thwarts the triumphal march of the best race and hence also the precondition for all human progress, and remains, in consequence, burdened with all the sensibility of man, in the animal realm of helpless misery.[13]

## [Corporatism]

This self-sacrificing will to give one's personal labor and if necessary one's own life for others is most strongly developed in the Aryan. The Aryan is not greatest in his mental qualities as such, but in the extent of his willingness to put all his abilities in the service of the community. In him the instinct of self-preservation has reached the noblest form, since he willingly subordinates his own ego to the life of the community and, if the hour demands, even sacrifices it.

Not in his intellectual gifts lies the source of the Aryan's capacity for creating and building culture. If he had just this alone, he could only act destructively, in no case could he organize; for the innermost essence of all organization requires that the individual renounce putting forward his personal opinion and interests and sacrifice both in favor of a larger group. Only by way of this general community does he again recover his share. Now, for example, he no longer works directly for himself, but with his activity articulates himself with the community, not only for his own advantage, but for the advantage of all. The most wonderful elucidation of this attitude is provided by

his word "work," by which he does not mean an activity for maintaining life
in itself, but exclusively a creative effort that does not conflict with the interests of the community. Otherwise he designates human activity, in so far as it
serves the instinct of self-preservation without consideration for his fellow
men, as theft, usury, robbery, burglary, etc.

This state of mind, which subordinates the interests of the ego to the
conservation of the community, is really the first premise for every truly human culture. From it alone can arise all the great works of mankind, which
bring the founder little reward, but the richest blessings to posterity. Yes, from
it alone can we understand how so many are able to bear up faithfully under a
scanty life which imposes on them nothing but poverty and frugality, but
gives the community the foundations of its existence. Every worker, every
peasant, every inventor, official, etc., who works without ever being able to
achieve any happiness or prosperity for himself, is a representative of this lofty
idea, even if the deeper meaning of his activity remains hidden in him.

What applies to work as the foundation of human sustenance and all human progress is true to an even greater degree for the defense of man and his
culture. In giving one's own life for the existence of the community lies the
crown of all sense of sacrifice. It is this alone that prevents what human hands
have built from being overthrown by human hands or destroyed by Nature.

Our own German language possesses a word which magnificently designates this kind of activity: *Pflichterfullung* (fulfillment of duty); it means not to
be self-sufficient but to serve the community.

The basic attitude from which such activity arises, we call—to distinguish it from egoism and selfishness—idealism. By this we understand only
the individual's capacity to make sacrifices for the community, for his fellow
men. . . .

Organizing the broad masses of our people which are today in the international camp into a national people's community does not mean renouncing
the defense of justified class interests. Divergent class and professional interests are not synonymous with class cleavage, but are natural consequences of
our economic life. Professional grouping is in no way opposed to a true national community, for the latter consists in the unity of a nation in all those
questions which affect this nation as such.

The integration of an occupational group which has become a class with
the national community, or merely with the state, is not accomplished by the
lowering of higher classes but by uplifting the lower classes. This process in
turn can never be upheld by the higher class, but only by the lower class
fighting for its equal rights. The present-day bourgeoisie was not organized
into the state by measures of the nobility, but by its own energy under its own
leadership.

The German worker will not be raised to the framework of the German
national community via feeble scenes of fraternization, but by a conscious rais-

ing of his social and cultural situation until the most serious differences may be viewed as bridged. A movement which sets this development as its goal will have to take its supporters primarily from this camp.[14] It may fall back on the intelligentsia only in so far as the latter has completely understood the goal to be achieved. This process of transformation and equalization will not be completed in ten or twenty years; experience shows that it comprises many generations.

The severest obstacle to the present-day worker's approach to the national community lies not in the defense of his class interests, but in his international leadership and attitude which are hostile to the people and the fatherland. The same unions with a fanatical national leadership in political and national matters would make millions of workers into the most valuable members of their nation regardless of the various struggles that took place over purely economic matters.

A movement which wants honestly to give the German worker back to his people and tear him away from the international delusion must sharply attack a conception dominant above all in employer circles, which under national community understands the unresisting economic surrender of the employee to the employer and which chooses to regard any attempt at safeguarding even justified interests regarding the employee's economic existence as an attack on the national community. Such an assertion is not only untrue, but a conscious lie, because the national community imposes its obligations not only on one side but also on the other.

Just as surely as a worker sins against the spirit of a real national community when, without regard for the common welfare and the survival of a national economy, he uses his power to raise extortionate demands, an employer breaks this community to the same extent when he conducts his business in an inhuman, exploiting way, misuses the national labor force and makes millions out of its sweat. He then has no right to designate himself as national, no right to speak of a national community; no, he is a selfish scoundrel who induces social unrest and provides future conflicts which whatever happens must end in harming the nation.

Thus, the reservoir from which the young movement must gather its supporters will primarily be the masses of our workers. Its work will be to tear these away from the international delusion, to free them from their social distress, to raise them out of their cultural misery and lead them to the national community as a valuable, united factor, national in feeling and desire.

If, in the circles of the national intelligentsia, there are found men with the warmest hearts for their people and its future, imbued with the deepest knowledge of the importance of this struggle for the soul of these masses, they will be highly welcome in the ranks of this movement, as a valuable spiritual backbone. But winning over the bourgeois voting cattle can never be the aim of this movement. If it were, it would burden itself with a dead weight which by its whole nature would paralyze our power to recruit from the broad masses. For regardless of the theoretical beauty of the idea of leading together the broadest masses from below and from above within the framework of the movement, there is the opposing fact that by psychological propagandizing of bourgeois masses in general meetings, it may be possible to create moods and even to spread insight, but not to do away with qualities of character or, better expressed, vices, whose development and origin embrace centuries.

## Notes

1. "*Spottgeburt aus Dreck und Feuer.*" Should be "*von Dreck und Feuer.*" Goethe's *Faust*, Part 1, 5356: Faust to Mephistopheles.

2. *Schaf[s]kopf* is a four-handed card-game widely played in Germany. *Tarock* [is a] three-handed card-game of Italian origin (*tarocco*), popular in Austria and southern Germany.

3. "*der Schlechteste unter den Anderen.*"

4. "*Volksgenosse.*" Brockhaus defines: In contrast to the concept of citizen which is based on the idea of legal equality in the state, the designation for all members of the same national community (*Volksgemeinschaft*), especially those who form a working association in the service of the nation as a whole. As used by the National Socialists, it might be translated as "racial comrades." I have chosen the more neutral term "national comrades" because the National Socialists did not coin the term and it occurs frequently in the speeches of parliamentarians who were not even noted for their anti-Semitism.

5. Bismarck's Anti-Socialist Law, put through the Reichstag on October 18, 1878, prohibited meetings, collections of funds, and publications of Social Democrats, Socialists, and Communists; it remained in force until 1890 when the new Emperor, William II, opposed it. Despite the law, Socialist deputies in the Reichstag retained their parliamentary immunity.

6. General Helmuth von Moltke (1800–91) became chief of the Prussian General Staff in 1859. He modernized the Prussian army and was the founder of the German General Staff.

7. Schwabing: the bohemian quarter of Munich, located near the university.

8. The German here has an untranslatable and rather elaborate pun. To sow wild oats is "*sich die Horner abstossen,*" to butt off one's horns. The word I have rendered as "worn-out" is *enthornt*, literally de-horned. Siegfried did not have horns; the reference is to the horny skin which made him invulnerable.

9. "... *in der Wahrung des letzten Naturrechtes, aber auch der letzten Natur-verpflichtung?*"

10. Second edition inserts "urge toward" before "racial purity."

11. Second edition: "so his action against Nature" instead of "this attack."

12. Second edition omits: "in this world."

13. "*und verbleibt in der Folge dann, belastet mit der Empfindlichkeit des Menschen, im Bereich des hilflosen Jammers der Tiere.*" Second edition has: "*Er begibt sich in der Folge, belastet mit der Empfindlichkeit des Menschen, ins Bereich des hilflosen Tieres.*" This would read: "In consequence, burdened with all the sensibility of man, he moves into the realm of the helpless beast."

14. Changed in second edition to "the workers' camp."

# A *KLANWATCH* SPECIAL REPORT

## *Domestic Terrorists: The KKK in the 'Fifth Era'*

*Klanwatch*, the source of the "Fifth Era," is a regular publication of the Southern Poverty Law Center in Montgomery, Alabama.

### 1984 Annual Review of the KKK, Neo-Nazis and Other White Supremacist Organizations

Visible Ku Klux Klan activity in the United States declined, for the second year in a row, in 1984. Fewer Klansmen rallied around burning crosses, marched in public parades or recruited on street corners, and incidents of KKK-related violence and intimidation reported to *Klanwatch* also dropped.

However, 1984 was the year a fringe element of the racist right quietly declared war on the federal government and began a violent initiative at establishing a whites-only nation in the United States and Canada.

Some KKK leaders have been writing and speaking for several years now of the need to move into a period of greater secrecy, referred to as the "Fifth Era" of the Klan. The four previous eras are Reconstruction, the 1920s–1930s, the 1950s–1960s, and the current resurgence, which began about 1972.

The chief advocates of the "Fifth Era" have included Robert Miles, a Michigan KKK chieftain who served time for firebombing schoolbuses, and Louis Beam, a former Texas Klan leader who has recently allied himself with the Idaho-based Aryan Nations.

They argue that the publicity-seeking of the Klan served racists well during the past decade by bringing in many new recruits and by "sensitizing" whites to "racialist" issues, but it has also brought increased prosecution, civil legal action, and opposition. Thus, they say, it is time for the Klan to take its committed members underground to begin work in earnest toward the white revolution they are certain is coming.

Terrorist-type activity toward this end dominated KKK news during 1984, overshadowing the more general decline in organized hate group activity and dwarfing the year's other significant developments, including:

- Indictment of 10 KKK leaders in Alabama for federal civil rights violations.
- Arrest and prosecution of five Georgia Klansmen for racially motivated attacks on two west Georgia families.
- Court-ordered bans on Klan paramilitary activity in North Carolina and Alabama.
- Attendance of Imperial Wizard Bill Wilkinson as a "reporter" at the Republican National Convention in Dallas.
- Wilkinson's resignation from the Klan.
- Acquittal of nine Klansmen and Nazis on civil rights charges arising out of the Greensboro killings in 1979.
- Arrests of several Klansmen in Montgomery, Ala., for arson of *Klanwatch* office and for conspiring to bomb a civil rights march.

Overall, the Klan spent much of 1984 in courtrooms, defending its members against civil lawsuits and state and federal criminal prosecutions.

### The Underground

Meanwhile, recent arrests indicate that a small cadre of Klansmen, Nazis and other radical white supremacists in the Northwest have been robbing banks and armored cars, counterfeiting money, and plotting assassinations.

This miscellaneous criminal activity is being conducted by what its perpetrators and the law enforcement community call the Underground. The terroristic nature of the crimes has led to an FBI domestic security investigation, and seventeen suspects had been arrested by late January.[1] The suspects are all connected in some fashion with the Aryan Nations, a white supremacist, pseudo-religious cult based near Hayden Lake, Idaho. Other names used by the underground include the Silent Brotherhood (or its German translation, Bruder Schweigen), The Order, the Aryan Resistance Movement and the White American Bastion.

The FBI has linked alleged Underground members to the murder of Jewish talk-show host Alan Berg in Denver in June 1984, to two armored car robberies in Washington and California, to a bank robbery in Washington in December 1983 and to counterfeiting operations throughout the region.

Evidence indicates that the robberies, netting more than $4 million of which little has been recovered, were to get money to buy weapons and equipment with which the group plans to overthrow the federal government. Underground members, like many white supremacists, believe the federal government is controlled by a Jewish-Communist conspiracy.

The armored car robberies were sophisticated, and recent arrests indicate that inside information was obtained.

The first holdup was 23 April in Seattle. At least six white males in disguises robbed a parked Continental Armored Car transport truck of $500,000 in cash.

The second, even more daring, raid was 19 July near Ukiah, Calif. A dozen men forced a Brink's truck off the road, shot out the vehicle's tires and sprayed it with automatic weapons fire. The thieves re-routed traffic along the highway while unloading $3.6 million in cash.

One suspect in the robberies was Underground leader Robert Mathews, who died 8 December in a shootout after the FBI tracked him to remote Whidbey Island near Seattle. Mathews was being sought after he wounded an FBI agent at a Portland, Ore., motel 24 November.[2] Holed up in a house on the island, Mathews exchanged shots with the FBI and died when he refused to leave the house after illumination flares fired from a helicopter set the ammunition-packed house ablaze.

Cary Yarbrough, who was arrested 24 November during the Portland shootout between Mathews and the FBI, is a suspect in the Denver ambush murder of Alan Berg, who had berated extremist groups like the Klan and Nazis on his radio show. Ballistics tests on a Mac–10 machine pistol found by the FBI in Yarbrough's Sand Point, Id., home matched the bullets taken from Berg's body.

Searches of the homes and safehouses of those arrested have turned up numerous illegal automatic weapons, explosives and white supremacist propaganda calling for a white revolution against federal authorities. Among the latter documents are copies of a "Declaration of War" against the "Zionist Occupational Government," or ZOG, the name by which Underground members refer to the national government. A number of those arrested recently had signed the document.

Underground documents plainly state that its members are committed to the overthrow of the government and to the purging of all nonwhites and Jews from the country. Ultimately, the goal is the establishment of a white people's state to replace the present system.

The Underground thus represents a complete radicalization of the traditional approach of the Klan to the "race problem" in the United States and an ideological marriage to Nazism.

KKK anti-Semitism is not new, but Klan leaders have mainly sought to preserve the status quo by putting or keeping blacks in "their place." Few Klansmen proposed that blacks, Jews or other minorities be exterminated. Even after segregation was outlawed by the Supreme Court in 1954, the Klan's violence was aimed at preventing integration from becoming a reality in the South.

The concept behind the Underground, however, is a new approach. Legal separation of the races or political repression are no longer acceptable answers to the radicals of the Underground. Today's "Fifth Era" white supremacists seek a new order based on the model of Nazi Germany. They want final solutions, not Jim Crow segregation.

For those who monitor white supremacist groups in the United States, the radicalization of certain elements of the Klan and their alliance with unabashed Nazis in an Underground terrorist army comes as no great surprise.

First, the stigma of Nazism has worn off with the passage of time and the older generation. Many of today's KKK leaders are too young to have a personal recollection of the Second World War.

In addition, Nazi ideology is simply the logical extension of the Klan's philosophy; that is, it is the doctrine of racism carried to its logical conclusion.

Finally, it is not surprising that the allied Klan and Nazi leaders who have been preaching the inevitability of armed conflict between whites and non-whites would eventually be forced to initiate the hostilities themselves if the race war was otherwise too slow in coming.

The FBI says the blueprint for the racist revolution is actually set out in *The Turner Diaries*, by National Alliance leader William Pierce. The fictional account of the "Great Revolution" is recounted through the "diary" of an Underground soldier.

In the book white racists go underground, form a revolutionary group known as "The Organization" and launch a terroristic campaign to topple the federal government. They support their activities through bank and armored car robberies and wide-scale counterfeiting operations. Their tactics include assassinations of key political and economic leaders, as well as guerrilla attacks on transportation systems and power facilities, all of which are meant to destabilize the government and polarize the population along racial lines.[3]

Already various Klan and Nazi publications are arguing the merits of the decision to openly revolt. It seems inevitable that the line between those who believe in a political struggle and those who subscribe to the "Fifth Era" strategy of secrecy and direct action will be drawn more distinctly.

One consequence already being seen from the decision to form the Underground is that the most extreme and violent radicals from various organizations appear to be entering into greater cooperation. Currently implicated in Underground activity are members of the various Aryan Nations and National Alliance factions previously mentioned, as well as members of Klan groups in Alabama, Georgia, North Carolina, California, Michigan and Canada.

Law enforcement officers nationwide are working overtime on the problem, but additional violence seems inevitable.

### The Legal Front

Through private civil litigation and criminal prosecution, several dozen Klansmen were called to accountability in 1984, resulting in a number of convictions, guilty pleas and court injunctions.

However, nine Klansmen and Nazis were exonerated for the second time of any criminal wrongdoing in the Greensboro killings and cannot be retried. A four-month federal civil rights trial ended in acquittals in May. Jurors later said they believed Communist Workers Party members started the violence by beating with sticks on the cars of the Klansmen as they drove by the CWP demonstration.

The Reagan Justice Department added to its impressive record of Klan prosecutions by bringing two more significant cases involving KKK violence in the Deep South.

Nine Klansmen were indicted last 17 May and a tenth pleaded guilty to charges they conspired to attack a black civil rights march in Decatur, Ala., on 26 May 1979. The prosecution came after a civil lawsuit filed by the Southern Poverty Law Center uncovered evidence which was hidden from the FBI's initial investigation shortly after the incident.

A grand jury acting on the new evidence returned indictments nine days before expiration of the five-year statute of limitations. Nine of the ten defendants were top state officials in the Alabama chapter of the Invisible Empire, Knights of the KKK in 1979, and the indictments represent the largest number of Klan leaders ever indicted on a single incident.

The trial is pending a federal appeals court ruling on the trial judge's decision to forbid government attorneys from using certain evidence gathered in the *Klanwatch* suit.

In August federal authorities in Atlanta announced the arrests of five members of the Invisible Empire for racially motivated attacks on two west Georgia families during late 1982 and early 1983.4

Both incidents were classic examples of KKK nightriding. The first attack, in November 1982, was prompted by the friendship of Peggy Jo French, a young white woman, and her black neighbors. After learning about the woman's interracial friendships, the Klansmen barged into French's home one night and flogged her with a strap while her children watched. As the Kluxers left, they warned French, who was bruised and sore but not seriously injured, not to associate with blacks in the future.

The second beating happened several months later. The victim this time was a black man, Warren Cokley, whose wife is white. Again the masked Klansmen burst into the victim's home at night, beat the victim, Cokley, and fled. But Cokley recognized one of his masked assailants and managed to stab one of them. The Klansmen were convicted and sentenced to terms of fifteen to forty years and given large fines. A Klansman who turned government witness was sentenced to six months in jail and a $2000 fine.

Other significant criminal prosecutions:

—Five members of the Knights of the KKK were arrested in Montgomery, Ala., in December on arson and explosives charges, including three Klansmen who were indicted for setting fire to the Southern Poverty Law Center and its *Klanwatch* offices. The indictments bring to at least 35 the number of Klansmen arrested in Alabama on federal civil right charges since 1979, far exceeding any other state.

—Henry Francis Hays, 30, the exalted cyclops of the Mobile, Ala., chapter of the United Klans of America, was sentenced last January to death for the brutal 1981 murder of Michael Donald, a black youth whom Hays and fellow Klansman James "Tiger" Knowles picked up off the street at random and killed. Benjamin F. Cox, a former exalted cyclops of the Mobile UKA chapter, has been indicted for conspiracy to commit murder in the same case.

—Bennie Jack Hays, 67, Titan of the Mobile, Ala., chapter of the United Klans of America, and his wife, Opal Hays, were convicted of federal mail and wire fraud charges in October for filing a false insurance claim in connection with a fire of mysterious origin which destroyed their home in July 1983. Hays is the father of Henry Hays and the father-in-law of Benjamin Cox.

—James Holder, a former den leader of the Carolina Knights of the KKK, was sentenced to 18 years in prison in July for killing fellow CKKKK leader David E. Wallace in November 1983 after an argument at a Klan meeting.

—William P. Brennan and Robert Alvarez of New York City were arrested in July and charged with the Christmas Eve 1977 murder of a black man who, minutes before his death, was seen embracing a white woman outside a church. The defendants were suspected white supremacists. Their photographs reportedly have appeared in *White Lightning,* a white supremacy magazine.

—Joseph Paul Franklin, a onetime member of the National States Rights Party and avowed white supremacist, was sentenced in July to 21–31 years in prison for the dynamite bombing of Beth Shalom synagogue in Chattanooga, Tenn., on 29 July 1977.

—Oddist J. Lambright, leader of a splinter faction of the KKK, pleaded guilty and received three years in federal prison in April on charges of planning a campaign of intimidation and terrorism aimed at forcing the ouster of a white Oakdale, La., radio station executive whose wife is black.

Civil litigation can also be an effective weapon in bringing KKK violence and intimidation under control. In 1984 several civil suits were concluded successfully against various Klan and white supremacist groups, and new lawsuits were filed. In addition, a Georgia television station and a Tennessee newspaper successfully defended against libel charges brought by Klansmen, and a North Carolina KKK leader dropped his lawsuit against a newspaper which refused to run an advertisement promoting a Klan rally.

—*Reed* v. *Handley.* Members of the Invisible Empire, Knights of the KKK Special Forces agreed in an out-of-court settlement not to operate a paramilitary group in Alabama in a suit brought by *Klanwatch.*

—*Hanna Elkon, et al.* v. *Brad Barry, et al.* A Jewish family which was subjected to three years of anti-Semitic harassment was awarded $550,000 in damages by a federal court in this lawsuit brought by the Washington, D.C.-based Jewish Advocacy Center. A permanent injunction against further acts by the defendants was entered and defendant Barry was ordered to stay at least 500 feet away from members of the family or their property. (E.D. of N.Y., CV 83–1898)

—*Bryant* v. *Barry Robinson.* Knights of the KKK leader Robinson was ordered by a federal judge in Pensacola, Fla., to pay three black men almost $100,000 in damages for injuries they suffered in a jailhouse attack set up by the Kluxer in the hope it would lead to the segregation of inmates by race in the county jail.

—*Royals* v. *Gray Communications Systems, Inc.* A jury found in favor of WALB-TV in Albany, Ga., in a $500,000 suit filed by KKK leader Clyde Wayne Royals who accused the station of libeling him.

—*White Knights of Liberty* v. *Wilkes Journal-Patriot Publishing Co.* Imperial Wizard Joe Grady of the North Carolina-based White Knights of Liberty dropped his suit against the newspaper, which he accused of discrimination because the paper refused to publish an advertisement promoting a KKK rally. Grady sued because he said the newspaper's decision was responsible for poor attendance at the rally, which drew only 50 Klansmen and spectators.

—*Donald* v. *UKA.* Civil suit brought by *Klanwatch* last summer on behalf of KKK murder victim's mother seeking damages and injunction against Klansmen who killed her son, Michael Donald. Plaintiff represents all blacks in Alabama. Victim lynched in tree to show black jury the consequences of letting off black defendant accused of killing policeman in a trial that ended in a hung jury the day of the murder. Suit seeks to have Klan specifically enjoined from intimidating blacks regarding jury duty.

—*Person* v. *Confederate Knights of the KKK. Klanwatch* suit on behalf of black prison guard who was harassed in attempt to obtain promotion. Suit also sought to close down CKKKK paramilitary operation in North Carolina. CKKKK leader Glenn Miller agreed to such a stipulation in a consent decree in January 1985.

—*Roland W. Torbert* v. *The Nashville Tennessean and Jerry Thompson.* Torbert, the former exalted cyclops of an Alabama IE klavern, claimed that reporter Jerry Thompson libeled him in a book Thompson wrote about his infiltration of Torbert's Klan group. A federal court jury in Birmingham found Thompson not guilty of libel.

*Trends of the KKK*

Generally speaking, Klan organizing on the scale of 1978–81 was rare in 1984, with the possible exceptions of Georgia and North Carolina, which continue to be the hotbeds of open KKK activity.

Public Klan functions are fewer and farther between, less well attended, and more and more isolated than in the recent past. Active membership today probably totals no more than 7500, and is confined mostly to the group's traditional Southern strongholds.

Easily the most active major Klan group last year—at least publicly—was the Carolina Knights of the KKK, led by Glenn Miller and based in Angier, N.C. Even so, the CKKKK, which changed its name to the Confederate Knights of the KKK toward year's end, achieved little net growth, if any, during 1984.

At the close of 1983, *Klanwatch* estimated that the CKKKK had about 500 members. Since that time, some members have quit in the aftermath of the James Holder-David Wallace shooting, and some of his older members have quit due to disagreements over tactics. Miller's current active membership is probably no more than 300.

The CKKKK's name change reflects a recent effort by Miller to expand into South Carolina, Georgia, Alabama, Tennessee, Kentucky, Virginia, Mississippi, Louisiana and Florida. He has established dens in Columbia, S.C., and Canton, Ga.

Miller played host to out-of-state Klan leaders. Illinois Knights of the KKK Grand Dragon K.A. Badynski and several Midwestern Klansmen attended a CKKKK rally at Siler City, N.C., in March, and Aryan Nations-KKK leader Louis Beam spoke to a private CKKKK rally in November.

In a recruitment and organizing ploy, Miller ran for governor in 1984, generating the expected cascade of publicity but attracting less than 1 percent of the vote in the primary.

One of the surprises of 1984 was the late-summer resignation of Imperial Wizard Bill Wilkinson of the Invisible Empire, Knights of the KKK. Once perhaps the largest faction in the country, the IE fell on hard times recently, and Wilkinson's resignation was nothing more than an admission of the inevitable. Membership in the group had sunk from a high of perhaps 3500 nationwide in 1980 to less than 500 last September, when he announced to the IEKKKK's national convention near Atlanta that he was throwing in the sheet.

Wilkinson was a victim of his own past violent rhetoric, which had inspired his followers to acts of vigilantism and in turn led to the legal and financial difficulties that made it impractical to go on. By the end of Wilkinson's nine years as Imperial Wizard, eighteen members of the group had been indicted for federal civil rights violations—fifteen of them last year.

In August, Wilkinson attended the Republican National Convention in

Dallas as an officially sanctioned reporter—complete with press credentials issued by the Republican National Committee to Empire Publishing Company, a Klan front. Wilkinson's reporter status allowed him to operate on the convention floor, and he claimed in *The Klansman* to have attended a news conference of Vice-President Bush.

Succeeding Wilkinson is James Blair of Five Points, Ala. Blair, formerly Alabama Grand Dragon of the IE, is an auto mechanic who claims his election as head Klansman is divinely ordained. But membership in the Invisible Empire is divided over Blair's leadership—his unpolished style is in stark contrast to Wilkinson's drawling good-old-boy charisma and publications issued under Blair are semi-literate. A source close to Wilkinson reports he is dismayed by Blair's actions since his succession.

A major shakeup in the Invisible Empire would not be surprising in 1985, with one or more of its state units realigning with other KKK factions. The Georgia chapter of the IE, with its young Grand Dragon, Ed Stephens, would be a prime candidate to do so.

For the third straight year, Georgia ranks alongside North Carolina as the hotbed of KKK activity in the country. Rallies and demonstrations were numerous there in 1984, especially in the west and north central areas of the state, and less intense organizing also was reported in the Savannah area and elsewhere downstate.[5]

Last April in Cedartown, fifty miles west of Atlanta, a black youth passing by a Klan demonstration was roughed up and maced by a robed Klansman wielding brass knuckles. A deputy sheriff who witnessed the incident said the attack was unprovoked, but to date no one has been arrested.

In other KKK news of 1984, Don Black, Grand Wizard of one faction of the Knights of the KKK, was released from federal prison in Texas 15 November and returned to Birmingham to set up operations of his dissension-wracked Klan. He had served two years on a three-year sentence for violating the United States Neutrality Act for plotting with other white supremacists to overthrow the island of Dominica in 1981.

Black, who faced a revolt in his ranks after going to prison in 1982, is in a stalemated fight for control of the Knights with Stanley McCollum, his former national office director. Both claim to be the legitimate wizard.

McCollum's faction was joined in 1984 by the Georgia-based Southern Knights of the KKK. This group was once called the New Order Knights and was forced by NSRP leader Ed Fields of Marietta.

On the political and organizing front, racist leaders rolled out two new educational tools in 1984 and, in so doing, thrust the Klan into the era of high-tech hate.

In California, longtime Klan leader Tom Metzger (who tried to drop the Klan label sometime ago and now peddles his ideology under the name of White American Resistance, or WAR) produced and began distributing a multi-part white supremacy "documentary" for showing on community-access cable television.

The program, titled "Race," aired for the first time in San Diego late in the summer and was shown on Qube Cable in Dallas last fall. White supremacists view community-access cable as a means of getting an uncensored message to the public.[6] The second development was the establishment of a national racist computer network. Actually, at least four separate bulletin boards were put on line, sponsored respectively by the Idaho-based Aryan Nations, the Confederate Knights of the KKK in North Carolina, Louis Beam in Texas and Metzger in California.

The networks, which are primarily an organizing tool, allow racists to send and receive electronic mail, to read and post messages and to have direct access to the public.

The Klan enjoyed no success at the ballot box in 1984 (a Falkville, Ala., Klansman running for mayor got fewer votes than he had family members), although Nazi Gerald Carlson won the Republican nomination and nearly 40 percent of the vote in a Michigan congressional race.

Carlson, who also ran in 1980 but lost badly in a primary runoff, conducted an openly white supremacist campaign with the slogan "Whites Have Rights, Too."

Finally, there was still the problem in 1984 of random racist violence —acts committed by individuals with no known KKK or other hate-group tie—which continued to be a serious but largely unnoticed phenomenon nationwide last year. For every act of KKK-related violence or intimidation there was at least one incident of random racist violence.

Reports of such activity came in to *Klanwatch* offices from around the country, without respect to sectional lines.

## Notes

1. Susan Merki Tornatzky has been charged with helping plot the Brink's robbery and for receiving a payment from the stolen currency. Tornatzky's husband, Eric, 30, was charged with passing counterfeit bills. A friend of the Tornatzkys, Jean Craig, 50, was also arrested for receiving a payment of $10,000 for helping plan the California robbery. Charged in the Seattle armored car robbery are Denver Daw Parmenter, Randolph George Duey, Andrew V. Barnhill, Robert J. Mathews, Gary Lee Yarbrough, and Bruce Carroll Pierce. Among those charged in the California robbery are Parmenter, Barnhill, Mathews, Yarbrough, James Dye, and Richard Harold Kemp. Authorities have declined to name several other individuals indicted by a federal grand jury in the Brink's robbery until the defendants are taken into custody.

2. Charged with harboring Mathews between 24 November and 7 December are Robert E. and Sharon K. Merki, and John Doe, aka Ian Stuart, aka Bartlett Duane Udell. The three had more than $50,000 when arrested. Also charged with harboring a fugitive are Randolph Duey, and Michael Stanley Norris and Mark Frank Jones, 26, both of

Northport, Ala. At the time of their arrest, the Merkis were wanted in Oregon on counterfeiting charges. The FBI says the participants in the Ukiah robbery fled to Boise, Id., after the heist and met at the Merki home, where they divided up the money.

3. There is a whole library of Underground literature the terrorists are using as reference guides, including *The Road Back, 33/5, Essays of a Klansman, Inter-Klan Newsletter and Survival Alert, Silencers, Snipers and Assassins* and *The Poor Man's James Bond* among them.

4. Arrested were Mailon Paul Wood, Winford Wood, James Kent Adams, Kenneth Davis, and William Deering.

5. The Atlanta metropolitan area was the scene of several acts of racial violence and intimidation, although no Klan connections to this activity have yet been established. Five youths were arrested last fall in a campaign of terroristic attacks against a black Lawrenceville, Ga., family which had moved into an all-white neighborhood shortly before. In two separate incidents, a cross was burned on the family's lawn and their car was firebombed and destroyed. Arrested in the firebombing were Floyd Cowen and Jimmy Hutcheson; charged in the cross burning were Albert Roebuck, Dennis Cain and Charles Medler. The victims have moved since the attacks. According to a member of the Atlanta Metro Fair Housing Board, other black families have been treated to similar, if less severe harassment in the Marietta area, which is the home of the National States Rights' Party.

6. Ironically, one of the racists, Frank Silva, profiled in "Race," is currently sought by the FBI in connection with alleged Underground criminal activity.

# Part Six

# Feminism

All of the ideologies in this book offer a vision of freedom. But with the possible exception of anarchism, it is freedom for the few. Which few is variously defined by class, gender, and/or race. Feminism is different. According to Catharine Stimpson, feminism offers "a moral vision of women, in all their diversity, and of social justice," and it enables "men and women to re-experience and re-form themselves."[1] Diversity and justice for men and women, rich and poor, black, brown, yellow, and white. Unlike the others, feminism is an inclusive ideology.

American feminism is often portrayed as a product of the 1960s, but it has a longer history. Our feminist movement originated, along with liberalism, when women demanded to be included in "the rights of man." In 1787 Abigail Adams warned her husband, John, a delegate to the Constitutional Convention, that "if particular care and attention is not paid to the ladies, we are determined to foment a rebellion, and will not hold ourselves bound by any laws in which we have no voice and representation!"[2] In 1848 women met for the first equal rights convention at Seneca Falls, New York. Paralleling the Declaration of Independence, they began their "Declaration of Sentiments" with these words: "We hold these truths to be self-evident: that all men and women are created equal."3 They demanded equal rights, among them the right to vote. Only in 1920 were women granted the suffrage. In America today women still lack equal rights. In 1983, the Equal Rights Amendment (ERA), which reads "equality of rights under the law shall not be denied or abridged by the United States or by any state on account of sex" missed ratification by three states.4

Feminists continue to debate the importance of the ERA. Was it a symbolic platform? A strategic error? In any case, its failure should remind Americans that sex discrimination persists. Other statistics confirm this. Sixty-six years after receiving the vote, women, who constitute 52 percent of the population, hold 5 percent of national offices. Working women average 64 cents for every dollar earned by men. The FBI estimates that a woman is raped every eight minutes. The list goes on and on. The question is: Why? Feminist answers to this question vary. The frameworks in this part provide different analyses of the nature and causes of women's oppression. They also offer different proposals for overcoming it.

As even this brief history suggests, liberal feminism predominates in the United States. The selections from Betty Friedan and Phyllis Schlafly represent the most recent debate over women's rights. In 1963, Friedan published *The Feminine Mystique* and identified "the problem that has no name." By acknowledging their shared sense of dissatisfaction, Friedan mobilized many women. Three years later, she founded the National Organization for Women (NOW). Two goals emerge in Friedan's and other liberal feminists' writings: the elimination of sex roles, and the extension of rights to women. Mary Wollstonecraft, the first liberal feminist, explained the logic that connects them. She insisted that women, if given the opportunity, would demonstrate equal rationality and deserve equal rights: "Let their faculties have room to unfold, and their virtues to gain strength and then determine where the whole sex must stand in the intellectual scale."5 Liberal feminists have continued to argue that natural sexual differences do not justify social sex roles.6 They have fought sex discrimination on two fronts, opposing discriminatory laws and using the law against discrimination. The NOW Bill of Rights outlines their demands: the ERA, nondiscriminatory employment practices, rights to maternity leave, child-care tax deductions, child-care centers, equal educational opportunities, job training, and reproductive rights.

Liberal feminists are also the most commonly criticized. Phyllis Schlafly, national chair of Stop ERA, has led the opposition. To Schlafly, liberal feminists' denial of sex differences and denigration of sex roles seems negative. Schlafly's "positive woman" "understands that men and women are different and that those very differences provide the key to her success as a person and fulfillment as a woman." Of course, Friedan would respond that many of Schlafly's "positive women" secretly suffer from "the problem that has no name." But Schlafly strikes a powerful chord in many women. Do liberal feminists respect wives and mothers? Do they propose a unisex society? Is this, many women ask, really liberation? According to Schlafly, "Our strength is in our diversity, not in our sameness." Again, Friedan has a response: Liberal feminists defend individuality, that is, "the right of every woman in America to become all she is capable of becoming."[7] This includes the freedom to choose marriage and motherhood. According to Friedan, "The real sexual revolution is the emergence of women from passivity, from thingness, to full self-determination, to full dignity."[8]

But can women ever "become all they are capable of becoming" in liberal, capitalist societies? Marxist feminists say no. Liberal feminists' emphasis on legal reform is naive. There is a deeper source of women's oppression: capitalism. To Marxist feminists, the traditional family (female homemaker and male breadwinner) is an economic unit. Women exchange sexual and domestic services for financial support. Marx and Engels even call bourgeois marriage legalized prostitution. As economic units, families are functional for capitalism. Monogamous marriage provides a clear line of descent, facilitating inheritance and, with it, capital accumulation. This is Engels's emphasis in *The Origin of the Family, Private Property and the State.* But the family also has other functions. It is a "haven in a heartless world," a place to take out and/or recover from frustrations at work. It creates artificially high consumption, that is, each family needs appliances, cars, a home, etc. It teaches sons to be good providers; daughters learn to perform socially necessary labor for free. Mothers also form a flexible labor force, available for part-time, temporary, and/or emergency work. Marxist feminists conclude that women's oppression in the family is integral to capitalism.

What, then, is to be done? Proletarian women and men must fight together for socialist revolution. This means that women must postpone their personal concerns with the transformation of marriage and family. These divide the proletariat and hence are counterrevolutionary. Only after the revolution does the real emancipation of women begin. Lenin distinguishes this emancipation from legal reform: "Not withstanding all the laws emancipating woman, she continues to be a domestic slave, because petty housework crushes, strangles, stultifies and degrades her. . . . The real emancipation of women, real communism, will begin only where and when an all-out struggle begins (led by the proletariat wielding the state power) against this petty housekeeping, or rather when its wholesale transformation into a large-scale socialist economy begins."[9] As Engels argued earlier, women must become producers, and to make this possible familial tasks must be socialized. Unfortunately, "real communism" has not emancipated women. Sexism pre- and postdates capitalism.

Radical feminism identifies a common problem with Marxist and liberal feminism. Both try to be gender blind, but they become gender biased. How? Radical feminists argue that the oppression of women is fundamental. Historically, women were the first oppressed group, and their oppression remains the broadest, deepest, and hardest to overcome. Radical feminists see every culture as two cultures, a male dominant and a female subordinate one. Whether through legal reform or economic revolution, liberals and Marxists fight only to include women in the dominant culture. They continue to define liberation in male terms. In contrast, in their quest for equality with men, radical feminists celebrate women's differences from men.

But conservatives, like Schlafly, also defend difference. How do radical feminist arguments differ? According to radical feminists, Schlafly's positive woman is a product of patriarchy. *Patriarchy* is their term for male domination, especially of women's bodies. This domination takes many forms. Monogamous heterosexuality reserves women's sexuality for men. Inadequate birth control and/or social pressure forces motherhood. Radical feminists do not merely invert this male culture; that is Schlafly's stance. Instead, they transform or reconceive it. For example, patriarchy encourages women to nurture husbands and children. Radical feminists tell women to nurture themselves.

Radical feminist proposals for social change vary. Many advocate lesbianism. For Charlotte Bunch, "To be a lesbian is to love oneself, woman, in a culture that denigrates and despises women."[10] According to Adrienne Rich, lesbianism may be as much a political statement as a sexual preference. She describes a "lesbian continuum" of "woman-identified experience," which includes many "forms of primary intensity between and among women."[11] Monique Wittig's vision of lesbianism, included here, is even more radical. She argues that man and woman are cultural categories. That is, men's control of women's bodies extends to the very definition of woman. It is not enough, she concludes, to replace patriarchy with matriarchy, since that inversion perpetuates "the oppressors' definition of us." True lesbianism moves "beyond the categories of sex." Man and woman disappear, and "we are for the first time in history confronted with the necessity of existing as a person."

Radical feminism is not acceptable or available to many women. Lesbianism minimizes sexual preferences and ignores economic realities binding women to men. Heidi Hartmann synthesizes radical and Marxist feminism to overcome their mutual limitations. The latter, she agrees, is sex blind, but the former is class blind. For Hartmann, the source of women's oppression, the link between class and sex, is men's control over women's productive and reproductive labor. She analyzes the reciprocal interactions between capitalism and patriarchy and concludes that women's liberation involves overcoming both. Her socialist feminist vision is reproductive freedom. This includes abortion services, birth control, child care, equal education, freedom of sexual choice, decent housing, good jobs, medical care, social welfare. This notion of reproductive freedom goes far beyond the liberals' reproductive rights. It not only affirms freedom of choice but also creates a context in which women can choose freely. Reproductive freedom also conveys the inclusive nature of feminism. Socialist feminists insist that "all these aspects of reproductive freedom must be available to all people—women, minorities, the disabled and handicapped, Medicaid and welfare recipients, teenagers, everyone."[12]

It goes without saying that women do not have reproductive freedom in this sense. Neither do men. House husbands are even less common than working mothers, and at present neither role is attractive. Yet many men and women choke on the sentence "I am a feminist." Catharine Stimpson has dubbed feminism "the new 'F' word."[13] That traditional voices choke on it is predictable. That women who have struggled and succeeded also do is more troubling. Many such women adopt what Betty Friedan calls a three-sex theory: there are men, other women, and me.[14] Statistics show, however, that exceptional women are just that—exceptions. Still others, Stimpson says, choke because they are overwhelmed. They say, "I am a feminist," and think "but I wish I did not have to be." For these voices, the lesson is that it is not possible to liberate one class, one race, one sex. Certainly, no one can do it alone. As one author puts it, "Black people alone cannot make a revolution in this country. Native American people alone cannot make a revolution in this country. Asians alone cannot make a revolution in this country. Chicanos alone cannot make a revolution in this country. White people alone cannot make revolution in this country. Women alone cannot make revolution in this country. Gay people alone cannot make revolution in this country. And anyone who tries it will not be successful."[15] Only as an inclusive ideology can feminism succeed.

## Notes

1. Catharine Stimpson, "The New 'F' Word," *Ms.* 16, nos. 1–2 (July/August 1987): 80.

2. Quoted in Jo Freeman, *The Politics of Women's Liberation* (New York: Longman, 1975), 12.

3. Elizabeth Cady Stanton, Susan B. Anthony, and Matilda Josephine Gage, "Declaration and Resolutions of the Seneca Falls Convention," in *Women Leaders in American Politics,* ed. James David Barber and Barbara Kellerman (Englewood Cliffs, N.J.: Prentice-Hall, 1986), 201–4.

4. See Jane Mansbridge, *Why We Lost the ERA* (Chicago: University of Chicago Press, 1986).

5. Mary Wollstonecraft, "A Vindication of the Rights of Woman," in *Philosophy of Woman,* ed. Mary Briody Mahowald, (Indianapolis: Hackett, 1983), 216.

6. The terminology used for this distinction is sex (biological characteristics) versus gender (social roles).

7. Betty Friedan, "Our Revolution Is Unique," in Mahowald, *Philosophy of Woman,* 14.

8. Ibid., 16.

9. V.I. Lenin, "The Emancipation of Women," in Mahowald, *Philosophy of Woman*, 119.

10. Charlotte Bunch, "Lesbians in Revolt," in *Feminist Frameworks*, ed. Alison Jaggar and Paula Rothenberg (New York: McGraw-Hill, 1984), 144.

11. Adrienne Rich, "Compulsory Heterosexuality and Lesbian Existence," in Jaggar and Rothenberg, *Feminist Frameworks*, 417.

12. Quoted in Alison Jaggar, *Feminist Politics and Human Nature* (Totowa, N.J.: Rowman and Allenheld, 1983), 318.

13. Stimpson, "The New 'F' Word."

14. Friedan, "Our Revolution Is Unique," 13.

15. Pat Parker, "Revolution: It's Not Neat or Pretty or Quick," in *This Bridge Called My Back: Writings by Radical Women of Color*, ed. Cherrie Moraga and Gloria Anzaldua; foreword by Toni Cade Bambara, 1st ed. (Watertown, Mass.: Persephone Press, 1981), 241.

# 30

## PHYLLIS SCHLAFLY

## *The Power of the Positive Woman*

Phyllis Schlafly (b. 1924) is best known for her work as national chair of "Stop ERA." Under her leadership, the Equal Rights Amendment was identified with unisex toilets and women in combat, contributing to its eventual defeat. Schlafly continues to argue that feminism "is no gain for women, for children, for families, or for America." Instead, she advocates the power of the positive woman.

The first requirement for the acquisition of power by the Positive Woman is to understand the differences between men and women. Your outlook on life, your faith, your behavior, your potential for fulfillment, all are determined by the parameters of your original premise. The Positive Woman starts with the assumption that the world is her oyster. She rejoices in the creative capability within her body and the power potential of her mind and spirit. She understands that men and women are different, and that those very differences provide the key to her success as a person and fulfillment as a woman.

The women's liberationist, on the other hand, is imprisoned by her own negative view of herself and of her place in the world around her. This view of women was most succinctly expressed in an advertisement designed by the principal women's liberationist organization, the National Organization for Women (NOW), and run in many magazines and newspapers and as spot announcements on many television stations. The advertisement showed a darling curlyheaded girl with the caption: "This healthy, normal baby has a handicap. She was born female."

This is the self-articulated dog-in-the-manger, chip-on-the-shoulder, fundamental dogma of the women's liberation movement. Someone—it is not clear who, perhaps God, perhaps the "Establishment," perhaps a conspiracy of male chauvinist pigs—dealt women a foul blow by making them female. It becomes necessary, therefore, for women to agitate and demonstrate and hurl demands on society in order to wrest from an oppressive male-dominated social structure the status that has been wrongfully denied to women through the centuries.

By its very nature, therefore, the women's liberation movement precipitates a series of conflict situations—in the legislatures, in the courts, in the schools, in industry—with man targeted as the enemy. Confrontation replaces cooperation as the watchword of all relationships. Women and men become adversaries instead of partners.

The second dogma of the women's liberationists is that, of all the injustices perpetrated upon women through the centuries, the most oppressive is the cruel fact that women have babies and men do not. Within the confines of the women's liberationist ideology, therefore, the abolition of this overriding inequality of women becomes the primary goal. This goal must be achieved at any and all costs—to the woman herself, to the baby, to the family, and to society. Women must be made equal to men in their ability *not* to become pregnant and *not* to be expected to care for babies they may bring into the world.

This is why women's liberationists are compulsively involved in the drive to make abortion and child-care centers for all women, regardless of religion or income, both socially acceptable and government-financed. Former Congresswoman Bella Abzug has defined the goal: "to enforce the constitutional right of females to terminate pregnancies that they do not wish to continue."

If man is targeted as the enemy, and the ultimate goal of women's liberation is independence from men and the avoidance of pregnancy and its consequences, then lesbianism is logically the highest form in the ritual of women's liberation. Many, such as Kate Millett, come to this conclusion, although many others do not.

The Positive Woman will never travel that dead-end road. It is self-evident to the Positive Woman that the female body with its baby-producing organs was not designed by a conspiracy of men but by the Divine Architect of the human race. Those who think it is unfair that women have babies, whereas men cannot, will have to take up their complaint with God because no other power is capable of changing that fundamental fact. On some college campuses, I have been assured that other methods of reproduction will be developed. But most of us must deal with the real world rather than with the imagination of dreamers.

Another feature of the woman's natural role is the obvious fact that women can breast-feed babies and men cannot. This functional role was not imposed by conspiratorial males seeking to burden women with confining chores, but must be recognized as part of the plan of the Divine Architect for the survival of the human race through the centuries and in the countries that know no pasteurization of milk or sterilization of bottles.

The Positive Woman looks upon her femaleness and her fertility as part of her purpose, her potential, and her power. She rejoices that she has a capability for creativity that men can never have.

The third basic dogma of the women's liberation movement is that there is no difference between male and female except the sex organs, and that all those physical, cognitive, and emotional differences you *think* are there, are merely the result of centuries of restraints imposed by a male-dominated society and sex-stereotyped schooling. The role imposed on women is, by definition, inferior, according to the women's liberationists.

The Positive Woman knows that, while there are some physical competitions in which women are better (and can command more money) than men, including those that put a premium on grace and beauty, such as figure skating, the superior physical strength of males over females in competitions of strength, speed, and short-term endurance is beyond rational dispute.

In the Olympic Games, women not only cannot win any medals in competition with men, the gulf between them is so great that they cannot even qualify for the contests with men. No amount of training from infancy can enable women to throw the discus as far as men, or to match men in pushups or in lifting weights. In track and field events, individual male records surpass those of women by 10 to 20 percent.

Female swimmers today are beating Johnny Weissmuller's records, but today's male swimmers are better still. Chris Evert can never win a tennis match against Jimmy Connors. If we removed lady's tees from golf courses, women would be out of the game. Putting women in football or wrestling matches can only be an exercise in laughs.

The Olympic Games, whose rules require strict verification to ascertain that no male enters a female contest and, with his masculine advantage, unfairly captures a woman's medal, formerly insisted on a visual inspection of the contestants' bodies. Science, however, has discovered that men and women are so innately different physically that their maleness/femaleness can be conclusively established by means of a simple skin test of fully clothed persons.

If there is *anyone* who should oppose enforced sex equality, it is the women athletes. Babe Didrickson, who played and defeated some of the great male athletes of her time, is unique in the history of sports.

If sex equality were enforced in professional sports, it would mean that men could enter the women's tournaments and win most of the money. Bobby Riggs has already threatened: "I think that men 55 years and over should be allowed to play women's tournaments—like the Virginia Slims. Everybody ought to know there's no sex after 55 anyway."

The Positive Woman remembers the essential validity of the old prayer: "Lord, give me the strength to change what I can change, the serenity to accept what I cannot change, and the wisdom to discern the difference." The women's liberationists are expending their time and energies erecting a make-believe world in which they hypothesize that *if* schooling were gender-free, and *if* the same money were spent on male and female sports programs, and *if* women were permitted to compete on equal terms, *then* they would prove themselves to be physically equal. Meanwhile, the Positive Woman has put the ineradicable physical differences into her mental computer, programmed her plan of action, and is already on the way to personal achievement.

Thus, while some militant women spend their time demanding more money for professional sports, ice skater Janet Lynn, a truly Positive Woman, quietly signed the most profitable financial contract in the history of women's athletics. It was not the strident demands of the women's liberationists that brought high prizes to women's tennis, but the discovery by sports promoters that beautiful female legs gracefully moving around the court made women's tennis a highly marketable television production to delight male audiences.

Many people thought that the remarkable filly named Ruffian would prove that a female race horse could compete equally with a male. Even with the handicap of extra weights placed on the male horse, the race was a disaster for the female. The gallant Ruffian gave her all in a noble effort to compete, but broke a leg in the race and, despite the immediate attention of top veterinarians, had to be put away.

Despite the claims of the women's liberation movement, there are countless physical differences between men and women. The female body is 50 to 60 percent water, the male 60 to 70 percent water, which explains why males can dilute alcohol better than women and delay its effect. The average woman is about 25 percent fatty tissue, while the male is 15 percent, making women more buoyant in water and able to swim with less effort. Males have a tendency to color blindness. Only 5 percent of persons who get gout are female. Boys are born bigger. Women live longer in most countries of the world, not only in the United States where we have a hard-driving competitive pace. Women excel in manual dexterity, verbal skills, and memory recall.

Arianna Stassinopoulos in her book *The Female Woman* has done a good job of spelling out the many specific physical differences that are so innate and so all-pervasive that

> even if Women's Lib was given a hundred, a thousand, ten thousand years in which to eradicate *all* the differences between the sexes, it would still be an impossible undertaking. . . .
>
> It is inconceivable that millions of years of evolutionary selection during a period of marked sexual division of labor have not left pronounced traces on the innate character of men and women. Aggressiveness, and mechanical and spatial skills, a sense of direction, and physical strength—all masculine characteristics—are the qualities essential for a hunter; even food gatherers need these same qualities for defense and exploration. The prolonged period of dependence of human children, the difficulty of carrying the peculiarly heavy and inert human baby—a much heavier, clumsier burden than the monkey infant and

much less able to cling on for safety—meant that women could not both look after their children and be hunters and explorers. Early humans learned to take advantage of this period of dependence to transmit rules, knowledge and skills to their offspring—women needed to develop verbal skills, a talent for personal relationships, and a predilection for nurturing going even beyond the maternal instinct.

Does the physical advantage of men doom women to a life of servility and subservience? The Positive Woman knows that she has a complementary advantage which is at least as great—and, in the hands of a skillful woman, far greater. The Divine Architect who gave men a superior strength to lift weights also gave women a different kind of superior strength.

The women's liberationists and their dupes who try to tell each other that the sexual drive of men and women is really the same, and that it is only societal restraints that inhibit women from an equal desire, an equal enjoyment, and an equal freedom from the consequences, are doomed to frustration forever. It just isn't so, and pretending cannot make it so. The differences are not a woman's weakness but her strength.

Dr. Robert Collins, who has had ten years' experience in listening to and advising young women at a large eastern university, put his finger on the reason why casual "sexual activity" is such a cheat on women:

A basic flaw in this new morality is the assumption that males and females are the same sexually. The simplicity of the male anatomy and its operation suggest that to a man, sex can be an activity apart from his whole being, a drive related to the organs themselves.

In a woman, the complex internal organization, correlated with her other hormonal systems, indicates her sexuality must involve her total self. On the other hand, the man is orgasm-oriented with a drive that ignores most other aspects of the relationship. The woman is almost totally different. She is engulfed in romanticism and tries to find and express her total feelings for her partner.

A study at a midwestern school shows that 80 percent of the women who had intercourse hoped to marry their partner. Only 12 percent of the men expected the same.

Women say that soft, warm promises and tender touches are delightful, but that the act itself usually leads to a "Is that all there is to it?" reaction. . . .

[A typical reaction is]: "It sure wasn't worth it. It was no fun at the time. I've been worried ever since. . . . "

The new morality is a fad. It ignores history, it denies the physical and mental composition of human beings, it is intolerant, exploitative, and is oriented toward intercourse, not love.

The new generation can brag all it wants about the new liberation of the new morality, but it is still the woman who is hurt the most. The new morality isn't just a "fad" —it is a cheat and a thief. It robs the woman of her virtue, her youth, her beauty, and her love—for nothing, just nothing. It has produced a generation of young women searching for their identity, bored with sexual freedom, and despondent from the loneliness of living a life without commitment. They have abandoned the old commandments, but they can't find any new rules that work.

The Positive Woman recognizes the fact that, when it comes to sex, women are simply not the equal of men. The sexual drive of men is much stronger than that of women. That is how the human race was designed in order that it might perpetuate itself. The other side of the coin is that it is easier for women to control their sexual appetites. A Positive Woman cannot defeat a man in a wrestling or boxing match, but she can motivate him, inspire him, encourage him, teach him, restrain him, reward him, and have power over him that he can never achieve over her with all his muscle. How or whether a Positive Woman uses her power is determined solely by the way she alone defines her goals and develops her skills.

The differences between men and women are also emotional and psychological. Without woman's innate maternal instinct, the human race would have died out centuries ago. There is nothing so helpless in all earthly life as the newborn infant. It will die within hours if not cared for. Even in the most primitive, uneducated societies, women have always cared for their newborn babies. They didn't need any schooling to teach them how. They didn't need any welfare workers to tell them it is their social obligation. Even in societies to whom such concepts as "ought," "social responsibility," and "compassion for the helpless" were unknown, mothers cared for their new babies.

Why? Because caring for a baby serves the natural maternal need of a woman. Although not nearly so total as the baby's need, the woman's need is nonetheless real.

The overriding psychological need of a woman is to love something alive. A baby fulfills this need in the lives of most women. If a baby is not available to fill that need, women search for a baby-substitute. This is the reason why women have traditionally gone into teaching and nursing careers. They are doing what comes naturally to the female psyche. The schoolchild or the patient of any age provides an outlet for a woman to express her natural maternal need.

This maternal need in women is the reason why mothers whose children have grown up and flown from the nest are sometimes cut loose from their psychological moorings. The maternal need in women can show itself in love for grandchildren, nieces, nephews, or even neighbors' children. The maternal need in some women has even manifested itself in an extraordinary affection lavished on a dog, a cat, or a parakeet.

This is not to say that every woman must have a baby in order to be fulfilled. But it is to say that fulfillment for most women involves expressing their natural maternal urge by loving and caring for someone.

The women's liberation movement complains that traditional stereo-typed roles assume that women are "passive" and that men are "aggressive." The anomaly is that a woman's most fundamental emotional need is not passive at all, but active. A woman naturally seeks to love affirmatively and to show that love in an active way by caring for the object of her affections.

The Positive Woman finds somebody on whom she can lavish her maternal love so that it doesn't well up inside her and cause psychological frustrations. Surely no woman is so isolated by geography or insulated by spirit that she cannot find someone worthy of her maternal love. All persons, men and women, gain by sharing something of themselves with their fellow humans, but women profit most of all because it is part of their very nature.

One of the strangest quirks of women's liberationists is their complaint that societal restraints prevent men from crying in public or showing their emotions, but permit women to do so, and that therefore we should "liberate" men to enable them, too, to cry in public. The public display of fear, sorrow, anger, and irritation reveals a lack of self-discipline that should be avoided by the Positive Woman just as much as by the Positive Man. Maternal love, however, is not a weakness but a manifestation of strength and service, and it should be nurtured by the Positive Woman.

Most women's organizations, recognizing the preference of most women to avoid hard-driving competition, handle the matter of succession of officers by the device of a nominating committee. This eliminates the unpleasantness and the tension of a competitive confrontation every year or two. Many women's organizations customarily use a prayer attributed to Mary, Queen of Scots, which is an excellent analysis by a woman of women's faults:

> Keep us, O God, from pettiness; let us be large in thought, in word, in deed. Let us be done with fault-finding and leave off self-seeking. . . . Grant that we may realize it is the little things that create differences, that in the big things of life we are at one.

Another silliness of the women's liberationists is their frenetic desire to force all women to accept the title *Ms.* in place of *Miss* or *Mrs.* If Gloria Steinem and Betty Friedan want to call themselves *Ms.* in order to conceal their marital status, their wishes should be respected.

But that doesn't satisfy the women's liberationists. They want all women to be compelled to use *Ms.* whether they like it or not. The women's liberation movement has been waging a persistent campaign to browbeat the media into using *Ms.* as the standard title for all women. The women's liberationists have already succeeded in getting the Department of Health, Education, and Welfare to forbid schools and colleges from identifying women students as *Miss* or *Mrs.*

All polls show that the majority of women do not care to be called *Ms.* A
Roper poll indicated that 81 percent of the women questioned said they prefer
*Miss* or *Mrs.* to *Ms.* Most married women feel they worked hard for the *r* in
their names, and they don't care to be gratuitously deprived of it. Most single
women don't care to have their name changed to an unfamiliar title that at
best conveys overtones of feminist ideology and is polemical in meaning, and
at worst connotes misery instead of joy. Thus, Kate Smith, a very Positive
Woman, proudly proclaimed on television that she is "Miss Kate Smith, not
Ms." Like other Positive Women, she has been succeeding while negative
women have been complaining.

Finally, women are different from men in dealing with the fundamentals
of life itself. Men are philosophers, women are practical, and 'twas ever thus.
Men may philosophize about how life began and where we are heading;
women are concerned about feeding the kids today. No woman would ever, as
Karl Marx did, spend years reading political philosophy in the British Museum while her child starved to death. Women don't take naturally to a search
for the intangible and the abstract. The Positive Woman knows who she is
and where she is going, and she will reach her goal because the longest journey
starts with a very practical first step.

Amaury de Riencourt, in his book *Sex and Power in History,* shows that a
successful society depends on a delicate balancing of different male and female
factors, and that the women's liberation movement, which promotes unisexual
values and androgyny, contains within it "a social and cultural death wish and
the end of the civilization that endorses it."

One of the two scholarly works dealing with woman's role, *Sex and
Power in History,* synthesizes research from a variety of disciplines—sociology,
biology, history, anthropology, religion, philosophy, and psychology. De
Riencourt traces distinguishable types of women in different periods in history, from prehistoric to modern times. The "liberated" Roman matron, who
is most similar to the present-day feminist, helped bring about the fall of
Rome through her unnatural emulation of masculine qualities, which resulted
in a large-scale breakdown of the family and ultimately of the empire.

De Riencourt examines the fundamental, inherent differences between
men and women. He argues that man is the more aggressive, rational, mentally creative, analytical-minded sex because of his early biological role as
hunter and provider. Woman, on the other hand, represents stability, flexibility, reliance on intuition, and harmony with nature, stemming from her pro-
creative function.

Where man is discursive, logical, abstract, or philosophical, woman tends
to be emotional, personal, practical, or mystical. Each set of qualities is vital
and complements the other. Among the many differences explained in de
Riencourt's book are the following:

Women tend more toward conformity than men—which is why they often excel in such disciplines as spelling and punctuation where there is only one correct answer, determined by social authority. Higher intellectual activities, however, require a mental independence and power of abstraction that they usually lack, not to mention a certain form of aggressive boldness of the imagination which can only exist in a sex that is basically aggressive for biological reasons.

To sum up: The masculine proclivity in problem solving is analytical and categorical; the feminine, synthetic and contextual. . . . Deep down, man tends to focus on the object, on external results and achievements; woman focuses on subjective motives and feelings. If life can be compared to a play, man focuses on the theme and structure of the play, woman on the innermost feelings displayed by the actors.

De Riencourt provides impressive refutation of two of the basic errors of the women's liberation movement: (1) that there are no emotional or cognitive differences between the sexes, and (2) that women should strive to be like men.

A more colloquial way of expressing the de Riencourt conclusion that men are more analytical and women more personal and practical is in the different answers that one is likely to get to the question, "Where did you get that steak?" A man will reply, "At the corner market," or wherever he bought it. A woman will usually answer, "Why? What's the matter with it?"

An effort to eliminate the differences by social engineering or legislative or constitutional tinkering cannot succeed, which is fortunate, but social relationships and spiritual values can be ruptured in the attempt. Thus the role reversals being forced upon high school students, under which guidance counselors urge reluctant girls to take "shop" and boys to take "home economics," further confuse a generation already unsure about its identity. They are as wrong as efforts to make a left-handed child right-handed.

## The Five Principles

When the women's liberationists enter the political arena to promote legislation and litigation in pursuit of their goals, their specific demands are based on five principles.

1. They demand that a "gender-free" rule be applied to every federal and state law, bureaucratic regulation, educational institution, and expenditure of public funds. Based on their dogma that there is no real difference between men and women (except in sex organs), they demand that males and females have identical treatment always. Thus, if fathers are not expected to stay home and care for their infant children, then neither should mothers be expected to

do so; and, therefore, it becomes the duty of the government to provide kiddy-care centers to relieve mothers of that unfair and unequal burden.

The women's lib dogma demands that the courts treat sex as a "suspect" classification—just as race is now treated—so that no difference of treatment or separation between the sexes will ever be permitted, no matter how reasonable or how much it is desired by reasonable people.

The nonsense of these militant demands was illustrated by the Department of Health, Education, and Welfare (HEW) ruling in July 1976 that all public school "functions such as father-son or mother-daughter breakfasts" would be prohibited because this "would be subjecting students to separate treatment." It was announced that violations would lead to a cutoff of federal assistance or court action by the Justice Department.

When President Gerald Ford read this in the newspaper, he was described by his press secretary as being "quite irritated" and as saying that he could not believe that this was the intent of Congress in passing a law against sex discrimination in education. He telephoned HEW Secretary David Mathews and told him to suspend the ruling.

The National Organization for Women, however, immediately announced opposition to President Ford's action, claiming that such events (fashion shows, softball games, banquets, and breakfasts) are sex-discriminatory and must be eliminated. It is clear that a prohibition against your right to make any difference or separation between the sexes anytime anywhere is a primary goal of the women's liberation movement.

No sooner had the father-son, mother-daughter flap blown over than HEW embroiled itself in another controversy by a ruling that an after-school choir of fifth and sixth grade boys violates the HEW regulation that bars single-sex choruses. The choir in Wethersfield, Connecticut, that precipitated the ruling had been established for boys whose "voices haven't changed yet," and the purpose was "to get boys interested in singing" at an early age so they would be willing to join coed choruses later. Nevertheless, HEW found that such a boy's chorus is by definition sex discriminatory.

The Positive Woman rejects the "gender-free" approach. She knows that there are many differences between male and female and that we are entitled to have our laws, regulations, schools, and courts reflect these differences and allow for reasonable differences in treatment and separations of activities that reasonable men and women want.

The Positive Woman also rejects the argument that sex discrimination should be treated the same as race discrimination. There is vastly more difference between a man and a woman than there is between a black and a white, and it is nonsense to adopt a legal and bureaucratic attitude that pretends that those differences do not exist. Even the U.S. Supreme Court has, in recent and relevant cases, upheld "reasonable" sex- based differences of treatment by legislatures and by the military.

2. The women's lib legislative goals seek an irrational mandate of "equality" at the expense of justice. The fact is that equality cannot always be equated with justice, and may sometimes even be highly unjust. If we had absolutely equal treatment in regard to taxes, then everyone would pay the same income tax, or perhaps the same rate of income tax, regardless of the size of the income.

If we had absolutely equal treatment in regard to federal spending programs, we would have to eliminate welfare, low-income housing benefits, food stamps, government scholarships, and many other programs designed to benefit low-income citizens. If we had absolutely equal treatment in regard to age, then seventeen-year-olds, or even ten-year-olds, would be permitted to vote, and we would have to eliminate Social Security unless all persons received the same benefits that only those over sixty-two receive now.

Our legislatures, our administrative departments, and our courts have always had and still retain the discretion to make reasonable differences in treatment based on age, income, or economic situation. The Positive Woman believes that it makes no sense to deprive us of the ability to make reasonable distinctions based on sex that reasonable men and women want.

3. The women's liberation movement demands that women be given the benefit of "reverse discrimination." The Positive Woman recognizes that this is mutually exclusive with the principle of equal opportunity for all. Reverse discrimination is based on the theory that "group rights" take precedence over individual rights, and that "reverse discrimination" (variously called "preferential treatment," "remedial action," or "affirmative action") should be imposed in order to compensate some women today for alleged past discriminations against other women. The word "quotas" is usually avoided, but it amounts to the same thing.

The fallacy of reverse discrimination has been aptly exposed by Professor Sidney Hook. No one would argue, he wrote, that because many years ago blacks and women were denied the right to vote, we should now compensate by giving them an extra vote or two, or by barring white men from voting at all.

But that is substantially what the women's liberationists are demanding—and getting by federal court orders—in education, employment, and politics when they ask for "affirmative action" to remedy past discrimination.

The Positive Woman supports equal opportunity for individuals of both sexes, as well as of all faiths and races. She rejects the theories of reverse discrimination and "group rights." It does no good for the woman who may have been discriminated against twenty-five years ago to know that an unqualified woman today receives preferential treatment at the expense of a qualified man. Only the vindictive radical would support such a policy of revenge.

4. The women's liberation movement is based on the unproven theory that uniformity should replace diversity—or, in simpler language, the federali-

zation of all remaining aspects of our life. The militant women demand that *all* educational institutions conform to federally determined rules about sex discrimination.

There is absolutely no evidence that HEW bureaucrats can do a better or fairer job of regulating our schools and colleges than local officials. Nor is there any evidence that individuals, or women, or society as a whole, would be better off under a uniform system enforced by the full power of the federal government than they would be under a free and competitive system, under local control, using diverse methods and regulations. It is hard to see why anyone would want to put more power into the hands of federal bureaucrats who cannot cope with the problems they already have.

The militant women demand the HEW regulations enforce a strict gender-free uniformity on all schools and colleges. Everything from sports to glee clubs must be coed, regardless of local customs or wishes. The militants deplore the differences from state to state in the laws governing marriage and divorce. Yet does anyone think our nation would be improved if we were made subject to a national divorce law devised by HEW?

The Positive Woman rejects the theory that Washington, D.C., is the fountainhead of all wisdom and professional skill. She supports the principle of leaving all possible control and discretion in the hands of local school and college officials and their elected boards.

5. The women's liberation movement pushes its proposals on the premise that everything must be neutral as between morality and immorality, and as between the institution of the family and alternate lifestyles: for example, that homosexuals and lesbians should have just as much right to teach in the schools and to adopt children as anyone else; and that illegitimate babies and abortions by married or single mothers should be accepted as normal behavior for teachers—and funded by public money.

A good example of the rabid determination of the militant radicals to push every law and regulation to the far-out limit of moral neutrality is the HEW regulation on sex discrimination that implements the Education Amendments of 1972. Although the federal statute simply prohibits sex discrimination, the HEW regulation (1) requires that any medical benefit program administered by a school or college pay for abortions for married and unmarried students, (2) prohibits any school or college from refusing to employ or from firing an unmarried pregnant teacher or a woman who has had, or plans to have, an abortion, and (3) prohibits any school or college from refusing admission to any student who has had, or plans to have, an abortion. Abortion is referred to by the code words "termination of pregnancy."

This HEW regulation is illogical, immoral, and unauthorized by any reasonable reading of the 1972 Education Act. But the HEW regulation became federal law on 18 July 1975, after being signed by the president and accepted by Congress.

The Positive Woman believes that our educational institutions have not only the right, but the obligation, to set minimum standards of moral conduct at the local level. She believes that schools and colleges have no right to use our public money to promote conduct that is offensive to the religious and moral values of parents and taxpayers.

## Neuterizing Society

A basic objective and tactic of the women's liberationists is to neuterize all laws, textbooks, and language in newspapers, radio, and television. Their friends in state legislatures are ordering computer printouts of all laws that use such "sexist" words as *man, woman, husband,* and *wife.* They are to be expunged and replaced with neuter equivalents. Some state legislators have acquiesced rather than face charges of "sexism." Others have rejected this effort and labeled it the silliness that it is.

The feminists look upon textbooks as a major weapon in their campaign to eliminate what they call our "sex-stereotyped society" and to restructure it into one that is sex-neutral from cradle to grave. Under liberationist demands, the Macmillan Publishing Company issued a booklet called *Guidelines for Creating Positive Sexual and Racial Images in Educational Materials.* Its purpose is to instruct authors in the use of sex-neutral language, concepts, and illustrations in order to conform to the new Macmillan censorship code. (The McGraw-Hill Book Company has issued a similar pamphlet, *Guidelines for Equal Treatment of the Sexes.*)

Henceforth, you may not say *mankind,* it should be *humanity.* You may not say *brotherhood,* it should be *amity. Manpower* must be replaced by *human energy; forefathers* should give way to *precursors. Chairman* and *salesman* are out; and "in" words are *chairperson* and *salesperson.*

You are forbidden to say "man the sailboat." The acceptable substitute is not given; presumably it is "person the sailboat." You must not say "the conscientious housekeeper dusts *her* furniture at least once a week"; you must say "*the* furniture," because otherwise you would imply that the housekeeper is a woman—and that would be intolerable. You may not say "the cat washed herself"; it must be "the cat washed itself," because it would be sexist to imply that the cat is female.

The section forbidding sexism in textbook illustrations is even more amusing. According to the Macmillan guidelines, males must be shown wearing aprons just as often as females. Father should be pictured doing household chores and nursing a sick child, mother working at her desk while dad clears the dining-room table, little girls reaching toward snakes instead of recoiling from them, boys crying or preening in front of a mirror, and fathers using hair spray.

Women must be shown participating actively "in exciting worthwhile pursuits," which, by apparent definition, do not include being a homemaker. The guidelines warn that books will not be tolerated that indicate that "homemaking is the true vocation for a woman."

The Macmillan guidelines reach the height of absurdity when they deliver a stern rebuke to the history book that refers to Sacajawea as "an amazing Shoshoni Indian woman" because she led the Lewis and Clark expedition through the Rockies "with a young baby strapped to her back." According to the Macmillan guidelines, the use of the word *amazing* is intolerable sexist propaganda that perpetuates "the myth of feminine fragility." It is a pity that our school children can no longer be told that Sacajawea was "amazing" because the historical fact is that her physical accomplishment was unique.

The Macmillan guidelines reserve their most stinging rebuke for the four-letter word *lady,* terming it "distasteful" specifically because it connotes "ladylike" behavior.

The Macmillan guidelines are not only a good source of laughs, but are a healthy exposure to the hypocrisy of the liberals who pilloried the West Virginia parents who tried to censor obnoxious four-letter words from their children's textbooks. It all depends on which four-letter words you want to censor.

Baby-care doctor Benjamin Spock was one of those whom the feminists targeted as obnoxious because of the alleged "sexism" in his bestselling baby books. His principal offense was that, in advising mothers how to care for their babies, he repeatedly used the pronoun *he* instead of *she*. Obviously, it would be a semantic hurdle of significant magnitude to write a baby book and say "he or she" every time the author refers to the baby. Until women's liberationists became so vocal, normal mothers understood that *he* is used in the generic sense to mean babies of both sexes.

The feminists continued their campaign against Dr. Spock's "sexism" until they finally convinced him that modern liberated society should treat males and females exactly the same. In his latest book he eliminated "sexist" language. The only trouble was, Dr. Spock bought the whole bag of "liberation." He walked out on his faithful wife Jane, to whom he had been married for forty-eight years, and took up with a younger woman. Dr. Spock was truly "liberated" from traditional restraints.

It is no gain for women, for children, for families, or for America to propel us into a unisex society. Our strength is in our diversity, not in our sameness.

31

BETTY FRIEDAN

*The Feminine Mystique*

Betty Friedan (b. 1921) was the "mother of the new feminist movement." *The Feminine Mystique,* which describes the pressures on
women to be wives and mothers, motivated 1960s feminist struggles.
By vocation a journalist and psychologist, Friedan also founded the
National Organization for Women in 1966. Her most recent book,
*The Second Stage,* identifies the problems of two-career families as
feminists' next major challenge.

## The Problem That Has No Name

The problem lay buried, unspoken, for many years in the minds of American
women. It was a strange stirring, a sense of dissatisfaction, a yearning that
women suffered in the middle of the twentieth century in the United States.
Each suburban wife struggled with it alone. As she made the beds, shopped for
groceries, matched slipcover material, ate peanut butter sandwiches with her
children, chauffeured Cub Scouts and Brownies, lay beside her husband at
night—she was afraid to ask even of herself the silent question—"Is this all?"

For over fifteen years there was no word of this yearning in the millions
of words written about women, for women, in all the columns, books and articles by experts telling women their role was to seek fulfillment as wives and
mothers. Over and over women heard in voices of tradition and of Freudian
sophistication that they could desire no greater destiny than to glory in their
own femininity. Experts told them how to catch a man and keep him, how to
breastfeed children and handle their toilet training, how to cope with sibling
rivalry and adolescent rebellion; how to buy a dishwasher, bake bread, cook
gourmet snails, and build a swimming pool with their own hands; how to
dress, look, and act more feminine and make marriage more exciting; how to
keep their husbands from dying young and their sons from growing into de-
linquents. They were taught to pity the neurotic, unfeminine, unhappy
women who wanted to be poets or physicists or presidents. They learned that

truly feminine women do not want careers, higher education, political rights
—the independence and the opportunities that the old-fashioned feminists
fought for. Some women, in their forties and fifties, still remembered painfully
giving up those dreams, but most of the younger women no longer even
thought about them. A thousand expert voices applauded their femininity,
their adjustment, their new maturity. All they had to do was devote their lives
from earliest girlhood to finding a husband and bearing children.

By the end of the 1950s, the average marriage age of women in America
dropped to twenty, and was still dropping, into the teens. Fourteen million
girls were engaged by seventeen. The proportion of women attending college
in comparison with men dropped from 47 percent in 1920 to 35 percent in
1958. A century earlier, women had fought for higher education; now girls
went to college to get a husband. By the mid-1950s, 60 percent dropped out
of college to marry, or because they were afraid too much education would be
a marriage bar. Colleges built dormitories for "married students," but the students were almost always the husbands. A new degree was instituted for the
wives—"Ph.T." (Putting Husband Through).

Then American girls began getting married in high school. And the
women's magazines, deploring the unhappy statistics about these young marriages, urged that courses on marriage, and marriage counselors, be installed in
the high schools. Girls started going steady at twelve and thirteen, in junior
high. Manufacturers put out brassieres with false bosoms of foam rubber for
little girls of ten. And an advertisement for a child's dress, sizes 3–6X, in the
*New York Times* in the fall of 1960, said: "She Too Can Join the Man-Trap
Set."

By the end of the 1950s, the United States birthrate was overtaking India's. The birth-control movement, renamed Planned Parenthood, was asked
to find a method whereby women who had been advised that a third or fourth
baby would be born dead or defective might have it anyhow. Statisticians were
especially astounded at the fantastic increase in the number of babies among
college women. Where once they had two children, now they had four, five,
six. Women who had once wanted careers were now making careers out of
having babies. So rejoiced *Life* magazine in the 1956 paean to the movement of
American women back to the home.

In a New York hospital, a woman had a nervous breakdown when she
found she could not breastfeed her baby. In other hospitals, women dying of
cancer refused a drug which research had proved might save their lives: its side
effects were said to be unfeminine. "If I have only one life, let me live it as a
blonde," a larger-than-life-sized picture of a pretty, vacuous woman proclaimed from newspaper, magazine, and drugstore ads. And across America,
three out of every ten women dyed their hair blonde. They ate a chalk called
Metrecal, instead of food, to shrink to the size of the thin young models. De-
partment-store buyers reported that American women, since 1939, had become

three and four sizes smaller. "Women are out to fit the clothes, instead of vice-versa," one buyer said.

Interior decorators were designing kitchens with mosaic murals and original paintings, for kitchens were once again the center of women's lives. Home sewing became a million-dollar industry. Many women no longer left their homes, except to shop, chauffeur their children, or attend a social engagement with their husbands. Girls were growing up in America without ever having jobs outside the home. In the late 1950s, a sociological phenomenon was suddenly remarked: a third of American women now worked, but most were no longer young and very few were pursuing careers. They were married women who held part-time jobs, selling or secretarial, to put their husbands through school, their sons through college, or to help pay the mortgage. Or they were widows supporting families. Fewer and fewer women were entering professional work. The shortages in the nursing, social work, and teaching professions caused crises in almost every American city. Concerned over the Soviet Union's lead in the space race, scientists noted that America's greatest source of unused brainpower was women. But girls would not study physics: it was "unfeminine." A girl refused a science fellowship at Johns Hopkins to take a job in a real-estate office. All she wanted, she said, was what every other American girl wanted—to get married, have four children and live in a nice house in a nice suburb.

The suburban housewife—she was the dream image of the young American women and the envy, it was said, of women all over the world. The American housewife—freed by science and labor-saving appliances from the drudgery, the dangers of childbirth and the illnesses of her grandmother. She was healthy, beautiful, educated, concerned only about her husband, her children, her home. She had found true feminine fulfillment. As a housewife and mother, she was respected as a full and equal partner to man in his world. She was free to choose automobiles, clothes, appliances, supermarkets; she had everything that women ever dreamed of.

In the fifteen years after World War II, this mystique of feminine fulfillment became the cherished and self-perpetuating core of contemporary American culture. Millions of women lived their lives in the image of those pretty pictures of the American suburban housewife, kissing their husbands goodbye in front of the picture window, depositing their stationwagonsful of children at school, and smiling as they ran the new electric waxer over the spotless kitchen floor. They baked their own bread, sewed their own and their children's clothes, kept their new washing machines and dryers running all day. They changed the sheets on the beds twice a week instead of once, took the rug-hooking class in adult education, and pitied their poor frustrated mothers, who had dreamed of having a career. Their only dream was to be perfect wives and mothers; their highest ambition to have five children and a beautiful house, their only fight to get and keep their husbands. They had no thought for the unfeminine problems of the world outside the home; they wanted the men to make the major decisions. They gloried in their role as women, and wrote proudly on the census blank: "Occupation: housewife."

For over fifteen years, the words written for women, and the words women used when they talked to each other, while their husbands sat on the other side of the room and talked shop or politics or septic tanks, were about problems with their children, or how to keep their husbands happy, or improve their children's school, or cook chicken or make slipcovers. Nobody argued whether women were inferior or superior to men; they were simply different. Words like "emancipation" and "career" sounded strange and embarrassing; no one had used them for years. When a Frenchwoman named Simone de Beauvoir wrote a book called *The Second Sex*, an American critic commented that she obviously "didn't know what life was all about," and besides, she was talking about French women. The "woman problem" in America no longer existed.

If a woman had a problem in the 1950s and 1960s, she knew that something must be wrong with her marriage, or with herself. Other women were satisfied with their lives, she thought. What kind of a woman was she if she did not feel this mysterious fulfillment waxing the kitchen floor? She was so ashamed to admit her dissatisfaction that she never knew how many other women shared it. If she tried to tell her husband, he didn't understand what she was talking about. She did not really understand it herself. For over fifteen years women in America found it harder to talk about this problem than about sex. Even the psychoanalysts had no name for it. When a woman went to a psychiatrist for help, as many women did, she would say, "I'm so ashamed," or "I must be hopelessly neurotic." "I don't know what's wrong with women today," a suburban psychiatrist said uneasily. "I only know something is wrong because most of my patients happen to be women. And their problem isn't sexual." Most women with this problem did not go to see a psychoanalyst, however. "There's nothing wrong really," they kept telling themselves. "There isn't any problem."

But on a April morning in 1959, I heard a mother of four, having coffee with four other mothers in a suburban development fifteen miles from New York, say in a tone of quiet desperation, "the problem." And the others knew, without words, that she was not talking about a problem with her husband, or her children, or her home. Suddenly they realized they all shared the same problem, the problem that has no name. They began, hesitantly, to talk about it. Later, after they had picked up their children at nursery school and taken them home to nap, two of the women cried, in sheer relief, just to know they were not alone.

Gradually I came to realize that the problem that has no name was shared by countless women in America. As a magazine writer I often interviewed women about problems with their children, or their marriages, or their houses, or their communities. But after a while I began to recognize the telltale signs of this other problem. I saw the same signs in suburban ranch houses and split-levels on Long Island and in New Jersey and Westchester County; in colonial houses in a small Massachusetts town; on patios in Memphis; in suburban and city apartments; in living rooms in the Midwest. Sometimes I sensed the problem, not as a reporter, but as a suburban housewife, for during this time I was also bringing up my own three children in Rockland County, New York. I heard echoes of the problem in college dormitories and semiprivate maternity wards, at PTA meetings and luncheons of the League of Women Voters, at suburban cocktail parties, in station wagons waiting for trains, and in snatches of conversation overheard at Schrafft's. The groping words I heard from other women, on quiet afternoons when children were at school or on quiet evenings when husbands worked late, I think I understood first as a woman long before I understood their larger social and psychological implications.

Just what was this problem that has no name? What were the words women used when they tried to express it? Sometimes a woman would say "I feel empty somehow . . . incomplete." Or she would say, "I feel as if I don't exist." Sometimes she blotted out the feeling with a tranquilizer. Sometimes she thought the problem was with her husband, or her children, or that what she really needed was to redecorate her house, or move to a better neighborhood, or have an affair, or another baby. Sometimes, she went to a doctor with symptoms she could hardly describe: "A tired feeling . . . I get so angry with the children it scares me . . . I feel like crying without any reason." (A Cleveland doctor called it "the housewife's syndrome.") A number of women told me about great bleeding blisters that break out on their hands and arms. "I call it the housewife's blight," said a family doctor in Pennsylvania. "I see it so often lately in these young women with four, five and six children who bury themselves in their dishpans. But it isn't caused by detergent and it isn't cured by cortisone."

Sometimes a woman would tell me that the feeling gets so strong she runs out of the house and walks through the streets. Or she stays inside her house and cries. Or her children tell her a joke, and she doesn't laugh because she doesn't hear it. I talked to women who had spent years on the analyst's couch, working out their "adjustment to the feminine role," their blocks to "fulfillment as a wife and mother." But the desperate tone in these women's voices, and the look in their eyes, was the same as the tone and the look of other women, who were sure they had no problem, even though they did have a strange feeling of desperation.

A mother of four who left college at nineteen to get married told me:

I've tried everything women are supposed to do—hobbies, gardening, pickling, canning, being very social with my neighbors, joining committees, running

PTA teas. I can do it all, and I like it, but it doesn't leave you anything to think about—any feeling of who you are. I never had any career ambitions. All I wanted was to get married and have four children. I love the kids and Bob and my home. There's no problem you can even put a name to. But I'm desperate. I begin to feel I have no personality. I'm a server of food and a putter-on of pants and a bedmaker, somebody who can be called on when you want something. But who am I?

A twenty-three-year-old mother in blue jeans said:

I ask myself why I'm so dissatisfied. I've got my health, fine children, a lovely new home, enough money. My husband has a real future as an electronics engineer. He doesn't have any of these feelings. He says maybe I need a vacation, let's go to New York for a weekend. But that isn't it. I always had this idea we should do everything together. I can't sit down and read a book alone. If the children are napping and I have one hour to myself I just walk through the house waiting for them to wake up. I don't make a move until I know where the rest of the crowd is going. It's as if ever since you were a little girl, there's always been somebody or something that will take care of your life: your parents, or college, or falling in love, or having a child, or moving to a new house. Then you wake up one morning and there's nothing to look forward to.

A young wife in a Long Island development said:

I seem to sleep so much. I don't know why I should be so tired. This house isn't nearly so hard to clean as the cold-water flat we had when I was working. The children are at school all day. It's not the work. I just don't feel alive.

In 1960, the problem that has no name burst like a boil through the image of the happy American housewife. In the television commercials the pretty housewives still beamed over their foaming dishpans and *Time*'s cover story on "The Suburban Wife, an American Phenomenon" protested: "Having too good a time . . . to believe that they should be unhappy." But the actual unhappiness of the American housewife was suddenly being reported—from the *New York Times* and *Newsweek* to *Good Housekeeping* and CBS television ("The Trapped Housewife"), although almost everybody who talked about it found some superficial reason to dismiss it. It was attributed to incompetent appliance repairmen (*New York Times*), or the distances children must be chauffeured in the suburbs (*Time*), or too much PTA (*Redbook*). Some said it was the old problem—education: more and more women had education, which naturally made them unhappy in their role as housewives. "The road from Freud to Frigidaire, from Sophocles to Spock, has turned out to be a bumpy one," reported the *New York Times* (28 June 1960). "Many young women—certainly not all—whose education plunged them into a world of ideas feel stifled in their homes. They find their routine lives out of joint with their training. Like shut-ins, they feel left out. In the last year, the problem of the educated housewife has provided the meat of dozens of speeches made by troubled presidents of women's colleges who maintain, in the face of complaints, that sixteen years of academic training is realistic preparation for wifehood and motherhood."

There was much sympathy for the educated housewife. ("Like a two-headed schizophrenic . . . once she wrote a paper on the Graveyard poets; now she writes notes to the milkman. Once she determined the boiling point of sulfuric acid; now she determines her boiling point with the overdue repairmen. . . . The housewife often is reduced to screams and tears. . . . No one, it seems, is appreciative, least of all herself, of the kind of person she becomes in the process of turning from poetess into shrew.")

Home economists suggested more realistic preparation for housewives, such as high-school workshops in home appliances. College educators suggested more discussion groups on home management and the family, to prepare women for the adjustment to domestic life. A spate of articles appeared in the mass magazines offering "Fifty-eight Ways to Make Your Marriage More Exciting." No month went by without a new book by a psychiatrist or sexologist offering technical advice on finding greater fulfillment through sex.

A male humorist joked in *Harper's Bazaar* (July 1960) that the problem could be solved by taking away woman's right to vote. ("In the pre–19th Amendment era, the American woman was placid, sheltered and sure of her role in American society. She left all the political decisions to her husband and he, in turn, left all the family decisions to her. Today a woman has to make both the family *and* the political decisions, and it's too much for her.")

A number of educators suggested seriously that women no longer be admitted to the four-year colleges and universities: in the growing college crisis, the education which girls could not use as housewives was more urgently needed than ever by boys to do the work of the atomic age.

The problem was also dismissed with drastic solutions no one could take seriously. (A woman writer proposed in *Harper's* that women be drafted for compulsory service as nurses' aides and baby-sitters.) And it was smoothed over with the age-old panaceas: "love is their answer," "the only answer is inner help," "the secret of completeness—children," "a private means of intellectual fulfillment," "to cure this toothache of the spirit—the simple formula of handing one's self and one's will over to God."

The problem was dismissed by telling the housewife she doesn't realize how lucky she is—her own boss, no time clock, no junior executive gunning for her job. What if she isn't happy—does she think men are happy in this world? Does she really, secretly, still want to be a man? Doesn't she know yet how lucky she is to be a woman?

The problem was also, and finally, dismissed by shrugging that there are no solutions: this is what being a woman means, and what is wrong with American women that they can't accept their role gracefully? As *Newsweek* put it (7 March 1960):

> She is dissatisfied with a lot that women of other lands can only dream of. Her discontent is deep, pervasive, and impervious to the superficial remedies which are offered at every hand.... An army of professional explorers have already charted the major sources of trouble.... From the beginning of time, the female cycle has defined and confined woman's role. As Freud was credited with saying: "Anatomy is destiny." Though no group of women has ever pushed these natural restrictions as far as the American wife, it seems that she still cannot accept them with good grace.... A young mother with a beautiful family, charm, talent and brains is apt to dismiss her role apologetically. "What do I do?" you hear her say. "Why nothing. I'm just a housewife." A good education, it seems, has given this paragon among women an understanding of the value of everything except her own worth....

And so she must accept the fact that "American women's unhappiness is merely the most recently won of women's rights," and adjust and say with the happy housewife found by *Newsweek*: "We ought to salute the wonderful freedom we all have and be proud of our lives today. I have had college and I've worked, but being a housewife is the most rewarding and satisfying role.... My mother was never included in my father's business affairs ... she couldn't get out of the house and away from us children. But I am an equal to my husband; I can go along with him on business trips and to social business affairs."

The alternative offered was a choice that few women would contemplate. In the sympathetic words of the *New York Times* : "All admit to being deeply frustrated at times by the lack of privacy, the physical burden, the routine of family life, the confinement of it. However, none would give up her home and family if she had the choice to make again." *Redbook* commented: "Few women would want to thumb their noses at husbands, children and community and go off on their own. Those who do may be talented individuals, but they rarely are successful women."

The year American women's discontent boiled over, it was also reported (*Look*) that the more than 21 million American women who are single, widowed, or divorced do not cease even after fifty their frenzied, desperate search for a man. And the search begins early—for 70 percent of all American women now marry before they are twenty-four. A pretty twenty-five-year-old secretary took thirty-five different jobs in six months in the futile hope of finding a husband. Women were moving from one political club to another, taking evening courses in accounting or sailing, learning to play golf or ski, joining a number of churches in succession, going to bars alone, in their ceaseless search for a man.

Of the growing thousands of women currently getting private psychiatric help in the United States, the married ones were reported dissatisfied with their marriages, the unmarried ones suffering from anxiety and, finally, depression. Strangely, a number of psychiatrists stated that, in their experience, unmarried women patients were happier than married ones. So the door of all those pretty suburban houses opened a crack to permit a glimpse of uncounted thousands of American housewives who suffered alone from a problem that suddenly everyone was talking about, and beginning to take for granted, as one of those unreal problems in American life that can never be solved—like the hydrogen bomb. By 1962 the plight of the trapped American housewife had become a national parlor game. Whole issues of magazines, newspaper columns, books learned and frivolous, educational conferences and television panels were devoted to the problem.

Even so, most men, and some women, still did not know that this problem was real. But those who had faced it honestly knew that all the superficial remedies, the sympathetic advice, the scolding words and the cheering words were somehow drowning the problem in unreality. A bitter laugh was beginning to be heard from American women. They were admired, envied, pitied, theorized over until they were sick of it, offered drastic solutions or silly choices that no one could take seriously. They got all kinds of advice from the growing armies of marriage and child guidance counselors, psychotherapists, and armchair psychologists, on how to adjust to their role as housewives. No other road to fulfillment was offered to American women in the middle of the twentieth century. Most adjusted to their role and suffered or ignored the problem that has no name. It can be less painful, for a woman, not to hear the strange, dissatisfied voice stirring within her.

It is no longer possible to ignore that voice, to dismiss the desperation of so many American women. This is not what being a woman means, no matter what the experts say. For human suffering there is a reason; perhaps the reason has not been found because the right questions have not been asked, or pressed far enough. I do not accept the answer that there is no problem because American women have luxuries that women in other times and lands never dreamed of; part of the strange newness of the problem is that it cannot be understood in terms of the age-old material problems of man: poverty, sickness, hunger, cold. The women who suffer this problem have a hunger that food cannot fill. It persists in women whose husbands are struggling interns and law clerks, or prosperous doctors and lawyers; in wives of workers and executives who make $5000 a year or $50,000. It is not caused by lack of material advantages; it may not even be felt by women preoccupied with desperate problems of hunger, poverty or illness. And women who think it will be solved by more money, a bigger house, a second car, moving to a better suburb, often discover it gets worse.

It is no longer possible today to blame the problem on loss of femininity:

to say that education and independence and equality with men have made American women unfeminine. I have heard so many women try to deny this dissatisfied voice within themselves because it does not fit the pretty picture of femininity the experts have given them. I think, in fact, that this is the first clue to the mystery: the problem cannot be understood in the generally accepted terms by which scientists have studied women, doctors have treated them, counselors have advised them, and writers have written about them. Women who suffer this problem, in whom this voice is stirring, have lived their whole lives in the pursuit of feminine fulfillment. They are not career women (although career women may have other problems); they are women whose greatest ambition has been marriage and children. For the oldest of these women, these daughters of the American middle class, no other dream was possible. The ones in their forties and fifties who once had other dreams gave them up and threw themselves joyously into life as housewives. For the youngest, the new wives and mothers, this was the only dream. They are the ones who quit high school and college to marry, or marked time in some job in which they had no real interest until they married. These women are very "feminine" in the usual sense, and yet they still suffer the problem.

Are the women who finished college, the women who once had dreams beyond housewifery, the ones who suffer the most? According to the experts they are, but listen to these four women:

> My days are all busy, and dull, too. All I ever do is mess around. I get up at eight—I make breakfast, so I do the dishes, have lunch, do some more dishes and some laundry and cleaning in the afternoon. Then it's supper dishes and I get to sit down a few minutes before the children have to be sent to bed. . . . That's all there is to my day. It's just like any other wife's day. Humdrum. The biggest time, I am chasing kids.

> Ye Gods, what do I do with my time? Well, I get up at six. I get my son dressed and then give him breakfast. After that I wash dishes and bathe and feed the baby. Then I get lunch and while the children nap, I sew or mend or iron and do all the other things I can't get done before noon. Then I cook supper for the family and my husband watches TV while I do the dishes. After I get the children to bed, I set my hair and then I go to bed.

> The problem is always being the children's mommy, or the minister's wife and never being myself.

> A film made of any typical morning in my house would look like an old Marx Brothers' comedy. I wash the dishes, rush the older children off to school, dash out in the yard to cultivate the chrysanthemums, run back in to make a phone call about a committee meeting, help the youngest child build a blockhouse,

spend fifteen minutes skimming the newspapers so I can be well-informed, then scamper down to the washing machines where my thrice-weekly laundry includes enough clothes to keep a primitive village going for an entire year. By noon I'm ready for a padded cell. Very little of what I've done has been really necessary or important. Outside pressures lash me through the day. Yet I look upon myself as one of the more relaxed housewives in the neighborhood. Many of my friends are even more frantic. In the past sixty years we have come full circle and the American housewife is once again trapped in a squirrel cage. If the cage is now a modern plate-glass-and-broadloom ranch house or a convenient modern apartment, the situation is no less painful than when her grandmother sat over an embroidery hoop in her gilt-and-plush parlor and muttered angrily about women's rights.

The first two women never went to college. They live in developments in Levittown, New Jersey, and Tacoma, Washington, and were interviewed by a team of sociologists studying workingmen's wives. The third, a minister's wife, wrote on the fifteenth reunion questionnaire of her college that she never had any career ambitions, but wishes now she had. The fourth, who has a Ph.D. in anthropology, is today a Nebraska housewife with three children. Their words seem to indicate that housewives of all educational levels suffer the same feeling of desperation.

The fact is that no one today is muttering angrily about "women's rights," even though more and more women have gone to college. In a recent study of all the classes that have graduated from Barnard College, a significant minority of earlier graduates blamed their education for making them want "rights," later classes blamed their education for giving them career dreams, but recent graduates blamed the college for making them feel it was not enough simply to be a housewife and mother; they did not want to feel guilty if they did not read books or take part in community activities. But if education is not the cause of the problem, the fact that education somehow festers in these women may be a clue.

If the secret of feminine fulfillment is having children, never have so many women, with the freedom to choose, had so many children, in so few years, so willingly. If the answer is love, never have women searched for love with such determination. And yet there is a growing suspicion that the problem may not be sexual, though it must somehow be related to sex. I have heard from many doctors evidence of new sexual problems between man and wife—sexual hunger in wives so great their husbands cannot satisfy it. "We have made woman a sex creature," said a psychiatrist at the Margaret Sanger marriage counseling clinic. "She has no identity except as a wife and mother. She does not know who she is herself. She waits all day for her husband to come home at night to make her feel alive. And now it is the husband who is not interested. It is terrible for the women, to lie there, night after night, waiting for her husband to make her feel alive." Why is there such a market for books and articles offering sexual advice? The kind of sexual orgasm which Kinsey found in statistical plenitude in the recent generations of American women does not seem to make this problem go away.

On the contrary, new neuroses are being seen among women—and problems as yet unnamed as neuroses—which Freud and his followers did not predict, with physical symptoms, anxieties, and defense mechanisms equal to those caused by sexual repression. And strange new problems are being reported in the growing generations of children whose mothers were always there, driving them around, helping them with their homework—an inability to endure pain or discipline or pursue any self-sustained goal of any sort, a devastating boredom with life. Educators are increasingly uneasy about the dependence, the lack of self-reliance, of the boys and girls who are entering college today. "We fight a continual battle to make our students assume manhood," said a Columbia dean.

A White House conference was held on the physical and muscular deterioration of American children: were they being overnurtured? Sociologists noted the astounding organization of suburban children's lives: the lessons, parties, entertainments, play and study groups organized for them. A suburban housewife in Portland, Oregon, wondered why the children "need" Brownies and Boy Scouts out here. "This is not the slums. The kids out here have the great outdoors. I think people are so bored, they organize the children, and then try to hook everyone else on it. And the poor kids have no time left just to lie on their beds and daydream."

Can the problem that has no name be somehow related to the domestic routine of the housewife? When a woman tries to put the problem into words, she often merely describes the daily life she leads. What is there in this recital of comfortable domestic detail that could possibly cause such a feeling of desperation? Is she trapped simply by the enormous demands of her role as modern housewife: wife, mistress, mother, nurse, consumer, cook, chauffeur; expert on interior decoration, child care, appliance repair, furniture refinishing, nutrition, and education? Her day is fragmented as she rushes from dishwasher to washing machine to telephone to dryer to station wagon to supermarket, and delivers Johnny to the Little League field, takes Janey to dancing class, gets the lawnmower fixed and meets the 6:45. She can never spend more than fifteen minutes on any one thing; she has no time to read books, only magazines; even if she had time, she has lost the power to concentrate. At the end of the day, she is so terribly tired that sometimes her husband has to take over and put the children to bed.

This terrible tiredness took so many women to doctors in the 1950s that one decided to investigate it. He found, surprisingly, that his patients suffering from "housewife's fatigue" slept more than an adult needed to sleep—as much as ten hours a day—and that the actual energy they expended on housework did not tax their capacity. The real problem must be something else, he decided—perhaps boredom. Some doctors told their women patients they must get out of the house for a day, treat themselves to a movie in town. Others prescribed tranquilizers. Many suburban housewives were taking tranquilizers like cough drops. "You wake up in the morning, and you feel as if there's no point in going on another day like this. So you take a tranquilizer because it makes you not care so much that it's pointless."

It is easy to see the concrete details that trap the suburban housewife, the continual demands on her time. But the chains that bind her in her trap are chains in her own mind and spirit. They are chains made up of mistaken ideas and misinterpreted facts, of incomplete truths and unreal choices. They are not easily seen and not easily shaken off.

How can any woman see the whole truth within the bounds of her own life? How can she believe that voice inside herself, when it denies the conventional, accepted truths by which she has been living? And yet the women I have talked to, who are finally listening to that inner voice, seem in some incredible way to be groping through to a truth that has defied the experts.

I think the experts in a great many fields have been holding pieces of that truth under their microscopes for a long time without realizing it. I found pieces of it in certain new research and theoretical developments in psychological, social and biological science whose implications for women seem never to have been examined. I found many clues by talking to suburban doctors, gynecologists, obstetricians, child-guidance clinicians, pediatricians, high-school guidance counselors, college professors, marriage counselors, psychiatrists and ministers—questioning them not on their theories, but on their actual experience in treating American women. I became aware of a growing body of evidence, much of which has not been reported publicly because it does not fit current modes of thought about women—evidence which throws into question the standards of feminine normality, feminine adjustment, feminine fulfillment, and feminine maturity by which most women are still trying to live.

I began to see in a strange new light the American return to early marriage and the large families that are causing the population explosion; the recent movement to natural childbirth and breastfeeding; suburban conformity, and the new neuroses, character pathologies and sexual problems being reported by the doctors. I began to see new dimensions to old problems that have long been taken for granted among women: menstrual difficulties, sexual frigidity, promiscuity, pregnancy fears, childbirth depression, the high incidence of emotional breakdown and suicide among women in their twenties and thirties, the menopause crises, the so-called passivity and immaturity of American men, the discrepancy between women's tested intellectual abilities in childhood and their adult achievement, the changing incidence of adult sexual orgasm in American women, and persistent problems in psychotherapy and in women's education.

If I am right, the problem that has no name stirring in the minds of so many American women today is not a matter of loss of femininity or too much education, or the demands of domesticity. It is far more important than anyone recognizes. It is the key to these other new and old problems which have been torturing women and their husbands and children, and puzzling their doctors and educators for years. It may well be the key to our future as a nation and a culture. We can no longer ignore that voice within women that says: "I want something more than my husband and my children and my home."

FRIEDRICH ENGELS

# The Origin of the Family, Private Property
# and the State

Although brief references to women are scattered throughout Marx's writings, he never thoroughly addressed "the woman question." It is Engels's *The Origin of the Family, Private Property and the State* (1884) that explores at length the relationship between sex and class —more specifically, between monogamy and capitalism. As other feminists are quick to mention, however, Engels privileges economic explanations of sexual oppression. For this reason, he cannot explain why sexism pre- and postdates capitalism.

According to the materialistic conception, the determining factor in history is, in the final instance, the production and reproduction of immediate life. This, again, is of a twofold character: on the one side, the production of the means of existence, of food, clothing and shelter and the tools necessary for that production; on the other side, the production of human beings themselves, the propagation of the species. The social organization under which the people of a particular historical epoch and a particular country live is determined by both kinds of production: by the stage of development of labor on the one hand and of the family on the other. The lower the development of labor and the more limited the amount of its products, and consequently, the more limited also the wealth of the society, the more the social order is found to be dominated by kinship groups. However, within this structure of society based on kinship groups the productivity of labor increasingly develops, and with it private property and exchange, differences of wealth, the possibility of utilizing the labor power of others, and hence the basis of class antagonisms: new social elements, which in the course of generations strive to adapt the old social order to the new conditions, until at last their incompatibility brings about a complete upheaval. In the collision of the newly developed social classes, the old society founded on kinship groups is broken up. In its place appears a new society, with its control centered in the state, the subordinate units of which are no longer kinship associations, but local associations; a society in which the system of the family is completely dominated by the system of property, and in which there now freely develop those class antagonisms and class struggles that have hitherto formed the content of all *written* history. . . .

## Stages of Prehistoric Culture

. . . Morgan was the first person with expert knowledge to attempt to introduce a definite order into the history of primitive man; so long as no important additional material makes changes necessary, his classification will undoubtedly remain in force.

Of the three main epochs—savagery, barbarism, and civilization—he is concerned, of course, only with the first two and the transition to the third. . . .

## The Family

. . . Reconstructing thus the past history of the family, Morgan, in agreement with most of his colleagues, arrives at a primitive stage when unrestricted sexual freedom prevailed within the tribe, every woman belonging equally to every man and every man to every woman. . . .

Lately it has become fashionable to deny the existence of this initial stage in human sexual life. Humanity must be spared this "shame.". . .

In my opinion, any understanding of primitive society is impossible to people who only see it as a brothel. We will return to this point when discussing group marriage.

According to Morgan, from this primitive state of promiscuous intercourse there developed, probably very early:

### 1. The Consanguine Family, the First Stage of the Family

Here the marriage groups are separated according to generations: all the grandfathers and grandmothers within the limits of the family are all husbands and wives of one another; so are also their children, the fathers and mothers; the latter's children will form a third circle of common husbands and wives; and their children, the great-grandchildren of the first group, will form a fourth. In this form of marriage, therefore, only ancestors and progeny, and parents and children, are excluded from the rights and duties (as we should say) of marriage with one another. Brothers and sisters, male and female cousins of the first, second, and more remote degrees, are all brothers and sisters of one another, and *precisely for that reason* they are all husbands and wives of one another.[1] At this stage the relationship of brother and sister also includes as a matter of course the practice of sexual intercourse with one another. In its typical form, such a family would consist of the descendants of a single pair, the descendants of these descendants in each generation being again brothers and sisters, and therefore husbands and wives, of one another. . . .

### 2. The Punaluan Family

If the first advance in organization consisted in the exclusion of parents and children from sexual intercourse with one another, the second was the exclusion of sister and brother. On account of the greater nearness in age, this second advance was infinitely more important, but also more difficult, than the first. It was effected gradually, beginning probably with the exclusion from sexual intercourse of one's own brothers and sisters (children of the same mother) first in isolated cases and then by degrees as a general rule (even in this century exceptions were found in Hawaii), and ending with prohibition of marriage even between collateral brothers and sisters, or, as we should say, between first, second, and third cousins. It affords, says Morgan, "a good illustration of the operation of the principle of natural selection." There can be no question that the tribes among whom inbreeding was restricted by this advance were bound to develop more quickly and more fully than those among whom marriage between brothers and sisters remained the rule and the law. How powerfully the influence of this advance made itself felt is seen in the institution which arose directly out of it and went far beyond it—the gens, which forms the basis of the social order of most, if not all, barbarian peoples of the earth and from which in Greece and Rome we step directly into civilization.

After a few generations at most, every original family was bound to split up. The practice of living together in a primitive communistic household which prevailed without exception till late in the middle stage of barbarism set a limit, varying with the conditions but fairly definite in each locality, to the maximum size of the family community. As soon as the conception arose that sexual intercourse between children of the same mother was wrong, it was bound to exert its influence when the old households split up and new ones were founded (though these did not necessarily coincide with the family group). One or more lines of sisters would form the nucleus of the one household and their own brothers the nucleus of the other. It must have been in some such manner as this that the form which Morgan calls the punaluan family originated out of the consanguine family. According to the Hawaiian custom, a number of sisters, natural or collateral (first, second or more remote cousins) were the common wives of their common husbands, from among whom, however, their own brothers were excluded. These husbands now no longer called themselves brothers, for they were no longer necessarily brothers, but *punalua*—that is, intimate companion, or partner. Similarly, a line of natural or collateral brothers had a number of women, *not* their sisters, as common wives, and these wives called one another *punalua*. This was the classic form of family structure (*Familienformation*), in which later a number of variations was possible, but whose essential feature was the mutually common possession of husbands and wives within a definite family circle, from which, however, the brothers of the wives—first one's own and later also collateral —and conversely also the sisters of the husbands, were excluded. . . .

In all forms of group family, it is uncertain who is the father of a child; but it is certain who its mother is. Though she calls *all* the children of the whole family her children and has a mother's duties toward them, she nevertheless knows her own children from the others. It is therefore clear that in so far as group marriage prevails, descent can only be proved on the *mother's* side and that therefore only the *female* line is recognized. And this is in fact the case among all peoples in the period of savagery or in the lower stage of barbarism. It is the second great merit of Bachofen that he was the first to make this discovery. To denote this exclusive recognition of descent through the mother and the relations of inheritance which in time resulted from it, he uses the term "mother right," which for the sake of brevity I retain. The term is, however, ill-chosen, since at this stage of society there cannot yet be any talk of "right" in the legal sense. . . .

### 3. The Pairing Family

A certain amount of pairing, for a longer or shorter period, already occurred in group marriage or even earlier; the man had a chief wife among his many wives (one can hardly yet speak of a favorite wife), and for her he was the most important among her husbands. This fact has contributed considerably to the confusion of the missionaries, who have regarded group marriage sometimes as promiscuous community of wives, sometimes as unbridled adultery. But these customary pairings were bound to grow more stable as the gens developed and the classes of "brothers" and "sisters" between whom marriage was impossible became more numerous. The impulse given by the gens to the prevention of marriage between blood relatives extended still further. Thus among the Iroquois and most of the other Indians and the lower stage of barbarism, we find that marriage is prohibited between *all* relatives enumerated in their system—which includes several hundred degrees of kinship. The increasing complication of these prohibitions make group marriages more and more impossible; they were displaced by the *pairing family*. In this stage, one man lives with one woman, but the relationship is such that polygamy and occasional infidelity remain the right of the men, even though for economic reasons polygamy is rare, while from the woman the strictest fidelity is generally demanded throughout the time she lives with the man and adultery on her part is cruelly punished. The marriage tie can, however, be easily dissolved by either partner; after separation, the children still belong as before to the mother alone. . . .

Thus the history of the family in primitive times consists in the progressive narrowing of the circle, originally embracing the whole tribe, within which the two sexes have a common conjugal relation. The continuous exclusion, first of nearer, then of more and more remote relatives, and at last even of relatives by marriage, ends by making any kind or group marriage practically impossible. Finally, there remains only the single, still loosely linked pair, the molecule with whose dissolution marriage itself ceases. This in itself shows what a small part individual sex love, in the modern sense of the word, played in the rise of monogamy. Yet stronger proof is afforded by the practice of all peoples at this stage of development. Whereas in the earlier forms of the family, men never lacked women but, on the contrary, had too many rather than too few, women had now become scarce and highly sought after. Hence it is with the pairing marriage that there begins the capture and purchase of women—widespread *symptoms,* but no more than symptoms, of the much deeper change that had occurred. . . .

The pairing family, itself too weak and unstable to make an independent household necessary or even desirable, in no wise destroys the communistic household inherited from earlier times. Communistic housekeeping, however, means the supremacy of women in the house; just as the exclusive recognition of the female parent, owing to the impossibility of recognizing the male parent with certainty, means that the women—the mothers—are held in high respect. One of the most absurd notions taken over from eighteenth-century enlightenment is that in the beginning of society woman was the slave of man. Among all savages and all barbarians of the lower and middle stages, and to a certain extent of the upper stage also, the position of women is not only free, but honorable. As to what it still is in the pairing marriage, let us hear the evidence of Ashur Wright, for many years missionary among the Iroquois Senecas:

> As to their family system, when occupying the old long houses (communistic households comprising several families), it is probable that some one clan (gens) predominated, the women taking in husbands, however, from the other clans (gentes). . . . Usually, the female portion ruled the house. . . . The stores were in common; but woe to the luckless husband or lover who was too shiftless to do his share of the providing. No matter how many children, or whatever goods he might have in the house, he might at any time be ordered to pick up his blanket and budge; and after such orders it would not be healthful for him to attempt to disobey. The house would be too hot for him; and . . . he must retreat to his own clan (gens); or, as was often done, go and start a new matrimonial alliance in some other. The women were the great power among the clans (gentes), as everywhere else. They did not hesitate, when occasion re-

quired, "to knock off the horns," as it was technically called, from the head of a chief, and send him back to the ranks of the warriors.

The communistic household, in which most or all of the women belong to one and the some gens, while the men come from various gentes, is the material foundation of that supremacy of the women which was general in primitive times, and which it is Bachofen's third great merit to have discovered. The reports of travelers and missionaries, I may add, to the effect that women among savages and barbarians are overburdened with work in no way contradict what has been said. The division of labor between the two sexes is determined by quite other causes than by the position of woman in society. Among peoples where the women have to work far harder than we think suitable, there is often much more real respect for women than among our Europeans. The lady of civilization, surrounded by false homage and estranged from all real work, has an infinitely lower social position than the hard-working woman of barbarism, who was regarded among her people as a real lady (lady, *frowa, Frau*—mistress) and who was also a lady in character. . . .

The first beginnings of the pairing family appear on the dividing line between savagery and barbarism; they are generally to be found already at the upper stage of savagery, but occasionally not until the lower stage of barbarism. The pairing family is the form characteristic of barbarism, as group marriage is characteristic of savagery and monogamy of civilization. To develop it further, to strict monogamy, other causes were required than those we have found active hitherto. In the single pair the group was already reduced to its final unit, its two-atom molecule: one man and one woman. Natural selection, with its progressive exclusions from the marriage community, had accomplished its task; there was nothing more for it to do in this direction. Unless new, *social* forces came into play, there was no reason why a new form of family should arise from the single pair. But these new forces did come into play.

We now leave America, the classic soil of the pairing family. No sign allows us to conclude that a higher form of family developed here or that there was ever permanent monogamy anywhere in America prior to its discovery and conquest. But not so in the Old World.

Here the domestication of animals and the breeding of herds had developed a hitherto unsuspected source of wealth and created entirely new social relations. Up to the lower stage of barbarism, permanent wealth had consisted almost solely of house, clothing, crude ornaments and the tools for obtaining and preparing food—boat, weapons, and domestic utensils of the simplest kind. Food had to be won afresh day by day. Now, with their herds of horses, camels, asses, cattle, sheep, goats, and pigs, the advancing pastoral peoples—the Semites on the Euphrates and the Tigris, and the Aryans in the Indian country of the Five Streams (Punjab), in the Ganges region, and in the steppes then much more abundantly watered by the Oxus and the Jaxartes—had acquired property which only needed supervision and the rudest care to reproduce itself in steadily increasing quantities and to supply the most abundant food in the form of milk and meat. All former means of procuring food now receded into the background; hunting, formerly a necessity, now became a luxury.

But to whom did this new wealth belong? Originally to the gens, without a doubt. Private property in herds must have already started at an early period, however. Is it difficult to say whether the author of the so-called first book of Moses regarded the patriarch Abraham as the owner of his herds in his own right as head of a family community or by right of his position as actual hereditary head of a gens. What is certain is that we must not think of him as a property owner in the modern sense of the word. And it is also certain that at the threshold of authentic history we already find the herds everywhere separately owned by heads of families, as are the artistic products of barbarism (metal implements, luxury articles and, finally, the human cattle—the slaves).

For now slavery had also been invented. To the barbarian of the lower stage, a slave was valueless. Hence the treatment of defeated enemies by the American Indians was quite different from that at a higher stage. The men were killed or adopted as brothers into the tribe of the victors; the women were taken as wives or otherwise adopted with their surviving children. At this stage human labor power still does not produce any considerable surplus over and above its maintenance costs. That was no longer the case after the introduction of cattle breeding, metalworking, weaving and, lastly, agriculture. Just as the wives whom it had formerly been so easy to obtain had now acquired an exchange value and were bought, so also with labor power, particularly since the herds had definitely become family possessions. The family did not multiply so rapidly as the cattle. More people were needed to look after them; for this purpose use could be made of enemies captured in war, who could also be bred just as easily as the cattle themselves.

Once it had passed into the private possession of families and there rapidly begun to augment, this wealth dealt a severe blow to the society founded on pairing marriage and the matriarchal gens. Pairing marriage had brought a new element into the family. By the side of the natural mother of the child it placed its natural and attested father with a better warrant of paternity, probably, than that of many a "father" today. According to the division of labor within the family at that time, it was the man's part to obtain food and the instruments of labor necessary for the purpose. He therefore also owned the instruments of labor, and in the event of husband and wife separating, he took them with him, just as she retained her household goods. Therefore, according to the social custom of the time, the man was also the owner of the new source of subsistence, the cattle, and later of the new instruments of labor, the slaves. But according to the custom of the same society, his children could not inherit from him. For as regards inheritance, the position was as follows:

At first, according to mother right—so long, therefore, as descent was reckoned only in the female line—and according to the original custom of inheritance within the gens, the gentile relatives inherited from a deceased fellow member of their gens. His property had to remain within the gens. His effects being insignificant, they probably always passed in practice to his nearest gentile relations—that is, to his blood relations on the mother's side. The children of the dead man, however, did not belong to his gens, but to that of their mother; it was from her that they inherited, at first conjointly with her other blood-relations, later perhaps with rights of priority; they could not inherit from their father because they did not belong to his gens within which his property had to remain. When the owner of the herds died, therefore, his herds would go first to his brothers and sisters and to his sister's children, or to the issue of his mother's sisters. But his own children were disinherited.

Thus, on the one hand, in proportion as wealth increased it made the man's position in the family more important than the woman's, and on the other hand created an impulse to exploit this strengthened position in order to overthrow, in favor of his children, the tradition order of inheritance. This, however, was impossible so long as descent was reckoned according to mother right. Mother right, therefore, had to be overthrown, and overthrown it was. This was by no means so difficult as it looks to us today. For this revolution —one of the most decisive ever experienced by humanity—could take place without disturbing a single one of the living members of a gens. All could remain as they were. A simple decree sufficed that in the future the offspring of the male members should remain within the gens, but that of the female should be excluded by being transferred to the gens of their father. The reckoning of descent in the female line and the matriarchal law of inheritance were thereby overthrown, and male line of descent and the paternal law of inheritance were substituted for them. As to how and when this revolution took place among civilized peoples, we have no knowledge. It falls entirely within prehistoric times. But that it *did* take place is more than sufficiently proved by the abundant traces of mother right which have been collected, particularly by Bachofen. . . .

The overthrow of mother right was the *world historical defeat of the female sex*. The man took command in the home also; the woman was degraded and reduced to servitude; she became the slave of his lust and a mere instrument for the production of children. This degraded position of the woman, especially conspicuous among the Greeks of the heroic and still more of the classical age, has gradually been palliated and glossed over, and sometimes clothed in a milder form; in no sense has it been abolished.

The establishment of the exclusive supremacy of the man shows its effects first in the patriarchal family, which now emerges as an intermediate form. Its essential characteristic is not polygyny, of which more later, but "the organization of a number of persons, bond and free, into a family under paternal power for the purpose of holding lands and for the care of flocks and herds.... (In the Semitic form) the chiefs, at least, lived in polygamy.... Those held to servitude and those employed as servants lived in the marriage relation."

Its essential features are the incorporation of unfree persons and paternal power; hence the perfect type of this form of family is the Roman. The original meaning of the word "family" (*familia*) is not that compound of sentimentality and domestic strife which forms the ideal of the present-day philistine; among the Romans it did not at first even refer to the married pair and their children but only to the slaves. *Famulus* means domestic slave, and *familia* is the total number of slaves belonging to one man. As late as the time of Gaius, the *familia, id est patrimonium* (family, that is, the patrimony, the inheritance) was bequeathed by will. The term was invented by the Romans to denote a new social organism whose head ruled over wife and children and a number of slaves, and was invested under Roman paternal power with rights of life and death over them all.

This term, therefore, is no older than the ironclad family system of the Latin tribes, which came in after field agriculture and after legalized servitude, as well as after the separation of the Greeks and Latins.

Marx adds:

> The modern family contains in germ not only slavery (*servitus*) but also serfdom, since from the beginning it is related to agricultural services. It contains *in miniature* all the contradictions which later extend throughout society and its state.
>
> Such a form of family shows the transition of the pairing family to monogamy. In order to make certain of the wife's fidelity and therefore of the paternity of the children, she is delivered over unconditionally into the power of the husband; if he kills her, he is only exercising his rights.

### 4. The Monogamous Family

... It develops out of the pairing family, as previously shown, in the transitional period between the upper and middle stages of barbarism; its decisive victory is one of the signs that civilization is beginning. It is based on the supremacy of the man, the express purpose being to produce children of undisputed paternity; such paternity is demanded because these children are later to come into their father's property as his natural heirs. It is distinguished from pairing marriage by the much greater strength of the marriage tie, which can no longer be dissolved at either partner's wish. As a rule, it is now only the man who can dissolve it and put away his wife. The right of conjugal infidelity also remains secured to him, at any rate by custom (the *Code Napoléon* explicitly accords it to the husband as long as he does not bring his concubine into the house), and as social life develops he exercises his right more and more; should the wife recall the old form of sexual life and attempt to revive it, she is punished more severely than ever.

We meet this new form of the family in all its severity among the Greeks. While the position of the goddesses in their mythology, as Marx points out, refers to an earlier period when the position of women was freer and more respected, in the heroic age we find the woman already being humiliated by the domination of the man and by competition from girl slaves. Note how Telemachus in the *Odyssey* silences his mother.[2] In Homer young women are booty and are handed over to the pleasure of the conquerors, the handsomest being picked by the commanders in order of rank; the entire *Iliad*, it will be remembered, turns on the quarrel of Achilles and Agamemnon over one of these slaves. If a hero is of any importance, Homer also mentions the captive girl with whom he shares his tent and his bed. These girls were also taken back to Greece and brought under the same roof as the wife, as Cassandra was brought by Agamemnon in Aeschylus; the sons begotten of them received a small share of the paternal inheritance and had the full status of freemen. Teucer, for instance, is a natural son of Telamon by one of these slaves and has the right to use his father's name. The legitimate wife was expected to put up with all this, but herself to remain strictly chaste and faithful. In the heroic age a Greek woman is, indeed, more respected than in the period of civilization, but to her husband she is after all nothing but the mother of his legitimate children and heirs, his chief housekeeper and the supervisor of his female slaves, whom he can and does take as concubines if he so fancies. It is the existence of slavery side by side with monogamy, the presence of young, beautiful slaves belonging unreservedly to *man,* that stamps monogamy from the very beginning with its specific character of monogamy *for the woman only,* but not for the man. And that is the character it still has today.

Coming to the later Greeks, we must distinguish between Dorians and Ionians. Among the former—Sparta is the classic example—marriage relations are in some ways still more archaic than even in Homer. The recognized form of marriage in Sparta was a pairing marriage, modified according to the Spartan conceptions of the state, in which there still survived vestiges of group marriage. Childless marriages were dissolved; King Anaxandridas (about 650 B.C.), whose first wife was childless, took a second and kept two households; about the same time, King Ariston, who had two unfruitful wives, took a third but dismissed one of the other two. On the other hand, several brothers could have a wife in common; a friend who preferred his friend's wife could share her with him; and it was considered quite proper to place one's wife at the disposal of a sturdy "stallion," as Bismarck would say, even if he was not a citizen. A passage in Plutarch where a Spartan woman refers an importunate wooer to her husband seems to indicate, according to Schörmann, even greater freedom. Real adultery, secret infidelity by the woman without the husband's knowledge, was therefore unheard of. On the other hand, domestic slavery was unknown in Sparta, at least during its best period; the unfree helots were segregated on the estates and the Spartans were therefore less tempted to take the helots' wives. Inevitably in these conditions women held a much more honored position in Sparta than anywhere else in Greece. The Spartan women and the elite of the Athenian *hetaerae* are the only Greek women of whom the ancients speak with respect and whose words they thought it worth while to record.

The position is quite different among the Ionians; here Athens is typical. Girls only learned spinning, weaving, and sewing, and at most a little reading and writing. They lived more or less behind locked doors and had no company except other women. The women's apartments formed a separate part of the house on the upper floor or at the back where men, especially strangers, could not easily enter and to which the women retired when men visited the house. They never went out without being accompanied by a female slave; indoors they were kept under regular guard. Aristophanes speaks of Molossian dogs kept to frighten away adulterers, and, at any rate in the Asiatic towns, eunuchs were employed to keep watch over the women—making and exporting eunuchs was an industry in Chios as early as Herodotus' time, and, according to Wachsmuth, it was not only the barbarians who bought the supply. In Euripides (*Orestes*) a woman is called an *oikurema*, a thing (the word is neuter) for looking after the house, and, apart from her business of bearing children, that was all she was for the Athenian—his chief female domestic servant. The man had his athletics and his public business from which women were barred; in addition, he often had female slaves at his disposal and during the most flourishing days of Athens an extensive system of prostitution which the state at least favored. It was precisely through this system of prostitution that the only Greek women of personality were able to develop, and to acquire that intellectual and artistic culture by which they stand out as high above the general level of classic womanhood as the Spartan women by their qualities of character. But that a woman had to be a *hetaera* before she could be a woman is the worst condemnation of the Athenian family.

This Athenian family became in a time the accepted model for domestic relations not only among the Ionians but to an increasing extent among all the Greeks of the mainland and colonies also. But, in spite of locks and guards, Greek women found plenty of opportunity for deceiving their husbands. The men, who would have been ashamed to show any love for their wives, amused themselves by all sorts of love affairs with *hetaerae*; but this degradation of the women was avenged on the men and degraded them also till they fell into the abominable practice of sodomy and degraded alike their gods and themselves with the myth of Ganymede.

This is the origin of monogamy as far as we can trace it back among the most civilized and highly developed people of antiquity. It was not in any way the fruit of individual sex love, with which it had nothing whatever to do; marriages remained as before marriages of convenience. It was the first form of the family to be based not on natural but on economic conditions—on the victory of private property over primitive, natural communal property. The Greeks themselves put the matter quite frankly: the sole exclusive aims of monogamous marriage were to make the man supreme in the family and to propagate, as the future heirs to his wealth, children indisputably his own. Otherwise, marriage was a burden, a duty which had to be performed whether one liked it or not to gods, state, and one's ancestors. In Athens the law exacted from the man not only marriage but also the performance of a minimum of so-called conjugal duties.

Thus when monogamous marriage first makes its appearance in history, it is not as the reconciliation of man and woman, still less as the highest form of such a reconciliation. Quite the contrary, monogamous marriage comes on the scene as the subjugation of the one sex by the other; it announces a struggle between the sexes unknown throughout the whole previous prehistoric period. In an old unpublished manuscript written by Marx and myself in 1846,[3] I find the words: "The first division of labor is that between man and woman for the propagation of children." And today I can add: The first class opposition that appears in history coincides with the development of the antagonism between man and woman in monogamous marriage, and the first class oppression coincides with that of the female sex by the male. Monogamous marriage was a great historical step forward; nevertheless, together with slavery and private wealth, it opens the period that has lasted until today in which every step forward is also relatively a step backward, in which prosperity and development for some is won through the misery and frustration of others. It is the cellular form of civilized society in which the nature of the oppositions and contradictions fully active in that society can be already studied. . . .

Thus, wherever the monogamous family remains true to its historical origin and clearly reveals the antagonism between the man and the woman expressed in the man's exclusive supremacy, it exhibits in miniature the same oppositions and contradictions as those in which society has been moving, without power to resolve or overcome them, ever since it split into classes at the beginning of civilization. I am speaking here, of course, only of those cases of monogamous marriage where matrimonial life actually proceeds according to the original character of the whole institution but where the wife rebels against the husband's supremacy . . .

Our jurists, of course, find that progress in legislation is leaving women with no further ground of complaint. Modern civilized systems of law increasingly acknowledge first, that for a marriage to be legal it must be a contract freely entered into by both partners and secondly, that also in the married state both partners must stand on a common footing of equal rights and duties. If both these demands are consistently carried out, say the jurists, women have all they can ask.

This typically legalist method of argument is exactly the same as that which the radical republican bourgeois uses to put the proletarian in his place. The labor contract is to be freely entered into by both partners. But is is considered to have been freely entered into as soon as the law makes both parties equal on *paper*. The power conferred on the one party by the difference of class position, the pressure thereby brought to bear on the other party—the real economic position of both—that is not the law's business. Again, for the duration of the labor contract, both parties are to have equal rights in so far as one or the other does not expressly surrender them. That economic relations compel the worker to surrender even the last semblance of equal rights—here again, that is no concern of the law.

In regard to marriage, the law, even the most advanced, is fully satisfied as soon as the partners have formally recorded that they are entering into the marriage of their own free consent. What goes on in real life behind the juridical scenes, how this free consent comes about—that is not the business of the law and the jurist. And yet the most elementary comparative jurisprudence should show the jurist what this free consent really amounts to. In the countries where an obligatory share of the paternal inheritance is secured to the children by law and they cannot therefore be disinherited—in Germany, in the countries with French law and elsewhere—the children are obliged to obtain their parents' consent to their marriage. In the countries with English law, where parental consent to a marriage is not legally required, the parents on their side have full freedom in the testamentary disposal of their property and can disinherit their children at their pleasure. It is obvious that in spite and precisely because of this fact freedom of marriage among the classes with something to inherit is in reality not a whit greater in England and America than it is in France and Germany.

As regards the legal equality of husband and wife in marriage, the position is no better. The legal inequality of the two partners bequeathed to us from earlier social conditions is not the cause but the effect of the economic oppression of the woman. In the old communistic household, which comprised many couples and their children, the task entrusted to the women of managing the household was as much a public, a socially necessary industry as the procuring of food by the men. With the patriarchal family and still more with the single monogamous family, a change came. Household management lost its public character. It no longer concerned society. It became a *private service*; the wife became the head servant, excluded from all participation in social production. Not until the coming of modern large-scale industry was the road to social production opened to her again—and then only to the proletarian wife. But it was opened in such a manner that, if she carries out her duties in the private service of her family, she remains excluded from public production and unable to earn; and if she wants to take part in public production and earn independently, she cannot carry out family duties. And the wife's position in the factory is the position of women in all branches of business, right up to medicine and the law. The modern individual family is founded on the open or concealed domestic slavery of the wife, and modern society is a mass composed of these individual families as its molecules.

In the great majority of cases today, at least in the possessing classes, the husband is obliged to earn a living and support his family, and that in itself gives him a position of supremacy without any need for special legal titles and privileges. Within the family he is the bourgeois, and the wife represents the proletariat. In the industrial world, the specific character of the economic oppression burdening the proletariat is visible in all its sharpness only when all special legal privileges of the capitalist class have been abolished and complete legal equality of both classes established. The democratic republic does not do away with the opposition of the two classes; on the contrary, it provides the clear field on which the fight can be fought out. And in the same way, the peculiar character of the supremacy of the husband over the wife in the modern family, the necessity of creating real social equality between them and the way to do it, will only be seen in the clear light of day when both possess legally complete equality of rights. Then it will be plain that the first condition for the liberation of the wife is to bring the whole female sex back into public industry, and that this in turn demands that the characteristic of the monogamous family as the economic unit of society be abolished.

## Notes

1. In a letter written in the spring of 1882, Marx expresses himself in the strongest terms about the complete misrepresentation of primitive times in Wagner's text to the *Nibelungen*: "Have such things been heard, that brother embraced sister as a bride?" To Wagner and his "lecherous gods" who, quite in the modern manner, spice their love affairs with a little incest, Marx replies: "In primitive times the sister *was* the wife, *and that was moral.*"

[*To the Fourth edition.*] A French friend of mine [Bonnier] who is an admirer of Wagner is not in agreement with this note. He observes that already in the Elder Edda, on which Wagner based his story, in the *Oegisdrecka*, Loki makes the reproach to Freya: "In the sight of the gods thou didst embrace thine own brother." Marriage between brother and sister, he argues, was therefore forbidden already at that time. The *Oegisdrecka* is the expression of a time when belief in the old myths had completely broken down; it is purely a satire on the gods, in the style of Lucian. If Loki as Mephistopheles makes such a reproach to Freya, it tells rather against Wagner. Loki also says some lines later to Njord: "With thy sister didst thou breed such a son" (*vidh systur thinni gaztu slikan mog*). Njord is not, indeed, an Asa, but a Vana, and says in the Ynglinga saga that marriages between brothers and sisters are usual in Vanaland, which was not the case among the Asas. This would seem to show that the Vanas were more ancient gods than the Asas. At any rate,

Njord lives among the Asas as one of themselves, and therefore the *Oegisdrecka* is rather a proof that at the time when the Norse sagas of the gods arose, marriages between brothers and sisters, at any rate among the gods, did not yet excite any horror. If one wants to find excuses for Wagner, it would perhaps be better to cite Goethe instead of the Edda, for in his ballad of the God and the Bayadere Goethe commits a similar mistake in regard to the religious surrender of women, which he makes far too similar to modern prostitution.

2. The reference is to a passage where Telemachus, son of Odysseus and Penelope, tells his mother to get on with her weaving and leave the men to mind their own business (*Odyssey*, Bk. 21, 11, 350*ff.*).

3. The reference here is to the *Deutsche Ideologie* (*German Ideology*), written by Marx and Engels in Brussels in 1845–46 and first published in 1932 by the Marx-Engels-Lenin Institute in Moscow. *See* Marx-Engels, 1970:51.

# MONIQUE WITTIG

## *One Is Not Born a Woman*

The French feminist Monique Wittig (b. 1935) is a novelist and a philosopher. She is the author of *L'Opponox* (1964), *Les Guerilleres* (1969), and *The Lesbian Body* (1984). An influential postmodern, she has created new meanings for the feminist movement.

A materialist feminist approach to women's oppression destroys the idea that women are a "natural group": "a social group of a special kind, a group perceived *as natural*, a group of men considered as materially specific in their bodies." A lesbian society destroys the artificial (social) fact constituting women as a "natural group." A lesbian society pragmatically reveals that the division from men of which women have been the object is a political one and shows how we have been ideologically re-built into a "natural group." In our case, ideology goes far since our bodies as well as our minds are the product of this manipulation. We have been compelled in our bodies and in our minds to correspond, feature by feature, with the *idea* of nature that has been established for us. Distorted to such an extent that our deformed body is what they call "natural," is what is supposed to exist as such before oppression. Distorted to such an extent that at the end oppression seems to be a consequence of this "nature" in ourselves (a nature which is only an *idea* ). What a materialist analisis does by reasoning, a lesbian society accomplishes in fact: not only is there no natural group "women" (we lesbians are a living proof of it) but as individuals as well we question "woman," which for us, as for Simone de Beauvoir thirty years ago, is only a myth. She said: "One is not born, but becomes a woman. No biological, psychological, or economic fate determines the figure that the human female presents in society; it is civilization as a whole that produces this creature, intermediate between male and eunuch, which is described as feminine."

However, most of the feminists and lesbian-feminists in America and elsewhere still believe that the basis of women's oppression *is biological as well as* historical. Some of them even claim to find their sources in Simone de Beauvoir. The belief in mother-right and in a "prehistory" when women would have created civilization (because of a biological predisposition), while the coarse and brutal men would have hunted (because of a biological predisposition), does not make the biological approach any better. It is still the same method of finding in women and men a biological explanation of their division, outside of social facts. For me this could never constitute a lesbian approach since it assumes that the basis of society or the beginning of society lies in heterosexuality. Matriarchies are no less heterosexual than patriarchies: it's only the sex of the oppressor that changes. Furthermore, not only is this conception still a prisoner of the categories of sex (woman and man), but it keeps to the idea that the capacity to give birth (biology) is what defines a woman. Although practical facts and ways of living contradict this theory in lesbian society, there are lesbians who affirm that "women and men are different species or races (the words are used interchangeably); men are biologically inferior to women; male violence is a biological inevitability." By doing this, by admitting that there is a "natural" division between women and men, we naturalize history, we assume that men and women have always existed and will always exist. Not only do we naturalize history, but also consequently we naturalize the social phenomena which express our oppression, making change impossible. For example, instead of seeing giving birth as a forced production, we see it as a "natural," "biological" process, forgetting that in our societies births are planned (demography), forgetting that we ourselves are programmed to produce children, while this is the only social activity "short of war" that presents such a great danger of death. Thus, as long as we will be "unable to abandon by will or impulse a lifelong and centuries old commitment to childbearing as *the* female creative act," having control of the production of children will mean much more than the mere control of the material means of this production. Women will have to abstract themselves from the definition "woman" which is imposed upon them.

A materialist feminist approach shows that what we take for the cause or origin of oppression is in fact only the *mark* imposed by the oppressor: the "myth of woman," plus its material effects and manifestations in the appropriated consciousness and bodies of women. Thus, the mark does not preexist oppression. Colette Guillaumin, a French sociologist, has shown that before the socio-economical reality of black slavery, the concept of race did not exist (at least not in its modern meaning: it was applied to the lineage of families). However, now, race, exactly like sex, is taken as an "immediate given," a "sensible given," "physical features." They appear as though they existed prior to reasoning, belonging to a natural order. But what we believe to be a physical and direct perception is only a sophisticated and mythic construction, an "imaginary formation" which reinterprets physical features through the network of relationships in which they are perceived. (They are seen *black,* therefore they *are* black; they are seen *women,* therefore they *are* women. But before being *seen* that way, they first had to be *made* that way.) A lesbian consciousness should always remember how "unnatural," compelling, totally oppressive, and destructive being "woman" was for us in the old days before the women's liberation movement. It was political obligation and those who resisted it were accused of not being "real" women. But then we were proud of it, since in the accusation there was already something like a shadow of victory: the avowal by the oppressor that "woman" is not something that goes without saying, since to be one, one has to be a "real" one (what about the others?). We were also confronted by the accusation of wanting to be men. We still are by certain lesbians and feminists who believe that one has to become more and more of a woman as a political obligation. But to refuse to be a woman does not mean that one has to become a man. And for her who does want to become a man: in what way is her alienation different from wanting to become a woman? At least for a woman, wanting to become a man proves that she escaped her initial programming. But even if she wants to, she cannot become a man. For becoming a man would demand from a woman having not only the outside appearance of a man but his consciousness as well, that is, the consciousness of one who disposes by right of at least two natural "slaves" during his life span. This is impossible since precisely one feature of lesbian oppression consists of making women out of reach for us, since women belong to men. Thus a lesbian *has* to be something else, a not-woman, not-man, a product of society not a product of "nature," for there is no "nature" in society.

The refusal to become heterosexual always meant to refuse to become a man or a woman, consciously or not. For a lesbian this goes further than the refusal of the role "woman." It is the refusal of the economic, ideological and political power of a man. This, we lesbians, and non-lesbians as well, have experienced before the beginning of the lesbian and feminist movement. However, as Andrea Dworkin emphasizes, many lesbians recently "have increasingly tried to transform the very ideology that has enslaved us into a dynamic, religious, psychologically compelling celebration of female biological potential." Thus, some avenues of the feminist and lesbian movement lead us back to the myth of woman which was created by men especially for us, and with it we sink back into a natural group. Thirty years ago Simone de Beauvoir destroyed the myth of woman. Ten years ago we stood up to fight for a sexless society. Now we find ourselves entrapped in the familiar deadlock of "woman is wonderful." Thirty years ago Simone de Beauvoir underlined particularly the false consciousness which consists of selecting among the features of the myth (that women are different from men) those which look good and using them as a definition for women. What the concept of "woman is wonderful" accomplishes is that it retains for defining women that best features which oppression has granted us and it does not radically question the categories "man" and "woman." It puts us in a position of fighting within the class "women" not as the other classes do, for the disappearance of our class, but for the defense of "woman" and its reinforcement. It leads us to develop with complacency "new" theories about our specificity: thus, we call our passivity "nonviolence." The ambiguity of the term "feminist" sums up the whole situation. What does "feminist" mean? Feminist is formed with the word "femme," "woman," and means "someone who fights for women." For many of us it means "someone who fights for women as a class and for the disappearance of this class." For many others it means "someone who fights for woman and her defense"—for the myth then and its reinforcement. But why was the word "feminist" chosen? We chose to call ourselves "feminists" ten years ago, not in order to identify ourselves with the oppressor's definition of us, but rather to affirm that our movement had a history and to emphasize the political link with the old feminist movement.

It is, then, this movement that we can question for its meaning of "feminism." It so happens that feminism in the last century could never resolve its contradictions on the subject of nature/culture, woman/society. Women started to fight for themselves as a group and rightly considered that they shared common features. But for them these features were natural and biological rather than social. They went so far as to adopt pseudo-Darwinist theories of evolution. They did not believe like Darwin, however, "that women were less evolved than men, but they did believe that male and female natures had diverged in the course of evolutionary development and that society at large reflected this polarization. . . . The failure of early feminism was that it only attacked the Darwinist charge of female inferiority, while accepting the foundations of this charge—namely, the view of woman as 'unique'." And finally it was women scholars—and not feminists—who scientifically destroyed this theory. But the early feminists had failed to regard history as a dynamic process which develops from conflicts of interests. Furthermore, they still believed that the cause (origin) of their oppression lay within themselves (among black people only the Uncle Toms believed this). And therefore feminists, after some astonishing victories, found themselves at an impasse for lack of reasons for fighting. They upheld the illogical principle of "equality in difference," an idea now being born again. They fell back into the trap which threatens us once again: the myth of woman.

Thus it remains historically for us to define our oppression in materialist terms, to say that women are a class, which is to say that the category "woman," as well as "man," is a political and economic category, not an eternal one. Our fight aims to suppress men as a class, not through a genocidal, but a political struggle. Once the class "men" disappears, women as a class will disappear as well, for there are no slaves without masters. Our first task, it seems, is to always thoroughly disassociate "women" (the class within which we fight) and "woman," the myth. For "woman" does not exist for us: it is only an imaginary formation, while "women" is the product of social relationship. Furthermore we have to destroy the myth within and outside ourselves. "Woman" is not each one of us, but the political and ideological formation which negates "women" (the product of a relation of exploitation). "Woman" is there to confuse us, to hide the reality "women." In order to become a class and to be aware of it, we have first to kill the myth "woman" even in its most seductive aspects. . . .

To destroy "woman" does not mean to destroy lesbianism, for a lesbian is not a woman and does not love a woman, given that we agree with Christine Delphy that what "makes" woman is a personal dependency on a man (as opposed to an impersonal dependency on a boss). Lesbian is the only concept that I know of which is beyond the categories of sex (woman and man), because lesbian societies are not based upon women's oppression and because the designated subject (lesbian) is *not* a woman either economically or politically or ideologically. Furthermore, what we aim at is not the disappearance of lesbianism, which provides the only social form that we can live in, but the destruction of heterosexuality—the political system based on women's oppression, which produces the body of thought of the difference between the sexes to explain women's oppression.

Beyond or within this class consciousness, this science/experience, while in the separateness of one's ego, do we still have to fight to exist as an autonomous entity? There is no doubt that we have to fight for this entity, since we are left with nothing, once we reject the basic determination "woman" and "man," once we have no more attributes by which to identify ourselves (I am this or that). We are for the first time in history confronted with the necessity of existing as a person.

HEIDI HARTMANN

*The Unhappy Marriage of Marxism and*
*Feminism: Towards a More*
*Progressive Union*[1]

Heidi Hartmann (b. 1945) is the director of the Institute for Women's
Policy Research in Washington, D.C. An expert on issues involving
women and work, she is the author of *Women, Work, and Wages*
(1981), *Comparable Worth* (1985), and *Women's Work, Men's Work*
(1986). Her essay included here helped define socialist feminism.

The "marriage" of marxism and feminism has been like the marriage of husband and wife depicted in English common law: marxism and feminism are
one, and that one is marxism.[2] Recent attempts to integrate marxism and feminism are unsatisfactory to us as feminists because they subsume the feminist
struggle into the "larger" struggle against capital. To continue our simile further, either we need a healthier marriage or we need a divorce.

The inequalities in this marriage, like most social phenomena, are no accident. Many marxists typically argue that feminism is at best less important
than class conflict and at worst divisive of the working class. This political
stance produces an analysis that absorbs feminism into the class struggle.
Moreover, the analytic power of marxism with respect to capital has obscured
its limitations with respect to sexism. We will argue here that while marxist
analysis provides essential insight into the laws of historical development, and
those of capital in particular, the categories of marxism are sex-blind. Only a
specifically feminist analysis reveals the systemic character of relations between
men and women. Yet feminist analysis by itself is inadequate because it has
been blind to history and insufficiently materialist. Both marxist analysis, particularly its historical and materialistic method, and feminist analysis, especially the identification of patriarchy as a social and historical structure, must

be drawn upon if we are to understand the development of Western capitalist societies and the predicament of women within them. In this essay we suggest a new direction for marxist feminist analysis. . . .

## I.
## Marxism and the Woman Question

The woman question has never been the "feminist question." The feminist question is directed at the causes of sexual inequality between women and men, of male dominance over women. Most marxist analyses of women's position take as their question the relationship of women to the economic system, rather than that of women to men, apparently assuming the latter will be explained in their discussion of the former. Marxist analysis of the woman question has taken (several) forms. All see women's oppression in our connection (or lack of it) to production. Defining women as part of the working class, these analyses consistently subsume women's relation to men under workers' relation to capital. . . . All attempt to include women in the category working class and to understand women's oppression as another aspect of class oppression. In doing so all give short shrift to the object of feminist analysis, the relations between women and men. While our "problems" have been elegantly analyzed, they have been misunderstood. The focus of marxist analysis has been class relations; the object of marxist analysis has been understanding the laws of motion of capitalist society. While we believe marxist methodology *can* be used to formulate feminist strategy, these marxist feminist approaches discussed above clearly do not do so; their marxism clearly dominates their feminism.

As we have already suggested, this is due in part to the analytical power of marxism itself. Marxism is a theory of the development of class society, of the accumulation process in capitalist societies, of the reproduction of class dominance, and of the development of contradictions and class struggle. Capitalist societies are driven by the demands of the accumulation process, most succinctly summarized by the fact that production is oriented to exchange, not use. In a capitalist system production is important only insofar as it contributes to the making of profits, and the use value of products is only an incidental consideration. Profits derive from the capitalists' ability to exploit labor power, to pay laborers less than the value of what they produce. The accumulation of profits systematically transforms social structure as it transforms the relations of production. The reserve army of labor, the poverty of great numbers of people and the near-poverty of still more, these human reproaches to capital are by-products of the accumulation process itself. From the capitalist's point of view, the reproduction of the working class may "safely be left to itself."[3] At the same time, capital creates an ideology, which grows up alongside it, of individualism, competitiveness, domination, and in our time, consumption of a particular kind. Whatever one's theory of the genesis of ideology one must recognize these as the dominant values of capitalist societies.

Marxism enables us to understand many aspects of capitalist societies: the structure of production, the generation of a particular occupational structure, and the nature of the dominant ideology. Marx's theory of the development of capitalism is a theory of the development of "empty places." Marx predicted, for example, the growth of the proletariat and the demise of the petit bourgeoisie. More precisely and in more detail, Braverman among others has explained the creation of the "places" clerical worker and service worker in advanced capitalist societies.[4] Just as capital creates these places indifferent to the individuals who fill them, the categories of marxist analysis, class, reserve army of labor, wage-laborer, do not explain why particular people fill particular places. They give no clues about why *women* are subordinate to *men* inside and outside the family and why it is not the other way around. *Marxist categories, like capital itself, are sex-blind.* The categories of marxism cannot tell us who will fill the empty places. Marxist analysis of the woman question has suffered from this basic problem.

### Towards More Useful Marxist Feminism

Marxism is also a *method* of social analysis, historical dialectical materialism. By putting this method to the service of feminist questions, Juliet Mitchell and Shulamith Firestone suggest new directions for marxist feminism. Mitchell says, we think correctly, that

> It is not "our relationship" to socialism that should *ever* be the question—it is the use of scientific socialism [what we call marxist method] as a method of analyzing the specific nature of our oppression and hence our revolutionary role. Such a method, I believe, needs to understand radical feminism, quite as much as previously developed socialist theories.[5]

As Engels wrote:

> According to the materialistic conception, the determining factor in history is, in the final instance, the production and reproduction of immediate life. This, again, is of a twofold character: on the one side, the production of the means of existence, of food, clothing, and shelter and the tools necessary for that production; on the other side, the production of human beings themselves, the propagation of the species. The social organization under which the people of a particular historical epoch live is determined by both kinds of production.[6]

This is the kind of analysis Mitchell has attempted. In her first essay, "Women: The Longest Revolution," Mitchell examines both market work and the work of reproduction, sexuality, and childrearing.[7]

Mitchell does not entirely succeed, perhaps because not all of women's work counts as production for her. Only market work is identified as production; the other spheres (loosely aggregated as the family) in which women work are identified as ideological. Patriarchy, which largely organizes reproduction, sexuality, and childrearing, has no material base for Mitchell. *Women's Estate,* Mitchell's expansion of this essay, focuses much more on developing the analysis of women's market work than it does on developing the analysis of women's work within the family. The book is much more concerned with women's relation to, and work for, capital than with women's relation to, and work for, men; more influenced by marxism than by radical feminism. . . .

Shulamith Firestone bridges marxism and feminism by bringing materialist analysis to bear on patriarchy.[8] Her use of materialist analysis is not as ambivalent as Mitchell's. The dialectic of sex, she says, is the fundamental historical dialectic, and the material base of patriarchy is the work women do reproducing the species. The importance of Firestone's work in using marxism to analyze women's position, in asserting the existence of a material base to patriarchy, cannot be overestimated. But it suffers from an overemphasis on biology and reproduction. What we need to understand is how sex (a biological fact) becomes gender (a social phenomenon). It is necessary to place all of women's work in its social and historical context, not to focus only on reproduction. Although Firestone's work offers a new and feminist use of marxist methodology, her insistence on the primacy of men's dominance over women as the cornerstone on which all other oppression (class, age, race) rests, suggests that her book is more properly grouped with the radical feminists than with the marxist feminists. Her work remains the most complete statement of the radical feminist position. . . .

## 2.
## Radical Feminism and Patriarchy

The great thrust of radical feminist writing has been directed to the documentation of the slogan "the personal is political." Women's discontent, radical feminists argued, is not the neurotic lament of the maladjusted, but a response to a social structure in which women are systematically dominated, exploited, and oppressed. Women's inferior position in the labor market, the male-centered emotional structure of middle-class marriage, the use of women in advertising, the so-called understanding of women's psyche as neurotic—popularized by academic and clinical psychology—aspect after aspect of women's lives in advanced capitalist society was researched and analyzed. The radical feminist literature is enormous and defies easy summary. At the same time, its focus on psychology is consistent. The New York Radical Feminists' organizing document was "The Politics of the Ego." "The personal is political" means for radical feminists, that the original and basic class division is between the sexes, and that the motive force of history is the striving of men for power and domination over women, the dialectic of sex.[9]

Accordingly, Firestone rewrote Freud to understand the development of boys and girls into men and women in terms of power.[10] Her characterizations of what are "male" and "female" character traits are typical of radical feminist writing. The male seeks power and domination; he is egocentric and individualistic, competitive and pragmatic; the "technological mode," according to Firestone, is male. The female is nurturant, artistic, and philosophical; the "aesthetic mode" is female.

No doubt, the idea that the aesthetic mode is female would have come as quite a shock to the ancient Greeks. Here lies the error of radical feminist analysis: the dialectic of sex as radical feminists present it projects male and female characteristics as they appear in the present back into all of history. Radical feminist analysis has greatest strength in its insights into the present. Its greatest weakness is a focus on the psychological, which blinds it to history.

The reason for this lies not only in radical feminist method, but also in the nature of patriarchy itself, for patriarchy is a strikingly resilient form of social organization. Radical feminists use patriarchy to refer to a social system characterized by male domination over women. Kate Millett's definition is classic:

> Our society . . . is a patriarchy. The fact is evident at once if one recalls that the military, industry, technology, universities, science, political offices, finances—in short, every avenue of power within the society, including the coercive force of the police, is entirely in male hands.[11]

This radical feminist definition of patriarchy applies to most societies we know of and cannot distinguish among them. The use of history by radical feminists is typically limited to providing examples of the existence of patriarchy in all times and places.[12] For both marxist and mainstream social scientists before the women's movement, patriarchy referred to a system of relations between men, which formed the political and economic outlines of feudal and some pre-feudal societies, in which hierarchy followed ascribed characteristics. Capitalist societies are understood as meritocratic, bureaucratic, and impersonal by bourgeois social scientists; marxists see capitalist societies as systems of class domination.[13] For both kinds of social scientists neither the historical patriarchal societies nor today's Western capitalist societies are understood as systems of relations between men that enable them to dominate women.

### Towards a Definition of Patriarchy

We can usefully define patriarchy as a set of social relations between men, which have a material base, and which, though hierarchical, establish or create interdependence and solidarity among men that enable them to dominate women. Though patriarchy is hierarchical and men of different classes, races, or ethnic groups have different places in the patriarchy, they also are united in their shared relationship of dominance over their women; they are dependent on each other to maintain that domination. Hierarchies "work" at least in part because they create vested interests in the status quo. Those at the higher levels can "buy off" those at the lower levels by offering them power over those still lower. In the hierarchy of patriarchy, all men, whatever their rank in the patriarchy, are bought off by being able to control at least some women. There is some evidence to suggest that when patriarchy was first institutionalized in state societies, the ascending rulers literally made men the heads of their families (enforcing their control over their wives and children) in exchange for the men's ceding some of their tribal resources to the new rulers.[14] Men are dependent on one another (despite their hierarchical ordering) to maintain their control over women.

The material base upon which patriarchy rests lies most fundamentally in men's control over women's labor power. Men maintain this control by excluding women from access to some essential productive resources (in capitalist societies, for example, jobs that pay living wages) and by restricting women's sexuality.[15] Monogamous heterosexual marriage is one relatively recent and efficient form that seems to allow men to control both these areas. Controlling women's access to resources and their sexuality, in turn, allows men to control women's labor power, both for the purpose of serving men in many personal and sexual ways and for the purpose of rearing children. The services women render men, and which exonerate men from having to perform many unpleasant tasks (like cleaning toilets) occur outside as well as inside the family setting. Examples outside the family include the harassment of women workers and students by male bosses and professors as well as the common use of secretaries to run personal errands, make coffee, and provide "sexy" surroundings. Rearing children, whether or not the children's labor power is of immediate benefit to their fathers, is nevertheless a crucial task in perpetuating patriarchy as a system. Just as class society must be reproduced by schools, work places, consumption norms, etc., so must patriarchal social relations. In our society children are generally reared by women at home, women socially defined and recognized as inferior to men, while men appear in the domestic picture only rarely. Children raised in this way generally learn their places in the gender hierarchy well. Central to this process, however, are the areas outside the home where patriarchal behaviors are taught and the inferior position of women enforced and reinforced: churches, schools, sports, clubs, unions, armies, factories, offices, health centers, the media, etc.

The material base of patriarchy, then, does not rest solely on childrearing in the family, but on all the social structures that enable men to control women's labor. The aspects of social structures that perpetuate patriarchy are theoretically identifiable, hence separable from their other aspects. Gayle

Rubin has increased our ability to identify the patriarchal element of these so-cial structures enormously by identifying "sex/gender systems":

> A "sex/gender system" is the set of arrangements by which a society transforms biological sexuality into products of human activity, and in which these trans-formed sexual needs are satisfied.[16]

We are born female and male, biological sexes, but we are created woman and man, socially recognized genders. *How* we are so created is that second as-pect of the *mode* of production of which Engels spoke, "the production of hu-man beings themselves, the propagation of the species."

How people propagate the species is socially determined. If, biologically, people are sexually polymorphous, and society were organized in such a way that all forms of sexual expression were equally permissible, reproduction would result only from some sexual encounters, the heterosexual ones. The strict division of labor by sex, a social invention common to all known soci-eties, creates two very separate genders and a need for men and women to get together for economic reasons. It thus helps to direct their sexual needs to-ward heterosexual fulfillment, and helps to ensure biological reproduction. In more imaginative societies, biological reproduction might be ensured by other techniques, but the division of labor by sex appears to be the universal solution to date. Although it is theoretically possible that a sexual division of labor not imply inequality between the sexes, in most known societies, the socially ac-ceptable division of labor by sex is one which accords lower status to women's work. The sexual division of labor is also the underpinning of sexual subcul-tures in which men and women experience life differently; it is the material base of male power which is exercised (in our society) not just in not doing housework and in securing superior employment, but psychologically as well.

How people meet their sexual needs, how they reproduce, how they in-culcate social norms in new generations, how they learn gender, how it feels to be a man or a woman—all occur in the realm Rubin labels the sex/gender sys-tem. Rubin emphasizes the influence of kinship (which tells you with whom you can satisfy sexual needs) and the development of gender specific personali-ties via childrearing and the "oedipal machine." In addition, however, we can use the concept of the sex/gender system to examine all other social institu-tions for the roles they play in defining and reinforcing gender hierarchies. Rubin notes that theoretically a sex/gender system could be female dominant, male dominant, or egalitarian, but declines to label various known sex/gender systems or to periodize history accordingly. We choose to label our present sex/gender system patriarchy, because it appropriately captures the notion of hierarchy and male dominance which we see as central to the present system.

Economic production (what marxists are used to referring to as *the* mode of production) and the production of people in the sex/gender sphere both determine "the social organization under which the people of a particular historical epoch and a particular country live," according to Engels. The whole of society, then, can be understood by looking at both these types of production and reproduction, people and things.[17] There is no such thing as "pure capitalism," nor does "pure patriarchy" exist, for they must of necessity coexist. What exists is patriarchal capitalism, or patriarchal feudalism, or egalitarian hunting/gathering societies, or matriarchal horticultural societies, or patriarchal horticultural societies, and so on. There appears to be no necessary connection between *changes* in the one aspect of production and changes in the other. A society could undergo transition from capitalism to socialism, for example, and remain patriarchal.[18] Common sense, history, and our experience tell us, however, that these two aspects of production are so closely intertwined, that change in one ordinarily creates movement, tension, or contradiction in the other.

Radical hierarchies can also be understood in this context. Further elaboration may be possible along the lines of defining color/race systems, arenas of social life that take biological color and turn it into a social category, race. Racial hierarchies, like gender hierarchies, are aspects of our social organization, of how people are produced and reproduced. They are not fundamentally ideological; they constitute that second aspect of our mode of production, the production and reproduction of people. I might be most accurate then to refer to our societies not as, for example, simply capitalist, but as patriarchal capitalist white supremacist. In Part 3 below, we illustrate one case of capitalism adapting to and making use of racial orders and several examples of the interrelations between capitalism and patriarchy.

Capitalist development creates the places for a hierarchy of workers, but traditional marxist categories cannot tell us who will fill which places. Gender and racial hierarchies determine who fills the empty places. *Patriarchy is not simply hierarchical organization,* but hierarchy in which *particular* people fill *particular* places. It is in studying patriarchy that we learn why it is women who are dominated and how. While we believe that most known societies have been patriarchal, we do not view patriarchy as a universal, unchanging phenomenon. Rather patriarchy, the set of interrelations among men that allow men to dominate women, has changed in form and intensity over time. It is crucial that the hierarchy among men, and their differential access to patriarchal benefits, be examined. Surely, class, race, nationality, and even marital status and sexual orientation, as well as the obvious age, come into play here. And women of different class, race, nationality, marital status, or sexual orientation groups are subjected to different degrees of patriarchal power. Women may themselves exercise class, race, or national power, or even patriarchal power (through their family connections) over men lower in the patriarchal hierarchy than their own male kin.

To recapitulate, we define patriarchy as a set of social relations which has a material base and in which there are hierarchical relations between men and solidarity among them which enable them in turn to dominate women. The material base of patriarchy is men's control over women's labor power. That control is maintained by excluding women from access to necessary economically productive resources and by restricting women's sexuality. Men exercise their control in receiving personal service work from women, in not having to do housework or rear children, in having access to women's bodies for sex, and in feeling powerful and being powerful. The crucial elements of patriarchy as we *currently* experience them are: heterosexual marriage (and consequent homophobia), female childrearing and housework, women's economic dependence on men (enforced by arrangements in the labor market), the state and numerous institutions based on social relations among men—clubs, sports, unions, professions, universities, churches, corporations, and armies. All of these elements need to be examined if we are to understand patriarchal capitalism.

Both hierarchy and interdependence among men and the subordination of women are *integral* to the functioning of our society; that is, these relationships are *systemic*. We leave aside the question of the creation of these relations and ask, can we recognize patriarchal relations in capitalist societies? Within capitalist societies we must discover those same bonds between men which both bourgeois and marxist social scientists claim no longer exist, or are, at the most, unimportant leftovers. Can we understand how these relations among men are perpetuated in capitalist societies? Can we identify ways in which patriarchy has shaped the course of capitalist development?

## 3.
## The Partnership of Patriarchy and Capital

How are we to recognize patriarchal social relations in capitalist societies? It appears as if each woman is oppressed by her own man alone; her oppression seems a private affair. Relationships among men and among families seem equally fragmented. It is hard to recognize relationships among men, and between men and women, as *systematically* patriarchal. We argue, however, that patriarchy as a system of relations between men and women exists in capitalism, and that in capitalist societies a healthy and strong partnership exists between patriarchy and capital. Yet if one begins with the concept of patriarchy and an understanding of the capitalist mode of production, one recognizes immediately that the partnership of patriarchy and capital was not inevitable; men and capitalists often have conflicting interests, particularly over the use of women's labor power. Here is one way in which this conflict might manifest itself: the vast majority of men might want their women at home to personally service them. A smaller number of men, who are capitalists, might want most women (not their own) to work in the wage labor market. In examining the tensions of this conflict over women's labor power . . . we will be able to identify the material base of patriarchal relations in capitalist societies, as well as the basis for the partnership between capital and patriarchy.

### Industrialization and the Development of Family Wages

. . . Family wages may be understood as a resolution of the conflict over women's labor power which [occurred] between patriarchal and capitalist interests [in the nineteenth century].

Family wages for most adult men imply men's acceptance, and collusion in, lower wages for others, young people, women and socially defined inferior men as well (Irish, blacks, etc., the lowest groups in the patriarchal hierarchy who are denied many of the patriarchal benefits). Lower wages for women and children and inferior men are enforced by job segregation in the labor market, in turn maintained by unions and management as well as by auxiliary institutions like schools, training programs, and even families. Job segregation by sex, by insuring that women have the lower paid jobs, both assures women's economic dependence on men and reinforces notions of appropriate spheres for women and men. For most men, then, the development of family wages secured the material base of male domination in two ways. First, men have the better jobs in the labor market and earn higher wages than women. The lower pay women receive in the labor market both perpetuates men's material advantage over women and encourages women to choose wifery as a career. Second, then women do housework, childcare, and perform other services at home which benefit men directly.[19] Women's home responsibilities in turn reinforce their inferior labor market position.[20]

The resolution that developed in the early twentieth century can be seen to benefit capitalist interests as well as patriarchal interests. Capitalists, it is often argued, recognized that in the extreme conditions which prevailed in the early nineteenth-century industrialization, working-class families could not adequately reproduce themselves. They realized that housewives produced and maintained healthier workers than wage-working wives and that educated children became better workers than noneducated ones. The bargain, paying family wages to men and keeping women home, suited the capitalists at the time as well as the male workers. Although the terms of the bargain have altered over time, it is still true that the family and women's work in the family serve capital by providing a labor force and serve men as the space in which they exercise their privilege. Women, working to serve men and their families, also serve capital as consumers.[21] The family is also the place where dominance and submission are learned, as Firestone, the Frankfurt School, and many others have explained.[22] Obedient children become obedient workers, girls and boys each learn their proper roles.

While the family wage shows that capitalism adjusts to patriarchy, the changing status of children shows that patriarchy adjusts to capital. Children, like women, came to be excluded from wage labor. As children's ability to earn money declined, their legal relationship to their parents changed. At the beginning of the industrial era in the United States, fulfilling children's need for their fathers was thought to be crucial, even primary, to their happy development; fathers had legal priority in cases of contested custody. As children's ability to contribute to the economic well-being of the family declined, mothers came increasingly to be viewed as crucial to the happy development of their children, and gained legal priority in cases of contested custody.[23] Here patriarchy adapted to the changing economic role of children: when children were productive, men claimed them; as children became unproductive, they were given to women. . . .

With respect to capitalism and patriarchy, the adaptation, or mutual accommodation, took the form of the development of the family wage in the early twentieth century. The family wage cemented the partnership between patriarchy and capital. Despite women's increased labor force participation, particularly rapid since World War II, the family wage is still, we argue, the cornerstone of the present sexual division of labor—in which women are primarily responsible for housework and men primarily for wage work. Women's lower wages in the labor market (combined with the need for children to be reared by someone) assure the continued existence of the family as a necessary income pooling unit. The family, supported by the family wage, thus allows the control of women's labor by men both within and without the family.

Though women's increased wage work may cause stress for the family (similar to the stress Kautsky and Engels noted in the nineteenth century), it would be wrong to think that as a consequence, the concepts and the realities of the family and of the sexual division of labor will soon disappear. The sexual division of labor reappears in the labor market, where women work at women's jobs, often the very jobs they used to do only at home—food preparation and service, cleaning of all kinds, caring for people, and so on. As these jobs are low-status and low-paying, patriarchal relations remain intact, though their material base shifts somewhat from the family to the wage differential, from family-based to industrially based patriarchy.[24]

The prediction of nineteenth-century marxists that patriarchy would wither away in the face of capitalism's need to proletarianize everyone has not come true. Not only did marxists underestimate the strength and flexibility of patriarchy, they also overestimated the strength of capital. They envisioned the new social force of capitalism, which had torn feudal relations apart, as virtually all-powerful. . . .

If the first element of our argument about the course of capitalist development is that capital is not all-powerful, the second is that capital is tremendously flexible. Capital accumulation encounters preexisting social forms, and both destroys them and adapts to them. The adaptation of capital can be seen as a reflection of the *strength* of these preexisting forms to persevere in new environments. Yet even as they persevere, they are not unchanged. The ideology with which race and sex are understood today, for example, is strongly shaped by the particular ways racial and sexual divisions are reinforced in the accumulation process. . . .

Industrially based patriarchal relations are enforced in a variety of ways. Union contracts which specify lower wages, lesser benefits, and fewer advancement opportunities for women are not just atavistic hangovers—a case of sexist attitudes or male supremacist ideology—they maintain the material base of the patriarchal system. While some would go so far as to argue that patriarchy is already absent from the family (see, for example, Stewart Ewen, *Captains of Consciousness*),[25] we would not. Although the terms of the compromise between capital and patriarchy are changing as additional tasks formerly located in the family are capitalized, and the location of the deployment of women's labor power shifts,[26] it is nevertheless true, as we have argued above, that the wage differential caused by extreme job segregation in the labor market reinforces the family, and, with it, the domestic division of labor, by encouraging women to marry. The "ideal" of the family wage—that a man can earn enough to support an entire family—may be giving way to a new ideal that both men and women contribute through wage earning to the cash income of the family. The wage differential, then, will become increasingly necessary in perpetuating patriarchy, the male control of women's labor power. The wage differential will aid in *defining* women's work as secondary to men's at the same time it necessitates women's actual continued economic dependence on men. The sexual division of labor in the labor market and elsewhere should be understood as a manifestation of patriarchy which serves to perpetuate it.

Many people have argued that though the partnership between capital and patriarchy exists now, it may *in the long run* prove intolerable to capitalism; capital may eventually destroy both familial relations and patriarchy. The argument proceeds logically that capitalist social relations (of which the family is not an example) tend to become universalized, that women will become increasingly able to earn money and will increasingly refuse to submit to subordination in the family, and that since the family is oppressive particularly to women and children, it will collapse as soon as people can support themselves outside it.

We do not think that the patriarchal relations embodied in the family can be destroyed so easily by capital, and we see little evidence that the family system is presently disintegrating. Although the increasing labor force participation of women has made divorce more feasible, the incentives to divorce are not overwhelming for women. Women's wages allow very few women to support themselves and their children independently and adequately. The evidence for the decay of the traditional family is weak at best. The divorce rate has not so much increased, as it has evened out among classes; moreover, the remarriage rate is also very high. Up until the 1970 census, the first-marriage age was continuing its historic decline. Since 1970, people seem to have been delaying marriage and childbearing, but most recently, the birth rate has begun to increase again. It is true that larger proportions of the population are now living outside traditional families. Young people, especially, are leaving their parents' homes and establishing their own households before they marry and start traditional families. Older people, especially women, are finding themselves alone in their own households, after their children are grown and they experience separation or death of a spouse. Nevertheless, trends indicate that the new generations of young people will form nuclear families at some time in their adult lives in higher proportions than ever before. The cohorts, or groups of people, born since 1930 have much higher rates of eventual marriage and childrearing than previous cohorts. The duration of marriage and childrearing may be shortening, but its incidence is still spreading.[27]

The argument that capital destroys the family also overlooks the social forces which make family life appealing. Despite critiques of nuclear families as psychologically destructive, in a competitive society the family still meets real needs for many people. This is true not only of long-term monogamy, but even more so for raising children. Single parents bear both financial and psychic burdens. For working-class women, in particular, these burdens make the "independence" of labor force participation illusory. Single-parent families have recently been seen by policy analysts as transitional family formations which become two-parent families upon remarriage.[28]

It could be that the effects of women's increasing labor force participation are found in a declining sexual division of labor within the family, rather than in more frequent divorce, but evidence for this is also lacking. Statistics on who does housework, even in families with wage-earning wives, show little change in recent years; women still do most of it.[29] The double day is a reality for wage-working women. This is hardly surprising since the sexual division of labor outside the family, in the labor market, keeps women financially dependent on men—even when they earn a wage themselves. The future of patriarchy does not, however, rest solely on the future of familial relations. For patriarchy, like capital, can be surprisingly flexible and adaptable.

Whether or not the patriarchal division of labor, outside the family and elsewhere, is "ultimately" intolerable to capital, it is shaping capitalism now. As we illustrate below, patriarchy both legitimates capitalist control and delegitimates certain forms of struggle against capital.

### Ideology in the Twentieth Century

Patriarchy, by establishing and legitimating hierarchy among men (by allowing men of all groups to control at least some women), reinforces capitalist control, and capitalist values shape the definition of patriarchal good. . . .

If we examine the characteristics of men as radical feminists describe them

—competitive, rationalistic, dominating—they are much like our description of the dominant values of capitalist society.

This "coincidence" may be explained in two ways. In the first instance, men, as wage laborers, are absorbed in capitalist social relations at work, driven into the competition these relations prescribe, and absorb the corresponding values.[30] The radical feminist description of men was not altogether out of line for capitalist societies. Secondly, even when men and women do not actually behave in the way sexual norms prescribe, men *claim for themselves* those characteristics which are valued in the dominant ideology. So, for example, the authors of *Crestwood Heights* found that while the men, who were professionals, spent their days manipulating subordinates (often using techniques that appeal to fundamentally irrational motives to elicit the preferred behavior), men and women characterized men as "rational and pragmatic." And while the women devoted great energies to studying scientific methods of childrearing and child development, men and women in Crestwood Heights characterized women as "irrational and emotional."[31]

This helps to account not only for "male" and "female" characteristics in capitalist societies, but for the particular form sexist ideology takes in capitalist societies. Just as women's work serves the dual purpose of perpetuating male domination and capitalist production, so sexist ideology serves the dual purpose of glorifying male characteristics/capitalist values, and denigrating female characteristics/social need. If women were degraded or powerless in other societies, the reasons (rationalizations) men had for this were different. Only in a capitalist society does it make sense to look down on women as emotional or irrational. As epithets, they would not have made sense in the Renaissance. Only in a capitalist society does it make sense to look down on women as "dependent." "Dependent" as an epithet would not make sense in feudal societies. Since the division of labor ensures that women as wives and mothers in the family are largely concerned with the production of use values, the denigration of these activities obscures capital's inability to meet socially determined needs at the same time that it degrades women in the eyes of men, providing a rationale for male dominance. An example of this may be seen in the peculiar ambivalence of television commercials. On one hand, they address themselves to the real obstacles to providing for socially determined needs: detergents that destroy clothes and irritate skin, shoddily made goods of all sorts. On the other hand, concern with these problems must be denigrated; this is accomplished by mocking women, the workers who must deal with these problems.

A parallel argument demonstrating the partnership of patriarchy and capitalism may be made about the sexual division of labor in the work force. The sexual division of labor places women in low-paying jobs, and in tasks thought to be appropriate to women's role. Women are teachers, welfare workers, and the great majority of workers in the health fields. The nurturant roles that women play in these jobs are of low status because capitalism emphasizes personal independence and the ability of private enterprise to meet social needs, emphases contradicted by the need for collectively provided services. As long as the social importance of nurturant tasks can be denigrated because women perform them, the confrontation of capital's priority on exchange value by a demand for use values can be avoided. In this way, it is not feminism but sexism that divides and debilitates the working class.

4.
## Towards a More Progressive Union

Many problems remain for us to explore. Patriarchy as we have used it here remains more a descriptive term than an analytic one. If we think marxism alone inadequate, and radical feminism itself insufficient, then we need to develop new categories. What makes our task a difficult one is that the same features, such as the division of labor, often reinforce both patriarchy and capitalism, and in a thoroughly patriarchal capitalist society, it is hard to isolate the mechanisms of patriarchy. Nevertheless, this is what we must do. We have pointed to some starting places: looking at who benefits from women's labor power, uncovering the material base of patriarchy, investigating the mechanisms of hierarchy and solidarity among men. The questions we must ask are endless.

Can we speak of the laws of motion of a patriarchal system? How does patriarchy generate feminist struggle? What kinds of sexual politics and struggle between the sexes can we see in societies other than advanced capitalist ones? What are the contradictions of the patriarchal system and what is their relation to the contradictions of capitalism? . . .

### Feminism and the Class Struggle

. . . The struggle against capital and patriarchy cannot be successful if the study and practice of the issues of feminism is abandoned. A struggle aimed only at capitalist relations of oppression will fail, since their underlying supports in patriarchal relations of oppression will be overlooked. And the analysis of patriarchy is essential to a definition of the kind of socialism useful to women. While men and women share a need to overthrow capitalism they retain interests particular to their gender group. It is not clear—from our sketch, from history, or from male socialists—that the socialism being struggled for is the same for both men and women. For a humane socialism would require not only consensus on what the new society should look like and what a healthy person should look like, but more concretely, it would require that men relinquish their privilege.

As women, we must not allow ourselves to be talked out of the urgency

and importance of our tasks, as we have so may times in the past. We must
fight the attempted coercion, both subtle and not so subtle, to abandon feminist objectives.

This suggests two strategic considerations. First, a struggle to establish
socialism must be a struggle in which groups with different interests form an
alliance. Women should not trust men to liberate them after the revolution, in
part, because there is no reason to think they would know how; in part, because there is no necessity for them to do so. In fact their immediate self-interest lies in our continued oppression. Instead we must have our own organizations and our own power base. Second, we think the sexual division of labor
within capitalism has given women a practice in which we have learned to understand what human interdependence and needs are. While men have long
struggled *against* capital, women know what to struggle *for*.[32] As a general rule,
men's position in patriarchy and capitalism prevents them from recognizing
both human needs for nurturance, sharing, and growth, and the potential for
meeting those needs in a nonhierarchical, nonpatriarchial society. But even if
we raise their consciousness, men might assess the potential gains against the
potential losses and choose the status quo. Men have more to lose than their
chains.

As feminist socialists, we must organize a practice which addresses both
the struggle against patriarchy and the struggle against capitalism. We must
insist that the society we want to create is a society in which recognition of interdependence is liberation rather than shame, nurturance is a universal, not
an oppressive practice, and in which women do not continue to support the
false as well as the concrete freedoms of men.

## Notes

1. Earlier drafts of this essay appeared in 1975 and 1977 co-authored with Amy B.
Bridges. Unfortunately, becuse of the press of current commitments, Amy was unable to
continue with this project, joint from its inception and throughout most of its long and
controversial history. Over the years many individuals and groups offered us comments,
debate, and support. . . . This is a substantially abridged version of the essay as it appeared
in *Women and Revolution*, ed. Lydia Sargent (Boston: South End Press, 1981). A more
complete version was also published in *Capital and Class* in the summer of 1979. . . .

2. Often paraphrased as "the husband and wife are one and that one is the husband,"
English law held that "by marriage, the husband and wife are one person in law: that is,
the very being or legal existence of the women is suspended during the marriage, or at least
is incorporated and consolidated into that of the Husband." I. Blackstone, *Commentaries,*
1965, 442–45, cited in Kenneth M. Davidson, Ruth B. Ginsburg, and Herma H. Kay, *Sex
Based Discrimination* (St. Paul: West, 1974), 117.

3. This is a paraphrase. Karl Marx wrote: "The maintenance and reproduction of the
working class is, and must ever be, a necessary condition to the reproduction of capital.

But the capitalist may safely leave its fulfillment to the labourer's instincts of self-preservation and propagation." *Capital* (New York: International Publishers, 1967), 1:572.

4. Harry Braverman, *Labor and Monopoly Capital* (New York: Monthly Review Press, 1975).

5. Juliet Mitchell, *Women's Estate* (New York: Vintage Books, 1973), 92.

6. Frederick Engels, *The Origin of the Family, Private Property and the State,* ed. Eleanor Burke Leacock (New York: International Publishers, 1972), "Preface to the First Edition," 71–72. The continuation of this quotation reads, "by the stage of development of labor on the one hand and of the family on the other." It is interesting that, by implication, labor is excluded from occurring within the family; this is precisely the blind spot we want to overcome in this essay.

7. Juliet Mitchell, "Women: The Longest Revolution," *New Left Review,* no. 40 (November-December 1966): 11–37; reprinted by the New England Free Press.

8. Shulamith Firestone, *The Dialectic of Sex* (New York: Bantam Books, 1971).

9. "Politics of Ego: A Manifesto for New York Radical Feminists" can be found in *Rebirth of Feminism,* ed. Judith Hole and Ellen Levine (New York: Quandrangle, 1971), 440–43. "Radical feminists" are those feminists who argue that the most fundamental dynamic of history is men's striving to dominate women. "Radical" in this context does *not* mean anti-capitalist, socialist, counter-cultural, etc., but has the specific meaning of this particular set of feminist beliefs or group of feminists. Additional writings of radical feminists, of whom the New York Radical Feminists are probably the most influential, can be found in Ann Koedt, ed., *Radical Feminism* (New York: Quadrangle, 1972).

10. Focusing on power was an important step forward in the feminist critique of Freud. Firestone argues, for example, that if little girls "envied" penises it was because they recognized that little boys grew up to be members of a powerful class and little girls grew up to be dominated by them. Powerlessness, not neurosis, was the heart of women's situation. More recently, feminists have criticized Firestone for rejecting the usefulness of the concept of the unconscious. In seeking to explain the strength and continuation of male dominance, recent feminist writing has emphasized the fundamental nature of gender-based personality differences, their origins in the unconscious, and the consequent difficulty of their eradication. See Dorothy Dinnerstein, *The Mermaid and the Minotaur* (New York: Harper Colophon, 1977); Nancy Chodorow, *The Reproduction of Mothering* (Berkeley: University of California Press, 1978); and Jane Flax, "The Conflict between Nurturance and Autonomy in Mother-Daughter Relationships and within Feminism," *Feminist Studies* 4, no. 2 (June 1978): 141–89.

11. Kate Millett, *Sexual Politics* (New York: Avon, 1971), 25.

12. One example of this type of radical feminist history is Susan Brownmiller, *Against Our Will: Men, Women, and Rape* (New York: Simon and Schuster, 1975).

13. For the bourgeois social science view of patriarchy, see, for example, Weber's distinction between traditional and legal authority: *Max Weber: The Theories of Social and Economic Organization,* ed. Talcott Parsons (New York: Free Press, 1964), 328–57. These views are also discussed in Elizabeth Fee, "The Sexual Politics of Victorian Social Anthropology," *Feminist Tradition* (New York: Basic Books, 1966), esp. chap. 3, "Community."

14. See Viana Muller, "The Formation of the State and Oppression of Women: Some Theoretical Considerations and a Case Study in England and Wales," *Review of Radical Political Economics* 9, no. 3 (Fall 1977): 7–21.

15. The particular ways in which men control women's access to important economic resources and restrict their sexuality vary enormously, both from society to society, from

subgroup to subgroup, and across time. The examples we use to illustrate patriarchy in this section, however, are drawn primarily from the experience of whites in Western capitalist countries. The diversity is shown in Rayna Rapp Reiter, ed., *Toward an Anthropology of Women* (New York: Monthly Review Press, 1975); Michelle Rosaldo and Louise Lamphere, eds., *Woman, Culture and Society,* (Stanford, Calif.: Stanford University Press, 1974); and Liba Leibowitz, *Females, Males, Families: A Biosocial Approach* (North Scituate, Mass.: Duxbury, 1978). The control of women's sexuality is tightly linked to the place of children. An understanding of the demand (by men and capitalists) for children is crucial to understanding changes in women's subordination.

Where children are needed for their present or future labor power, women's sexuality will tend to be directed toward reproduction and childrearing. When children are seen as superfluous, women's sexuality for other than reproductive purposes is encouraged, but men will attempt to direct it towards satisfying male needs. The Cosmo girl is a good example of a woman "liberated" from childrearing only to find herself turning all her energies toward attracting and satisfying men. Capitalists can also use female sexuality to their own ends, as the success of Cosmo in advertising consumer products shows.

16. Gayle Rubin, "The Traffic in Women," in Reiter, *Anthropology of Women,* 159.

17. Himmelweit and Mohun point out that both aspects of production (people and things) are logically necessary to describe a mode of production because by definition a mode of production must be capapble of reproducing itself. Either aspect alone is not self-sufficient. To put it simply, the production of things requires people, and the production of people requires things. Marx, though recognizing capitalism's need for people, did not concern himself with how they were produced or what the connections between the two aspects of production were. See Himmelweit and Mohun, "Domestic Labour and Capital," *Cambridge Journal of Economics* 1, no. 1 (March 1977): 15–31.

18. For an excellent discussion of one such transition to socialism, see Batya Weinbaum, "Women in Transition to Socialism: Perspectives on the Chinese Case," *Review of Radical Political Economics* 8, no. 1 (Spring 1976): 34–58.

19. The importance of the fact that women perform labor services for men in the home cannot be overemphasized. As Pat Mainardi said in "The Politics of Housework," "the measure of your oppression is his resistance." See *Sisterhood is Powerful,* ed. Robin Morgan (New York: Vintage, 1970), 451. Her article, perhaps as important for us as Firestone on love, is an analysis of power relations between women and men as exemplified by housework.

20. Libby Zimmerman has explored the relation of membership in the primary and secondary labor markets to family patterns in New England. See her "Women in the Economy: A Case Study of Lynn, Massachusetts, 1760–1974," Ph.D. dissertation, Heller School, Brandeis, 1977. Batya Weinbaum is currently exploring the relationship between family roles and places in the labor market. See her "Redefining the Question of Revolution," *Review of Radical Political Economics* 9, no. 3 (Fall 1977): 54, 78; and *The Curious Courtship of Women's Liberation and Socialism* (Boston: South End Press, 1978). Additional studies of the interaction of capitalism and patriarchy can be found in Zillah Eisenstein, ed., *Capitalist Patriarchy and the Case for Socialist Feminism* (New York: Monthly Review Press, 1978).

21. See Batya Weinbaum and Amy Bridges, "The Other Side of the Paycheck: Monopoly Capital and the Structure of Consumption," *Monthly Review* 28, no. 3 (July-August 1976): 88–103, for a discussion of women's consumption work.

22. For the view of the Frankfurt School, see Max Horkheimer, "Authority and the

Family," in *Critical Theory* (New York: Herder and Herder, 1972) and Frankfurt Institute of Social Research, "The Family," in *Aspects of Sociology* (Boston: Beacon, 1972).

23. Carol Brown, "Patriarchal Capitalism and the Female-Headed Family," *Social Scientist* (India), nos. 40–41 (November-December 1975): 28–39.

24. Brown, in "Partriarchal Capitalism," argues, for example, that we are moving from "family based" to "industrially based" patriarchy within capitalism.

25. Stewart Ewen, *Captains of Consciousness* (New York: Random House, 1976).

26. Jean Gardiner, "Women's Domestic Labour," *New Left Review*, no. 89 (January-February 1975): 47–58, clarifies the cause for the shift in location of women's labor, from capital's point of view. She examines what capital needs (in terms of the level of real wages, the supply of labor, and the size of markets) at various stages of growth and of the business cycle. She argues that in times of boom or rapid growth it is likely that socializing housework (or more accurately capitalizing it) would be the dominant tendency, and that in times of recession, housework will be maintained in its traditional form. In attempting to assess the likely direction of the British economy, however, Gardiner does not assess the economic needs of patriarchy. We argue in this essay that unless one takes patriarchy as well as capital into account one cannot adequately assess the likely direction of the economic system.

27. For the proportion of people in nuclear families, see Peter Uhlenberg, "Cohort Variations in Family Life Cycle Experiences of U.S. Females," *Journal of Marriage and the Family* 36, no. 5 (May 1974): 284–92. For remarriage rates, see Paul C. Glick and Arthur J. Norton, "Perspectives on the Recent Upturn in Divorce and Remarriage," *Demography* 10 (1974): 301–14. For divorce and income levels, see Arthur J. Norton and Paul C. Glick, "Marital Instability: Past, Present, and Future," *Journal of Social Issues* 32, no. 1 (1976): 5–20. Also see Mary Jo Bane, *Here to Stay: American Families in the Twentieth Century* (New York: Basic Books, 1976).

28. Heather L. Ross and Isabel B. Sawhill, *Time of Transition: The Growth of Families Headed by Women* (Washington, D.C.: Urban Institute, 1975).

29. See Kathryn E. Walker and Margaret E. Woods, *Time Use: A Measure of Household Production of Family Goods and Services* (Washington, D.C.: American Home Economics Association, 1976); and Heidi I. Hartmann, "The Family as the Locus of Gender, Class, and Political Struggle: The Example of Housework," *Signs: Journal of Women in Culture and Society* 6, no. 3 (Spring 1981).

30. This should provide some clues to class differences in sexism, which we cannot explore here.

31. See John R. Seeley et al., *Crestwood Heights* (Toronto: University of Toronto Press, 1956), 382–94. While men's place may be characterized as "in production," this does not mean that women's place is simply "not in production" —her tasks, too, are shaped by capital. Her nonwage work is the resolution, on a day-to-day basis, of production for exchange with socially determined need, the provision of use values in a capitalist society (this is the context of consumption). See Weinbaum and Bridges, "The Other Side of the Paycheck," for a more complete discussion of this argument. The fact that women provide "merely" use values in a society dominated by exchange values can be used to denigrate women.

32. Lise Vogel, "The Earthly Family," *Radical America* 7, nos. 4–5 (July-October 1973): 9–50.

# ABOUT THE AUTHOR

Nancy S. Love is an associate professor in the department of political science at Pennsylvania State University, where she received the Christian R. and Mary F. Lindback Award for Distinguished Teaching in 1991. She has also taught at Swarthmore College and Cornell University.

Professor Love received her A.B. degree from Kenyon College and her Ph.D. from Cornell University.

She is the author of *Marx, Nietzsche, and Modernity*, published by Columbia University Press in 1986. Her articles have appeared in *differences: A Journal of Feminist Cultural Studies*, *New German Critique*, *Polity*, and *Women and Politics*.

Professor Love is currently at work on a book entitled *Discourse and Democracy: Rethinking Power*.